1st Edition 2007

Singapore

The Complete **Residents'** Guide

Passionately Publishing...

EXPLORER

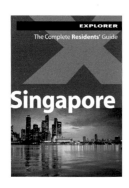

Singapore Explorer 1st Edition ISBN 13 - 978-976-8182-80-7 ISBN 10 - 976-8182-80-6

Copyright © Explorer Group Ltd 2007
All rights reserved.

Front Cover Photograph: Pete Maloney

Printed and bound by Emirates Printing Press, Dubai, United Arab Emirates.

Explorer Publishing & Distribution
PO Box 34275, Zomorrodah Bldg, Za'abeel Rd, Dubai
United Arab Emirates
Phone   (+971 4) 335 3520
Fax   (+971 4) 335 3529
Email   Info@Explorer-Publishing.com
Web   www.Explorer-Publishing.com

Welcome...

Congratulations. By buying this book, you've made your new life in Singapore as neat and tidy as the city itself. We've taken all the essentials, the nitty gritty, fun and active stuff and put it into an easy to read format (with pretty pictures too). Whether you're looking to hire a car, find your local park or a good place to get your wig chopped, it's all here.

The **General Information** chapter gives an overview of Singapore including history, geography, transport system, climate and culture. The **Residents** chapter will have the whole family settled in no time. With information on visas, work, housing, residential areas, schools and hospitals, this section will tell you your rights and how to get your life started in Singapore.

Once you've got all that done and dusted, start **Exploring**. You'll discover museums, galleries, islands and more – and don't forget to tick off the checklist of our must dos. If you can still find the time, the **Activities** chapter tells you where to destress, revitalise and get energised. Find out about the many sports clubs, social groups or check out your local beauty salon, learn the language or find new ways to relax.

Our **Shopping** chapter won't disappoint. Singapore is a shopper's paradise and we've got the lowdown. As well as the glitz of Orchard Road, the bazaars and markets will give you a taste of the old town. All this action has probably made you hungry, so figure out what's hip and happening with **Going Out**. We have reviewed a selection of the best restaurants, cafes, bars and nightclubs to keep your belly full and your feet tapping.

So now you know where you want to go, look at the street maps and MRT rail map at the back of the book and start navigating.

Finally, we'd like to say a big thanks to all of you for buying this book – without you, we wouldn't have had to endure the terrible task of shopping, eating out, partying and exploring this wonderful city.

The Explorer Team

Explorer online

Life can move pretty fast so make sure you keep up at **www.explorerpublishing.com.** Register for updates on the latest happenings in your city, or let us know if there's anything we've missed out by filling in our reader response form. You can also check out city info on various destinations around the world - whether you're planning a holiday or making your next big move, we've got it covered. All our titles, from residents' guides to mini visitors' guides, mini maps to photography books are available to purchase online so you need never be without us!

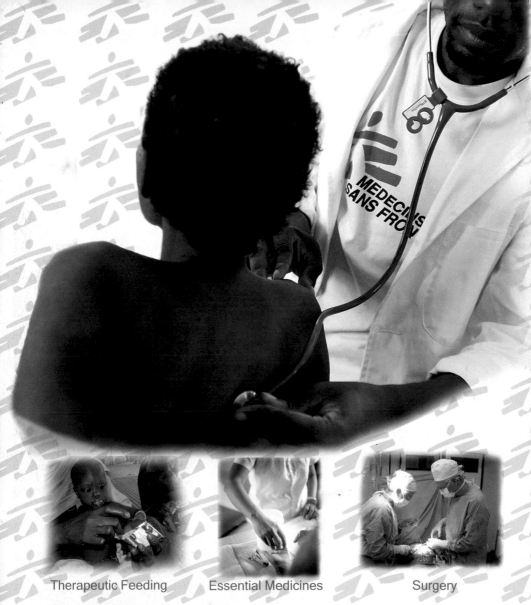

Therapeutic Feeding   Essential Medicines   Surgery

MEDECINS SANS FRONTIERES
أطـبـاء بـلا حـدود

Providing emergency medical
relief in over 70 countries.

help us help the helpless

Raw power, refined.

The new Chevrolet Tahoe refines the raw power of a 355 horsepower Vortec V8 engine and couples it with smooth handling and a quiet ride. Examine Tahoe's luxuriously appointed interior and you'll find refinement in every detail.

CHEVROLET

Tahoe 2007

from

S$**190**⁺⁺

The new face of Clarke Quay

For that ultimate experience in the vibrant entertainment hub of Clarke Quay, the newly renovated Novotel Clarke Quay is the perfect place to stay. Packages start from S$190+++.

Discover our sleek modern facilities.

Novotel Clarke Quay, Singapore
177A River Valley Road, Singapore Tel: (65) 6 338 3333 Fax: (65) 6339 2854
Email: info@novotelclarkequay.com.sg website: www.novotel.com/asia

Accor operates over 70 Novotel Hotels & Resorts in Asia Pacific

For reservation and information, contact Accor reservation services in Indonesia 0807 1 777 777 or Thailand (02) 237 6064. Or toll Free in China 800 830 2688, Hong Kong 800 93 8768, Japan 00531 61 6353, Singapore 800 6161 367, Malaysia 1800 802 578 and South Korea 0079 8611 1288. If calling from countries other than those listed please phone (61-2) 8584 8666 or e-mail: accorres.bkk@accor.com

NOVOTEL

Accor hotels

ACCOR ▶ **A new perspective on our Hotels and Services**

BIGGEST CHOICE OF BOOKS

 MAGIC CHOICE OF BOOKS

EXCITING CHOICE
OF *BOOKS*

 Phenomenal choice of books

UNBEATABLE CHOICE OF BOOKS `IN FULL COLOUR`

SPECIAL CHOICE of books

THRILLING CHOICE OF BOOKS

Encyclopedic choice of Books

BALANCED CHOICE OF BOOKS

  # FANTASTIC
CHOICE OF BOOKS

BORDERS.

Jeanne Leong

'Ask Jeanne' is what everyone knows this girl as. She knows everything about everything from celeb gossip to the best shops. Having spent most of her life in Singapore (she studied in Canada and spent some years in Malaysia), she has nine years experience in regional marketing and communications, starting her career with Singapore Tourism Board. She loves the city, travel, yoga, dining out with friends, and dreaming!

Karsten Cramer

Karsten graduated from Queen's University in Kingston, Canada, with a Bachelor of Commerce and after several successful years specialising in commercial research, went on to create his own company, Outlook Editorial and Research, together with brother Steinar in 2005. He's been in Singapore just over three years, and is making the most of all the opportunities the city has to offer. He loves being outdoors and active, and is an aspiring chef.

Luke Clark

Having spent a decade in Singapore, this New Zealander somehow manages to juggle work with serious play and is a keen DJ, dragon boater and confessed food obsessive. His top tip for living in Singapore is 'add chilli to everything'. Now three years into a freelance career, Luke shares his time between magazine, book and online projects, and has written for the likes of *Discovery*, *Conde Nast* and *FHM*.

Abdul Gafoor
AKA: Ace Circulator
After a successful stint on Ferrari's Formula One team Gafoor made a pitstop at our office and decided to stay. He has won our 'Most Cheerful Employee' award five years in a row – baffling, when you consider he spends so much time battling the traffic.

Andrea Fust
AKA: Mother Superior
By day Andrea is the most efficient manager in the world and by night she replaces the boardroom for her board and wows the pants off the dudes in Ski Dubai. Literally. Back in the office she definitely wears the trousers!

Ahmed Mainodin
AKA: Mystery Man
We can never recognise Ahmed because of his constantly changing facial hair. He waltzes in with big lambchop sideburns one day, a handlebar moustache the next, and a neatly trimmed goatee after that. So far we've had no objections to his hirsute chameleonisms, but we'll definitely draw the line at a monobrow.

Cherry Enriquez
AKA: Bean Counter
With the team's penchant for sweets and pastries, it's good to know we have Cherry on top of our accounting cake. The local confectioner is always paid on time, so we're guaranteed great gateaux for every special occasion.

Claire England
AKA: Whip Cracker
No longer able to freeload off the fact that she once appeared in a Robbie Williams video, Claire now puts her creative skills to better use – looking up rude words in the dictionary! A child of English nobility, Claire is quite the lady – unless she's down at Jimmy Dix.

Ajay Krishnan R
AKA: Web Wonder
Ajay's mum and dad knew he was going to be an IT genius when the found him reconfiguring his Commodore 64 at the tender age of 2. He went on to become the technology consultant on all three Matrix films, and counts Keanu as a close personal friend.

David Quinn
AKA: Sharp Shooter
After a short stint as a children's TV presenter was robbed from David because he developed an allergy to sticky back plastic, he made his way to sandier pastures. Now that he's thinking outside the box, nothing gets past the man with the sharpest pencil in town.

Alex Jeffries
AKA: Easy Rider
Alex is happiest when dressed in leather from head to toe with a humming machine between his thighs – just like any other motorbike enthusiast. Whenever he's not speeding along the Hatta Road at full throttle, he can be found at his beloved Mac, still dressed in leather.

Enrico Maullon
AKA: The Crooner
Frequently mistaken for his near-namesake Enrique Iglesias, Enrico decided to capitalise and is now a regular stand-in for the Latin heartthrob. If he's ever missing from the office, it usually means he's off performing for millions of adoring fans on another stadium tour of America.

Alistair MacKenzie
AKA: Media Mogul
If only Alistair could take the paperless office one step further and achieve the officeless office he would be the happiest publisher alive. Wireless access from a remote spot somewhere in the Hajar Mountains would suit this intrepid explorer – less traffic, lots of fresh air, and wearing sandals all day - the perfect work environment!

Firos Khan
AKA: Big Smiler
Previously a body double in kung fu movies, including several appearances in close up scenes for Steven Seagal's moustache. He also once tore down a restaurant with his bare hands after they served him a mild curry by mistake.

Hashim MM
AKA: Speedy Gonzales
They don't come much faster than Hashim – he's so speedy with his mouse that scientists are struggling to create a computer that can keep up with him. His nimble fingers leave his keyboard smouldering (he gets through three a week), and his go-faster stripes make him almost invisible to the naked eye when he moves.

Jane Roberts
AKA: The Oracle
After working in an undisclosed role in the government, Jane brought her super sleuth skills to Explorer. Whatever the question, she knows what, where, who, how and when, but her encyclopaedic knowledge is only impressive until you realise she just makes things up randomly.

Helen Spearman
AKA: Little Miss Sunshine
With her bubbly laugh and permanent smile, Helen is a much-needed ray of sunshine in the office when we're all grumpy and facing harrowing deadlines. It's almost impossible to think that she ever loses her temper or shows a dark side... although put her behind the wheel of a car, and you've got instant road rage.

Jayde Fernandes
AKA: Pop Idol
Jayde's idol is Britney Spears, and he recently shaved his head to show solidarity with the troubled star. When he's not checking his dome for stubble, or practising the dance moves to 'Baby One More Time' in front of the bathroom mirror, he actually manages to get some designing done.

Henry Hilos
AKA: The Quiet Man
Henry can rarely be seen from behind his large obstructive screen but when you do catch a glimpse you'll be sure to get a smile. Lighthearted Henry keeps all those glossy pages filled with pretty pictures for something to look at when you can't be bothered to read.

Kate Fox
AKA: Contacts Collector
Kate swooped into the office like the UK equivalent of Wonderwoman, minus the tights of course (it's much too hot for that), but armed with a superhuman marketing brain. Even though she 's just arrived, she is already a regular on the Dubai social scene - she is helping to blast Explorer into the stratosphere, one champagne-soaked networking party at a time.

Ieyad Charaf
AKA: Fashion Designer
When we hired Ieyad as a top designer, we didn't realise we'd be getting his designer tops too! By far the snappiest dresser in the office, you'd be hard-pressed to beat his impeccably ironed shirts.

Katie Drynan
AKA The Irish Deputy
Katie is a Jumeirah Jane in training, and has 35 sisters who take it in turns to work in the Explorer office while she enjoys testing all the beauty treatments available on the Beach Road. This Irish charmer met an oil tycoon in Paris, and they now spend the weekends digging very deep holes in their new garden.

Ingrid Cupido
AKA: The Karaoke Queen
Ingrid has a voice to match her starlet name. She'll put any Pop Idols to shame once behind the mike, and she's pretty nifty on a keyboard too. She keeps us all ticking over and was a very welcome relief for overworked staff. She certainly gets our vote if she decides to go pro; just remember you saw her here first.

Kiran Melwani
AKA: Bow Selector
Like a modern-day Robin Hood (right down to the green tights and band of merry men), Kiran's mission in life is to distribute Explorer's wealth of knowledge to the fact-hungry readers of the world. Just make sure you never do anything to upset her – rumour has it she's a pretty mean shot with that bow and arrow.

Ivan Rodrigues
AKA: The Aviator
After making a mint in the airline market, Ivan came to Explorer where he works for pleasure, not money. That's his story, anyway. We know that he is actually a corporate spy from a rival company and that his multi-level spreadsheets are really elaborate codes designed to confuse us.

Times NewsLink

With 7 TimesNewslink & 2 Kaboom speciality children's stores located conveniently throughout Singapore Changi Airport, you're sure to find something for your journey from our extensive range of the latest international magazines, newspaper and books as well as a wide selection of stationery and children's products.

Terminal 1
- Departure/Transit Lounge East *24 hrs*
- Check-in-Hall West
- Departure/transit Lounge West *24 hrs*

Terminal 2
- Departure/Transit Lounge North *24 hrs*
- Departure/Transit Lounge South
- Departure/Check-in Hall South

Times NewsLink

Chia Ming Chien

Ming Chien's our native Singaporean with 30 years of city life under his belt. Although he spent his early childhood in London and his university days in Australia, he loves Singapore for its diversity and rich multicultural society. He's quite a nature lover, and enjoys swimming, martial arts and yoga. And he's even set up his own company, with an office in India, despite the fact that he's never even set foot there.

Steinar Cramer

This Canadian charges about on his bike, doing his best to avoid crazy taxi drivers and heavy monsoon downpours. He knows the city well, having spent six years here. He has worked for the Economist Intelligence Unit, and as head of the research department for the Singex Group. In 2005 he started Outlook Editorial and Research with his brother, Karsten. He's fluent in Dutch and loves listening to the local Singlish.

Thanks...

As well as our star team of authors, whose expert advice and incredible research have ensured the Singapore Explorer is the most up-to-date and comprehensive guide to expat life for Singapore, there are a number of other people without whom this book would not have been the success it is. Massive thanks go to the godfather of the Singapore Explorer, Ben Zelazny, for all his assistance at various stages of the book; thanks to our team of food reporters who assisted with the Going Out chapter: Abie Sutherland, Jean Fung, Mark Newton, Naeema Ismail, Nik Lee, Seah Siew Hua, and thanks also to the following for lending a hand: John Marriott, John Morgan at the British Chamber of Commerce Singapore, Singapore Tourism Board, Phillip Overmyer at Singapore International Chamber of Commerce, Aya Yamamoto and Sabastian Tan at ASTA Projects and all at Maps Geosystems. And special thanks to Miki and the Junior Explorers, Dan and Amy, for all their support!

Rafi VP
AKA: Party Trickster

After developing a rare allergy to sunlight in his teens, Rafi started to lose a few centimeters of height every year. He now stands just 30cm tall, and does his best work in our dingy basement wearing a pair of infrared goggles. His favourite party trick is to fold himself into a briefcase, and he was once sick in his hat.

Shyrell Tamayo
AKA: Fashion Princess

We've never seen Shyrell wearing the same thing twice – her clothes collection is so large that her husband has to keep all his things in a shoebox. She runs Designlab like clockwork, because being late for deadlines is SO last season.

Roshni Ahuja
AKA: Bright Spark

Never failing to brighten up the office with her colourful get-up, Roshni definitely puts the 'it' in the IT department. She's a perennially pleasant, profound programmer with peerless panache, and she does her job with plenty of pep and piles of pizzazz.

Sunita Lakhiani
AKA: Designlass

Initially suspicious of having a female in their midst, the boys in Designlab now treat Sunita like one of their own. A big shame for her, because they treat each other pretty damn bad!

Sean Kearns
AKA: The Tall Guy

Big Sean, as he's affectionately known, is so laid back he actually spends most of his time lying down (unless he's on a camping trip, when his ridiculously small tent forces him to sleep on his hands and knees). Despite the rest of us constantly tripping over his lanky frame, when the job requires someone who will work flat out, he always rises to the editorial occasion.

Tim Binks
AKA: Class Clown

El Binksmeisterooney is such a sharp wit, he often has fellow Explorers gushing tea from their noses in convulsions of mirth. Years spent hiking across the Middle East have given him an encyclopedic knowledge of rock formations and elaborate hair.

Tissy Varghese
AKA: PC Whisperer

With her soft voice and gentle touch, Tissy can whip even the wildest of PCs into submission. No matter how many times we spill coffee on our keyboards she never loses her temper – a real mystery, especially as she wakes at 3am every day to beat the Sharjah traffic.

Shabsir M
AKA: Sticky Wicket

Shabsir is a valuable player on the Indian national cricket team, so instead of working you'll usually find him autographing cricket balls for crazed fans around the world. We don't mind though – if ever a retailer is stumped because they run out of stock, he knocks them for six with his speedy delivery.

Tom Jordan
AKA: The True Professional

Explorer's resident thesp, Tom delivers lines almost as well as he cuts them. His early promise on the pantomime circuit was rewarded with an all-action role in hit UK drama Heartbeat. He's still living off the royalties – and the fact he shared a sandwich with Kenneth Branagh.

Shefeeq M
AKA: Rapper in Disguise

So new he's still got the wrapper on, Shefeeq was dragged into the Explorer office, forced to pose in front of a camera, and put to work in the design department. The poor chap only stopped by to ask for directions to Wadi Bih, but since we realised how efficient he is, we keep him chained to his desk.

Zainudheen Madathil
AKA: Map Master

Often confused with retired footballer Zinedine Zidane because of his dexterous displays and a bad head-butting habit, Zain tackles design with the mouse skills of a star striker. Maps are his goal and despite getting red-penned a few times, when he shoots, he scores.

Laura Zuffa
AKA: Travelling Salesgirl
Laura's passport is covered in more stamps than Kofi Annan's, and there isn't a city, country or continent that she won't travel to. With a smile that makes grown men weep, our girl on the frontlines always brings home the beef bacon.

Mohammed T
AKA: King of the Castle
T is Explorer's very own Bedouin warehouse dweller; under his caring charge all Explorer stock is kept in masterful order. Arrive uninvited and you'll find T, meditating on a pile of maps, amid an almost eerie sense of calm

Mannie Lugtu
AKA: Distribution Demon
When the travelling circus rode into town, their master juggler Mannie decided to leave the Big Top and explore Dubai instead. He may have swapped his balls for our books but his juggling skills still come in handy.

Motaz Al Bunai
AKA: Car Salesman
Motaz starts every day with a tough decision, namely, which one of his fleet of exotic cars he's going to drive to work. If he ever takes a break from his delightful designing, he could always start his own second-hand car garage – Motaz's Motors.

Maricar Ong
AKA: Pocket Docket
A pint-sized dynamo of ruthless efficiency, Maricar gets the job done before anyone else notices it needed doing. If this most able assistant is absent for a moment, it sends a surge of blind panic through the Explorer ranks.

Noushad Madathil
AKA: Map Daddy
Where would Explorer be without the mercurial Madathil brothers? Lost in the Empty Quarter, that's where. Quieter than a mute dormouse, Noushad prefers to let his Photoshop layers, and brother Zain, do all the talking. A true Map Daddy.

Matt Farquharson
AKA: Hack Hunter
A career of tuppence-a-word hackery ended when Matt arrived in Dubai to cover a maggot wranglers' convention. He misguidedly thinks he's clever because he once wrote for some grown-up English papers.

Pamela Grist
AKA: Happy Snapper
If a picture can speak a thousand words then Pam's photos say a lot about her - through her lens she manages to find the beauty in everything – even this motley crew. And when the camera never lies, thankfully Photoshop can.

Mimi Stankova
AKA: Mind Controller
A master of mind control, Mimi's siren-like voice lulls people into doing whatever she asks. Her steely reserve and endless patience mean recalcitrant reporters and persistent PR people are putty in her hands, delivering whatever she wants, whenever she wants it.

Pete Maloney
AKA: Graphic Guru
Image conscious he may be, but when Pete has his designs on something you can bet he's gonna get it! He's the king of chat up lines, ladies – if he ever opens a conversation with 'D'you come here often?' then brace yourself for the Maloney magic.

Mohammed Sameer
AKA: Man in the Van
Known as MS, short for Microsoft, Sameer can pick apart a PC like a thief with a lock, which is why we keep him out of finance and pounding Dubai's roads in the unmissable Explorer van – so we can always spot him coming.

Rafi Jamal
AKA: Soap Star
After a walk on part in The Bold and the Beautiful, Rafi swapped the Hollywood Hills for the Hajar Mountains. Although he left the glitz behind, he still mingles with high society, moonlighting as a male gigolo and impressing Dubai's ladies with his fancy footwork.

Experience the latest attractions at Imbiah!

Imbiah is the latest attraction cluster on Sentosa and a great introduction to what you can see and do here. Boasting a collection of attractions, dining and retail outlets, this exciting zone lets you relish a full day's enjoyment of varying experiences.

Butterfly Park & Insect Kingdom
Stroll through the lush surroundings of the Butterfly Park as 1,500 live butterflies flutter around you at the cool outdoor conservatory. It also has one of the largest collections in Asia with 3,000 species of some of the world's most beautiful and rarest insects.

Cable Car
Enjoy magnificent views when you ride hundreds of metres above the harbour, sea and rainforest in a cable car. Glass-bottomed cars present Singapore in a whole new perspective!

Fort Siloso
Singapore's only surviving preserved coastal fortification is an important window to our colonial past and a poignant reminder of the war years. Life-sized replicas, interactive exhibits, photographs, documents and film clips are on display. Get to handle real-life historical guns and cannons, or explore the old tunnels too.

Images of Singapore (Must see)
Journey through the history of Singapore where cultural diversity, unity of values and adventures come together for an enchanting trip.

Sentosa 4D Magix (New)
The latest attraction in Sentosa lets you be the 'star' in a movie! Combining 3D film with a variety of '4D' special effects that synchronise with events that occur throughout the film, you will be dodging bullets and jumping over cliffs like it is done in the movies!

Sentosa Luge & Skyride (New)
The Sentosa Luge, the first facility in Southeast Asia, lets you race down or cruise leisurely along a 650m paved track in a luge cart that combines a unique steering and braking system. Then, transfer to a Skyride for a scenic ride among the tropical rainforest back to the starting point.

Sky Tower
Singapore's tallest public viewing tower at 131m above sea level offers panoramic views across Singapore, Sentosa and the Southern Islands. Day or night, views from the tower promise to be both scenic and breathtaking.

The Merlion
Venture into Singapore's tallest icon at 37m high, and discover the secret of this lion city, in an animated theatre show. Enjoy spectacular views of Singapore's city skyline and Sentosa at the Merlion's top. Toss a gold coin into a Mercub's mouth and bring home a unique Merlion souvenir!

www.sentosa.com.sg

sentosa

Singapore's Island Resort

*MOTO*RAZR *maxx V6*

*Move faster with 3.5G HSDPA high speed mobile broadband, external touch music keys and a 2 mega-pixel camera with flash. **The new MOTORAZR maxx V6. Cutting-edge speed for cutting-edge style.***

hellomoto.com

Residents' Guides

All you need to know about living, working and enjoying life in these exciting destinations

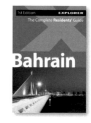

* Covers not final. Titles available Winter 2007.

Activity Guides

Drive, trek, dive and swim... life will never be boring again

Mini Guides
The perfect pocket-sized
Visitors' Guides

* Covers not final. Titles available Winter 2007.

Mini Maps
Wherever you are,
never get lost again

* Covers not final. Titles available Winter 2007.

Photography Books
Beautiful cities caught through the lens

Contents

Contents

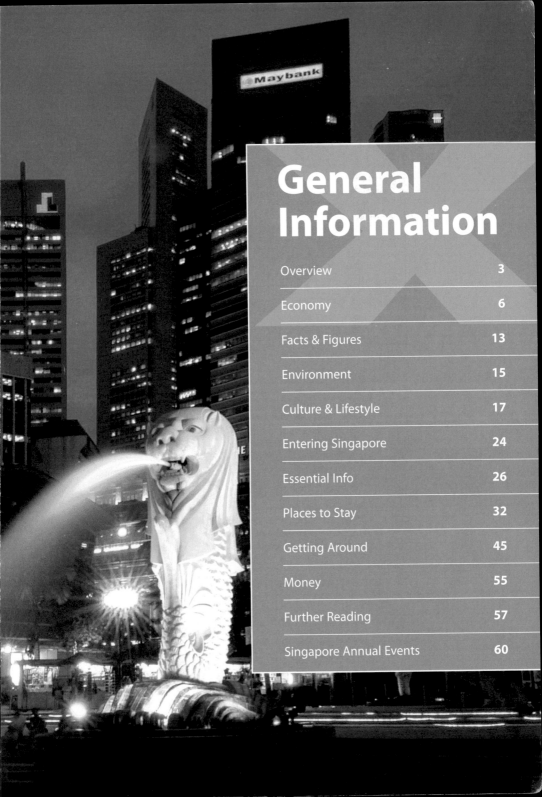

General Information

Geography

The Republic of Singapore is situated just north of the equator between the Indian Ocean and South China Sea, a strategically vital location where major sea lanes between east and west converge. Nestled at the southern tip of the Malayan Peninsula, the country is made up of one main island surrounded by about 60 small isles, mostly to the south. To the north, it is separated from West Malaysia by the one kilometre-wide Johore Strait. Two causeways link the countries to provide access by road. To the south, the island is separated from Indonesia by the Singapore Strait.

Singapore's total land area is 697 square kilometres and the main island is 617 square kilometres. Spanning 42 kilometres from east to west and 23 kilometres north to south, Singapore is also known as the Red Dot because that's all you see on the world map. For over 30 years, Singapore has been diligently reclaiming land from the sea. The total land area in 1960 was 581.5 square kilometres and it's targeted to reach 733 square kilometres by 2030. Among other areas, the housing estate of Marine Parade and the extensive East Coast Parkway sit on reclaimed land. The main island, composed of a granite core, is essentially flat with the highest point, Bukit Timah, rising a mere 166 metres (540 feet) above sea level. Relentless urbanisation has reduced the rainforests to a few modest nature reserves forming a catchment area for its precious reservoirs. Singapore has just 10 square kilometres of water and is completely dependent on Johore in Malaysia for water. Half the area on the main island is used for residential, commercial and industrial purposes, with agriculture taking up just an 11 square kilometre sliver of land. Along the 193 kilometre coastline there is little in the way of beautiful, natural, sandy beaches. The few popular beaches were man-made as part of the land reclamation programme.

First time visitors are often struck by the overwhelming number of high-rise buildings. About 90% of the population lives in high-rise flats or condominium apartments. But the concrete jungle has been transformed into a garden city by an enlightened initiative started some 30 years ago to grow trees and tropical plants throughout the state.

Singapore Fact Box

Coordinates – 1° 22' North, 103° 48' East.
(More precisely: between latitudes 1°09'N and 1°29'N and longitudes 103°36'E and 104°25'E)

Total land area – 697 sq km

Mainland – 617.1 sq km

Total coastline – 193 km

Highest point – 166 m

Percentage of inhabited land – 50%

History

The earliest record of Singapore is a third century account by the Chinese who referred to the tiny island as Puluozhong, a transliteration of Pulau Ujong, Malay for 'island at the end' of the peninsula. In the 1300s the island was known as Temasek (sea town), and was a focal point for trade – and a haven for pirates preying on the busy sea lanes. According to legend, Sang Nila Utama, ruler of Palembang in the 14th century, sought shelter from a storm in a tranquil fishing village on Temasek. He spotted an animal resembling a lion and renamed the island Singa Pura (lion city).

Singapore Overview

Modern Singapore

Modern Singapore was founded in 1819 when Englishman Sir Stamford Raffles of the British East India Company claimed Singapore as a regional base. After some political manoeuverings, which included reinstating an exiled Sultan, Singapore, as part of the Straits Settlements, became a British colony. Realising the economic potential afforded by Singapore's naturally deep harbour and the convergence of trade routes at this seaport, Raffles declared the colony a free port. Consequently, Singapore flourished as traders, merchants and migrants from Malaya, Indonesia, China, India, the Middle East and Europe took advantage of its tax-free status. Within 50 years of Raffles' arrival, this trading post of a few thousand had grown into a busy, cosmopolitan seaport of 85,500. The Chinese, mainly immigrants from southern China, became the dominant ethnic group in an ethnically diverse population.

Independence

During World War Two, the British governing the colony of Singapore suffered a humiliating defeat and surrendered to the Japanese who then occupied the island from 1942-45. Post-war, Singapore reverted to British rule. In 1959, Singapore achieved the constitution of a self-governing state and Lee Kuan Yew became the first prime minister after his People's Action Party won the elections. With a population of 1.5 million people, a land area of 581.5 square kilometres and devoid of natural resources, Lee believed Singapore's future lay in joining the Federation of Malaya, formed in 1963. Friction in this marriage was intense and the differences proved irreconcilable. On August 9, 1965, Singapore declared its independence and become the Republic of Singapore, a parliamentary democracy with a legal system based on British law.

Post Independence

This was a momentous period in its history. Britain was grappling with its own domestic issues and had little attention to spare for Singapore. The communists were a force in the region; a cohesive national identity among the disparate races, mostly migrants from completely different countries and culture, did not exist; unemployment was high; the population was largely uneducated and housing was manifestly lacking. The prime minister, a lawyer, was only 35 years old. Matters were further exacerbated by the unexpected withdrawal of British troops leaving the nascent nation defenceless and with a loss of 50,000 jobs.

Prime minister Lee and a core group of leaders rallied to tackle the most pressing issues. Top of the agenda was unifying the different races and minority groups into a single multi-racial, multi-cultural 'Singaporean identity'. The government was adamant the race riots of the 1960s would never be repeated. Four national languages were designated (Malay, Chinese, Tamil and English) and the first elected head of state, President Yusof bin Ishak, was Malay. Led by Lim Kim San, the government tackled the problem of housing its citizens. The Housing and Development Board built high-rise flats that were leased to the public at subsidised cost. Today, over 80% of the population lives in HDB flats.

Goh Keng Swee, architect of Singapore's economy and Minister of Finance (1959), moved to industrialise Singapore. Several industrial estates were created and the largest, Jurong, had port and shipbuilding facilities to facilitate the efficient movement of trade. Lee and several ministers went on a world tour to market Singapore as a viable base to do business in Asia. Concomitantly, legislation was enacted to ensure stable relations between employers and the workforce, until then wracked by labour disputes and strikes. By 1972, one quarter of Singapore's manufacturing firms were either foreign-owned or joint-venture companies.

Lee Kuan Yew (1923-)
Singapore's success is synonymous with Lee Kuan Yew and its citizens view him as their founding father. A graduate in law from Cambridge University, Lee formed the socialist People's Action Party and, at age 35, became the first prime minister of Singapore. After leading the PAP in seven victorious elections, Lee stepped down in 1990, with no loss in stature or influence. Lee has never been apologetic for being an autocrat; rather he saw it as necessary to steer the nation out of its dire straits to become an Asian tiger respected around the world. Revered, Lee's influence in major decisions affecting Singapore is still evident. Lee still serves the government as Minister Mentor.

In 1967, a conscription army was constituted and all able-bodied males served two to two and a half years of National Service. Today, the army, navy and air-force have matured into a technologically advanced and formidable defence force.

Model of Success

In the 40 years since Independence, Singapore's free market economy has accomplished phenomenal progress and has often been cited as a model of success for emerging nations. A stable political and industrial climate, reliable legal system, sophisticated banking and financial services, highly educated workforce and technologically advanced infrastructure made Singapore the favoured location for multinationals to base their headquarters and manufacturing plants in Asia. Riding on this affluence, arts and culture have blossomed; in 2002 the $650 million performing arts centre Esplanade – Theatres on the Bay was opened and a fledgling film industry has emerged.

In response to China and India's accelerating influence in the 21st century, Singapore began investing heavily in life-sciences, bio-technology and providing high-end services in a global economy where knowledge is capital.

Passing the Torch

In 1990, after 31 years as prime minister, Lee Kuan Yew passed on the leadership to Goh Chok Tong. The citizens were housed, educated, affluent and morale was high. There was only the slightest tinge of concern Singapore may falter under the second generation of leaders. Two dire events, the Asian financial crisis in 1997 and SARS in 2003, allowed the government to prove its mettle and maturity. Then in 2004, the mantle was passed on to Lee Hsien Loong, eldest son of Lee Kuan Yew.

Since 2000, the economy has experienced a major recession, its highest rate of unemployment in decades, and the emergence of China and India as major economic forces. An extraordinary platform of success carries PM Lee and the third generation of leaders into a new and uncertain era.

Singapore Timeline

3rd Century	Earliest recorded account of Singapore.
13th Century	Sang Nila Utama renames the island Singa Pura.
1819	Sir Stamford Raffles, founder of modern Singapore, establishes Singapore as a crown colony.
1942-45	British surrender and the Japanese Occupation.
1955	David Marshall elected first Chief Minister of Singapore.
1959	Lee Kuan Yew becomes prime minister after People's Action Party wins the general elections.
1960	Housing and Development Board set up.
1963	Federation of Malaysia formed.
1965	Singapore separates from Federation to become independent republic.
1967	National Service commences.
1976	PAP wins every seat in parliament.
1979	Singapore is second busiest port in the world, by tonnage.
1981	JB Jeyaretnam, Worker's Party, becomes first opposition MP.
1984	Three PAP women MPs elected; first women to serve in parliament.
1990	Goh Chok Tong sworn in as prime minister.
1993	Ong Teng Cheong becomes the first directly-elected president.
1999	Singapore experiences recession resulting from Asian financial crisis.
2001-2003	Singapore economy languishes through another recession.
2002	Esplanade – Theatres on the Bay opens.
2003	Biopolis, a major bio-medical research center, opens.
2004	Lee Hsien Loong becomes Singapore's third prime minister.
2005	Approval given to build two casinos as part of multi-billion dollar integrated resorts.
2006	General Elections held. PAP returned to power with 66.6% of eligible votes, winning 82 of the 84 seats in parliament.

Singapore Overview

Singapore's free market economy has enjoyed almost uninterrupted growth since independence in 1965. The city-state has one of the highest per capital GDPs in the world ($44,666) with standard of living comparable to North America and western Europe. A stable political climate, disciplined unions and non protectionist trade policy has enabled a well-educated labour force of 2,183,000 to generate a GDP of $194 billion in 2005, which is a rise of 6.4% on the previous year. This looked set to continue as early figures for 2006 already showed around a 9% rise over the same period in 2005. Singapore's currency is also strong, with Fitch, Moody's and S&P all giving it triple A ratings.

Per Capita GDP
1965 – $1,567
2005 – $44,666

The building blocks of post-independent Singapore's economy were trade, manufacturing, shipbuilding, ship repair and oil refining. Total trade exceeded $580 billion, of which exports accounted for $303 billion. Total manufacturing output for all sectors exceeds $190 billion. Singapore is the world's busiest container port by tonnage and its 10 refineries make it one of the largest oil-refining centres in Asia.

GDP (adjusted
to current
market prices)
1965 – $42,948,000
2005 – $194,359,800,000

As the economy matured and a more highly skilled workforce grew, financial and business services, telecommunications, electronics and professional services transformed Singapore into the regional centre of operations and a manufacturing base for over 7,000 multinational companies across a broad spectrum of industries.

Typical of all sectors in the 90s, manufacturing moved up the technological ladder with electronics commanding a 30% global share of hard disk drive output volumes. Tourism has become increasingly important and 2005 saw a record 8.9 million visitors bring in $10.8 billion in receipts.

Gross Domestic Product

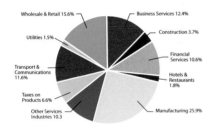

Wholesale & Retail 15.6%
Utilities 1.5%
Transport & Communications 11.6%
Taxes on Products 6.6%
Other Services Industries 10.3
Business Services 12.4%
Construction 3.7%
Financial Services 10.6%
Hotels & Restaurants 1.8%
Manufacturing 25.9%

In response to global competition, lower manufacturing costs in neighbouring countries and rising local wages, the government shifted the focus to higher value-added services catering to a global knowledge-based economy. The attention is on research and development, information technology, info-communication, e-business, media and digital entertainment, film-making and the arts. Life sciences, comprising pharmaceuticals, biotechnology and medical devices, are strategic to the next phase of economic growth. The telecommunications, financial services and power generation industries are in the process of liberalisation to encourage participation by foreign companies. The drive to be a regional arts hub was embodied in the opening of the $650 million Esplanade arts centre in 2002.

The government has never taken for granted its economic success, fully appreciating its vulnerability and dependence on regional and global events and this has resulted in a tightly managed economy.

Tourism

Tourism generated $10.8 billion in receipts from a record 8.94 million visitors in 2005, a 10% increase over the previous year. Plans are afoot by the government to triple spending on tourism to $2 billion and double the number of tourists to 17 million by 2015. Two groups are seen as key markets: the leisure and cruise group and MICE visitors (meetings, incentive travel, conventions and exhibitions). The top five visitor markets were Indonesia, China, Australia, Japan and India, which accounted for 50% of tourists. 36,300 rooms spread over 225 hotels in Singapore had an average occupancy of 84% in 2005.

The tourism industry is well developed and has won numerous international awards. In 2004, Singapore was voted Best Overseas City in Conde Nast Traveller UK's Readers' Travel

Awards, and in 2005 was awarded Top Convention City in Asia and Second Top Convention City in the World, by the International Congress and Convention Association. Singapore offers its visitors a cosmopolitan destination rich in cultural diversity and dynamic contrasts between old and new, east and west. In a single day, visitors can traverse seamlessly from heritage-protected ethnic enclaves to ultra-modern cityscapes, and shop for exotic handicrafts or Tiffany and Dior. Day and night the city-state offers a phenomenal array of local and international cuisines and dining experiences. Shopping is another reason people visit the city-state. Singapore Tourism Board works closely with retailers to create extraordinary shopping experiences for visitors (such as the annual Great Singapore Sale) who can be assured of variety, quality, competitive prices and honesty.

Singapore is a free port and duties for items going into Singapore are only charged for cars, gasoline, tobacco and alcohol. A goods and services tax is levied on all imported items but tourists are eligible for a GST refund when they leave the country. As a result, prices of popular retail items such as electronic products, cameras, cosmetics and perfumes are very competitive compared to many other countries. Shopping is still one of Singapore's main attractions for tourists.

Singapore Tourism Board is spearheading plans to make the city a venue for world-class events in entertainment, sports and the arts. After much public debate, the city will now have two casinos in the multi-billion dollar integrated resorts located at Sentosa and Marina Bayfront. Singapore is also being positioned as a destination for nature and themed attractions, lifestyle escapism and eco-adventure. Islands such as Bintan, Batam, the Southern Isles and Pulau Ubin are being developed accordingly. On the MICE front, Singapore is geared up to host mega events such as the International Olympic Council's 117th Session, where the host city for 2012 Olympics was decided; and the 2006 Annual Meetings of the Board of Governors of the IMF and the World Bank.

Key Singapore Projects

Two extensive projects are underway that will significantly change Singapore's commercial, residential, industrial and tourism landscape. The Marina Bay will be transformed into a new financial and business district, juxtaposed with residential and commercial properties, together with leisure, entertainment and cultural facilities. While Sentosa and the southern isles are being transformed into one of Asia's top family tourist destinations.

The Merlion

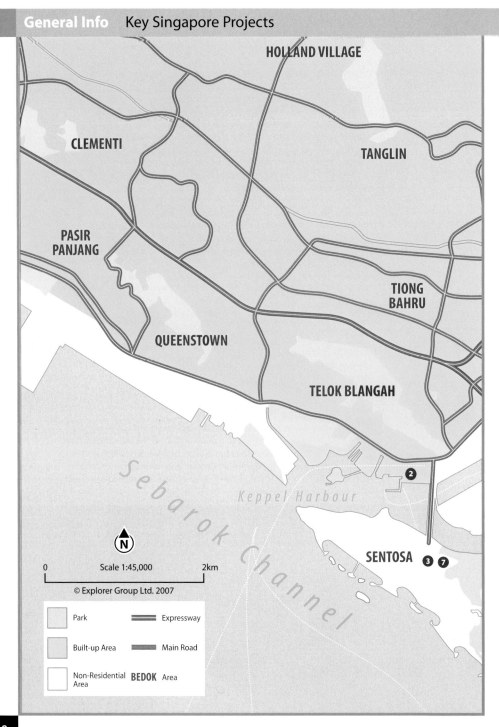

HOLLAND VILLAGE

CLEMENTI

TANGLIN

PASIR
PANJANG

TIONG
BAHRU

QUEENSTOWN

TELOK BLANGAH

2

Sebarok

Keppel Harbour

SENTOSA **3 7**

Channel

N

| 0 | Scale 1:45,000 | 2km |

© Explorer Group Ltd. 2007

	Park		Expressway
	Built-up Area		Main Road
	Non-Residential Area	**BEDOK**	Area

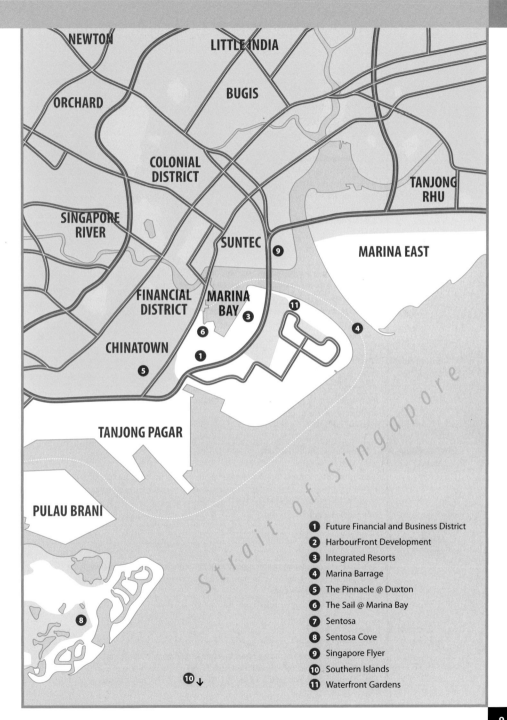

NEWTON

LITTLE INDIA

BUGIS

ORCHARD

COLONIAL
DISTRICT

TANJONG
RHU

SINGAPORE
RIVER

SUNTEC ⑨

MARINA EAST

FINANCIAL   MARINA
DISTRICT   BAY ③

CHINATOWN   ⑥

⑪

④

①

⑤

TANJONG PAGAR

PULAU BRANI

⑧

Strait of Singapore

① Future Financial and Business District
② HarbourFront Development
③ Integrated Resorts
④ Marina Barrage
⑤ The Pinnacle @ Duxton
⑥ The Sail @ Marina Bay
⑦ Sentosa
⑧ Sentosa Cove
⑨ Singapore Flyer
⑩ Southern Islands
⑪ Waterfront Gardens

⑩ ↓

Marina Bay ◀ *Map 17-D3*	## Future Financial and Business District *www.marina-bay.sg* The seamless extension of the existing commercial centre into Marina Bay is the centrepiece of the redevelopment of the present city area. It will host ultra-modern offices integrated with apartments, shops, entertainment and food outlets. **Completion** First phase – 2010
Telok Blangah ◀ *Map 16-F4*	## HarbourFront Development *www.sentosa.com.sg* This landmark development spans 24 hectares and lies at the foothills of Mount Faber along Singapore's southern waterfront overlooking Sentosa island. It will encompass cruise and ferry terminals, Singapore's only cableway system, and a multi-concept entertainment hub in a heritage building. **Completion** 2007
Marina Bay & ◀ **Sentosa Island** *Map 17-D3*	## Integrated Resorts *www.ura.gov.sg* There will be two Integrated Resorts (IRs), one at Marina Bay and the other on Sentosa Island, each a themed mega tourist destination. The plan is for the IRs to be iconic tourist destinations offering world-class entertainment and leisure facilities such as hotels, restaurants, retail outlets, theatres and themed attractions. The jewel in each of these super resorts will be a Las Vegas-styled casino. **Completion** 2009
Marina Bay ◀ *Map 17-F2*	## Marina Barrage *www.marina-bay.sg* A dam built across the Marina channel will turn Marina Bay into a reservoir providing a fresh water supply and a year-round stable water level for water-based activities, events and sports such as F1 powerboat racing. **Completion** 2007
Tanjong Pagar ◀ *Map 17-C3*	## The Pinnacle@Duxton *www.ura.gov.sg* Built by the Housing and Development Board, these will be the tallest public housing buildings in Singapore. Providing 1,800 new homes, they comprise seven 48 storey blocks linked by sky parks at the 26th storey and roof level. **Completion** 2007
Marina Bay ◀ *Map 17-D2*	## The Sail *www.thesail.com.sg* Two luxurious residential towers providing 1,111 units with spectacular waterfront views are set to be a new icon for the city. The 70 storey block will be among the world's 10 tallest residences. **Completion** 2009
Sentosa ◀ *Map 19-C2*	## Sentosa ▶ p.197 *www.sentosa.com.sg* This 500 hectare resort island is geared towards family-themed leisure and entertainment. It will be home to one of the Integrated Resorts and a casino. When completed, Sentosa expects more than eight million visitors a year and over $1 billion in revenue. **Completion** 2010

Sentosa◀
Map 19-E3

Sentosa Cove

www.sentosacove.com.sg

A unique development for Singapore, it offers a marina-oriented lifestyle encompassing upmarket residential bungalows and condominium living, quayside retail and a magnificent marina. The $4 billion Sentosa Cove will be home to Singapore's only oceanfront residences.

Completion 2008

Marina Bay◀
Map 17-E2

Singapore Flyer

www.stb.com.sg

Gracing Marina Bay, the 170m observation wheel will give a 45km unobstructed view stretching to Malaysia and Indonesia. 35m higher than the Millennium Wheel in London, this tourist attraction is expected to attract 2.5 million visitors in the first year.

Completion 2008

Map 1-D4◀

Southern Islands

The southern islands of Kusu, Lazarus, Seringat, Sisters and St. John's, lying one kilometre off Sentosa, are being developed to provide a broad range of high-end entertainment venues, theatres, exclusive restaurants, health spas, resorts, themed attractions and conference facilities. The islands cover 137 hectares.

Marina Bay◀
Map 17-E2

Waterfront Gardens

www.marina-bay.sg

Landscaped waterfront gardens spread across 90 hectares at Marina Bay will provide a green sanctuary for those living and working in the area, with thematic gardens and concert bowls.

Completion First phase – 2009

International Relations

When Singapore gained independence in 1965, the 581.5 square kilometre country had no illusions about its place in the region or the world. With nothing in terms of natural resources to offer, and surrounded by unfriendly neighbours, diplomacy was key to its survival. Copying Switzerland's model of neutrality and non-alignment, Singapore's stated foreign policy was 'we are friends with all those who wish to be friends with us'.

Diplomatic ties were readily established with countries from the USA to the then Soviet Union, Israel to Egypt. To this day, Singapore holds fast to this delicate balance of neutrality and is a member of the Non-Aligned Movement. Singapore was a founding member of the Association of Southeast Asian Nations (ASEAN) and Asia-Pacific Economic Cooperation (APEC). Relations with the USA and Europe are particularly warm and Singapore is a member of the Commonwealth and United Nations, where it served on the UN Security Council in 2001- 2002. An advocate of free trade, Singapore is a member of the World Tourism Organization (WTO).

There are 55 resident foreign embassies and high commissions, 39 foreign consular posts, eight international organisations in Singapore and over 60 accredited non-resident foreign ambassadors.

Relations with Malaysia

Since independence, Singapore's relationship with her nearest and most important neighbour has remained delicate, seeing highs and lows. Malaysia is Singapore's most important trade partner and the latter relies on Johore for its water and thus its survival. Both countries have had a history of rivalry and tiffs yet remain inextricably bound by cultural and family ties. Many Singaporeans and Malaysians have relatives in the others' country. This 'sibling rivalry' between the two countries remains, but with the benefit of over four decades of interaction with genuine efforts towards amicable relations.

Government & Politics

Singapore is a parliamentary republic based on a unitary state, with a number of similarities to the Westminster system in the UK, a legacy from its colonial past. It has a unicameral parliament with the president as head of state. A cabinet of ministers headed by the prime minister forms the government which answers to parliament. The cabinet collectively decides government policies. The head of state, appointed by cabinet, was a ceremonial role until 1991, when the constitution was amended to allow citizens to elect their head of state. While executive powers remain with the cabinet, the elected president has responsibilities to oversee the government's use of financial reserves and has veto powers over the budget and appointments to public office. President SR Nathan, the sixth president, was re-elected in 2005 to serve a second six-year term.

Each parliament has a term of five years, after which general elections are held. The constitution of Singapore is the supreme law and can be amended only by a two-thirds majority vote in parliament, which

Sir Stamford Raffles

comprises 84 elected members. Provision has been made to allow the appointment of six Non-Constituency Members of Parliament and up to nine Nominated Members of Parliament with limited voting rights (see 'NCMP & NMP' on the left).

General elections are held on a 'first past the post' system and represent either single-member constituencies (electoral divisions) or Group Representation Constituencies where political parties field a team of between three and six candidates spanning several previously single electoral divisions. Voting is compulsory for all citizens once they reach the legal voting age of 21.

The ruling People's Action Party has overwhelmingly dominated politics winning all the past ten elections. The incumbent prime minister, Lee Hsien Loong, took office in 2004, succeeding Goh Chok Tong whose predecessor Lee Kuan Yew held office for 31 years. Both remain in government with Goh as Senior Minister and Lee as Minister Mentor. PAP experienced it's lowest majority vote, 65%, in 1997. In the 2001 elections, PAP rebounded with a 75% majority taking 82 of the 84 seats. In 2005, there were nine appointed NMPs and one NCMP. General elections held in May 2006 saw the PAP returned to power with 66.6% of the vote, again taking 82 seats.

There are five major opposition political parties and another 12 minor parties that have contested past elections. The two opposition MPs are Chiam See Tong, MP for Potong Pasir since 1984 and leader of the Singapore Democratic Alliance, an alliance of four political parties, and Low Thia Khiang, who has been MP for Hougang since 1991 and leads the Worker's Party. In the 2006 elections, both received an increase in votes over previous elections.

The role of women in politics has traditionally been minor, though lately it is on the rise. In 1984, three female PAP candidates were elected to Parliament, its first ever women MPs. Women have been increasingly encouraged to participate in politics and in 2001 there were three women MPs and several female NMPs in parliament.

NCMP and NMP

Responding to the dearth of opposition MPs in parliament, the government introduced a scheme in 1984 to give voting rights, subject to a few exceptions, to a maximum of six unelected Non-Constituency Members of Parliament. NCMP seats are offered to the top opposition losers who obtained more than 15% of the votes in their constituencies, providing there are less than three opposition MPs. In 1990, a scheme was introduced to allow appointed Nominated Members of Parliament representation in parliament. The rationale was to enable non-partisan citizens an opportunity to debate policies and contribute to the country without the necessity of the electoral process. The quota is nine NMPs. NCMPs and NMPs can vote on all issues, except matters pertaining to:
- *amendment of the constitution*
- *public funds*
- *vote of no confidence in the government*
- *removal of the president*

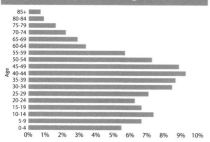

Singapore Population - Age Breakdown

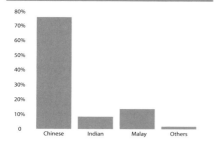

Singapore Population by Ethnic Origin

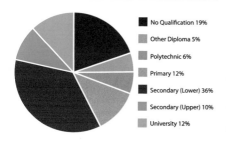

Education Levels

- No Qualification 19%
- Other Diploma 5%
- Polytechnic 6%
- Primary 12%
- Secondary (Lower) 36%
- Secondary (Upper) 10%
- University 12%

Population

The total population of Singapore, including residents and expats, was 4,351,400 in 2005, compared to 3,047,100 in 1990. The resident population was 3,553,500.

- The population density is 6,066 per square kilometre.
- Median age of population: 35.7 years.
- The growth rate is 1.4% and there were 988 males for every 1,000 females.
- The life expectancy is 77.4 years for males and 81.3 years for females.
- Approximately 43% have been married with a mean age at first marriage of 30.5 for men and 27.3 for women.
- 55% of residents have secondary or higher educational qualification. The literacy rate is 95%.

Detailed official statistics can be found at: http://www.singstat.gov.sg/keystats/people.html#demo

National Flag

Singapore acquired its flag in 1959 when it was accorded self-government. The flag has two horizontal halves, red above white. The red signifies universal brotherhood and equality, with the white symbolising purity and virtue. In the upper left corner, a white crescent moon and five white stars form a circle. The crescent moon denotes a young nation on the rise and the five stars represents democracy, peace, progress, justice and equality. The flag is treated with utmost respect by residents and there are strict laws against defiling it. During National Day, many buildings and residential flats can be seen proudly flying the flag.

Local Time

Singapore is eight hours ahead of UCT (Universal Coordinated Time – formerly known as GMT). The clocks remain constant throughout the year as no adjustments are made for daylight saving. The Time Zones table on the next page shows time differences between Singapore and various cities around the world (not allowing for any daylight savings hours in those cities).

Social & Business Hours

Singapore is moving towards a Monday to Friday week although about 50% of companies (the more traditional ones) still tend to work a half-day on Saturday mornings too. Sunday is the official day off for everyone, although this is not mandated by law or religious imperative. And because Sunday is the free day for Singaporeans, for whom eating and shopping are favourite leisure activities, many retail, hospitality and entertainment outlets remain open. For these businesses, Monday usually becomes their day off. Some organisations, including the civil service and public services, are open for a half day every Saturday, with employees taking turns to work alternate weekends.

13

Time Zones

Abu Dhabi	-4
Amsterdam	-7
Auckland	+5
Bandar Seri Begawan	0
Bangalore	-2.5
Bangkok	-1
Beijing	0
Canberra	+3
Hanoi	-1
Ho Chi Minh	-1
Hong Kong	0
Jakarta	-1
London	-8
Los Angeles	-16
Moscow	-5
Mumbai	-2.5
New York	-13
Paris	-7
Perth	0
Phnom Penh	-1
Riyadh	-5
Rome	-7
San Francisco	-16
Shanghai	0
Sydney	+3
Taipei	0
Tel Aviv	-6
Tokyo	+1
Wellington	+5

The official working day is eight hours with a one-hour lunch break, but working one or two hours overtime a day is commonplace. Government offices operate from 08:00 to 17:00 and private companies vary their start time between 08:00 and 09:00. Retail outlets, in particular the large department stores and supermarkets, usually open at 10:00 and close at 21:30. Banking hours differ slightly between banks and vary between opening at 08:30 to 09:30 and closing at 15:30 to 16:30. Office hours for embassies usually start between 08:30 and 09:30 and end at 16:30 or 17:30. Most have specific times for handling passport and visa matters, so check before going.

Food and beverage hours vary considerably between outlets with restaurants tending to close by 23:00 and bars closing between 24:00 and 04:00. Food is the ranking passion among Singaporeans and there is no lack of shops serving food 24 hours a day. Typically, most Chinese and Malay families have their evening meal around 19:00 or 19:30, whereas Indian families eat later at around 21:00.

Public Holidays

There are 10 public holidays a year, celebrating key religious events or new year festivals on the Chinese, Muslim, Hindu, Buddhist and Christian calendars, as well as Labour Day and National Day. Chinese New Year, Hari Raya Puasa (Aidilfitri), Hari Raya Haji, Vesak Day and Easter follow the lunar calendar and change accordingly each year. Nevertheless, these dates are fixed many months in advance. Some international schools also celebrate some of their own key days such as Thanksgiving.

Hari Raya Haji (Feast of the Sacrifice) is the new year for Muslims who follow a lunar calendar. Hari Raya Puasa (Aidilfitri) marks the end of Ramadan, a month of fasting and purification. Vesak Day commemorates the birth, enlightenment and death of Buddha. Deepavali (Festival of Lights) is celebrated by Hindus and symbolises the victory of good over evil.

If a public holiday falls on a Sunday, the following Monday becomes a holiday. Public holidays falling on a Friday or Monday afford a long weekend, which many residents use to make short trips to neighbouring countries – especially since budget airlines began offering low cost fares. The causeway linking Singapore and Malaysia is invariably packed with motor vehicles on such weekends.

Public Holidays

1 Jan	New Year's Day
6 Apr	Good Friday
1 May	Labour Day
31 May	Vesak Day
9 Aug	National Day
13 Oct	Hari Raya Puasa (Aidilfitri)
8 Nov	Deepavali (Diwali)
20 Dec	Hari Raya Haji
25 Dec	Chinese New Year
25 Dec	Christmas Day

Photography

Photography is hugely popular in Singapore and people are accustomed to the ubiquitous shutterbug capturing magic moments and favourite sights. You might encounter the odd coy person, but people seldom take offence at being photographed. Places forbidding photography will have signs indicating so. Generally, supermarkets, department stores and interiors of government buildings prohibit photography without permission.

Climate

Singapore has an equatorial climate characterised by little variation in temperature throughout the year, high humidity and plenty of rain Average daily temperatures vary between highs of 31-32°C and lows of 23-24°C, although it can get as hot as 36°C and as cool as 19°C. The mean relative humidity is 84%, though during heavy rain it frequently sits at 100%. The average annual rainfall is 2,300mm. Due to a rain shadow effect, the eastern side of the island is much drier and slightly hotter than the western side. There are two monsoon seasons. The north-east monsoon, known as the wet season, lasts from December to early March. It brings squally conditions with winds up to 20km/h and frequent heavy showers occurring mostly in the afternoons – though at times they can last for days at a stretch. The south-west monsoon from June to September is milder, usually bringing scattered showers at midday. Maximum rainfall occurs in December and April while February and July are the driest months.

The Fog

One of Singapore's major environmental concerns is the 'haze' caused by the illegal burning of forests in Indonesia. In 1997 and 1998, severe haze resulted in serious health problems and a huge drop in tourist numbers. The economic loss was estimated at $9.3 billion. The government was quick to respond and led regional initiatives to address the problem. Since then, the haze has never been as severe, but it remains a threat every year between June and September when the south-west monsoon blows across from Indonesia.

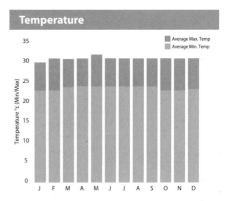

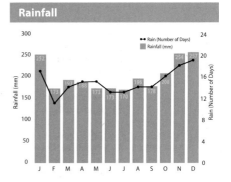

Due to the high temperatures, raincoats are seldom worn but everyone keeps an umbrella or two handy (they're good for protecting you against the sun on hot, sunny days too). Many buildings provide plastic bags to sheath your wet umbrella on entering. Rainfall can be so heavy it severely limits visibility for motorists; driving with the headlights on is highly recommended.

Flora & Fauna

A photograph in the Raffles Hotel depicts a tiger shot dead in its Bar & Billiards Room. In August 1902, tigers became extinct in Singapore – as have so many other species of fauna and flora in the course of the island's tranformation into an intensely urbanised city-state. There are virtually no natural habitats left to support wildlife, apart from 3,000 hectares of nature reserves. The 164 hectare Bukit Timah Nature Reserve is home to the only primary rainforest remaining, while the beautifully conserved Sungei Buloh Wetland Reserve, encompassing 130 hectares of mangrove swamps, is an internationally important site for migratory birds.

Fauna

Save for smaller species such as monkeys, macaques, flying lemurs, squirrels, snakes, bats, monitor lizards and the rare pangolin or anteater, Singapore has lost most of its fauna to urbanisation and deforestation. There are 85 known species of mammals. On rare occasions, usually in less populated and heavily vegetated parts of the island, the odd snake can be spotted, usually non-venomous grass snakes or pythons, although cobras too have been seen.

Flora

Little is left of Singapore's rainforests and what remains is mainly secondary re-growth regenerated from deforestation during the colonial period. There are some 500 hectares of mangrove wetlands scattered along the coast, most notably at the nature reserve of Sungei Buloh. There are 2,282 known species of plants in Singapore and the Botanic Gardens, an oasis of green near the city centre, is a pleasant place to see much of the island's indigenous flora.

Birds

There are over 142 resident bird species in Singapore. However, more than 180 species can be seen at Sungei Buloh Wetland Reserve where migratory birds from as far north as Japan come to feed and rest en route to Australia. Singapore's most common birds are the Javan mynah, house crow (often a nuisance), starling and bulbul.

Marine Life

Singapore's entire coast has been extensively modified through land reclamation, damming and construction. The ecology of the surrounding waters has been subjected to heavy shipping traffic and the silt churned out by land reclamation and regular dredging has literally smothered much of the coral to death. To enjoy what remains of Singapore's marine life a trip to the southern isles is more promising, as local divers have spotted turtles, nurse sharks, rays, barracudas and even pink dolphins, but don't hold your breath!

Saving Water
Where water is concerned, Singaporeans are hyper aware of the fact that they depend on another country for this life-sustaining commodity. Wherever possible, water is recycled. To avoid water wastage, all taps, other than those in a private residence, must automatically shut off.

Environmental Issues

Environmental issues rank high on the government's priorities because the island is tiny and densely populated (6,066 people per square kilometre) – so a little can harm a lot. There is keen awareness that environmental progress is sustainable only if matters are viewed from economic, social and health perspectives. Singapore's experiences show that environmental protection and economic growth are mutually supportive. The National Environment Agency, a major government body tasked to ensure a quality environment for Singapore, awards individuals and organisations for outstanding contributions to the protection of the environment. Over the next decade, NEA aims to have the population incorporate environmental protection practices into everyday life. For instance, recycling has become part of the household rubbish disposal process. Care of the environment takes place at numerous levels – from industrial waste management, emission controls and water recycling, down to littering; Singapore is renowned as being possibly the cleanest city in the world. To combat air-pollution, the government has strict vehicular exhaust emission controls; the sight of black fumes pouring out of a car, common in the 70s, has been completely eradicated. Furthermore, most cars use unleaded fuel.

There is a growing environmental consciousness among citizens evidenced by the initiatives taken by ad-hoc citizen groups and non-governmental organisations to protect the environment. The government also plays an active role in educating the public: the Green Labelling Scheme, for example, has been implemented to promote 'green' consumerism among the public and to encourage manufacturers to produce eco-friendly products. This growing awareness is also seen in the building industry where public recognition is accorded to 'intelligent' buildings designed to reduce electricity consumption by way of better insulation materials, automatic dimmers and similar innovations.

Culture

Singapore has succeeded wonderfully in creating a multi-cultural society with remarkable tolerance for racial and religious differences. In the 19th and early 20th centuries, the island was substantially populated by immigrants and ethnically, Singapore is inherently diverse; Chinese, Malays, Indians and Europeans have lived side by side for many generations. The race riots of the 60s spurred the government to inculcate a singular Singaporean identity, transcending race and religion: one is first and foremost a Singaporean, and then a Chinese, Indian, Christian or whatever. In the last 30 years, Singapore has actively solicited foreigners to work here and the city-state has become truly cosmopolitan.

The country's history has given it a unique culture. While 76% of residents are of Chinese origin, the primary medium of instruction is English. Singapore has a fundamentally Chinese culture; yet delving deeper you will detect a westernised and modern flavour. Television and cinema is overwhelmingly imported from the west. Over the past 30 years, a substantial number of Singaporeans have studied or worked in western countries; their impact on the consciousness of the Singaporean identity has, in some form or other, diluted the Chinese-ness of the culture.

There is no predominant religion and the separation of state from religion is enshrined by the constitution. The main religions practiced are Buddhism, Islam, Christianity, Hinduism and Taoism, and generations of close proximity between these has afforded an empathy towards other races. For example, when Chinese (who love pork) have a party that includes Muslim friends, the host may well have a pork dish on the table, but will ensure the pork never touches any utensil their Muslim friends may use. No offence is taken that pork is on the table: there is a fundamental understanding that each is different and a little adjustment is accordingly made. Singaporeans are generally easy-going and accommodating.

A common trait is the importance given to family, respect for elders, and priority of communal interests over the individual's. Though culturally tolerant, Singaporeans are relatively conservative and wary of 'western liberal attitudes', in particular regarding sex and self-expression. Characteristic of the culture is the concept of 'face', which, loosely translated, means personal dignity/respect. Be careful not to cause someone to 'lose face' – you may not be readily forgiven. While still a male-dominated society, institutionalised gender inequalities are uncommon. Women are highly respected and expect equality. The glass ceiling protecting traditionally male-only positions at multinational corporations and major organisations has been repeatedly breached. In marriage, it can no longer be said men are automatically the head of the household. Singapore's culture is hard to define as it is a unique amalgam of diverse ethnicities, east and west, ancient and modern, conservative yet open to a global influence.

Language

Other options **Language Schools** p.276, **Learning Mandarin** p.158

Singapore has four official languages : Malay, Chinese, English and Tamil. Malay is the national language but English is the unifying language between all the various ethnic groups. Only the elderly may

Singlish

Singlish is a colloquial pidgin-like form of English widely used among local residents. It's formulation is a combination of Chinese syntax literally translated into English and also mixed up with, more often than not, Hokkien (a Chinese dialect) and/or Malay words. For instance: 'Why you so like that?' (grammatically perfect if spoken in Mandarin) means 'Why are you behaving in such a manner?'

Singlish words are sometimes an admixture of Chinese and English; for instance the Hokkien word for sleep is 'koon' and you might find someone saying: 'Ah, you are kooning, eh' to mean, 'Ah, you are sleeping, eh?' Some Singlish words defy translation, such as the common favourite 'shiok' which loosely means 'really nice', 'what a great feeling', 'wonderful'. Other Singlish words are simply badly pronounced English words: a 'helicopter' is a Chinese educated person (educated > helicated > helicopter).

Most Singaporeans either can or do speak Singlish, and certainly all understand it. For a while its usage was very popular because it served as a cultural badge of identity; it is uniquely Singaporean. However, in recent years, a policy of minimising its use has taken place because widespread use has undermined the learning of standard English.

Mandarin for Beginners

Yes	shì [shir]	Toilet	cè suǒ [cher swore]
No	bú [boo]	Hello	nǐ hǎo [nee how]
Correct	duì [dway]	How are you?	nǐ hǎo [nee how]
Wrong	bú duì [boo dway]	Fine	hěn hǎo [hern how]
Please	qǐng [cheeng]	Good morning	zǎo ān [chao arn]
Sorry	duì bù qǐ [dway boo chee]	Good afternoon	wǔ ān [woo arn]
Thank you	xiè xiè [sieh sieh]	Good night	wǎn ān [warn arn]
You are welcome	bú kè qǐ [bu ker chee]	Goodbye	zài jiàn [chai chian]
Good	hǎo [how]		

Basic Mandarin

General	
Yes	duì
No	bú duì
Please	qǐng
Sorry	duì bù qǐ
Thank you	xiè xiè
You are welcome	bú kè qǐ
Good	hǎo
Toilet	cè suǒ
Greetings	
Hello	nǐ hǎo
How are you?	nǐ hǎo
Fine	hěn hǎo
Good morning	zǎo ān
Good afternoon	wǔ ān
Good night	wǎn ān
Goodbye	zài jiàn
Introduction	
My name is...	wǒ jiào
What is your name?	qǐng wèn níng guì xìng
Where are you from?	nǐ cóng nǎ lǐ lái
I am from...	wǒ cóng (country) lai
America	měi guó
England	yīng guó
Europe	ōu guó
India	yìn dù
Questions	
How much?	duō shǎo
Where?	nǎ lǐ
When?	hé shí
Which?	nǎ yī ge
Why?	wèi shěn me
What?	shén me
Who?	hé rén
Bachelor's Essentials	
You are beautiful	nǐ hěn piào liàng
I love you	wǒ ài nǐ
Do you love me?	nǐ ài wǒ ma
I will love you forever	wǒ huì yǒng yuǎn ài nǐ
Accidents	
Accident	shì gù
Police	jǐng fāng
Permit/Licence	zhúan zhèng
Insurance	bǎo xiǎn

Taxi / Car Related	
Stop	tíng
Right	yòu biān
Left	zuo biān
Straight ahead	zhí zǒu
North	běi
South	nán
East	dōng
West	xī
Turning	guǎi wān
First	dì yī
Second	qí cì
Road	mǎ lù
Traffic lights	hóng lǜ dēng
Close to	jiē jìn
Petrol station	yóu zhàn
Beach	hǎi tān
Airport	fēi jī chǎng
Hotel	lǔ gǔan
Bank	yín háng
Restaurant	càn gǔan
Slow down	fàng màn diǎn
Calendar Related	
Today	jīn rì
One day	yī tiān
Tomorrow	míng rì
One week	yī zhōu
Next week	xià gè xīng qī
Year	nián
Next year	lái nián
Date	rì qī
Numbers	
One	yī
Two	èr
Three	sān
Four	sì
Five	wǔ
Six	liù
Seven	qī
Eight	bā
Nine	jiǔ
Ten	shí
Hundred	bǎi
Thousand	qiān

18

Common Singlish Words:

Ang mor:	caucasian – literally, red hair (he got ang mor girlfriend)
Blur:	confused (don't ask him to drive, he very blur)
Batang:	man
Char bor:	girl
Kiasu:	someone who goes to extremes to make sure that they do not miss out on something. (he very kiasu)
-lah:	a common suffix (don't do that, lah)
Makan:	eat (let's makan)
Obiang:	off-beat as in taste (his clothes are so obiang)
Tackle:	to court a girl (he's trying to tackle her)
Talk cock:	talking nonsense (you talk cock, lah)

For an excellent Singlish dictionary, visit www.talkingcock.com and click on Dictionary.

not understand any English and pretty much everyone under 40 years old speaks some. Road signs and all signage are in English, while official public notices are either in English and Chinese or in all four official languages. English is the language of business and government administration and while it is the first language in most schools, bilingualism is compulsory; students must learn English and their mother tongue. Many Singaporeans speak English in public and their mother tongue at home. In 1979, the Speak Mandarin campaign was launched to create a unified Chinese language environment because most Chinese spoke in dialects, effectively different languages. Hanyu pinyin, the common system of romanisation of Mandarin, is adopted by Singapore. While not a simple representation of Mandarin in Roman type, learning the basics will allow you to get to grips with the sounds and be able to read it. And with over three quarters of the population speaking Mandarin as their mother tongue, it's always appreciated if you make the effort to communicate in the local language, even if it is only the basic pleasantries.

Religion

Chinese Names

The family name comes first followed by the given name, usually made up of two characters. Please note the given name has two characters but it is one name. Thus prime minister Lee Hsien Loong's surname (family name) is Lee. If you are on first name basis with him, you would call him Hsien Loong. If you are a close buddy (or terribly rude) you might call him Loong for short.

No dominant religion prevails in Singapore, and the many religions co-existing mirror the country's racial diversity. Singapore is officially secular and prohibits religious teachings in public schools. The main religions are Buddhism, Islam, Christianity, Hinduism and Taoism but there's also a small number of Sikhs and Jews. Of Singapore's 10 public holidays, six celebrate key religious events.

Major Religions	
Buddhism	42.5%
Islam	14.9%
Christianity	14.6%
Taoism	8.5%
Hinduism	4%
Other Religions	0.7%
No Religion	14.8%

The various religions co-mingle with remarkable harmony and many Singaporeans take pleasure in this cultural montage of religious influences. The rapport has been carefully nurtured over decades and the government is quick and unequivocal in its response to any activity threatening the concord. While the constitution provides for religious freedom, this right is restricted in some instances. The Jehovah's Witness and Unification Church are banned, the former because members refuse to perform National Service. Christmas is the most visible religious celebration because 'the season of giving' has been commercialised to the extent that festivities begin in early December to include Christians and non- Christians alike. Another occasion bringing the various races together is Hari Raya Puasa or Aidilfitri, celebrated at the end of Ramadan, the month-long fasting period for Muslims. Malays customarily invite friends home to feast together. Vesak Day, commemorating the birth, enlightenment and death of Buddha, is the most important day for Buddhists, who make up over 40% of the population. It's a relatively subdued affair with devotees going to a temple in the morning to chant sutras and make offerings; followed by the ritual of releasing of captured animals like birds, turtles and fish. Deepavali (Diwali) or the Festival of Lights celebrates the victory of

Places of Worship		
Central Sikh Temple	Toa Payoh	6299 3855
Kong Meng San Phor Kark See Monastery	Bishan	6458 4454
Maghain Aboth Synagogue	Colonial District	6337 2189
Novena Church	Novena	6255 2133
Sri Mariamman Temple	Chinatown	6223 4064
Sultan Mosque	Arab Street & Kampong Glam	6293 4405
Thian Hock Keng Temple	Chinatown	6423 4616
Wesley Methodist Church	Colonial District	6336 1433

good over evil and marks the new year for Indians. Serangoon Road, the main road passing through Little India, is decorated with lights, much like Orchard Road during Christmas. Families wake at 03:00 to take a traditional oil bath and light lamps, candles and incense in their home. For the business community, it's a time for settling debts. The opportunity to celebrate the religious event of a friend from a different faith is taken as an honour and reciprocated with great warmth and goodwill.

National Dress

For most part, the Singaporean dress code closely follows western attire. For men, trousers, shirt and tie are expected of working professionals, a jacket or suit for formal dress and a tuxedo for glitzy occasions. There are no

rules that women must wear skirts for any occasion; dress etiquette is very much North American and European in form and cosmopolitan in fashion. Guys, Singapore's women are very fashion conscious!

The Chinese, Malays and Indians have their own traditional costumes which are worn on formal occasions or on a daily basis by the older generation. The traditional Chinese dress for women is the cheongsam, a one-piece dress typified by a high collar, long skirt (or mid-calf) in silk, embroidered satin or other fabric. It's often tightly fitted with a high slit up the side. Very elegant and sensuous, it's a splendid alternative to the little black dress for special events where men would wear a suit or tuxedo.

Malay women have at least two traditional costumes. The baju kurung comprises a blouse worn over a long skirt or sarong. Female Malay office workers frequently wear this on Fridays as a sign of respect for the day, even if they wear modern clothing the rest of the week. Their other traditional dress is the figure-hugging sarong kebaya, made up of a tight blouse and skirt of fine batik wrapped around the body. It's the uniform of the Singapore Airlines stewardess. Men wear the baju melayu, a shirt worn over a sarong or trousers.

Southern Indian women wear the sari, a long strip of fabric wrapped around the body in various styles, most commonly around the waist with one end draped over the shoulder. Northern Indian women typically wear a shalwar kurta, a long blouse over loose trousers. Men wear the dhoti or the shalwar kurta for daily wear and for formal occasions, the achkan consisting of normal trousers worn with a collarless jacket often richly embroidered.

Reiterating the desire for a unified Singaporean identity, the government invented a national costume. This is simply a dress or sleeved shirt of no particular design as long as it features the Vanda Miss Joaquim orchid motif, but it is seldom seen.

Food & Drink

Other options **Eating Out** p.386

If there's one thing that can stop a Singaporean from going to live somewhere else, it's the local food! The easy access to such a stunning variety of food, day and night, and at reasonable prices is irresistible. A lot of people simply eat all their meals out because it's so convenient and affordable. Unless you live in a remote part of the island, you're likely to find something to eat within a 20 minute radius 24 hours a day.

Food is an obsession with Singaporeans, and people think nothing of travelling across the island for their favourite bowl of noodles. The most popular mealtime conversation is food; people will enthusiastically exchange discoveries of a new food outlet or a superior version of the dish they are eating. And much of the culture revolves around food; it's central to bonding, entertaining, recreation, the prelude to business and the conclusion to a deal. Singaporean cuisine essentially refers to food from the country's predominant ethnic groups, primarily Chinese, Malay and Indian. There's also Peranakan (or nonya) food, a unique cuisine that is the result of the marriage of Chinese and Malay culture. Chinese food can be sub-divided by dialect group; Szechuan, Cantonese and Hakka cuisine each have distinctive flair. The variety extends from fine dining (with dishes such as double-boiled shark's fin) to hawker fare at $3 a meal. Singaporeans' can't-live-without dishes tend to be the hawker food.

Eating Out

Cultural Norms
Eating is often a communal affair where several dishes are placed in the centre of the table and everyone shares from it. For casual meals at a restaurant or food court, the dishes are chosen by consensus. It's considered very good form to serve one another. It is usual to eat Malay and Indian food with fingers and not doing so is also perfectly acceptable. If you do, use the right hand only, unless left-handed. There is an elegant way to go about it – observe your host. Chilli is to Chinese cuisine what wine is to French cuisine. There's a matching chilli sauce for different foods; the variety is endless and a chilli sauce can make or break a dish!

There are three main types of places to eat out at: Singapore's famous hawker centres or food courts, coffee shops or restaurants. Hawker centres consist of anything from 20 to 100 individual stalls that collectively serve a wide variety of local favourites that cost about $3 per dish, each a meal on its own. Typically, the choice will range from Chinese, Malay and Indian to western grilled food. Food courts are the modern version of these centres, and can be found inside all the main shopping malls. Serving up economical meals in air-conditioned comfort, the food courts are popular with office workers at lunch time.

Kopi tiams, the vernacular for coffee shops, are small shophouses with a few individual stalls serving up similar dishes to what you find in the food courts. Restaurants come in all shapes and sizes and are totally cosmopolitan. Quality runs from mediocre to world class and you get everything from global franchises like McDonald's and Burger King to three star Michelin chefs whipping up magic.

Chinese restaurants are varied and many specialise along ethnic lines; Cantonese, Hokkien, Teochew and so on. The more popular international cuisines are American, French, Italian, Japanese, Mediterranean, Thai and Vietnamese but you'll find food from numerous nationalities available including African, Mexican, Mongolian, Nepalese and others. If it's food-related, Singaporeans are game to try anything; there's a perennial search for something new or exotic.

Malay food is also very popular among Chinese, but it doesn't offer anywhere near the variety of Chinese cuisine. Food consumed by Muslims must be halal, which means that the animal had to have been slaughtered in a particular manner. Muslims do not eat pork or food that has been in contact with it or any derivative such as lard. Lately, an increasing number of restaurants have begun offering halal Chinese food. Indian restaurants are sub-divided into northern and southern cuisine. Northern Indian food tends to use milder combination of spices and the curries are thicker. Southern Indians love their food hot and very spicy.

Vegetarians

With the vast choice of cuisine available, Singapore is a great place for vegetarians. Although many Chinese dishes have meat mixed in with the other ingredients, there's usually enough on the menu in most places for a good choice. There are also some dedicated vegetarian restaurants, including some that even serve mock meat! You can get anything from duck to a whole suckling pig, fairly close in taste and resemblance to the real thing, but made entirely of gluten. Many Hindus are vegetarian at least one day a week so you'll find a concentration of vegetarian restaurants in Little India. If you are invited to eat at home with local people and are vegetarian, it's not likely to be a problem as the range of cultures here has made Singaporeans very accommodating, but do inform your host beforehand.

Supermarkets

The majority of residents cook at home and buy their food either at 'wet' markets or at supermarkets. The wet markets offers fruit, vegetables, freshly slaughtered meats and fish at more or less the same price as for the supermarket. Supermarkets are very well stocked and one stop will get you pretty much everything you may want. Speciality supermarkets such Jason's and Tierney's target expats and stock familiar or hard-to-find foods.

Alcohol

Alcohol is readily available though a licence is required to sell or serve it. There are thousands of bars and pubs of all description; people love meeting over a drink. Because of taxes and high rental costs, drinks are expensive, averaging about $12 a standard drink. Most bars have happy hours where drinks are heavily discounted or sell at two-for-the-price-of-one. The minimum legal age for buying or drinking alcohol is 18 years old and Singapore is strict about not drinking and driving.

Local Beverages

For many locals, nothing beats a teh tarik or kopi o, drunk at a favourite kopi tiam (coffee shop). Teh is tea and tarik is to pull, a technique of pouring tea from one cup into another and 'pulling' it in order to aerate it. Kopi is coffee and 'o' means empty, as opposed to with milk. The type of tea and coffee used is a cheap grade but when mixed with condensed or evaporated milk it produces a cuppa that's hard to beat. A popular variation of tea, usually served at Malay drink stalls, is teh alia where fresh ginger juice is mixed with tea. Fresh fruit juices are very popular, cheap and available in most food courts. Pick the combination of fruit you want and it will be juiced on the spot. Local fruits like papaya, watermelon, sugar cane and pineapple are deliciously cooling on a hot day. Canned drink companies have produced a wide variety of local fruit flavours, carbonated and non-carbonated. Although dedicated Chinese tea drinking shops have not caught on, Chinese tea is invariably offered with Chinese food at restaurants. There is usually a house-pour, which will be served if you simply ask for tea. Bear in mind though, tea drinking is as intricate an art as wine drinking; with an equally overwhelming variety of teas to choose from. Thus, when you go into a fine-dining Chinese restaurant and the waiter asks if you'd like tea and you say 'Yes, please,' he will ask 'And what would that be?' in exactly the same way as if you were in a French restaurant and were asked if you wanted wine. In a Chinese restaurant just say 'poh lay char' (a common Chinese tea) and you'll save the day!

Top Nosh

There's eternal bickering about what Singapore's favourite local dishes are, but here's a list of the top 12 (in no particular order), to give you an idea of the real must-try dishes:

Char kway teow – fried flat noodles in sweet black sauce

Laksa – noodles in a spicy coconut gravy

Hokkien mee – fried noodles

Wanton mee – thin noodles with slices of pork and dumplings

Chicken rice – slices of steamed chicken with rice boiled in chicken stock

Chilli crabs – mud crabs in a thick spicy sauce

Chai tau kueh or 'carrot cake' – actually white carrot/radish fried with egg

Oh luak – oyster omelette

Mee pok – yellow noodles

Roti prata – Indian flatbread

Nasi padang – mixed Malay food

Satay – barbequed slices of meat on a skewer

Visas

Other options **Residence Visa** p.71, **Entry Visa** p.70

Nationalities Requiring a Visit Visa

Afghanistan, Algeria, Armenia, Azerbaijan, Bangladesh, Belarus, Egypt, Georgia, India, Iran, Iraq, Jordan, Kazakhstan, Kyrgyzstan, Lebanon, Libya, Moldova, Morocco, Myanmar, Pakistan, People's Republic of China, Russia, Saudi Arabia, Somalia, Sudan, Syria, Tajikistan, Tunisia, Turkmenistan, Ukraine, Uzbekistan, Yemen. Nationals of some countries may not require a visa if holding a diplomatic or official passport.

Visitors of many nationalities do not require a visa to enter Singapore, and will be given a visa (referred to as a social visit pass) for 30 days upon arrival by air or 14 days if they enter overland from Malaysia. These countries include Australia, Canada, Japan, New Zealand, most EU countries, Norway, South Africa, Switzerland and the USA. For a list of countries that do require either a business or social visit visa, see the column on the left. Visas for these nationalities cannot be obtained at any immigration checkpoint in Singapore, application and approval must be processed prior to arrival. If you are in any doubt, check with an embassy or a travel agent before travelling, or visit the website of the Singapore Immigration & Checkpoints Authority (app.ica.gov.sg) for further details.

Because of the discrepancy between visas issued at the airport and at the causeway, visitors sometimes get caught out and inadvertently overstay which can have very unpleasant consequences in Singapore. For example, if you fly in and get a 30 day pass and two days later drive across to Malaysia for a short trip your 30 day pass becomes void the moment you cross the causeway. When you return to Singapore (via the causeway) you will only have a 14 day pass. Check the date that is stamped in your passport to be on the safe side, as one of the punishments open to the authorities for overstay of visas is caning. Visitors can apply for a longer pass, say 90 days, and applications are considered on the merits of the case.

Visa Run

The social visit pass can be easily renewed by a quick trip across into Johore, Malaysia. People often combine it with a shopping trip or a seafood dinner, which is delicious and cheap. There is no guideline as to how many times you can renew: some people have managed 10 months of renewals, others a couple of times. You can also renew at the Immigration and Checkpoint Authority office; but for this you will require a local sponsor who is a citizen or permanent resident. The social visit pass is free, renewable subject to approval and must be done before it expires. Again, authorities are strict about overstaying and, depending on the charge, an offender may be fined, or jailed or even caned. So cover your ass and don't overstay your welcome!

Requirements for a Visit Visa

• *Valid passport with a minimum validity of six months*
• *Visa for Singapore (if applicable)*
• *Onward/return ticket*
• *Entry visa for next destination (if applicable)*
• *Sufficient funds to stay in Singapore*

Changi Airport

The total area of Changi Airport is 1,300 hectares of which 870 hectares consists of land reclaimed from the sea. There are two parallel runways, each 60m wide and 4,000m long. Terminal 1 covers 276,100 square metres and can handle 21 million passengers a year, while Terminal 2, covering 358,000 square metres, can handle 23 million. The airport can handle 18,000 bags per hour for departures and 10,000 bags per hour for arrivals. There are 114 aircraft parking bays.

Facilities and services are mind-boggling: 30,000 square metres are dedicated to over 160 duty-free shops and 50 eateries. You have everything from children's playgrounds to hair salons, manicures, spa and shower facilities, reflexology, massage, gym, free wireless broadband, supermarket, medical clinics, entertainment centre and more here.

Terminal 3, costing S$1.5 billion and planned to be operational in 2008, will add a capacity of 20 million passengers a year, giving Changi Airport a total capacity of 64 million passengers.

In March 2006, a Budget Terminal was opened to cater for the growing number of budget airlines. Comprising two single-storey buildings for departure and arrival, it's able to handle about 2.7 million passengers per year initially with scope for expansion should need arise (www.btsingapore.com).

E-tickets and Electronic Immigration Clearance

Most airlines use e-tickets and charge $35 to issue traditional printed tickets. Budget airlines only issue e-tickets. The Immigration Automated Clearance System uses an electronic access card to enable travellers to speedily clear immigration through automated lanes at these checkpoints: Changi Airport, Singapore Cruise Centre, Tanah Merah Ferry Terminal and the bus passenger halls at Woodlands and Tuas Checkpoints. Citizens, permanent residents and holders of an employment pass, work permit or dependant's pass are eligible.

Meet & Greet

Both terminals at Changi Airport provide meet and greet services. Staff can help passengers clear immigration and escort them through the airport. The normal service costs $10.50 and VIP service is $31.50; the difference being one member of staff attends to only one VIP. A surcharge applies outside the hours of 07:00 to 23:30. For reservations, call 6546 8168 for Terminal One and 6542 2848 for Terminal Two, at least three days in advance.

Customs

The government views customs offences very seriously. Customs officers will be polite and the whole process of clearing may appear cursory, but there are always eyes about, observing passengers. Some of Singapore's laws are very strict, and certain offences can result in corporal punishment or even the death penalty. Be particularly careful not to bring in any of the following prohibited items:

- Controlled drugs and psychotropic substances. (The sentence is the death penalty.)
- Liquors and cigarettes marked with the words 'Singapore duty not paid'.
- Chewing tobacco and imitation tobacco products
- Chewing gum
- Any imitation firearm including cigarette lighters in pistol or revolver shapes
- Endangered species of wildlife and their by-products
- Firecrackers
- Obscene articles and publications in any form
- Pirated software, DVDs and music CDs
- Seditious and treasonable materials

Food items such as poultry, seafood and beef may be brought in for personal consumption, up to a combined total limit of five kilograms after which an import permit is needed. A 'reasonable amount' of vegetables are permitted. Medicines that require a prescription under Singapore law, for example, sleeping pills and stimulants must be accompanied by a doctor's prescription.

The government is spearheading regional intellectual property initiatives and to set an example, enforces strict anti-piracy laws: do not bring in pirated software, videos, DVDs, music, books and the like. If caught, you're not likely to be let off with just a warning. There are no limits on the amount of currency you may bring in or out of Singapore.

Leaving Singapore

Checking in at the airport one and a half hours before your flight is usually sufficient; if you like cutting things fine, an hour is still ok. Immigration procedures are simple and straightforward. If you booked your ticket online, remember to bring the credit card you used. Most airlines don't require you to reconfirm your flights but it's always safer to check.

Going Home Alone

Unaccompanied children under 16 years old have to be escorted to and from the plane by ground staff. You will need to inform counter staff at check-in if your child is flying alone and some airlines charge a fee for the escort.

Meeting People is Easy

The layout of the arrival terminal makes it easy to meet someone. Numerous TV monitors provide flight arrival details including the baggage claim row. The glass panel separating you from arriving passengers allows you to spot them collecting their luggage. There are no porters, but trolleys are aplenty. Once out, it's a few meters to the taxi stand.

Duty-Free Allowances

Applies to persons over 18 years old and arriving from a country other than Malaysia.
• Spirits: 1 litre
• Wine or port: 1 litre
• Beer, stout or ale: 1 litre
There are no concessions on cigarettes and other tobacco products. Perfume is non-dutiable.

Fill Her Up

Singapore registered cars driving into Malaysia must have at least three-quarters of a tank of petrol when leaving Singapore. Depending on the luck of the draw, you will either get a customs officer who asks you to go back and fill up (which means rejoining the queue all over again), or you will be fined about $150 to $200, or both.

25

Electricity
The electricity supply is very reliable and comes in 220/240 volts, 50Hz using a square three pin plug, the same as the British system. Many electrical appliances now come with two pin plugs requiring adapters which are easily available at sundry shops. Many hotels will loan you a suitable adaptor or transformer for appliances with a different voltage, such as 110/20 volts, 60Hz.

In Emergency

All of Singapore's emergency services are very efficient and all phone receptionists speak English.

Police

Singapore's police pride themselves on being a force with a heart. They are polite, keen to assist, and sincere in their endeavour to care for and serve the public. However, it would be silly to mistake kindness for weakness; the police are accorded much power and they apply it without hesitation. Singapore's low crime rate is due in part to even petty crimes being taken seriously.

The police will not stand for any disrespect. At the same time, the government discourages rude, abusive or dishonest police. A cop would be deeply offended if you offered a bribe; it won't work and there'll be another charge to face!

There are two main police forces and their presence is a common sight. Typically, the general police force wears dark blue uniforms while the traffic police have blue and white uniforms. Both forces use white cars and motorbikes, in addition to some unmarked vehicles. Although armed violence is uncommon, all police carry side arms. For a crime-related emergency or road accident, call the police on 999.

Hospitals

Singapore's hospitals are excellent by world standards and are staffed by well-trained physicians using the very latest equipment. For urgent but non-life threatening cases, go directly to the accident & emergency ward of a hospital. Identification is required and payment by cash or credit card is expected immediately. US health insurance is generally not recognised. In this case, you will have to settle with cash and claim reimbursement from your insurance company. For emergencies and ambulances call 995, and you will be taken to the nearest general hospital in your area.

Post
Singapore's postal service is very efficient – post a letter to a local address before 17:00 and it usually arrives the next day. Postal rates for a 20gm letter are $0.22 for local mail, while international mail ranges between $0.60-1.00 and takes 7-12 days. To find out postage rates see www.singpost.com. Post boxes are common and often located at petrol stations.

The difference in cost for expats between private and government hospitals is relatively small so most people opt for private care. Foreign residents usually have medical insurance, and all hospitals will ask for this before treatment although in an emergency, they will treat the injury and stabilise the problem, and then talk money. If you have no applicable insurance cover, you will normally have to settle with cash. In cases where a patient cannot pay for the emergency treatment, costs may be waived. But if you can afford to pay, you will normally be required to do so. Any follow-up post emergency treatment will be provided according to what you can afford.

Car Accidents

If someone suffers injury, you must call the police (999) immediately as they'll want to inspect the accident site. They will also arrange an ambulance if required. If an insurance claim is intended, you need to personally file a police report within 24 hours. For vehicle breakdown services, see Recovery Services/Towing on p168.

Lost Property

If you lose something in a hotel, mall or department store, report it to the lost property department. If it was a handbag, chances are you'll get it back minus cash and mobile phone. If you think you left it behind in a shop, it's worth the trip back because staff will often hold it for you. All public transport and taxi companies have a lost property department. Taxi fare receipts include the taxi number for reference (for telephone numbers of taxi companies, see p.52). For enquiries about lost and found items on the MRT (subway or underground), call 1800 336 8900. If you drop something valuable on the street, report it at any police station or neighbourhood police post – there is a chance you'll get it back.

Telephone

Telephone

Telephone services are excellent and comparatively cheap. Public phones used to be found everywhere but are gradually declining because of high mobile phone ownership. They use either coins (10 cents per three minutes) or phone cards, which are available at all post offices and many convenience shops. Overseas calls can be made from these phones. Dial 001 for IDD access. Pre-paid phone cards are easily available. However, as an anti-terrorism measure, everyone must register their personal particulars to purchase this card.

Emergency Services

Alexandra Hospital	6472 2000	Public Hospitals
Changi General Hospital	6788 8833	Public Hospitals
Electricity Service	1800 778 8888	Emergency Services
Fire/Ambulance	995	Emergency Services
Gleneagles Hospital	6473 7222	Private Hospitals
Mount Elizabeth Hospital	6731 2218	Private Hospitals
Mt Alvernia Hospital	6347 6688	Private Hospitals
National University Hospital	6779 5555	Public Hospitals
Raffles Hospital	6311 1111	Private Hospitals
Samaritans of Singapore	1800 221 4444	General Services
Singapore General Hospital	6222 3322	Public Hospitals
Singapore Police Emergency	999	Emergency Services
STB 24 Hr Tourist Hotline	1800 736 2000	General Services
Tan Tock Seng Hospital	6256 6011	Public Hospitals
Thomson Medical Centre	6256 9494	Private Hospitals

For a suspected theft, file a report in person at a police station. Do not call 999 unless it's an emergency or for a serious crime such as burglary. If a mobile phone is lost or stolen, call your service provider to cancel the phone line or you'll end up paying for all calls made from it.

Lost Passport

For lost or stolen passports, you should make a police report immediately then go to your embassy or high commission to obtain the necessary travel documents. For a listing of embassies and high commissions, see p.28.

To avoid a great deal of hassle if your personal documents go missing, make sure you keep one photocopy with friends or family back home and one copy in a secure place, such as your hotel room safe, along with a note of any IDs you might need and telephone numbers for cancelling credit cards and mobile phones if they are from your home country.

Water

Tap water is very safe and most residents drink it. Bottled water is commonly available in shops and restaurants. Although Singapore imports over 50% of its water from Malaysia, it has avoided the need to ration water for over 30 years.

Health Requirements

The only vaccination certificate required for Singapore is if you have been in a country where yellow fever is endemic in the six days preceding arrival. For a list of Yellow Fever endemic countries go to: http://app.ica.gov.sg/travellers/entry /entry_requirements.asp

However, it is recommended that you get vaccinated against Hepatitis A and B, which are common in Singapore. While the island is malaria-free, this is not the case in Batam and Bintan, popular holiday destinations for residents. Also, a dengue fever epidemic recently hit Singapore and as there is no vaccine against this, beware of mosquitoes. Although SARS claimed over 30 lives in 2003, government agencies now have rigorous systems in place to prevent or manage any recurrence.

Travel Insurance

As everyone has to pay for all medical services in Singapore, it's essential for both visitors and residents to have health insurance. If you are going to work, chances are your employer will arrange it for you. But if you are just visiting, you should arrange cover with an international company in your home country before travelling. Most standard travel insurance policies do not cover 'extreme sports' such as motor sports or bungee jumping, so check carefully what the fine print says before signing up.

Female Visitors

Singapore is about as safe as it gets in the world for a woman to move around alone day or night. Most long-time residents don't think twice about going out alone and take this safety for granted. There is, however, no substitute for common sense. Avoid taking a short cut through a construction site at night or using unlit paths in deserted areas. If you are being harassed or threatened, scream for help; chances are someone will aid you by calling the police – almost everyone has a mobile phone. If you must take a taxi to a really remote destination, let the driver hear you telling someone the taxi's licence number (it's visible inside the cab) on your mobile phone. The penalties for sexual harassment and molestation act as successful deterrents. When entering a mosque, your arms and legs should be covered.

Travelling with Children

As well as being one of the safest cities in the world, Singapore is very family oriented and children receive tremendous attention and pampering. With 20% of the resident population under the age of 15, this city-state is geared for children. Restaurants will normally have a children's menu and baby chairs. Virtually all condominiums have a children's playground and swimming pools usually have a separate shallow pool for young children.

Sentosa Island, East Coast Park, West Coast Park, Pasir Ris Park and Singapore Zoo are fabulous places for children, offering themed amusement parks, water parks and plenty of child-friendly activities. Many families employ full-time maids so babysitting services are uncommon, but working couples can leave children in a daycare centre, of which there are many.

Embassies & Consulates

Name	Phone	Map
Australia	6836 4100	13-F4
Bangladesh	6255 0075	14-C3
Brunei Darussalam	6733 9055	13-E4
Cambodia	6341 9785	17-E1
Canada	6854 5900	17-B3
China	6418 0224	13-F3
Denmark	6355 5010	14-C3
France	6880 7800	13-E2
Germany	6533 6002	14-A4
India	6737 6777	17-B1
Indonesia	6737 7422	13-F4
Ireland	6238 7616	14-A4
Italy	6250 6022	14-C3
Japan	6235 8855	13-F3
Laos	6250 6044	14-C3
Malaysia	6235 0111	17-C1
Myanmar	6735 0209	13-F4
Netherlands	6737 1155	14-A4
New Zealand	6235 9966	14-B4
Norway	6220 7122	17-C2
Pakistan	6737 6988	14-A4
Philippines	6737 3977	13-F3
Russia	6235 1834	13-F3
South Africa	6339 3319	17-D1
South Korea	6256 1188	14-B3
Spain	6725 9220	17-C2
Sri Lanka	6254 4595	14-B3
Sweden	6415 9720	14-B4
Switzerland	6468 5788	6-D4
Thailand	6737 2158	14-A4
United Kingdom	6424 4270	13-F4
United States	6476 9100	13-F4
Vietnam	6462 5938	13-C3

Physically Challenged Visitors

Although progress has been made with regard to facilities for the physically challenged, there's still considerable room for improvement and growing awareness is prompting action to make life easier for people with special needs. Changi Airport is ahead of the game in these matters and no problems should be encountered here. The MaxiCab airport shuttle service (6456 4222) offers proper wheelchair facilities while Citycab Taxis (6552 2222) also cater for wheelchair users.

Elsewhere, all car parks have some spaces reserved, most major buildings have special toilet facilities and newly renovated food courts come with wheelchair friendly tables. Wheelchair ramps are becoming a standard feature of new buildings and some cinemas have special wheelchair lifts.

Accessible Attractions

CHIJMES p.185
How Par Villa p.228
Jurong Bird Park p.230
Most museums p.203
Night Safari p.230
Sentosa Island p.196
Singapore Cable Car p.226
Singapore Discovery Centre p.212
Singapore Science Centre p.212
Singapore Zoo p.231

28

International Calls

International direct dialling access code: 001 Standard trunk dialling access code for Malaysia: 02 There are many service providers offering cheap international calls using VOIP (voice over internet protocol). These companies will have their own specific IDD (international direct dialing) access code.

Before going to a hotel or restaurant, check if it has facilities for people with special requirements, because chances are most won't. For hotels with specially adapted facilities for the physically challenged, please refer to the table on p.33.

Dress

People are generally free to dress as they please and with the fairly constant temperatures all year round, seasonal wardrobes are not required. Singaporeans are very fashion conscious and closely follow North American and western European styles. Attire for work is formal and a 'corporate' look is necessary if you expect to be taken seriously.

In the evening, people take greater pains to dress up. Nightclubs and bars vary widely from anything-goes-so-long-as-you-drink-plenty to those with a 'no jeans' rule and requirements for 'smart casual wear' – trousers and a collared shirt. Fine-dining restaurants require men to wear trousers and, usually, a collared shirt. Some hotels refuse entry to men wearing shorts, vests or sandals. Cinemas can get uncomfortably cold, so take an extra layer.

When visiting a mosque or temple, it's expected of women not to expose their arms and legs. Topless sunbathing is forbidden anywhere in Singapore, even in the privacy of your garden if your neighbour can see you.

Dos and Don'ts

There are plenty of don'ts in Singapore – which is sometimes referred to as 'a fine city'. Yes, you can get fined for spitting, littering or using abusive language. Smoking is banned in all government buildings, air-conditioned restaurants, shopping malls, sports complexes, and at taxi stands and bus stops. On the other hand you can walk down the street with a can of beer in your hand. Contrary to popular belief, chewing gum is not prohibited, but bringing it into the country or selling it is.

Do not 'jaywalk' (cross a road within 50m of a pedestrian crossing or amble across anything other than a perpendicular path to the pavement). Vandalism, such as graffiti, may be considered a prank or misdemeanor in many countries; in Singapore it carries a mandatory three strokes of the cane and jail.

Do not be rude to the police – they are accustomed to being treated with respect. Then again, don't tolerate any impolite behaviour from them either; if you are ill-treated it is worth making a complaint as rude behaviour by any public servant is not tolerated by the government.

There is a sense among foreigners (who haven't lived here) that this 'fine city' might be uncomfortably uptight. On closer examination, most of these rules are about treating the country and its citizens with respect and having consideration for other people. For those who appreciate these values, Singapore may come as a refreshing breath of fresh air.

If you are contemplating consuming illegal drugs, you must be mad! Singapore has an absolutely zero tolerance policy – you will not get away with a warning, even if you are an expat. The courts have set a sentencing policy of at least six months to a year's imprisonment for first time drug users; recent cases indicate there are no mitigating factors. There is also legislation to convict someone who fails a drug test in Singapore,

Urban Myth

According to legend, if an expat got caught for something to do with drugs, they would be quietly allowed to leave Singapore within 24 hours. However, two recent drug busts in which several expats – some in senior management positions – were caught for possession and consumption of drugs proved that there's no basis for this myth. Whatever truth there may have been, it's now strictly historical.

Area Codes & Useful Numbers	
Billing Information (SingTel)	1688
Directory Enquiries	100
Fault Reporting	1608
International Call Assistance	104
M1 Customer Service (Mobile)	1627
Singapore Country Code	65
SingTel Customer Service	1609
SingTel Mobile General Hotline	1626
Speaking Clock	1711
StarHub Customer Care (Mobile)	1633
To dial a typical Singapore number from overseas	00 65 XXXX XXXX

even if they consumed the drugs in another country. Minors are sometimes prosecuted as adults for drug offences. Because the penalties are so severe, some people who've been arrested agree to be informers and turn in their friends. In addition, if you are found to be illegally importing controlled drugs such as heroin, marijuana or morphine into Singapore, the offence is punishable by death.

Crime & Safety

Other options **In Emergency** p.26

In an international quality of life survey, Singapore ranked second after Luxembourg, and alongside Helsinki, Zurich, Geneva and Bern in the personal safety category. Its crime rate is also one of the lowest in the world. While 2005 saw an increase in the overall crime rate, it was mostly as a result of minor crime like theft from homes, or of mobile phones and bags. It's silly to leave valuables unattended in public places, especially laptops. Travelling by public transport and taxis, however late at night, even if you are female and alone, is safe.

While not commonplace, women in bars and nightclubs have had their drinks spiked, so don't leave them unattended. A reliable way to start a fight is to stare at someone; men interpret it as an affront and the customary response is belligerence.

On the road, watch out for motorcyclists as they often don't follow road lanes and squeeze in between cars to overtake or get to the front of the traffic. Singaporeans are so accustomed to following explicit rules that when lane markings are absent (due to road works), they become befuddled and lane discipline breaks down.

Tourist Information

For tourist information, the Singapore Tourism Board (STB) is a great source of things to do and see in Singapore. Their main office is at 1, Orchard Spring Lane, just off Orchard Road (6736 6622), where staff will provide you with general information and brochures. Additional locations include Liang Court Shopping Centre, Suntec City Mall, at the Singapore Cruise Centre on the HarbourFront and booths at Changi Airport in the arrivals hall at both terminals. They also have a 24 hour tourist hotline (1800 736 2000), and their website is rich with information: www.visitsingapore.com.

For a list of errant retailers or to file a complaint against a retailer, call the hotline number. If you are looking for guided tours, try a travel agent (See Travel Agencies p.233) or ask the concierge of your hotel.

Singapore Tourist Info Abroad

The Singapore Tourism Board (STB) is also charged with promoting Singapore to overseas business travellers and tourists alike. Meetings, incentive travel, conventions and exhibitions are an important segment of the country's tourism business. Check out their website at: www.visitsingapore.com.

Singapore Tourism Offices Overseas

Australia	Sydney	(61-2) 9290 2888
Germany	Frankfurt	(49-69) 920 7700
Hong Kong SAR	Wanchai	(852) 2598 9290
India	Chennai	(91-44) 5213 9995
	Mumbai	(91-22) 2380 2202/03/06/07
	New Delhi	(91-11) 4168 3070/71/72
Indonesia	Jakarta	(62-21) 5799-2276
Japan	Tokyo	(81-3) 3593 3388
Korea	Seoul	(82-2) 399 5570
Malaysia	Johor Bahru	(60-7) 222 3355
	Kuala Lumpur	(60-3) 2142 7133
New Zealand	Auckland	(64-9) 262 3933
People's Republic of China	Beijing	(86-10) 5879 3388
Philippines	Manila	(632) 813 0946
Taiwan	Taipei	(886-2) 2718 5280
Thailand	Bangkok	(662) 630 4774
United Arab Emirates	Dubai	(971) 4 329 0898
United Kingdom	London	(44-20) 7437 0033
USA	New York	(1-212) 302 4861
Vietnam	Ho Chi Minh City	(84) 8 277 646

Esplanade – Theatres on the Bay

Riverside

Places to Stay

Singapore offers a whole spectrum of accommodation, with everything from deluxe hotels to backpacker lodges. The competition in the hotel industry, from one-star to five-star establishments, is intense and owners have to innovate and keep on their toes to survive. In the last few years, several boutique hotels have opened, offering cosy, luxurious accommodation in old, converted shophouses with personality as a primary selling point, underpinned by high services standards and modest prices.

Backpackers, once sneered at by mainstream hoteliers are now welcomed. Numerous guesthouses have sprung up to cater to this market and the standards generally leave little room for complaint. The serviced apartment sector is growing as new companies enter the market and as established ones expand. Some hotels are converting some of their existing rooms into serviced apartments.

Hotels

Other options **Main Hotels** p.34, **Weekend Break Hotels** p.234

Get Out Of Town

If the pace of living gets too much for you, Singapore has a multitude of options for easy getaways from the city, accessible by a quick boat trip or even by taxi! For more information on hotels on Sentosa Island and the Outer Islands see Resorts on p.41, Island Resorts on p.225 and Outer Islands on p.201.

Singapore has about 225 registered hotels, providing approximately 36,300 rooms, and average hotel occupancy hovers around 80%. The hotel industry is well monitored by the hotel association and the Singapore Tourism Board. There are about 30 internationally rated five-star hotels and these, along with the four-star hotels, are mostly concentrated in the prime Orchard Road entertainment belt and around the Raffles City/Marina Square civic and business district. There are only two hotels with beach access, Shangri-La's Rasa Sentosa Resort and The Sentosa, both on Sentosa Island. The average hotel room rate in Singapore is around $120 per night, relatively cheap compared to the equivalent in North America and Europe, yet service standards are as high, or higher. When the two multi-billion dollar Integrated Resorts open in 2009, the pressure on the upmarket hotels is going to intensify further.

Virtually all hotels offer, and in fact prefer, online reservations. Booking online saves you money and some hotels list two prices – normal and internet rates. Most hotels have booking arrangements with online hotel and travel portals and the rate you'll get through them is usually better than the price offered directly by the hotel online reservation system. A large number of Singapore's tourists are here for business and therefore all hotels have facilities for business, ranging from a desk in your room to secretarial services, meeting and conference rooms. Internet access goes without saying, most having broadband access and some offering wireless connectivity. A gym or fitness centre is pretty standard with some hotels going the full hog with an in-house spa. Swimming pools are common, varying only in the size and scale of the surrounding landscaping.

Hotels

Five Star	Phone	Website	Map
Conrad Centennial	6334 8888	http://conradhotels1.hilton.com	17-D1
Four Seasons Hotel	6831 7131	www.fourseasons.com/singapore	14-A4
Goodwood Park Hotel	6737 7411	www.goodwoodparkhotel.com	14-B4
Grand Copthorne Waterfront Hotel	6733 0880	www.grandcopthorne.com.sg	17-B1
Grand Hyatt Singapore	6738 1234	www.singapore.grand.hyatt.com	14-A4
Hilton Singapore	6737 2233	www.singapore.hilton.com	14-A4
Hotel InterContinental	6338 7600	www.ichotelsgroup.com	17-D1
M Hotel Singapore	6421 6120	www.m-hotel.com	17-C3
Marina Mandarin	6845 1000	www.marina-mandarin.com.sg	17-D1
Meritus Mandarin Singapore	6737 4411	www.mandarin-singapore.com	14-B4
Pan Pacific Hotel	6336 8111	www.panpacific.com	17-D1
Raffles Hotel	6337 1886	www.raffleshotel.com	17-D1
Raffles the Plaza	6339 7777	www.singapore-plaza.raffles.com	17-D1

Hotels

Five Star	Phone	Website	Map
Ritz-Carlton, Millenia	6337 8888	www.ritzcarlton.com	17-D1
Royal Plaza on Scotts	6737 7966	www.royalplaza.com.sg	14-A4
Scarlet Boutique Hotel	6511 3333	www.thescarlethotel.com	17-C2
Shangri-La Hotel	6737 3644	www.shangri-la.com	14-A3
Shangri-La's Rasa Sentosa Resort	6275 0100	www.shangri-la.com	19-A1
Sheraton Towers	6737 6888	www.sheratonsingapore.com	14-B3
Singapore Marriott Hotel	6735 5800	www.marriott.com/sindt	14-A4
Swissôtel Merchant Court	6337 2288	www.singapore-merchantcourt.swissotel.com	17-C2
Swissôtel The Stamford	6338 8585	www.singapore-stamford.swissotel.com	17-D1
The Fullerton Singapore	6733 8388	www.fullertonhotel.com	17-D2
The Oriental Mandarin Singapore	6338 0066	www.mandarinoriental.com/singapore	17-D1
The Regent	6733 8888	www.regenthotels.com	13-F4
The Sentosa Resort & Spa	6275 0331	www.thesentosa.com	19-C2
Traders Hotel Singapore	6738 2222	www.tradershotels.com	13-F4
Four Star			
Allson Hotel	6336 0811	www.allsonhotelsingapore.com	17-D1
Amara Hotel	6879 2555	http://singapore.amarahotels.com	17-C3
Berjaya Duxton Hotel Singapore	6227 7678	www.berjayaresorts.com	17-C3
Carlton Hotel	6338 8333	www.carlton.com.sg	17-D1
Changi Village Hotel	6379 7111	www.changivillage.com.sg	8-D3
Copthorne King's Hotel Singapore	6733 0011	www.millenniumhotels.com	17-B2
Copthorne Orchid Hotel	6415 6000	www.millenniumhotels.com	13-F2
The Elizabeth Singapore	6738 1188	www.theelizabeth.com.sg	14-B4
Furama RiverFront Hotel	6739 6405	www.riverfront.furama.com	17-C2
Gallery Hotel	6849 8686	www.galleryhotel.com.sg	17-B1
Grand Mercure Roxy Hotel	6344 8000	www.accorhotels-asia.com	15-D4
Grand Plaza Parkroyal	6336 3456	grandplaza.singapore.parkroyalhotels.com	17-C1
Hotel Phoenix	6737 8666	www.hotelphoenixsingapore.com	14-B4
Meritus Negara	6737 0811	www.meritus-negara.com.sg	14-A4
Novotel Clarke Quay ▶ p.43, p.391	6338 3333	www.accorhotels.com/asia	17-C1
Orchard Hotel	6734 7766	www.orchardhotel.com.sg	14-A4
Orchard Parade Hotel	6737 1133	www.orchardparade.com.sg	14-A4
Rendezvous Hotel	6336 0220	www.rendezvoushotels.com/singapore	17-C1
York Hotel	6737 0511	www.yorkhotel.com.sg	14-B4
Three Star			
Albert Court Hotel	6339 3939	www.albertcourt.com.sg	14-C4
Chinatown Hotel	6225 5166	www.chinatownhotel.com	17-B3
Harbour Ville Hotel	6271 2771	www.harbourvillehotel.com	17-A3
Oxford Hotel	6332 2222	www.oxfordhotel.com.sg	17-C1
River View Hotel	6732 9922	www.riverview.com.sg	17-B2
Robertson Quay Hotel	6735 3333	www.robertsonquayhotel.com.sg	17-B1
Royal Peacock Hotel	6223 3522	www.royalpeacockhotel.com	17-B2
Sijori Resort Sentosa	6271 2002	www.sijoriresort.com.sg	19-C2
Summer View Hotel	6338 1122	www.summerviewhotel.com.sg	14-C4
Two Star			
Dickson Court Hotel	6297 7811	www.dicksoncourthotel.com.sg	14-D4
Fragrance Hotel	6844 7888	www.fragrancehotel.com	15-D4
Hotel 81	6476 8181	www.hotel81.com.sg	15-A3
Hotel Bencoolen	6336 0822	www.hotelbencoolen.com	17-C1

33

Main Hotels

Albert Court Hotel

180 Albert St
Colonial District
🚇 **Little India**
Map 14 C4

6339 3939 | www.albertcourt.com.sg
This hotel was built on a heritage conservation plot and captures an era from the past with guestrooms that were once pre-war shophouses, outfitted with teakwood furniture and intricate Peranakan carvings. Facilities are modern and cosy meeting rooms present an ideal setting for business presentations. It's across the road from Little India and within walking distance of the Mustafa super mall.

Allson Hotel

101 Victoria St
Colonial District
🚇 **City Hall**
Map 17-D1

6336 0811 | www.allsonhotelsingapore.com
Conveniently located for shopping and entertainment attractions, this hotel is spacious with an oriental ambience. The 450 rooms are furnished with rosewood and Connolly's leather furniture to add a touch of extra comfort. Facilities include an outdoor swimming pool, gym and health centre with sauna, steambath, Jacuzzi and massage.

Amara Hotel

165 Tanjong Pagar Rd
Telok Blangah
🚇 **Tanjong Pagar**
Map 17-C3

6879 2555 | www.singapore.amarahotels.com
Balinese decor and soothing surroundings greet guests at this hotel situated in the business district. Amara's recently refurbished rooms have spacious bathrooms, high ceilings, broadband internet access and other modern amenities. There's a Balinese-style resort pool and fully-fledged spa. The hotel's Japanese, Thai, Vietnamese and Chinese restaurants are highly acclaimed.

Changi Village Hotel

1 Netheravon Rd
Chinatown
🚇 **Somerset**
Map 8-D3

6379 7111 | www.changivillage.com.sg
With its chic, contemporary interior and impressive landscaped gardens, this hotel is set far from the madding crowd, close to Changi beach and is a good option for both leisure and business guests. Modern rooms feature telephones with voicemail, a desk with internet and fax connection, and there's a rooftop pool and gym facilities.

Conrad Centennial

Two Temasek Blvd
Suntec
🚇 **City Hall**
Map 17-D1

6334 8888 | www.conradhotels1.hilton.com
Superlative luxury marks this award-winning hotel. The ambience is a stylish combination of Asian influences and contemporary chic, warm and elegant yet clearly designed for fast-paced corporate executives. The well-equipped fitness centre is open 24 hours and the landscaped swimming pool offers panoramic views of the city.

Copthorne Orchid Hotel

214 Dunearn Rd
Bukit Timah
🚇 *Newton*
Map 13-F2

6415 6000 | *www.millenniumhotels.com*
Located in an exclusive residential district, this hotel is ensconced in lush greenery. Resort-style in architecture, it is a retreat from the city's bustle, yet only five minutes by car to Orchard Road. Guests can enjoy a landscaped outdoor pool, a gym and a health centre offering massage and sauna services.

The Elizabeth Singapore

24 Mount Elizabeth
Orchard
🚇 *Orchard*
Map 14-B4

6738 1188 | *www.theelizabeth.com.sg*
The Elizabeth Hotel is situated close to Orchard Road and next door to major shopping centres. The neo-classical architecture speaks of grandeur and exclusivity. All 256 guestrooms and suites are beautifully furnished and there are both recreational and business facilities. Baby-sitting services also available.

Four Seasons Hotel

190 Orchard Blvd
Orchard
🚇 *Orchard*
Map 14-A4

6831 7131 | *www.fourseasons.com/singapore*
Beyond the exquisite luxury of the decor and comfort of the rooms, this hotel is defined by its exceptional and highly personalised 24 hour service. Innovative, but never at the expense of elegance and sophistication, the Four Seasons is also famed for its exclusive club with Singapore's only air-conditioned tennis courts. Facilities also include an outdoor lap pool with poolside whirlpool, saunas and steam rooms.

The Fullerton Singapore

1 Fullerton Square
Chinatown
🚇 *Raffles Place*
Map 17-D2

6733 8388 | *www.fullertonhotel.com*
Located on Singapore River in the heart of the civic district, this neo-classical building built in 1928, was formerly the General Post Office during the colonial era. Transformed into a deluxe hotel, the Fullerton is considered to be a six-star property, offering old world charm with ultra-modern amenities and exceptional service.

Golden Landmark Hotel

390 Victoria St
Arab Street &
Kampong Glam
🚇 *Bugis*
Map 14-D4

6297 2828 | *www.goldenlandmark.com.sg*
Close to the CBD and just a short walk away from the roadside eateries of Arab Street and Bugis Village, the Golden Landmark Hotel is a good choice for business travellers. It's close to Sim Lim Square, Parco Bugis Junction and an MRT station that puts you within reach of the rest of the city too. The hotel has an outdoor pool, a health club, an executive club lounge and conferencing facilities.

22 Scotts Rd
Orchard
◎ **Orchard**
Map 14-B4

Goodwood Park Hotel

6737 7411 | *www.goodwoodparkhotel.com*
This Preferred Heritage Hotel was built in 1900 in classical
European style, and as a historic Singapore landmark, it has
been designated a national monument. There are two
swimming pools, a cutting-edge fitness centre and spa
facilities. Its fine dining restaurants are long-time favourites
among local residents.

Havelock Rd
Riverside
◎ **Outram Park**
Map 17-B1

Grand Copthorne Waterfront Hotel

6733 0880 | *www.grandcopthorne.com.sg*
Situated next to Singapore River, this hotel has an elegant
resort-like ambience with river or city views. Geared for the
business traveller, it provides wireless connectivity,
meeting rooms, secretarial services and audio-visual
equipment. It also has a pool and outdoor Jacuzzi, health
and leisure facilities, award-winning restaurants and bars.

10 Scotts Rd
Orchard
◎ **Orchard**
Map 14-A4

Grand Hyatt Singapore

6738 1234 | *www.singapore.grand.hyatt.com*
Luxurious five-star hotel with superbly appointed rooms, a
fabulous array of facilities and exceptional F&B outlets
frequented by Singapore residents. Leisure facilities
include a pool, gym and health club, night golfing range,
and squash and tennis courts. BRIX nightclub offers live
entertainment and is very popular with single people.

581 Orchard Rd
Orchard
◎ **Orchard**
Map 14-A4

Hilton Singapore

6737 2233 | *www.singapore.hilton.com*
Located in the heart of Orchard – close to the shopping
malls – this 5 star hotel is popular with business executives,
for whom a buffet breakfast and use of the well-facilitated
gym, among other benefits, is included in the cost. There
are several fine dining options, including the Harbour Grill
and Oyster Bar, the Glow Juice Bar and Checkers Brasserie.
For a spot of jazz in the evening, try the Kaspia Bar.

80 Middle Rd
Colonial District
◎ **Bugis**
Map 17-D1

Hotel InterContinental

6338 7600 | *www.ichotelsgroup.com*
A landmark in the civic and cultural district of Bugis, this
hotel boasts a graceful, elegant and contemporary
Peranakan style, designed to create a city sanctuary with
modern amenities and excellent facilities, which include an
outdoor pool and a fitness centre with sauna. Voted as one
of the Top Seven 'Best Business Hotels in the World' by
Business Traveller, Asia Pacific in 2004.

36

100 Orchard Rd
Orchard
🚇 **Somerset**
Map 14-B4

Le Meridien Singapore

6733 8855 | www.lemeridien.com

A stay at Le Meridien Singapore places you right in the heart of Orchard and all its shopping centres, food and entertainment options. The hotel has 407 rooms each with high-speed internet access and a wide selection of cable channels. Facilities include a fitness centre, business centre (for a fee), an outdoor swimming pool and 11 conference halls. Access to public transport is easy.

81 Anson Rd
CBD
🚇 **Tanjong Pagar**
Map 17-C3

M Hotel Singapore

6421 6120 | www.m-hotel.com

Function with luxury best describes this hotel, which is located in the centre of the business district within walking distance of the major commercial, financial and government offices. Rooms are equipped with executive desks, 21 inch TVs, wireless keyboards, a leather chair and the business centre offers professional secretarial services. Leisure facilities include a gym and a swimming pool.

6 Raffles Blvd
Marina Bay
🚇 **City Hall**
Map 17-D1

Marina Mandarin

6845 1000 | www.marina-mandarin.com.sg

The Marina Mandarin has a long-standing reputation for excellence, as a result of their philosophy of providing elegance and efficiency together with a high level of service and customer care. For recreation, there's a 25m mineral water pool, a 24 hour fitness centre and the new upmarket St Gregory Spa.

333 Orchard Rd
Orchard
🚇 **Somerset**
Map 14-B4

Meritus Mandarin Singapore

6737 4411 | www.mandarin-singapore.com

Voted one of *Condé Nast Traveller*'s Gold List Hotels in 2005, this five-star hotel is geared towards meeting the business traveller's every whim. Its location on Orchard Road puts it in easy proximity to shops, restaurants and entertainment, but with all its own facilities, you may not want to leave the hotel. It has a gymnasium, squash courts, a pool, a host of award-winning restaurants and, full business facilities.

442 Orchard Rd
Orchard
🚇 **Orchard**
Map 14-A4

Orchard Hotel

6734 7766 | www.orchardhotel.com.sg

This medium size hotel is cosmopolitan in design, with 670 rooms, and is well situated on a popular part of Orchard Road. It has an excellent Cantonese restaurant, Hua Ting, and there's a poolside where you can enjoy snacks and cocktails.

1 Tanglin Rd
Orchard
🚇 **Orchard**
Map 14-A4

Orchard Parade Hotel

6737 1133 | www.orchardparade.com.sg
Another hotel for those with shopping on their minds, the Orchard Parade is located – as the name might suggest – in the middle of the shopping district. The Mediterranean-styled hotel offers quiet hospitality as well as services and facilities including a hair, nail and body care salon and a range of restaurants. You can also chill out at the Lobby Bar or burn off any extra energy at the pool.

5 Raffles Ave
Marina Bay
🚇 **City Hall**
Map 17-D1

The Oriental Mandarin Singapore

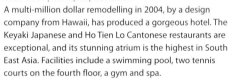

6338 0066 | www.mandarinoriental.com/singapore
Accentuating the luxurious comfort synonymous with the Oriental are some of the best views of the city skyline and the harbour. The facilities reflect the hotel's philosophy; to pamper guests with superlative service – which saw it voted in the top three 'Best Overseas Business Hotels' for 2005 by *Condé Nast Traveller*. There is a magnificent 25m outdoor pool set in lush verdant gardens and a Fitness & Yoga Studio.

7 Raffles Blvd
Marina Square
Marina Bay
🚇 **City Hall**
Map 17-D1

Pan Pacific Hotel

6336 8111 | www.panpacific.com
A multi-million dollar remodelling in 2004, by a design company from Hawaii, has produced a gorgeous hotel. The Keyaki Japanese and Ho Tien Lo Cantonese restaurants are exceptional, and its stunning atrium is the highest in South East Asia. Facilities include a swimming pool, two tennis courts on the fourth floor, a gym and spa.

Beach Rd
Colonial District
🚇 **City Hall**
Map 17-D1

Raffles Hotel

6337 1886 | www.raffleshotel.com
Established in 1887, the Raffles Hotel is the legendary crown jewel in Singapore's hotel industry. Originally a sprawling colonial bungalow, it has retained the inimitable style of that era, and suites come with high ceilings, elegant period furnishings, oriental carpets and marble floors. It is home to the luxurious Amrita Spa and 14 food and beverage outlets. For more on the hotel, see p.210 in Exploring.

80 Bras Basah Rd
Colonial District
🚇 **City Hall**
Map 17-D1

Raffles the Plaza

6339 7777 | www.singapore-plaza.raffles.com
Voted in the 'Top 50 Asia Hotels' and 'Top 100 in the World' in the Condé Nast Traveler Readers' Choice Awards 2005', this hotel has long been associated with sophistication, intimacy and elegance. It is situated at the crossroads of Singapore's business, cultural, entertainment and shopping districts. There are 17 distinctive restaurants and bars, and Amrita Spa – one of the finest spa facilities in Asia.

1 Cuscaden Rd
Orchard
🚇 **Orchard**
Map 13-F4

The Regent

6733 8888 | *www.regenthotels.com*

Subtle, elegant and sophisticated, the Regent offers a different class of luxury from the usual five-star hotel. The warm and refined Asian theme follows through into the opulent rooms and suites with private balconies. The F&B outlets are creative and exceptional. The Bar was voted one of the 'World's Best Bars' by *Newsweek*. Facilities include private offices, translation services, a pool and a spa.

7 Raffles Ave
Marina Bay
🚇 **City Hall**
Map 17-D1

Ritz-Carlton, Millenia

6337 8888 | *www.ritzcarlton.com*

Quiet sophistication, ultra modern facilities and the most impeccable and personalised service make this deluxe hotel a favourite with discerning business travellers and Singapore residents alike. Surrounded by seven acres of gardens, the hotel is only a few minutes from the commercial and entertainment district. Recreation facilities include a swimming pool, whirlpool, spa and sauna.

25 Scotts Rd
Orchard
🚇 **Orchard**
Map 14-A4

Royal Plaza on Scotts

6737 7966 | *www.royalplaza.com.sg*

Innovative excellence distinguishes this hotel. You will be escorted to a beautifully appointed room within a minute of your arrival – no need to check in at reception. And it's the only hotel in Singapore to provide a free mini-bar in all rooms. Guests enjoy special discounts at the DFS (Duty Free Shopping) Galleria adjacent to the hotel. Facilities include a pool, gym and sauna, and a fully-equipped business centre.

33 Erskine Rd
Chinatown
🚇 **Chinatown**
Map 17-C2

Scarlet Boutique Hotel

6511 3333 | *www.thescarlethotel.com*

Sensual, daring, funky and highly individualistic, this small boutique hotel offers five-star quality and style. It was listed on *Condé Nast Traveller UK* 2005 Hot List for 'Best New Hotels in the World' and on the *DestinAsia* 2005 Luxe List. Facilities include an outdoor Jacuzzi, gym and business centre. Mostly, the action is left for you to create in the indulgently sexy bedrooms.

22 Orange Grove Rd
Orchard
🚇 **Orchard**
Map 14-A3

Shangri-La Hotel

6737 3644 | *www.shangri-la.com/singapore*

The name Shangri-La is synonymous with paradise and grandeur, and this hotel, one of the world's most renowned, lives up to the hype. The extensive landscaped gardens, complete with waterfalls and exotic pools, have won numerous awards and the hotel's service sets the bar for the rest of the industry; as do its food and beverage outlets. Facilities include a fitness centre, pools, Jacuzzi, and a sauna.

39

39 Scotts Rd
Newton
🚇 **Newton**
Map 14-B3

Sheraton Towers

6737 6888 | www.sheratonsingapore.com
A deluxe hotel that has won many awards for its service, including awards from *Condé Nast Traveller* and *Travel & Leisure* magazines. The hallmark of the hotel is its residential charm combined with the modern facilities demanded by corporate hi-flyers, and all guests enjoy personalised butler service. Its Chinese and Italian restaurant are famous. Facilities include a gym, sauna and swimming pool.

320 Orchard Rd
Orchard
🚇 **Orchard**
Map 14-A4

Singapore Marriott Hotel

6735 5800 | www.marriott.com/sindt
Renowned for its warm hospitality and efficiency, the Marriott commands a spectacular view of the city. Situated in the busiest part of Orchard, it is ideally placed for both leisure and business travellers. Facilities include excellent meeting rooms and amenities, an outdoor pool, a spa aptly named The Retreat, and the alfresco Crossroads Cafe – a favourite hangout among locals for people watching.

Clarke Quay
Riverside
🚇 **Clarke Quay**
Map 17-C2

Swissôtel Merchant Court

6337 2288 | www.singapore-merchantcourt.swissotel.com
Situated on the Singapore River next to the pubs, restaurants and nightclubs of Clarke and Boat Quay, this hotel stands out for its convenience, efficiency and comfort. There's a free-form pool and gym for recreation. However, the real gem is the exceptional Amrita Spa, which offers a full array of services.

2 Stamford Rd
Colonial District
🚇 **City Hall**
Map 17-D1

Swissôtel The Stamford

6338 8585 | www.singapore-stamford.swissotel.com
Right in the centre of the CBD, this hotel, (previously the world's tallest), is located in Raffles City Shopping Complex. You have a choice of 16 restaurants and lounges, many of them exceptional. The business and meeting facilities range from the executive conference centre to the award-winning Raffles City convention centre, all under one roof. Facilities include two pools, six tennis courts and a spa.

1A Cuscaden Rd
Orchard
🚇 **Orchard**
Map 13-F4

Traders Hotel Singapore

6738 2222 | www.tradershotels.com
Just around the corner from Orchard Road and within walking distance of Singapore's famed Botanic Gardens, Traders Hotel has 546 superbly-furnished guestrooms, tastefully decorated and equipped with modern amenities. Facilities include a business centre, an outdoor pool and there is a link to the mall next door, which offers various shops and boutiques, small restaurants and a food court.

21 Mount Elizabeth
Orchard
🚇 *Orchard*
Map 14-B4

York Hotel

6737 0511 | *www.yorkhotel.com.sg*

The York Hotel is a quiet haven away from the city bustle. It's located just minutes away from the buzzing Orchard Road, but when guests walk in, they're surrounded by tranquility, comfort and personalised service. An outdoor swimming pool, Jacuzzi and fitness centre provide further ways to relax.

Resorts

Other options **Island Resorts** p.225

Singapore doesn't really have any truly themed resorts such as an eco-tourist or mountain resort. Two multi-billion dollar Las Vegas-styled integrated resorts have been approved for development and the focus will be on entertainment. See Integrated Resorts on p.435.

Pulau Ubin
🚇 *Punggol*
Map 8-B2

Marina Country Club Ubin Resort

6388 8388 | *www.marinacountryclub.com.sg*

Rustic like the rest of the island, Ubin Resort is suited for those who want action, action, action rather than creature comforts. Chalets are air-conditioned and have comfortable beds, but few frills. The Sports, Leisure & Recreation Centre offers kayaking, rock climbing, archery, flying fox, abseiling, Leap of Faith, guided trekking and canoeing.

2 Bukit Manis Rd
Sentosa
🚇 *HarbourFront*
Map 19-C2

The Sentosa Resort & Spa

6275 0331 | *www.thesentosa.com*

A putt away from the beach, surrounded by tropical woodlands, The Sentosa is a deluxe beach resort offering serenity, tranquility and recreation. The Spa Botanica is an award-winning tropical spa set to pamper and indulge your senses. As well as access to two of Asia's best golf courses at Sentosa Golf Club, there are tennis courts, an indoor gym, volleyball and pétanque.

101 Siloso Rd
Sentosa
🚇 *HarbourFront*
Map 19-A1

Shangri-La's Rasa Sentosa Resort

6275 0100 | *www.shangri-la.com*

Situated on the beautiful, sandy white shores of Sentosa Island, this is Singapore's only beach front hotel. It has deluxe facilities including a superb pool area, a luxurious health spa as well as a range of restaurants and bars. Part of the famous Shangri-La group, it is just 10 minutes from the business district, yet in a world of its own.

Serviced Apartments

Serviced apartments can be a more affordable alternative to a hotel room; convenience without the commitment of a long-term lease. They can be rented on a daily, weekly, monthly and even yearly basis and save you the hassle of utility connections, furnishings and domestic chores. The serviced apartment industry is currently expanding and most developments are new and of a similar quality to four or five-star hotels. Laundry, housekeeping and concierge are usual services offered, the more luxurious ones have a gym, spa and swimming pool.

Serviced Apartments			
Ascott Singapore	Orchard	6735 6868	www.the-ascott.com
Cairnhill Towers	Orchard	6839 1233	www.fareastsvcapts.com.sg
Central Place	Hougang	6881 7520	www.fareastsvcapts.com.sg
Fraser Place	Riverside	6270 0800	www.fraserhospitality.com
Great World Serviced Apts	River Valley Rd	6722 7000	www.greatworld.com.sg
Lanson Place	Orchard	6834 0880	www.lansonplace.com
Leonie View	Orchard	6839 1233	www.fareastsvcapts.com.sg
Lotus at Jervois	Tanglin	6838 7489	www.lotus-sanctuary.com.sg
Orchard Parksuites	Orchard	6839 1233	www.fareastsvcapts.com.sg
Park Avenue Suites	River Valley Rd	6732 8200	www.parkavenuesuites.com
Shangri-La Apartments	Orchard	6213 4635	www.shangri-la.com
Somerset Bencoolen	Colonial District	6849 4688	www.somersetbencoolen.com
Somerset Liang Court	Riverside	6337 0111	www.somersetliangcourt.com
Treetops Executive Residences	Orchard	6233 7336	www.treetops.com.sg
Wilby Bukit Timah	Bukit Timah	6233 7336	www.wilby.com.sg

Hostels

In the last few years the increase in budget travel, along with the realisation of the economic potential afforded by backpackers, has created a niche of hostels and guesthouses catering for this market. They provide just the essentials: clean accommodation, decent service, security and internet access. Most are independently-run single establishments, though a few chains are beginning to emerge, most notably the Hotel 81 chain that even offers two or four-hour rentals.

Backpacking

For a long time backpackers were viewed as terribly downmarket and overlooked by the hotel industry proper; accommodation was in dingy dormitories hidden from the public eye. After the deep recession of the late 90s though, hungry entrepreneurs spotted the growing market of backpackers and numerous little hostels sprouted up to tap into this source of revenue. With competition came better service and facilities – backpackers are welcome! Standards you can expect are clean rooms with air con, a communal lounge, internet access, and a communal kitchen with coffee and tea readily available. Food is cheap everywhere on the island; there is lots to see and do and it needn't cost much more than your bus fare.

Hostels				
Name	Area	Phone	Website	Map
Betel Box Backpacker Hostel	Geylang	6247 7340	www.betelbox.com	15-C3
Dickson Court Hotel	Little India	6297 7811	www.dicksoncourthotel.com.sg	14-D4
Fern Loft Backpacker Hostel	Various locations	6449 9066	www.fernloft.com	–
Fragrance Hotel	Geylang	6844 7888	www.fragrancehotel.com	15-D4
The Hive	Little India	6341 5041	www.thehivebackpackers.com	14-D3
Hotel 81	Various locations	6476 8181	www.hotel81.com.sg	–
The Inn at Temple Street	Chinatown	6221 5333	www.theinn.com.sg	17-C2
InnCrowd Backpackers Hostel	Little India	6296 9169	www.the-inncrowd.com	14-C4
New 7th Storey Hotel	Colonial District	6337 0251	www.nsshotel.com	17-D1
PBG Backpacker Hostel	Tiong Bahru	6271 3296	www.bootsnall.com	17-A2
Perak Lodge	Little India	6299 7733	www.peraklodge.net	14-D4
Sleepy Sam's Bed & Breakfast	Arab Street & Kampong Glam	9277 4988	www.sleepysams.com	14-D4
YMCA	Orchard	6336 6000	www.ymcaih.com.sg	17-C1

from

S$190+++

The new face of Clarke Quay

For that ultimate experience in the vibrant entertainment hub of Clarke Quay, the newly renovated Novotel Clarke Quay is the perfect place to stay. Packages start from S$190+++.

Discover our sleek modern facilities.

Novotel Clarke Quay, Singapore
177A River Valley Road, Singapore Tel: (65) 6 338 3333 Fax: (65) 6339 2854
Email: info@novotelclarkequay.com.sg website: www.novotel.com/asia

Accor operates over 70 Novotel Hotels & Resorts in Asia Pacific

For reservation and information, contact Accor reservation services in Indonesia 0807 1 777 777 or Thailand (02) 237 6064. Or toll Free in China 800 830 2688, Hong Kong 800 93 8768, Japan 00531 61 6353, Singapore 800 6161 367, Malaysia 1800 802 578 and South Korea 0079 8611 1288. If calling from countries other than those listed please phone (61-2) 8584 8666 or e-mail: accorres.bkk@accor.com

NOVOTEL
ACCOR hotels

► **A new perspective on our Hotels and Services**

Campsites

Other options **Camping** p.250

Campers have a choice of five parks on the mainland where overnight camping is permitted, all located on or close to the beach. As a form of backpacker's accommodation, camping is discouraged, with the parks being promoted more for overnight trips and a modest form of getting away from the urban jungle. On weekends, no permit is necessary, but weekday camping is allowed only in designated areas of these parks and a permit is required, issued daily and on the spot by park rangers patrolling the area (some form of personal identification is needed). Campers are only allowed to stay a maximum of three consecutive week nights.

Campsites		
Changi Beach Park	Changi	8-E4
East Coast Park	East Coast	18-C1
Pasir Ris Park	Pasir Ris	8-B4
Sembawang Park	Sembawang	4-D2
West Coast Park	Pasir Panjang	10-C3

Facilities for camping are limited: barbecue pits (which you need to book separately), toilets and showers. For washing, you need to bring your own water or use water from the toilet/showers.

For more information and enquiries about camping in these parks you can either call the National Parks Board (1800 471 7300), who manage all Singapore's parks, or check out their website which has all the information you'll need to know before you go; www.nparks.gov.sg. Barbeque pits can only be booked via AXS machines located in many places: see www.axs.com.sg.

The camping policy on Pulau Ubin (map 8-C2), an isle north of the main island, is more liberal; you can camp anywhere without a permit. For more information on this island and what there is to do there, see p.251.

CBD

Elgin Bridge

Getting Around

Other options **Maps** p.441, **Exploring** p.171

Singapore is possibly the most expensive place in the world to own a car – a situation created in order to control the car population and reduce traffic jams. The result is that the vast majority of residents use public transport and to this end the government has provided superbly.

Between the bus service, ultra-modern MRT (subway) and taxis, the public transport system is excellent, comparatively cheap, comfortable and really convenient. A combination of bus and MRT is by far the most common way to commute but taxis are plentiful and for a number of people, travelling just by taxi is still affordable and, yes, cheaper than owning a car!

Motorcycles provide a popular low-cost alternative to cars. However, they can be dangerous, with more than half of all road fatalities involving motorcyclists. Cycling is also dangerous because of the lack of consideration given to cyclists by motorists on Singapore's crowded roads. The city is very pedestrian friendly and all roads have proper pedestrians pathways. But due to the high temperatures and humidity, walking can be an energy-sapping way to get around, and you are likely to arrive sweaty.

The island is served by several key arterial expressways that criss-cross the island. The main ones are the Ayer Rajah Expressway (AYE), Bukit Timah Expressway (BKE), Central Expressway (CTE), East Coast Parkway (ECP) and Tampines Expressway (TPE).

The traffic system is well planned and is continually being improved on, with new flyovers to ease traffic, road widening and traffic flow management through the Electronic Road Pricing scheme (ERP), where motorists pay to use certain roads during peak hours. New MRT stations are being constructed along with a Light Rail Transit system (LRT) connecting commuters from the MRT station to more convenient stops within housing estates.

Air

Other options **Meet & Greet** p.25

Year after year, Changi International Airport has won international awards for Best Airport in the world. The airport serves over 80 airlines flying to more than 180 cities in over 50 countries, making Singapore an ideal place from which to travel. Tourism is vital to the economy and the authorities meet the needs of travellers with exceptional efficiency. The airport comprises two modern terminals with a combined

Airlines

Air Asia	6733 9933	www.airasia.com
Air China	6225 2177	www.airchina.com.cn
Air France ▶ p.5	6415 5111	www.airfrance.com/sg
Air India	6220 5277	www.airindia.com
Air New Zealand	6532 3846	www.airnewzealand.com
Air Niugini	6250 4868	www.airniugini.com.pg
All Nippon Airways	6323 4333	www.anaskyweb.com/sg/e
Asiana Airlines	6225 3866	http://sg.flyasiana.com
British Airways	6589 7000	www.britishairways.com
Cathay Pacific	6533 1333	www.cathaypacific.com
China Airlines	6737 2211	www.china-airlines.com
Delta Airlines	6339 5500	www.delta.com
Emirates	6735 3535	www.emirates.com
EVA Airways	6226 1533	www.evaair.com
Finnair	6733 3377	www.finnair.com
Garuda Indonesia	6250 5666	www.mas.com.my
Japan Airlines	6221 0522	www.sg.jal.com
Jetstar Asia Airways	6822 2288	www.jetstarasia.com
KLM Royal Dutch Airlines ▶ p.5	6823 2220	www.klm.com
Korean Air Lines	6534 2111	www.koreanair.com
Lufthansa	6835 5933	www.lufthansa.com
Malaysia Airlines	6336 6777	www.malaysiaairlines.com
Philippine Airlines	6336 1611	www.philippineairlines.com
Qantas	6589 7000	www.qantas.com.au
Royal Brunei Airlines	6235 4672	www.rba.com.bn
SilkAir	6542 8111	www.silkair.com
Singapore Airlines	6223 8888	www.singaporeair.com
SriLankan Airlines	6223 6026	www.srilankan.aero
Thai Airways	1800 224 9977	www.thaiair.com
Tiger Airways	1800 388 8888	www.tigerairways.com
The Travel Market Place	6534 0187	www.natastravel.com
United Airlines	6873 3533	www.united.com
Valuair	6822 2288	www.valuair.com
Wotif.com	1800 186 1023	www.wotif.com.sg
Zuji	6246 1234	www.zuji.com.sg

capacity to handle 44 million passengers. In 2005, 32 million passengers passed through Changi. Terminal 3, under construction, will raise the airport's capacity to comfortably serve 64 million passengers. And the operative word is comfortably.

Even at peak traffic, it typically takes 30 minutes to clear immigration, collect your baggage and clear customs. Downtown is 20km away, a 20 minute drive; but there's no need to hurry and many a reason to tarry. Passengers can avail themselves of a marvellous range of amenities from spa services, massages, manicures, a swimming pool, fitness centre, shower facilities, hotel accommodation, banks, ATMs, multi-faith prayer rooms, wireless internet...the list is long. To top it off, 30,000 square metres are

Meet me at Terminal...?

Terminal 1 services all airlines except the following which are at Terminal 2:
Air Canada (AC)
Air Macau (NX)
Air New Zealand (NZ)
Austrian Airlines (OS)
Lufthansa German Airlines (LH)
Malaysia Airlines (MH)
Philippine Airlines (PR)
Royal Brunei Airlines (BI)
Silk Air (MI)
Singapore Airlines (SQ)
Virgin Atlantic Airways (VS)

Duty-Free Allowances

Applies to persons over 18 years old and arriving from a country other than Malaysia.
• Spirits: 1 litre
• Wine or port: 1 litre
• Beer, stout or ale: 1 litre
There are no concessions on cigarettes and other tobacco products. Perfume is non-dutiable.

dedicated to 160 duty-free shops and 50 eateries; from Chanel to MacDonald's and everything in between. Prices are guaranteed to be no higher than at a retailer's downtown outlet. In addition, shops at the airport offer a 'no questions asked money back guarantee' on all items, valid up to 30 days from purchase.

The national carrier is Singapore Airlines, renowned for its in-flight service excellence. SIA boasts a string of numerous 'firsts'; such as the first airline to fly the new Airbus A380 and the world's longest commercial flight with its non-stop daily service between Singapore and New York. Since deregulation in the airline industry, several budget airlines now operate in Asia. It's possible to buy air tickets to popular destinations (Bali, Bangkok, Darwin, Hanoi, Ho Chi Minh, Manila, Phuket and more) for less than $10 excluding airport taxes. Most require you to book online and e-tickets are the norm. Transportation to and from the airport is easy. The most convenient option is by taxi and it should cost about $20 to the city. For alternatives, see Airport Transport below.

Except for the specially designated smoking rooms, no smoking is allowed in the airport, not even in the taxi queue.

Airport Transport

Bus

Service 36 runs from Terminals 1 and 2 to Orchard Road. The fare is $1.70 and you should have the exact amount ready as no change is given. This is a normal bus service and stops en route to Marina Square and Orchard Road, looping back to the airport.

MRT

The MRT (subway) goes from Terminal 2 to Orchard station with regular stops at stations along the way. Fare is $1.70.
The frequency of buses and the MRT is less than every 15 minutes. Generally, services operate from 05:30 to 00:00.

Shuttle Cab

From the airport: the MaxiCab, shared by seven passengers, has flexible routing and goes to all major hotels and MRT stations downtown. Frequency varies from 15 minutes (peak) to 30 minutes (off peak). Book at airport shuttle counters in the arrival halls in either terminal. Operating hours are 06:00 to 00:00. Adults: $7. Child: $5. Wheelchair friendly.

To the airport: the service also runs from these pickup points: Concorde Hotel, Mandarin Hotel, Excelsior Hotel and Marina Mandarin, book with the hotel's concierge. Operating hours are 08:00 to 22:00.

Boat

Singapore is a popular port of call for international cruise ships from all over the world and several companies use the island as a base for their South-East Asia cruises. Singapore itself is made up of many islets and lies a short distance from the thousands of islands that make up the Riau archipelago in Indonesia. Together they provide a pleasant respite from the city's bustle.

To get to Singapore's southern isles of Kusu, St. John's, Lazarus and Sister Islands, use the Sentosa Ferry Terminal at Clifford Pier; regular trips run daily. Ferries to Pulau Ubin, a popular isle just 10 minutes away from the main island and 40 years back in time, operate from Changi Point Ferry Terminal. Except for independently run water taxis, ferries are operated by different companies, charge almost the same prices and leave at regular departure times. To reach the shores of Batam and Bintan, the two most popular Riau islands, use Singapore Cruise Centre at Maritime Square or the Tanah Merah Ferry Terminal.

Sailing is fairly popular and there are several marinas dotting the coast of Singapore where you can berth your yacht and sail to where whim and wind takes you. If you leave Singapore and enter international waters, certain immigration procedures are applicable. A departure advice must be submitted to the Brani Ops Centre (6377 5882) a day before and on the day of departure, a Customs officer will come down to the yacht club and stamp your passport and similarly so on return. Your yacht club will probably handle these formalities on your behalf.

Batam and Bintan

Depending on the ferry operator, fares are approximately $30-50 for a return trip. There are several scheduled trips every day from Singapore Cruise Centre (www.singaporecruise.com), which operates from HarbourFront Passenger Terminal, Maritime Square (6513 2200) map 16-F4, and Tanah Merah Ferry Road. (6540 8000) map 12-E3.

Desaru

Various operators offer ferries leaving at regular departure times from Chang Ferry Terminal (6546 8518) map 8-E4, to Tanjung Belungkor for about $22 a return trip. From there, hire a taxi or mini-van to take you to Desaru for around $20 per person, two-way.

Southern Isles

There are several scheduled trips every day to Kusu Island from $9 return and St. John's from $10 return.

Lazarus and Sister Islands

Hire an independently operated water taxi (bumboat) at approximately $50 an hour from Clifford Pier in Marina Bay (map 17-D2).

Pulau Ubin

Share a water taxi, $2 per person for a one-way trip, or hire the whole water taxi for $24 per one way trip. The taxi leaves when there are 12 passengers and runs from Changi Point Ferry Terminal (not to be confused with Changi Ferry Terminal) map 8-E4.

Mini Map

This is the perfect companion for trips around Singapore – small enough for your pocket but big enough to expand your horizons. Keep the Mini Map handy and you'll be navigating your way around the city like a local in no time.

Bus

The bus transportation system caters to a highly mobile population where less than 10% of people own cars. Bus routes have been planned in conjunction with MRT routes so you can efficiently commute to almost every part of Singapore, usually in air-conditioned comfort. Dedicated bus lanes ensure timely arrival even during peak hour traffic jams. Depending on the bus route and time of day, service frequency ranges from 8 to 30 minutes. Buses provide both seats and standing room but the number of passengers allowed to stand is strictly monitored.

Even during peak hours you'll seldom have to wait for another bus. For the most part, seats are available. Because the bus is Singapore's primary mode of public transportation, the level of service is high and constantly monitored and it's impressive by world standards. To get home after a late night out on Friday, Saturday or on the eve of a public holiday, the Night Owl and Night Rider services (00:00 to 04:00, flat fare of $3) run from the city to various outlying suburbs.

Exact fares are required as no change is given. For convenience use an ezLink card (www.ezlink.com.sg), where a discounted fare will be automatically deducted. It also works for the MRT. Buy one, or top it up, at any bus terminal or MRT station where bus guides are also available, or at surrounding convenience shops.

Normal bus services operate 05:30 to 23:45 and the maximum fare is $1.90.

Bus Information

SBS Transit (including Night Owl): www.sbstransit.com.sg
SMRT Bus (Night Rider): www.smrt.com.sg/buses/night_rider.html

Car

Other options **Transportation** p.159

On the whole, driving is Singapore is relatively safe, disciplined and (if you can afford it!) the best way to commute. The road and traffic system is meticulously planned. Roads are excellent and suited to wet weather conditions. As can be expected of a densely populated city caught in the rat race of ambitious progress, there are a few quirks, such as a reluctance for drivers to give way to someone trying to filter into their lane. Expect local drivers to be law-abiding but no more. To curb road rage, courts almost without exception hand out jail terms to those convicted of physical violence.

The Highway Code is a legacy from colonial British rule, along with vehicles being right-hand drive and driving on the left-hand side of the road. Unless otherwise stated, the speed limit is 50km/h on roads and 70-90km/h on expressways. Cameras at traffic lights, speed detectors and traffic police patrols work to keep motorists in check. Bribing a cop out of a traffic ticket will guarantee an appearance in court so don't even think about it!

The government is determined to prevent the crippling traffic jams commonly associated with some Asian cities. Numerous mechanisms to avoid traffic congestion make Singapore possibly the most expensive place in the world to own a car. Typically, the same car in the USA costs 75% less to buy. About 10% of the population own cars and already traffic is bumper to bumper on main arterial roads during peak hours. For this reason, the government has built a marvellous public transport system that makes car ownership unnecessary.

Useful Numbers

Traffic Police 6547 0000
Land Transport Authority (LTA) 1800 225 5582
Automobile Association Of Singapore (AAS) 6737 2444
Accidents involving injuries – emergency 995

Dry Cleaners p.74
Divorce Lawyers p.108

Written by residents, these unique guidebooks are packed with insider info, from arriving in a new destination to making it your home and everything in between.

Explorer Residents' Guides
We Know Where You Live

ERP

Motorists driving into the CBD and on some major roads and expressways must pay an Electronic Road Pricing fee, another scheme to manage traffic flow. Fees vary according to the road and time of day, and range between $0.50 and $3.50. The correct fee is automatically deducted from a CashCard inserted in an In-Vehicle Unit (IU), installed in every car, when you pass an ERP gantry. CashCards can be purchased and topped up at banks, post offices, petrol stations, some ATMs and at the many car parks that use CashCards to collect fees.

Parking

Parking is rarely a problem but with a few exceptions, you'll have to pay for it. The exceptions are side streets in residential suburbs, on Sundays and public holidays in some car parks, and after 17:00 on some roads. All car parks have signboards showing rates. A coupon system is used for public parking. The standard rate is $0.50 per half hour (white parking lots) and double that in the CBD (yellow parking lots). Parking coupons are displayed on the dashboard. Coupons are available from some petrol stations and supermarkets, and convenience stores such as 7-11. Increasingly, public car parks use traffic wardens from private companies who earn a commission on fines collected. Be warned, this incentive to find and fine works!

All shopping centres, commercial buildings, hotels and some public car parks have a paid parking system where you pay for the time parked. Charges vary and can cost $2 per half hour. A variety of payment systems are used: parking attendant, ticket, IU or CashCard.

Demerit Points

Some traffic violations carry demerit points in addition to fines. Accumulate more than 24 demerit points in a two year period and your driver's licence will be suspended. Demerit points have a 12 month shelf life after which they are automatically cleared. A suspended driver must re-sit and pass the Basic Theory Test before their licence is be reinstated.

Accidents

For accidents where no injuries occurr and damage to the vehicle is minor, both parties can choose to settle the matter without involving the police. Nonetheless, exchange particulars with the other driver and note the vehicle's licence number. If in doubt, you should file a police report. If you do intend to claim, your insurance company will

Car Rental Agencies

ATS Rent-a-Car	6732 0304	www.atsrentacar.com
Avis	6737 1668	www.avis.com.sg
C&P Rent-A-Car	6736 6666	www.candp.com
CityLimo	6882 0882	www.citylimo.com.sq
DownTown Travel Services	6334 1700	www.dts.com.sg
Expat Motors	6722 8420	www.expatmotorsingapore.com
Falcon-Air	6452 0880	www.falconair.com.sg
Hertz Rent A Car	1800 734 4646	www.hertz.com
Motorway	6468 2200	www.motorway.com.sg
ORIX Car Rentals	6319 8000	www.orix.com.sg
Popular Rent A Car	6742 8888	www.popularcar.com
Premier Rent A Car	6732 3375	www.premier-rentacar.com
Samly Limousine	6746 2692	www.samlylimousine.com.sg
San's Car Rentals	6734 9922	www.sanstours.com
Siang Hock	6256 8888	www.sianghock.com.sg
Smart Car Rental	6485 7788	www.smartcarrental.com.sg

require a police report, made within 24 hours, to accompany any claim. For accidents involving injuries, a police report is mandatory. Call 995 immediately for on-site assistance.

Car Hire

There are many car rental companies, from the well-known large international names to small local companies, and between them you can choose from 1.3 litre budget sedans, SUVs, Mercedes and BMWs to exotic sports cars. For a standard 1.6 litre saloon car, average prices range from $70-150 per day. Not all companies accept an International Drivers Permit. Check the Damage Excess payable in the event of an accident. Consider buying a Collision Damage Waiver, which can reduce the payable amount from, for example, $2,000 to $300. Most rental companies restrict driving to within Singapore only.

Cycling

Other options **Cycling** p.254

Not a recommended way to getting around – it's either hot (average 32°C) and humid (84%), or it's raining. Commuting by bicycle is uncommon, due to the lack of facilities for cyclists. Expressways are off limits and footpaths are for pedestrians, so cyclists have to ride on the road where the attitude of most motorists is 'might is right'! However, cycling does have a following among avid sportsmen. Outlying areas like Sembawang Road, Changi Coast Road and East Coast Parkway offer nice stretches of roads where cycling can be a pleasurable experience. For off-road riding, there are some great trails at Bukit Timah Nature Reserve and on Pulau Ubin Island, and a 'bike hash' group (p.281).

Motorcycles

This is possibly the cheapest mode of transportation and definitely the quickest way to get around – provided you survive. Riding a motorcycle in Singapore is dangerous compared to Australia, western European countries and the US. You will get no respect from car drivers. When it comes to the rules of the road, the choice is yours; you can make like the local motorcyclists and weave your way through the cars, especially when the traffic comes to a halt – which brings its own perils, or follow traffic rules and ride properly behind a car, but this would be so unexpected that you're changes of being rear-ended are high. With over 50% of traffic fatalities involving motorcyclists, riding in Singapore requires focus, concentration and a defensive posture. But owning and maintaining a bike is temptingly cheap, it's an exciting way to see Malaysia and there are motorbike clubs that arrange road trips all the way to Thailand.

Taxi

Taxis are an excellent way to get around Singapore. There are over 20,000 of them, plenty for a city of this size, and as many ply the roads during the day as at night. The

51

business is well regulated and efficient, from computerised booking systems to paying fares by credit card, and fares are very reasonable. Tipping is not normally required.

Catching a taxi is easy – wave one down from the roadside or go to one of the taxi stands located outside most major shopping centres and hotels. Alternatively, book a taxi and it will usually arrive within 5 to 10 minutes. A booking fee applies ($2-5).

Some companies have computerised booking systems that locate an available taxi within minutes, remember the last two locations from where you booked a taxi, and call you when they've arrived.

Fares and surcharges vary slightly among taxi operators, but expect a flag down fare of approximately $2.40 including the first kilometre, increasing at about $0.50 per kilometre. A 50% midnight surcharge applies until 06:00. The metered fare automatically includes any applicable surcharges such as travel from the airport and toll charges for certain expressways or for entering the CBD. As all charges are registered on the meter, it's almost impossible to be cheated.

Road knowledge varies considerably among drivers; it's best to have some idea of your destination, or at least a landmark. Speak clearly and slowly because English is not many drivers' first language. All said, Singapore's taxi service is excellent and in many ways beats owning a car.

Taxi Companies	
Citycab	6552 2222
Comfort	6552 1111
Premier/Silver Cab	6363 6888
SMART	6485 7700
SMRT	6555 8888
TRANScab	6555 3333

Train

Malaysia

The close proximity of Malaysia makes it a popular weekend break destination from Singapore, and taking the train can be a pleasant way to see the sights as you make the journey. You can head north to Johor Bahru, just over the causeway, or up to the capital city, Kuala Lumpur. For more information on the country, see Weekend Breaks on p.232 and Holidays from Singapore on p.236.

There's no train service in Singapore but there is an excellent underground system called the MRT (Mass Rapid Transit) that covers the island. For more details, see Underground on p.52. Connecting into the MRT network, there are also three short LRT (Light Rail Transport) lines, linking outlying residential areas to MRT stations, but this is more of a 'people mover' system than a train network.

If you are planning a holiday in Malaysia, there is a train service to Johore Bahru and Kuala Lumpur that runs daily from the Tanjong Pagar Railway station (11-A4). Trains are air-conditioned with basic amenities and the night train to Kuala Lumpur offers sleeping berths. For more information contact Malayan Railway (6222 5165).

Alternatively, for the romance of five-star luxury railway travel from a bygone era, you can book a railway journey by Eastern & Oriental Express (E&O, 6392 3500) to Penang and the River Kwai in Thailand.

Underground

The MRT (Mass Rapid Transit) is Singapore's equivalent to the London Underground or New York's subway. It's an excellent way to get around: modern, safe, reliable, air-conditioned, fast and inexpensive ($0.80-1.70). Operating hours are from 05:30-00:30 (but vary slightly between stations), and while it can get crowded during peak hours, train frequencies are adjusted accordingly and you can expect another train to arrive in just three to eight minutes.

Single trip tickets valid for a day can be purchased from vending machines in every station. A $1 deposit for the smart card is automatically deducted and refunded via the vending machines. Remember to collect your deposit when you reach your destination. Three main lines span the island, and feeder services by the bus network and LRT system (Light Rail Transport) make it even easier to get to an MRT station. For regular commuting, buy an ezLink fare card ($15) which works seamlessly between the three transport systems. It is available at all stations. For further information on the MRT, visit www.smrt.com.sg.

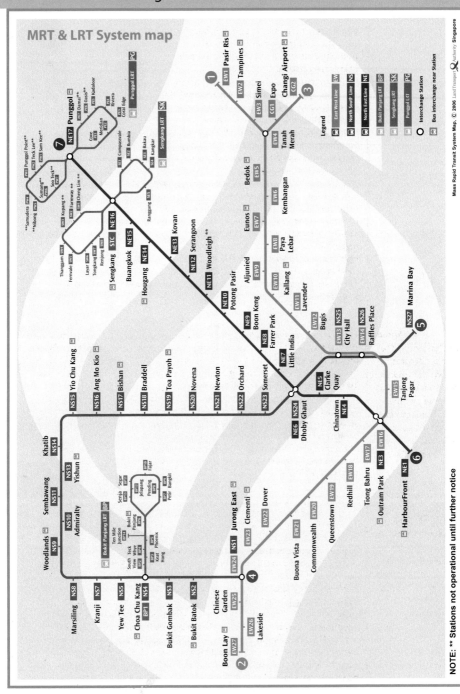

MRT & LRT System map

NOTE: ** Stations not operational until further notice

Mass Rapid Transit System Map, © 2006 Land Transport Authority, Singapore

Walking

Other options **Hiking** p.270

Other options **Hiking** p.270

Beware the Drains
They are everywhere,
and too often
uncovered. There is no
legal recourse if you fall
into one and hurt
yourself; it's presumed
to be your second
nature to avoid them.

Singapore's equatorial climate – with frequent rain, average daytime temperatures of around 32°C and a mean relative humidity of 84% – can make walking for any length of time rather uncomfortable. Perspire you will. The singlet (vest) is commonly worn by executives wishing to avoid the 'wet look' at business meetings. Also, everyone owns an umbrella or two.

That said, Singapore is very pedestrian friendly, particularly around popular shopping and tourist areas. There are footpaths alongside most roads and pedestrian crossings or footbridges are suitably placed for safety. In fact, it's against the law to jaywalk and you must use bridges or crossings, or cross at a traffic light. Car drivers are generally mindful of pedestrians, or at least, the severe repercussions should they knock one down! When crossing a road, it's incumbent on the pedestrian to look out for cars – don't just assume that they will stop at a pedestrian crossing for you.

Money

While cash is still the preferred mode of payment, the use of credit cards is extensive and commonplace – even taxis accept them. Many smaller shops and retail outlets that don't accept credit cards often use the popular NETS card (Network for Electronic Transfers), a direct debit card linked to your bank account. Apart from hotels, which accept some of the major foreign currencies, all other transactions should be in Singapore's currency. Most shops, department stores, supermarkets and restaurants do not accept cheques.

Local Currency

The local currency is the Singapore dollar, which is usually referred to by just the dollar sign, or by S$ or SG$. Its full international currency code is SGD. Notes come in denominations of $1, $2, $5, $10, $50, $100, $500, $1000 and $10,000, with coins in 1 cent, 10 cent, 20 cent, 50 cent and $1 denominations. New polymer $2 and $10 notes are now in circulation and the $1 coin is replacing the $1 note, which is fast disappearing. The $20 note was discontinued in 1984 though a few may still be in circulation. The Singapore dollar is pegged to the Brunei dollar and the Currency Interchangeability Agreement between the two countries allows for the currency notes of one country to be used in the other.

Banks

Singapore is a global financial hub with a network of local and international merchant, investment and retail banks. International banks are concentrated in the CBD, while local banks are spread across the island with branches in major suburbs and housing estates. All local banks offer a comprehensive range of services including private banking, foreign exchange remittance, investments and loans. For information on opening a bank account, please refer to Bank Accounts on p.87 of the Residents section.

Banks are open Monday to Friday and half a day on Saturday. Operating hours differ from bank to bank, with opening times varying between 08:30 and 09:30, and closing times between 15:30 to 16:30. Some banks have late closing branches. On Saturdays, banks close between 12:00 and 13:00.

Main Banks

ABN AMRO Consumer Bank	1800 226 2676	www.abnamro.com.sg
BNP Paribas	6210 1288	www.bnpparibas.com.sg
Citibank ▶ p.IFC	6225 5225	www.citibank.com.sg
DBS Bank (Development Bank of Singapore)	1800 111 1111	www.dbs.com.sg
HSBC ▶ p.89	1800 786 6666	www.hsbc.com.sg
Maybank	1800 629 2265	www.maybank.com.sg
Overseas Chinese Banking Corporation (OCBC)	1800 438 3333	www.ocbc.com.sg
Post Office Savings Bank (POSB)	1800 111 1111	www.dbs.com.sg
Standard Chartered Bank	1800 747 7000	www.standardchartered.com.sg
United Overseas Bank (UOB)	1800 222 2121	www.uob.com.sg

ATMs

An extensive network of ATMs is spread across the island. ATMs can be found at MRT stations, supermarkets, shopping malls, government buildings where payments are made, HDB estates, cinemas and wherever there's a dense concentration of human traffic. In general, ATMs accept AMEX, Cirrus, Mastercard, Overseas' Plus, Visa and Visa Electron, though the precise service provided depends on the bank's ATM; look for the logos displayed at top of the machine. Some ATMs allow you to top up the CashCard for paying ERP charges, see Driving in Singapore in the Residents section p.160.

Money Exchanges

Singapore has numerous independent money exchanges, also know locally as money changers. They must be licenced and operate from a registered location. Tiny booths can be found in many malls and shopping complexes popular with tourists, and there's usually more than one. The bulk of them are concentrated in the CBD – around Orchard Road and

Exchange Rates

Foreign Currency(FC)	1 Unit FC = x $	$1 = x FC
Australia	1.20	0.83
Brunei	1.0	1.0
Canada	1.30	0.76
China	0.19	5.08
Denmark	0.26	3.73
Euro	1.99	0.50
Hong Kong SAR	0.19	5.07
India	0.03	28.9
Indonesia	0.00	5.89
Japan	77.5	0.01
Malaysia	0.43	2.28
New Zealand	1.06	0.94
Pakistan	0.02	39.6
Philippines	0.03	31.8
South Korea	0.0016	610.0
Switzerland	1.23	0.80
Taiwan	0.04	21.3
Thailand	0.04	23.41
UAE	0.41	2.38
UK	2.98	0.33
UK	2.98	0.33
USA	1.53	0.65

the Shenton Way area – though some suburbs and housing estates also have them, and their rates are comparable to the ones downtown. Exchange rates at a money changer are invariably better than at a bank or hotel, plus they handle a wider range of currencies. They follow the same operating hours as the building they're located in, usually from 10:00 to 18:00 for an office building or until 21:00 if it is a shopping centre. Do not change money with someone who walks up to you on the street – it'll be a con.

Credit Cards

Paying by credit card is a way of life here, and shops that do not accept credit cards are at a disadvantage. A lot of smaller shops won't take credit cards, certainly none in the markets, and retailers selling goods with very low profit margins, such as electronic products, may ask to add the card commission to the selling price. Some places have a minimum purchase amount, usually $20, for payment by credit card.

Almost all restaurants and cafes take credit cards, but food courts and hawker centres don't. At pubs or nightclubs it's common practice to leave an open or running tab, where your credit card is held by the cashier until you are ready to leave. This practice is generally safe, but can leave you vulnerable to 'card skimming'. How much of this goes on is hard to tell, but syndicates have been busted. The credit card slip you sign has a space for a tip to be included – remember, a 10% service charge is automatically included in all bills.

Another word of caution: at a pub or nightclub, always check your bill before paying. These places get so crowded that it's normal for strangers to share a table. Quite naturally, you might strike up a conversation with another party. The waiter has no idea if they are your friends or perfect strangers and may well put their drinks on your tab since bills are usually charged to a table! This is partly because it's a Singaporean custom for one person to pay first and later split the bill among themselves. On the other hand, thanks to the influx of expats, waiters these days are used to making out separate bills for one table so if you're with a large group of friends, it's fine to ask for separate bills – before you order, not at the end of the night.

Keep your credit card safely. Cashiers often do not check the signature signed against the one on the credit card, making it easier for someone who found or stole the card to use it. If you lose your card, call your issuing bank immediately to cancel it.

Tipping

While it isn't obligatory to tip in Singapore, it is an acceptable practice and definitely welcomed by recipients. It is left entirely to your discretion, as in any industry it's unacceptable to ask for a tip. While not required to tip taxi drivers, tour guides and hotel staff, it's customary (though not compulsory) to tip car park valets and porters a dollar or so. At food and beverage outlets, a 10% service charge in place of tips is automatically included in the bill. Ask to take it off the bill if the service was horrendous. How this gets distributed to the staff, if at all, differs widely among companies. A fairly common practice is for the company to distribute 50% of the service charge among the service staff and keep the rest. The tip on your credit card slip goes to the company first and is pooled together with the service charge. Tips do not go to specific waiters. If you wish to thank a particular waiter, give them cash and let them know the tip is personally for them.

Newspapers/Magazines

Singapore has seven major daily newspapers in three languages. They are all published by Singapore Press Holdings. *The Straits Times* is the main English language daily, with a circulation of 400,000 and a readership of one million. *The Business Times*, *The New Paper* (an afternoon tabloid) and *Today* (circulated free), are also in English. The other three are in Chinese (*Lianhe Zaobao*), Malay (*Berita Harian*) and Tamil (*Tamil Murasu*). Newspapers are available by subscription and delivered to your door, or you can pick one up just about anywhere; many shops and most petrol stations sell them. Larger supermarkets and specialist magazine shops carry foreign newspapers such as the *International Herald Tribune*.

From a technical perspective, local newspapers are excellent in quality, especially the coverage of world news. A board of censors is responsible for all media including broadcast and the arts. However, the newspapers have a custom of self-censorship based on second-guessing government sensibilities or on experience. Culturally, Singaporeans prefer to err on the safe side and to avoid rocking the boat. The ban on *Cosmopolitan* was recently lifted – an indication the government is gradually loosening its tight control. However, *Playboy* and *Penthouse* remain out of circulation. There are numerous locally published magazines in different languages, covering a wide spectrum of subjects from parenting, teens, computers, sports, wine, dining and architecture to, of course, dozens of women's fashion titles. Popular local magazines are *Her World*, *Female*, *Women's Weekly*, *Simply Her*, *New Man*, *Young Parents*, *Family*, *Wine & Dine*, *8 Days* and *Home & Décor*. The foreign magazines such as *Vogue*, *Marie Claire*, *Elle*, *Harper's Bazaar*, *Cleo*, *Tatler*, *FHM*, *Time*, *Newsweek* and *The Economist* are abundant and many magazine stands carry them. On the whole, because of the limited readership compared to broadcast or dailies, magazines can get away with much more in terms of editorial content. Articles about sex, once taboo, are now virtually de rigueur in many of the popular publications.

Most bookshops and hotels carry entertainment, shopping and sightseeing guides. *The Singapore Visitor* can be found at the airport and most hotels. The free magazine *IS* keeps locals up-to-date on what's happening in town and is available at many pubs and restaurants and at the tourist information centres. Other popular resources for expats include *Expat* and *Expat Living* magazines.

At the time of writing, it was announced that *Time Out* would be launching *Time Out Singapore* – a monthly entertainment and listings magazine – in March 2007. Popular in many other cities worldwide, it could be worth checking out for the lowdown on the entertainment and nightlife scene.

Recommended Reads

Singapore English in a Nutshell: An Alphabetical Description of its Features by Brown, Adam. A good reference guide to Singapore English, a quirky admixture of English, Chinese dialect and Malay.

Makansutra 05/06 Singapore: Die, Die Must Try by Seetoh, KF. In it's fifth edition, this 'bible' of foodies is a guide to 1,000 of the best eating places, typically hawker stalls and mid-priced restaurants. The author is an acknowledged food guru.

Culture Shock! Singapore by Joann Craig, covers the cultural norms of Singapore's different ethnic groups, business etiquette, and good tips for expats.

Singapore City Scoops by CityScoops Media. A team of savvy urbanites let you in on some of the city's best experiences, from tucked-away eateries, to boutique hotel bars, yoga retreats and little-known side-street galleries.

Mini Explorer

Don't be fooled by the size of this little star – it's full of insider info, maps, contacts, tips and facts about this vibrant city. From shops to spas, bars to bargains and everything in between, the Mini Explorer helps you get the most out of your stay in Singapore, however long you're staying.

Books

Other options **Websites** p.58

There are a whole host of travel guides on Singapore from all the main publishers, most of which are widely available in the country's bookshops, or in your home country. In Singapore, most bookshops and hotels carry entertainment, shopping and sightseeing guides. In addition, there are a good number of independant publishers producing guides, photography books and a variety of other publications on all aspects of life in Singapore. For some recommendations, see Recommended Reads on p.57.

Websites

Singapore Information

http://sg.movies.yahoo.com	Movie guide
www.asiaone.com	Local and world news
www.cancerstory.com	Singapore based cancer support website
www.cia.gov/cia/publications/factbook/geos/sn.html	CIA's factbook on Singapore
www.city.net/regions/asia	Info on Asian countries
www.elibraryhub.com	National Library
www.getforme.com	Anything and everything on Singapore
www.holisticliving.com.sg	Guide for all things holistic in Singapore
www.hotels.online.com.sg	Singapore hotels
www.lawonline.com.sg	Legal portal
www.livelife.ecitizen.gov.sg	Culture, recreation and sports events
www.nparks.gov.sg	Public parks
www.nvpc.org.sg	Volunteering
www.pzlabs.com/aulenti	English-Chinese dictionary
www.sbstransit.com.sg	Singapore bus guide
www.sentosa.com.sg	Sentosa island – great place for recreation
www.sg	Comprehensive portal of links and info
www.singnet.com.sg	Links to govt, travel & food sites
www.sistic.com.sg	Concerts and events (Online Ticket Booking)
www.smrt.com.sg	MRT and bus guide
www.ssc.gov.sg	Sports activities
www.ticketcharge.com.sg	Book concert tickets online
www.visitsingapore.com	Singapore Tourism Board website for visitors
www.wholivesnearyou.com	Website to help people socialize with like-minded people living nearby
www.wildsingapore.com	Wild places, activities, animals and people in Singapore
www.yellowpages.com.sg	Yellow pages, residential phone directory

Government/Business/Industry

http://polyclinic.singhealth.com.sg	Government outpatient clinics
www.acra.gov.sg	Portal for setting up a business
www.aseansec.org	Home page of the Asian Secretariat
www.ecitizen.gov.sg	Gateway to all government services
www.marina-bay.sg	New business and entertainment hub
www.mfa.gov.sg	Ministry of Foreign Affairs, list of embassies
www.nhgp.com.sg	Government outpatient clinics
www.nmsg-singapore.com	Mothers' support group
www.singpost.com	Singapore Post
www.singstat.gov.sg/	Statistics
www.sna.org.sg/cms/publish/article_94.shtml	List of hospitals
www.ste.com	Bulletin board for businesses & advertisements
www.ura.gov.sg	Urban Redevelopment Authority

Embassies

www.embassyworld.com	Phone Numbers of Singapore Embassies Abroad and Foreign Missions in Singapore

Great things can come in small packages…

Perfectly proportioned to fit in your pocket, this marvellous mini guidebook makes sure you don't just get the holiday you paid for, but rather the one that you dreamed of.

Singapore Mini Visitors' Guide
Maximising your holiday, minimising your hand luggage

Suntec Singapore
4-8 Oct

ARTSingapore
www.artsingapore.net
Over 50 leading art galleries gather to network and showcase the works of more than 400 contemporary Asian artists from the region. Corporate and individual buyers welcome.

Singapore Expo
Nov - tbc

Asian Children's Festival
www.asianchildrenfest.com
An opportunity for story-tellers, dramatists, performers and educators to both stimulate and inspire creative thinking and learning in children. The aim is for professionals to network and develop creative Asian content, products and services for children.

Singapore Expo
Nov - tbc

Big Boyz Toyz
www.bigboyztoyz.com.sg
Toys for adults who still haven't grown up. Mostly related to cars, there's a chance to ogle the latest from Lamborghini, Lotus and Ferrari, as well as electronics, games and beer.

Various locations
7-17 Mar

Children First!
www.childrenfirst.com.sg
The Singapore International Festival for Children is recognised as the premier children's art festival in the region. It presents high quality performing arts experiences to inspire, nurture and showcase children's arts.

Singapore Expo
7-9 Sep

Fitness Asia
www.fitnessasia.com.sg
Find out the latest trends and developments in sports, fitness and spa products. Topics covered include sporting activities, exercise regimes, fitness apparel, sports equipment and technologies, wellness spas, massage treatments, health and nutrition.

Various locations
Oct

Navaratri
www.heb.gov.sg
Navaratri, meaning 'nine lights' in Tamil, celebrates three Hindu goddesses with song and dance for three nights each. Visitors are welcome to join the prayers and classical dance and music performances held in different Indian temples.

Republic Plaza
25 Feb

National Vertical Marathon 2007
www.ntusportsclub.com
This is a stair-climbing competition to see who can summit Republic Plaza the fastest. Tougher than it seems!

Laguna National
Golf and Country Club
8-11 Mar

OSIM Singapore Masters
www.osimsingaporemasters.com
Part of the Asian and European professional golf circuits, this professional golf tournament with a purse of US$1,000,000 is a highly prestigious event attracting the top golfers in the world. Vijay Singh and Colin Montgomerie are past winners.

East Coast Park
July - tbc

OSIM Singapore Triathlon
www.singaporetriathlon.com
The premier triathlon event in Singapore, it attracts top competitors from the region. Last year's competition had 1,500 participants.

Various locations
25 May - 24 Jun

Singapore Arts Festival
www.singaporeartsfest.com
The major festival is truly international and features world premieres. The core programme has over 75 performances of dance, theatre and music from around the world.

Toa Payoh
Sports Hall
Nov - tbc

Singapore Basketball Challenge
www.bas.org.sg
Excellent event for recreational players with a competitive streak. Expats teams get to square off against top local basketball teams.

East Coast Park
17 Mar

Singapore Biathlon
www.safra.sg/singaporebiathlon
The largest and most competitive biathlon event in Southeast Asia, it attracts thousands of participants who want to compete in a 1.5km swim followed by a 10km run.

Various locations
Sep - tbc

Singapore Biennial
www.singaporebiennale.org
Organisers promise 'a unique and exciting experience through interfaces and encounters between city life and art that will inspire dialogue among citizens and visitors within the multicultural state of Singapore.' Get an insight into the edge of Singapore's contemporary art scene.

Raffles City
Convention Centre
11 Mar

Singapore Dancesport Championships
www.dancesport.org.sg
140 couples representing around 25 countries will come together for this fiercely contested ballroom and Latin dance competition. Includes Open World Ranking and special guest appearances.

Various locations
1-30 Apr

Singapore International Film Festival
www.filmfest.org.sg
A world film festival offering over 250 films showcasing the best in Asian and world cinema, with an emphasis on regional documentaries and Singaporean short films.

Sentosa Golf Club
1-4 Nov

Singapore Open
www.singaporeopen.org
With a purse of US$2 million, this is by far the richest golf event in Singapore. The tournament will bring together the cream of Asian golfers and a select group of star players from overseas.

Singapore Expo
Nov - tbc

SITEX
www.sitex.com.sg
A major infocom and consumer electronic event with over 500 exhibitors. See the latest innovative technologies in computer hardware and software, digital products, wireless applications, digital photography, gaming and animation. Great bargains!

The Regent
Apr - various dates

Sotheby's Paintings Auction
www.sothebys.com
Auction of south-east Asian paintings by mostly regional and some international artists.

Various locations
11 Feb

Thaipusam
A colourful, spectacular Hindu festival where devotees carry a beautifully decorated kavadi (yoke of burden) weighing 20-60 kilograms for about 5km along Serangoon Road to Thendayuthapani Temple. Parts of the devotees' bodies are pierced with metal spikes.

61

Fort Canning Park
Aug - tbc

WOMAD

www.womadsingapore.com

A festival of world music and dance featuring award-winning artistes from the UK, USA, Cuba, Algeria, France, South Africa, South Pacific, India, Italy and other countries. Set in a beautiful outdoor venue at Fort Canning Park. Pack a picnic and bring the family.

Singpapore Expo
14-16 Sep

Women Expo

www.womenexpo.com.sg

All things female. A regional event showcasing the latest in beauty, glamour, fashion, health & wellness, jewellery and wine from Singapore.

Suntec City
May - tbc

World Book Fair

www.bookfair.com.sg

The largest and best known book fair in the region, it is the ultimate browsing and book experience for the 700,000 book lovers that come. Get to see the latest publications and electronic book products.

Various locations
tbc

The Mana Mana Amslam/Air Blast kitesurfing event

www.bintan-resorts.com

The Bintan Resort hosts two banner events in January and February each year, timed with the annual north-east monsoon. January sees the exciting international windsurfing competition, the Mana Mana Amslam, showcasing some of the world's best windsurfers. In February is the annual Air Blast kitesurfing event, a competition format event spread over two days and showcasing the range of kitesurfing skills and tricks from the region and around the world.

Singapore's Public Art

Singapore Annual Events Calendar 2007

January

1	New Year's Day	Public holiday	na

February

11	Thaipusam	Serangoon Road	www.sttemple.com
18-19	Chinese New Year	Public holiday	na
25	National Vertical Marathon	Republic Plaza	www.ntusportsclub.com

March

7-17	Children First!	Various	www.childrenfirst.com.sg
8-11	OSIM Singapore Masters	Laguna Golf & Country Club	www.singaporemasters.com
11	Singapore Dancesport Championships	Raffles City Convention Ctr	www.dancesport.org.sg
17	Singapore Biathlon	East Coast Park	www.safra.sg/singaporebiathlon
tbc	Sun Sports/STTA Table Tennis Championships	Sun Sports Club	www.ssc.gov.sg

April

1-30	Singapore International Film Festival	Various	www.filmfest.org.sg
6	Good Friday	Public holiday	na
29	Sotheby's Paintings Auction	The Regent Hotel	www.sothebys.com

May

1	Labour Day	Public holiday	na
25-24/6	Singapore Arts Festival	Various	www.singaporeartsfest.com
31	Vesak Day	Public holiday	na
tbc	Singapore Cup Men Basketball Invitation	Toa Payoh Sports Hall	www.ssc.gov.sg
25-3/6	World Book Fair	Suntec City	www.bookfair.com.sg

June

tbc	Aviva Open Singapore 2007 (Badminton)	Singapore Indoor Stadium	www.singaporebadmintonopen.com
tbc	Basketball Association of Singapore Open	Various	www.bas.org.sg
tbc	CSC-STTA Table Tennis Championships 2007	Chinese Swimming Club	www.stta.org.sg

July

tbc	OSIM Singapore Triathalon	East Coast Park E2	www.singaporetriathlon.com

August

9	National Day	Public holiday	na
tbc	WOMAD	Fort Canning Park	www.womadsingapore.com

September

7-9	Fitness Asia	Singapore Expo Centre	www.fitnessasia.com.sg
14-16	Women Expo	Singapore Expo Centre	www.womenexpo.com.sg
tbc	Singapore Biennale	Various	www.singaporebiennale.org

October

4-8	ARTSingapore	Suntec City	www.artsingapore.net
13	Hari Raya Puasa	Public holiday	na
25-27	Wine for Asia	Singapore Expo Centre	www.wineforasia.com
tbc	Navaratri	Various temples	na
tbc	SENI Singapore	Singapore Art Museum	www.nhb.gov.sg/SAM

November

1-4	Singapore Open (Golf)	Sentosa Golf Club	www.singaporeopen.org
8	Deepavali	Public holiday	na
tbc	Asia Fashion Week	Singapore Expo	na
tbc	Asian Children's Festival	Various	www.asianchildrenfest.com
tbc	Big Boyz Toyz	Singapore Expo	www.bigboyztoyz.com.sg
tbc	Corporate Triathlon 2007	East Coast Park E2	jsp.triathlonsingapore.org
tbc	Singapore Basketball Challenge	Various	www.bas.org.sg
tbc	SITEX	Singapore Expo	www.sitex.com.sg

December

20	Hari Raya Haji	Public holiday	na
25	Christmas Day	Public holiday	na

63

exPat LIVING

Easter Treats

Cheaper Calls
Home Office Ideas

Vietnam · Shanghai · Macau

Expat Living Magazine Singapore *Your guide to the perfect tropical lifestyle.*
Be the first to see inside the beautiful homes of expats in Singapore each month, plus practical and striking interior design ideas; property insights; unique regional travel features, food & wine reviews, health & beauty tips and lots of events and new products. **www.expatlivingsingapore.com**

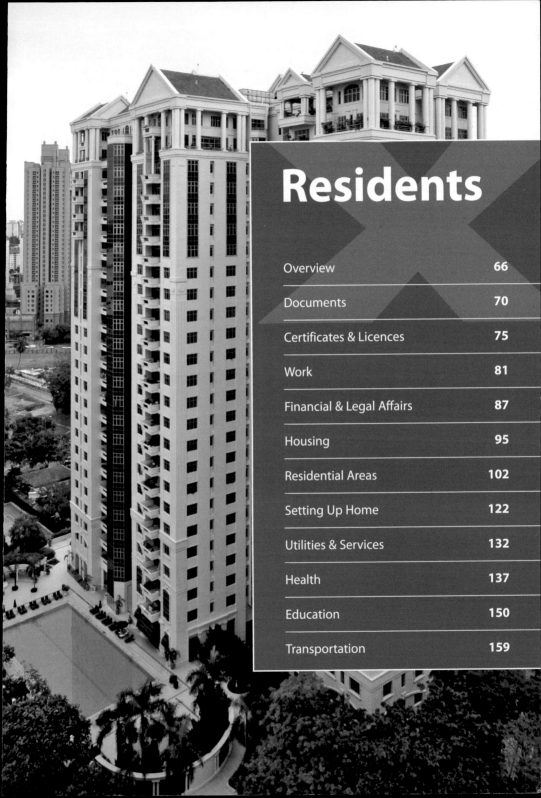

Residents

Residents

Overview

Singapore is a great place to live, offering a taste of Asia in a clean, modern and safe environment. Life here moves at a bit more of a 'tropical' pace than that of its neighbours Japan and China, but still offers plenty of buzz and excitement.

That may surprise you as Singapore has a reputation for being a rather boring country with too many rules and too little fun. This is a huge misconception: you can do pretty much whatever you want in Singapore. Many of the strict rules that were in place 30 years ago have been relaxed as Singapore has been transformed from a sleepy village community to a bustling international business centre. As for the things you're not allowed to do… well, you probably shouldn't be doing them anyway.

Singaporeans have eagerly adopted the driving commercial and business sensibilities of their early leaders and the island is now a regional business hub that offers many exciting work and travel opportunities for expats. The government continues to push economic development and there are always opportunities to get in on the latest initiative; most recently biotechnology, healthcare and tourism have jumped to the fore, while finance, marketing and the hi-tech sectors continue to be open to qualified expats.

Arriving in Singapore as an expat can be a pleasant experience. The procedures for obtaining residency are clearly explained and aimed at making Singapore attractive to highly skilled expat professionals.

Urban Myths

Most people know very little about Singapore unless they've actually visited the city – and even then there are a few misconceptions that just won't go away.

Fines for all sorts of minor infractions
While it's true that there are signs posted everywhere warning of fines for littering, smoking and eating, drinking or taking durians on the train, it's extremely rare to hear of someone who has actually been fined. The fines are there to deter and in general they do just that.

Chewing gum is illegal in Singapore
Not true! See more information about this particular myth on p.93 but yes, you can have your spearmint and chew it.

Singapore's nightlife is tame and boring
That may have been the case 10 or 15 years ago, but one look at the Going Out chapter from p.386 and you'll realize that Singapore has transformed itself into a great place to party.

It's a foreign country so no one speaks English
There's an amazing array of languages and dialects spoken in Singapore but almost everyone, from taxi drivers to shop assistants, speak English. Sometimes it morphs into Singlish (see p.17) but most locals tone it down when speaking to foreigners. Communication won't be a problem in Singapore.

Considering Singapore

As with any city in the world, there are pros and cons to living here. By and large the pros outweigh the cons but individual tastes will ultimately decide if this is the place for you.

A big plus for many is the weather, which doesn't vary much throughout the year. Temperatures hover around 30°C (82°F) every day and humidity can regularly reach 80-90%. If you don't handle the heat well or take particular pleasure in the changing of the seasons, this could be a negative. The travel possibilities here are also a great positive; jetting off to the beaches, jungles or cities of Southeast Asia for a long weekend is not uncommon. You'll also be able to enjoy countless restaurants and nightspots and a growing arts scene. And on the whole life can be quite comfortable with the services of a maid; a large, modern residence with all the facilities; and a commute that probably won't exceed 15 minutes.

From a work and business perspective, Singapore offers many opportunities for expats with the right qualifications. Salaries may not be as high as they once were but taxes remain low and entrepreneurs will love the excitement that comes with being in the fastest growing economic region in the world. You'll probably arrive in Singapore with a job already lined up, but if you're looking to explore new opportunities here it's worth a preliminary visit to meet people face-to-face and to build up an initial network. (See Finding Work Before You're Here on p.83 as well as the rest of the Work section for tips on working in Singapore and finding a job.)

You'll get a social visit pass when you first arrive. A residence visa can only be obtained once you or your spouse have employment and are approved for an employment pass.

Before You Arrive

If you've decided to move to Singapore for work, it helps to do your homework before you rush off to the airport. The more preparations you complete, or at least start, before moving, the easier the transition will be. If you have the luxury of time, consider a trip to Singapore before you move in order to scope out residential areas, visit schools and get a feel for what to expect. Things you should try to sort out before you arrive include: Selling or renting your property – depending on how long you expect to stay in Singapore you may want to sell or rent out your house in your home country before you move.

Shipping your possessions – if you're bringing more than you can fly over with, enquire about sending your belongings over in advance so that you aren't left waiting for months while your furniture it out at sea (see p.122).

Financial matters at home – it will make life much easier for you later on if you can sort out your financial affairs before you move. Things to check up on include pension plans, insurance payments and mailing addresses held by banks and other institutions. Tax status and payments – make sure that you clearly understand your tax obligations in your home country before you leave and ensure that you've made all the necessary payments to the taxman.

Book a flight – consider whether you plan to make a trip back home during your first year abroad and whether it makes more sense to book a one-year open return ticket or a one-way flight.

Start your job search – if you're coming to Singapore to look for a job, do as much networking prior to your arrival as possible. Get in touch with friends and business contacts and be sure to post your CV on Singapore-specific internet job sites and monitor job postings regularly. (See Work on p.81 for more information.)

Accommodation – if possible, arrange temporary accommodation for the first few weeks after your arrival so that you have time to find your dream home. See Serviced Apartments on p.42 for a list of furnished apartments or estate agents on p.96.

Schools for your children – start enquiring about schools right away as some schools have lengthy waiting lists. Some parents pick a school then find a home nearby, while others do it the other way around (see Education on p.150).

When You Arrive

The list of things to do once you arrive may seem endless – but the sooner you get them over with, the sooner you'll be enjoying all Singapore has to offer. Here are some of the main tasks you'll have to tackle:

- **Residency/visas** – if you're coming to Singapore for work you'll need to submit your employment pass application, get an approval-in-principle letter and have a medical test (if applicable) before submitting your passport for them to process your residency application.

Expat Websites on Singapore

Getting to know about life in the country you're moving to will definitely help reduce the culture shock once you get there. This book, of course, is one of the most comprehensive sources of information but logging on to expat websites could be helpful too. You'll often find chat rooms or email addresses and you could find yourself building a support network before you've even arrived.

- www.entersingapore.info
- www.expatlivingsingapore.com
- www.expatsingapore.com
- www.singapore.alloexpat.com
- www.singapore.asiaxpat.com
- www.singaporeexpats.com
- www.theexpat.com

Mini Explorer

Don't be fooled by the size of this little star – it's full of insider info, maps, contacts, tips and facts about this vibrant city. From shops to spas, bars to bargains and everything in between, the Mini Explorer helps you get the most out of your stay in Singapore, however long you're staying.

- **Make a home** – for information about residential areas see p.102, for accommodation options see p.97, and where to furnish your home see p.124.
- **Find schools for your children** – choosing a school is always a long process, more so when you're in a foreign country. Start the process early and bear in mind that as there could be waiting lists, any research you do in advance (on the internet or by asking other expats with school-going children) will stand you in good stead. See the Education section on p.150.
- **Get connected** – find out how to get a mobile phone on p.134 and how to get your utilities up and running (p.132).
- **Licences** – see p.75 to find out about the licences you need to drive a car or p.136 for your TV.
- **Register with your embassy** – it's a good idea to let your embassy know you're living in Singapore.
- **Settle in** – start to enjoy your new home by exploring the country (p.172) and getting involved in sports or other activities (p.242). Start meeting members of your new community through social groups (p.294) and at places of worship (p.20).

Essential Documents

The official documents required for applications generally need to be originals, although in most cases all that's required is for someone to see the original and make a copy of it. It's a good idea to make copies of all of your documents and keep them somewhere safe in case you ever lose the originals.

Your original passport, valid for at least six months from your date of arrival in Singapore, is absolutely essential. Any forms that you complete will ask for your passport number so memorising it or keeping it close at hand will make things easier. To obtain an employment pass or a dependant's pass you'll also need:

- Marriage certificate
- Educational certificates (highest level only – no need to bring your primary school certificate)
- Children's birth certificates

Passport photos are required for your employment or dependant's pass application, but not usually for other applications. The instant photo shop passport photos taken against a white background are fine and they don't need to be signed by a witness.

Other documents such as your birth certificate, divorce or annulment certificates, driving licence, university transcripts, professional certification certificates, and employment contracts could also become necessary at some point, so bring them along. Any forms or applications that you submit to the government

> ### Beat The Heat
> *The heat and humidity may seem stifling when you first arrive in Singapore, but most people do acclimatise – to the point where 26°C will seem cold! Until you reach that point, air conditioning will be your best friend. Ceiling fans and a breezy residence with windows at the front and back can also help you survive the heat.*

and other institutions in Singapore will be in English, and any of your official documents that are not in English will require a certified translation to be submitted along with the original. Certified translations are usually easier to get in your home country, but your home country's embassy in Singapore will probably provide this service for a fee.

When You Leave

Departure from Singapore involves a bit more than a plane ticket and packed suitcase. First and foremost, the government wants to be sure you've paid your taxes. Beyond that there are services to terminate, accounts to close and property to sell up, ship out or dispose of.

- **Taxes** – your company is responsible for filing your Form IR21 with the Internal Revenue Authority of Singapore, but it's worth confirming with HR that they've taken care of it. Many people want to know if they can reclaim taxes when they leave, particularly if they've only lived there for part of a year. The short answer is no. Tourists are entitled to a GST refund, but EP holders, permanent residents and citizens cannot claim the refund. If you work in Singapore for less than 60 days of the year, you usually don't have to pay any tax. If you've worked for anything from 60 days to six months (in a calendar year) you will play a flat rate of 15%. Anything longer than six months makes you a tax resident and you will pay taxes according to the standard graduated tax rates. This is all detailed in the Taxation section (see p.90).
- **Residence Permit** – you will need to go to the Ministry of Manpower to cancel your residence permit and to receive a social visit pass in exchange. Make sure you're out of the country before it expires!
- **Rent deposit** – your landlord will inspect your rental property and, hopefully, return the deposit. A quick but thorough clean usually ensures you get your deposit back.
- **Utilities** – don't forget to cancel all services such as water, lights, phone, internet, cable TV and your newspaper service.
- **Change of address** – if you know what your address at your new destination will be, you can pay a small fee to have SingPost redirect your mail for the first few months after your departure.
- **Shipping** – it's amazing how much you can collect in a short time in Singapore. You'll need to arrange a shipping address at your next destination for anything you're not taking on the plane.
- **Moving sale** – you can donate things you don't need or want anymore to a charity, hold a garage sale or give it away to friends. There will always be takers if the price is right.

69

Moving to Singapore is fairly straightforward in terms of the official documents that you will need to get. The vast majority of expats enter the country on a social visit pass that's issued by immigration when you enter the country. The next step then is to apply for an employment pass or a dependant's pass. If approved, this will generally be the only official document you will need – there are no separate health cards or identity cards. Your company may help you with submitting your EP or DP application and collecting the pass when it is ready, but even if they don't the process isn't particularly arduous.

Entry Visa
Other options **Visas** p.24

All travellers entering Singapore must pass through immigration clearance whether you're entering by land, sea or air. Foreigners with travel documents issued by European countries or the United States generally don't need a visa to enter Singapore. Those holding passports from various countries in the Middle East, North Africa, south Asia and south-east Asia may need to apply for a visa prior to their arrival in Singapore. A full list of countries requiring visas can be found on the Immigration & Checkpoints Authority website (www.ica.gov.sg). Regardless of your nationality, you must have a passport valid for at least six months from the date that you enter Singapore. For more information about entering Singapore as a tourist or visitor, see the General Information chapter (p.1).

Visa Problems
Singapore takes visa offences very seriously. If you overstay the period of your visa, you will be detained by Immigration & Checkpoints Authority officials when you leave the country, and you may be fined or face a jail sentence depending on how long you have overstayed your welcome.

Regardless of whether you're entering Singapore to look for work, to take up a pre-arranged job or to accompany your spouse who is moving here to work, you will initially enter on a social visit pass, or SVP. SVPs are valid for 14 to 30 days and can be renewed for up to three months.

Armed with an SVP you will now be able to sort out your residence visa, which you must do while the SVP is still valid. You aren't allowed to work while you only hold a SVP unless you've received an approval-in-principle letter from the Ministry of Manpower in response to your employment pass application. However, SVP holders are permitted to go to job interviews and participate in business negotiations. If you need to leave the country while you're an SVP holder it's best to confirm the validity of your pass before leaving in order to avoid any confusion on your return.

When your residence visa – whether it's an employment or a dependant's pass – is issued, it will replace your SVP and you will need to produce it when leaving and returning to Singapore.

Health Card
Singapore does not have a public healthcare system, so you don't need a health card. Medisave is a national programme that requires Singaporeans to set a portion of their income aside in a medical savings scheme, but this only applies to Singapore citizens and permanent residents; expats living in Singapore on an employment pass or dependant's pass are not eligible.

When using the healthcare services, such as government and private hospitals and clinics, you should bring along your passport and green card (employment pass, dependant pass or long-term social visit pass). If you have health insurance through your employer or a personal insurance plan, make sure that you know what steps you should take to be reimbursed by your insurance company. In some cases you are required to notify your insurance company prior to undertaking any medical services, while in other cases you must notify the insurer within a maximum number of days following medical treatment. See Health Insurance on p.71 for more information. Both public and private hospitals generally provide emergency medical treatment before dealing with matters of insurance and payment. But if your situation isn't deemed to be critical, you will probably need to provide payment or prove that your medical insurance will cover costs before you will be treated. For more information, see Emergency Services on p.138.

Health Insurance

Health insurance is not mandatory for expats, but since you must pay for medical services in Singapore it's definitely a good idea to have insurance. Most expats receive health insurance through their employer, but if you have a spouse and children you should definitely check whether your family is covered under any insurance you receive through work. If you're being transferred to Singapore by your employer, check whether the health insurance you have in your home country will cover you while living in Singapore – this may be the case if your insurer has a branch in Singapore. If you are starting a new job in Singapore and you are offered a contract with no health insurance included, try to negotiate to have it added to your contract – it will be one less thing for you to arrange and the cost to your employer is relatively low.

As one of Asia's top financial services centres, Singapore is home to many major international insurance companies offering insurance plans similar to those you would find at home. Insurance benefits vary depending on the insurer and plan that you choose, but in general the following things are covered in standard health insurance: hospital treatment and services, including day surgery, home nursing following hospitalisation, accident dental services and local ambulance; outpatient services, including visits to specialists, outpatient laboratory and x-ray services, and outpatient prescription drugs; organ transplants; emergency medical evacuation; and travel personal accident coverage. Just as the benefits of health insurance plans can range from basic to fully loaded, so can the cost. You can pay anywhere from a few hundred to many thousands of dollars per year, with premiums increasing the older you are. Coverage for children can be considerably lower if one of the parents is covered by the insurer. Some insurers have family health insurance plans that offer discounts when all members of a family are covered under the same plan. Premiums are generally paid annually.

Residence Visa
Other options **Visas** p.24

Depending on your employment and living circumstances, you will be issued with one of several different types of visas in order to live in Singapore. However this visa is only issued at the Ministry of Manpower office so you will first enter the country on a social visit pass following the same entry process as tourists. This applies both if you'll be looking for work once here and if you have already lined up a job and submitted an employment visa application through your new employer. See the Entry Visa section on p.70 for more information.

If You Are Looking For Work
You can attend job interviews while holding a social visit pass (SVP). If the SVP isn't valid for long enough for you to land a job and you don't want to do visa runs, you can apply for an 'employment pass eligibility certificate'. The EPEC is intended for highly qualified expats with advanced degrees, specialised skills or professional qualifications. If granted, the EPEC allows you to apply for a six-month social visit pass. You'll need to submit an application form, copies of your academic or professional qualifications and transcripts, a recent passport photo and a copy of your passport showing the page with your personal details. Your application will be processed within three working days at no charge. The EPEC is only issued once and cannot be renewed.

If You Have a Job
To work in Singapore you must have either a professional visa or a visa for entrepreneurs. These act both as a residence visa and as a labour card. Other options are the professional visit pass for foreigners undertaking short-term professional assignments in Singapore; or the long-term social visit pass for entrepreneurs. The latter allows foreigners to reside in Singapore for up to six months while exploring business opportunities, or for up to a year if they're supported by the Singapore Economic Development Board or the Agency for Science, Technology and Research. While these visas may be useful for individuals in specific situations, the vast majority of expats have an employment pass.

Employment Pass

There are three categories of employment pass (or EP): P1, P2 and Q1.

- To qualify for a P1 EP you must earn more than $7,000 per month and have professional qualifications or skills in a professional, administrative, executive or managerial capacity.
- To qualify for a P2 EP, you must earn between $3,500 and $7,000 per month.
- To qualify for a Q1 EP you must earn more than $2,500 per month and hold degrees or other qualifications that are deemed acceptable by the Ministry of Manpower.

If you hold either a P1 or P2 EP, you can apply for long-term social visit passes for your parents, parents-in-law, step children, common-law spouse, handicapped children and unmarried daughters older than 21 years.

Employment Pass Application and Renewal

The EP application process is fairly straightforward and can be started before you arrive in Singapore. You need the following documents:
- A completed EP application form (Form 8), signed by you and your prospective employer.
- A passport photo taken within the last three months.
- A copy of your highest educational certificate.
- A copy of your passport showing your personal details.

If applicable, a copy of your registration with the necessary professional body or accreditation agency (see Registration of Professionals on p.73).

You can submit these documents either at a SingPost post office or over the internet if your employer is a registered user of the EP Online system. The $10 application fee is payable by cash, cashcard or NETS (NETS is the point-of-sale debit system used in Singapore) at the post office or by Visa, MasterCard or eNETS debit if you're doing this online. The Ministry of Manpower (MOM) will take about three weeks to process your EP application. (Just by the by, although we know you'd never do it, making false statements in an EP application is a serious offence, and you could face a fine of up to $4,000 and a jail term of up to one year if found guilty of doing so.)

Professional Bodies and Accreditation Agencies		
Nurses	Singapore Nursing Board	6372 3082
Doctors	Singapore Medical Council or	6372 3061
	Traditional Chinese Medicine Practitioners Board	6236 1080
Teachers	Singapore Ministry of Education	6872 2220
Lawyers	Singapore Attorney-General's Chambers	6336 1411
Dentists	Singapore Dental Council	6372 3076

If your application meets the ministry's requirements, an approval-in-principle letter is sent to your employer, allowing you to start working while you complete the final steps of the application process. The letter will tell you whether you need to have a medical test and will include a form to be filled in by the doctor. You will probably have to have a chest x-ray for tuberculosis and an HIV test, which can be done at any medical clinic and will cost $25-50.

Once this is done, take the medical results, the approval-in-principle letter and your original passport to the MOM office at 18 Havelock Road (map 17-C2). The office is open from 8:00 to 16:00 from Monday to Friday and 8:00 to 12:00 on Saturday. (It's best to go first thing in the morning.) Take a number to submit your documents to an officer who will then give you a receipt and ask you to return about three hours later to collect your passport and EP (assuming there are no problems with your medical test). When you return for collection, take another queue number and then pay $30 for every year that the EP is valid.

Employment passes are usually valid for one to two years, although three years can be granted at the discretion of MOM. When the employment pass expiry date approaches, your employer will receive a renewal form to fill out and mail back to MOM. The notification may include a health declaration form for you to fill out and return with the renewal form. Any dependant's passes linked to your EP will come up for renewal at the same time. Once the renewal is approved, an approval-in-principle letter will be sent to your employer. Take this, along with your passport and existing EP to MOM. Leave it there for about three hours and return in the afternoon to pay the renewal charges and collect your new EP. You should bring your dependants' passports and passes along at the same time. Renewal costs $30 per year or part thereof for every EP or Dependant's Pass.

Employment Pass Through Self-Employment

The EntrePass is an EP for entrepreneurs who want to set up their own business in Singapore. Application for this is more involved, requiring, among other things, a 10 page business plan with pro-forma financial statements. The renewal process will assess the performance of your company and whether it will continue to be viable. See also Setting Up a Business on p.81.

Registration of Professionals

Expats working in the nursing, medical, teaching or legal professions have to register with the relevant body or accreditation agency and provide a certificate of registration when applying for their employment pass.

Dependant's Pass

If you hold a P1, P2 or Q1 EP you can apply for dependant's passes for your spouse and unmarried children under 21 years old. Dependant's passes (or DP's) are linked to your EP and you can submit their application at the same time as you submit your EP application, or once your EP application has been submitted. Anyone applying for a dependant's pass must hold a valid social visit pass and the following documents must be submitted:

- A completed dependant's pass application form (Form 12) signed by you and your prospective employer.
- A copy of your official marriage certificate (if applying for your spouse or if your spouse is a Singapore citizen).
- A copy of an embassy-certified document confirming the relationship between you and your common-law spouse (if applying for a DP for a common-law spouse).
- A copy of your children's birth or adoption certificates if applying for a DP for your children.
- A copy of your spouse and/or children's passports showing their personal details.
- Passport photos of your spouse and/or children taken within the last three months.
- DP holders are not allowed to work. If they would like to they will have to apply for an EP (see p.72).

The application and renewal procedures for DPs are the same as those for EPs. A DP costs $30 per year or part thereof to renew, and will have the same renewal timeline as the EP to which it's linked. Children with DPs don't require a student pass to attend a Ministry of Education approved school. If you and your spouse have a baby while living in Singapore, your child will automatically be granted a social visit pass valid for 42 days from the date of birth, during which time you'll need to apply for a DP for your baby. If your application is still pending at the end of the 42 days, you may apply for an extension of the baby's SVP.

Sole Custody/Single Parents

Single parents or parents with sole custody of their children should not have any difficulty in gaining dependant's passes for their children as long as they have the children's birth certificates identifying them as one of the birth parents. In the case of step children or adopted children, a single parent or parent with sole custody must submit a certified letter from a court confirming that they have been granted sole custody of the children.

Sponsoring a Maid

Expats usually hire a maid through an agency. Using an agency means that you don't have to deal with the administrative hassles of bringing a maid into the country, such as arranging a work permit, health check, security bond and travel arrangements. As long as you have a minimum annual income of $30,000, you can hire a maid. See Domestic Help, p.126.

Student Pass

Student passes are available to foreigners who want to study fulltime at an institution that's registered with the Ministry of Education (MOE) or with the Ministry of Community Development, Youth and Sports (MCYS) to operate as a childcare centre. Student passes may also be issued for non-registered institutions provided that the Immigration & Checkpoints Authority has given them permission to accept foreign students. Children of expats who have valid DPs do not require a separate student pass to study at a school that's registered with MOE or MCYS. However they will require a student's pass once they want to apply to study at a Singapore university or college. See Education, p.150.

Citizenship ◄	*Permanent Residence*
If you've been a permanent resident for two years or more and you're at least 21 years old you can apply for citizenship, although not many expats take this major step. For more information about citizenship contact the Immigration & Checkpoints Authority at 6391 6100.	Expats can apply for permanent residence if they hold a P1, P2 or Q1 EP or if they are the spouse or unmarried child (below 21 years old) of a Singapore permanent resident (SPR) or Singapore citizen (SC). In assessing your application, the Immigration & Checkpoints Authority will consider how long you have lived in Singapore, your age, your educational and professional qualifications, your income and whether you have any family residing in Singapore.

There are mixed feelings among expats regarding the benefits of PR. On the plus side you will become part of the Central Provident Fund scheme, a national pension fund to which you and your employer will contribute. It's also easier for you to set up a company and as an SPR you can remain in the country if you lose your job whereas EP holders have to leave. One of the drawbacks though is that sons of SPRs have to perform two years of fulltime National Service when they're 16 and fulfill other NS duties each year until they're in their 40s or 50s.

The Global Investors Programme is another option for those seeking PR. The programme targets foreign investors and entrepreneurs who are willing to invest a minimum of $1 million in a new or existing business in Singapore and helps them to acquire PR. For more information contact the Singapore Economic Development Board at 6336 2288.

ID Card

Singapore citizens and permanent residents have a national registration identity card (NRIC) but there's no ID card for expats, who tend to use their passport as their primary identity document. When asked for an identification number on an official form you can either fill in your passport number or your foreign identification number. The FIN is the nine-digit alpha-numeric number that's given to you when your employment or dependant's pass is issued.

Driving Licence

Other options **Transportation** p.159

For the Record

Your foreign licence must have been obtained at least six months prior to your Singapore EP being issued. If you have demerits on your home country licence it's not much of a problem – these are only taken into consideration if you hold a Malaysian licence.

Singapore has a relatively simple driving licence system for foreigners. You can drive in Singapore for 12 months with a valid foreign driving licence and an international driving permit (IDP). If your original licence isn't in English you will need to carry an official English translation of it too. The translation can usually be done by your embassy in Singapore for $100-200. The 12 month period is based on your first arrival in Singapore and counts from then even if you leave the country in the meantime. After 12 months you'll have to convert your licence to a Singaporean one. The legal age for driving is 18. If you have a valid driving licence from your home country but are under 18, you may not drive in Singapore. You should always have your driving licence and IDP (if applicable) on you when driving as you'll need it if you're in an accident or are caught breaking a traffic rule.

Once you reach 12 months in Singapore, you will have to convert your home country licence to a Singapore driving licence, which will be valid for five years.

Converting Your Home Country Licence

To convert your driving licence you will need to take the basic theory test, which is administered by computer at one of the three government-sanctioned Driving Centres in Singapore (see table on p.76). No practical test is required. Register for the BTT at any of the Driving Centres to be given a test date. Tests are held daily, but high demand means you'll probably have a three-week wait.

The BTT is taken with the traffic police who, conveniently, have offices at each of the Driving Centres. The test costs $11.25 and you'll know your result immediately after completing the test. Reading through the $3.20 study book for the test is recommended and if you want to get in some practice before sitting for the test, you can take a trial BTT at the Driving Centres for $5.25. Once you've successfully completed the BTT you can apply for licence conversion with the traffic police. You need your passport and employment pass (EP), a valid foreign driving licence, a valid IDP, an official translation if your original licence is not in English and an extract of your driving licence record showing the date of first issue of your foreign licence and its class.

Health Check For Two

If you're over 65 and are planning to apply for licence conversion immediately upon arrival in Singapore, it's worthwhile getting the checklist and having it completed at the same time as your medical test for your EP.

If you're over 65 you will have to take a medical test before the licence conversion is granted. The traffic police will give you a checklist that you'll have to take to a doctor to be completed. Once you reach 70 you have to provide medical test results annually. Your driving licence is linked to your EP so if you change jobs you have to notify the traffic authorities. If you cancel your EP and leave the country, your licence becomes invalid. Your Singapore driving licence is valid for five years (except if your circumstances change as mentioned above). As long as your EP is still valid your driving licence can be renewed at the Traffic Police Headquarters at Ubi Avenue 3 (6547 0000). Take your passport, EP, existing driving licence, a passport photo and $50.

Driving Test

If you don't have a valid driving licence from your home country you'll have to sit for the full driving test in Singapore. You'll start with the BTT, as described above, then take a final theory test for $11.25. You can then enroll for the practical test at the driving centre. Enrolment costs $80 plus $154.40 to take the test (the fee includes the use of a car). There's usually a two-month wait from when you complete the theory tests to the time when you can take the practical. There are numerous driving schools (often just one-man operations with a car) that can provide you practice time behind the wheel.

Driving Schools

Bukit Batok Driving Centre	Bukit Batok	6561 1233	www.bbdc.sg
Comfort Driving Centre	Geylang	6841 8900	www.comfortdrivingcentre.com.sg
Singapore Safety Driving Centre	Ang Mo Kio	6482 6060	www.ssdcl.com.sg

Motorcycle Licence

The BTT and conversion process for a motorcycle licence are the same as for a car licence. If you want to convert to a dual car/motorcycle licence in Singapore, your home country licence must indicate that you are licensed to drive both. Singapore has three classes of motorcycle licence, the lowest being for bikes below 200cc. All foreigners, regardless of what their home country licence allows, are given the lowest class of Singapore motorcycle licence to begin with. After a year you can take a practical test and apply for a higher class licence.

Birth Certificate & Registration

Births in Singapore should be registered within 14 days, although there is an official grace period of up to a month. A birth can be registered at the Registry of Births and Deaths or, if it takes place at one of the following hospitals, at the birth registration centre there: KK Women's Hospital, East Shore Hospital, Gleneagles Hospital, Mt Alvernia Hospital, Mt Elizabeth Hospital, National University Hospital, Singapore General Hospital, Thomson Medical Centre, Raffles Hospital. The Registry of Births and Deaths is located in the ICA Building (10 Kallang Road, 6391 6343). The registration fee is $18 but some hospitals may charge an additional administrative fee. Documents required for registration are: the notification of live birth issued by the hospital, both parents' passports and EP cards and the original marriage certificate. The child's name must be furnished upon registration. If someone other than the parents registers the birth, a letter of authorisation from the parents of the child is also required.

Once the birth is registered, a Singapore birth certificate is issued. This is not a certificate of citizenship – that's only available to the children of Singapore citizens. You must apply for residency (in the form of a dependant's pass) within 42 days of your child's birth. The process is the same as for any other person requesting a DP (see p.73). You will first need to apply for a passport with your home country's embassy. Procedures vary so contact your embassy to find out what is required and how long it takes to process a passport. If the parents are of different nationalities you'll need to go to the relevant embassies to find out whether their regulations allow dual citizenship.

Unmarried women who give birth won't face any problems but will have to register the birth at the ICA Building.

Adoption

Adoption is not as common in Singapore as it is in the west. Local culture lends itself more to informal adoption where friends or members of the extended family take responsibility for a child. That said, it is possible to adopt both local and foreign children and the procedures are well documented. For Singaporean children first priority is given to placing them with a Singaporean family, then with a permanent resident family and finally expats on an employment pass will be considered. The starting point for adoption would be to contact the Ministry of Community Development, Youth and Sports (www.mcys.gov.sg, MCYS Adoption Hotline 6355 6388), the government agency that oversees adoptions. From there a good next step is to contact TOUCH Adoption Services (www.tcs.com.sg, 6317 9988) who run adoption workshops and who can guide you through the process. It's also recommended that you appoint a lawyer to help you through the paperwork and prepare you for your required appearance before a judge. An adopted child is generally not given Singapore citizenship when adopted by foreign or PR parents.

Christenings

Catholic baptisms are held on Sundays at any of the Catholic churches in Singapore (see www.veritas.org.sg for a list of churches). Some churches hold a preparation session for parents and godparents before the christening. Both godparents must be confirmed Catholics and parents must have been married in a Catholic church. There's a form to be filled out at the church but it's fairly straightforward and there's no fee involved.

Marriage Certificate & Registration

Getting Married in Singapore

It's not common for expats to get married in Singapore, unless one half of the couple is Singaporean. Otherwise, it's more likely that the wedding will take place in their home country, among old friends and family, followed by a reception or party for their friends in Singapore once the newlywed couple returns. However island weddings are becoming an increasingly popular option too.

Back in Singapore, popular venues for weddings tend to be the major hotels, along with the Singapore Botanic Gardens, Chjimes and the Sentosa Resort and Spa on Sentosa Island. Most weddings are a mix of western-style wedding with some elements of Asian style. This is either to pay homage to the fact that the couple met in Singapore, or to meet the wishes of the Singaporean half of the couple, if there is one. Regardless of their style or the venue, weddings are big business in Singapore, and there's a wide range of wedding service providers to choose from. Jonathan Goh at Wedding Acts (www.weddingacts.com, 9186 5536) is an experienced planner who can take the entire process out of your hands and present you with a spectacular experience on the day. If you want to take care of the details yourself, www.singaporebrides.com lists local product and service providers and hosts a chat room where you can ask questions of other brides. Gift registries aren't typical, but a wedding planner should be able to tell you which few stores do offer the service. See also Wedding Services on p.354.

Found the One?
Lucky you. Now you've just got to sort the invitations, the tailor-made wedding dress, the shoes, the cake, the dinner, the flowers, the music, the seating plan… But don't stress it! Turn to p.354 for information on Singapore's very finest wedding professionals.

The Paperwork

Marriages are overseen by the Registry of Marriages, but Muslim marriages come under the Registry of Muslim Marriages (see further on in this section). ROM is located at 7 Fort Canning Rise, between City Hall and Dhoby Ghaut MRT stations. The process for getting married is relatively straightforward and is fully explained on the ROM website (www.rom.gov.sg). If you're using a wedding consultant they'll be able to guide you through the procedure as well.

It begins with filing a 'notice of marriage' online at ROM's website. You will need to include information about your marriage official or solemniser at the same time, so you need to choose this person first. You will also need the passport information (or NRIC information for Singaporeans) for both parties and the two witnesses. You then have to wait a minimum of 21 days before

Chinese Weddings

Chinese weddings are more about the style in which the wedding is held rather than any strict religious rituals. Often hundreds of people are invited to a lavish Chinese-style dinner. Guests are as likely to be close friends of the bride and groom as they are distant business associates of the bride's father. Essentially, the wedding is a chance for the parents of the couple to show off. Red packets containing money, or ang pows, are presented by guests to the couple with the idea that the value should hopefully cover the cost of the dinner and wedding arrangements. Chinese weddings are compatible with most Christian denominations.

you can solemnise your marriage (take your vows).
When you do take your vows you have to go to ROM
three to five days before the ceremony for the
'verification of documents and a statutory declaration'
(VD/SD). This requires both parties and the witnesses,
and you will need to present all your documents.
Upon completing the VD/SD you'll receive your
marriage licence and you can go ahead and proceed
with your wedding on the appointed day (again, both
parties and two witnesses need to be present for this).
Note that the notice of marriage expires after three
months, so you need to solemnise the marriage
before then or re-file.

After the vows have been taken and the registry has
been signed you will receive your marriage certificate. Congratulations! You're now
officially married.

Your documents must be in English and you must have the originals or certified
translations if the originals are not in English. If either party does not speak English,
Malay, Mandarin or Tamil, you will need an official translator with you for the VD/SD
and solemnization.

The procedure is easiest if both parties are at least 21 and your witnesses must be 21 or
older. For details on marriage when one or both parties are under 21 see the ROM
website. If both parties are foreigners, at least one of you will have to have been
resident in Singapore for 15 days before being able to file.

Wedding fees are $26 if one of the parties is Singaporean. If both are foreigners the
cost ranges from $128 to $298 depending on the day you solemnise your marriage.
For a list of legal solemnisers in Singapore see the ROM website. If you choose to be
married at the Registry Office a solemniser will be appointed for you. Marriages
registered in Singapore are generally recognised elsewhere in the world, but it's worth
confirming this with your home country embassy. You may also have to register your
wedding with your embassy.

If you decide to take your husband's name you will have to change your documents to
match your new name. Changes to make include your bank accounts, passport, driving
licence and any government agencies you deal with. Changing your name can usually be
achieved with a copy of your marriage certificate, your passport and residence permit.

> ### Island Style I Dos
> A growing number of couples
> are opting to take a select
> group of friends and family to
> exotic locations like Bali,
> Indonesia or islands in Malaysia
> or Thailand for an idyllic beach
> wedding. Wedding planners in
> Singapore will take care of all
> the arrangements – from hotel
> bookings and paperwork, to
> decorations and catering.

Shotgun Weddings
*If you're looking for a
shotgun wedding in
Singapore, you're out of
luck. The minimum time
it would take for you to
be formally married
after making the
decision is 21 days, and
that's if you act fast.*

Catholics and Anglicans

Catholics are required to take a marriage preparation course through the Marriage
Encounter House in Punggol. Prior to the wedding they will also have to sign a
prenuptial enquiry form. Once this is completed and all the ROM procedures have
been followed, the marriage can be solemnised. It's best to contact your parish or
priest about six months before the wedding date so that everything can run smoothly.
For Anglican couples wishing to be married at a cathedral in Singapore, one of the
parties must have been an active member of the church in question for more than a
year. The couple is required to take a marriage preparation course which is free, but the
course book costs about $15. It's also suggested that the couple has an interview with
the pastor in order to develop a closer relationship with the person who will play an
important part in the proceedings.

Muslims

Muslims wishing to be married in Singapore follow the same process as non-
Muslims, but with the following differences: registration is done at the Registry of

Muslim Marriages (7 Fort Canning Place, www.romm.gov.sg) either in person or online. Registration requires a Wali, the bride's guardian, to be present. From registration the minimum time before solemnisation is seven days and the registration expires after 150 days.

The VD/SD again requires the presence of both parties and the Wali. The solemnisation will have to be witnessed by two practicing Muslim males and the groom must give a gift with a minimum value of $100 to the bride.

Couples must take a marriage guidance course before solemnisation. These are available through ROMM and a schedule of courses is on their website. If the prospective groom is a non-Muslim, he will have to take a conversion course with the Islamic Religious Council of Singapore (Majlis Ugama Islam Singapura). For more information on conversion, call MUIS at 6256 8188 or visit www.muis.gov.sg.

Hindus

There are many temples around Singapore where Hindu weddings can be held. For information on the procedures involved you can contact the Hindu Endowments Board at 6296 2469, or go to a temple and ask for guidance.

Death Certificate & Registration

In the Event of a Death

When someone dies outside of a hospital, the police should be notified by dialling 999. They will arrange for a Ministry of Health officer to examine the body. Assuming the officer is satisfied that the cause of death is natural, a certificate of cause of death will be issued. If the death takes place in a hospital, the attending doctor will provide you with a certificate (the CCD). The embassy of the deceased's home country should also be contacted to register the death with them. The embassy will want to see the Singapore death certificate and they will be able to provide support and guidance on any issues relating to repatriation of the corpse and obtaining a death certificate from the home country.

Investigation & Autopsy
In the event of a suspicious death, or where the attending doctor or MOH officer is not satisfied that the death was natural, an investigation will be launched by the police. This may involve an autopsy and will delay the issuing of a death certificate. It's best to inform the relevant embassy of the investigation so that they can collaborate with the police as necessary.

Registering a Death

Deaths are required to be registered within 24 hours. Registration is free of charge. Deaths occurring at government-run hospitals can be registered at the hospital itself and they will issue the death certificate. Government-run hospitals include Alexandra Hospital, Changi General Hospital, Tan Tock Seng Hospital, KK Women's Hospital, Ang Mo Kio Community Hospital, National University Hospital, Singapore General Hospital and the Centre for Forensic Medicine. For a death occurring in a private hospital or outside of a hospital you are required to register the death at any neighbourhood Police Centre/Post or at the Registry of Births & Deaths (ICA Building, 10 Kallang Road, 6391 6343). The documents required are the CCD, the deceased's passport and EP and the informant's passport and EP.

Returning the Deceased

The deceased's home country embassy and an undertaker will help you with the repatriation process. The embassy will help you with the country-specific guidelines and requirements for the home country to accept the corpse. You will need to engage an undertaker, who will deal with most of the paperwork. The undertaker will take a copy of the death certificate and passport of the deceased, together with the embalming and sealing certificates that he will provide, to the Port Health agency. Port Health will then provide an export permit. With the export permit, the undertaker will liaise with the relevant embassy and arrange a flight. Packing requirements vary by country and will affect the cost. A rough estimate of the total cost of repatriation is $5,000-10,000. The entire repatriation process can be completed in two to three days, depending on available flights. No export permit is required for the ashes if a corpse is cremated, although the destination country may require some paperwork.

Organ Donation

Singapore has an active organ donation system that Singaporeans must opt out of if they do not want to take part. For expats though, it's an opt-in system. You can download an organ donation pledge form from the Ministry of Health website (www.moh.gov.sg) and send it in. Within three weeks you'll receive your donor card and you will have been added to the organ donor database. (See also Donor Card on p.138.)

Working in Singapore

Singapore is a great place to work as an expat. While working and living conditions are perhaps not as glamorous as they were in the boom years of the 1980s and early 1990s, the vast majority of expats still have luxurious standards of living and Singapore should certainly not be looked upon as a hardship posting. It has a vibrant, international business environment and provides excellent opportunities for regional exposure and career advancement. Taxes are low, services and infrastructure are first rate and the pace of life, while not totally relaxed, is certainly less intense than in Tokyo, Hong Kong, London or New York.

The expat population is large, and the government is very supportive of it as they fashion Singapore into a global city along the lines of New York and London. There are sizeable communities of Americans, British, Japanese and Australians, but just about every western and Asian country has some presence here. Singapore has four official languages – English, Mandarin, Malay and Tamil – but English is the language of government and business and you won't need to speak another language to be able to conduct business effectively here. However, it never hurts to try and learn a few phrases that can be used to show your respect and break the ice at a meeting.

Close Community

Despite the large expat population, there's still a good chance that you're only once or twice removed via common friends from most other expats in Singapore. You can play this to your advantage for connections and job opportunities, but also be careful what you say; news and gossip travel quickly!

Employment Pass

The employment pass is your initial ticket to reside in Singapore, either directly as an employee, or indirectly as the dependant of an EP holder. The EP is tied to your job, so changing companies requires the cancellation of your existing EP and applying for a new one. As an EP holder you will not be allowed to take on any work outside the scope of work defined by your EP, which can sometimes be limiting if you see an interesting sideline business opportunity that you want to pursue.

Setting Up a Business in Singapore

Singapore can be a great place to set up a business. It has excellent business infrastructure, a strong legal system with intellectual property rights enforcement and low corporate taxes. If you're setting up a business in one of the government-targeted growth industries, you'll most likely be eligible for numerous tax incentives, grants and other benefits. For more information on this see the Economic Development Board website at www.edb.gov.sg.

The government has recognised the importance of attracting businesses and entrepreneurs to Singapore, given that it has no natural resources and a small population. The result is that setting up a business here is an easy, straightforward process. For Singapore citizens and permanent residents it can be a matter of 48 hours and $65 to set up a company. For foreigners, the process is slightly more complex, but still a breeze compared to most other countries.

You will have to apply for an EP in tandem with your business start-up, as it will be the basis on which you gain employment and residency in Singapore. Download an Entrepass application form from the Ministry of Manpower website (www.mom.gov.sg) and fill it out. You will need to submit this to MOM, along with supporting documentation as listed in the form and a business plan of a maximum of 10 pages. The business plan and application will be evaluated to assess whether the business is a viable one and whether you are capable of operating the business. Unless you're a chiropractor trying to set up an engineering firm (or something similarly irrelevant to your education and experience) you should have little problem getting approval.

Once you have in-principle approval for your plan, you need to get a bankers guarantee for $3,000 and register your business with the Accounting and Corporate Regulatory Authority (www.acra.gov.sg). The banker's guarantee is the government's safeguard against you leaving the country without paying your taxes. If you can find a reputable

Singapore-registered company to sponsor you, no banker's guarantee is required. You'll likely have to have a direct relationship with a company, or someone in its management, in order for them to consider sponsoring you. With these two pieces of paper you can return to MOM to collect your EP – and you've set up your business!

Networking

The saying 'it's not what you know, but who you know' is particularly relevant in Singapore. While skills and experience are certainly not discounted, it is immeasurably important to be plugged into the local business scene for your industry or profession. The right connection is often the key to a new business opportunity or job. There is no shortage of opportunities to network in Singapore. The American, British and Singapore International Chambers of Commerce – among many others – are all very active and provide numerous networking activities every month. Trade shows, conferences, seminars and social events are all prime opportunities to keep yourself in the loop, meet the right people and hear about the latest opportunities.

Business Culture & Etiquette

Singapore's business culture is somewhat more relaxed than in Northern Asia, but at times more formal than in the West. The concept of 'face' – not losing face in public – is still evident, although not as strongly as you'll see in China or Japan. Maintaining a respectful attitude and not directly contradicting someone in front of others is still appropriate in many situations. You will also find that the senior person at a meeting will often be deferred to for any decisions or statements of opinion. However, a more western style of business is slowly taking hold and you are unlikely to find yourself feeling out of place or at a loss for what to do during a business transaction.

In terms of business attire, a full suit is usually not required, unless you are meeting very senior people or work in industries such as banking or law. A shirt and tie or blouse and skirt will suffice for most occasions – if you are unsure, just ask your colleagues what is appropriate for a given situation. Casual Fridays have been adopted at some companies and creative industries like marketing and advertising can have very relaxed corporate cultures.

Business cards, known as name cards locally, are a crucial tool for meetings and networking. English language cards are sufficient for local business, but if you regularly conduct business around the region, it can be useful to get the flip side of your card printed in the relevant language.

Meetings generally start on time, so it is good to be punctual. Before a meeting gets under way name cards will be exchanged between everyone present. These should be proffered with two hands and an introduction, followed by a handshake. The cards should be left out on the table during the meeting so you can refer to them as required, and to show interest in who you are meeting.

Drinks such as tea, coffee or water will be offered at most meetings and it's polite to accept, even if you're not particularly thirsty. Note that if you ask for water, it's worth specifying if you want it warm or cold. If you don't, you'll most likely get warm water.

While the above guidelines should see you through most business situations, keep in mind that Singapore is a truly international business city and you can easily find yourself at a meeting with a room full of Japanese, Thai or British executives, so be prepared for different cultures as you navigate the corporate landscape here.

Work Ethic in Singapore

There is a strong work ethic in Singapore, but also a definite difference between here and some other countries in Asia. The fact is, you're in the tropics, and elements of a more relaxed lifestyle are evident. If you've got your work done at the end of the workday, you can go home; no need to stay in the office just because your boss is still there.

Working Hours

Standard office hours are 09:00 to 18:00 with maybe a half hour variation on either side depending on the company you work for. Teachers are usually at school from 07:30 to 15:00 but invariably stay longer to complete work or oversee extra-curricular activities. Retail stores are open from 10:00 to 22:00 in most places although some will close one or two hours earlier. Split shifts are virtually unheard of in Singapore and most lunch hours are, as the name suggests, an hour long and are taken anywhere from 12:00 to 14:00.

The working week is almost universally Monday to Friday, and even government ministries went from a six to a five-day week in 2004. Government legislation limits the official working week to 44 hours, although certain exceptions allow for a 48 hour week.

Annual leave allowances start at 15–18 days and can increase with long service to around 25 days. Exceptions to this rule are possible with some expat packages and are more likely in European companies where home-country leave allowances can stretch to six or even eight weeks. Public holidays are determined by the government and religious holidays, often corresponding with moon cycles, are set by respective religious authorities. The major religions in Singapore are Buddhism, Christianity, Islam and Hinduism and their religious holidays are honoured. See p.14.

Finding Work

Singapore's desire to be a truly international city means that the government is very open to international workers. As long as you have strong qualifications and there's a job opening for you, getting an employment pass shouldn't be difficult. On the corporate side, a huge number of MNCs are present in Singapore with many using the country as their regional headquarters. This bodes well for international job seekers, as does the fact that local companies are starting to see expats as a way to internationalise their companies in preparation for overseas expansion. The days when you could walk into Singapore with a bachelor's degree and find work are over and most workers will arrive in Singapore with a job or move to new jobs once they are there and have an employment pass. There are always exceptions to this rule, but you'll need a good network or excellent qualifications to be able to pull this off.

Finding Work Before You Come

The majority of expats working in Singapore will have initially been posted here by a company in their home country. Securing a job from overseas can be difficult and it's highly unlikely that you'll be able to sign a contract without a trip to Singapore. Most companies will look to fill positions from the pool of employees available in Singapore. However, there are opportunities for highly qualified individuals to solicit positions from overseas. Singapore is working hard to create centres of excellence in industries such as biotechnology, education and digital content, and these present opportunities for qualified foreigners. If you're recruited from overseas, the company will probably pay for your flights and perhaps assist with relocation costs.

Business Councils & Groups	
American Chamber of Commerce	6235 0077
Australian Chamber of Commerce	6738 7917
British Chamber of Commerce	6222 3552
Canadian Chamber of Commerce	6233 6816
French Chamber of Commerce	6735 5523
Indian Chamber of Commerce & Industry	6224 6634
Japanese Chamber of Commerce & Industry	6221 0541
New Zealand Chamber of Commerce	6235 7119
Prime Time	6234 0973
Singapore Business Federation	6827 6828
Singapore International Chamber of Commerce	6224 1225

A good start to finding a job from overseas is to look at job websites such as www.jobsdb.com, www.monster.com.sg and www.jobstreet.com. There are also many recruitment agencies in Singapore (see table on p.84) and a call to one of these should give you a better idea of the current state of the market and the opportunities in your industry. Most recruitment agencies will have departments that specialize in areas such as finance, IT, marketing and sales and if you speak to someone in the relevant department you'll get more in-depth information. Checking company websites for job vacancies is also an avenue worth pursuing, although inevitably you will need to come to Singapore for an interview or preliminary meeting. If you can schedule a number of meetings around the same time, it's probably worth a trip to Singapore to get some quality face-time with the companies you're interested in joining.

Following Your Partner or Spouse

Not relishing staying at home while your partner or spouse heads off to work every day? The American Association of Singapore (AAS) runs the Career Resource Center for Expatriates (CRCE), which helps to place Dependent's Pass holders in suitable positions in Singapore. You will need to be an AAS member to use the service. For details, see www.aasingapore.com.

Finding Work While You're Here

Finding new work is relatively easy if you already have a job in Singapore and are just looking to switch companies; it's then just up to the job market in your chosen job field. However, if you're arriving in the country on a tourist visa and then start to look for work, things can be a bit more difficult. This is odd, given that employment passes are evaluated on a case-by-case basis by the Ministry of Manpower and whether you currently have an EP is not taken into consideration. In some instances this can be explained as a company's reluctance to take on 'travellers' who they perceive as transient and less committed to long-term employment. Highly qualified individuals can apply for an Employment Pass Eligibility Certificate before coming to Singapore that will allow them to extend their Social Visit Pass for up to six months while they look for work (see p.85). It is also possible to look for work while on a social visit pass, but make sure you don't overstay your welcome.

Once in the country, networking is of utmost importance as you're more likely to find a job opening through someone you meet than through the classifieds (see Networking on p.82). That said, read the newspapers for announcements of company expansion plans and classified job listings. The Straits Times is the best, with the Saturday edition having the most listings. If you have a specific company in mind, try to set up a meeting with a relevant person in their HR department to discuss any opportunities they may have.

Recruitment Agencies

There are many recruitment agencies in Singapore, and they can be a good avenue for finding work. Some recruitment agencies specialise in an industry, or will have departments dedicated to a specific sector. A little research can help you to approach the right ones and target your job search more effectively. Most agencies are open to an initial phone call, but will then want you to either sign up via their website or send in your CV for a particular position.

Others agencies lean more towards the head-hunter role and focus on middle to senior management positions. A headhunter's fee is based on a percentage of the salary paid to the successful candidate. A headhunter will screen likely candidates and pass the most promising ones on to the client. They will assist the candidate in negotiations if required, but generally take a back seat in the proceedings.

Recruitment Agencies

A.T. Kearney	6298 7200	www.executivesearch.atkearney.com
Adecco	6737 1333	www.adecco-asia.com
Amrop Hever	6225 3188	www.amrophever.com.sg
Aquent	6336 7444	www.aquent.com
Drake	6225 5809	www.drakeintl.com
Heidrick & Struggles	6332 5001	www.heidrick.com
Hudson	6339 0355	www.hudson.com/sg
Kelly Services	6223 3362	www.kellyservices.com.sg
Korn Ferry	6224 3111	www.kornferry.com
Michael Page	6533 2777	www.michaelpage.com.sg
Robert Walters	6538 3343	www.robertwalters.com
Spencer Stuart	6586 1186	www.spencerstuart.com

Voluntary & Charity Work

Doing volunteer and charity work on a dependant's pass is allowed as long as the organisation you're involved with is a non-profit one and there is no employee-employer relationship. It's still a good idea though to check with MOM before commencing any volunteer work to ensure that the ministry agrees that the work you plan to do is considered charity work.

Send an email to mom_wpd@mom.gov.sg or call 6438 5122 to explain the nature of the work, identify the non-profit organisation and provide your foreign identification number (FIN). MOM will then assess your case and inform you whether the ministry has any objections. There's no official list of non-profit organisations that you are permitted to volunteer at – situations are assessed on a case-by-case basis.

Working as a Freelancer/Contractor

Generally speaking you need an employment pass in order to work in Singapore for any period longer than one month, be it at a full time job, on a short-term consultancy or freelance basis. Some short-term engagements are covered by a professional visit pass, but this is usually limited to performing artists, professional speakers or journalists. The short-term employment pass (STEP) covers professionals with project or contract work in Singapore for the duration of less than a month. The STEP is issued on a strictly non-renewable basis – if you need to extend your stay, you will have to apply for a regular employment pass. An employment pass can usually be secured in two weeks. A STEP can be arranged in as little as three days if it's urgent.

Maternity Leave ◀

With a rapidly ageing population, Singapore's government is trying to make having children an attractive proposition. Maternity leave is usually for a minimum of three months, although each company will have its own policies in this regard. Once you return to work, you'll be happy to know that live-in nannies are cheap, reliable and easy to find. For more information, check out Domestic Help on p.126.

Employment Contracts

Employment contracts are crucial in Singapore as they will be the sole legal basis for your employment terms and conditions; Singapore's labour laws do not apply to expats (see Labour Law on p.86). So it's worthwhile getting a lawyer to look at your employment contract to check for loopholes or any glaring omissions (see Recommended Labour Lawyers on p.86) before you sign anything.

Negotiating an expat employment contract is usually more difficult than a local one. There are many more aspects to consider, and if you haven't lived in Singapore before, it may be a challenge to assess the salary level and benefits you'll need to maintain your lifestyle. Common elements of an expat contract include a housing allowance, car allowance, education, home leave and flights home, relocation expenses, medical coverage and temporary living costs while you search for a permanent residence. You will also have to take into account the currency you're paid in, tax implications and Singapore's tax regime. Another thing worth checking is whether you will receive the excess if your rental costs are below your housing allowance. Some companies will pay the excess to you, but others will only pay out the value of your rent. See the Cost of Living Table on p.88 and Setting up Home on p.122 for some details on potential expenses and what you might need when settling in.

Singapore law doesn't require a company to offer a severance payment, so it's really up to the terms of your contract. Many MNCs will offer a severance package as part of their global HR policy, but it's worth keeping an eye out for this and negotiating one if it's not offered at first. Also look at the probation period – usually three months – and whether there are any limitations on your benefits during this time. While an employment pass is required from the moment you start work, some companies will hold off on as many expenses as they can until the probation period is over and your appointment is confirmed.

Many companies offer a standard 13th month bonus scheme. This, along with the fact that performance bonuses are often calculated as a multiple of your monthly pay, means it's important to consider whether you want housing and other allowances stripped out of your base salary, or all lumped together. It can take some careful calculations and an understanding of Singapore's tax structure to come to an arrangement that's most beneficial for you. For details on Singapore's tax structure see the IRAS website at www.iras.gov.sg. In an effort to become more flexible in times of economic downturn, some local companies have introduced a monthly variable component into employment contracts. Essentially, the MVC means that a percentage of your salary, usually 5-10%, is seen as variable and can be withheld when the business is facing difficulties. This practice is not common among MNCs but you may find it in your contract if you work for a local company.

Labour Law

Recommended **Labour Lawyers***
Most major international law firms have long-standing practices and partnerships in Singapore, so you'll have no shortage of choice for representation should you find yourself in an employment-related dispute. Esquire Law Corporation (6733 5011) and Rodyk & Davidson (6225 2626) are both respected law firms that can assist with drafting of contracts and other labour issues.

Labour law in Singapore is fully documented in the Employment Act and available online at www.mom.gov.sg. Unfortunately it's unlikely that the Employment Act will be relevant to you as it doesn't cover managers or consultants, or anyone making more than $1,600 per month. This means that everything comes down to your employment contract. This will be the legal document that governs any disputes between you and your employer, so it's important that you get it right. It's highly recommended that you consult with a lawyer to review your employment contract before signing it. Ultimately, you shouldn't be scared off by this situation; expats rarely have stories of employment disputes or abuse of contracts.

Changing Jobs

Changing jobs is a common occurrence in Singapore and a relatively simple procedure. Your employment pass is directly tied to your job, so a change of employment will require the cancellation of your EP and an application for a new one.

You have to go to the Ministry of Manpower within one week of your last day of employment to cancel your EP. You can apply for a new EP while you're still employed at your current job, but it will only be issued (if it is approved) once you've cancelled your current EP. Luckily, you can receive the approval-in-principle letter (see p.72) before you cancel your current EP, which essentially means that you can safely leave your job with the knowledge that it's all systems go for you to take up the new one.

In general, EPs will be approved, as long as you're well-qualified for the job you're applying for. It's important to note that a two-week social visit pass is issued when you cancel your EP. This means that for the period between your current EP being cancelled and the new one being issued, you are not entitled to work in Singapore.

In principle, when a foreigner leaves a job in Singapore, he is required to pay all taxes owing up to that point. However, it is possible to appeal to the Internal Revenue Authority of Singapore (6356 8233, www.iras.gov.sg) for your tax obligations to be carried through to your next position, so you will only be liable for tax payment at the end of the tax year. In line with global practices, employment contracts in some industries will have a no-compete clause, especially at the senior management level. However there is some question as to how enforceable these are, and the clause may only be invoked in the most sensitive or competitive of situations.

*Job Hopping***
Changing jobs is a breeze in Singapore. Just cancel one EP and collect your new one. To make things even easier, you're allowed to apply for your next EP while still holding your current EP. This gives you the safety of knowing whether your next EP will be approved or not before you leave your current job.

Company Closure

In the unfortunate event that the company you're working for closes down, you will have to check your employment contract to see what you're entitled to in terms of termination notice period, severance pay and benefits. It is legislated that a company must pay out your salary and unused annual leave. But any additional benefits are only required to be paid out if they are included in the employment contract. EP holders who lose their job due to company closure are treated the same as EP holders who lose their job for other reasons or who resign from their job: you have to cancel your EP with the Ministry of Manpower within one week of your final day of work. You will then receive a social visit pass and will have to comply with its terms.

Bank Accounts

As one of Asia's main financial centres, Singapore has an abundance of local and foreign banks. The three main local banks are United Overseas Bank, Development Bank of Singapore and Overseas Chinese Banking Corporation and all offer similarly comprehensive services and an extensive branch and ATM network. There are six foreign banks with 'qualifying full bank' status. This allows them to offer the same services as the local banks but with restrictions on the number of branches and ATMs they can have. (There are many other foreign banks in Singapore, but their activities are focused on commercial rather than consumer banking.)

Opening a bank current or savings account is fairly straightforward if you have an employment or dependant's pass. You'll have to take your passport and EP to open the account and you usually need an initial deposit, which can range from a few hundred to several thousand Singapore dollars. Dependant's pass holders will also need to bring in the EP to which their pass is linked. Some banks will only allow an EP holder to open an account if your employer has a corporate account at the bank, but this varies depending on the class of the employment pass. The minimum age for opening a standard account is 21 but several banks offer accounts for students or savings accounts for children. It's always best to call and find out exactly what the bank requires before going to open an account.

Some banks, including UOB and DBS, allow you to open an account without an EP or other residence visa. In addition to your passport, you'll need to furnish a letter of introduction from a friend, relative or colleague who is an existing account holder at the bank. The letter is simply to indicate that the person knows you and that they would like to introduce you to the bank – it's not a guarantee of any sort. You may also be asked to produce a national identification card from your home country (like a social security card) and a letter of reference from a bank where you hold an account stating that you have a relationship with the bank.

Regular banking hours tend to be 09:30 to 16:00 from Mondays to Fridays and 09:30 to 13:00 on Saturdays, although several banks open earlier or close later at some of their branches. Banks charges vary; some charge a small monthly fee, while others only charge if your average daily balance for the month dips below the minimum account balance.

Bounced Cheque Penalties

The penalties for bounced cheques vary from bank to bank, ranging from $20 to $40 per cheque. A penalty is incurred if you have insufficient funds in your account to clear a cheque or if a post-dated cheque is deposited or cashed before the stated date. You won't normally be penalised if a cheque is returned for a technical reason, such as the amount written in words and numbers not matching up.

Banking Comparison Table

Bank	Phone	Website	Online Banking	Phone Banking
ABN AMRO Consumer Bank	1800 226 2676	www.abnamro.com.sg	✓	✓
BNP Paribas	6210 1288	www.bnpparibas.com.sg	–	–
Citibank ▶ p.IFC	6225 5225	www.citibank.com.sg	✓	✓
DBS Bank (Development Bank of Singapore)	1800 111 1111	www.dbs.com.sg	✓	✓
HSBC ▶ p.89	1800 786 6666	www.hsbc.com.sg	✓	✓
Maybank	1800 629 2265	www.maybank.com.sg	✓	✓
Overseas Chinese Banking Corporation (OCBC)	1800 438 3333	www.ocbc.com.sg	✓	✓
Standard Chartered Bank	1800 747 7000	www.standardchartered.com.sg	✓	✓
United Overseas Bank (UOB)	1800 222 2121	www.uob.com.sg	✓	✓

Financial Planning

Singapore's low tax rates make it an attractive place for expats to work for a few years to save money for retirement. While expat salaries may not be as high as they were, there's a good chance that you'll earn a comfortable income here and have money to put away besides. Financial planners abound, many of them specialising in helping expats, and they are a good way for you to navigate the complexities of financial planning. One of the largest groups offering financial services in Singapore is Professional Investment Advisory Services. PIAS are independently owned and offer a broad range of services and have qualified advisers from a range of expatriate nationalities.

It's highly recommended that you deal only with financial advisors who are licensed by the Monetary Authority of Singapore. While many financial institutions provide financial planning services they will only try to sell you their products. Independent advisors are better placed to act in your best interest because they can source financial products from the global market and they are generally not paid on commission. An independent financial advisory firm will give you access not only to a financial advisor, but also to the firm's tax lawyers, fund managers and other financial services professionals. There are no restrictions on expats opening savings accounts in Singapore (see Bank Accounts on p.87), so most expats save here, especially as the Singapore dollar is a relatively stable currency. Alternatively, you may want to use your home country savings account or set up an off-shore savings account, which can be done through most major banks in Singapore. If you plan to use either of these options, you should consider the bank charges involved in moving your money and the possible tax implications in your home country.

Expats may invest in approved condominium developments. Foreigners wanting to buy restricted residential property (vacant plots or landed property such as semi-detached houses or

How Much?

If the costs listed in the table opposite mean nothing to you, refer to the Currency Exchange Table (p.56) to work out the equivalent in your home country's currency.

Cost of Living

Apples (per kg)	$2.75
Bananas (per kg)	$1.50
Barber haircut (male)	$10.00
Bottle of house wine (restaurant)	$40-60
Bottle of wine (supermarket)	$20-30
Burger (takeaway)	$4.00
Bus (maximum single-journey fare)	$1.90
Camera film	$5.00
Can of dog food	$2.50
Can of soft drink	$1.00
Cappuccino	$3.50
Car rental (per day)	$140.00
Carrots (per kg)	$2.00
CD album	$20.00
Chocolate bar	$1.20
Cigarettes (pack of 20)	$10.00
Cinema ticket	$9.00
Dozen eggs	$4.00
Film developing (colour, 36 exp)	$16.00
Fresh beef (per kg)	$30-40
Fresh chicken (per kg)	$8.00
Fresh fish (per kg)	$15-20
Golf (18 holes)	$100-200
House wine (glass)	$12.00
Large takeaway pizza	$23.00
Loaf of bread	$2.00
Local postage stamp	$0.31
Milk (1 litre)	$2.50
New release DVD	$30.00
Newspaper (international)	$3.00
Newspaper (local)	$0.80
Orange juice (1 litre)	$2.00
Pack of 24 aspirin/paracetamol tablets	$3.00
Petrol (per litre)	$1.70
Pint of beer	$12.00
Postcard	$2.00
Potatoes (per kg)	$2.00
Rice (1 kg)	$2.00
Salon haircut (female)	$60.00
Salon haircut (male)	$30.00
Six pack of beer	$16.00
Strawberries (per punnet)	$8.00
Sugar (2 kg)	$2.25
Taxi (10km journey)	$8.00
Text message (local)	$0.05
Tube of toothpaste	$2.50
Water 1.5 litres (supermarket)	$1.00
Watermelon (per kg)	$0.75

However you view your life abroad, HSBC can help you make the most of it.

If you live and work outside your home country, the Expatriate Team at HSBC Singapore understands your experience and can offer a wide range of financial solutions to help you make the most of your money.

Talk to us today.

Call (65) 6731 5698

Email expatriateteam@hsbc.com.sg

Click www.offshore.hsbc.com

HSBC

The world's local bank

Financial Advisors

The Fry Group	6225 0825	www.wtfry.com
Global Strategies	6297 0150	www.gsworldwide.com
IPP Financial Advisers	6511 8800	www.ippfa.com
Professional Investment Advisory Services ▶ See insert opposite p.92	6866 1477	www.profinvest.com.sg

Financial Checklist
Tidying up loose ends will help you to make the most of your financial gain in Singapore:

- Keep your bank account in your home country topped up to cover outgoing expenses

- Ensure you have medical cover

- Build an emergency fund of about three months' salary

- Review your insurance policies (and make any necessary changes)

- Start a savings plan

bungalows) have to apply for permission to do so. The real estate market is down from a peak in 1996 and remains quite affordable, but it doesn't currently offer the growth prospects being seen in some other countries in the region, such as Hong Kong. For more information, see also Buying Property on p.99. Expats also invest in property in nearby countries but this often carries a higher risk as the legal environment in these countries can be ambiguous, so it's buyer beware!

Expats commonly hold pensions in their home countries. Singapore only has two pension schemes that offer tax concessions – the Central Provident Fund and the Supplementary Retirement Scheme – but these are only available to Singapore citizens and permanent residents. Some companies allow you to identify a savings scheme to which the company will contribute on your behalf. The Monetary Authority of Singapore has a list of approved funds and savings schemes, and a financial advisor would be able to assist you in selecting something suitable.

Taxation

Singapore levies personal income tax, although the rates are lower than in most western countries. Rates vary according to whether you're a tax resident (if you're present in Singapore for at least 183 days in a calendar year or if you've worked in Singapore for at least three consecutive years) or not. If you're not considered a tax resident, you're taxed at a flat 15% or at the tax resident rate, whichever results in a higher tax income. Income from short-term employment of 60 days or less isn't usually taxed.

As a tax resident your income will be taxed from 0-21% depending on how much you earn, (see the Income Tax Rates for Tax Residents table below). Income tax is paid for the calendar year and you have to file a tax return by April 15 for the previous year. Income tax matters fall under the domain of the Inland Revenue Authority of Singapore. Their website, www.iras.gov.sg, has useful information including details on Singapore's tax treaties with other countries which are intended to avoid citizens of those countries who work in Singapore being taxed twice. There's also information on tax relief. Income from a variety of sources is taxable, including employment income, dividends, interest, and income from property rental, but there are exemptions and exceptions so it's worth contacting IRAS for more information. Although personal income tax rates are the same for expats as they are for citizens and permanent residents, the latter groups are eligible for more tax relief. This is one reason why expats who intend to stay in Singapore long-term become permanent residents.

In addition to personal income tax, there's also goods and services tax (GST). This 5% tax is levied on imported goods and most goods and services sold in Singapore. One important exception is the sales and lease of residential land and buildings. Prices in shops are inclusive of GST, so what you see is what you pay but sales receipts will often also indicate the amount of GST that you paid on your purchase. Other than GST, there is no additional tax levied on alcohol or tobacco products.

Income Tax Rates for Tax Residents

On the first $20,000	0%
On the next $10,000	0.75%
On the next $10,000	5.75%
On the next $40,000	8.75%
On the next $80,000	14.5%
On the next $160,000	18%
Above $320,000	21%

Legal Issues

Singapore's legal system is based on English common law. A judiciary, a legislature and an executive form the three main pillars of Singapore's constitutional democracy. The judiciary has two main courts: the Supreme Court, which consists of the High Court and the Court of Appeal; and the Subordinate Courts, which comprise sub-courts such as District Courts, Small Claims Tribunals and the Juvenile Court. Court proceedings are conducted in English. Crime is not tolerated in Singapore and it's one of the few developed countries where capital punishment is used, and caning remains a punishment in common use. Fines are frequently used as deterrents for behaviour that is considered undesirable or antisocial, such as eating on the subway or failing to wear a seatbelt in a taxi, but it's uncommon to see these

Singapore Supreme Court

actually being handed out. The main legal issues likely to affect expats are work and tax related and possibly corporate law if you're involved in any entrepreneurial ventures.

Divorce

In order for expats to divorce in Singapore, you or your spouse must have resided here for at least three years prior to commencing divorce proceedings. You can also file for a divorce if either you or your spouse is a permanent resident or citizen. Divorce after less than three years of marriage can only be filed on the grounds of suffering exceptional hardship or having a spouse who is exceptionally unreasonable or cruel. If one spouse holds a dependant's pass linked to the other party's employment pass, the dependant's pass will become invalid on the granting of the divorce and the pass holder will have to leave the country or apply for their own residence visa.

If you have children, both parties can apply for custody. The judge will consider the parties wishes as well as those of your children if they're deemed old enough to comment. The decision is based upon the best interests of the children. In some cases custody may be granted to a family member or guardian other than you or your spouse. Whoever is granted custody of the children may apply for maintenance. The children's needs and the parties' financial situations will be taken into consideration when determining maintenance. In general, custody and maintenance continue until the children turn 21 or are deemed to be financially independent.

Wives may apply for maintenance. The judge will consider factors such as the length of the marriage, the spouses' ages, standard of living and earning capacities. The judge may set maintenance payments intended to allow the wife to enjoy the same standard of living that she enjoyed while married. Payments usually continue until either the husband or wife dies or until the wife remarries.

Law Firms

Alban Tay Mahtani & de Silva	6534 5266	www.atmdlaw.com.sg
Allen & Gledhill	6890 7188	www.gledhill.com.sg
Baker & McKenzie.Wong & Leow	6338 1888	www.bakernet.com
Drew & Napier	6535 0733	www.drewnapier.com
KhattarWong	6535 6844	www.khattarwong.com
Ramdas & Wong	6236 9229	www.ramdwong.com.sg
Rodyk & Davidson	6225 2626	www.rodyk.com.sg
Tan Rajah & Cheah	6532 2271	www.trc.com.sg

Making a Will

Anyone who is 21 or older can write a will. Although you may write your own will, it's recommended that you seek a lawyer's assistance to ensure that your will gives clear instructions that can be carried out easily upon your death. Any lawyer licensed to practice in Singapore can help you, but it makes sense to find a lawyer who deals with personal legal matters. In addition to identifying the beneficiaries of your will, you should also nominate an executor. Your will must be signed in the presence of two witnesses (both present at the same time) who may not be beneficiaries or spouses of beneficiaries. To amend your will, you should rewrite a new will or prepare a supplemental one as changes to the original will could render it invalid. Your will is nullified if you marry or remarry, so you will have to rewrite or reinstate it. You don't need to have your will attested by a court or registered at your local embassy.

Adoption

Expats are allowed to adopt foreign and Singaporean children, although different procedures apply. Adopting a local child can be difficult because preference is given to Singaporean parents, while adopting a foreign child can also be difficult because the process involves multiple organisations and jurisdictions. Expats commonly adopt children from Indonesia and Malaysia as procedures there are slightly less complicated than in other countries.

To adopt a local child you must to file a petition at the Family Court in Singapore. The Ministry of Community Development, Youth and Sports will then assess whether the proposed adoption meets certain criteria. To adopt a foreign child you'll have to undergo a home study report, to be carried out by an MCYS accredited agency. Regardless of where the child is from, you will need to find out how to acquire citizenship for your adopted child with your home country's embassy. See Certificates and Licences on p.76.

Myths & Truths ◀

While there are no laws prohibiting a woman from getting pregnant out of wedlock it does run counter to local social norms.

Crime

Singapore is one of the safest major cities in the world, thanks largely to its high standard of living and effective policing. Mention Singapore to a foreigner and there's a good chance that one of their first comments will be that they've heard it's safe (and clean). It would be unwise to take personal safety for granted, just as it would be anywhere else in the world, but both men and women can feel comfortable riding the subway (called the MRT) or taking a taxi alone late at night. If you're ever unlucky enough to lose your wallet on a bus or in a taxi, there's a decent chance that some friendly passer-by will hand it over to the authorities and that you'll get it back. Most crime in Singapore is relatively minor, such as theft of mobile phones or other property-related offences. Violent crimes such as murder, rape and muggings are very uncommon.

Singapore has a stigma of being overly strict. While certain laws are undoubtedly tough, most expats will have no problem if they behave in the same manner here as they would in their home country. The Singapore authorities wouldn't look kindly upon you if you decided to graffiti a building, but this is probably not something you would do at home either. The high profile case of American teenager Michael Fay, who received a caning for vandalism in 1994, shouldn't put you off – countless expats have lived here for decades without incident.

There are some cultural differences though and failing to adjust to local norms could get you into trouble. While being homosexual is not illegal, engaging in homosexual acts is. Homosexual activity in a private residence is illegal but the chances of being caught are small. Homosexual activity in public though can have serious consequences. These laws focus more on gay men than women, and in general lesbians enjoying a greater degree of social acceptance than gay men.

YES, please open my eyes to quality advice.

Name: .... Tel: .... Email: ....

Address: ....

.... Postcode: ....

**BUSINESS REPLY SERVICE
PERMIT NO. 07962**

Professional Investment Advisory Services Pte Ltd
12th Floor, 4 Robinson Road,
Singapore 048543

Public nudity is also against the law in Singapore. While going topless on a beach in your home country may be normal, doffing your top (or bottom) in Singapore is likely to attract a visit from the police. If you're desperate to avoid tan lines, it's essential to do so in your own garden or on your balcony, out of view of passers-by.

Driving under the Influence

If you're arrested for drunk driving you'll be taken to a police station and your car will be impounded while the police investigate the matter. If charged and convicted in court, you could lose your driving licence for 12 months or more. If you want to drive again, you will have to retake all of the tests to obtain a new driving licence.

Drugs Possession

Consuming or dealing in illegal narcotics is considered one of the most serious offences in Singapore, and punishment can be severe. A common misconception is that foreigners charged with drug offences are treated more leniently than locals, but several recent cases suggest that this is not the case. If you're found guilty of taking and dealing in illegal narcotics, you could face a lengthy prison term, a caning, or even the death penalty. Certain medications that are available in your home country may be illegal in Singapore, so you should check with the Health Sciences Authority (6866 3400) before bringing medication into the country, or at least to carry a copy of your prescription from a doctor.

Public Nuisance

Being drunk and disorderly after a big night on the town could get you a warning from the police or a trip to the police station. If it's the latter, you can be held for up to 48 hours (although it's usually less) while the police decide whether to release you or press charges. If you're clever, you'll sober up smartly and be on your best behaviour.

Assault

Assault is not taken lightly in Singapore. If you're caught fighting with someone you may be taken to a police station and held for up to 48 hours while police investigate. Depending on the seriousness of the incident, an assault conviction could lead to a fine or time in prison.

Traffic Accidents & Violations

If you're involved in a traffic accident that results in a fatality, you'll be taken to a police station while police investigate the accident. If the police determine that you're at fault, you will be formally charged in court and released on bail at the discretion of the judge. It will be

up to the courts to decide whether you're responsible and if so, to determine if you must compensate the victim's family. See p.166 for more about fines and what to do in the event of a traffic accident.

You're Nicked!

If you're arrested, the police may hold you for up to 48 hours before they are required to bring you to court and formally charge you. Upon arrest, you may request to make a telephone call to your family, a lawyer or your embassy, although your request may be deferred if the police believe that it will interfere with their investigation. If the police lay charges against you in court, a judge will decide whether you may be granted bail and what the amount and conditions will be. If you are granted bail, you may ask one or more individuals to pay it on your behalf. If you're charged with a crime, you may be fingerprinted and photographed for records kept by the Criminal Investigation Department. If

No smoking	No eating and drinking
Fine $1000	Fine $500
No flammable goods	No durians
Fine $5000	

acquitted you may request that your fingerprints and photos be returned to you; if you are convicted, the crime will be reflected in your criminal record. If you've been convicted of a crime in Singapore, the privacy laws in some western countries may prevent your criminal record from showing up in your home country. However, this can vary by country and according to the nature of the crime, so you'll need to check this with your embassy.

Foreigners with a criminal record in their home country may enter Singapore as long as their home country hasn't restricted them from traveling, they don't have a previous criminal record in Singapore and they meet the usual entry requirements. However, EP applications require you to indicate whether you've ever been convicted of a crime and if so to furnish details, which could lead to your application being turned down. Having a criminal record in your home country will not prevent you from opening a bank account in Singapore if you meet the standard criteria.

Doing Time

The Singapore Prison Service manages 14 prisons and drug rehabilitation centres around the country. Conditions in these facilities are better than those in most other countries in the region, but it is hardly easy living. Inmates are put through rehabilitation programmes that may include social and religious counselling, work, recreation, foot drills, and education. Inmates' next of kin are provided with a visit card, which they must bring along every time that they visit the inmate. Other family members and friends may also visit but must be accompanied by the next of kin carrying the visit card. Visits are usually scheduled once every two weeks, although a request for an urgent visit may be made in writing to the facility concerned. Certain Singapore Prison Service institutions offer an internet home tele-visit (IHT) service, allowing online meetings during scheduled timeslots.

Chewing Gum in Singapore

After 12 years of being banned in Singapore, chewing gum was partially legalised in 2004. The ban was imposed to combat litter problems but loosened as part of series of liberalisations aimed at improving the country's image and meeting its obligations under a free trade agreement with the US. Actually chewing gum, however, remains controlled as only gum that is considered therapeutic can be sold in pharmacies, and then only to buyers who provide their name and identification number.

94

Housing

Housing is a major consideration when you move to Singapore. Do you want to rent or buy? Would you like a house with a garden or a condo with a pool? Should you live near the downtown entertainment district or near the beach? There are plenty of factors to consider, and you'll probably have to make some tough choices, but wherever you end up you're bound to love it as you turn it into your home.

Renting in Singapore

It's fairly common for expat employment contracts to include an accommodation allowance, providing you with a set amount of money to put towards the rent at a residence of your choice. It is unlikely your contract will specify your accommodation unless the contract is a short-term one, in which case your employer may arrange a hotel suite or serviced apartment for you.

Finding a Home

Expats commonly use a real estate agent to help them find accommodation. The process is straightforward:

- You find an agent to work with (see Real Estate Agents on p.96).
- You discuss your needs and wants.
- Your agent shortlists options for you and arranges viewings.
- You view the options and make a choice.
- Your agent prepares a letter of intent and submits it to the landlord along with a cheque from you for the first month's rent as a deposit. The landlord then decides whether to rent the place to you and if not, he returns the cheque.
- Your agent helps you negotiate the details of the lease with the landlord or the landlord's agent.
- You sign the lease and provide a copy of your passport and employment pass.
- Your agent helps to arrange the stamp duty for the lease.
- You pay your agent for their services (see Other Rental Costs on p.98 for an explanation of this and the stamp duty).

If you have time and patience to spare you can find accommodation on your own. You'll need to identify possible places, arrange viewings, submit a letter of intent, negotiate with the landlord and sort out the stamp duty. Searching for shared accommodation without the help of an agent is easier than searching for a condo or house to rent. If you are searching on your own, the classified section of *The Straits Times* or a website such as www.singaporeexpats.com is a good place to start. You could also check the notice boards at Cold Storage supermarkets for listings or even just stroll around the neighbourhoods you're interested in and look for 'to rent' signs. Most locals live in Housing Development Board apartments, a distinctive feature of Singapore's cityscape, these consist of large blocks clustered together. While they might appear uninspiring from the outside, they're often done up nicely inside. While expats can rent an HDB apartment, or a room in one, few actually do. (See Main Accommodation Options on p.97 for the types of accommodation where expats generally live.) But if you are interested in checking out an HDB apartment, a real estate agent or a look through the classified section of *The Straits Times* will give you some leads.

Rent Terms and Conditions

As of 2006, Singapore's housing market was doing well and landlords have been increasing rents by 5-10%. Demand is high in many areas and accommodation is being snapped up quickly so you need to be prepared to make a quick decision if you find something you like. Hesitate too long and someone else will squeeze in ahead of you. Although rents are rising they are often negotiable, so there's no harm trying. Leases

Maintain a Poker Face

Don't show too much interest when you view a property, even if you love the place. If you show too much enthusiasm during the viewing, you may find yourself bidding against a mysterious other buyer who just happened to make a higher offer. It's best to deal with your agent (if you have one) rather than with the landlord or landlord's agent during a viewing, as your agent can usually negotiate on your behalf more effectively than you can.

usually run for one or two years, but shorter and longer leases can be arranged. Rent is almost always paid in advance on a monthly basis. You could probably arrange to pay your rent quarterly or even in one lump sum, but this isn't advisable as you'll lose any leverage you may have if the landlord doesn't meet the terms of the lease. Rent can be paid either by cheque or by electronic bank transfers, a choice that's usually at the discretion of the landlord. There are no regulations

about rent increases, so this is between you and the landlord. Once the rent has been set in the lease and the lease has been stamped, a rent increase is all but impossible unless it has been accounted for in the lease. If you do have a dispute with your landlord you could try the arbitration services of the Singapore Mediation Centre (www.mediation.com.sg). Failing that, you could resort to legal action involving lawyers and the courts.

For almost all accommodation, utilities (electricity, water and gas) are not included in your rent, so you will have to pay for your usage. The one exception is serviced apartments (see Main Accommodation Types on p.97), which are more like hotels and often include the utilities in the rent. Your lease will often require you to pay for regular (bi-monthly or quarterly) air conditioning maintenance, but you may be able to negotiate to have this included in your rent. You are responsible for any other minor maintenance work. Your lease may state that you must pay a deductible (like the first $150) and that the landlord will pay any charges above this for major maintenance or repair work.

Some accommodation may have its own parking area – like a garage at a condo or a driveway at a house – and this is included in your rent. But parking may not be included if you rent a private apartment or a house with no driveway. Rules vary and there are sometimes prohibitions on pets.

Real Estate Agents

Many expats opt to use a real estate agent. While most people grumble about having to pay agent's fees (see Other Rental Costs on p.98), the truth is that an agent can help you sift through the many options and narrow down your choices. The key is to find an agent who you can trust, which is best done through word of mouth. If you're new to Singapore and don't know anyone to ask for referrals, try contacting one of the companies on the Real Estate Agents table on the left. Agents don't need a licence to operate, although there is a

Quick Decisions
Singapore's rental market is currently strong, so properties don't remain available for long. If you find a place that you like, consider issuing the landlord with a letter of intent and one month's deposit right away. If you cannot come to a subsequent agreement about the lease, you will get the deposit back (although admittedly it can be a hassle sometimes).

Real Estate Agents		
CB Richard Ellis	6224 8181	www.cbre.com.sg
Century 21 Singapore	6291 2121	www.century21singapore.com
CityState Singapore ▶ p.viii ▶ p.125	6235 5652	www.citystate.com.sg
Coldwell Banker	6226 2000	www.coldwellbanker.com
Colliers International	6223 2323	www.colliers.com/singapore
ERA	6226 2000	www.era.com
Far East Organization	6235 2411	www.fareast.com.sg
FPDSavills	6536 5022	www.fpdsavills-singapore.com
Great World Serviced Apartments	6722 7000	www.greatworld.com.sg
Jones Lang Lasalle	6220 3888	www.joneslanglasalle.com.sg
Orangetee.Com	6471 8888	www.orangetee.com
SE Realty	6733 3503	www.singaporeexpats.com
United PREMAS	6876 6288	www.premas.com

Housing Abbreviations

BR	Bedroom
B&W	Black and white (colonial housing)
Bunglw	Bungalow
Ensuite	Bedroom has private bathroom
F/facilities	Full facilities (swimming pool, tennis courts, etc.)
F/furn	Fully furnished (comes with all major appliances and major furniture items)
flr	Floor, as in 'high floor' and 'low floor'
Lift level	The unit is on a floor with elevator access
P/furn	Partially furnished (usually comes with major appliances but no bed, sofa, table, etc.)
rm	Room
Semi-d	Semi-detached house
Terr	Terrace house
Unfurn	Unfurnished (comes without any major appliances or major furniture items)

voluntary accreditation through the Institute of Estate Agents (www.iea.org.sg). Accreditation isn't a guarantee though, just as a lack of accreditation doesn't mean the agent is lousy either. Go with your instinct here and use an agent you feel you can trust.

The Lease

Lease agreements are written in English and must be signed by both the landlord and tenant. You have to pay stamp duty – a tax on certain legal documents to ensure that they are recognised by the local courts – on your lease (see Other Rental Costs on p.98 for details). If there's any chance you may need to leave Singapore before the end of your rental period, you should ask for a diplomatic clause to be included in your lease (only an option for leases of two years or more). A diplomatic clause allows for the early termination of the lease if you are transferred out of Singapore for work. For a diplomatic clause to take effect you are usually required to live in the place for a minimum of a year and you must give two months notice before leaving Singapore, so you will have to pay for at least 14 months out of a 24 month lease. To renew your lease you may be required to inform the landlord of your desire to stay a few months before it expires (check your lease to see if this is stipulated). There are no regulations that require the landlord to allow you to renew, so you will have to negotiate new terms with him. Feel free to try to negotiate a lower rent if the rental market is down, but be aware that your landlord is likely to raise the rent if the rental market is booming.

Main Accommodation Options

Condos

Condos are usually upscale developments of one to four (or more) bedroom units. They usually have facilities, which may include a pool, gym, sauna, tennis courts, squash courts, barbecue pits, function rooms and security. The downside is that condos often have smaller rooms and lower ceilings than the older apartment buildings that they probably replaced.

Private Apartments

Private apartments are similar to condos but do not have any facilities, except perhaps for security. Private apartments are more likely to be in older buildings than condos, which can mean bigger rooms and higher ceilings. There are some drawbacks though, including the fact that older apartment buildings are sometimes not hooked up to the cable television network (see Television on p.136) and that they may not have an elevator if they are only a few stories high.

Shophouse/Terrace House/Semi-Detached Townhouse

Shophouses and terrace houses are similar in that they consist of several attached units in a row. Shophouses though are usually narrower and taller with smaller windows and a more traditional appearance, while terrace houses are usually wider with bigger windows and tend to be more modern. Semi-detached townhouses consist of two units that share a common wall, with each unit usually having a small garden.

Detached Houses

Detached houses, sometimes called landed houses or bungalows, don't share a wall with another house and have a garden. Some detached houses can be great value rentals, as the lack of facilities you would get with a condo is more than made up for by their size and privacy. The luxury of a large garden also comes with a responsibility to maintain it, so you may find yourself forking out money for a gardener if you're not willing to cut the grass yourself.

Black and Whites

Black and whites are colonial houses and apartments that previously served as housing for British army officers. Now considered heritage housing, the name black and white is derived from their distinctive white walls and black woodwork. There are black and whites in many parts of Singapore, but a few of the main enclaves are in Newton, Portsdown Road, Rochester Park and Mount Pleasant. Black and whites tend to be stylish, with big rooms and high ceilings. The houses often have a large garden. They're not modern buildings though which means they often lack central air conditioning and cable television connections (see Television on p.136).

Shared Accommodation

Shared accommodation is readily available, although it may take a while to find something that meets your needs if you have specific criteria. Cold Storage supermarkets have noticeboards near the entrance where you'll find messages about rooms to rent which are usually located in the same area as the store. You'll find a useful section on www.singapore.asiaxpat.com called 'Share Flats' where people post room for rent notices for free; you can sort listings by area, price and date of posting. The classified section of *The Straits Times* is another good place to look for shared accommodation ads as they are grouped by area. Depending on the location, type of accommodation and number of people living there, shared accommodation can cost anywhere from $300 to $1,500 per month.

Other Rental Costs

When planning your budget you should factor in costs, other than your monthly rent, associated with renting. It's common practice for landlords to ask for one or two month's rent as a security deposit, which will be paid back at the end of your lease after damages (if any) have been deducted. If you used an agent to find your accommodation, you will also be charged an agent's fee. The standard agent's fee is the equivalent of two week's rent if you sign a one-year lease, or a month's rent if you sign a two-year lease. However, these are merely guidelines, and you can negotiate the agent's fee before you start house hunting. Just make sure the amount is agreed before the agent starts to work for you! Any fee charged by an agent that the landlord hires to find prospective renters should be paid by the landlord, not the tenant.

Arab Street

To ensure that your lease is recognised as a legal document by Singapore's Courts you have to pay stamp duty to the Inland Revenue Authority of Singapore. This is something the landlord or your agent will arrange but which you will be charged for. The stamp duty is calculated as $1 for every $250 or part thereof of annual rent for a one-year lease, or $2 for every $250 or part thereof of annual rent for a two or three-year lease.

Unless utilities are included in your rent, you will also have to pay a deposit to SP Services for your electricity, water and gas supply (see Utilities & Services on p.132). There are no deposits required for hooking up a phone line if you hold an employment pass, but a dependant's pass holder must pay a $200 deposit. There is also a once-off connection fee for your phone line – see the Telephone section on p.133.

You don't have to pay any municipality or community tax when renting.

To avoid unexpected costs associated with your rental accommodation, ensure that you read the lease carefully before signing and don't be shy about asking for clarifications or changes.

Property Agents ◀

It's definitely a good idea to use a property agent to assist you with either buying or selling property – you want to be sure that everything is carried out according to local regulations.

Buying Property

Expats are allowed to buy property in Singapore, but they are limited to units in approved condo developments or apartment buildings. Expats have to apply for, and receive, permission to buy restricted residential property such as vacant plots, semi-detached houses or bungalows.

The real estate market is down from a peak in 1996 and remains quite affordable, but it doesn't currently offer the growth prospects being seen in some other countries in the region, such as Hong Kong. Expats also invest in property in nearby countries but this often carries a higher risk as the legal environment in these countries can be ambiguous, so it's buyer beware!

After living in Singapore for a while and deciding to stay long-term, you may decide to buy rather than to continue paying monthly rent. Alternatively, you may buy investment properties to rent out, although the returns are unlikely to be as high as those on some of your other investment options.

Residential properties are divided into three categories: 99-year leasehold, 999-year leasehold and freehold. While expats tend to shy away from leasehold properties because they dislike the idea that their ownership has a limited lifespan, you shouldn't think that ownership could be taken away at the government's fancy. Leasehold can be a good option as prices tend to be much lower than those of similarly-sized and located freehold properties. The leasehold period starts from the date that a developer purchases a piece of land, and there will probably be a few years between this date and the time that units are sold to the public. So it's common for 6 or 7 of the 99 or 999 years to have elapsed by the time you buy a new unit.

Expats tend to buy properties in the main expat enclaves (see Residential Areas on p.102) but new condos are constantly springing up so finding a new development in which to buy shouldn't be a problem.

The Process

Once you've found a property that you would like to buy, the purchasing process takes two to three months to complete. These are the general steps involved in purchasing a property:

- Negotiate a price with the owner
- Make a verbal offer to the owner
- Issue an Offer to Purchase to the owner along with a cheque for 1% of the purchase price

Continue to negotiate until a final price and terms are agreed upon (there's usually a limit of three days to do this from the date of the Offer to Purchase). If the price has increased from what was initially discussed, you may have to top up the amount that you paid before so that it's still equal to 1% of the revised purchase price. If an agreement cannot be reached, the 1% payment will be returned to you.

If an agreement is reached the owner will issue an option to purchase to you, after which you have 14 days to make a final decision about whether you want to go through with the purchase. To exercise the option to purchase, you must pay the

Property Developers

CapitaLand	6820 2188	www.capitaland.com
Centrepoint Homes	6273 2122	www.centrepointhomes.com
City Developments Limited	6877 8228	www.cdl.com.sg
Far East Organization	6235 2411	www.fareast.com.sg
GuocoLand Limited	6535 6455	www.guocoland.com.sg
JTC Corporation	1800 568 7000	www.jtc.gov.sg
Keppel Land Limited	6338 8111	www.keppelland.com.sg
MCL Land	6221 8111	www.mclland.com.sg

owner another 4% of the purchase price within the 14 days; if you fail to do so, you forfeit the initial 1% that you paid.

Once the Option to Purchase has been exercised, your lawyer will launch a caveat to prevent the owner from selling the property to another buyer.

The Singapore Land Authority will then investigate to ensure that the owner has the right to sell the property (meaning that the owner isn't involved in bankruptcy proceedings that may preclude the sale of the property).

The details of the mortgage needs to be finalised with your bank.

A handover will take place with lawyers present to ensure that the property being handed over meets the terms of the sale.

Buying to Rent

Expats are allowed to buy properties in Singapore in order to rent them out. The purchasing process is the same as if you were buying the property to live in yourself. You may choose to make your own arrangements for renting out the place, but you can also pay a property management company to manage this for you. Their fees are usually around 5 to 10% of the gross monthly rent.

You should carefully consider your mortgage costs, the state of the property market (current and future) and how much rent you can reasonably expect when deciding whether buying a property to rent out is a sound investment. Rental income is taxed in the same way as employment income.

Selling Property

As with buying, it's recommended that you hire a real estate agent to assist you in the sale of your propery. Resale values depend on numerous factors, such as the type of property (freehold vs. leasehold), the location, the condition that the property is in, and the state of the property market in general.

Mortgages

Most major banks in Singapore offer mortgages and if you have a relationship with one of the banks in your home country, it may be easier for you to get a mortgage through the same bank here. In deciding whether to extend a mortgage to you, the bank will assess your assets and income to decide whether you have the means to repay the mortgage. Banks will conduct their own valuation of the property to determine the amount of the mortgage. The banks often base the valuation largely on the last transacted price for the property (if it's not new) rather than on the proposed purchase price, which can leave you paying more out of your own pocket if property values have increased since the previous sale of the property. Banks can loan expats a maximum of

Mortgage Providers

ABN AMRO Consumer Bank	1800 226 2676	www.abnamro.com.sg
Citibank ▶ p.IFC	6225 5225	www.citibank.com.sg
DBS Bank (Development Bank of Singapore)	1800 111 1111	www.dbs.com.sg
HSBC ▶ p.89	1800 786 6666	www.hsbc.com.sg
Maybank	1800 629 2265	www.maybank.com.sg
Overseas Chinese Banking Corporation (OCBC)	1800 438 3333	www.ocbc.com.sg
Standard Chartered Bank	1800 747 7000	www.standardchartered.com.sg
United Overseas Bank (UOB)	1800 222 2121	www.uob.com.sg

80% of the purchase price (locals can get 90%), so you will have to come up with at least 20% of the purchase price on your own. The maximum repayment period for a mortgage is 35 years. Most banks will penalise you about 1% of the total loan amount if you pay the mortgage off within the first year, but if you do so after three years there's no penalty.

Other Purchasing Costs

In addition to the purchase price of the property, there are several other costs involved in purchasing a property. First you have to pay stamp duty equal to about 3% of the purchase price to the Inland Revenue Authority of Singapore to ensure that the purchase contract is recognised by the courts. Legal fees will probably set you back $2,000 to $3,000. Property insurance, including fire insurance, could cost you anywhere from a few hundred to a few thousand dollars. If you used an agent you will have to pay a 1% agent fee – although if the purchase price is high you may be able to negotiate that the seller pays this fee instead of you. The seller also has to pay his agent a 2% commission. If you purchase a condo with facilities you will have to pay a maintenance fee that ranges from $200 to $500 per month.

Real Estate Law

The basic legal proceedings required when purchasing a property include the following (see The Process on p.99 for more details):
Offer to Purchase – the buyer issues a letter to the owner indicating their desire to purchase the property. This is submitted together with 1% of the purchase price.
Option to Purchase – an option issued by the owner to the buyer giving the buyer the right to purchase the property at the agreed price if the buyer exercises that right within 14 days by paying the owner 4% of the purchase price.
Launching of a caveat – once the option to purchase has been exercised, the buyer's lawyer will launch a caveat to prevent the owner from selling the property to another buyer.

Approval by Singapore Land Authority

Approval from SLA is required to ensure that the owner has the right to sell the property.
Residential properties in Singapore are either freehold or leasehold. In theory freehold properties can be owned indefinitely as ownership doesn't expire at any point. However, should the government one day decide that the property would better serve the country in some other way, there would be little you could do about it. Leasehold properties are either 99 or 999 year leaseholds, indicating the number of years that the property can be privately held before being returned to the government. Seeing as you're not likely to blow out the candles on your thousandth birthday cake, 999 year leasehold is effectively the same as freehold. For information about freehold versus leasehold, see Buying Property on p.99.
It's important to appoint a lawyer when buying a property to ensure that all the legal documents are correct and valid. Once you've bought a property it's also advisable (although not mandatory) that you write a new or revised will that includes your new purchase. See Certificates & Licences on p.75.

Residential Areas

Other options **Exploring** p.172

Once you've made the decision to live in Singapore it can be difficult to choose which residential area you would prefer to live in – especially if your knowledge of the city is still limited. Of course, other factors could narrow down your options. A landed house or a luxury condominium may not be within the budget, particularly if you consider your other start-up costs. If you have children, the proximity of your home to their school may be an issue and you'll need to consider how easy it will be to get to the office given the available public transport if that's what you're relying on. The area's proximity to leisure and entertainment facilities is also important.

Every area in Singapore has its attractions and its downsides, so no matter where you choose to live you should find that the benefits outweigh the negatives. The following pages will give you some insight into the various residential areas and should help you to narrow down your list, but nothing beats getting out there and exploring them for yourself.

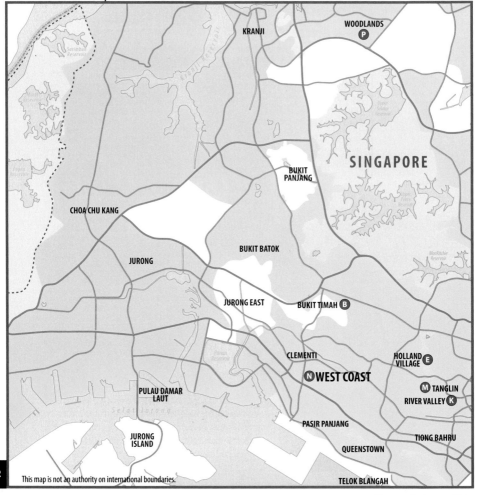

This map is not an authority on international boundaries.

Singapore Explorer 1st Edition

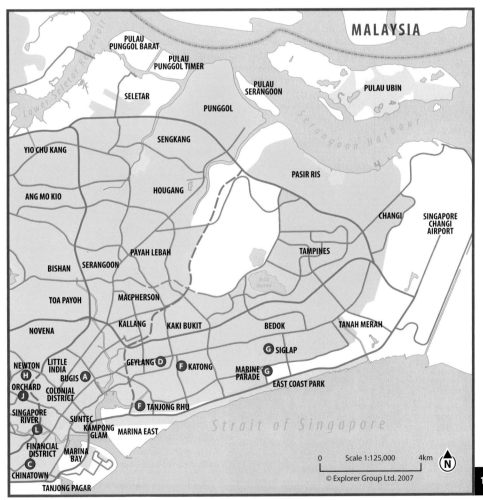

© Explorer Group Ltd. 2007

Map 14-D4

Bugis

Centred around Bugis MRT station, this area primarily consists of office buildings and shopping malls, but there are some intriguing residential options nestled in the side streets. It's not ideal for families, but the buzz around the shopping malls, cool restaurants and movie theatres appeals to singles or couples without children. All your amenities are within a short walk and transportation links are excellent. If you work around Bugis, City Hall or Raffles, it's a great location with a short commute.

Best Points
Bugis is in the middle of the action and sports interesting neighbourhoods such as Arab Street, Little India and the Colonial District around Raffles Hotel.

Worst Points
It's busy and there's little green space. Depending on where your apartment is, it can be noisy.

Accommodation

Although it's not one of the primary residential areas of Singapore, Bugis does have a number of unique shophouses and smaller apartment complexes, especially in the streets between North Bridge Road and Beach Road. Purvis, Liang Seah and Tan Quee Lan Streets all have shophouses with small restaurants at ground level and residential apartments on the upper floors. While they generally aren't spacious, most are modern and rent is reasonable – from $2,000 to $4,000. Don't expect facilities at any of the apartments in the area.

Shopping & Amenities

Parco Bugis Junction, with its shops, department stores, cinemas and a Cold Storage grocery store, is a large mall right at the Bugis MRT station. Down the road towards the river is Raffles City Shopping Centre, which has a Marketplace grocery store, and in the opposite direction you have Arab Street area and its many small shops.

Entertainment & Leisure

There's plenty to do around Bugis. The major hotels in the area all have top quality dining, there are cinemas at Parco Bugis Junction and Shaw Towers and hours of reading pleasure to be had at the recently opened National Library.

Healthcare

Raffles Hospital on the same block as the MRT station is one of Singapore's top private hospitals. It has specialist outpatient clinics as well as an emergency services and general outpatient care. Many of the office buildings and shopping malls in the area have small private dental and GP clinics.

Education

There aren't really any schools in the area. The closest ones are Chatsworth and the Overseas Family School, both just off Orchard Road.

Traffic & Parking

Traffic can be a major headache here at the weekends and during peak periods, although taxis are readily available and buses and the MRT are also easily accessible. Parking can be tricky, especially if your apartment doesn't have a parking lot.

Safety & Annoyances

Despite being in the heart of the city Bugis is fairly safe. The reality is that there aren't many places in Singapore where you aren't safe at any time of the day or night. The main annoyance here is the traffic and noise associated with such a busy area.

Map 6-C4

Bukit Timah

This area encompasses the streets on either side of Bukit Timah Road from Newton Circus up to the Bukit Timah and Bukit Batok Nature Reserves. It's definitely one of Singapore's more upscale neighbourhoods and once you get off Bukit Timah Road and into the back streets it has a distinctly suburban feel. There are no huge malls here, but rather a number of smaller strip malls with upscale restaurants and stores. The nature reserves on either side of Upper Bukit Timah Road and the Botanic Gardens nearer to town offer great escapes for nature lovers.

Best Points

Off the main road, the area has a very quiet, suburban feel to it, yet most of the amenities you'll need are close at hand and great parks are just a short run or ride away.

Worst Points

Transportation options are quite limited. Buses do run down Bukit Timah and into town, but there's no MRT and you will have to walk out to the main road to get a taxi.

Accommodation

Bukit Timah Road itself has a mix of low-rise and larger luxury condominiums with all the amenities you could wish for. The real appeal to expats may be the landed houses in the streets off the main road. Most are two or three storey houses with anything ranging from a small area to park your car out front to sprawling gardens with a pool and space to kick around a football. Rents are at the higher end of the scale here, with apartments going for $3,000-6,000 and landed houses starting at $5,000, but quickly jumping up to over $10,000 per month.

Shopping & Amenities

While it's not a shopping hub, Bukit Timah has its share of strip malls, many with boutique stores and grocers. These malls are located at the main crossroads, including Balmoral Road, Farrer Road, Coronation Road, Sixth Avenue and Clementi Road. There are also a number of car dealerships and garages at Turf City.

Entertainment & Leisure

Bukit Timah is a great place to get outdoors. The Botanic Gardens has many walking paths, ponds and some nice restaurants. Bukit Timah Nature Reserve is the mountain biking hub of Singapore, with some good trails through the jungle also used for hiking. The British and Hollandse Clubs and the Japanese Association and Alliance Française are nearby.

Healthcare

The nearest hospitals are the Thomson Medical Centre and Mount Elizabeth Hospital, near the eastern end of Bukit Timah Road. There are some stand-alone private clinics along Bukit Timah, but no major medical centres.

Education

There is a cluster of international schools near where Clementi Road meets Bukit Timah. The Canadian, German European and Hollandse Schools are all in the area. Further east along Bukit Timah is the Hwa Chong International School. There are a number of nurseries in the area, including Willow Nursery directly opposite the Canadian School.

Traffic & Parking

Bukit Timah Road is a major thoroughfare and can be very busy at the weekends and peak periods during the week. But once you get off the main road it's very quiet and traffic is limited to local residents going about their daily business. Parking is generally not a problem, as most condos have ample resident and visitor parking, while houses will have a drive at the front. Parking on the residential roads is also fine.

Safety & Annoyances

Bukit Timah is a clean, safe area with few, if any, annoyances. You may find the traffic a bit loud if you live on Bukit Timah Road and your apartment faces the street. Otherwise, it's as relaxed and secure as can be.

105

Map 17-C2

Chinatown

Chinatown is not the most obvious choice for expat housing, but it does have an interesting vibe and can add more of a cultural feel to your time in Singapore. Its location right near Raffles Place is definitely a plus if that's where you work. There are a few suitable apartment buildings in the area, but the real attraction is its heritage shophouses. It's not a great location if you have a family, with little in the way of parks, schools or kids activities. For younger singles and couples though, the great restaurants and little bars around Club Street and Tanjong Pagar Road are very appealing.

Best Points

Culturally interesting and centrally located, living in Chinatown is an alternative to the large condo districts that expats generally flock to.

Accommodation

Large complexes such as the Riverwalk on the Singapore River and Emerald Gardens on Club Street are the main expat housing options. The apartments are not particularly spacious, but the selling point is their location close to Raffles Place and the business district. A two-bedroom apartment will set you back $2,500-4,000. There are some beautiful heritage shophouses along Blair Road and Spottiswoode Park which may seem a bit out of the way, but if you can afford the rent you can also afford a car or taxi fares. Rents start at $8,000 and can reach close to $20,000.

Worst Points

Since it's not a real expat area, there are few stores catering to their needs. Western grocery stores are absent, as are large shopping malls.

Shopping & Amenities

There isn't a real expat shopping mall in Chinatown, but you can get a lot of your day-to-day necessities from the smaller shops in the area and China Square Central has a Cold Storage. The Amara Hotel has a small shopping centre next to it and an NTUC Fairprice across the road for groceries. For anything you can't get in Chinatown, it's only a few stops on the MRT or a five-minute taxi ride to City Hall, Bugis or Orchard Road where you can shop till you're giddy.

Entertainment & Leisure

There's not much in the way of parks, malls or cinemas in Chinatown but there's no shortage of restaurants to choose from. Far East Square has great al fresco dining and pubs with a good vibe even on weekdays. Tanjong Pagar Road and the surrounding small streets have some of Singapore's top restaurants and there are countless little local restaurants and stalls to be discovered in the side streets between New Bridge and South Bridge Roads. Club Street and Ann Siang Road are also home to a number of excellent restaurants.

Education

There are no schools in this area but it's not too far to the Orchard area and its schools. You can also get onto the Ayer Rajah Expressway fairly easily from here and that will take you to the ISS Senior Campus, United World College and Tanglin Trust School.

Healthcare

Singapore General Hospital is located across from Outram MRT station. It provides a full range of health services, including a number of specialist treatment centres and an accident and emergency service. Chinatown is also good if you're interested in alternative therapies such as acupuncture.

Traffic & Parking

Parking is available at all the condos and apartment blocks in the area. Parking in the heart of Chinatown can be scarce, but you'll probably only be walking from home if you need to go somewhere in the area anyway. Traffic runs smoothly most of the time, with only occasional delays during peak periods. The area's well-served by public transport with the Chinatown, Outram and Tanjong Pagar MRT stations and many bus routes running down New Bridge Road and Eu Tong Sen Street.

Safety & Annoyances

While some of the backstreets of Chinatown may seem a bit dodgy they are really quite safe. Annoyances are minimal, as most of the residential zones here are set back from the main roads and enjoy relative peace and quiet.

Map 15-B3

Geylang

Geylang has a distinctive feel to it that you won't find elsewhere. Part of this stems from the many establishments catering to gentlemen in search of amorous adventures, that line a number of the side streets (called 'lors') off Geylang Road. It also comes from the traditional shophouse architecture, the clan association headquarters and the mix of nationalities found on the streets. As a residential area, it's not great for families, but for singles or young couples it can be interesting place and there are a few unique housing options.

Best Points
The vibe and the great food.

Worst Points
Not great for amenities and definitely not family-friendly.

Accommodation

There are a couple of condo blocks towards the eastern part of Geylang along Lors 26-33. They're not top-of-the-line and are appropriately priced at around $1,500 to $3,000. The more interesting option in Geylang is the opportunity to live in a heritage shophouse. There are a couple of lors that have rows of residential shophouses for rent. It's worth hunting these down just to see the inside. Who knows, you may be taken by one and decide to move in.

Shopping & Amenities

The shopping is nothing like what you see in town. For the most part it's just a dizzying array of ground-level shophouse stores selling most of what you need and a lot of what you don't. At the far eastern end of Geylang is City Plaza, which is a bit more of a proper shopping mall. But if you can't find what you're looking for in the area, it's only a short hop across the Kallang Basin to the shopping malls of Bugis.

Entertainment & Leisure

Geylang offers plenty of leisure, but it may not be the kind that you're comfortable with. In that case, there are services, albeit limited ones. Geylang East Community Library is next to the Aljunied MRT station. The National Stadium complex is just to the west of Geylang and has a number of sports centres and pitches. Directly west of Geylang is also the main area for dragon boating, with many clubs putting their boats into the Kallang Basin at weekends for training.

Healthcare

East Shore Hospital is the nearest medical facility. There are some traditional Chinese medicine practitioners in the area where you can get acupuncture and reflexology done. Raffles Hospital is also not too far away, just across the Kallang Basin in the Bugis area.

Education

There are no international schools in Geylang and the nearest one is the East Campus of Chatsworth International School. It's most likely that children will be sent off to schools in town or in the west, which makes for a longer commute.

Traffic & Parking

The many side streets off Geylang Road offer space for parking, but can fill up quickly in the evenings, when driving can be a bit of a challenge thanks to the pedestrian and vehicle traffic. From Geylang it's a straight shot across the Kallang Basin on Nicoll Highway to the Beach Road and Bugis areas. Public transportation links are good, with buses running along Geylang Road and Aljunied and Kallang MRT stations close at hand. Taxis are everywhere, but you may have to wait for one in the evenings when demand increases.

Safety & Annoyances

While threats to your actual safety are minimal, this is one of the edgier parts of town and there are times when women may feel uncomfortable.

Map 13-C3 ◀

Holland Village

With great restaurants, bars and amenities, it's no surprise Holland Village is one of the main expat areas. A mix of landed houses and condo blocks provide a good range of accommodation options. The area directly around Holland Avenue is like a small self-contained community and could be termed Holland Village proper. You'll see familiar faces at the grocery store or at the cafes along the street. There's a lot of construction going on right now to connect Holland Village to the MRT Circle Line. Once completed it will be yet another of the area's pluses.

Best Points ◀

Holland Village has a unique character, combining a cosy neighbourhood feel with a mix of classy boutiques, restaurants and cafes.

Worst Points ◀

Access to public transport isn't great, although this will improve when the MRT Circle Line is completed in a year or two.

Accommodation

Immediately north of Holland Road are modern condo blocks with full facilities that range from $2,500 to $4,500. Set further back from Holland Road are many luxurious landed houses that rent out for between $12,000 and $30,000 per month. You'll find many embassies among these too. There are some smaller – and generally older – low-rise condo blocks south of Holland Drive. These range from $2,000 up to $5,000 depending on the size of the apartment and the facilities included. Further west along Holland Road is Sixth Avenue, one of the more sought-after locations in Singapore. The landed houses that line Sixth Avenue and its side streets rent out for anything from $5,000 to $20,000.

Shopping & Amenities

Furniture and clothing boutiques, a fine foods store, an excellent electronics store and a petshop can all be found in Holland Village. Holland Road Shopping Centre has a Cold Storage grocery store and there's a wet market off Lorong Mambong. Several banks have branches in Holland Village, including HSBC and DBS. A few health spas offer massage and beauty services.

Entertainment & Leisure

Holland Village has a profusion of restaurants and bars along Jalan Merah Saga, Lorong Mambong and Lorong Liput. Dining options range from hawker stalls and fast food joints to elegant restaurants serving western, Asian and fusion food. Many restaurants and bars have outdoor seating, creating an ambience reminiscent of European cafes.

Healthcare

There are a number of small medical clinics in Holland Village and the Camden Medical Centre is close by. The public National University Hospital and the private Gleneagles Hospital are nearest, and both have full services and accident and emergency departments.

Education

Anglo-Chinese School (International) is located in Holland Village, while Dover Court Preparatory School, Tanglin Trust School, and United World College of South East Asia are close by. Holland Village is also near the National University of Singapore and INSEAD campuses. The Canadian School and British, Hollandse and German European Schools are also easily accessible.

Mini Map

This is the perfect companion for trips around Singapore - small enough for your pocket but big enough to expand your horizons. Keep the Mini Map handy and you'll be navigating your way around the city like a local in no time.

Traffic & Parking

Traffic can be bad along Holland Road heading towards Orchard and downtown, and the construction of the new Circle Line MRT station at Holland Village has slowed traffic down too. This should improve once construction in completed in two or three year's time, and the MRT station will provide a welcome new link to the rest of the island. Taxis are easy to catch, but you may have to wait in line during peak periods.

Safety & Annoyances

Construction of the new MRT Circle Line does create traffic bottlenecks in and around Holland Village and there's also construction noise to contend with. But the area is safe and you can walk around at any time and feel comfortable.

Map 15-D3 & 15-B4

Katong & Tanjong Rhu

The western part of the larger East Coast area, Katong & Tanjong Rhu has everything from huge resort-style condo complexes to landed houses with spacious yards. While Tanjong Rhu may seem to be stranded out in the Kallang Basin, the Katong area is a bustling neighbourhood with plenty of life. East Coast Park, which runs along much of the shoreline from Tanjong Rhu all the way up to Changi Airport, is perfect for the outdoors fitness buff. It has paths for running, biking and inline skating and beaches for relaxing.

Best Points

The proximity to East Coast Park and the neighbourhood feel that comes from the lack of malls and five-star hotels.

Worst Points

Tanjong Rhu and the area nearer the coast are not convenient for public transport.

Accommodation

Tanjong Rhu is home to some of the largest condo complexes in Singapore. Many have great views of the East Coast and the downtown skyline. However, their size means that many units share the same facilities. An apartment can go for anything from $2,500 to $8,000 depending on size and the floor it's on. Further east in Katong, there are some beautiful landed houses with large yards. These infrequently come up for rent, but when they do, can cost over $12,000 per month. There are also numerous smaller condo complexes and low-rise buildings along the ECP and near Haig and Joo Chiat Roads. These vary in price, but are noticeably cheaper than similar buildings in town. Expect to pay anything from $1,500, with modern luxury condos still commanding a hefty sum.

Shopping & Amenities

There are few amenities in Tanjong Rhu; for anything resembling a shopping mall you'll have to head into Katong and the stretch of East Coast Road between Haig and Joo Chiat Roads. The new Parkway Parade Shopping Mall is a bit further south, and has just about everything you might need, with the exception of high-end boutiques. The nearest major shopping district is Suntec City, 10 minutes into town.

Entertainment & Leisure

At Tanjong Rhu, you're right on the Kallang Basin, a great venue for watersports. Most dragon boat teams practice here and there's also kayaking to be done. East Coast Park offers plenty of outdoor recreation, a long-grass bird sanctuary and some good seafood restaurants. There's more than enough to keep you outdoors and active, but for real excitement or nightlife you'll have to head into town.

Healthcare

The East Shore Hospital, which provides accident and emergency services, is not far away. There are also a number of private medical clinics in the malls along East Coast Road, including Katong Mall.

Education

The only school in the area is the East Campus of the Chatsworth International School, on Jalan Tembusu, just off Haig Road. It can be quite a trek from here to the international schools in town or out west.

Traffic & Parking

Easy access to the ECP (an expressway running along the entire East Coast) makes getting to Changi Airport and into town fairly straightforward if you have a car or take taxis. Public transportation options are more limited. With the MRT line running further inland the area is reliant on buses. Taxis are available on the main roads.

Safety & Annoyances

The only concern may be the slightly seedy reputation of a few of the hotels along East Coast Road. But, unless you go inside and are easily offended, there are really no problems here.

Map 15-E4 & 12-B3

Marine Parade & Siglap

The eastern section of Singapore's East Coast area, Marine Parade and Siglap have a comfortable community atmosphere about them. Life is definitely a bit more laidback here. The location is great if you're a frequent flyer, but might be a drawback if you have children to send to school, as there aren't any in the area. Most needs are catered to with the existing amenities, but they're not on par with the malls further west.

Best Points
A great community feel in a laidback atmosphere; difficult to find elsewhere in Singapore.

Worst Points
Far from schools and the malls in town.

Accommodation

Accommodation here tends to be older, bigger and have more character than the new blocks in town. That said, the mix of landed houses, terrace houses and older condo blocks is slowly giving way to new, larger condos. Landed houses range from $3,000 to $8,000 per month. Condos start at $1,500 and go up to around $5,000 for the newer blocks.

Shopping & Amenities

There are plenty of smaller shops and stalls in Marine Parade and Siglap, but for proper shopping you'll have to head up to Changi Road or west to Katong. It really is a residential area and malls are kept to a minimum.

Entertainment & Leisure

This area is great if you enjoy being outdoors and on or near the water. East Coast Park runs the full length of the coastline and is dotted with facilities. These include the Singapore Tennis Centre, Pasta Fresca Sailing Club and the East Coast Seafood Centre. There are also the walking, biking and inline skating paths that wind through the park. While it can be crowded at weekends, you'll have it all to yourself during the week.

Healthcare

East Shore Hospital is the main medical facility servicing the Marine Parade/Siglap area. Further to the east is the government-run Changi Hospital. Both provide a full range of services including accident and emergency care. There is also the smaller St. Andrew's Community Hospital.

East Coast Park

Education

There are no international schools in this area and a significant commute is required to get to any of the schools in town or in the west.

Traffic & Parking

Traffic is usually fairly smooth in the area and easy access to the ECP makes for relatively fast travel times into town or to Changi Airport. The MRT line runs along Sims Avenue and is convenient for those living further inland, near Eunos and Kembangan MRT stations.

Safety & Annoyances

The main disturbance comes from the construction sites where older buildings are being torn down and new condos put up. The noise can continue into the weekends, which doesn't make for a relaxing day by the pool if you're next door to a site.

111

Map 14-B3

Newton

Best Points

Families will enjoy the quiet back streets and foodies will appreciate the hawker food at Newton Circus.

Worst Points

If you're looking for excitement on your doorstep, this is not the place to be.

The Newton area, centred around the Newton and Novena MRT stations, is a relatively sleepy part of town, with not much in the way of entertainment other than the Novena Square and United Square shopping centres. The only place open late is the Newton Circus hawker centre. Housing is primarily in large high-rise condos, but there are a number of landed houses in the streets west of Newton Road. It's centrally located and enjoys quick access to Orchard, Bukit Timah and Little India.

Accommodation

The Newton area is chock-a-block with modern condos, and new ones are being built all the time. There are also a couple of unique black and white apartment buildings on Monk's Hill Road and a row of older black and white terrace houses on Monk's Hill Terrace. Hooper Road, on the other side of Bukit Timah, also has a great little community of black and white bungalows. Rents for these go from $1,500 to $3,000. There are also landed houses along Gentle Road and Chancery Lane that go for between $5,000 and $15,000.

Shopping & Amenities

For shopping, the focus is firmly on Novena Square and United Square, both large malls with the usual array of shops and services. Novena Square has a Cold Storage, and there's one at Chancery Court on Bukit Timah as well. Beyond this there really isn't much on offer.

Entertainment & Leisure

With Orchard Road not far away, Newton is close to a lot of entertainment options, but doesn't actually have many of its own. There is the Newton Circus hawker centre (p.427), one of Singapore's largest and most famous with undeniably good food, although it is accused of being a bit of a tourist trap at times. Novena Square and United Square have a few dining options, but they're really not all that exciting. Francophiles will be happy to know that the Alliance Francaise is just a few minutes walk from Newton MRT station.

Healthcare

With three hospitals in the area, medical assistance is never far away – all have accident and emergency departments. Tan Tock Seng Hospital is right next to Novena Square and KK Women's and Children's Hospital (the top paediatric hospital) is a few minutes from Newton Circus. The privately run Thomson Medical Centre is a two-minute drive from Novena Square and has a full range of outpatient and specialist clinics.

Education

Beyond The Kiddiewinkie Place, a nursery just next to the carpark at Newton Circus, there are no schools in the immediate area. But it's a straight shot to the Australian School at Bishan and an easy drive down Bukit Timah to the British, Hollandse and German European Schools. The Overseas Family School and International School Singapore's elementary and middle schools aren't that far away either.

Traffic & Parking

Traffic is reasonable, although Newton Circus roundabout can get busy at peak times, as can Newton Road. MRT stations at Novena and Newton make public transport an easy option and there are bus routes along the major roads. Taxis are easy to flag down, but you'll have to walk to a main road if you live in one of the smaller back streets.

Safety & Annoyances

The Newton area is safe and pleasant for families. The main hindrance will come from occasional traffic noise and construction as new condos are put up.

Chinatown

Bugis

Mount Faber

Rooms with a view

Map 14-B4 ◀

Orchard

Lined with malls, Orchard Road is the shopping mecca of Singapore and offers no residential options. But you'll find many high-end condo complexes – often full of expats – in the streets within walking distance from Orchard Road. Everything you need is pretty much on your doorstep here and your transportation, dining and entertainment options are excellent. The only thing missing is some green space, although a walk to Fort Canning Park is not out of the question.

Best Points ◀

The amenities are second to none. Some of the best shopping in the world lines Orchard Road and it can be pleasant to wander down there on a weekend morning to sit at a cafe sipping your coffee and watching the world go by.

Worst Points ◀

Getting in and out of the area can be a real hassle at weekends as it's packed with shoppers. Taxis are hard to come by at peak times.

Accommodation

There are many condos on Cairnhill Road, St. Thomas Walk, Stevens Road and Grange Road. Most of the buildings are large, modern high-rises but there are still some older buildings that haven't given in to rampant redevelopment. These are generally more spacious and have a bit more character, but won't have facilities. Rents can start at $2,500 and rocket up to $10,000 depending on how luxurious you need your home to be. There are also two areas of stunning conservation shophouses in Emerald Hill and Cairnhill Road that are worth checking out if your budget allows: they start at $8,000 and go up to $18,000 per month.

Shopping & Amenities

The difficulty you have at Orchard lies not in finding what you need, but rather in deciding at which of the many malls you're going to get it. The Heeren and Orchard Cineleisure cater to the younger generation, with an HMV and all the latest styles. Paragon and Ngee Ann City Shopping Centres are upscale malls where all the major luxury brands from Europe and the US are well represented. Paragon has a Marketplace grocery store and Ngee Ann City has a Cold Storage. Further down the road, Plaza Singapura is another major development with a cinema. Lucky Plaza is generally the domain of tourists but it can be a fun place to go hunting for a bargain and it also boasts two of the best bookstores in Singapore, Borders and Kinokuniya.

Entertainment & Leisure

There are three major cinemas along Orchard Road, at Shaw House, Orchard Cineleisure and Plaza Singapura. Restaurants abound at street level, in the shopping malls and at the major hotels, including the Grand Hyatt, Marriott, Goodwood Park and Meritus Mandarin. Sitting at one of the many cafes lining Orchard Road can be a nice break from shopping, or a good way to while away a weekend morning reading the paper. The Youth Park next to Somerset MRT station has a skate park and regular performances and activities to keep youngsters entertained, while for the older set Emerald Hill has some excellent bars in beautiful shophouses that are perfect for after work drinks on a Friday.

Healthcare

Mount Elizabeth Hospital is a private hospital tucked behind Paragon Shopping Centre. It offers a full range of services including outpatient care and accident and emergency department. Paragon's top floors house a variety of specialist private clinics for everything from paediatrics to plastic surgery.

Education

Chatsworth School is on Emerald Hill while the Overseas Family School and International School Singapore's Elementary and Middle Schools are on Paterson Road, near Wheelock Place and Borders.

Traffic & Parking

All condos have parking spaces for residents and the shophouses in the area have designated street parking in front of each house. On Orchard Road itself, each shopping mall has a huge parking lot and there are a few independently run lots too. Traffic can be hectic, as everyone in Singapore seems to converge on the area at weekends. It can be difficult to get a taxi during peak periods, and you may have to walk down to a taxi stand at one of the shopping malls, where there's often still a queue. But public transport links are great, with Orchard, Somerset and Dhoby Ghaut MRT stations in the area and many bus routes running down Orchard.

Safety & Annoyances

The only threat here is the traffic swarming around Orchard. Annoyances include the crowds at the weekends, though you can always choose to stay by your condo's pool rather than venture out. Construction noise can be a problem at times, as developers work seven days a week tearing down old buildings in the area and putting up new luxury condos.

Map 17-B1 ◀

River Valley

River Valley is one long stretch of condominiums from Clemenceau Avenue all the way to the Alexandra Road. The buildings range from older high-rises to brand new condos with all the facilities. Many of the older buildings are prime targets for en bloc sale, after which they will be torn down and a new condo put up in their place. While it's not a shopping area, it is walking distance to Orchard Road and has some great little restaurants. Many expats choose to make their home here as they'll be near schools and amenities.

Best Points ◀

It's in the heart of the city, within walking distance of the Singapore River and Orchard areas.

Worst Points ◀

Not much in the way of parks or greenery unless you live down near the Fort Canning end. Some areas are also a bit cut off from public transport.

Accommodation

There are two big condo developments at the far eastern end of River Valley, UE Square and Aspen Heights. Moving west takes you into the heart of condo-country, with high-rises and older walk-ups lining River Valley and its surrounding roads all the way to Alexandra Road. You can find anything from an old no-facilities walk-up to some of the most luxurious condos in the country here. Prices for walk-ups can start at $1,500 while newer condos won't go for less than $3,500 and then keep on going.

Shopping & Amenities

You won't find many shops along River Valley. There's an NTUC Fairprice on Killiney Road and a Cold Storage in UE Square, but that's about it. Luckily, Orchard Road and Great World City are close at hand.

Entertainment & Leisure

River Valley has some good entertainment options. At its far eastern end is Clarke Quay, which is fast turning into one of the hottest restaurant and nightlife spots. Fort Canning, a green refuge from the malls and condos, is just across the road. Further west is the bar-lined Mohamed Sultan Road, but things have toned down here considerably since its heyday five or ten years ago. Killiney Road has an interesting stretch of smaller restaurants leading down to Orchard Road. At the far western end of River Valley, near the corner with Zion Road, is a row of locally famous eating establishments. And if that's not enough, there's always Orchard Road just a short walk away.

Healthcare

There are no medical clinics or hospitals on River Valley Road, but it's a short walk or taxi ride to the medical centres at Orchard Road and Tanglin. These include Camden Medical Centre, Gleneagles and Mount Elizabeth Hospitals and the clinics in Tanglin and Paragon Shopping Centres.

Education

The Brighton Montessori School is right on River Valley Road at the corner with Oxley Road (where former prime minister Lee Kuan Yew lives). Within walking distance are the International School Singapore (elementary and middle schools) and the Overseas Family School.

Traffic & Parking

Traffic on River Valley rarely gets backed up outside of short delays at peak periods. Parking for residents and visitors is available at all the condos and roadside parking is possible outside many of the older walk-ups, though you may have to wait for a spot to open up.

Safety & Annoyances

The only disturbance here may come from late night revellers leaving the bars on Mohamed Sultan Road, but that only affects two or three condos in the area.

Is getting lost your usual excuse?

Whether you're a map person or not, this pocket-sized marvel will help you get to know the city like the back of your hand… so you won't feel the back of someone else's.

Singapore Mini Map
Putting the city in your pocket

EXPLORER

Map 17-B2

Singapore River

The Singapore River residential area is a long strip that runs on either side of the river from Boat Quay to Robertson Quay. It's popular among tourists who come to ride the bumboats that fare up and down the river, or to chill at the countless restaurants and bars. The area is lively and colourful, and if you work in the central business district it's just a short commute away. Though not typically thought of as a residential area, Singapore River does have a few major condos and more are being built.

Best Points

If you like to party and you love being where the action is, you couldn't find a better place to live.

Worst Points

The area is very tourist-oriented so you'll have to put up with higher prices for food and drink in the restaurants and bars.

Accommodation
Accommodation is limited to a handful of condos, including River Place, Riverside View, and Riverwalk Apartments. Rent in one of these popular developments can start as low as $2,500 for a one bedroom unit, but quickly rises to $8,000 for three bedrooms.

Shopping & Amenities
Shopping options tend to target tourists. Liang Court at Clarke Quay is a small-scale shopping mall that doesn't hold too much of interest aside from its Kinokuniya bookstore and a Meidi-Ya Supermarket. If you prefer Cold Storage grocery stores, there's one just a short walk from Clarke Quay at UE Shopping Mall.

Entertainment & Leisure
Living in the Singapore River area, you're surrounded by Singapore's most active nightlife spots. Boat Quay is home to a number of pubs and clubs that attract the after-work crowd from the financial district, while Clarke Quay has experienced a transformation over the past year or two and is now home to some of the country's hottest clubs. Robertson Quay has a handful of trendy drinking and dining spots. Venture a bit further up-river and you'll reach Singapore's legendary Zouk nightclub. If partying is not your thing, you'll be happy to know that both the Asian Civilisations Museum (Empress Place) and the Singapore History Museum are in the area.

Healthcare
While there isn't a hospital directly in this area, a five to ten-minute drive will get you to a number of medical centres and hospitals. On the south side of the river, Singapore General Hospital is the nearest medical facility. To the north, the medical centres and hospitals in Tanglin and Orchard are close at hand.

Education
There are no schools in the Singapore River area but it's only a short trip to the schools around Orchard and quick access to the AYE gets you out to the ISS Senior Campus, United World College and Tanglin Trust School fairly easily.

Traffic & Parking
Traffic in this area can be a bit hectic around peak periods, but it's manageable the rest of the time. Parking can be a bit of an issue at some of the buildings on the north side of the river near Robertson Quay and Zion Road. Clarke Quay and Redhill are the two main MRT stations serving this area. Getting a taxi is generally not a problem..

Safety & Annoyances
The Singapore River area is fairly safe and free of disturbances. The only concern may be rowdy partiers emerging from the bars that line the river at its eastern end.

Map 13-F4 ◀

Tanglin

Situated between Holland Village and Orchard, Tanglin is a quiet, sophisticated neighbourhood characterised by grand houses, often with sizeable gardens and tall fences for privacy. The area is home to a number of foreign embassies and high commissions, some housed in stately mansions that add to the opulent feel of the neighbourhood. The Singapore Botanic Gardens are in the area but you'll have to venture outside its boundaries to find much in the way of eating, drinking and entertainment.

Best Points ◀

Tanglin's quiet streets are wonderful for evening strolls in beautiful surroundings. The Singapore Botanic Gardens are in the area and provide a relaxing backdrop for jogging or dog walking.

Worst Points ◀

Tanglin is not very accessible by public transport as there's no MRT line nearby and buses only ply a few main routes. If you live on one of the neighbourhood's back streets you might find yourself walking out to the main roads or calling taxis more often than not.

Accommodation

Here you're looking at landed houses with large gardens and even larger rents. When you're rubbing shoulders with foreign diplomats and Singapore's well-to-do, you have to be prepared to pay for the privilege. Rents for a small bungalow start at $8,000 but rapidly rise to $16,000 and up for larger houses. There are plenty of modern condos on the eastern side of the Tanglin area along Nassim, Cuscaden and Grange Roads, where rents range from $4,000 to $16,000.

Shopping & Amenities

Tanglin Mall is the main shopping location in the neighbourhood, with a full range of clothing stores, restaurants, a Market Place supermarket and a few great antique shops. Nearby is Tanglin Shopping Centre and a strip of stores that includes a good bicycle shop (Treknology Bikes). The laid-back yet trendy Dempsey Road area is a great place for poking around in antique stores or picking up a few bottles of wine.

Entertainment & Leisure

With a few small exceptions, Tanglin doesn't have much happening in terms of nightlife. There are a few hip wine bars and tasty eateries in the Dempsey Road area and the Botanic Gardens are home to lovely restaurants surrounded by greenery. The Gardens themselves are excellent for walking in, particularly if you're interested in the local plant life. Also in the neighbourhood is the Tanglin Golf Course, a members-only club.

Healthcare

Tanglin is one of the hubs of medical services. Gleneagles Hospital is one of Singapore's top private hospitals and has specialist outpatient clinics as well as an accident and emergency department. The Camden Medical Centre houses a number of specialist clinics. There are also many service providers on the upper floors of the Tanglin Shopping Centre, including physical therapy and chiropractic clinics.

Education

Both the Overseas Family School and International School Singapore (elementary and middle school campus) are on nearby Paterson Road. The Chatsworth International School is a bit further down Orchard, but still only a short drive away. The schools along Bukit Timah Road are also easily accessible.

Traffic & Parking

Traffic around Tanglin is mostly limited to residents. Tanglin and Holland Roads are the main thoroughfares, and neither are particularly busy outside of peak periods. Parking isn't an issue for the landed houses and the condos in the area all have ample carparks.

Safety & Annoyances

One of the most affluent neighbourhoods in Singapore, Tanglin is also one of the safest. And with so many of the embassies here it's bound to be secure. There are simply no major annoyances – even construction work isn't as rampant as it is elsewhere.

119

Maps 9 & 10

West Coast

The area is an excellent location if you have kids or work in Jurong or at the National University of Singapore. It's got plenty of schools and the West Coast Park has open space and an excellent playground for your kids to run around in. For additional greenery there are the Kent Ridge and Telok Blangah Parks, both situated up on hills with views of the sea. The amenities along the coast are surprisingly good and it's not far to Alexandra Road where you can find just about everything you need.

Best Points
Great location for families with schools and parks. Rents are cheaper than in town too.

Worst Points
It's not that far out of town, but can feel like it at times.

Accommodation

The main housing options are clustered along Pasir Panjang and South Buona Vista Roads, where condos and houses rent out at $2,500 to $7,000 per month. There are two areas of unique black and whites, one at Portsdown Road and the other at Bury and Preston Roads, near Alexandra Road. The community around Portsdown Road is an interesting mix of locals and expats with a common affection for older colonial housing and the desire to be set back from the hustle and bustle of Singapore.

Shopping & Amenities

Pasir Panjang Hill Village and the Village Centre next door cater to quite a few of the day-to-day needs of local residents. When they don't suffice, Alexandra Road, the Harbourfront Centre and VivoCity should be able to pick up the slack. There's an IKEA at Alexandra Road, as well as Anchor Point providing all the usual amenities found in a suburban mall. Alexandra Road is also one of the main car showroom strips in Singapore.

Entertainment & Leisure

If you like to be outdoors, West Coast is one of the better places to live. West Coast Park is much less crowded than its East Coast counterpart, and Telok Blangah, Mount Faber and Kent Ridge Parks are all pleasant green spaces. For the golfer, there's the Transview Golf Course and Keppel Golf Links. It's also hard to overlook the nearby Sentosa Island, with beaches, golf courses and various attractions. Restaurants in the area are mostly little local secrets and include Singapore's premier biker hangout, The Handle Bar.

Healthcare

There's the National University Hospital on the campus of the National University of Singapore (NUS) and Alexandra Hospital on the north side of the AYE, near Queensway Shopping Centre. Both hospitals offer specialist and outpatient services as well as accident and emergency care.

Education

The West Coast is a hub of educational institutions. Both NUS and INSEAD have their campuses here, as do United World College, Dover Court Preparatory School, Tanglin Trust School, ISS International School Singapore (Senior Campus) and the Japanese School. It's also a relatively quick trip up Clementi Road to the Canadian, British, Hollandse and German European Schools.

Traffic & Parking

Except for the West Coast Highway and the AYE, traffic is quite light. Getting in and out of town is easy – you can be home from Raffles Place in about 15 minutes. Buses run along the West Coast Highway and there's an MRT station at Harbourfront, across from Sentosa.

Safety & Annoyances

The only disturbance is the many trucks carrying containers to the terminals along the West Coast whose presence on the roads can be unnerving for less experienced drivers.

Map 4-A3

Woodlands

At first glance Woodlands seems an unlikely place for expats to live. It's located at the northern tip of Singapore, where the causeway connects Singapore to Malaysia. It's not near any great amenities or locations where expats work. The real draw is the Singapore American School. An expat community has sprung up around the sprawling campus on Woodlands Street 41, and while it may have its inconveniences, it continues to draw expat families.

Accommodation

Accommodation around the American School is limited to a compact area along Woodgrove Avenue and its side streets. This mainly has landed houses to offer with a couple of condo buildings in between. Houses rent for between $4,500 and $10,000 per month while the condo units start at $1,500 and go up to $5,000.

Shopping & Amenities

Woodlands' one major shopping mall is Causeway Point, which has everything you'd expect to find in a suburban mall including a Cold Storage grocery, a bookshop and cinemas. Several smaller shopping plazas are dispersed around the neighbourhood but for anything more, you have to head into town.

Entertainment & Leisure

There are numerous small parks spread throughout Woodlands, so wherever you live you won't have to walk too far to reach a green patch. The Woodlands Swimming Complex is great for those days when all you want to do is submerge yourself to escape the heat. There's also the Woodlands Regional Library at the Woodlands Civic Centre, just across the road from Causeway Point.

Healthcare

Woodlands has two clinics: the Woodlands Polyclinic on Woodlands Street 31 and the SATA Woodlands Clinic at the Woodlands Civic Centre. The area isn't particularly well-served by hospitals: the nearest private one is Adam Road Hospital and the closest public hospital is at Mount Alvernia near Braddell. The Raffles Group has a private dental clinic as well as a Women's Centre at the Causeway Point Shopping Centre in Woodlands.

Education

The real reason that Woodlands is popular with expats is that it's home to the Singapore American School (p.155). The vast, modern campus houses everything from pre-school through to high school. SAS is one of the top schools in Singapore and the region.

Traffic & Parking

The main problem is that Woodlands is near the causeway that crosses over to Malaysia. This means heavy traffic during peak periods and nightmarish line-ups on the eve of long weekends as labourers and Singaporean tourists wait to cross over to Johor Bahru. Marsiling and Woodlands MRT stations service the area, but be prepared for a long ride if you're using the train to get into town.

Safety & Annoyances

Woodlands is safe and pleasant but the traffic associated with the causeway to Malaysia is a major drawback.

Best Points
You're close to the causeway, so you can cross over to Johor for cheap food and shopping. Just avoid the massive queues on public holidays! Because you are further from downtown, accommodation is generally cheaper.

Worst Points
You're far from the malls of Orchard Road, the offices of the CBD and the beaches of East Coast and Sentosa. Count on it taking 20 minutes to an hour to get into town depending on your mode of transportation.

121

You've collected your employment pass, opened a bank account and found an apartment. Now what? There are still plenty of little details to sort out to make life in Singapore more comfortable. These include everything from decorating your new home to finding out where you can rent a good movie. If you're coming to Singapore with a job already waiting for you, your employer may help you with some of the aspects of moving and setting up a home, either with practical or financial assistance. If not, you'll find all the information you need from your new friends and colleagues and from this guide.

Emerald Hill

Smooth Moves

Before you start packing for your move to Singapore, check the Singapore Customs website (www.customs.gov.sg) to see whether any of the items you plan to bring are prohibited. If you will be moving in or out of a condo, be aware that some prohibit tenants from moving at certain times during the week, such as Saturday afternoons or Sundays.

Moving Services

If you know you will be staying in Singapore long-term you may want to ship your furniture and belongings over. But if you're only here for a year it might make more sense to rent furnished accommodation, or to buy furniture here. Fortunately, appliances and furniture are reasonably priced in Singapore so starting from scratch is do-able.

You'll find plenty of moving companies that will help you move within Singapore by packing, loading, transporting, unloading and unpacking your worldly goods. Depending on whether you're moving overseas or down the road, you can opt for different levels of service. If all you need is a truck and some able bodies to help you carry things, you're probably best off with a local company. Fees start at around $50 per hour for a mid-sized truck and a driver who will help with loading, but quickly rise as you add more movers and increase the size of the truck. Of course a cheaper moving arrangement does mean you're less likely to receive compensation for any damages incurred during the move.

For an overseas move, an international moving company is a better option as its employees are better equipped to properly pack your belongings for what could be a bumpy ride. You can also place the entire move in someone else's hands and use a relocation specialist company. In addition to looking after the packing and moving, a relocation specialist can help with arranging visas, clearing your belongings through customs and scouting out schools for your children. Service like this does come at a price, so first check whether your employer will be subsidising your move. Before the movers arrive with your goods decide how you're going to organise your belongings so you can direct them as they carry their heavy loads in. It's a good idea to start on the bedrooms first.

Relocation Companies

Asian Welcome	6733 0233	www.asianwelcome.com
Asta Projects	6891 2812	www.astaprojects.com.sg
Cendant Mobility	6557 0039	www.cendantmobility.com
CityState Singapore ▶ p.v ▶ p.125	6235 5652	www.citystate.com.sg
Collin's Movers	6873 9595	www.collinsmovers.com.sg
Cross Roads	6425 2086	www.crossroads.com.sg
Crown Worldwide	6861 6818	www.crownrelo.com
Estin Movers	6388 8887	na
GMAC Global Relocation Services	6535 0010	www.gmacglobalrelocation.com
No Stone Unturned	9855 8501	www.nostone-unturned.com
OCSC Global	6238 0777	www.ocsc.com.sg
Pricoa Relocation	6536 1966	www.pricoarelocation.com
RelocationsPlus Network	6487 6256	www.relocationsplus.com
Santa Fe Relocation Services	6398 8588	www.santaferelo.com

moving?

relax.
we carry
the
load.
SM

Door to door moving with Allied Pickfords

Allied Pickfords are one of the largest and most respected providers of moving services in the world, handling over 50,000 international moves every year.

We believe that nothing reduces stress more than trust, and each year thousands of families trust Allied Pickfords to move them. With over 800 offices in more than 40 countries, we're the specialists in international moving and have the ability to relocate you anywhere anytime. Move with Allied to Allied worldwide.

Call us now on +65 6862 4700
www.alliedpickfords.com

ALLIED PICKFORDS

Removal Companies

Allied Pickfords ▶ p.123	6862 4700	www.alliedpickfords.com.sg
Crownline	6261 0880	www.crownline.com.sg
Family Movers	6266 5225	www.familymovers.com
Interdean Interconex International Movers	6266 5525	www.interdeaninterconex.com
Interport Executive Movers	6264 2622	www.interport.com.sg
K.C. Dat (Asian Tigers K.C. Dat)	6261 8116	www.asiantigers-kcdat.com
Raffles Movers International	6894 3720	www.rafmover.com
Rhema Movers	6542 0201	www.rhemamovers.com.sg
Vanpac International	6262 1300	www.vanpac.com.sg

Furniture Leasing

A nice compromise between not being forced to live with what's in a furnished apartment and not having to drain your bank account on buying stuff you like is furniture leasing. It's also a great option if you don't want the hassle of shipping furniture home at the end of your stay. Find out more from Gallery 278 (www.gallery278.com).

Furnishing Your Home

Rental accommodation can be fully, partially or unfurnished. A fully furnished home will come equipped with all the major appliances (fridge, oven, washing machine, television, air-conditioning units and sometimes even a microwave) and major furniture items (beds, bedside tables, sofas, dining table and chairs). A partially furnished home usually has some major appliances (fridge, stove, washing machine and air conditioning units) and a few items of furniture. An unfurnished home is normally bare. Furniture allowances from employers are not common, but see if you can get one.

If you choose partially furnished or unfurnished accommodation there's a broad range of options to choose from when shopping for your new home. There's everything from simple and affordable items at IKEA to pricey pieces of sophisticated teak furniture. To get your bearings, check out Home Furnishings & Accessories in the Shopping chapter on p.342. If buying pre-made furniture isn't your thing, wander down to Gallery 278 on River Valley Road (www.gallery278.com) to discuss custom-made furniture with the sales staff.

If you don't know the difference between pastel and parquet, you may want to get some professional assistance in decorating your new home. Interior designers have a knack of turning ideas into tangible things you can sit and eat on, and as they get trade prices for furniture and fittings, it might even cost you less than if you try to do it yourself. Try Audrey Lee of Audrey Lee Interiors (6474 7150) who has helped many expats create their new homes.

Second-Hand Items

With expats coming and going, there are many opportunities to buy second-hand items. Good places to find out about moving sales are from notice boards at Cold Storage supermarkets, word of mouth from friends and colleagues, or social and sports clubs' online forums.

Tailors

Regardless of whether you've moved into a furnished or unfurnished place, you may want to add your

Tailors

Romanez	Bukit Timah	6468 0183
Your's Furnishing	River Valley Road	6887 3317

personal touch. Tailor-made curtains, cushions and other soft furnishings can be a great way to influence the style of a home without charging ahead with major renovations. If you've got the time and the money, a tailor will be happy to create bespoke soft furnishings for you. For more options, check out the Tailoring (p.353) and Textiles (p.354) sections in the Shopping chapter.

CITYSTATE
SINGAPORE

for a lifestyle of excellence

elevating the level of services in real estate and relocation

With our years of experience and exposure to the Expatriate's lifestyle we understand your needs and will be able to find the right home for you and your family.We pride ourselves in keeping our customers satisfied, which is made possible by our holistic approach in integrating real estate and relocation with high quality service and intelligent research.
Contact us now!

CITYSTATE (SINGAPORE) PTE LTD
282D River Valley Road, Singapore 238323
Tel: (65) 6235 5652 Fax: (65) 6235 5962
email: info@citystate.com.sg | website: www.citystate.com.sg

Household Insurance

Housebreaking is uncommon in Singapore but household insurance is still a good idea. A home contents insurance policy will cover your furniture, appliances, clothing and books from theft or damage from fire, lightning or explosion. Some insurers also offer separate coverage for valuable items such as jewellery, art pieces, antiques and collectables. Most of these policies only provide 'within location' coverage but some insurers extend the coverage to goods that are stolen or damaged outside the boundaries of your home.

Household Insurance		
Allianz Insurance Co of Singapore	6297 2529	www.allianz.com.sg
American Home Assurance Company	6419 1000	www.aig.com.sg
AXA Insurance Singapore	1800 880 4741	www.axainsurance.com.sg
Federal Insurance	6333 8113	www.chubb.com
Liberty Insurance	6221 8611	www.libertyinsurance.com.sg
NTUC Income Insurance Co-operative	6788 1122	www.income.com.sg
Royal & Sun Alliance Insurance	6423 0888	www.royalsunalliance.com.sg

Rates vary but you can expect to pay annual premiums of $2.50 per $10,000 sum insured for a building; $2.50 per $10,000 sum insured for fixtures, fittings and renovations and $15 per $10,000 sum insured for home contents.

Laundry Services

Most expats have a washing machine at home although dryers aren't as common. Houses and apartments often have a laundry area with a drying rack or long bamboo poles from which to hang clothes. There are also many laundry and dry cleaning companies in Singapore that offer a full range of services for clothing and household items such as curtains, carpets and cushions. Every shopping mall has a laundry and dry cleaning outlet that can usually provide a next day express service or a two to

Laundry Services		
Cotton Club	Home pickup/delivery	6747 7844
Homemaker	Home pickup/delivery	6241 0028
Just Relax Home Service	Home pickup/delivery	6256 0171
M21 Drycleaners	Home pickup/delivery	6883 2321
Presto Drycleaners	Novena	6256 5886
	Orchard (Paragon)	6738 6145
	Orchard (Starhub Centre)	6737 0668
	Orchard (Ngee Ann City)	6735 7477
	Tanjong Pagar	6220 4525

three-day regular service. Home pickup and delivery is also quite popular and several companies offer an island-wide service with competitive prices. Costs vary, but they're in the region of $2-4 per shirt or pair of trousers or $6-8 per dress for laundry service, while dry cleaning costs about $1-2 more per item. Larger laundry companies may offer some compensation for lost items, but reimbursement amounts are often capped at $100 or less per item. Presto Drycleaners has multiple shopping mall outlets. For home pickup and delivery, try Cotton Care, Just Relax Home Service, Homemaker and M21 Drycleaners.

Domestic Help

Other options **Entry Visa** p.70

It is very common for expats and locals alike to employ a full or part-time maid. The eight approved source countries for foreign domestic workers are Bangladesh, India, Indonesia, Malaysia, Myanmar, Philippines, Sri Lanka and Thailand. There are many maid agencies in Singapore that can provide you with a domestic helper while taking care of the details, including your maid's work permit, insurance, travel arrangements, medical screening and security bond. The best way to find a maid is to ask for referrals from friends or colleagues for a reliable maid agency. Alternatively, you may be able to take over a maid from someone who no longer requires her services.

Sponsoring a Live-in Maid

Live-in full-time maids are quite common, especially for families with children. The obvious benefit is that your time, that might otherwise have been spent cleaning or minding your children, is freed up. The main drawback is that you will lose a degree of privacy, which isn't always easy. A maid agency can short-list candidates for you to interview. It's important to ask about childcare experience, English proficiency, cooking abilities and any other area that is relevant to your personal situation.

Wages for a live-in maid vary but you will probably have to pay a monthly salary of $300-500. In addition to this, you have to pay a monthly $345 levy to the government for hiring a foreign domestic worker. You are also obligated to pay for your maid's mandatory medical check-up every six months, which costs about $50.

Foreign maids must obtain a work permit from the Ministry of Manpower but your maid agency will look after this. The agency will also provide a contract outlining the employee-employer relationship. As part of the work permit application process, the maid must complete a multiple choice test in English to check her numerical and literary skills. When your maid ceases her employment with you, her work permit will be cancelled and you will have to pay for her trip home. You also need to post a $5,000 bond with MOM, which you forfeit if you fail to pay for your maid's return home upon the cancellation of her work permit.

Part-Time Domestic Help

If you don't need a full-time maid you may want a part-time domestic worker to come in once a week or so to clean and do the ironing. Word of mouth is a good option as there are many maids in Singapore who are happy to take on a few extra hours of work per week for about $10 per hour. Ask around among your neighbours, friends and colleagues. Although it's technically illegal for a live-in maid to be employed outside of her employer's home, it's a common practice and unlikely to cause a problem.

There are also many companies that offer part-time maid services on either a regular or ad hoc basis, starting at about $15-20 per person per hour (a company may send more than one person at a time to clean your place). Try Just Relax Home Service, Amahs on Wheels, or Homemaker.

Domestic Help Agencies

121 Personnel Services	6733 8121	www.121personnel.com
AJS Manpower Consultants	6463 0990	www.ajsmanpower.com
Amahs On Wheels	6837 2708	www.amahsonwheels.com
FMP Manpower Consultant	6238 1466	www.fmp.netmaid.com.sg
Homemaker	6241 0028	www.homemaker.com.sg
Just Relax Home Service	6256 0171	www.justrelax.sg
Laundry Maid	6466 6423	www.laundry-maid.com.sg
Reliance Consultancy & Resources	6338 8728	www.reliance.netmaid.com.sg
Sincere Manpower Management	6538 1192	www.sincere.netmaid.com.sg
Workforce Recruitment Centre	6342 1211	www.workforce.com.sg

Babysitting & Childcare

With live-in maids so common in Singapore, babysitting is not as prevalent as it is in many western countries. Still, there are a number of places you can look if you want someone to babysit for you on an ad hoc basis.

To find someone you can trust, the best approach is referrals from other parents. Live-in maids are often willing to do some babysitting on the side for about $10 per hour; officially it is illegal for them to work outside of their employer's home but it's a fairly common practice all the same.

If you don't know other parents to ask for referrals, you can post a message on www.motherhood.com.sg. Social clubs are another good source. The Australian and New Zealand Association maintains a register of people available for casual babysitting work, but it's only available to ANZA members. It's also worth checking out the supermarket notice boards, particularly those at Cold Storage.

Domestic Services

If you're renting, minor maintenance work is usually your responsibility while the landlord may help to cover the expense of major maintenance or repairs (see Rent in Singapore on p.95). It's fairly common for people to sign an annual contract with a maintenance company to provide regular service throughout the year. Unless there's a clause in your lease stating which company to use, you're free to choose a company of your liking. Your lease may state that you must have the air conditioning units serviced quarterly or bi-monthly. The cost depends on the number of units and how often they need to be maintained. To service two aircon units every second month you can expect to pay an annual fee of $270-300. Try Sky-Mac Services or Just Relax Home Service.

Singapore's tropical climate means that ants and other pests tend to flourish if not kept in check. For regular pest control services or for emergency extermination, contact PestBusters or Major's Pest Management Services.

Communal swimming pools will likely be cleaned by building management, but if you have your own pool you will probably need to arrange your own regular cleaning. Give Clean & Clear Pool Service or Hydro-Pool Engrg a call and you'll be swimming happily in no time.

If the garden looks like you could lose your kids in it, you may be in need of gardening services such as Horti Green Garden or Jobmiles Cleaning & Gardening. And if plumbing or electrical work is causing you stress, give Just Relax Home Service a call. As their name suggests, they should be able to put you at ease.

Domestic Services			
Amahs On Wheels	Kallang	6837 2708	Professional home cleaning
Clean & Clear Pool Service	Hougang	6289 3526	Pool cleaning and maintentance
De Hygienique	Ubi	6749 1950	Carpet and rug cleaning
Furniture Hygiene Experts	Kallang	6296 3456	Furniture drycleaning
Horti Green Garden	West Coast	6872 2555	Gardening services
Hydro-Pool Engrg	Toa Payoh	6254 3880	Pool cleaning and maintentance
Jobmiles Cleaning & Gardening Services	Kallang	6299 1767	Gardening services
Just Relax Home Service	Toa Payoh	6256 0171	Air-conditioning servicing, plumbing, electrical work, handyman services, painting, house cleaning,
Major's Pest Management Services	Bukit Timah	6464 7455	Pest control services
Mrs Sparkles	Serangoon	6298 2923	Housekeeping services
PestBusters	Geylang	6288 2828	Pest control services
Sky-Mac Services	Geylang	6744 1904	Air-conditioning servicing

DVD & Video Rental

Singapore has several options for DVD and video rental, with the latest Hollywood blockbusters readily available alongside a wide range of films from the region. Video EZY is the main chain of rental shops, with 25 locations around the island. Hollywood Clicks and HomePal are online DVD rental stores that allow you to select movies on their websites and receive the DVDs by mail within one to two working days. For $35 a month, you can rent up to three movies at a time and as many times as you wish for the month. Check out www.hollywoodclicks.com or www.homepal.com.sg for details.

Some libraries also carry a decent selection of DVDs and videos, although not usually the new releases. The Alliance Française is a good source of French films; see Libraries on p.277.

DVD & Video Rental			
Hollywood Clicks	Mail delivery	6836 9445	www.hollywoodclicks.com
HomePal	Mail delivery	6559 9016	www.homepal.com.sg
Video Ezy	Various locations	6440 9331	www.videoezy.com.sg

Pets

Pets are generally well-liked and accepted in Singapore, and dogs in particular are commonly kept as pets. However Singapore has a large Muslim community and it's important to respect that for religious reasons, Muslims won't want to come into physical contact with dogs. Cats are also kept as pets, but the large population of stray cats suggests that, sadly, abandonment is not uncommon.

The accommodation you choose will have an impact on the type of pet, if any, that you can keep. If you're renting you might find that only certain types of pets, or even no pets, are allowed. This is at the property owner's discretion so check your lease to make sure you're not breaking any rules.

Dogs and cats are happier with more space, so take this into consideration before buying a pet or bringing one over from your home country.

Major pet shows are held from time to time. The Singapore Cat Club and the Singapore Kennel Club organise shows and competitions which are often held at the Singapore Expo exhibition facility.

Animal Rescue ◀
The Society for the Prevention of Cruelty to Animals is an animal rescue organisation that runs an Adopt-a-Pet programme for abandoned dogs, cats, rabbits, guinea pigs and hamsters if they meet certain health, age and temperament criteria. The society is always looking for volunteers, so give them a call if you love animals and would like to help. For more information, check out www.spca.org.sg or call 6287 5355.

Cats & Dogs

If your rented accommodation allows you to keep dogs you must still abide by a government regulation that limits the number of dogs in residential premises to three. All dogs older than three months must be licensed with the Agri-Food & Veterinary Authority and must have an identification tag attached to a collar on their neck. Dog licences are available at the AVA Animal Control Section, which is located at 75 Pasir Panjang Road, or you can apply by mail or on www.ava.gov.sg. Your dog licence must be renewed annually and you must notify the AVA of any changes in ownership or address, or if your dog is lost or dies. Dogs must be confined to their owner's premises, or must be leashed and supervised when out in public. The AVA website also has a list of which breeds must be muzzled when out in public. You also have to scoop up your dog's poo so don't leave home without a plastic bag or three when you take your dog for a walk.

When buying a dog or bringing one to Singapore, you should take the tropical climate into consideration. Dogs with thick fur that are used to cold climates may suffer in the heat and humidity. Leaving a dog outdoors in a garden without sufficient shade and water in the hot equatorial sun could cause them to suffer from heat stroke.

Dogs are generally allowed in any outdoor public places but not in shopping malls or on public transport. Some taxi drivers will be happy to pick you and your dog up, but others will simply drive past, particularly if it's raining. There are plenty of good parks for walking your dog, such as the Botanical Gardens, Bishan Park and Tanjong Beach on Sentosa Island.

Cats do not need a licence and there are no government restrictions on the number of cats that you can own. If you're renting you should check with your landlord whether you're allowed to keep a cat.

Fish & Birds

Singapore is a top exporter of ornamental fish, which are popular as pets. There are several hundred pet shops carrying a rainbow of species in all colours and sizes. A popular choice among locals is the flower horn fish, also called luo han which has markings that some believe represent lucky lottery numbers. Birds are also common pets, with an abundance of colourful species from around the region available in most pet shops.

Pet Shops

Singapore has hundreds of pet shops selling a wide variety of small mammals, fish and birds. Most shops operate legally and treat their animals humanely but

Singapore does have its share of illegal trade in endangered animals. Some pet shops carry everything from endangered turtles to rare birds and illegal snakes and lizards. Raids are conducted from time to time by the Agri-Food & Veterinary Authority but enforcement is insufficient to stem the trade entirely. Pet shops must have a licence from AVA in order to operate, so make sure that a shop is licensed before you buy a pet.

Vets & Kennels

Veterinary clinics are scattered across the island but a number are clustered in the Bukit Timah area. Some clinics charge heavily for service outside of regular weekday work hours, so if your pet has a minor health problem at a weekend it may be worth your while to wait until Monday morning to take it to a vet. Rates do vary so shop around. Kennels usually offer both non air-conditioned and slightly more expensive air-conditioned facilities. Pet Movers offer two sizes of kennels, ranging from $20 to $25 per day for air-conditioned units and $15 to $20 per day for units without aircon. Cats can be booked into an air-conditioned cattery for $12 per day, but they have to have a $30 preventative external paraciticide treatment upon arrival.

Grooming & Training

Unless you come from a country with a climate similar to Singapore's, your pet may take time to adjust to the heat and humidity. You can make this transition easier for your pet by ensuring that it has access to an air-conditioned area in your residence. Due to the heat, dogs and cats tend to shed more here. Fleas are uncommon in Singapore, but you should be vigilant for ticks, especially if you have a garden. There are many pet grooming companies in Singapore (see the Pets Services table below). Prices vary, but you can pay around $50 to $100 for a full grooming session for your dog or cat. Obedience training services are also available and cost from $150 to $400 for a multi-week course.

Bringing Your Pet to Singapore

Some breeds of dogs are prohibited in Singapore, including pit bulls, akitas and Neapolitan mastiffs. You should check with the Agri-Food & Veterinary Authority to ensure that you can bring your pet into the country before making any arrangements. There are four main requirements for importing your pet into Singapore:

- Health certificate – An original certificate from a vet in your home country indicating that your pet is healthy must be issued no more than seven days from the date of entry into Singapore.

Pet Services

Amy's Grooming Salon	River Valley Road	6733 0017	Grooming
Dog Care Singapore	Bukit Timah	6252 2326	Grooming
Mitchville K-9 Kennels	Yio Chu Kang	6482 0084	Kennelling, relocation services
The Pampered Pet Corner	East Coast	6345 5345	Grooming, obedience training
Pet Movers	Pasir Ris	6581 3688	Kennelling, obedience training, relocations, quarantine station, pet ambulance
Shiloh Dawg School	Chinatown	1800 474 4564	Grooming, obedience training
Singapore Kennel Club	Bukit Timah	6469 4821	Obedience training, pedigree inspection
Snips & Clips	Clementi	6469 4239	Pet grooming
Sookee Kennel	Toa Payoh	6254 6037	Grooming, obedience training, kennelling
Suds & Scissors Pet Parlour	Clementi	6468 1904	Grooming

- Vaccination card – Dogs and cats must have a record showing that they have had various vaccinations; contact AVA for specifics (www.ava.gov.sg).
- Microchip – Dogs and cats must have an ISO-compatible microchip for identification; if they do not have one, AVA officials may issue them one.
- Import permit – You have to get an import permit from AVA at least two weeks prior to importation and pay an importation fee of $50 per pet.
- Reserve quarantine space – Your pet must be quarantined for 30 days upon arrival in Singapore (except those from Australia, UK, Ireland and New Zealand) so you need to reserve a space for your pet at the official quarantine facility by submitting the 'application and acceptance for quarantine space' form to AVA. All cats and dogs will be given a mandatory rabies vaccination.
- Pet Movers offers a wide range of pet services, including assistance with bringing your pet to Singapore and exporting it out again. To find out more visit www.petmovers.com.sg.

Pet Transport

Singapore Airlines accepts pets in appropriate containers as excess baggage and will transport them in the cargo hold. Only seeing-eye dogs are allowed in the passenger compartment. The airline will not carry certain types of pets, including puppies and kittens less than six months old. For more information, check out www.singapore air.com.

Taking Your Pet Home

You will need an export permit from AVA to take your pet out of Singapore. You must apply for the permit at least seven working days before the date of export, and the permit is valid for 30 days from the date of issue. You will probably also need permission to import your pet into your destination country. You should check out the new country's requirements well in advance because there are often stipulations such as vaccinations should have been done no less than 30 days before the animal is to travel.

Veterinary Clinics

The Animal Clinic	Clementi	6776 3450
Holland Village Veterinary Clinic	Holland Village	6472 1003
James Tan Veterinary Clinic Centre	Bukit Timah	6253 1122
Mount Pleasant Animal Clinic	Yishun	6452 5770
	East Coast	6448 8153
	Serangoon	6287 1190
Mount Pleasant Animal Hospital	Bukit Timah	6250 8333
Mount Pleasant Animal Medical Centre	Clementi	6776 8858
Namly Animal Clinic	Bukit Timah	6469 1122
PAW Veterinary Centre	Telok Blangah	6273 7573
The Veterinary Clinic	Holland Village	6468 6312

Electricity & Water

SP Services is the only electricity, water and mains gas supplier for residential customers. They are the commercial arm of electricity provider Singapore Power and the billing agent for the Public Utilities Board and City Gas, the suppliers of water and gas respectively. Supply is excellent and shortages are almost unheard of.

The connection process is quite simple and water, electricity and gas can all be done with one application. Full details on how to apply are on the SP Services website, www.spservices.sg. You can apply by phone (1800 222 2333), fax (6823 8229), mail, online or by going to one of the three customer service centres. The main centre is at 111 Somerset Road, Singapore Power Building and is open Monday to Friday from 08:00 to 18:00 and Saturdays from 08:00 to 13:00. The other two centres are in Toa Payoh and Woodlands and have slightly shorter hours.

When you apply by phone, online or in person you can arrange for the meter reader or technician to turn on your services within a day or two. There are no connection fees but you will have to pay a security deposit. The deposit amount is determined by your residence type and whether you are paying your bills by GIRO (direct deposit) or not. It ranges from $300 for an apartment with GIRO payment to $800 for a bungalow without GIRO payment. The size of a household's utility bill varies greatly depending on how much you use the air conditioning and whether someone is home during the day or not.

Maintain Your Cool ◀

Make sure you maintain your air conditioning units and clean the filters regularly. Air conditioning is a major source of energy usage, and having it work efficiently can reduce your monthly bills, extend the life of the units and keep you cooler.

Electricity

Electricity is generated by fuel oil and natural gas generator plants so tariffs are pegged to the price of fuel oil. The power supply is 230 volts and 50 cycles and the most common socket type is the three-pin one with flat blades (the same as in the UK). Round two-pin sockets are also used for lamps and small appliances and converters for these are available at most department stores or hardware shops. There have been significant changes to the electricity supply system in recent years, but they have yet to trickle down to the residential customer. Currently, only commercial customers with usage over 120kW/year are eligible to choose their electricity provider from the six or seven private suppliers in the market.

Water

The water supply comes from two sources: pipelines from Malaysia's Johor Province and from the local reservoir system which captures rain and groundwater. The water is moderately soft, fluoridated and the quality is well within the guidelines for drinking water set out by the World Health Organisation. Still many people choose to use bottled water and dispensers. You'll need to put down a refundable deposit of $200 for a dispenser and a package of four 20 litre bottles per month works out to $12 per bottle. Many companies require that you use them for minimum of a year and will withhold some of the deposit if you return the dispenser before that year is up.

Sewerage

All of Singapore is now linked to a modern sewer system. Waste water is treated at Singapore's six Water Reclamation Plants and either discharged into the sea or redirected for non-potable (usually industrial) use. The NEWater project is a highly advanced membrane treatment process that turns waste water into ultra-clean water that's made available for non-potable use. In order to increase Singapore's water self-sufficiency there are plans to slowly introduce NEWater into the island's reservoirs, albeit at a small fraction of the total volume of water. The cost of sewerage is built into your water utility bill.

Water Suppliers	
Arista Water	6455 2822
Candid Water Cooler	6221 3533
Pere Ocean	6253 5888
Polar Water	6292 1078
Prolife Water	6283 0638
Sunshield	6346 6325

132

Gas

Most of Singapore is on the mains gas network, supplied by City Gas and administered by SP Services. The application for connecting your gas is included in your overall utilities application to SP Services (see Electricity & Water p.132). The only difference is that you need to arrange a separate appointment for someone to come and turn on your gas supply. There's no connection fee.

Apartments in older buildings may not be connected to the mains gas network, in which case you'll probably have to get a gas canister as in almost all cases cookers run on gas. The actual suppliers of these gas canisters and the refills are large companies like Shell, ESSO and SPC, but they use a network of hundreds of delivery agents to distribute their product. Deliveries are available at short notice, so if your gas runs out just before a big dinner party or BBQ, you may still

Gas Suppliers	
Huasoon L P Gas Suppliers	6256 2786
Shell Gas	6383 0808
Sunny L P Gas Supplier & Trading	6543 2020
Union Energy	6287 5555

have time to get a replacement. Gas canisters cost $25-30 and you can get them in 12.7kg or 14kg bottles. If there's an existing canister at your residence, it's easiest to call the same company that supplied it, as that guarantees that the regulator will be compatible with your stove. Canisters usually have a sticker on them with the phone number of the supplier.

Rubbish Disposal and Recycling

All rubbish in Singapore is either recycled or incinerated at one of the country's four incineration plants. Non-incinerable items like rubble and the ashes from incineration are disposed of at the offshore Semakau Landfill. There are four government-designated waste collection companies in Singapore, each assigned to a different geographical area of the island. Rubbish disposal billing commences when you activate your utilities services through SP Services. Costs will vary slightly depending on your service provider.

Given Singapore's limited land area and the ever-increasing burden on its solid waste disposal system, there is strong support for waste minimisation and recycling. The government-run National Recycling Programme is operated by the four waste collection companies. The service is available in most areas and designated recycling bins and bags are collected every two weeks. You can recycle most items, including paper, plastic, aluminium cans and glass. For more details on recycling programmes in Singapore visit the National Environment Agency's website at www.nea.gov.sg or the Singapore Environment Council's website at www.sec.org.sg.

Telephone

Singtel is the main landline service provider in Singapore. An application for a landline can be done at any Singtel Customer Service Centre or at SingPost outlets. Foreigners must be 21 or older to apply for a line and you'll need to take your passport, employment or dependant's pass and your tenancy agreement along. The cost of setting the service up is $52.50.

Your line will be connected within four days of you submitting your application. Fees for the landline are $26.25 per quarter or $105 per year. Local calls are charged at 74 cents per 30 second block from Monday to Friday, 08:00 to 18:00. Outside of these times, the cost is 74 cents for a full minute. Add-on services such as call waiting, caller ID, three-way calling and voicemail are also available. For full details see www.singtel.com. You could also set up a landline service through Starhub (www.starhub.com), but this is a digital voice service run through your home's cable point. Setup fees are about $300 and the monthly fee is $10.29. International calls are charged in addition to the monthly fee.

Telephone & Internet Suppliers

Pacific Internet (internet only)	6336 6622	www.pacific.net.sg
Singnet	1610	welcome.singtel.com
Starhub	1633	www.starhub.com

Once you have a landline from Singtel, you still have the option of selecting a different international call provider, such as Starhub. You then receive two bills, one for your landline with Singtel and one from Starhub for international calls.

Coin-operated payphones are disappearing and almost all payphones now use cards for payment. Prepaid phone cards are available from SingPost branches and 7-Eleven stores.

Getting a Phone Line

It's a good idea to take an employment pass holder with you when you apply for a phone line if you don't hold an EP yourself. EP holders won't need to pay a deposit but dependant's pass holders have to pay a deposit of $200 in addition to the other start-up costs.

Mobile Phones

Mobile phones are almost a necessity in Singapore, or at least an important contributor to maintaining an active social life. For teens and the fashion conscious, mobile phones are very much an important accessory and the choice of phone is not taken lightly. The three mobile phone operators in Singapore are Singtel, Starhub and M1 (www.m1.com.sg). The competition between the three is fierce and new services and packages are regularly introduced, so it's worth shopping around to find the best deal. The cost of using a mobile phone is relatively low. A basic service package that includes 150 minutes of outgoing calls, caller ID and voicemail costs around $25-40 per month, with a one-off sign-up fee of around $40. Additional local calls are charged at around 21 cents per minute during peak times (Monday to Saturday, 09:00 - 21:00) and half that during off-peak hours. SMS messaging is widely used and most packages include up to 300 free text messages per month.

Mobile Service Providers

M1	1627	www.m1.com.sg
Singtel Mobile	1626	welcome.singtel.com
Starhub	1633	www.starhub.com

Prepaid services are also available but if you're going to be in Singapore for more than six months it's probably best to go for a package. Heavy discounts on mobile phones are given when you buy a service package, often cutting 40-70% off the price of the phone. Some models can even be included free of charge if you're willing to be seen with a bulky model that's one or two years old.

While all the networks offer roughly the same level of coverage and quality, some people prefer M1 for its service levels, while others like to keep all their bills with one company and go for Starhub or Singtel.

Internet

Other options **Websites** p.58, **Internet Cafes** p.426

Other options **Websites** p.58, **Internet Cafes** p.426

Singapore is one of the most connected countries in the world and is 99% wired for broadband internet. As a result there are few internet cafes, save in the backpacker areas around Little India and Beach Road. But most cafes have Wi-Fi hubs so you can log in wirelessly if you have a subscription with the respective internet provider at your cafe of choice. Three companies provide internet access in Singapore: Singtel, Starhub and Pacific Internet. A dizzying array of service packages are available, ranging from dial-up to cable internet at 35Mbps. Broadband can be accessed through cable points or phone lines and provides unlimited usage. There are options that include regular or wireless modems in the package or you can buy your own and just link in to the network.

When you apply for a service you'll need your passport, EP and proof of tenancy. The deposit is usually waived for EP holders. A basic broadband package costs $40-50 per month and your initial sign-up fee is usually an amount equal to the monthly fee. Contact the individual service providers to find out the exact details on their application and connection processes.

The government doesn't censor internet access but it does discourage the setting up of local mirror sites for content providers that deal mostly in pornography or other objectionable content.

Bill Payment

Phone bills with itemised calls and charges are mailed out monthly. You can pay by internet, post, credit card, at SingPost outlets and by GIRO which is an automatic direct debit from your bank account. If you miss a payment you'll be sent a warning letter. After this your line will be suspended and you'll need to pay a reconnection fee of $30-40 depending on the service provider. Most providers have a service that allows you to see the status of your phone bill online, so you can keep track of usage and fees.

Post & Courier Services

The country's efficient and reliable postal services are provided by SingPost. Branches are spread across the island and post boxes can be found on most major commercial and residential roads, at shopping centres and near office buildings. Post boxes usually have a slot for Singapore mail and one for other countries. Stamps can be bought at any post office outlet or at the self-service automated machines (SAMs) that can be found all over the island, including outside most post offices. You can even weigh packages, get rates and buy stamps from the SAMs.

Delivery is done directly to residences. Apartments and condos have a bank of letterboxes in the lobby. Post to houses is delivered right to the door or put into the letterbox. Letters and packages take 7 to 12 days to reach almost any destination in the world by airmail. Surface mail can take six to nine weeks. Airmail postage rates for a letter are 60 cents for most of Asia, 70 cents for Australia and $1 for Europe and North America. A 5kg parcel costs $60-90 for delivery to Australia, Europe or North America by air and reaches its destination in 7 to 15 days. Mail redirection services are available when you move at a cost of $21 for one month or $52.50 for two.

Courier Companies

Locally, there's an endless supply of courier services to get urgent packages and documents across town quickly. You can call up and have someone at your door in

Courier Companies

DHL International	1800 285 8888	www.dhl.com.sg
Federal Express	1800 743 2626	www.fedex.com.sg
OCS Courier Services	6225 1366	www.ocscourier.com.sg
TNT Express Worldwide	1800 745 3122	www.tnt.com
United Parcel Services (UPS)	1800 738 3388	www.ups.com

about an hour for a pick up. Your parcel will be delivered shortly thereafter, or at most within half a day. All the major international courier services are present in Singapore, including FedEx, UPS, DHL and TNT. SingPost also has its own courier service called SpeedPost.

Radio

There are numerous radio stations broadcasting in English, Mandarin, Tamil and Malay in Singapore. The BBC World Service is broadcast in English on 88.9FM. MediaCorp Radio's The International Channel at 96.3FM has programming in Japanese and relays of Deutsche Welle and Radio France Internationale.

Many of the stations run competitions, especially during the morning drive to work and at lunchtime, so keep your ears peeled

English Radio Stations

Gold	90.5FM	Golden oldies
Symphony	92.4FM	Classical
938LIVE	93.8FM	News and talk
Class	95FM	Adult contemporary
Perfect Ten	98.7FM	Contemporary hits
Lush	99.5FM	Electronic, dance

and your phone ready and you could walk away with some good prizes, including cash, free tickets or gift vouchers. Most stations also provide a traffic update service during peak periods, warning of jams on the expressways, accidents and other delays.

Censorship & Blocking

The Singapore government has greatly relaxed media and entertainment censorship over the years and the focus is now on limiting content intended to incite racial or religious conflict. There are 'out of bounds markers' for the media, but no one really knows where they are until they cross them. IS Magazine publishes a weekly OB Index that charts the week's events in relation to the out of bounds markers.

Television

You have to have a residential TV licence if you have a TV set capable of receiving broadcasting services in your residence, even if you don't use it. A TV licence is valid for a calendar year and it costs $110 to renew it each year. You can pay online through the Media Development Authority website (www.mda.gov.sg) or at post offices (take your passport and EP along). The licence is assigned to a residence, so one licence will cover all the TVs you might have at home.

Singapore has a reasonable selection of local TV channels but only two of them, both run by MediaCorp, are in English. Channel 5 consists mainly of western programming with an emphasis on the latest dramas, comedies and reality TV shows from the US. It also shows movies, European football, golf and talk shows like Oprah. ChannelNewsAsia (CNA) is a local version of CNN and you'll find it on channel 32. CNA covers business and news in a short form format. Other local channels are in Mandarin, Malay and Tamil and have a definite slant towards local programming which can provide an interesting glimpse into local culture, but may not be everyone's cup of tea. Channel 8 shows many local dramas in Mandarin with English subtitles.

Satellite TV & Radio

Satellite services are not permitted for private households, so you'll have to go with cable to get your fix of international programming. Certain establishments, such as embassies, gazetted hotels, education institutions and some financial institutions can have TV receive-only satellite systems.

The sole cable TV provider is Starhub (1633, www.starhub.com), and they provide a full range of channels in both analogue and digital TV formats. Digital TV gives you access to a number of channels not available in analogue. Basic cable starts at around $25 per month, but additional channels and services can quickly increase this to over $60. All the major international channels are available including BBC, CNN, CNBC, Discovery Channel, MTV, Cartoon Network, Disney Channel, HBO and Cinemax.

General Medical Care

Singapore has a world-class healthcare system comparable to anything found in Europe and North America. While it's not likely to become a premier destination for medical tourism, this is not due to quality, but rather to cost (which, while still reasonable, can't really compete with the price of medical services in cities like Bangkok).

Where Singapore does occasionally fall a bit short of western standards is in its nursing and ambulance standards, but this is only evident if you've had a lot of interaction with them back home for comparison.

There are both public and private hospitals, with customer service levels rather than quality of medical care being the real difference. As an expat, your healthcare is not subsidised by the government, so it's important to make sure you have coverage of some sort, either privately or through your company. In general, any kind of medical treatment you might require is available in Singapore.

Government Healthcare

Singapore's Ministry of Health (www.moh.gov.sg) provides healthcare services through two integrated delivery networks: National Health Group and Singapore Health Services. Between them, the two networks run a number of government hospitals including KK Women's and Children's Hospital, National University Hospital, Singapore General Hospital and Tan Tock Seng Hospital.

KK Hospital is widely regarded as the top paediatric hospital in Singapore, if not the region, and most complicated cases will be referred there from other hospitals. Tan Tock Seng offers a full range of services and specialises in managing communicable diseases. There are also numerous government polyclinics that provide outpatient services, although these are not commonly used by expats and waiting times can be lengthy.

Private Healthcare

Private healthcare in Singapore is of an excellent standard and service levels are very high. The difference in cost between private and public hospitals is relatively small so most expats opt for private care. The main private hospitals are Gleneagles, Mt Elizabeth and Raffles. Private clinics are also spread across the island and provide outpatient services. Fee structures can vary significantly, so it's worth calling to check what the estimated cost of a treatment is going to be. Most private hospitals have a department that deals with this type of enquiry. The Camden Medical Centre on Grange Road has a wide range of clinics and services for expats. Gleneagles and Mt Elizabeth Hospitals both have extensive private clinics on their premises and Paragon Shopping Centre has many expat-oriented medical clinics on its medical floors (access is via the elevators near the back of the shopping centre). Raffles Medical Group (www.rafflesmedical.com) runs over 25 private medical clinics all over the island and has seven dental clinics.

Health Insurance

Almost all expats will have comprehensive health insurance provided by their company but you should check that your spouse and children are also covered by the plan and whether additional private coverage is needed. If you're self-employed you'll definitely want to take up health insurance for yourself and will probably have to look into coverage options for any employees you might have.

Surviving the Heat
With daytime temperatures averaging about 30°C (86°F) and humidity near 90% most of the time, it's worth taking a moment to make sure you have a full water bottle and a hat with you when you head outdoors for exercise. While you're never far away from shade and facilities in Singapore, it also doesn't take long for dehydration or heat-stroke to take hold if you're exerting yourself at midday without rehydrating.

Health Insurance Companies

Company	Phone	Website
Allianz Insurance Co of Singapore	6297 2529	www.allianz.com.sg
American International Assurance Co	1800 248 8000	www.aia.com.sg
Aviva General Insurance	6827 7888	www.aviva-gi.com.sg
AXA Insurance Singapore	1800 880 4741	www.axainsurance.com.sg
HSBC Insurance (Singapore) ▶ p.89	6225 6111	www.insurance.hsbc.com.sg
NTUC Income Insurance Co-operative	6788 1122	www.income.com.sg
Prudential Singapore	1800 333 0333	www.prudential.com.sg
Royal & Sun Alliance Insurance	6423 0888	www.royalsunalliance.com.sg

137

Emergency Services

All public and private hospitals in Singapore have an accident and emergency department. In case of a medical emergency you have two options. You can call 995 and be picked up by a Civil Defence Force's emergency ambulance. They will take you to the nearest public hospital at a charge of $60 during office hours and $80 outside of office hours. Response time is relatively good (around 10 to 15 minutes), but the ambulance attendees aren't up to western standards. Here, their main job is to stabilise a patient as best they can and get them to the hospital quickly. Your second option is to call the emergency department of a private hospital to be picked up by one of their ambulances or to call a private ambulance service that will take you to the hospital of your choice. If this is your preferred course of action, it's a good idea to have a couple of the numbers written out and post it on your fridge, as well as saving the numbers on your mobile phone. If you have a maid, especially one that looks after your children, make sure to brief her on the procedures you want followed in case of an emergency.

Private Hospital A&E Departments	
Mt Elizabeth Hospital	6731 2218
Gleneagles Hospital	6470 5688
Mt Alvernia Hospital	6347 6210
Raffles Hospital	6311 1555
East Shore Hospital	6340 8666

Both public and private hospitals will generally provide emergency medical treatment before dealing with matters of insurance and payment. However, if you arrive at a hospital and your situation is not deemed to be critical, you will probably need to provide payment or prove that your medical insurance will cover your costs before you are treated.

Pharmacies

All hospitals and many clinics have an in-house pharmacy to dispense prescribed medication and to give you advice. For less complex requirements there are independent pharmacies in most shopping malls. Guardian, Watson's and Apex are three of the more extensive pharmacy chains and they're good for more common ailments and pharmaceutical needs.

Many of the drugs you would get over the counter in Europe and North America are only available on prescription in Singapore. This includes oral contraceptives, sedatives and sleeping pills. Even painkillers with ibuprofen in them, such as Advil, are not supposed to be given out without a prescription, although pharmacists might provide them to expats in limited quantities if you ask nicely.

Drugs are also generally more expensive than back home, so if you have a standing prescription, or a drug that you regularly require, bring a good supply when you come to Singapore. But make sure you have the prescription or a doctor's letter with you when you bring them into the country.

Health Check-Ups

You can go to the private clinic or government polyclinic of your choice for a full medical check-up. It's a good idea to make an appointment ahead of time and mention what you'd like to cover at your appointment. Some clinics have packages offering different levels of service, from basic check-ups to more in-depth testing.

Donor Cards

Organ donation is strongly supported in Singapore. The government has implemented an opt-out system for organ donation, rather than an opt-in system which was found insufficient to meet demand. Foreigners are not covered under the opt-out system, but are able to pledge their organs on an opt-in basis through the Ministry of Health. Expats can download an organ donation pledge form from www.moh.gov.sg, fill it out and send it to MOH. This will add you to the donor database in about three weeks and you will be sent a pledge card indicating that you have opted in to the donor programme.

Dengue Fever in Singapore

Dengue fever, a virus spread by a certain type of mosquito, is a serious concern in Singapore and has drawn increasing attention from health officials in recent years. The number of dengue fever cases approached 14,000 in 2005 – 19 of which were fatal. However, the government campaign to boost public awareness, fog mosquito breeding areas and fine residents who have standing water around their homes is helping to minimise the risk. Check out www.dengue.gov.sg to find out how to protect yourself from dengue fever.

138

Giving Blood

Blood donation is overseen by the Health Sciences Authority but all blood drives and donor recruitment are administered by the Singapore Red Cross. It's estimated that a minimum of 250 donors a day are needed to meet the needs of the healthcare system so blood drives are continually taking place. The Red Cross runs mobile donation units and you'll probably find one at your office building a couple of times each year. Watch for posters in the lobby and go on the specified day to donate. You can also call the Red Cross on 6220 0183 to find out where the latest drive is taking place, or go to HAS opposite the Outram MRT station to donate blood.

Giving Up Smoking

There are numerous government sponsored initiatives to help people stop smoking. The QuitLine (1800 438 2000) is manned by trained counsellors who will provide you with advice on quitting smoking or helping someone to quit smoking. Many hospitals and polyclinics run programmes called Quit Services. You can call the QuitLine to find out more about these. Some alternative healthcare service providers also offer services to assist in quitting smoking, such as acupuncture and meditation. See Acupuncture on p.146.

Main Government Hospitals

Government hospitals in Singapore provide high quality medical treatment, although the level of customer service is a bit below that of private hospitals. Expats are not eligible for any subsidies, but prices are still a bit lower than at private hospitals. See Government Healthcare on p.137 for more information.

KK Women's and Children's Hospital

6293 4044 | www.kkh.com.sg

KK Womens' and Children's Hospital on Bukit Timah Road is located halfway between the Newton and Little India MRT stations. It's a truly world-class women's and children's hospital and a major referral centre for high-risk obstetrics, gynaecological cancer treatment, neonatal care and paediatrics, including paediatric open-heart surgery. Additionally, it has a number of specialist outpatient centres and an accident and emergency (A&E) department.

Government Health Centres/Clinics

Ang Mo Kio Polyclinic	Ang Mo Kio	6458 2116
Bedok Polyclinic	Bedok	6243 6740
Bukit Batok Polyclinic	Bukit Batok	6560 3400
Bukit Merah Polyclinic	Tiong Bahru	6271 3911
Choa Chu Kang Polyclinic	Northwest Singapore	6765 9641
Clementi Polyclinic	Clementi	6777 5051
Geylang Polyclinic	Geylang	6842 2440
Hougang Polyclinic	Hougang	6386 2377
Jurong Polyclinic	Jurong	6562 3011
Marine Parade Polyclinic	Marina Bay	6345 0049
Outram Polyclinic	Tiong Bahru	6435 3980
Pasir Ris Polyclinic	Pasir Ris	6585 5390
Queenstown Polyclinic	Queenstown	6471 9530
Sengkang Polyclinic	Sengkang	6315 3500
Tampines Polyclinic	Tampines	6786 4070
Toa Payoh Polyclinic	Toa Payoh	6259 6833
Woodlands Polyclinic	Woodlands	6367 7880
Yishun Polyclinic	Yishun	6757 7790

National University Hospital

5 Lower Kent Ridge Rd
Pasir Panjang
🚇 **Commonwealth**
Map 16-A1

6779 5555 | *www.nuh.com.sg*

National University Hospital offers a full range of services including A&E. Located on the campus of the National University of Singapore, NUH has a strong track record in cardiac, obstetrics and gynaecology, oncology, orthopaedic and gastroenterology services. Singapore's only university hospital, NUH has a good reputation for clinical research and advanced treatments.

Other Government Hospitals		
Alexandra Hospital	Queenstown	6472 2000
Changi General Hospital	Changi	6788 8833
Institute of Mental Health	Hougang	6389 2000

Singapore General Hospital

1 Hospital Drive
Tiong Bahru
🚇 **Outram Park**
Map 17-A3

6222 3322 | *www.sgh.com.sg*

Located opposite the Outram MRT station, just outside of Chinatown, Singapore General Hospital offers outpatient services, an A&E department and a wide range of specialist clinics. It houses the National Heart Centre, National Eye Centre and the Department of Pathology. Specialist clinics are open to the public by appointment only and it's recommended that you get a referral from a general practitioner before trying to see a specialist here.

Tan Tock Seng Hospital

11 Jalan Tan Tock Seng
Novena
🚇 **Novena**
Map 14-C2

6256 6011 | *www.ttsh.com.sg*

Tan Tock Seng Hospital was established in 1884, and is now the second largest hospital in Singapore. In addition to outpatient services, A&E and a range of specialist services, it's also home to the centres specialising in rehabilitation medicine and communicable diseases. Its travel health centre may be useful if you travel to some of the more remote areas of south-east Asia and need vaccinations.

Main Private Hospitals

Singapore's private hospitals offer world-class care and service. Expats often talk of how they can't get the quality of service they receive here, in their home country. Private hospitals generally have a variety of specialist clinics and provide a complete range of services. See Private Healthcare on p.137 for more information.

East Shore Hospital

321 Joo Chiat Place
Katong
🚇 **Tanah Merah**
Map 15-E3

6340 8688 | *www.eastshore.com.sg*

East Shore is a smaller private hospital serving the east coast area. It offers general outpatient care and specialist services in surgery, paediatrics and obstetrics and gynaecology. It has an A&E department as well as intensive and neo-natal intensive care units.

Private Health Centres/Clinics		
ACJ Women's Clinic	Novena	6256 9494
Australia Clinic	Bishan	6452 1205
Bethesda Medical Centre	Suntec	6337 8933
Integrative Medical Clinic	Orchard	6836 0808
International Medical Clinic	Tanglin	6733 4440
International Women's Clinic	CBD	6323 2266
Raffles Medical Clinic	Orchard	6734 7355
	Siglap	6422 0488
	Tanjong Pagar	6323 5212
	Suntec	6337 6000
	Colonial District	6339 6911

6A Napier Rd
Tanglin
🚇 *Orchard*
Map 13-F4

Gleneagles Hospital

6473 7222 | *www.gleneagles.com.sg*

Set in lush greenery opposite the US Embassy and Tanglin Golf Course, Gleneagles is a full-service private hospital and regional referral centre for complex cases. A free shuttle for patients runs between Mount Elizabeth Hospital and Gleneagles as there are often cross-referrals or tests that get taken at one or the other. Gleneagles also has an accident and emergency department.

Other Private Hospitals

Adam Road Hospital	Bukit Timah	6466 7777
Ang Mo Kio Community Hospital	Ang Mo Kio	6453 8033
St Andrew's Community Hospital	Siglap	6586 1000
Thomson Medical Centre	Novena	6256 9494
Westpoint Family Hospital	Jurong	6268 7555

820 Thomson Rd
Toa Payoh
🚇 *Braddell*
Map 7-A4

Mt Alvernia Hospital

6347 6688 | *www.mtalvernia-hospital.org*

Mount Alvernia Hospital was founded in 1961 by a group of sisters from a Franciscan missionary. Located near Braddell MRT station at the eastern end of MacRitchie Reservoir, it provides general outpatient care, and specialist services from its 45 specialist clinics. It has a neo-natal critical care unit and an accident and emergency department.

3 Mount Elizabeth
Orchard
🚇 *Orchard*
Map 14-B4

Mt Elizabeth Hospital

6737 2666 | *www.mountelizabeth.com.sg*

Mount Elizabeth is one of Singapore's premier private hospitals and a favourite with expats. Conveniently located behind the shopping malls of Orchard Road, it has a wide range of specialist and outpatient services, including maternity, accident and emergency and a neonatal intensive care department. It also has comprehensive radiology and diagnostic services, including MRI scans and mammography.

585 North Bridge Rd
Colonial District
🚇 *Bugis*
Map 14-D4

Raffles Hospital

6311 1111 | *www.raffleshospital.com*

Opened in 2001, Raffles Hospital is Singapore's newest private hospital. It offers a full range of outpatient and specialist services in state-of-the-art facilities. Located in the centre of town, just down the road from Bugis MRT station, Raffles includes a Japanese clinic, women's centre, aesthetics centre and acupuncture clinic. It also has a family medicine centre and an accident and emergency department.

Maternity

Other options **Maternity Items** p.346

Pain Relief
Epidurals are available and, in general, a doctor will not hesitate to administer one if it's deemed necessary. The additional cost is around $300, but this will vary from hospital to hospital.

It's not unusual for expats to choose to have their babies in Singapore. The quality of maternity and neonatal care is very high – in fact, many expats say it's much better than the service they receive at home. So the decision usually comes down to whether the mother wants to be among extended family during and after the birth.

If you choose to stay in Singapore, there's no problem with having your husband in the delivery room at time of birth, in fact, it's encouraged.

Having a baby in Singapore is relatively straightforward from an administrative and legal point of view and there's no problem with single mums.

You will need to register the birth with the Registry of Births and Deaths. Depending on which hospital you deliver in, it may be possible to do this at the hospital but if not you'll have to go to the ICA Building at the Lavender MRT station to file the necessary papers (see Birth Certificate & Registration on p.76).

Maternity Hospitals & Clinics

Antenatal Diagnostic Centre and Well Women Clinic	Tanglin	6333 8621	Private
Gleneagles Hospital	Tanglin	6473 7222	Private
KK Women's and Children's Hospital	Newton	6293 4044	Government
Mt Elizabeth Hospital	Orchard	6737 2666	Private
Raffles Hospital	Colonial District	6311 1111	Private

Postnatal Depression

Postnatal depression can stem from any number of sources including thinking about the increased responsibility that you've just taken on by having a child. Luckily there are clinical treatments and countless support groups that can help you see the brighter side of your bundle of joy. Inquire about groups and counselling services offered by the hospital where you gave birth.

Government Hospitals

You can deliver a baby in any of the government hospitals but if there's any chance of complications you'll probably be referred to KK Women's and Children's Hospital (KKH), one of the best maternity and paediatric hospitals in the region. At KKH maternity packages start at $2,250 for a normal delivery and two-day stay. A premier package for a caesarean delivery and three-day stay costs $3,915 and includes a dedicated obstetrician instead of care by a pool of doctors. Antenatal care packages are offered for women in their 16th week of pregnancy and range from $330-620, including 10 antenatal visits and 10 urine tests.

Private Hospitals

The private hospitals in Singapore offer world-class maternity services. Mount Elizabeth hospital has an excellent maternity package that starts at $1,600 for a normal birth and two-day stay in a two-bed room. If an epidural is required the price goes up by $300. An emergency epidural and three-day stay in a single-bed room costs $3,800. On top of this are the doctor's fees which start at $1,500 and can go up to $4,800 if there are complications. Doctor's fees vary, so make sure you check your selected specialist's rates. If you opt for a single room arrangements can be made for your husband to stay overnight in the room for a 'lodger's fee', which includes meals. You can pre-register at the hospital about a month before your due date so that you won't have to worry about this when you come in and are in labour. Remember to take your passport with you for pre-registration. The hospitals also have everything from antenatal, breastfeeding and baby care classes available – there's even a free ride home in a limousine when you and your new arrival leave the hospital!

Mammograms

About 1,100 women are diagnosed with breast cancer annually in Singapore. Early detection methods and treatments are greatly improving the chances of defeating breast cancer and Raffles Hospital offers an MRI breast and mammogram package. Contact 6311 1222 for more details.

Antenatal Care

Antenatal care is very good in Singapore. You can go to any gynaecologist you choose, but it doesn't hurt to start the relationship with your specialist at the same place that you plan to give birth. There's a certain level of comfort in knowing that you will receive consistent service

Shot Scheduler

At KK Women's and Children's Hospital the recommended vaccination schedule is as follows:

At birth	BCG (for tuberculosis), hepatitis B first dose
2 months	Hexa (includes diphtheria, tetanus, pertussis, haemophilus iInfluenza type B, inactivated polio and hepatitis B)
4 months	Hexa, without the Hepatitis B
6 months	Hexa
12 months	Hepatitis B Booster for children of hep B carrier mothers
15 months	Measles, mumps, rubella
18 months	Hexa, without hepatitis B, first booster
6 years	Diphtheria and tetanus, second booster oral Sabin, second booster (oral polio vaccine)
12 years	Diphtheria and tetanus, third booster, oral Sabin, third booster, measles, mumps, rubella, second dose

from the same source all the way through your pregnancy. Most clinics and hospitals offer antenatal classes and services. Elective caesareans are possible, but should be discussed with your specialist.

Maternity Support Groups

Having a baby can be quite a rollercoaster ride, and there are support groups in Singapore for most of the ups and downs of parenthood. Twins Plus (www.twinsplussing.com) is a support group for parents of multiple birth children. Child Bereavement Support (www.childbereavementsupport.org.sg) is a group to help parents who have lost a child, either before or after birth.

Postnatal Care

Home visits from nurses can be arranged through most private hospitals but it's less usual to have a specialist pay you a home visit. There are a number of support groups too. The New Mothers' Support Group – Singapore provides its members with educational talks, reading material and the opportunity to meet other new mothers. See www.nmsg-singapore.com for more information. There's also the Breastfeeding Mothers' Support Group (www.breastfeeding.org.sg, 6339 3558) and the La Leche League of Singapore (http://lllsg.tripod.com).

Child with High Temperature

It is not unusual for an infant to run a high temperature and it's generally a sign that he is fighting a virus. Measures you can take include giving the child paracetamol syrup and sponging him off with cool (not cold) water. If the high temperature continues for an extended period you should contact your paediatrician for advice.

Maternity Leave

Maternity leave for Singaporeans is legislated at three months. However, this law does not apply to expats so the length of your maternity leave will depend on the terms of your employment contract. Your contract should also cover paternity leave but expect three to five days as a rough guide.

Gynaecology & Obstetrics

You don't really want the process of finding the right gynaecologist to be one of trial and error so a good way to keep the process simple is to ask friends who they would recommend. You could also start your search at the private hospitals, particularly Raffles, Mount Elizabeth or Gleneagles. Staff there provide excellent service and are well-versed in dealing with expats. Remember that you'll need a prescription from a gynaecologist to get oral contraceptives.

Gynaecology & Obstetrics

BH The Obs-Gyn Clinic for Women	Orchard	6732 8313
Christopher Chen Centre for Reproductive Medicine	Tanglin	6474 3900
Dr Ann Tan – Women and Fetal Centre	Orchard	6887 1102
Dr LK Yap Surgery for Women	Orchard	6734 3328
International Women's Clinic	CBD	6323 2266
Lien Clinic for Women	Orchard	6736 3331
O&G Partner's Clinic for Women & Fertility Centre	Tanglin	6479 7267
Parkway Women & Fertility Clinic	East Coast	6345 0060
PS Lui Clinic & Surgery for Women	Orchard	6737 3366
Women's Health Professionals	Orchard	6732 7337

Paediatrics

While everyone has their own idea of what makes a good paediatrician, a good place to start is to ask friends who have kids for their recommendations. Generally though, you'll find good paediatricians at the KK Women's and Children's Hospital, at specialist clinics within the private hospitals or with private paediatric clinics such as the Kinder Clinic at Paragon Shopping Centre which receives good reviews and offers excellent service. Your insurance should cover the cost of visits but check the fine print.

Paediatrics		
Babies and Children Specialist Clinic	Orchard	6736 4511
The Child and Allergy Clinic	Orchard	6736 0533
The Kidz Clinic	Tanglin	6471 6808
Kinder Clinic	Orchard	6732 4718
	Tanglin	6472 6018
	Toa Payoh	6478 5925
KK Women's and Children's Hospital	Newton	6293 4044
Paediatric Centre (Hospital)	Novena	6250 2474
Singapore Baby & Child Clinic	Tanglin	6235 6706
Wonderland Children's Clinic	Toa Payoh	6356 3133

Children with Disabilities

The diagnosis and treatment of children with disabilities and learning difficulties is continually improving. Efforts to treat children early on and integrate them into a normal social environment often meet with good success. There are many specialist clinics in Singapore that can provide treatment for children with disabilities. For a list of psychologists that can help with ADHD and other disabilities, see the Counsellors/ Psychologists table on p.148.

Dentists/Orthodontists

Dental care in Singapore is first-class and many of the dentists have been trained overseas. There are hundreds of dentists offering their services and some of the best can be found in smaller private clinics. A basic check-up and cleaning will set you back about $80. Dental coverage is not always provided by your company or its insurance plan, so it's worth checking on this before you decide on a more expensive dental procedure. Cosmetic dentistry, which is widely available in Singapore, is less likely to be covered.

Dentists/Orthodontists		
Aaron Dentalcare	Holland Village	6466 7313
Aesthete Smilestudio	CBD	6438 3811
Aloha Dental Clinic	Orchard	6733 2268
Corporate Dental Clinic	Tiong Bahru	6272 4858
Creation Dentalworks @ The Smile	River Valley Road	6533 4200
Dental Excellence	Tanglin	6834 0877
Dental Wellness	Novena	6250 6997
Dentalcare @ Tanglin	Tanglin	6732 8908
International Dental Centre	Chinatown	6372 0082
Killiney Dental Centre	River Valley Road	6235 1638
Omni Dental Centre	Orchard	6737 7375
Scotts Dental Centre	Orchard	6887 0380
Smilefocus	Tanglin	6733 9882
Tangs Dental Group	Tanglin	6479 9883
White Dental Group	Bukit Timah	6733 0268

Opticians & Opthamologists

You'll find an optician in just about every shopping mall in Singapore. Contact lenses are readily available and lens solution can be found at any pharmacy or optician and even at many grocery stores.

Laser eye surgery is available and gaining popularity. The LASIK laser eye surgery centre at Mount Elizabeth Hospital (6737 2666) has state-of-the-art equipment and uses the latest techniques. Raffles Hospital (6311 1111) has a specialist eye and ENT centre that offers everything from eye screenings and general ophthalmology to cataract surgery and corneal disorder treatment.

Eye Tests

An eye test is required in order to get a driving licence, but it's administered at the driving centre and doesn't require a trip to the optician.

Cosmetic Treatment & Surgery

Cosmetic treatments and surgery are becoming more acceptable as Singaporeans continually strive to look their best. There are clusters of cosmetic surgery clinics at Mount Elizabeth Hospital, Camden Medical Centre and on the medical floors at Paragon Shopping Centre. All the latest treatments are available including Meso Botox, which is said to extend the effectiveness of a Botox treatment by almost 100%. Other common procedures include nose, cheek and chin jobs and breast enhancement. If you're not ready for a full surgical procedure, many spas offer peeling and cellulite treatments.

Cosmetic Treatment & Surgery		
The Aesthetics Clinic	Orchard	6223 6394
The Cosmetic Surgery Clinic	Orchard	6733 3372
Dr Marco Faria Correa Plastic Surgery	Tanglin	6464 8075
Plastic Surgery Associates	Orchard	6472 1221
	Orchard	6732 8682
TLC Medical Centre - Aesthetics & Family	Holland Village	6462 0083
Woffles Wu Aesthetic Surgery & Laser Centre	Tanglin	6733 9771
Wong's Plastic Surgery Centre	Tanglin	6479 7173
Yeap Plastic, Reconstructive & Cosmetic Surgery	Orchard	6734 0061

Alternative Therapies

Alternative therapies are quite well-established in Singapore – traditional Chinese medicine has contributed to having other alternative therapies become widely accepted. If you log on to www.holisticliving.com.sg you'll find information about the Holistic Living Angel Card; a membership card that gets you up to 50% off regular prices at over 40 holistic and healthy lifestyle clinics and establishments in Singapore. Through the same website you can also find out more about the Holistic Living Festival held annually at the Fort Canning Centre. It's a good place to go and get a feel for what's available in Singapore and to meet the actual practitioners.

Dermatologists		
CT Lee Skin & Laser Clinic	Orchard	6738 6178
Joyce Lim Skin & Laser Clinic	Orchard	6834 9159
K B Lim Sink Clinic	Tanglin	6471 0965
LL Cheong Skin & Laser Clinic	Orchard	6836 1480
Mallika's Clinic for Hair & Skin	Tanglin	6474 0112
Mount Elizabeth Skin Clinic	Orchard	6734 5655
National Skin Centre	Novena	6253 4455
The Skin Clinic	East Coast	6447 2388
Specialist Skin Clinic	Orchard	6734 2511
Tham Siew Nee Skin Clinic	Tanglin	6476 6821
W K Wong Skin Clinic	Orchard	6738 9792

Acupressure & Acupuncture

Acupressure and acupuncture are forms of traditional Chinese medicine, which have a relatively large following among the local population. As acupuncture has become a more accepted therapy in the West, many expats in Singapore are taking the opportunity to explore its benefits. Traditional Chinese medicine clinics can be found all over the island, with some of the more expat-friendly ones to be found along Orchard Road

Acupressure/Acupuncture		
Chiang Acupuncture Specialist	Orchard	6737 7390
Chinese Nature Cure Institute	Orchard	6738 3861
Chinese Physician Christopher Lee	East Coast	6345 7980
Daren Chinese Physician	Tanglin	6736 1686
Eastern Clinic	Katong	6478 0762
Eu Yan Sang	Chinatown	6223 6333
Laser Acupuncture Centre	Serangoon	6742 9883
Ma Kuang Chinese Medicine & Research Centre	Colonial District	6884 4772
Raffles Acupuncture Clinic	Colonial District	6311 2350
Shen Centre	Chinatown	6438 6238
TCMS Health	Orchard	6836 3637

and on the East Coast. Recognising the increasing popularity of acupuncture and acupressure, the government has taken some steps to ensure that practitioners receive proper training.

Aromatherapy

Aromatherapy, the practice of bringing harmony to your mind and body through natural oils, is popular in Singapore. Many spas offer aromatherapy massages, which are a

Aromatherapy		
Charakas Ayurvedic & Aroma Therapeutic Health Centre	Bukit Timah	6836 7666
Earth Sanctuary	Chinatown	6324 7933
Heaven & Earth Aromatherapy	Colonial District	6337 3175
Holistic Approach	Bukit Timah	6463 7404
Therapeutic Bodywork	Tanglin	6887 4544

wonderful way to relax and experience the benefits of aromatherapy, while some clinics provide a wider range of aromatherapy treatments and counselling. And if you want to take the benefits home with you, Nature's Essences has two outlets at Great World City and Suntec City. They carry nebulisers, aroma necklaces, aromatherapy oils, organic candles and more. See their website (www.naturesessences.com) for details.

Healing Meditation

While many health centres offer meditation courses and services, The Golden Space in Tanjong Pagar takes things a step further. Here you'll be able to attend courses and workshops on healing meditation. To find out more about their services call 6222 5114.

Homeopathy

The government recognises homeopathy as an alternative medical practice, although it's not regulated by any specific legislation. The industry is represented by the Registered Professional Homeopathy Association, Singapore, which was set up in 1992. Homeopathic treatments have gained more acceptance in recent years, but still take a back seat to more traditional Chinese therapies. You'll find a number of homeopathic clinics clustered around Little India.

Homeopathy		
Arbor Vitae Healing Therapy	Bukit Timah	6467 0783
Bethesda Homeopathy Centre	Little India	6292 9206
Fundamental Homeopathic Centre	Tanglin	6235 1220
Hahnemann Homeopathy Centre	Little India	6291 9440
Sai Homeopathy Centre	Little India	6299 4502

Reflexology & Massage Therapy

Other options **Massage** p.313

Reflexology and massage therapy are very popular here. Between all the spas and clinics you can find services ranging from a basic massage to professional reflexology based on ancient Chinese pressure points in the body. Foot reflexology in particular has a big following, with many centres and clinics offering treatments and therapies. Many condominium and Housing Development Board complexes have a reflexology path – a walkway of raised stones for you to walk barefoot on. If you're not used to it, it can feel quite uncomfortable at first and you may have to lean rather heavily on the railing along the path. After a few sessions though it's virtually guaranteed that you'll come to love it and you'll enjoy a wonderfully relaxed feeling after walking the path.

Reflexology/Massage Therapy		
The Body Clinic	CBD	6438 2900
Body System Therapy	Tanglin	6732 1005
David Lee, Massage Therapist	Tanglin	6734 6990
Earth Sanctuary	Chinatown	6324 7933
Health Step	Holland Village	6468 2655
Kenko Healthy Family Foot Reflexology	Suntec	6336 7117
Qi Mantra	Chinatown	6221 5691
Shiatsu Foot Reflexology	Orchard	6733 0826
The Shiatsu School	River Valley Road	6836 1231

Rehabilitation & Physiotherapy

Singapore has many excellent rehabilitation and physiotherapy clinics providing custom services to get you back in action. Some physiotherapists specialise in pushing you to the limit so you can get back to the sports and activities you love as quickly as possible, while others take a more conservative approach. Camden Medical Centre and Tanglin Shopping Centre both have a number of physiotherapy clinics, while Physionique offers a full range of services at 8 Claymore Hill, next to the American Club.

Rehabilitation & Physiotherapy		
Body System Therapy	Tanglin	6732 1005
Chiropractic Care	Tanglin	6738 9142
Core Concepts	Tanjong Pagar	6226 3632
Emmanuel Physiotherapy	Tanglin	6235 2757
Orchard Physiotherapy Centre	Orchard	6737 1118
Phsyiofocus	Tanglin	6734 8151
Physionique	Orchard	6734 0245
Podiatric Sports Medicine	Orchard	6733 9522

Back Treatment

Long hours in an office chair, a mattress with poor support, strain from a long weekend of golf or an imbalance in your feet, knees or hips are all things that can cause back pain. Luckily, there are loads of clinics that can treat your discomfort with a variety of approaches. Tanglin Shopping Centre has a good selection of chiropractors, including Robert Wasserman at Chiropractic Care (www.chiropractic-care.com.sg), one of Singapore's longest-established chiropractic clinics. The Osteopathic Treatment Centre (www.osteopathy.com.sg) is also located at the Tanglin Shopping Centre. An initial consultation there will cost $100 and subsequent treatments are $80. Less intense back treatments are available in the form of massage from one of the many spas (see p.311). A good hour or two of massage can do wonders for a stiff back.

Back Treatment		
Back and Neck Centre	Orchard	6735 7796
The Brain and Spine Clinic	Orchard	6887 5123
Chiropractic Care	Tanglin	6738 9142
Holistic Chiropractic	Tanglin	6733 1805
Island Spine and Scoliosis	Tanglin	6474 5488
Orchard Clinic	Orchard	6884 4123
Osteopathic Treatment Centre	Tanglin	6734 6440

147

Nutritionists & Slimming

Whether you are looking to lose a few of the extra pounds you gained over the holidays or want to drop six dress sizes, Singapore has the slimming services to get you there. *The Straits Times* is crammed full of slimming ads promoting the latest techniques and technologies to help you keep a slim and trim figure. Marie France Bodyline offers over

Nutritionists & Slimming		
Elements	6737 6466	www.elements.com.sg
Expressions	6235 9890	www.expressions.com.sg
Marie France Slimming Salon	6235 8030	www.mariefrance-transformation.com
Mary Chia Beauty & Slimming Specialist	1800 250 2001	www.marychia.com
Petite Elites, British Association	6339 8229	www.britishassociation.org.sg
Slimming Sanctuary	6355 6161	www.slimming-sanctuary.com
SPA Valley	6235 4341	spavalley.com

40 different slimming programmes that can be tailormade to your needs and body type. Their methods are 100% natural and do not involve heavy exercise, extreme dieting or drugs.

Petite Elites is part of the British Association. Members meet on Monday mornings for exercise, motivation and, yes, to get weighed. A walking group meets on Wednesday and Friday mornings at the Singapore Botanic Gardens.

At Slimming Sanctuary, you can choose from a number of treatments to help you lose weight and tone flabby skin. Options include the Sono-Slim programme, ginger slimming therapy and 'near infrared radiation'.

At Mary Chia's they use the latest technology from France to help you attain a firm, trim body in a short period of time. Combined with a healthy diet, their anti-cellulite and weight loss treatments can give you fast and lasting results.

Most of the private hospitals have specialist clinics offering weight management programmes. Raffles Hospital has a 14 session course over six months that includes exercise therapy and dietary modification. Mount Elizabeth and Gleneagles Hospitals also have weight management centres that offer a full range of dietary, exercise and medical therapies.

Counselling & Therapy

While Singapore is a great place to live, it's still not home, and this can get some expats down. Whether it's a minor case of homesickness or a deeper bout with depression, Singapore has a very good network of psychological and psychiatric clinics and specialist services to help you through the difficult times. Mount Elizabeth Hospital works in tandem with Charter Behavioural Health Services from the US to run a psychiatric and behavioural care service. They treat children and adults with emotional, behavioural and psychiatric disorders and addictions. The Institute of Mental Health at Woodbridge Hospital has specific services dealing with everything from eating disorders and sexual dysfunction to sleep and mood disorders. The Institute's Child Guidance Clinic provides assessment and treatment of learning disabilities, development disorders and behavioural problems. The Singapore American Community Action Council (SACAC, www.sacac.com) has an excellent counselling service. Its team of professionals offers counselling for marital concerns, stress management, eating disorders and more. They also run occasional workshops on parenting, menopause, adjustment, transitions and other topics.

Counsellors/Psychologists		
Centre for Effective Living	Tanglin	6338 3383
Goslings	Novena	6256 7710
Inez Psychological Well Being Clinic	Tanglin	6474 7552
Institute of Mental Health	Hougang	6389 2000
Leonardo Talpo	Holland Village	9088 0146
Lifesteps Counselling	Holland Village	6735 5612
The Psychological Medicine Practice	Tanglin	6476 0493
The Psychotherapy Clinic for Adults and Children	Tanglin	6732 7557
Wee Care	Orchard	6836 1450

Addiction

Most psychologists and counsellors at clinics will provide addiction treatment services. There are also a number of organisations in Singapore that provide support for beating addictions. Alcoholics Anonymous Singapore meets regularly at various locations. Information is available by calling 6475 0890, or on their website at sg.geocities.com/aa_singapore. Narcotics Anonymous Singapore provides peer support for recovering drug addicts. You can email nasingapore@hotmail.com for more information or visit www.geocities.com/nasingapore. There's also a chapter for Overeaters Anonymous (call 9827 3089), a help group for compulsive shopping (call 6389 2387) and Gamblers Anonymous (www.gamblersanonymous.org).

Psychiatrists		
Bose Psychiatric & Stress Disorder Clinic	Orchard	6738 7155
Brian Yeo Clinic Psychiatry Consultancy	Orrchard	6887 3378
Kok & Tsoi Psychiatric Clinic	Tanglin	6472 8924
The Psychiatric & Behavioural Medicine Clinic	Orchard	6737 3663
Psychiatric Care Clinic	Orchard	6733 5565
The Psychological Medicine Practice	Tanglin	6476 0493
Sharon Chan Child Guidance Clinic	Tanglin	6475 7811
Yeo Seem Huat Psychiatric Clinic	Orchard	6734 5537

Support Groups

Living overseas can take you away from your most important support group, your family. Luckily, Singapore has a good network of support groups and services to help you through any difficult times you might face here.

- The Asthma Club (6394 3016) at the KK Women's and Children's Hospital helps asthmatic children and their parents learn how to manage bronchial asthma and how asthmatics can lead a normal and active life.
- The Diabetes Support Group (6850 2310) helps diabetics to cope with the disease. The group meets for talks in English on the first and third Wednesdays of the month at Changi General Hospital.
- Action for Aids (www.afa.org.sg) is a support group providing assistance to people living with HIV and AIDS. AfA operates the only anonymous HIV-testing facility in Singapore.
- Organised by the Thomson Medical Centre, the Anti-Ageing Support Group (6358 0055) aims to help people cope with the ageing process.
- The Autism Association Parent Support Group (www.autismlinks.org.sg) provides support and advice for parents with autistic children, especially those whose children are newly diagnosed as autistic.
- The Breast Cancer Foundation Expat Support Group (6352 5400, www.bcf.org.sg) meets on the first Monday of every month.
- The Down's Syndrome Association (6278 3907) offers support for families with children who have Down's syndrome.
- Reach-To-Recovery (6421 5803) is a support group for women with breast cancer.
- SPARK (www.spark.org.sg, 6467 2329) helps adults, children and parents of children with DDD/ADHD cope with the disorder. It holds meetings at the Child Guidance Clinic at Singapore General Hospital.
- The Infertility Support Group helps couples to deal with (www.sacac.com, 6733 9249) the difficulties of infertility by providing information and mutual support. A trained facilitator leads weekly discussions.

Social Groups
There are numerous expat social groups and societies in Singapore that welcome new residents and make you feel right at home. These groups are a great way to meet new friends and get tips on settling in. See Social Groups on p.294.

Internet Support

As well as the groups above, information and support can also be found on a number of websites. For Singapore's top expat websites and other resources for expatriates on the web, see Expat Websites on Singapore on p.67.

Schooling is compulsory for children from the age of 6 to 15 and Singapore has an excellent education system that offers a wealth of options. The government education system is known internationally for producing talented students strong in maths and the sciences. But while government schools are open to children of expats with valid dependant's passes, most expats send their kids to one of the numerous international schools here. If you do want to enroll your child in a government school, visit the Ministry of Educations website for foreign student information – www.moe.gov.sg/esp/foreign. Another good online source is www.singaporeedu.gov.sg which is Singapore Education's website. Students in the government school system sit for Singapore-Cambridge PSLE and GCE (N, O and A level) examinations.

At the primary and secondary school level, the majority of expat children attend one of the international schools, which generally offer an excellent standard of education. In addition to their internationally recognised curricula, most of these schools have extensive extracurricular programmes and facilities to provide students with a comprehensive and enjoyable educational experience. International schools usually accept foreign students and permanent residents, although sometimes local students do enrol. Some schools have additional entry requirements, such as a minimum enrolment quota for students of a particular nationality (British citizens have to make up 70% of Tanglin Trust School's student population, for example).

English is the language of instruction for most international schools in Singapore. Some schools require a minimum level of English proficiency for admission; others, like the Canadian International School and the Overseas Family School, are known for their strong 'English for speakers of other languages' (ESOL) programmes, designed to help students whose mother tongue is not English make the transition into an English language learning environment. Schools like The Japanese School and the Lycée Français de Singapour have a specific national affiliation and teach primarily in their home country language.

There are no regulations about having to live in a catchment area in order to enrol your child in an international school. Most parents don't want their children, particularly those in primary school, to spend a long time commuting each day on a school bus or in a car. Some parents choose their school based on its proximity to their home, while others prefer to choose a school first and then find somewhere to live nearby. But do bear in mind that living two blocks from a school is no guarantee that your child will have a short bus ride; depending on the bus routes, your child may be picked up early and first taken further away to pick up other kids before going to the school.

Choosing a school can be difficult as you are probably considering a number of factors such as location, curriculum, costs and the dreaded waiting list. If you can, try to visit a number of

---

Little Johnny Been A Good Boy?

To reward good performance at school, turn to p.151 in the Activities chapter for details of Kids' Activities in Singapore, or look out for the Kid Friendly icon 😊 in the Going Out chapter for which restaurants welcome families. For an extra special present, see Kids Toys in the Shopping chapter on p.344.

ISS International School

schools and speak to other expat parents before making your decision. When you're ready to enroll your child you'll need the following:

- Application form
- Application fees (if applicable)
- Child's birth certificate
- Child's passport and dependant's pass
- Parents' passport and employment pass and/or dependant's pass
- Child's immunisation certificates or records (if available)
- Passport photos of child
- Child's transcripts or report cards from previous school
- Other documents required by certain schools

Nurseries & Pre-Schools

With its abundance of top quality nurseries and pre-schools, your children will be well looked after in Singapore. Nurseries and pre-schools are great places for your children to meet others their age and develop social skills that will set their path for lifelong learning. Your children will have fun and a creative environment in which to play and learn, while you'll have a bit more time in your day for work, chores or relaxing.

Before enrolling your child in a facility, you should confirm that it's licensed by the Ministry of Community Development, Youth and Sports (for child care centres) or registered with the Ministry of Education (for kindergartens). Staff at the better nurseries and pre-schools are usually qualified in teaching or childcare.

Admission criteria vary, but in general nurseries and pre-schools accept children aged two to six, as primary education normally starts at age seven. A number of services are available, allowing you to choose between a full or half day, or just a few days a week. You'll also find different teaching styles on offer. Some nurseries and pre-schools are Montessori-accredited, some focus on bilingual teaching (usually English and Mandarin) and others take a themed learning approach. For example, the Julia Gabriel Centre offers EduDrama for children aged 2 to 18 years, using drama as an educational tool to help develop everything from communication skills to confidence and creativity.

Kindergartens are usually open Monday to Friday, with daily sessions of two-and-a-half to four hours depending on how old your child is. You generally have to enroll your children and pay for a term – for drop-off services see Babysitting & Childcare on p.127. Fees for full-day child care range from $300 to $1,000 per month. Fees for kindergarten range from $400 to $1,000 for a three-month term.

Demand for nurseries and pre-schools can be quite high, so you should contact the place of your choice as far in advance as possible.

In addition to the nurseries and pre-schools listed below, take a look at the primary and secondary schools on p.153, as some of those also have pre-school facilities.

Brighton Montessori

370 River Valley Rd
River Valley Road
Map 17-A1

6341 9336
Brighton Montessori has both nursery and pre-school facilities for children aged from 18 months to 6 years old. The centre offers a full-day programme that runs from 08:30 to 17:30, as well as half-day sessions in the mornings and afternoons. Afternoon sessions tend to be less busy than those in the morning.

Carpe Diem Schoolhouse

144A/146 Jalan
Jurong Kechil
Bukit Timah
Map 6-C4

6468 0368
Carpe Diem Schoolhouse offers full-day and half-day care as well as before and after-school care. The centre is part of the Carpe Diem Group which also runs childcare

facilities in other areas of Singapore. At the Carpe Diem Schoolhouse you can also enroll your child in a music enrichment programme called Kindermusik, which encourages childhood development through music.

Various locations

Julia Gabriel Centre

6733 4322 | www.juliagabriel.com

The Julia Gabriel Centre is best known for its EduDrama programmes, which are designed to help children to develop creativity and self-confidence through drama activities. But also on offer are various play groups and early childhood programmes that cater to children aged six months to five years. There are two Julia Gabriel Centres, one on Orchard Road at Forum the Shopping Mall and the other at 26 Evans Road near Bukit Timah Road.

420 Clemenceau
Ave North
River Valley Road
🚇 Newton
Map 17-B1

The Kiddiewinkie Place

6734 0390

The Kiddiewinkie Place accommodates children aged 18 months to 6 years old. They offer full-day and morning sessions as well as before and after school care for children up to 12 years old. Academic lessons focusing on reading and math skills are usually conducted in the morning, while enrichment activities such as crafts and cooking are held in the afternoon.

Various locations

Kinderland Educare Services

6881 8818 | www.kinderland.com.sg

Kinderland has an extensive network of childcare and pre-school facilities located across Singapore, as well as branches in other countries in the region. Kinderland centres offer childcare for children from the ages of 2 months to 12 years, as well as pre-school and kindergarten classes. Call their enquiries and enrolment hotline on 6881 8818 to find out about their facilities nearest to where you live.

9 Winchester Rd
Pasir Panjang
🚇 Redhill
Map 16-B2

Lorna Whiston Pre-School

6272 8826 | www.lornawhiston.com.sg

The Lorna Whiston Pre-School is part of the respected Lorna Whiston education group that also runs English language training and speech and drama education programmes. The pre-school is located in the West Coast area off Alexandra Road. Both full-day and half-day programmes are available and they're taught using a bilingual English and Mandarin approach. Children are accommodated from as young as 18 months up to age 6.

03-06 Great
World City
River Valley Road
🚇 Outram Park
Map 17-A1

Periwinkle Nurture Centre

6732 4821

The Periwinkle Nurture Centre is located in the Great World City shopping mall in the River Valley Road area. The centre offers full-day and half-day programmes in the mornings for children aged 18 months to 6 years. Academic lessons for the older children are taught in the morning, with the afternoon usually reserved for play and napping. Speech, drama and music sessions are held regularly throughout the week.

26A Toh Tuck Rd
Bukit Timah
🚇 Bukit Batok
Map 6-C4

Willow Nursery

www.willownursery.edu.sg

Conveniently located across the road from the Canadian International School, Willow Nursery caters primarily for expat children and is run by expatriate teachers. The nursery offers a toddler group for two and three year olds and a pre-school programme for three to five year olds. The toddler group boasts a 1:5 staff to student ratio, while ratio for the pre-school programme is 1:7. The nursery operates on a two-semester calendar, the first semester running from January to June and the second running from August to December. Email them for more information on info@willownursery.edu.sg.

Primary & Secondary Schools

Singapore has an array of excellent primary and secondary schools. Most expats opt to enrol their kids in an international school as these have foreign curricula and teachers. Attending an international school can be a valuable opportunity for your child to learn alongside students from other cultures and backgrounds. In general, the teaching standards are excellent and students come away with enriching experiences.

Parents are conscious of the fact that they will probably return to their home country at some point and that their children will have to fit in with the local education system. This is less of a concern at the primary school level but parents often choose a secondary school that offers the same curriculum as in their home country. Another option is to have your child attend a school that follows the International Baccalaureate Diploma programme as this is taught and recognised around the world. The admission staff at the international schools are familiar with these concerns, so it's a good idea to discuss your situation with them.

International schools' hours are usually Monday to Friday, 8:30 to 15:30. Some, such as The Japanese School, also have classes on Saturday mornings, and it's not uncommon for extracurricular events to be scheduled for Saturdays and weekday evenings. School holidays vary, with nationally aligned schools often following the holiday schedule of the country to which they are aligned (so the Australian International School follows the holiday schedule of schools in Australia). Many of Singapore's international schools have a summer holiday around June and July and a holiday in late December to early January.

International schools range in size from a few hundred students up to about 3,000 students. In general, they have pleasant classrooms and at least some outdoor areas for sports, possibly a pool and an air-conditioned gymnasium. Class sizes vary, but they're usually capped at about 25 students. Many schools offer excursions to other countries in the region for sporting or cultural events or volunteering experiences. With their extensive infrastructure and foreign teachers, international schools don't come cheaply. Fees vary widely but generally the bigger the school and the more facilities it has, the heftier your bill. You can expect to pay anywhere from $4,500 to $18,000 in annual fees per child for primary schooling and from $6,000 to $23,000 for secondary schooling. In addition to tuition fees, you should also factor in uniforms, school supplies, transport and excursions. Most schools have an application fee ranging from $100 to $2,800 but sometimes it's set off against the tuition fees if your child is accepted.

The Race Is On
Some of the top schools have lengthy waiting lists so, no pressure, but the sooner you make a decision about where to apply, the better.

Australian International School

1 Lorong Chuan
Katong
🚇 *Clementi*
Map 15-B4

6883 5155 | *www.ais.com.sg*

The Australian International School accommodates about 1,300 students from pre-school to secondary school. The school teaches the New South Wales (Australian) curriculum, but it's also phasing in the International Baccalaureate curriculum. The majority of students are from Australia and New Zealand, although the student population is made up of over 40 nationalities. AIS follows the Australian school calendar, which differs from the typical northern hemisphere school calendar.

Canadian International School

Various locations

6467 1732 | *www.cis.edu.sg*

The Canadian International School is split into three campuses; an elementary campus for pre-school to grade 3, a Middle School campus for grades 4 to 8, and a High School campus for grades 9 to 12. It has about 1,300 students split over the three sites. CIS offers a full International Baccalaureate curriculum from grade 1 to 12, as well as the Ontario secondary school curriculum for high school students. The school's excellent primary school programme is well-known. The campuses are located on Toh Tuck Road, Bukit Tinggi Road and Kampong Bahru.

Various locations ◄

Chatsworth International School

6737 5955 | www.chatsworth-international.com
Chatsworth International School provides schooling from kindergarten to high school for about 630 children. The curriculum is based on both the American and British education systems and it offers the International Baccalaureate in grades 11 and 12. There are three campuses: Chatsworth International School (Emerald Hill Rd, 6737 5955); East Campus (Jalan Tembusu, 6344 5955); and Chatsworth Kindergarten (Jalan Kayu, 6481 5585).

Opp Singapore ◄
Polytechnic
Queenstown
🚇 *Dover*
Map 13-A4

Dover Court Preparatory School

6775 7664 | www.dovercourt.edu.sg
Dover Court Preparatory School provides schooling from pre-school to middle school (up to age 14) for about 900 children. The school is most popular for its primary and pre-schools and follows the British curriculum. Dover Court also accepts children with special needs and integrates them into regular classes (see Special Needs Education on p.158 for more information).

Various locations ◄

EtonHouse International School & Preschool

6346 6922 | www.etonhouse.com.sg
EtonHouse International has seven campuses across Singapore with its newest addition to the list being the Mountbatten Road EtonHouse Infant and Toddler Centre. The school provides schooling from pre-school to year seven for about 750 children. For children aged 3 to 5 it follows the UK Early Years curriculum and children from 6 to 11 are taught in accordance with the British national curriculum. Special provision is made for those who want their children to follow a Mandarin curriculum and Mandarin is available to all the students here. Primary school children who want to learn Japanese or French can do so through the school's language clubs that operate after normal school hours. Enquiries can be made via email at enquiry@etonhouse.com.sg.

72 Bukit Tinggi Rd ◄
Bukit Timah
Map 6-E4

German European School Singapore

6469 1131 | www.gess.sg
The German European School has two sections. Classes in the German Section are taught in German and follow the German curriculum. The European section teaches the International Baccalaureate curriculum from primary to diploma level. Although the language of instruction in the European Section is English, all students have to study German as well.

65 Bukit Tinggi Rd ◄
Bukit Timah
🚇 *Buona Vista*
Map 6-D4

Hollandse School

6466 0662 | www.hollandseschool.org
The Dutch have a long history in Singapore and the Hollandse School was born out of a need for Dutch and Flemish expats to have a school that taught their children their culture and language. This was either because parents knew they would be returning to the Netherlands at some point or because they wanted their children to know and understand their cultural heritage. The Hollandse School provides schooling from pre-school to grade eight for about 170 students and follows the international primary curriculum. Lessons are taught in Dutch and nearly all of the student population holds Dutch or Belgian citizenship. Your child will have a Dutch proficiency evaluation before being admitted. English is a compulsory subject.

Hwa Chong International School

663 Bukit Timah Rd
Bukit Timah
Map 13-D2

6464 7077 | *www.hcis.edu.sg*
The Hwa Chong International School is affiliated with the Hwa Chong Institute, a top independent school in Singapore. The international school opened in 2005 and currently caters to about 90 students from 12 countries. The school offers grades 7 to 10, and by 2008 classes will be added for grades 11 and 12. Students will finish grade 12 with Cambridge GCE A Levels and in the interim years they'll sit for the IGCSE and the SAT.

ISS International School Singapore

Various locations

6235 5844 | *www.iss.edu.sg*
ISS International School Singapore has two campuses: an elementary and middle school at 25 Paterson Road and a high school campus at 21 Preston Road (6475 4188). The school offers three different curricula, namely the International Baccalaureate, the American high school diploma and the British IGCSE. There are about 500 students from over 40 nationalities split over the two campuses and no one dominant culture.

The Japanese School, Singapore

Various locations

6775 3366 | *www.sjs.edu.sg*
The Japanese School has three campuses and follows the Japanese curriculum. The primary school campuses – one in Clementi and one in Changi – cater to students in years one to six in primary school. The campus on the West Coast caters to students in secondary years one to three. The secondary school curriculum includes an English immersion programme in which subjects such as physical education, art and home economics are taught in English. The campuses have a total of about 2,500 students.

Lycée Français de Singapour

3000 Ang Mo Kio Ave 3
Seragoon
🚇 *Hougang*
Map 7-C3

6488 1160 | *www.lyceefrancais.edu.sg*
Lycée Français de Singapour provides schooling from pre-school up to grade 12. The curriculum followed is that set out by the French Ministry of Education. Classes are given in French, although a limited amount of English instruction is given to assist students whose first language is not French.

Overseas Family School

25F Paterson Rd
Orchard
🚇 *Orchard*
Map 14-A4

6738 0211 | *www.ofs.edu.sg*
The Overseas Family School is conveniently located just off Orchard Road. The school has over 2,000 students in classes from kindergarten to high school. OFS offers the International Baccalaureate primary years and middle years diploma programmes. A multicultural school, OFS is known for its strong 'English for speakers of other languages' (ESOL) programme. The school's facilities include two swimming pools and a sports field.

Singapore American School

40 Woodlands St 41
Woodlands
🚇 *Marsiling*
Map 3-F4

6363 3403 | *www.sas.edu.sg*
The Singapore American School is considered one of the top choices by many expat parents here. The school is home to about 3,400 students in classes from pre-school up to grade 12. In addition, it also has an Early Childhood Center. About 60% of the students here are American passport holders and the curriculum is based on the US education system. SAS has excellent facilities and a broad range of extracurricular activities.

Tanglin Trust School

Portsdown Rd
Queenstown
🚇 *Commonwealth*
Map 16-C1

6778 0771 | *www.tts.edu.sg*
The Tanglin Trust School caters to nearly 2,000 children from pre-school to high school. TTS follows the British curriculum, offering the 'general certificate of secondary

education' (GCSE) and 'general certificate of secondary education at advanced level' (A Levels). The school uses a quota system to maintain a school population in which about 70% of the students hold a British passport. There's no ESOL (English for speakers of other languages) programme, so your child will need to speak English in order to be considered for enrolment.

United World College of South East Asia

1207 Dover Rd
Clementi
🚇 *Dover*
Map 13-A4

6775 5344 | www.uwcsea.edu.sg

The United World College of South East Asia, usually called UWC for short, offers schooling from kindergarten to grade 12. The school has about 2,700 students and offers both International Baccalaureate and GCSE curricula. UWC has extensive facilities and offers a wide variety of extracurricular activities and excursions. The school is notorious for having long waiting lists (up to a year in some cases!), so if you have your heart set on sending your children here you should apply as soon as possible.

University & Higher Education

Adult Education

Numerous institutions in Singapore offer night classes, part-time studies and online learning. The National University of Singapore has a continuing education arm called NUS Extension that has a thick catalogue of courses offered through one of its three centres. See www.nus.edu.sg/nex for details. Nanyang Technological University's NTU Centre for Continuing Education offers short courses that are primarily business-related. Check out www.ntu.edu.sg/cce for more information.

Children of expats often return to their home countries once they've completed secondary school. But for those who stay, Singapore has a number of excellent options in tertiary education. There are three local universities, each of which has its own strengths. The National University of Singapore is popular for its science, arts and social science courses and is the only local university to offer law and medicine. The Nanyang Technological University is best known for its engineering and business programmes and Singapore Management University, the newest of the three, offers mainly business-related courses. There is also a wide variety of other higher education options. Numerous local institutions offer post-secondary programmes in arts and business fields. Two leading foreign business schools, INSEAD and the University of Chicago Graduate School of Business, have established campuses here, while many other foreign universities offer courses through local partners.

Australia's University of New South Wales will open a campus in Singapore in March 2007. Called UNSW Asia, it will be the first full foreign university in Singapore. The university will offer undergraduate, postgraduate and research degrees in a variety of business, science and arts fields as well as foundation degrees, as of 2008. UNSW Asia will have a quota of 30% Singaporean student enrolment and promises to be a truly international campus. Children of expats in Singapore who wish to study further here will need to apply as international students. Requirements vary but in general your children must have taken at least 12 years of primary and secondary schooling, meet minimum English proficiency requirements, and in some cases provide scores for internationally recognised tests like the SAT, ACT or GMAT. Once their application for enrolment in a local university or other post-secondary institution has been accepted, they must apply for a student pass as the privileges of a dependant's pass don't extend past their secondary education. Your children must apply through the student's pass online application and registration (SOLAR) system, and will require the following items:

- A valid passport
- A letter of offer from a university in Singapore
- A notification from the university with information needed for the online application

For more information about applying for a student pass, see the Immigration & Checkpoints Authority's website (www.ica.gov.sg).

INSEAD, Asia Campus

Ayer Rajah Avenue
Queenstown
🚇 *Buona Vista*
Map 16-B1

6799 5388 | www.insead.edu

INSEAD is a large international business school founded in 1957. It has a campus in France and in Singapore and affiliation with the Wharton School of America. Here students can pursue MBAs, executive education and PhDs. The Singapore campus has over 110 faculty members along with administrative and research staff. Importance is placed on the networking opportunities that an education at INSEAD offers.

90 Goodman Rd
Katong
🚇 *Aljunied*
Map 15-A4

LASALLE-SIA College of the Arts

6344 4300 | www.lasallesia.edu.sg
LASALLE-SIA College of the Arts provides arts education to about 1,300 students. The college is affiliated with several foreign universities and students are able to pursue both undergraduate and graduate degree studies. The college offers courses in a broad range of arts disciplines, including design, fine arts, media arts and performing arts. The college attracts international students from the region and beyond.

Nanyang Avenue
Jurong
🚇 *Boon Lay*
Map 5-D4

Nanyang Technological University

6791 1744 | www.ntu.edu.sg
Nanyang Technological University is best known for its strong science and technology courses. The university is home to about 18,000 undergraduate students and 8,000 graduate students. Business and engineering are two popular courses of study at NTU. The university has forged strong relationships with universities, institutes and companies around the world to provide its students with excellent learning opportunities. International student applicants must submit SAT test scores and must meet minimum levels of English proficiency.

21 Lower Kent
Ridge Rd
Queenstown
🚇 *Dover*
Map 16-A1

National University of Singapore

6516 6666 | www.nus.edu.sg
The National University of Singapore has about 23,000 undergraduate and 8,600 graduate students. The university offers a wide range of courses in 13 faculties and schools and is currently the only university to offer degrees in law and medicine. The university is a major centre for research, with 13 national-level and 12 university-level research institutes and centres located within it. Depending on the academic credentials that they hold, international students may be required to submit SAT test scores and English proficiency test scores along with their application.

81 Victoria St
Colonial District
🚇 *Dhoby Ghaut*
Map 17-C1

Singapore Management University

6828 0101 | www.smu.edu.sg
Singapore Management University was established in 2000, and has relocated to a downtown campus that was opened in 2005. The university has a youthful image that helps attract talented and ambitious students who are keen to launch themselves into the business world. SMU has four schools with a combined enrolment of about 3,800 that offer full-time undergraduate programmes in business, accountancy, information systems, economics and social sciences. International student applicants are required to submit SAT, ACT or GMAT test scores with their application and they must be proficient in English.

101 Penang Rd
Orchard
🚇 *Dhoby Ghaut*
Map 17-C1

University of Chicago Graduate School of Business
6835 6482 | *www.gsb.uchicago.edu*
Founded in 1898, the Chicago GSB is the second oldest business school in the world. Today it has four campuses – two in the United States, one in London and one in Singapore. The Singapore campus serves as the Asian home for the school's executive MBA programme and has a number of student-friendly facilities including an online library and a conference centre.

Special Needs Education
Singapore has a number of schools that cater to the needs of children with physical, mental and social difficulties. A few mainstream schools such as Dover Court Preparatory School accept children with special needs, but you should speak to admissions staff for details. While you can arrange for home visits from private psychologists, there are no official home schooling programmes for special needs children in Singapore.

The Association for Persons with Special Needs operates five schools (three primary, one middle and one high school). Although the vast majority of the students are citizens or permanent residents of Singapore, the schools do accept expat children at considerable tuition fees. For more information call 6479 6252 or see www.apsn.org.sg.

The National Council of Social Service is Singapore's leading organisation for social services. NCSS has a website about education for children with special needs and it includes a directory of special needs schools (www.ncss.org.sg/sped/index.asp).

Dover Court Preparatory School is a mainstream international school (see its entry under Primary & Secondary Schools on p.153) that accepts children with some special needs. For more information contact 6775 7664 or visit www.dovercourt.edu.sg.

Genesis School for Special Education is a non-profit private school that provides schooling for children with a variety of special needs, including autism, Asperger's syndrome, and attention deficit hyperactivity disorder. For further details, call 6733 1172 or check out www.geocities.com/genesis_singapore

Learning Mandarin
Other options **Language Schools** p.276

You'll have no problem getting by in Singapore entirely on English, but some expats like to use their time here as an opportunity to learn a local language. Mandarin is the most common choice, and there are numerous language schools offering one-to-one and group lessons during the day or at night. Most international schools offer Mandarin lessons, either as a required course or as an elective, so your children will be able to enhance their language skills too. Pretty soon the whole family will be chatting away in Mandarin.

Learning Mandarin		
Berlitz	6733 7472	www.berlitz.com
Eduplus Language Centre	6837 2538	www.eduplus.com.sg
Hua Language Centre	6255 5060	www.hua.com.sg
inlingua School of Languages	6737 6666	www.inlinguaasia.com/singapore.htm
Linguaphone Language Centre	6235 1855	www.linguaphoneasia.com
Singapore Chinese Chamber Institute of Business	6334 1080	www.scciob.edu.sg

Transportation

Other options **Getting Around** p.45, **Car** p.48

Going Underground
*For more information
on using the MRT
system as well as
detailed map to get you
around Singapore faster
than a speeding bullet,
see p 53.*

Singapore's transportation runs like a well-oiled machine – for the most part. A modern, integrated public transportation system includes buses, mass rapid transit (MRT or the subway) and light rail. Taxis are everywhere and still reasonably cheap, making cars a luxury rather than a necessity, unless you have a family to drive around or live well off the main road.

The road system can be congested during peak hours, but generally functions well. Parking can be a frustration, but no more than it is in any other major city around the world. Singapore is also small enough for you to travel just about anywhere in not much more than 30 minutes, even when using public transport.

Buses

Buses are probably the least frequently used mode of transportation for expats, yet they can be useful if a route runs directly from your residence to your office. Given the extensive bus system, that's not as unlikely as it might sound.

Almost all buses are now air-conditioned and have comfortable seats. They're also cheap and run regularly between 06:00 and 23:30, seven days a week. In addition to bus numbers and route information posted at most bus stops, each bus has its number and destination on the front and a list of major stops on a panel by the door. Detailed information on routes can be found on the SBS website (www.sbstransit.com.sg), including maps and a routefinder function that explains how best to get from point to point.

Bus fares can be paid by exact change, but it's far more convenient to use an EZLink card, which acts as a debit card for both buses and the MRT. EZLink cards are available at major bus stations and all MRT ticket offices.

MRT

Singapore's MRT system is world-renowned for its efficiency. Three main lines take people from the centre of town to the far reaches of the island in air-conditioned comfort. Once they're beyond the central part of the island the lines move above ground, giving you an interesting glimpse of some areas you might not regularly see. Every station has a ticket counter where you can get help with finding your route or paying for a ticket. The MRT runs on the same EZLink cards as the buses and all you have to do is touch your card to the reader as you pass the turnstile to get through.

The current lines run west from the city centre to Jurong, east to Changi Airport and north up the centre of the island to Woodlands, before taking a turn to the west and coming down to Jurong. The Circle Line is under construction and should be completed in 2010. It will serve expat areas such as Holland Village, Bukit Timah, Pasir Panjang and Suntec. The light rail systems are located well outside the city centre and go to less accessible local residential areas, so you're not really likely to make use of them.

159

Taxi

Taxis are modern, safe, relatively cheap and the best way to get around if you don't have a car. Many people's budgets accommodate the use of a taxi for their daily commute. Usually all it takes is a wave of the arm on any street curb and you'll have a taxi pull up in seconds, but during peak periods and on rainy days it

might be best to book one over the phone.

There are a number of taxi companies (see Taxi Companies on p.52), but they all have the same general level of service and drive the same model of car. City Cab and Comfort have the largest fleets. Rates are regulated by the government and have stayed fairly static in the last 15 years, although booking rates recently went up. The starting fare for a ride is $2.40 up to the first kilometre, with every additional 225m costing 10 cents. There are surcharges for peak periods, public holidays, passing through the Electronic Road Pricing gantries, pickups at certain locations (airport, Singapore Expo, the Central Business District) and telephone bookings. Rides from 23:00 onwards are subject to increased fare rates, with rides from 01:00 to 06:00 increasing by 50% over regular fares.

Phone bookings are available for all taxi companies and some are also automated, keeping addresses you have previously been picked up from in their database and giving them as options for you to choose from. It generally takes 5 to 10 minutes to book a taxi and have it show up at your pickup location. Some companies are linked to satellite tracking systems, making the booking process that much faster. A phone booking costs $4 from 07:30 to 09:30 and 17:00 to 23:00 on weekdays and $2.50 for all other times. Premier Taxis, which are all Mercedes-Benz cars, have the same rates as normal taxis but booking fees are a bit higher. If you have a lot of baggage to take on your trip, you can call and request a Maxi-Cab, which is an eight-seater van.

Hiring a driver is usually the realm of the ultra-rich but if you're particularly high up in your company, it could be one of the perks, or at least the arrangements will have been made on your behalf.

Driving in Singapore

While the cost of owning and operating a car has come down significantly in recent years, Singapore is still not a cheap place to be a car-owner. Petrol isn't particularly cheap; electronic road pricing (ERP) charges can add up if you drive in and out of the CBD or on expressways regularly and the cars themselves are expensive to get on the road. Add to this a limited resale market for used cars and a cheap and efficient public transport system, and it may be worth careful consideration as to whether you really need a car.

That said, driving in Singapore can be quite easy compared to other major cities around the region, or even back home, for that matter. Singapore traffic drives on the left side of the road. There are traffic lights at all major intersections and few roundabouts to negotiate. Singapore drivers are generally thoughtful, although there is a tendency to float across lanes and not to signal. Navigating the roads can be a breeze once you get used to which signs to look out for. There are few cyclists, pedestrians know their place and roads are well marked and signed. Singapore uses an electronic road pricing system to control traffic congestion and every vehicle has an ERP card reader on the dashboard. Overhead gantries will indicate when an ERP is in operation and the charge will be automatically deducted from the ERP CashCard inserted in your reader. You can top up at ATMs displaying the CashCard logo, most gas stations and 7-Eleven stores.

ERP Card Reader

Graduated ERP

A graduated electronic road pricing system has been introduced to try and avoid the mad rush as drivers raced to get through the gantries before they turned on. While there's still some incentive to make it through by a certain time, the ERP pricing now increases gradually around the turn-on times, rather than just switching from zero to full-price.

Traffic Rules & Regulations

Speed limits in Singapore are 50km/h unless otherwise posted. On expressways the speed limit is generally 90km/h, although sections of certain expressways still have an 80km/h limit. There are automatic speed cameras, marked with a blue and white sign with a camera on it, set up at various points around the island in order to enforce speed limits. The traffic police also set up laser speed cameras so it's best to respect the speed limit.

If you're caught on camera you'll receive a ticket in the mail within a week. If you've hired a car and are ticketed, you will have to pay the fine. A speeding ticket starts at $130 for going anything up to 20km/h over the limit and progresses to $170 plus a court appearance. Demerit points are also noted on your licence, which can lead to its suspension if you accumulate enough of them.

If you're in an accident, you have to stop your car and assess the situation. If there's significant damage, injury or damage to public property, call the police on 999. If it's a minor fender bender you can take pictures if you have a camera, take down the details of the other parties involved and agree to a course of action, be it to register the accident with the police or take it up with your respective insurance companies.

Driving Licence

As a foreigner, you'll need a valid driving licence from your home country and an international driving permit to drive a rental or private car. Once you've been in Singapore for more than 12 months you'll have to convert your licence to a local one. This requires only a simple theory test and a small fee. (See Driving Licence on p.75).

Parking

Parking is generally not a problem. Shopping malls and office and apartment buildings generally have ample carparks, almost all of which are paid lots. Most of these run on an electronic system that can be paid using your ERP CashCard. Some systems read the card directly from the unit on your dashboard, while others require you to insert the card in the gantry machine at the entrance and exit of the carpark. Other carparks and most street-side parking work on a pre-purchased coupon system. The coupons have partly perforated holes so you can punch out the date and time that you're parking for and display the coupon on your dashboard. Parking coupons can be purchased at most gas stations, SingPost outlets, NTUC Supermarkets and Cheers convenience stores. Parking generally costs around $1-1.50 for the first hour and $1 per hour thereafter, although prices can vary and are generally cheaper outside the CBD.

161

Petrol Stations

SPC, Shell and Esso are the major petrol station operators here. Low-sulphur diesel, as well as a range of unleaded gasoline, from standard to ultra-premium, is available at most stations. Diesel fuel is quite cheap in Singapore, at around $1.20 per litre, while unleaded fuels cost from $1.50 1.80 per litre depending on the grade. Almost all stations are full-service and you can often pay at the pump with a debit card.

Most stations also have a convenience store where you can buy snacks, drinks and car-related products. Manual car washes are also common at petrol stations. Car service centres at petrol stations aren't as common in the centre of town, where space is at a premium, but can be found at many of the stations a bit further out.

Say it Hands-Free or Call Back Later

Driving while talking on your mobile phone is a serious offence in Singapore and even first time offenders face fines of up to $1,000 and jail time of up to six months. If you need to be on the phone while you're on the move, get a hands-free or Bluetooth connection so that you can at least have two hands on the wheel as you make your way down the expressway.

Vehicle Leasing

There's not really much call for short-term vehicle leasing in Singapore. The public transport and taxi network is cheap and good enough so it doesn't make much sense to lease unless you're looking at doing so for a year or more. While long-term leases are pricier than buying a car, they can be advantageous on a couple of levels. First, car resale values are very low, so if you leave Singapore after a couple of years, you won't recoup much on a car you bought. Leasing

Vehicle Leasing Agents		
AutoFleet Pacific	6311 9728	–
Avis	6737 1668	www.avis.com.sg
C&P Rent-A-Car	6736 6666	www.candp.com
Classic Auto Rental	6553 3511	–
DownTown Travel Services	6334 1700	www.dts.com.sg
Expat Motors ▶ p.163	6722 8420	www.expatmotorsingapore.com
Hawk Rent A Car	6469 4468	www.hawkrentacar.com.sg
Hertz Rent A Car	1800 734 4646	www.hertz.com
Motorway	6468 2200	www.motorway.com.sg

also removes most of the hassle of getting a car on the road. Long term leases are available for just about any model and make of car you can think of, and packages usually include insurance, road tax and servicing. A year-long lease can cost from $1,500 per month for a small Japanese hatchback to $4,000 for a luxury car or SUV.

Company Cars

It's not unusual for expats, especially senior managers, to have a company car included in their contract. The car will invariably be leased by the company and you will have to return it when you leave. Arrangements for leasing will be made through the company, so there's little for you to do on the administrative end beyond ensuring you can legally drive in Singapore (see Driving Licence on p.75). Alternatively, you could negotiate for a transportation allowance to be included in your contract. This can be used any way you see fit, whether it's to catch a taxi, put the money towards leasing a car or to buy a vehicle.

Buying a Vehicle

The reality is that few expats buy cars unless they're committed to being in Singapore for five or more years – it just doesn't make much financial sense otherwise. Cars aren't cheap, although prices have slowly come down in recent years. Still, you'll end up paying $85,000 for a Toyota Camry as compared to US $20,000 ($32,500) in the US. Similarly, a BMW 5-series costs a whopping $200,000 in Singapore, but only US $42,000 ($68,350) in the US.

ExpatMotor
www. Singapore .com

Driven to Service all your Motoring Needs

BUY, LEASE NEW OR USED
Professional Service to your Door whether Buying or Leasing New and Used Vehicles.

COMPETITIVE PRICE SEARCH
Experienced Brokers search and deliver based on your selection criteria and budget.

ONE-STOP FINANCE PLANS
Lease, Finance and Insurance arranged, tailored to meet your personal requirements.

WORRY FREE MOTORING
Maintenance Packages guaranteed to provide exceptional after sales customer service.

PRO-ACTIVE ASSIST SELLING
Pro-active advice and assistance when selling to upgrade, changeover or depart Singapore.

TAKE YOUR CAR WITH YOU
Import, Export Service to and from your home country or destination of choice.

Expat Motor Singapore Pte Ltd
219 River Valley Road
#03-01 Singapore 238277
tel   +65 6732 6248
fax   +65 6732 6757
admin@expatmotorsingapore.com
www.expatmotorsingapore.com

Driven to Service all your Motoring Needs

New Car Dealers

Audi	Premium Automobiles	6566 1111	www.audi.com.sg
Bentley	Malayan Motors	6378 2662	www.malayan-motors.com.sg
BMW	Performance Motors	6319 0100	www.pml.com.sg
Citroen	Advance Auto	6476 7131	na
Ford	Regent Motors	6376 2288	www.fordsingapore.com
Honda	KAH Motor	6841 3333	www.honda.com.sg
Hyundai	Komoco Motors Pte LTD.	6475 8888	singapore.hyundai-motor.com
Jaguar	Malayan Motors	6378 2662	www.malayan-motors.com.sg
KIA	Cycle & Carriage	6471 9111	www.jcclgroup.com
Lexus	Borneo Motors	6475 1288	www.borneomotors.com.sg
Mazda	Mazda Motor @ MacPherson	6395 8888	www.mazda.com.sg
Mercedes-Benz	Cycle & Carriage	6471 9111	www.jcclgroup.com
MG Rover	Auto Eurokars	6749 4333	www.opelcars.com.sg
Mini	Trans Eurokars	6473 3777	www.mini.com.sg
Mitsubishi	Cycle & Carriage	6471 9111	www.jcclgroup.com
Nissan	Tan Chong Motors	6466 7711	www.nissan.com.sg
Opel	Auto Eurokars	6749 4333	www.opelcars.com.sg
Peugeot	Regent Motors	6376 2288	www.fordsingapore.com
Porsche	Auto Eurokars	6749 4333	www.opelcars.com.sg
Proton	Proton Motors	6472 5885	www.proton.com.sg
Saab	Stuttgart Auto	6363 3003	www.saab.com.sg
Ssangyong	Ssangyong Motors	6476 5805	www.ssangyong.com.sg
Subaru	Motor Image	6475 5333	www.motorimage.net/sg
Suzuki	Champion Motors	6778 4412	www.championmotors.com.sg
Toyota	Borneo Motors	6475 1288	www.borneomotors.com.sg
Various	Automobile Megamart	6347 7777	www.aml.com.sg
Various	Expat Motors ▶ p.163	6722 8420	www.expatmotorsingapore.com
Volkswagen	Cars & Cars	6474 1111	www.vwasia.com
Volvo	SM Motors Private Limited	6473 1488	www.smmotors.com.sg

Private Sales ◀

Private sales are not all that common in Singapore, although there's a selection to be found in the classifieds section of The Straits Times. *Once you've found a car that you want, you and the owner need to register for a transfer of vehicle with the LTA (www.lta.gov.sg) at their offices at 10 Sin Ming Drive (Map 7-B4). There are a number of vehicle inspection centres clustered around the LTA office, and it's a good idea to take the car into one of these first to get a professional assessment of what sort of shape it's in.*

The vast majority of cars on the road are Japanese or European. Toyota, Nissan and Honda hold a strong position in the market for economy and family cars, while Mercedes and BMWs rule the luxury car segment. Most other brands are available as well, including Hyundai, Opel, Peugot, Renault and Ford. Once you've made the commitment to buy a new car, a dealer will do pretty well everything for you, from obtaining the certificate of entitlement (COE) and insurance to financing and vehicle registration – all you need to do is be in possession of a valid residence permit. Almost all new car buyers take the dealers up on this package offer as it is genuinely a good deal.

The process starts when you sign a sales contract agreeing on the terms and conditions. You then pay a deposit and the dealer will start bidding on a COE for your vehicle. Once this is secured, registration and insurance can be finalised, and you'll get a call to come and pick up your new wheels.

The best showrooms are clustered around two locations, one on Alexandra and Leng Kee Road, just down from IKEA and the other at the East Coast's Automobile Megamart at Ubi Avenue 2, near Eunos. The strip along Alexandra Road has flagship showrooms for most of the major car brands, including Cycle & Carriage – which sells Mercedes-Benz – and Performance Motors for BMWs.

Buying a Used Car

Buying a used car can be tricky, as more of the administrative burden can fall on you, especially if it's a private sale. But legitimate used car dealers can provide all the administrative services that a new car dealer would, and they usually do. The price will

Used Car Dealers

Auto Touch	Ubi	6746 0606	www.pinnaclemotors.com
Benz Direct	Clementi	6776 0012	www.benzdirect.com.sg
Capital Motor Enterprises	Ubi	6846 8488	na
Car One	Marina Bay	6440 0330	na
Car Times	Ubi	6841 5111	na
Expat Motors ▶ p.163	River Valley Rd	6722 8420	www.expatmotorsingapore.com
Forward Motors	Bukit Timah	6465 4466	www.forward.com.sg
Greatdeal Motors Trading	Ubi	6280 3373	na
Happy Motoring	Ubi	6844 2228	na
Hua Heng Motoro Trading	Bukit Timah	6280 2453	na
Jie Heng Motoring	Bukit Timah	6469 3350	na
Kheng Keng Motors	Ubi	6844 3333	na
L & D Ideal Motor	Bukit Timah	6467 5186	na
Leco Motor	Ubi	6846 0020	www.lecomotor.com.sg
Pinnacle Motors	Ubi	6746 0606	www.pinnaclemotors.com
Raymond Auto Trading	Ubi	6741 3392	na
Three Crowns Auto Enterprise	Orchard	6532 0777	na
Vincar	Ubi	6749 1119	na
Yokawa Motors	Jurong	6285 0023	www.yokawamotoring.com

almost always include the cost of the transfer fees payable to the Land Transport Authority, which are set at 2% of the vehicle's assessed value. The value is determined at the time of transfer by the Registrar of Vehicles. Used car dealers are spread out across Singapore, but a couple of good places to look are at Turf City, just off Bukit Timah, and at the Automobile Megamart. Like anywhere else in the world, be careful when buying a used car; have someone knowledgeable about cars come along with you and make sure all the paperwork is in order before you hand over any money.

Certificate of Entitlement

The Certificate of Entitlement, or COE as it is commonly referred to, was implemented by the government in 1990 in an attempt to control the number of vehicles on the road. Car owners must purchase a COE before registering a car. Each month the government releases a quota of COEs, the amount of which depends on prevailing traffic conditions and the number of cars scrapped. COEs are bought through a tendering process; but all car dealers package their cars with COEs for convenience. The COE is valid for 10 years after which the car must be scrapped, or the COE renewed.

In the late 1990s COE prices could get up as high as the actual price of a car. Since then they have moderated somewhat and the prices have stabilised. The COE will be included in the price of any new car and you'll often see two prices listed for new cars: one for the car with a guaranteed COE and the other with a confirmed COE. A guaranteed COE basically means that you'll pay an extra couple of thousand dollars to get the COE right away by bidding at a higher cost. For the confirmed COE, you may have to wait for a week or two while the dealer waits for the right COE price to come along. COEs are auctioned off on the first and third Mondays of every month, with the bidding period lasting three days. A COE is good for 10 years and stays with the car if it changes owners but must be renewed after the 10 year period. For detailed information visit www.lta.gov.sg.

ERP Gantry

Vehicle Finance

All car dealers will offer financing as part of the package when you buy a car. The current trend is to offer a flat rate of around 3-3.5%. In most cases the deal is pretty good, but it's always worth checking what kind of rates or alternative financing structures you can get from the banks.

Vehicle Finance		
DBS Bank (Development Bank of Singapore)	1800 111 1111	www.dbs.com.sg
GE Money	6410 3100	www.gemoney.com.sg
Hong Leong Finance	6416 2777	www.hlf.com.sg
United Overseas Bank (UOB)	1800 222 2121	www.uob.com.sg

Vehicle Insurance

All cars on the road need to be insured. Comprehensive insurance is usually sold with your car and most buyers of new cars take up this option as it works out cheaper than buying directly from insurance companies. Vehicle insurance is based on the model and age of the car as well as the owner's age and driving record. Expect to pay about $3,500 per year in insurance for a $100,000 car, but this can vary depending on your age and driving record.

Most insurance schemes have a no-claims bonus, so for every year that you don't have an insurance claim, you could end up paying 10% less on your premiums (up a maximum of 50% off). Some packages cover driving outside the country, usually in Malaysia and Thailand, but this isn't always the case so do check this out if you're planning a road trip.

Vehicle Insurance		
American Home Assurance Company	6419 1000	www.aig.com.sg
AXA Insurance Singapore	1800 880 4741	www.axainsurance.com.sg
Mitsui Sumitomo Insurance	6220 9644	www.ms-ins.com.sg
NTUC Income Insurance Co-operative	6788 1122	www.income.com.sg
United Overseas Insurance	6222 7733	www.uoi.com.sg
Zurich Insurance	6220 2466	www.zurich.com

Registering a Vehicle

Your new vehicle will be registered by the dealer you buy it from. There is a registration number bidding process administered by the Land Transport Authority that gives you some say in what number appears on your licence plate. If the number is of no interest to you let the dealer know and he'll take a computer-assigned number for you. If you're set on having many 8s (auspicious in Chinese culture) or want to avoid 4s (bad luck) you can bid for a specific number. Your dealer will help you through this process and the price of registration is usually included in the total price of the car, unless you're bidding for a particularly expensive registration number. The registration will transfer to you when you process the deal at the LTA (www.lta.gov.sg, 1800 225 5582). Before the transfer can take effect you'll have to have car insurance in place, so make sure you've organised this before you head down to the LTA at 10 Sin Ming Drive (Map 7-B4).

Traffic Fines & Offences

The rules of the road are enforced in Singapore through a network of speed cameras, random checkpoints and roving patrols. Speed cameras are set up around the island, and are marked with blue and white signs with a picture of a camera on them. Mobile speed camera units are also deployed.

Most offences net you a fine of $120-150 and a few demerit points. More severe infractions can land you in court, where you face higher fines and the possibility of jail. The Driver Improvement Points System assigns demerit points for various infractions.

Vehicle Radio Licence

A Vehicle Radio Licence is required for any radio receiver installed in a vehicle. The annual fee is $27 and you can pay online through the Media Development Authority website (www.mda.gov.sg) or at post offices as long as you produce your passport and EP. The licence should be applied for under the name of the vehicle's registered owner.

Babywear p.98
Bank Loans p.22

Written by residents, these unique guidebooks are packed with insider info, from arriving in a new destination to making it your home and everything in between.

Explorer Residents' Guides
We Know Where You Live

Accumulate 24 demerit points in 24 months and your licence will be suspended for three months. If you notch up a further 12 points in 12 months after your first suspension, you'll lose your licence for up to three years. New drivers who accumulate more than 13 demerits in the 12 months after they receive their licence, will have it revoked. If your licence is suspended or revoked you'll have to re-sit all the tests in order to get your licence again.

DIPS Offences and Penalties

3 demerit points and $120 fine
Driver or passengers failing to wear a seatbelt
Parking in a Demerit Points No Parking Zone
Stopping in a Demerit Points No Stopping Zone

4 demerit points and $130 fine
Exceeding speed limit up to 20km/h
Crossing double white lines
Failing to give way to traffic at controlled junction

6 demerit points and $150 fine
Driving on the shoulder of an expressway
Exceeding speed limit by 20-30km/h
Failing to give way at a pedestrian crossing

All the rules apply to foreigners and local alike, but in order to close the loophole that allowed foreigners to drive on their foreign licence and IDP if their local licence was suspended, foreigners receive a prohibition order rather than having their licence suspended. A prohibition order means you may not drive, no matter what licence you hold/DIPS penalties range from 3 to 6 demerit points and fines from $120 to $150, but can be higher for driving at more than 30km/h over the limit (8-24 points), running a red light (12 points), driving while using a hand-held mobile phone (12 points) or reckless and dangerous driving (24 points). Some of these offences also carry fines and possible jail terms.

You can pay your fines at traffic police offices, at SingPost Self-Service Automated Machines, AXS terminals and on the internet via DBS, OCBC and UOB Banks.

Tinting of car windows is allowed to 30% and no more.

Breakdowns

In the event of a breakdown, it's best to try and get your vehicle off the road, or at least to a safe area where you won't be obstructing traffic. If this isn't possible you should set up a cone, safety triangle or other marker about 15 to 20m behind the car so that traffic will realise there's a stalled car on the road and have time to change lanes. If you're a member of the Automobile Association of Singapore, you can call them on 6749 9911 for a tow truck. Otherwise you can try your garage or any of the towing services listed in the Recovery Services/Towing table to the right.

When Cars Die

There's a limited market for used cars in Singapore, and old ones that don't run well anymore command even less interest. Your best bet is to go to a used car dealer (see p.165) who will either ship it to an eager new owner in the region, or scrap it for spare parts. The dealer will guide you through the necessary paperwork.

Recovery Services/Towing (24 hour)	
Auto Expert	6841 6566
Automobile Association of Singapore	6748 9911
People's Vehicle Recovery Service	6743 8552
Riverview Auto Services	6481 2025
STAR Automotive Service	9718 9999
UTS Towing Service	6844 4938

Traffic Accidents

Other options **Car** p.48

Traffic accidents are fairly common in Singapore, although most are just fender benders. The more serious accidents tend to involve motorcycle riders, as they try to squeeze between cars and the bikes are also easier to lose control of.

You have to file a police reports for any accidents involving injury, damage to public property, foreign vehicles, pedestrians or cyclists. If someone has been injured call the police on 999 and wait for them to arrive. Make sure not to move any of the vehicles until the police arrive unless absolutely necessary, as they will need to take measurements and assess the situation. You should note down the date and time, place, particulars of witnesses, damage and position of vehicle(s), registration numbers and road conditions. In the case of a non-injury accident involving damage to public property, a foreign vehicle, pedestrians or cyclists, you have to file a police accident report within 24 hours at any Neighbourhood Police Centre or Post. For all

In 2004 there were 6,842 fatal and injury traffic accidents in Singapore. Of these 183 were fatal and 72 were serious injury accidents. The vast majority were termed slight injury accidents. Of the fatal accidents, just over half of the victims were motorcycle riders or passengers, one quarter were pedestrians and 24 were car drivers or passengers.

other non-injury accidents (your basic fender-bender) you just need to lodge a report with your insurance company.

Repairs (Vehicle)

When you take your vehicle in for repair you'll need your driving licence and vehicle

Repairs (Vehicle)		
Autoplus	Serangoon	6487 2727
Hock Wah Motor Workshop	Tampines	6785 3933
Riverview Auto Services	Ang Mo Kio	6481 2025
Sin Ming Autocare	Bishan	6455 0600
STAR Automotive Service	Queenstown	6562 0000
Su Brothers' Motor Workshop	Ang Mo Kio	6482 4355
Ubi Automobile Services	Ubi	6748 3377

registration. Some garages will want to see a copy of your insurance company report or police report if the damage is the result of an accident, so it's best to bring these along if this is the case. Many insurance companies will give you a list of garages that you can use if you're making a claim. The deductible for claims depends on your insurance coverage, but it's generally around $500. If your car is under warranty you'll be able to use the agency garage, usually without having to pay a premium to your insurance company.

In Singapore much of the wear and tear on your car is weather related: your aircon will work hard; overheating engines aren't uncommon if you don't watch your radiator fluid levels; and the rain, sun, heat and humidity can be tough on your car's exterior. Otherwise, your car should age at a normal rate, with the usual repairs, check-ups and maintenance along the way. Most agency garages are quite good. Other garages worth considering include STAR Automotive (www.star.com.sg) which has a branch in Queensway and another in Bedok, and Riverview Auto Services in Ang Mo Kio.

"It's that Volkswagen feeling!"

It Gets Me.

I can't quite say why I'm so madly attracted to my Volkswagen. It's like we share an uncommon passion. Sure, it feels so safe and sound on the road, while also looking sleek and styled on the outside. It also feels nice and comfortable on the inside, too!
But it's really more than all that. It's another dimension. A real connection – it's like a soul mate. I guess I can say it's the ONE for me. So why do I always go for a Volkswagen? Because it simply gets me.

For the love of automobiles

Exploring

Exploring

Exploring

For a nation of just 682 square kilometres, Singapore has had to take a tactical approach to gain its considerable prosperity. For visitors this means a compelling mixture of attractions, in a city that has been carefully planned to allow easy movement.

Dubbed the Lion City, Singapore has long been an important hub of commerce and trade. Today it has the world's busiest port and one of its most notable airports. While it would never make such a bold claim, Singapore's unofficial positioning is as a capital city of south-east Asia – a carefully planned commercial crossroads and jumping-off point into the greater Asia Pacific region.

Tourism is a key industry for Singapore, and the government is forever planning new ways of positioning the country as a hub for everything from IT and research to soft industries like retailing and the arts. This has meant ongoing lobbying for new foreign-based attractions to spice up the tourism offerings and encouragement for new local businesses to seed.

Singapore is famed for its diversity: leafy tracts of virgin rainforest and manicured tropical gardens; gleaming malls and tall towers; shady riverside restaurant shophouses and bars; and all the rich colours and aromas of the ethnic quarters.

For residents, what at first appears to be an over-emphasis on planning and cleanliness, later reveals itself to be a city reaching to find its soul. Singapore's famed efficiency can be a blessing, but so is the new emphasis on arts, theatre, historical preservation, youth culture and entertainment. Just as the country has rushed to its present position in 40 years, so its determination to perfect the blueprint for an ideal city experience should continue to make it attractive to foreign residents.

The city's best images begin with its most visible attractions. Start with the ethnic quarters of Chinatown, Little India and Arab Street, and enjoy the bustle of tradition and daily commerce. A detour down the back streets will present you with a number of hidden worlds away from the traffic and dust. Here the traditional multi-coloured shophouses provide a more human scale to the scenery and the mixture of businesses, from spice merchants, fabric sellers and herbalists to sidewalk cafes, provides a lot to see and take in. (Unique to Singapore, shophouses are two or three storey-high buildings that originally had a shop on the ground floor, with living quarters above. Many have now been converted and they've become sought-after spaces for living, playing and exhibiting art or fashion in.) There are Indian and Chinese temples and Muslim mosques here, often side by side, and they're open for respectful visitors to explore.

On South Bridge Road and Boat Quay, from out of an undisturbed row of shophouses, grow the sharp and clean lines of the financial district's buildings. Sir Stamford Raffles' clear demarcation of zones has resulted in a city in which different worlds lie literally side by side.

The centre of the city is defined by a zone known for its heritage, and dotted with early 20th century schools and convents now used as museums and leisure areas. One version of the city's heritage walk stretches roughly from the leafy escapes of Fort Canning, down past the Singapore Art Museum, Raffles Hotel and the grass-lined Padang to the riverfront. Thanks to a project to light up the city's trees and building, this makes particularly good exploring in the cool of the evening.

Get Into The Mix

While its residents may not be as effervescent as their Thai neighbours or as culturally diverse as those of the Indonesian archipelago, Singapore is certainly one the region's most cosmopolitan cities. The easy mix of different cultures, tradition and modernity, and western and Asian influences help to make life here an experience for new residents. While anxious and industrious, its people are also eclectic – slipping easily from their high rise offices, to their favourite cafes, bars and restaurants and on to traditional family lives of ceremony and ritual.

Focal Point

In much of the city, the attraction for photographers is in the bizarre viewshafts - the glimpses you get of another facet of the city in the spaces between the ultra-modern lines of highrise buildings.

Chinatown p.180

Visit a Chinese herbalist in Chinatown to learn about more about your chi and whether you're naturally more 'heated' or 'cooling' by nature. He will tell you what foods you should eat, and mix an aromatic concoction of teas especially for you. Then you can soothe those aching feet, and possibly your internal organs, with a sometimes painful but ultimately satisfying session of foot reflexology.

Raffles Hotel p.210

Once on the edge of the beach, the revered Raffles Hotel complex is situated rather more inland today, thanks to land reclamation, but it remains a must-see. While the iconic Singapore Sling in the Long Bar may not be to everyone's taste, roaming through the hotel complex is a pleasant way to enjoy its hushed, leafy courtyards, the museum filled with memorabilia, and the Writer's Bar where Kipling and Maugham collected morsels of gossips and travel tales for their novels.

Festive Lights

From Chinese New Year to Hari Raya, Deepavali to Christmas, the festive season in Singapore stretches from November to January. This is when Orchard Road and the ethnic quarters glitter with intricate light displays and activity. As shoppers come in to spend for their celebrations, the areas become more atmospheric.

Riverside Meal

For early Singaporeans the centre of life and trade was at the busy shophouses and godowns or dockside warehouses along the Singapore River. Now they come to life in the cool of the evenings with wafting aromas of food and jugs of cool amber liquid, not unlike the colour of the river. You'll find a good variety of cuisines and prices, and everything from loud rock music and sports bars to hushed, romantic dining among the quays. Competition is hot for drinks prices, so don't give in to the first offer.

Sentosa p.196

From the cable car to beach volleyball, underwater discoveries to laser shows, Sentosa is positioned as the city's leisure island. First styled as a resort about 30 years ago, it's currently undergoing a bit of an upgrade and the new 'grown-up' entertainment of beach bars and destination spas will broaden its appeal.

Red Lights

Just to disprove its squeaky-clean reputation, the seamier sides of Singapore are to be found in Geylang, inner Chinatown, Changi Point and Orchard Towers. They're worth exploring at night for their cheeky humour, cheap food and beer, and cultural insights you won't find in travel guides. Being Singapore, the risk level is fairly low, and it's good to see evidence of 'old Asia'.

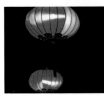

Shophouses

Whether morphed into food and beverage outlets, design studios, brothels, boutique hotels or posh housing, the last protected tracts of shophouses are Singapore's most attractive heritage buildings. In areas containing long stretches of them, they are often painted in bright colours and the restaurants among them offer good alfresco dining. Duxton Hills, Emerald Hill and Neil Road make for great exploring and photographing.

173

Hawker Centres p.427

Forget the sanitised and air-conditioned food courts, the real eating action is still under a fan in an open-air hawker centre. Featuring anything from 5 to 50 separate stalls, and offering cool beer at decent prices, the best centres have a congregation of old men telling tall stories in their own dialect, and drinks ladies barking orders in rough Hokkien. You can eat for as little as two or three dollars, or pay more at certain 'cult hawkers' that dish up gourmet numbers like the famed Crab Bee Hoon.

Orchard Road p.194

Big malls and bright lights, sometimes flashy and often tacky, the wide tree-lined boulevard of Orchard Road is the place to suck in your cheeks, don sunglasses and designer shopping bags and play the age-old sport of 'see and be seen'. While you should avoid the place on Sundays, a wander up Singapore's shopping mile is a must, if only to enjoy some of the outfits being worn and to remind yourself that teenagers are indeed strange creatures in any culture.

Asian Civilisations Museum p.211

A catch-all for Asian culture, this riverside museum is attractively located in The Empress Place Building, a former colonial government office. Worth exploring for both its regular and travelling exhibitions, here you can learn about the spread of rice cultivation in the region and check out the 1,300 artefacts that fill its rooms. These include Islamic art, bronze Buddhas, Javanese shrines and jewellery characteristic of the region.

Chijmes p.185

While it's not exactly conventional to dine and drink in a former convent, Chijmes somehow pulls its new incarnation off. Dotted with food and beverage venues and meeting places, the design of the courtyard and the wonderfully restored church has maintained the integrity of the complex and its restaurants offer a pleasant, quiet evening in the balmy night air.

Little India p.190

Henna tattoos and banana leaf curry, anyone? Perhaps the most-loved ethnic quarter among expats of all nationalities, Little India still serves a large and active South Asian community. On Sundays it hums with the chatter of thousands of men on their day off who gather to gossip and hang out. Delicious South Indian cuisine is the rule, and there's worthwhile exploring to be done on the back streets. Don't miss 24 hour retail sensation Mustafa's which stocks everything under the sun, new models and old at amazing prices.

Chicken Rice

More so even than chilli crab, the Singapore variation on Hainanese chicken rice is rightfully the island's most loved and unique dish. Roasted or steamed, with bones or without, the dish of salty fragrant rice and moist, succulent chicken is usually served with cucumber and broth, doused in a bright red chilli sauce and thick, sweet soy. Meet a Singaporean abroad and, chances are, this is what he craves.

Bukit Timah p.229

Hiking in the nature reserves is one of the most loved escapes for the fit and intrepid, and Bukit Timah is the most noted of the city's numerous parks and reserves. Hiking in virgin rainforest as monkeys leap overhead, it's easy to forget how populated the city is – until you see another edge of the reserve being subdivided into condominiums, that is. Rule number one with a Singapore park: use it or lose it.

Fort Canning p.215

Built to protect the harbour from invasion, the history of Fort Canning is tinged with sad irony, since the invaders arrived via the back door through Malaysia. Today though, its gardens, gorgeous old trees and open spaces make a great urban escape from the traffic and noise. Used regularly for outdoor events, notably Ballet Under the Stars, WOMAD and movie night, the grassy sloping lawn, stage, trees and skyline backdrop make for one of the nicest views in the city. Bring your camera along.

Arab Street p.178

The area around Arab Street and Kampong Glam are defined as the city's Muslim quarter. Aside from the mosques, they are dotted with stalls selling interesting fabrics, basket ware and Malay and Arabic food. Stop by one of the area's cafes after dinner for Middle-Eastern desserts and sweets, and smoke an orange or apple-flavoured shisha in the cool night air.

Zouk p.436

Arguably Singapore's most successful home grown entertainment brand, superclub Zouk carries its One Dance mantra through four distinct clubs and bars in this protected riverside warehouse. Recently refurbished and refreshingly friendlier thanks to new competition, Zouk also opens later due to liberalised drinking laws. Live music may still be at a premium in Singapore, but Zouk brings some of the hottest global DJs to town each weekend.

Night Safari p.230

The world's first dedicated night zoo, this atmospheric evening arm of the Singapore Zoo is among the country's most innovative attractions. Board a tram that takes you through zones that represent the world's different jungle areas. The magic is in the good condition of the animals, the lack of visible bars, thoughtful lighting and carefully orchestrated feeding times. The result is natural and highly visible displays of nocturnal animals at their most awake.

Holland Village p.200

Jokingly dubbed 'the expat quarter', Holland Village is the most cosmopolitan of the neighbourhood retail and dining areas, and its hairdressers, spas, magazine stalls, restaurants, bars and cafes attract people here in the evenings and weekends. It's all about chilling out, exploring arts and crafts stores, eating and socialising here. Its proximity to the universities and the mix of wealthy and more modest housing areas lends 'Holland V' a diverse, lightly bohemian neighbourhood feel.

Esplanade p.188

This $600 million landmark is nicknamed 'the durians' for its two spiky spheres resembling the notorious tropical fruit. Although it stirred up grumblings when construction started (this is a culture still new to the idea of the arts as an important part of society), with its large theatre and chamber halls, the venue offers a year-round diet of acts, from the high brow to the accessible, Asian and imported and the regular free shows on the promenade have significantly improved the range of free weekend entertainment options.

River Boat Ride

Taking a 'bumboat' ride along the Singapore River is undeniably touristy, yet worthwhile all the same. Named because they would take goods at the aft of trading ships, the presence of bumboats on the river is one of its enduring charms, and the inexpensive ride gives you a good insight into the linkages and contrasts that form the lifeblood of the city.

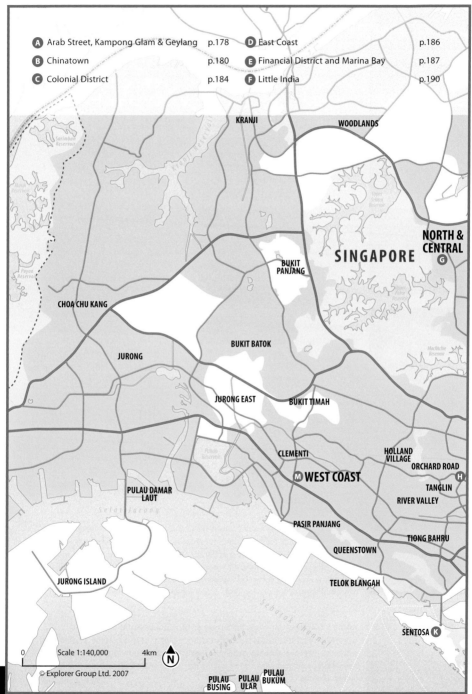

A   Arab Street, Kampong Glam & Geylang   p.178
B   Chinatown   p.180
C   Colonial District   p.184
D   East Coast   p.186
E   Financial District and Marina Bay   p.187
F   Little India   p.190

KRANJI

WOODLANDS

NORTH & CENTRAL
G

SINGAPORE

BUKIT PANJANG

CHOA CHU KANG

BUKIT BATOK

JURONG

JURONG EAST

BUKIT TIMAH

CLEMENTI

HOLLAND VILLAGE

ORCHARD ROAD
H

M WEST COAST

TANGLIN

RIVER VALLEY

PULAU DAMAR LAUT

PASIR PANJANG

TIONG BAHRU

QUEENSTOWN

JURONG ISLAND

TELOK BLANGAH

SENTOSA K

0   Scale 1:140,000   4km   N

© Explorer Group Ltd. 2007

PULAU BUSING   PULAU ULAR   PULAU BUKUM

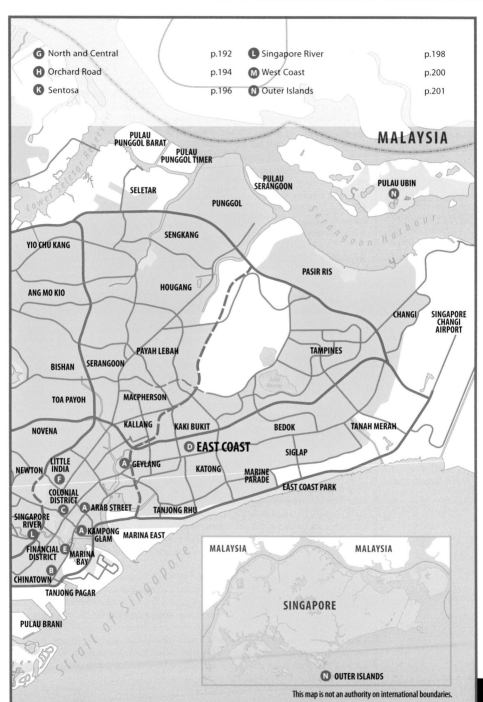

G North and Central   p.192   **L** Singapore River   p.198

H Orchard Road   p.194   **M** West Coast   p.200

K Sentosa   p.196   **N** Outer Islands   p.201

MALAYSIA

PULAU PUNGGOL BARAT
PULAU PUNGGOL TIMER
SELETAR
PULAU SERANGOON
PULAU UBIN **N**
PUNGGOL
SENGKANG
YIO CHU KANG
Serangoon Harbour
ANG MO KIO
HOUGANG
PASIR RIS
CHANGI
SINGAPORE CHANGI AIRPORT
PAYAH LEBAH
TAMPINES
BISHAN
SERANGOON
TOA PAYOH
MACPHERSON
NOVENA
KALLANG
KAKI BUKIT
BEDOK
TANAH MERAH
D EAST COAST
SIGLAP
NEWTON
LITTLE INDIA **F**
A GEYLANG
KATONG
MARINE PARADE
COLONIAL DISTRICT **C**
A ARAB STREET
TANJONG RHU
EAST COAST PARK
SINGAPORE RIVER **L**
A KAMPONG GLAM
MARINA EAST
FINANCIAL DISTRICT **E** MARINA BAY
B
CHINATOWN
TANJONG PAGAR
PULAU BRANI

Strait of Singapore

Lower Seletar Reservoir

MALAYSIA   MALAYSIA

SINGAPORE

N OUTER ISLANDS

This map is not an authority on international boundaries.

Map 14-D4 ◄

Arab Street, Kampong Glam & Geylang: The Malay Quarter

Kampong Glam (or Gelam) literally means 'village of eucalyptus'. Gelam is a eucalypt variety that grew nearby and was used in oils for medicines and for making boats watertight. Previously home to Singapore's Malay aristocracy before colonial rule, Kampong Glam and Arab Street area remain a relaxing and interesting area to eat, explore and learn about the city's Malay roots. Under the Raffles Plan, Kampong Glam was set aside for the Sultan of Singapore and the Malay and Arab communities. This, and the number of important mosques in the district, means this area is also often referred to as the 'Muslim Quarter'.

While much of the Malay community later moved to Geylang and other suburbs, the area is still an important one for the community. It buzzes with activity during the fasting month of Ramadan, when many Muslims break their fast here, and buy food and traditional wares for the feast that follows, Hari Raya Puasa. The area is a great place to eat and explore, tucked nicely away from much of the bustle of the central city. Stroll around its famous textile shops, and check out the stores selling fishing tackle, jewellery and rattan furniture. Later, stop by one of the cafes for tea and to smoke a shisha pipe.

Residential

Expatriates seeking cheap residential accommodation will have to put up with the area being slightly frenetic at night, but the sense of living in Asia is greater than you'll get in a shiny new condominium.

Retail

The Geylang Serai Wet Market (map 15-C3) is a traditional Asian market crammed with stalls selling meat, fish, food and fabrics. During Ramadan, this area is the place to be in the evenings, with seasonal market stalls. Sadly though, the original market will soon be torn down to be replaced by a new multi-million dollar market complex. The retail streets of neighbouring Katong are interesting for their strong Peranakan architectural influence. The Peranakan are the indigenous Straits Chinese who lived in Singapore before the various waves of migration, and their mixed heritage is embraced as a symbol of modern Singapore. There are Peranakan-style terraces along Koon Seng Road and restaurants sell delicious Peranakan food – arguably the first example of fusion food in Singapore. The culturally rich Joo Chiat area includes daytime businesses, night restaurants and music lounges and Katong Antique House – a good place to buy authentic Peranakan artifacts.

Places of interest

Apart from its red-light district to one side, Geylang is charming, if slightly scruffy, and a great place for a late supper. Eating outdoors near the roadside is closer to a 'real' Asian experience than dining in many of Singapore's shining modern areas, and the food is typically excellent. Organised into lorongs or lanes, word has it that ladies of the night (strictly-speaking, not all are ladies) operate only in alternating lorongs – those without closed circuit TV cameras.

Some of Singapore's most noted mosques are in the area, including Sultan Mosque (p.204); Hajjah Fatimah Mosque (map 14-E4) on Beach Road, a mosque that was built in 1846 featuring British-influenced architecture and a minaret that leans six degrees off centre, and was named after a Malakan-born Malay woman who once lived on the site and married a wealthy Bugis sultan; and Abdul Gaffoor Mosque, finished in 1910, with a unique sundial believed to be the only one of its kind in the Islamic world – inscribed with the names of 25 chosen prophets in Arabic calligraphy. There is also Istana Kampong Glam, the palace of the former Sultan of Singapore and now the Malay Heritage Centre (p.209).

The Lowdown
Small but worth exploring. Begin your discovery of the area by wandering down Arab Street, then making your way over to what is now the real Malay cultural centre in Geylang.

The Good
The huge variety of materials and cane goods, atmospheric backstreets and cafes, the size and atmosphere of Sultan Mosque and great streetside food in Geylang.

The Bad
Arab Street can feel empty at times, a little lacking in hustle and life.

The Must Dos
Visit Sultan Mosque, dig into a fabric stall, eat at a busy Malay stall and smoke shisha at a sidewalk cafe.

Sultan Mosque

Bussurah Street

Map 17-C2

Chinatown: Hustle and Heritage

A mixture of temples, markets, specialist shops and tourist traps, Chinatown is a vibrant commercial and cultural area for Singapore's Chinese population and the city's many visitors. With bustling shops and good hawker food, Chinatown lies within walking distance of the Financial District. Centred around South Bridge Road and spanning several blocks either side, Chinatown is in fact a series of less distinct areas, each with its own appeal. Offering noisy open air markets and festive decorations here in the weeks leading up to Chinese New Year, foot reflexology and a variety of massages at other times, Chinatown's many faces reflect traditional and modern Singapore life at the same time – which is very much a reflection of how the country's people embrace these different facets of their environment in their everyday lives.

Enter Chinatown by train and you'll rise up from the underground onto Pagoda Street to see shophouses looming above you on either side. While not to everyone's liking, Pagoda Street and its interconnecting streets is now Singapore's tourist centre. Search among the hawker stalls and cafes and you will find gems, but you may still have to wade through a good deal of tat first. The success of the area is that the authorities have been able to limit the amount of traffic flowing through it. Someone may have to look at the quality of offerings and the touts next.

Socially and architecturally speaking, there are many Chinatowns – the design houses, cosy cafes and bars of Club Street and Duxton Hill; North Bridge Road's expanses of 1970s malls and retail oddities; colourful Tanjong Pagar with its eclectic range of bridal salons by day, gay bars by night. Beyond this are the fancy residences and hushed elegance of the Tanjong Pagar conservation area, and then, if you double back toward the Outram Park MRT, you'll stumble into streets that sport a combination of brothels, boutique hotels and bars. Whichever part of Chinatown you're in though, you'll find wonderful local food – oily, cheap, strange and delicious. Spend a good half day here getting purposefully lost. The magic here often starts where you hadn't been planning on looking.

The Lowdown

The centre of tourism and traditional Chinese activity, you'll either love or hate Chinatown, depending on which of its many contrasts you are witness to. But it's well worth visiting.

The Good

Fantastic for food and a laidback atmosphere. Central Chinatown buzzes over the lunar New Year and its back streets make for great exploring at night.

The Bad

The touts in the arcade area are getting worse, while a lot of the wares on sale are junk.

The Must Dos

A reflexology session, followed by a curbside meal.

Residential

While Chinatown on the city side of South Bridge Road is still very much downtown, to the other side it becomes distinctly more mixed, with more of a selection of HDBs, apartment blocks and reconditioned shophouses that are especially popular with expatriates. Depending on the condition they're in, shophouses range from the affordable to the deluxe and renting rooms upstairs from a Chinese family is a good way for expats to get affordable indoor-outdoor accommodation that's full of character. The shophouse area off Neil Road is particularly attractive, and fetches high rents. Some expats enjoy living in the older private apartments on the outskirts of Chinatown that still command a charming view of shophouse rows and tall trees.

Far East Square

Located between Amoy and China Street, the Fuk Tai Chi Museum at Far East Square Mall is the site of the first temple built in Singapore. Meanwhile, the Chui Eng Free School, one of the first free schools in Singapore, now rather mischievously houses bars and restaurants. When Chinese immigrants arrived in Singapore, many joined clan associations whose membership consisted of people from the same area in China. Nearby Ying Fo Fui Kun was built in the 1880s for the Hakka community.

Retail

The central streets of Chinatown are packed with stalls selling all sorts of Chinese trinkets, ceramics and kitchenware. Chinese tourists shop for sweet red bak kwa, or barbecued pork – try the Bee Cheng Hiang brand – and every kind of weird and wonderful, from pungent mushrooms to frogs, red crabs, flavoursome teas and medicinal cure-alls. The Tanjong Pagar market is especially good for fresh fruit, vegetables and flowers. On South Bridge Road are attractive – but expensive – antique shops.

Places of Interest

Most obvious in Chinatown is the fact that it isn't just filled with Chinese people. Much of the reason for this is the mixture of temples and mosques. And it's this quiet level of cultural chaos that makes Singapore interesting. The Sin Chor Kung Temple on Amoy Street, built in 1869, is dedicated to the Tua Pek Kong deity, popular among the Teochews. The Nagore Durgha Shrine, built in 1830 in Telok Ayer, is an Indian temple that features a mix of styles – moulded arches with Indian Muslim motifs, Doric columns and Palladian doors. The Telok Ayer Chinese Methodist Church, a national monument, was built between 1924 and 1925, and used as a base by English and American Methodist missionaries. Also, the Jamae Chulia Mosque is one of three Islamic hertiage buildings in Chinatown erected by early immigrants (see p.204).

On South Bridge Road you'll find Sri Mariamman Temple, the islands oldest Hindu place of worship which is slap bang in the middle of Chinatown and still very much in use today (see p.206).

Beyond North Bridge Road at the top of Eu Tong Sen Street, is the shadowy yet elegant Thong Chai Medical Institute, built in 1892, that is reputed to have dispensed free medical help to all, regardless of race. A national monument with its Serpentine gables and wooden carved pillars, it's now a bar-restaurant complex.

Over on Neil Road, beyond Tanjong Pagar, is Tea Chapter, a tea museum and shop. A pot of tea and an introduction to Chinese tea drinking costs around $8. Tea Chapter features one of the biggest Zisha teapots in Singapore – an estimated 380kg of purple clay was used to make it. The venue also hosts a pottery workshop.

Other interesting spots in Chinatown include Nei Xue Tang on Cantonment Road with its collection of Buddhist art works and the Tiong Bahru bird area. You'll also find Speaker's Corner here: once billed as the next Hyde Park, it's now rather dead as a result of a general reluctance to speak strongly and publicly about controversial issues.

And if you still feel you need some orientation, visit the Singapore City Gallery (p.212), which is home to a 100 square metre architectural model of the city, as well as two floors of exhibits.

Tanjong Pagar Conservation Area

Once a nutmeg plantation, this charming area now boasts some of Singapore's most elegant shophouses, especially along Tanjong Pagar Road and around Duxton Road. Spice today comes in the form of numerous bars, some slightly seedy KTV (karaoke) joints, clubs and boutique hotels. In the last few years a number of young local fashion designers have set up shop in the area too.

The Caged Birds of Singapore

Shrilly tweeting birds in ornamental cages are a feature of Singapore life, and in certain areas owners gather with their birds, and while away the day drinking coffee. One of the few remaining areas where this happens is Tiong Bahru where you'll find owners - and their birds - gather every day of the week, but particularly on Sundays. Nearby coffee shops keep everyone plied with refreshments and the birds' bamboo cages are hung from hooks in groups according to type, while their occupants sing and socialise.

Are you always taking the wrong turn?

Whether you're a map person or not, these pocket-sized marvels will help you get to know the city… and its limits.

Explorer Mini Maps
Putting the city in your pocket

Abu Dhabi • Amsterdam • Bahrain • Barcelona • Dubai • Dublin • Geneva • Hong Kong • Kuwait
London • New York • New Zealand • Oman • Paris • Qatar • Shanghai • Singapore • Sydney

EXPLORER
www.explorerpublishing.com

Map 17-C1

Colonial District: The Historical Heart of Singapore

At the base of Orchard Road leading down to the harbour and river's edge is the colonial or civic district. Home to colonial buildings, museums and galleries and parks, the area has witnessed many of the country's landmark moments in history. While necessity dictates that the historical buildings often sit alongside new office blocks and shopping centres, the government has still managed to protect a good number of its most attractive structures.

In some cases inspired urban redevelopment has seen attractive buildings being given a new life as places for people – the Singapore Art Museum (see p.203) and Chijmes being two notable examples. In other cases, such as the Raffles Hotel, historic buildings were rebuilt and expanded in award-winning style.

Development wins occasionally too, as was the unfortunate case with the tree-lined park on Bras Basah Road that is now the site of the new and rather ugly Singapore Management University. Put this aside though when you explore the city's heritage buildings – your presence and feedback will help to preserve them further, as will the district's dual purpose as a training and tourism centre.

The Lowdown

Singapore's most noted historic buildings are found in a five-block square here. From cathedrals to forts, hotels to convents, the buildings here reflect Singapore's new concern for conserving its heritage, and provide a soulful link with the past.

The Good

Easy access and nominal entrance fees for some superb spaces. Highlights include Fort Canning, Raffles, Chijmes and the Singapore Art Museum.

The Bad

Traffic, construction, heat and poor pedestrian access makes it difficult to string these places along in a self-styled walking tour.

The Must Dos

An exhibition at SAM, high tea at Raffles, a game of frisbee on the Padang, and a quiet afternoon in the gardens at Fort Canning.

Residential

Little residential space is available in this downtown area, although Killiney and River Valley Roads nearby are popular with expatriates, and offer a good range of apartments within a short walk of the CBD. Closer to the water, new corporate apartments are being built near the Marina area, but these are not yet complete.

Retail

The Raffles Hotel complex contains a large range of boutique stores, including a tasteful range of Raffles souvenirs and gift ideas including food and kitchenware. The largest mall in the area is Raffles City, built on the former site of Raffles Institution, and linked to Raffles The Stamford, the island's tallest hotel. City Hall MRT is downstairs.

The multi-storied Raffles City includes the gourmet supermarket Jason's, Guardian, Robinsons and Marks & Spencer. Towards the river along North Bridge Road is the Funan IT Mall (or, more properly, Funan DigitaLife after its 2005 upgrade).

Peninsula Plaza, also on North Bridge Road, specialises in camera stores, including Cathay Photo.

National Library

Places of Interest

You can start a day's exploration of the area at Fort Canning (see p.215), one of Singapore's nicest urban parks, just above the heart of the city. More wild in feeling than the Botanic Gardens and defined by its height above the city, Fort Canning also hosts some memorable arts and culture events under the stars – everything from Ballet Under The Stars and WOMAD to Deep Purple and Fatboy Slim.

It was from here in World War II that Singapore's British forces carefully watched the harbour, cannons trained for evidence of the Japanese invasion – unaware of the enemy's rapid progress through Malaysia behind them. Today its cafes and spice gardens provide a place for you to briefly forget about the realities of business. The Padang (see p.216) also saw its share of memomrable wartime moments, although today it plays host to much lighter, happier events. Meanwhile, you can learn all about the war itself at The Battle Box (see p.211).

From here, head down the hill and move from building to building along Bras Basah Road in the direction of Beach Road and Raffles (see p.210). Worth a detour up to Middle Road is Sculpture Square, which features modern three dimensional works by local and regional artists. When you see Suntec City in front of you, take a moment to remember that this was once the sea's edge before the land reclamation process began. Find somewhere cool to chill out in the heat of the day - The Arts House (see p.203) is the city's oldest government building by the river hosting art exhibits, plays, movie screenings or brush up on your history at Singapore History Museum (see p.212) or at the Singapore Philatelic Museum (see p.212); then as the sun sets and lights illuminate many of the historic places, head towards the Padang and the Cricket Club or try an aerial view with the DHL Balloon (see p.226).

Chijmes

Having spent 131 years as the Convent of the Holy Infant Jesus, Chijmes on Victoria Street is now an atmospheric complex of restaurants, bars and special events venues. Its walled compound and grass lawns make it a perfect venue for weekend jazz events and recitals. The attractive chapel, now the multi-purpose Chijmes Hall, and Caldwell House, now an art gallery, are both national monuments. For the history buff, the Chijmes Service Centre runs 40 minute tours of the complex from Mondays to Fridays, from 11:00 to 15:00. Tours can be booked by calling 6338 2529 and cost $6 per person, including afternoon tea. For more details on all the venues at Chijmes, log onto www.chijmes.com.sg or call 6332 6273.

Chijmes

Raffles Hotel

East Coast: The Leisure Coast

Map 15 & 18 ◄

For those Singaporeans who have always lived on the East Coast, there's no better place. With a little more space and perhaps a more laidback attitude to life than the CBD, the East Coast has the added benefit of ready access to the beach. And in such a small city state, nothing is really that far away – despite what some may say.

The Lowdown ◄
Breezy beach parks, good condos, great chilli crab.

While the West Coast is more industrial and shipping-orientated, the East Coast is very much the leisure coast of Singapore, and the East Coast Park in particular offers a long stretch of perfect coastline for running, cycling or just enjoying the sea breeze. There are also some excellent places for food; whether it's chilli crab near the beach or local food in some of the city's oldest neighbourhoods, like historic Geylang and Katong. These are traditional Malay and Peranakan neighbourhoods, and outside of festive seasons like Hari Raya, they are also refreshingly light on tourists.

The Good

Singapore's leisure coast – East Coast Park is a great place to eat (delicious!) seafood and get some exercise.

Residential

The East Coast is extremely popular with expatriates. Those on good pay packets favour the sea views, palm trees and ocean breezes of the condominiums that hug the coastline almost all the way to Changi airport. For edgier urban living, the areas around Geylang, Kallang and Katong may be more 'colourful' in the evenings, but they also offer great dining and fabulous restored buildings. For fans of Siglap, meanwhile, theirs is the 'Holland Village of the East', only with a slightly more residential, more family oriented feel and still full of good eating options. Cafes, restaurants, pubs, a shopping mall and a tailor who makes traditional Malay blouses or kebayas are also attractions.

The Bad

Lacking somewhat in soul and history, the East Coast is more about exercise than excitement.

Retail

The Must Dos

Eat chilli crab by the sea, rollerblade in East Coast Park.

Each neighbourhood has its own shopping malls, but the East is known more for its leisurely living than its retail therapy.

Places of Interest

Changi

The original kampongs in Changi have been replaced with housing estates and reclamation projects, the gigantic Singapore Expo Centre and Changi Business Park. Changi Village offers fantastic nasi lemak (a Malay dish of fish, chicken and peanuts) at its popular and inexpensive hawker centre while its carpark offers the curious a chance to ogle the friendly transsexual men.

If you're into outdoor sports you'll find plenty of space to pursue your passion here. Apart from East Coast Park (p.214), there's also Kallang, the home of Singapore's Indoor Stadium. A rather sterile, but functional venue, it's been the site of many mid-size concerts and events like badminton tournaments, street soccer and ice skating shows. The Kallang basin is also a popular area for watersports like kayaking and dragon boating, while many people jog or walk their dogs around the inlet. It's also a good place to watch the national day parade at the National Stadium. Kallang Theatre is still the venue for plays and musicals that aren't quite grand enough for the Esplanade.

The small Changi Chapel & Museum (see p.213) will give you a lesson in war history. You can then complete the trip by taking a bumboat to Johor where you'll find the Johor Battery (see p.209), a remote labrinth of tunnels that was the largest artillery hold during WWII outside of Britain. For lighter entertainment, the Katong Antique House (see p.209) is loaded with all sorts of treasures and over in Pasir Ris Park (see p.216), home to the mangrove forests, there's lots to see and do.

If architecture is your thing, make the detour to Koon Seng Road (just of Joo Chiat Road) with its row of ornately-decorated Peranakan terrace houses. The Malay Cultural Village at 39 Geyland Road is a complex of traditional Malay houses. It is supposed to recreate the kampong life of early Singapore and on weekends it has free dance displays and Malaysian food for sale. Sadly though, it's poorly run and not widely recommended. Changi is home to a many of the traditional black & white bungalows, and if you're heading further afield you'll find the ferry terminal for bumboats to Pulau Ubin and Johor here.

Map 17 ◀

Financial District and Marina Bay: Old Business, New Leisure

The Lowdown
Singapore's two highrise downtown business clusters include malls, hotels, and are rapidly being joined by a new wave of waterside entertainment venues.

The Good
Views of Singapore, Malaysia and Indonesia. Great upmarket hotels such as the Ritz Carlton, Conrad and the Oriental. The evening buzz and seaside access of Esplanade and One Fullerton, and the hum of Raffles City.

The Bad
Suntec in particular gets terribly congested at peak hours, and parking is always challenging. Can feel a little dead at weekends, and lacks atmosphere in comparison to some other areas.

The Must Dos
A sunset meal up high at Equinox, the Stamford Plaza or a Moët Sunday brunch at the Ritz-Carlton. Meander among renowned artists' work on the downtown sculpture walk. Catch an opera performance at The Esplanade.

Depending on where you see them from, Singapore's two imposing high-rise clusters of the Financial District and Suntec City appear to rise dramatically out of the Singapore River, the shophouse bars of Boat Quay or the attractive shop frontages of North Bridge Road in Chinatown. The financial and corporate pulse of the city beats here, yet the centre of each cluster is relatively small – one encompassing Raffles Place and Shenton Way, the other at the north-eastern edge of the CBD on three blocks of reclaimed land around Suntec.

It used to be that the high-rise clusters hugging either side of the harbour mouth had little to offer for leisure, save a little fishing. But this has changed in the last decade, thanks to major urban redevelopment that has made the harbour and river mouth an entertainment focal point. This has included the construction of the Esplanade and One Fullerton developments – and has continued inland past Empress Place and along the Singapore River with the continuing upgrade of the city's riverside areas. In local marketing speak, the river is rapidly becoming a place to 'live, work and play' once again. Further attractions are being built across the water in Marina South. These include a revolving wheel called The Singapore Flyer, landscaped waterfront gardens and tourist development that will house one of the nation's first two casinos. A project that's due to be completed in 2007 is a dam across that Marina Channel that will turn the bay into a fresh water reservoir and a year-round arena for events and sports like powerboat racing.

Residential

Aside from in a few penthouses, not many people live right in the hub of the Financial District or Suntec City. Just to the east of Suntec and across the water, Tanjong Rhu's condominiums are popular with expat urbanites wanting proximity to the city and the inlet seaside lifestyle. There is more apartment accommodation inland from the Financial District, especially in some of the older buildings, but in general neither district offers great shops (of the day-to-day variety) or facilities for residents.

Retail

The major mall in the area is Suntec City, opened in 1995 along with the Suntec Development. Until the arrival of VivoCity in 2006, it was the largest shopping centre in Singapore. Together with the CityLink Mall that links Suntec with Raffles City Mall, this stretch is the major retail rival to Orchard Road. Featuring 360 outlets over three floors, the cluster is anchored by the Carrefour hypermarket, and includes Nike by BIRD, Tower Records, an Adidas Concept Store, Toys R Us, Courts and Harvey Norman.

The Merlion

Places of Interest

Photo Opportunity

From Marina South (catch the MRT), Singapore's money shot is of the tall towers rising out of Boat Quay's shophouses, with the gleaming river mouth and Esplanade in the foreground.

Tour the Durians

Theatre buffs will enjoy the 45 minute tours of the Esplanade - Theatres on the Bay. These run daily at 11:00 and 14:00 on weekdays and at 11:00 only on weekends, and take in the special features that make this a world class venue. Tickets cost $8 for adults and $5 for children of 12 and younger. For more details call 6828 8377 or check out www.esplanade.com.

Start a walking tour of the district by taking the MRT to Raffles Place, the financial heart of Singapore. Known as Commercial Square when it was first built in 1823, it was dubbed Raffles Place in 1858. From the early 1900s, the area became a banking centre, with flagship buildings for Shell Tower, Clifford Centre, Ocean Building and Republic Plaza.

Dotted among the gleaming towers are still some interesting national monuments. The riverside Tan Si Chong Su Temple on Magazine Road was built in 1876 and arrived in Singapore as ballast. Said to have excellent feng shui, this Hokkien temple was a focal point for Singapore's large Tan clan. Across from Capital Square on the corner of Church and Philip Streets, is the Wak Hai Cheng Temple, built in 1850. Mixing Buddhism and Taoism, its roof is decorated with pictures of life in China. Another temple with beautiful artwork is Thian Hock Keng Temple (see p.206). Among the antiquities are some modern sculptures that are worth tracking down too. These include Salvadore Dali's Homage to Newton and Fernando Botero's typically chubby Bird, both in and just outside the UOB Plaza. While you're there, take a look at Kenzo Tange's building, one of the more striking pieces of architecture in the Financial District.

From here, walk towards the harbour, and cross the river via the underground tunnel to One Fullerton. Here a number of atmospheric restaurants and bars occupy the promenade next to the big white Merlion statue. Spouting water out of his mouth, the mythical Merlion is meant to be the city's protector at the mouth of the river.

Now cross the bridge towards the Esplanade and Suntec City, where one of the major attractions is the Fountain of Wealth (see p.226). By the pencil-shaped Millenia Tower at Millenia Promenade, you'll find another modern sculpture, this time the colourful and cartoon-like Singapore Brushstrokes by Roy Lichtenstein. Head back by foot towards the harbour to browse around another valuable collection of contemporary art at the Ritz Carlton Singapore.

For a bite to eat in the area, Lau Pa Sat (see p.209) is a protected building and home to some of the finest food in town.

If you're still up for some walking, Marina City Park (see p.215) offers great views of the skyline and some interesting sculptures.

Singapore's Merlion

The Merlion is almost to Singapore what the Eiffel Tower is to Paris. Designed by Fraser Brunner for the Singapore Tourism Board in 1964, it has become a trademark symbol for the island-state. It's a statue with a head of a lion and the body of a fish, inspired by the story of the discovery of Singapore by the legendary Sang Nila Utama who saw a lion while hunting on the island. There are five official Merlions - the original being the one at the mouth of the Singapore River, and its smaller companion at Merlion Park. A taller replica stands on Sentosa Island and there are two others at Mount Faber and Tourism Court at Orchard Spring Lane. A fake Merlion at Ang Mo Kio has since been removed, and for some reason China has many imitation Merlions dotted about its housing estates and commercial areas.

Esplanade - Theatres on the Bay

Nicknamed 'the durians' by Singaporeans for the way its hedgehog-like roof structure resembles two durian halves laid flat, the $600 million Esplanade - Theatres by the Bay waterfront complex is Singapore's unofficial headquarters for performing arts, and the place to watch Broadway musicals, concerts, plays and dance performances.

While rather conservatively decorated inside, the structure saves its best for the concert halls, where the acoustics are excellent. Esplanade houses three visual art spaces and another two smaller exhibition venues. The fourth floor roof garden offers an attractive view of the city skyline and the river at sunset. There are several good bars and restaurants in and around the building that are popular in the evenings with the office crowd. The Esplanade organises free outdoor concerts regularly, so check the website for listings, www.esplanade.com. A tour of the Esplanade complex is available, see 'Tour the Durians' above.

The Complete **Residents'** Guide

Map 14-D4

Little India: The Exotic East

Culturally, Little India is one of the richest districts in Singapore, offering you experiences ranging from savouring fish-head curry and masala tea along Racecourse Road to getting a henna tattoo or visiting a parrot fortune teller. Whether it's due to fear, respect or a little of both, Little India has retained an identity all its own and a sense of independence that goes beyond simply being a cultural heart for South Asians. This is partly because the place hasn't yet been over-themed or dressed up.

Apparently Little India developed around a former settlement for Indian convicts. Its location on the Serangoon River made it attractive for raising cattle and it became known for its trade in livestock. As more immigrants moved in from Chulia Kampong – an area that had been put aside for Indian immigrants under the Raffles Plan of Singapore – and as other economic activity in Little India developed, it began to look like a real Indian town.

Such is the way in which a slice of urban Indian has been transplanted here that you could be wandering the streets of Madras or Hyderabad. Ironically, the district is vibrant in the same way as a 'Chinatown' is vibrant in the West; it's made all the more distinct by the stark differences all around it.

Walk down Little India's streets signposted in Tamil, Hindi and Bengali and shop for colourful saris, spices and Indian Barbie dolls – it's all here in colourful abundance. On Saturday nights and all day on Sundays, homesick Indian workers converge on the area to shop, eat and catch up on gossip. While it can be chaotic at times, it's also one of the more authentic experiences an outsider can enjoy in what can be a rather 'Asia-lite' Singapore. Like a real Indian city, what keeps this area so vibrant is the force of population it serves – not only several generations of resident Indians, mainly Tamils from southern India, but also large groups of South Asian labourers and tourists from the now booming homeland.

Residential

Some of the more traditional Singaporeans are somewhat wary of Little India, yet the more casual and expressive aspects of the area make it attractive to many foreigners. The terrace houses of Townerville, the nearby condominiums and the restored shophouses close to or within Serangoon are popular with expats, and the proximity to food outlets and the city is an additional plus factor.

Retail

Singapore's Chinese community is not the only one that's shopping mad. The stores of Little India are packed with all manner of Indian goods, from music to fruit. Two giant shopping centres dominate. The first of these is the Mustafa Centre on Syed Alwi Road, a mecca for bargains and the sheer range of goods. If you haven't been there a while, the centre will seem to have grown in your absence. From Rolex watches to bags of lentils and tailored suits, it's all here, all the time – the centre is open 24 hours. Sim Lim Square, technically speaking, is across the street from Little India, on 1 Rochor Canal Road. Filled with electronics, you'll find plenty of competitive pricing here, not to mention a good degree of fast talking. The centre is also known for selling pirated software, but this practice is stamped down on periodically. The other shopping options in the area cater more to the Indian market.

The Lowdown

The eastern corner of town is where the centre of retail action and culture for Singapore's Indian community can be found.

The Good

The most consistently interesting and authentic of Singapore's ethnic enclaves, Little India is bustling, friendly and colourful.

The Bad

Too often crowded and congested with traffic, especially on a Sunday. Rather visit the area early on weekday mornings.

The Must Dos

Masala prawns on a banana leaf or fish head curry. Exploring the back streets. The gadget shop at Mustafa's.

Tekka Mall at 2 Serangoon Road is Little India's first and only modern air-conditioned shopping mall, and rather soulless when compared to the bustle outside. Tekka Centre on the other hand is a wet market for fresh produce, hawker food, traditional Indian clothing and jewellery.

Places of Interest

Little India's main thoroughfare is Serangoon Road, and there's network of streets that run off it. As ever, the real life and intrigue is in the back streets, and wandering through them in the early morning or at dusk offers you a captivating sampling of some of the cultural richness missing in the westernised corners of town. The fact that Little India has been allowed to go its own way is something of a blessing – while you'll see hip cafes and boutiques where once there were backpackers' hostels, this happens at a pace that allows the district to retain its identity. Even its new MRT is set off to one side – whereas Chinatown's cut right into the heart of it. Head to Little India Arcade (p.209) for a real taste of life down here.

Meanwhile, Singapore's common languages, food and shopping, are what bring non-Indian residents back to Little India each time – the lure of heavily spiced vegetarian fare, or red-pasted prawns served on a banana leaf and washed down with fresh lassi is too much to resist for too long. As is the thought of bargains galore at retail sensation Mustafa's. While it may look chaotic at times, it's very possibly Singapore's most successful centre. Waiving the niceties of display and comfort for the benefits of a lot of stock, Mustafa's is the most likely place to have what you're looking for.

But it's not all food and shopping here, Leong San See Temple is a beautiful Taoist Temple and is well worth a look (p.205) as are the Sakaya Muni Buddha Gaya Temple (p.205), the Sri Srinivasa Perumal Temple and the Sri Veeramakaliamman Temple (p.206).

Map 6 ◀

North and Central: The Green Belt

The central and northern parts of Singapore are havens for wildlife, and they draw tourists, runners, hikers, mountain bikers and nature enthusiasts to their quiet green escapes. When you take into account the tracts of primary rainforest at Bukit Timah, scenic reservoirs such as MacRitchie, and superb natural attractions like Night Safari, you gain a greater appreciation for the planning that allows a heavily populated city state to set aside such extensive portions of land for nature and recreation. This green belt also serves an important role as the island's lung that absorbs carbon emissions coming from the city's maze of motorways. When exploring, be sure to bring ample water, bug spray and a mobile phone.

The Lowdown ▶

Home to some of the island's best reserves, reservoirs and sports fields, the central belt northward is where many residents play and unwind at weekends.

Residential

The Bukit Timah area is a particularly prominent location with a high land value. It has extensive flora and contains the Bukit Timah Nature Reserve, which is part of the reason for its high land value. The area includes educational institutions such as the Hwa Chong Institution, Raffles Girls' Primary School, Methodist Girls' School and others, as well as many bungalows – traditionally expensive in land-scarce Singapore – and high rise condominiums. It's a popular location for expats and well heeled Singaporeans. The Keretapi Tanah Melayu from Malaysia has a passing loop station here along its rail network from Johor Bahru to Tanjong Pagar.

The Good

Get back to nature in Bukit Timah and MacRitchie or go on a night safari to discover the jungle dweller within.

Retail

In terms of retailing, the area's proximity to the city tends to limit the need, although Novena is the best bet for neighbourhood shops.

The Bad

Not many interesting older neighbourhoods, and a myriad of motorways.

Places of Interest

Among the numerous natural attractions such as Bishan Park (see p.215), there's the Bukit Timah Nature Reserve (see p.229) and the MacRitchie Reservoir (see p.230), not to mention the Sungei Buloh Wetland Reserve in the northwest which, in 2002, became the first wetlands reserve to have been gazetted in Singapore. A stopover point for migratory birds, it's 1.3 square kilometres of birding pleasure. Orchid enthusiasts will enjoy the Mandai Orchid Gardens, a short walk from the Singapore Zoo (see p.231).

The Must Dos

Hiking, walking and mountain biking . . . or just watching the birds.

Bukit Timah

Kranji in the north makes a nice scenic drive. A military camp prior to the Japanese invasion, Kranji is now home to the Kranji War Cemetery and the memorial at 9 Woodlands Road (map 3-E4). The Kranji War Memorial's walls are inscribed with the names of 24,346 British men and women from Singapore, Malaya, Java and Sumatra who died in the war. Further along the winding road are a series of organic farms and lifestyle farms, perhaps the closest to 'alternative lifestylers' that Singapore has. Ivy Singh-Lim runs Bollywood Veggies, a lovely organic farm that has short guided tours and a cafe that serves home-cooked Asian cuisine (made from organic ingredients, of course). Call them first before visiting (6898 5001). For some outdoor amusement, dress up and head to the races at the Singapore Turf Club (see p.228). Also this side of town is the largest Buddhist Temple in the country can be found, Kong Meng San Phor Kark See Temple (see p.205).

193

Map 14-B4

Orchard Road: The Shopping Mile

Orchard Road is easily Singapore's most identifiable street. As the name suggests, the road was originally the site of nutmeg plantations, pepper farms and fruit orchards. Now this four-lane, each-way street is dominated by shopping malls and hotels. It connects with Tanglin at the top western end and the Colonial or Civic District near the river at its far end. Scotts Road, which intersects Orchard, is the second main street in this district.

The Singapore Government estimates that Orchard Road is visited by three-quarters of the tourists who visit Singapore each year. This street's importance is in part a reflection of the retail sector's health. As such, the buzz is returning to the street after a five year downturn, and new arrivals – like the 10,000 square foot Massimo Dutti flagship store – indicate that retailing is on the rebound. In the mid term, Singapore plans to spend nearly US$1 billion of public and private investment on upgrading the street, with plans for a new 218 metre skyscraper, four new shopping malls and improvements to pedestrian access and street features.

While most of the Orchard is dominated by shops, restaurants and entertainment spots, there are points of cultural and social interest in between. The Goethe Institute Art Gallery (6735 4555, 163 Penang Road #05-01 Winsland House II) and Opera Gallery in Ngee Ann City are examples of specialist art galleries in the area. Noted places of worship in the area include the turn of the century Chesed-El Synagogue off Tank Road on Oxley Rise which is no longer in use. And also on Tank Road is one of Singapore's oldest Roman Catholic churches, Church of the Sacred Heart which was founded in 1910.

Residential

Living on or near Orchard Road has serious cache and usually costs big dollars. Luxury apartments and large historic houses abound on this stretch and on its side streets, including Nassim Road, Orange Grove, Grange Road and Tanglin. While proximity to the city is the attraction, neighbourhood facilities remain rather limited, and traffic can be constant. Cheaper accommodation with good floor space but limited facilities is available in some of the older apartment buildings near Orchard Road.

Retail

You'll find branded stores galore in this consumer's paradise, including a large HMV, Borders, Kinokuniya, Mango, Calvin Klein and Zara outlets. Orchard has some of Singapore's biggest and best known malls – Wisma Atria, The Paragon, The Heeren, Takashimaya, Centrepoint and the iconic home-grown department store Tangs. With its distinctive tiled Chinese roof and columns next door to the Mandarin Hotel, Tangs remains one of the most recognisable shop buildings on the street. Many of the malls are now joined by underground air-conditioned links, and connect with the MRT at Orchard, Somerset and Dhoby Ghaut stations.

The Lowdown

Singapore's main street for shopping malls also has many restaurants and hotels for you to refuel at. A planned upgrade could mean more noise and congestion in the short term.

The Good

Shopping, movies, restaurants and cafes are all close at hand. Good for enjoying the glitz and urban buzz, the wide tree-lined boulevard makes for a pleasant morning or evening stroll, particularly when there's a light breeze.

The Bad

Parts of Orchard Road can feel over-commercial and soulless, while others are distinctly run down. It also features a disproportionate number of teenagers. During weekends and rush hours Orchard's sidewalks and underground links are congested.

The Must Dos

Relax at the Botanic Gardens or window shop at Takashimaya and The Paragon. Enjoy cold beer and tapas al fresco at Emerald Hill. Brunch at mezza9 in the Grand Hyatt.

Places of Interest

When you arrive in Singapore, Orchard Road tends to be your first and most convenient stop. With its restaurants, shopping and movies and quick access to the MRT, it's an ideal place for you to find your bearings and to soak up the urban tropical atmosphere. Emerald Hill (see p.208) offers the only original shophouse architecture left. You'll see more colonial architecture at the Goodwood Park Hotel (see p.208), the tower of which is a national monument and The Istana, the President's official residence (see p.209). For a step back in time of the outdoor variety, head to the Singapore Botanic Gardens (see p.216).

For many longer-term residents though, the area is often avoided at busy times unless you're well primed to brave the crowds, the heat and the slow-moving traffic, both foot and motor powered. During office hours however, its malls are well worth exploring, and they do feature some hidden gems and off-beat corners.

Orchard has a cluster of top-line hotels too, including Shangri-La, Marriott, Hilton, Grand Hyatt and Meritus Mandarin. As a result, there are also some big name restaurants, bars and night spots here that can offer a good night out.

Map 19

Sentosa: An Easy Escape ▶ p.197

From cable car rides to beach volleyball, underwater discoveries to laser shows, Sentosa is positioned as the city's leisure hotspot. It's ideal for a day of fun in the island's gardens and on the white, sandy beaches. The island is currently undergoing a transformation and 'grown-up' entertainment such as beach bars, new restaurants and destination spas have broadened the appeal. The good times here are easily accessible: simply drive over to the island or catch a taxi. In time, the MRT will be an option too.

Despite the ease of access, Singapore's 'leisure island' certainly feels different to Singapore proper, with its five-star hotels and fine dining restaurants. For information about any aspect of the island, visit www.sentosa.com.sg or call 1800 736 8672.

Residential

The next phase of development on Sentosa will see its first high-end residential community being built – a development with exclusive condos, a marina, hotels and so forth. The core development is at Sentosa Cove which also offers the only oceanfront residences currently available in Singapore.

Retail

Since VivoCity (p.363) opened up at the entrance to Sentosa in late 2006, there has been a quantum leap in the range of retail options available within easy reach of Sentosa. Together with the new St James Powerstation club opening soon, the aim is to make this a more vibrant area for leisure and entertainment.

Places of Interest

With a mixed offering of attractions – some hits, some misses – this resort and theme park island will keep you busy. There are a number of themed attractions that kids enjoy, including Underwater World (p.229), Dolphin Lagoon, the Sentosa Luge (see 'Sentosa Luge and Skyride' on p.225), the Magical Sentosa musical fountain laser show in the evening, and the Carslberg Sky Tower that gives you an aerial view of the island. There's also Fort Siloso (p.208), the free Nature Walk (livened up with plastic dragons), the Sentosa Golf Club (p.268 in the Activities chapter) and Sijoro Wondergolf. Added to this, Images of Singapore (p.212) will transport you through the ages of Singapore's History.

Some of the sights worth missing are the 37 metre Merlion that comes alive with changing neon colours, Volcano Land's rather fairly feeble interpretations of the real thing every half hour and the Butterfly Park and Insect Kingdom where the netted enclosure of 50 species of butterflies and the museum filled with dead bugs don't offer great value for money.

The Lowdown

The city's favourite resort getaway, Sentosa's got everything from beaches, cycling, golf and good museums to luxurious spas, cocktail bars and cheesy tourist attractions.

The Good

A short drive from the city but a world apart thanks to its resort feel and laidback atmosphere. An easy island escape for a day of beaches, brunch, rides, bars and a tan.

The Bad

Some of the attractions are a little tame and it can feel a little sterile and over-planned at times. Crowds at weekends can make the journey home slow.

The Must Dos

Scream down the Luge then recover your cool with cocktails at beach bar KM8 (p.431), or a massage at Spa Botanica. Meet friends for a Sunday brunch at Sentosa Resort and Spa.

Sentosa's Beaches

Sentosa's three beaches are all along the south-western side of the island with Siloso Beach (map 19-A1) on the western end, Tanjong Beach (map 19-C4) and Palawan Beach in the middle (map 19-B3). Each beach is enhanced with imported sand and planted palm trees. While not quite Malaysia or Thailand, locals and tourists still enjoy the island life here, particularly at weekends, when they gather to play volleyball, swim, tan or have a beer at one of the many beach pubs (see KM8 on p.431 in Going Out for one favourite). The Singapore Strait's waters don't really make for inviting swimming so activities are mostly land-based. Check out www.sentosa.com.sg to find out more.

Experience the latest attractions at Imbiah!

Imbiah is the latest attraction cluster on Sentosa and a great introduction to what you can see and do here. Boasting a collection of attractions, dining and retail outlets, this exciting zone lets you relish a full day's enjoyment of varying experiences.

Butterfly Park & Insect Kingdom
Stroll through the lush surroundings of the Butterfly Park as 1,500 live butterflies flutter around you at the cool outdoor conservatory. It also has one of the largest collections in Asia with 3,000 species of some of the world's most beautiful and rarest insects.

Cable Car
Enjoy magnificent views when you ride hundreds of metres above the harbour, sea and rainforest in a cable car. Glass-bottomed cars present Singapore in a whole new perspective!

Fort Siloso
Singapore's only surviving preserved coastal fortification is an important window to our colonial past and a poignant reminder of the war years. Life-sized replicas, interactive exhibits, photographs, documents and film clips are on display. Get to handle real-life historical guns and cannons, or explore the old tunnels too.

Images of Singapore *Must see*
Journey through the history of Singapore where cultural diversity, unity of values and adventures come together for an enchanting trip.

Sentosa 4D Magix *New*
The latest attraction in Sentosa lets you be the 'star' in a movie! Combining 3D film with a variety of '4D' special effects that synchronise with events that occur throughout the film, you will be dodging bullets and jumping over cliffs like it is done in the movies!

Sentosa Luge & Skyride *New*
The Sentosa Luge, the first facility in Southeast Asia, lets you race down or cruise leisurely along a 650m paved track in a luge cart that combines a unique steering and braking system. Then, transfer to a Skyride for a scenic ride among the tropical rainforest back to the starting point.

Sky Tower
Singapore's tallest public viewing tower at 131m above sea level offers panoramic views across Singapore, Sentosa and the Southern Islands. Day or night, views from the tower promise to be both scenic and breathtaking.

The Merlion
Venture into Singapore's tallest icon at 37m high, and discover the secret of this lion city, in an animated theatre show. Enjoy spectacular views of Singapore's city skyline and Sentosa at the Merlion's top. Toss a gold coin into a Mercub's mouth and bring home a unique Merlion souvenir!

sentosa

Map 17-B2

Singapore River: Fun by the Water

Arranged into Boat Quay, Clarke Quay and Robertson Quay, the river district was once the site of Singapore's earliest trading activities, and now hosts some of its finest dining activity.

The Lowdown
Central to Singapore's history is its river district. Once a hub for trade, it's now the place for dining, nightlife and entertainment.

The Good
Cool evenings when the breeze is up. Good photo opportunities and a pleasant place to stroll about in the mornings or late evenings.

The Bad
The touts at Boat Quay and some overly commercial stretches.

The Must Dos
A beer by the water, a play at Kallang Theatre, a stroll around The Fullerton and bar hopping in Clarke Quay.

Residential

Although the river district was once the place where Singaporeans worked, lived and played, there's very little now in the way of residential or retail space. The Riverwalk apartments next to Boat Quay are the exception.

Retail

The new Central development at Clarke Quay will provide more upscale retail and residential options, and boost the area's tourist appeal and nightlife.

Places of Interest

The best place to start and finish a walking and boat tour of the area is at the river mouth, at 1 Empress Place where the marble statue of Sir Stamford Raffles, the founder of Singapore, marks the spot where he first set foot in Singapore on 29 January 1819.

Visit the Asian Civilisations Museum (see p.211), the city state's newest and most impressive museum which traces the history of the region's different cultural groups, with particular attention paid to Singapore's Malay, Chinese and Indian roots. Stop for a drink either at Empress Place to enjoy the view of Boat Quay and the high towers across the water, or in the Arts House, once the first House of Parliament. Walk past the attractive Victoria Theatre & Concert Hall, built in 1862 – once a town hall, it's now a venue for shows from Rent to Buena Vista Social Club. Note the original bronze work, cast by Thomas Woolner and unveiled on the Padang in 1887, in front of the theatre. Cross the historic Cavenagh Bridge, the oldest bridge in the country and only the second suspension bridge here. Built in 1869, it still sports an original sign forbidding cattle to cross. Carry on to the fabulous Fullerton (see p.35), once a post office and now a landmark hotel owned by the Far East Group. At night, especially when a breeze is up, this is one of Singapore's most magical and evocative walks.

Turn right, and walk towards Boat Quay, taking time to enjoy the brass People of the River sculptures that adorn both sides of the river: the five boys jumping into the water, Kucinta cats and the Chinese man and his workers talking to the colonial trader. Each gives a sense of the old life of the river. There are also modern art statues to be seen.

In Boat Quay, stop for an ale at Harry's, the closest bar to the Financial District and once rogue trader Nick Leeson's favourite watering hole. Continue along Boat Quay past the two and three-storey shophouses and cobbled

Clarke Quay

Named after Sir Andrew Clarke, the second governor of Singapore, this used to be a strip of dilapidated 19th century warehouses run mostly by Chinese traders. Redeveloped into a less successful counterpart to Boat Quay in the early 1990s, its most recent makeover took two years to transform this waterfront strip into a popular night haunt, featuring eccentric - some say ugly - pods and lily pads. For full details of what you can find in the area, check out www.clarke quay.com.sg.

One place worth a visit is the Royal Selangor Pewter Museum (6268 9600) at 3A River Valley Road, which has a private collection of pewter items ranging from tobacco boxes to oil lamps and Chinese lanterns with lotus motifs, as well as centuries old pewter-making tools.

paths. Now restaurant-central, these were once the homes and offices of the original Singapore traders. It may be touristy, but the river scene is still an evocative reminder of those often tough times.

Next, hop into a bumboat to take a tour of the remainder of the river. You'll pass under the Anderson, Elgin and Coleman bridges and follow the curve of the river around to Robertson and Clarke Quay. Clarke Quay is now the new hotspot for nightlife and entertainment, and regularly features new arrivals like Ministry of Sound and Crazy Horse. Robertson Quay at the furthest end of the river was once used to store goods. Now some of the old godowns function as clubs (like Zouk), restaurants, hip hotels and outdoor bars. Also worth a look whilst here is the Singapore Tyler Print Institute (see p.203). As the boat ride loops back on the same course, try and take it past The Fullerton and out to sea – passing the mythical Merlion spitting water at Esplanade Park.

199

Map 16-A2

West Coast: Live, Learn, Hang Out

While Singapore's West Coast is dominated by its port activities, it has a wide variety of interesting spots, from the expatriate enclaves and landed houses of Holland Village and Sixth Avenue, to the scenic stretch of Pasir Panjang and Jurong. While listed as an outer island, Sentosa is also part of this area, making the West the best area for family attractions. With the National University of Singapore campus and the ever-growing Science Park nearby, the West is also a centre of learning in Singapore.

The Lowdown
Cafe culture, expensive landed properties and a lightly bohemian neighbourhood vibe in Holland Village.

Residential

From Holland Village to Sixth Avenue to Pasir Panjang, the mid-West is extremely popular with expatriates, and as such attracts more adventurous dining and cafe concepts. These areas feature more tree-lined streets of landed properties or two-storey terrace houses than elsewhere on the island. You'll find more alfresco dining, magazine stores, wine bars and organic food outlets here than in the rest of the island too. A generous mix of HDB apartments gives the area a nice mixed feel despite some of the land values.

The Good
Excellent cafes, restaurants and bars, and some interesting retail concepts.

Retail

Holland Village is the current centre of retail for the west, specialising in arts, crafts, clothing and electronics. The next largest malls are towards Queensway, where the hugely popular IKEA store lives, and then further out to Jurong. The new VivoCity (p.363) opposite Sentosa, which opened near the end of 2006, is now the largest mall in Singapore and has boosted shopping in the West considerably.

The Bad
Somewhat pretentious in corners. Excessive construction recently.

Places of Interest

While National University of Singapore isn't the world's prettiest university, it does have good sports facilities and three small art museums on campus that are well worth exploring. West Coast Park next to Pasir Panjang Wharf is great for space to throw a frisbee in, while the isolated houses of Portsdown and Woking Road are a fascinating look at life in the 1930s. Right next to the railway line, they were army barracks back in the days of hushed neighbourhoods surrounded by trees and colourful parrots. As the Science Park spreads, this lovely area isn't likely to be here forever.

The Must Dos
Eat chilli crab by the sea. Rollerblade in West Coast Park.

Reflections at Bukit Chandu in Pasir Panjang (6375 2519) is worth a visit if you're interested in military history. It is built in memory of the 1,400 soldiers of the Malay regiment who fought 13,000 Japanese soldiers in World War II. Out in the Choa Chu Kang area are a number of farms where you can often spend a pleasant morning strolling around and maybe buy an ornamental fish, an exotic bird, hydroponic veggies, orchids or even a couple of frogs. Do make time to visit Jurong BirdPark, it's truly beautiful (see p.230) and Mount Faber Park (see p.215) will also give you a great panoramic of the island, as well as a great spot to dine and have a few drinks.

For something a little different, although not for the squeamish, take a visit to Haw Par Villa, an Asian mythology theme park (see p.228). For some history and some cutting edge technology and fun, head to teh Singapore Discovery Centre (see p.212) or the Singapore Science Centre (see p.212).

Holland Village

Recent years have seen Holland Village veer from artsy and alternative to more trendy and family-oriented, partly because its inhabitants have aged, and partly because the area is becoming gentrified. You'll find some of the nicest spots for alfresco dining outside of the beaches tucked in behind three rows of shophouses in the cluster of Lorong Mambong's restaurants and bars to one side, and Jalan Merah Saga's to the other. The Holland Village Shopping Centre (p.338) specialises in arts and crafts from around the region, and is one of the most easy-going shopping experiences in Singapore.

The beauty of Holland Village though lies in its neighbourhood feel, thanks to the mixture of housing here, from the HDB apartments all around, to the NUS student accommodation to the high-end houses nearby. A measure that came into place several years ago to block the streets from cars at night has made the area even more popular for evening socialising - and Wala Wala (p.432) would have to be one of Singapore's most successful bars.

Map 1 ◀ # Outer Islands: Sun and Sand

Since its extensive land reclamation began, Singapore has lost more than 20 of its outer islands, although over 50 remain. Of these, Pulau Ubin (Pulau is Malay for island) is the only one that is really still inhabited, with a few hundred villagers living there. Singapore's other outer islands, such as Saint John's Island and Kusu Island are genuinely remote, with little infrastructure to speak of. Many of these are popular with snorkellers and picnickers, and ferries link you to all the islands.

The Lowdown ◀

An escape to an outer island at the weekend is a great way to refresh your point of view.

Residential

The outer islands of Singapore are comparatively untouched by the modern lifestyles of Singapore mainland and therefore have very little in the way of residential property. Pulau Ubin, which can be reached by ferry from the Changi Village jetty, has a small community of villagers living in wooden houses but public pressure is keeping the island from being developed further in the near future. The only accommodation option for visitors is the upmarket Marina Country Club Ubin Resort.

The Good

Beaches, nature, fresh breezes – a good way to remind yourself that you do live in the tropics after all, especially after a hard week in the office.

Retail

This is where you come to get away from it all, remember?

Kusu Island

South of Singapore, is Kusu Island (map 1-D4). The name means Tortoise Island and legend has it that a giant turtle saved a Malay and Chinese sailor here by turning itself into a rock. The island is also a turtle sanctuary. From two tiny outcrops on a reef, the island has been enlarged and transformed into an island holiday resort of 85,000 square metres (but does not offer accommodation). The island has a popular Chinese temple, Da Bo Gong, and its hilltop hosts three Malay kramats, or shrines of saints dating from the 19th century. Many devotees climb the 152 steps leading to the kramats to pray and Taoists make an annual pilgrimage to the Tua Pekong Temple here during the ninth lunar month. A daily ferry

The Bad

Access can be infrequent and safety is not as assured as in the heart of Singapore. The islands can get crowded on weekends and, this close to the shipping lanes, some pollution is to be expected, although it's not always the case.

The Must Dos

Sunbathe, hike, swim and unwind.

service leaves the Sentosa Ferry Terminal for Kusu Island and the trip takes about 30 minutes. See www.nparks.gov.sg for more details or call 1800 471 7300.

Pulau Ubin

The island of Pulau Ubin (map 8-C2) to date has been preserved from urban development and concrete buildings. For visitors, its wooden villages and jetties and relaxed villagers and pristine nature recall the original kampong lives of the first Singaporeans. You can still find a traditional village atmosphere here, along with granite quarries, coconut and rubber plantations, mangrove swamps, fish and prawn farms, and traditional fishing done with 'kelongs' or nets. Ubin is popular for walking, camping and cycling, with bikes available for hire at the village.

201

Tanjung Chek Jawa, a virtually unspoilt reef around 5,000 years old, is a big attraction. A 10 minute bumboat ride takes visitors from Changi Village jetty to Pulau Ubin at an affordable cost. Marina Country Club Ubin Resort is the main accommodation option for visitors (www.marinacountryclub.com.sg/ubinresort.html) and provides a variety of activities, whether you want to relax and unwind or be active and adventurous. See www.npark.gov.sg or call 18004717300 for more details.

Saint John's Island

Lying 6.5km to the south of the main island of Singapore, off the Straits of Singapore, Saint John's Island (map 1-C4) was the site of Raffles' anchorage before meeting the Malay chief of Singapore in 1819. Reputedly haunted, it used to be a quarantine station for leprosy and cholera patients, political dissidents and heroin addicts. The remains of their housing litter the central island and there's still a detention centre for illegal immigrants here, as well as the Marine Aquaculture Centre.

In 1975 though, the 39 hectare island was transformed into a tranquil getaway with lagoons, beaches, picnic grounds, trekking routes and soccer fields. With a host of flora and fauna, it's popular for weekend visits.

While the island houses the Tropical Marine Science Institute, the Agri-Food & Veterinary Authority of Singapore's Marine Aquaculture Centre, as well as a detention centre for illegal immigrants, visitors will probably prefer to stay in the Holiday Bungalow. This accommodates up to 10 people and has a kitchen, while the dormitories at the Holiday Camps take up to 60 people. You will need to arrange accommodation through the Sentosa Development Corporation (6275 0388, www.sentosa.com.sg). A daily ferry service leaves the Sentosa Ferry Terminal for the 45 minute trip to St. John's Island.

Sisters Islands

The Sisters Islands lie to the south, off the Straits of Singapore. Big Sister's Island, also known as Pulau Subar Laut, is about 39,000 square metres in area, while Little Sister's Island, or Pulau Subar Darat, is roughly 17,000 square metres. The two are separated by a narrow channel that can be very dangerous to swimmers and divers. The Sisters Islands' beaches and warm blue waters make snorkelling, picnicking and camping a favourite activity here, and the islands have some of Singapore's richest reefs with sealife including giant clams, seahorses and octopus. Big Sister's Island is also home to long-tailed macaques. The Southern Islands are soon to be developed and will ultimately feature high-end entertainment options, exclusive restaurants, resorts, spas and conference facilities.

Other islands around Singapore to look up and possibly explore include Bukum, Hantu, Punggol Barat, Seletar, Semakau and Tekong (all preceded by the word 'Pulau').

Mini Map
This is the perfect companion for trips around Singapore – small enough for your pocket but big enough to expand your horizons. Keep the Mini Map handy and you'll be navigating your way the city around like a local in no time.

Art Galleries

Other options **Art** p.325, **Art & Craft Supplies** p.326

Singapore's fine arts scene is in its infancy, but it is certainly a well-funded childhood. Investment in arts venues like the Esplanade, coupled with the superb restoration and conversion of some heritage buildings into arts spaces, in particular the Singapore Art Museum, means Singapore now has a generous supply of excellent small and mid-sized galleries. Funded by an urbanised society keen to invest in new Asian art, a number of smaller galleries showcase regional artists, and while the prices are not quite as good as in Vietnam or Myanmar, the quality is often excellent. There are also more regional artists now based in Singapore who make a living from their art.

Arts House

As well as those listed below, you can find more information about private galleries such as the Goethe Institute Art Gallery and Opera Gallery on Orchard Road (p.325), the Soo Bin Art Gallery and Gajah Gallery (p.325) in the Shopping section.

1 Old Parliament Lane
Colonial District
🚇 **Raffles Place**
Map 17-C2

The Arts House

6332 6900 | www.theartshouse.com.sg

Singapore's oldest government building was reopened in 2004 as a superb riverside venue for art exhibits, plays, movie screenings and corporate events, and it's well worth regular visits. As a public space, people now get to hold meetings in the original House of Parliament, sitting in very seats in which the nation's first prime minister Lee Kuan Yew and his ministers sat. Originally a private mansion, the building became the island's first courthouse, then the Parliament House. Opening hours are from 10:00 to 20:00 Mondays to Fridays, 11:00 to 20:00 on Saturdays. It's closed on Sundays unless there's a special event on, in which case the box office opens 90 minutes before the show begins. The current Parliament House is just next door – and for those who are interested, sessions are open to the public (just take your passport or other identification along).

71 Bras Basah Rd
Colonial District
🚇 **Dhoby Ghaut**
Map 17-C1

Singapore Art Museum

6332 3222 | www.nhb.gov.sg/SAM

The former Catholic boys' school, St Joseph's Institution, is now the site of the inspiring Singapore Art Museum, thanks to reconstruction work overseen by local architect Wong Hooe Wai. SAM is a good place to spend a couple of hours, with its attractive white-washed walls, ample natural light, and hushed ambience. It has 13 galleries and resident works include those of Filipino artist Ramon Orlina and US artist Dale Chihuly. Exhibits range from Chinese calligraphy to contemporary art and in recent years their travelling exhibitions have included some major international collections. The museum also has a cafe and gelataria on its premises. Entrance fees are $3 per adult, $1.50 per child and SAM is open from 12:00 to 18:00 on Mondays, from 09:00 to 21:00 on Fridays and from 09:00 to 18:00 on other days.

41 Robertson Quay
Riverside
🚇 **Clarke Quay**
Map 17-B1

Singapore Tyler Print Institute

6336 3663 | www.stpi.com.sg

Established by American printmaker Kenneth E Tyler, the gallery holds printmaking exhibitions four times a year. It also serves as a paper mill and education facility. Although Ken Tyler has returned to the States, his master printmakers remain and they collaborate with artists from around the world to make unique, limited edition prints, some of which are for sale here. The institute is open from 13:00 to 17:00 on Sunday and Monday and from 09:30 to 18:00 from Tuesday to Saturday.

203

Churches & Cathedrals

60 Hill St
Colonial District
🔊 **City Hall**
Map 17-C1

Armenian Church of St Gregory the Illuminator
6334 0141
Singapore's first permanent place of worship was built in 1835 in neo-classical style by George Coleman. The grounds include graves of several Sarkies (although not those of the two Sarkies brothers who opened Raffles Hotel), and Agnes Joaquim, the Armenian who discovered Singapore's national flower, named Vanda Miss Joaquim. The church is open on Mondays to Fridays from 9:00 to 17:00 and from 09:00 to 12:00 on Saturdays.

4 Queen St
Colonial District
🔊 **City Hall**
Map 17-C1

Cathedral of the Good Shepherd
6337 9879 | *www.veritas.org.sg*
Singapore's oldest Catholic building, built between 1843 and 1847, was administered by French missionary Jean-Marie Beurel. Father Beurel also established St Joseph's Institution, now the Singapore Art Museum. A quick visit is interesting, because while the condition of the building is fading, it retains a more original feel than many of Singapore's restored buildings. Its Latin cross form includes doric columns and a crafted timber ceiling and its grounds include the Archbishop's bungalow.

Coleman Street
Colonial District
🔊 **City Hall**
Map 17-D1

St Andrew's Cathedral
6337 6104 | *www.livingstreams.org.sg/sac*
The elegant St Andrews is one of the most beautiful churches in Singapore. It is in fact the third church to have been built on this site. The first was built between 1835 and 1837 but two lightning strikes destroyed it and it was finally demolished in 1852. Work on the present neo-Gothic cathedral was begun by lieutenant colonel Ronald MacPherson in 1856 using convict labour from India, and completed in 1861. While it is an Anglican church, it was named after the patron saint of Scotland, as Scottish merchants contributed to its construction. The Visitors Centre has artefacts, memorials to soldiers, pictures and a video of its history. It is open daily and guided tours available on request.

Mosques

218 South Bridge Rd
Chinatown
🔊 **Chinatown**
Map 17-C2

Jamae Chulia Mosque
www.visitsingapore.com
Jamae Chulia is one of three Islamic heritage buildings in Chinatown that were erected by early immigrants, Tamil Muslims who were mostly traders and money changers. The other two are Al-Abrar Mosque and Nagore Durgha on Telok Ayer Street. The entrance gate to Jamae Chulia, which dates to 1826, is distinctively South Indian, while the two prayer halls and the shrine are built in neo-classical style. During Hari Raya Haji, which is the Festival of Sacrifice held in the last month of the Islamic lunar calendar, the mosque sacrifices goats and sheep in remembrance of Prophet Abraham and distributes the meat to the poor. The mosque was made a national monument in 1974.

3 Muscat St
Arab Street &
Kampong Glam
🔊 **Bugis**
Map 14-D4

Sultan Mosque
6293 4405
When Singapore was ceded to the British in 1819, part of the agreement with the island's chief, Temenggong Abdul Rahman, and its sultan, Hussain Shah of Johore, was the use of Kampong Glam for their residences. With a grant from Raffles and the East India Company, Singapore's most important, and biggest, mosque was built in the area in 1825. A century later, the old mosque was replaced by the larger one that you see today. Designed by an Irish architect from the company that designed Raffles Hotel, it incorporated Turkish, Persian and Moorish elements. A standout feature is the large golden dome that has

become a Kampong Glam focal point. The mosque, also known as the Masjid Sultan, has a prayer hall that accommodates 5,000 people, mosaic tiled walls with inscriptions from the Quran and a rug donated by a Saudi prince. While visitors may enter, they should only do so if they are modestly dressed, and if there isn't a prayer session taking place. Taking photographs of people in prayer is inappropriate.

Temples

15 Tank Rd
River Valley Road
Dhoby Ghaut
Map 17-C1

Chettiar Temple

6737 9393

This Shaivite Hindu temple was built in 1984 to replace the one built by Indian chettiars, or money lenders. It is dedicated to the six-headed Lord Subramaniam, and is officially known as the Sri Thandayuthapani Temple. This temple is at its most colourful and exciting during the annual Thaipusam festival (around January and February), as the memorable procession ends up here. Open from 08:00 to 12:00 and from 17:30 to 20:30.

88 Bright Hill Rd
Bishan
Map 7-A3

Kong Meng San Phor Kark See Temple

6453 4046 | www.kmspks.org

Venerable Zhuan Dao began to build this monastery in 1921 for the many monks who arrived in Singapore and didn't have any lodging. Built along the lines of a traditional Chinese forest monastery, it was the first of its kind in Singapore and it remains the largest Buddhist temple here.

The monastery's main function is as a crematorium and you're likely to witness a funeral ceremony here any day of the week. The remains of the dead are placed in an urn which is housed in a niche in the columbarium. There are also various halls to wander through in which you'll find Buddha in different guises. The Pagoda of 10,000 Buddhas has 9,999 images of Buddha lining the inside of its golden, cone-shaped stupa, with the final Buddha being the giant one inside the pagoda. Call in advance to enquire about a guided tour.

371 Race Course Rd
Little India
Farrer Park
Map 14-D3

Leong San See Temple

6298 9371

A quiet and peaceful Taoist temple, its name translates from Cantonese as Dragon Mountain Temple. Beautifully decorated, it is dedicated to the Goddess of Mercy, Kuan Yin. At the back of the temple there are hundreds of wooden tablets bearing the names and photographs of the deceased, and many parents bring their children here to pray for them before an image of Confucius.

366 Race Course Rd
Little India
Farrer Park
Map 14-D3

Sakaya Muni Buddha Gaya Temple

6294 0714

Popularly known as the Temple of 1,000 Lights, this Buddhist temple across the road from the Leong San See Temple, is dominated by a 15 metre-high Buddha. He sits alongside Kuan Yin, the Chinese goddess of mercy, as well as Hindu deities Brahma and Ganesh. The entrance is guarded by yellow tigers, symbols of vitality and protection.

Religious Sites

Singapore's cultural and religious roots remain strong despite the modern environment around them. Buddhist and Hindu temples, Islamic mosques and Christian churches sit almost side by side, and each welcomes guests, providing certain common courtesies are observed. You need to keep noise down and refrain from photographing worshippers. Before entering a Hindu temple you need to remove your shoes and for mosques you need to cover bare skin and women shouldn't enter when menstruating. Some interesting temples include the Sri Senpaga Vinayagar Temple on 18 Ceylon Road. Built in the mid-19th century and renovated in 2003, it features 32 forms of Lord Vinayagar, and is the only such Vinyagar Temple in the world. There are three fascinating temples along Race Course Road - Beo San Hood Chor, Leong San See (below) and the Temple of 1,000 Lights. The Kong Meng San Phor Kark See Temple (left) in Bishan is the country's largest temple complex.

205

Inside the temple is a two-metre long footprint made of mother-of-pearl and said to be a replica of a huge footprint on Adam's Peak in Sri Lanka (which Muslims believe to be that of Adam, Hindus that of the god Siva and Christians that of St Thomas). And for 50 cents you can spin the wheel of fortune and have your fortune told.

244 South Bridge Rd
Chinatown
🚇 *Chinatown*
Map 17-C3

Sri Mariamman Temple
6223 4064

One of the inspiring contrasts of Singapore is the way temples and mosques sit side by side. The island's oldest Hindu place of worship stands happily right in the heart of Chinatown, and is still much in use today. While you will find depictions of Brahma, Vishnu and Shiva here, the temple is dedicated to Sri Mariamman, a goddess known for her powers to cure epidemic disease. From the exterior you'll notice the Gopuram, or entrance gateway, a fascinating tower covered with striking pastel coloured statues of over 70 Hindu deities. The walls of the temple compound are topped with figures of sacred cows. Do remove your shoes before entering and hand over your 'tourist tax' to the caretaker at the door. Your entry will cost $3 for the use of a camera or $6 for a video camera. Tourists are asked not to enter the main worship area, but you can still marvel at the elaborate paint work of Hindu deities and traditional Indian floral designs on the ceiling of the main shrine. If you visit the temple during the annual Thimithi fire walking festival, usually in October or November, you'll witness Hindu devotees walking barefoot on hot coals as a form of penance or thanksgiving. Open daily from 07:00 to 12:30 and 18:00 to 20:30.

Kong Meng San Phor Kark See Tem

397 Serangoon Rd
Little India
🚇 *Farrer Park*
Map 14-D3

Sri Srinivasa Perumal Temple
6298 5771

One of the most important Indian temples in Singapore, Sri Srinivasa Perumal is the starting point for the annual walk to the Chettiar Hindu Temple during the Thaipusam Festival (see Annual Festivals, p.60). Built in 1855, it was originally a simple structure with a prayer hall and pond. Its impressive six-tier tower or gopuram was built in 1966. Major reconstruction of the temple, which is dedicated to Vishnu, took place in the 1990s.

141 Serangoon Rd
Little India
🚇 *Little India*
Map 14-C4

Sri Veeramakaliamman Temple
6293 4634

The goddess Kali, Lord Shiva's bloodthirsty consort who is portrayed as having many arms and hands, has always been popular in Bengal. This temple, built in 1855 by Bengali labourers, is dedicated to her. The temple doors are covered with little bells and devotees ask God to grant their requests by ringing the bells before entering. The temple's ceiling is rimmed with statues of Hindu gods, while the main shrine houses a black statue of Kali next to Ganesh and Murugan.

158 Telok Ayer St
Chinatown
🚇 *Chinatown*
Map 17-C2

Thian Hock Keng Temple
6423 4616

In the early 1800s crossing the South China Sea to arrive in Singapore was a feat in itself. Thian Hock Keng, the oldest Chinese temple in Singapore was built to allow early Hokkien migrants to thank the gods for delivering them safely and its name ('Temple of Heavenly Happiness') probably aptly describes the relief of being on dry land again. Initially built in 1819 and rebuilt in 1839, the temple was built in southern Chinese style, with a grand entrance featuring a high step in front. Guarding the doors are tigers, lions and door gods. The temple underwent a major renovation in 2000. Its most attractive feature, a calligraphic panel from the Emperor of China, Guang Xu of the Qing Dynasty, dates to 1907.

Heritage Sites – City

Other options **Art** p.325, **Museums – City** p.210, **Mosques** p.204

The majority of Singapore's inner-city attractions listed in this chapter are heritage sites, although most are restored and modernised versions of the original version and many of these are now used for quite different contemporary purposes. Singapore's Preservation of Monuments Board (PMB) has gazetted 58 buildings and structures in Singapore as national monuments. Deemed to be of special historic, traditional, archaeological, architectural or artistic value, these cannot be demolished, removed, altered or renovated or have any addition made without the permission of the PMB.

Most of the city's heritage sites are within three areas – the colonial or civic district, beside the Singapore River and waterfront, and in Fort Canning Park. While there are archaeological remains in a number of museums, particularly from the area around Fort Canning, there are no active sites.

As well as the sites listed below, see also Chijmes (see p.185), Clarke Quay (see p.198), Fort Canning (see Fort Canning Park p.215) and The Padang (see p.216).

Colonial District
🚇 *Bugis*
Map 14-D4

Bugis Street

Bugis Street is of more interest for its colourful past than its present day shopping and food outlets. In the mid 1960s this was the centre of much of the 'action' for western tourists. The area, with its transsexuals and transvestites, outdoor bars and food centres, was nicknamed 'Boogie Street' – and was once the subject of a Hong Kong movie. Little of this remains though, and apart from a night market and the large Bugis Junction mall (which includes some original facades and stairwells in its design), it's now a fairly soulless spot.

Highlights nearby include the fabulously gothic-looking Park View building, whose imposing exterior and lavish lobby wouldn't look out of place in Gotham City, or 1930s Manhattan. The nearby National Library was shifted to its present location in 2005. Its 58,000 square metres of floorspace house over 634,000 items, an attractive space-age dome and the Lee Kong Chian Reference Library with its Singapore and south-east Asian collections.

Pagoda Street
Chinatown
🚇 *Chinatown*
Map 17-C2

Chinatown Heritage Centre

6325 2878 | *www.chinatownheritage.com.sg*

An air-conditioned escape from the Chinatown heat, the Chinatown Heritage Centre is a museum within three restored shophouses. A short walk from the MRT station at Pagoda Street, the museum sits among stores selling sweets, barbequed meat and cheap souvenirs. A wander through its three storeys brings you up close with recreated scenes from early Chinatown: a teahouse, slaughtered and skinned snakes for sale in the wet market, a prostitute's boudoir, a Chinese funeral, and a chance to step into the rough communal bathrooms once typical of the living quarters inhabited by Chinese immigrants. You'll learn about Chinese society in the early days of Singapore, and the various professions these immigrants were involved in from the recorded aural and video accounts of local people. Open from 09:00 to 20:00 from Mondays to Thursdays, and from 9:00 to 21:00 on Fridays to Sundays. Entry costs $8.80 for adults, $5.30 for children.

207

Orchard
🚇 *Somerset*
Map 14-B4

Emerald Hill

www.landseer.com.sg/conservation

The only area of original shophouse architecture left in Orchard, the narrow streets around Emerald Hill and Peranakan Place offer a charming escape from the noise and traffic. Just off Orchard Road is a stretch of two-storey bars with indoor and outdoor seating, all popular with expats. Stroll beyond these and you'll find an attractive terrace of Peranakan-style shophouses dating from the 1920s. The area includes Cuppage Road, named after William Cuppage who owned the nutmeg estate originally on the site. This small area of highly sought-after shophouse residences reflects a blend of Chinese-influenced architecture and art deco style.

33 Allanbrooke Rd
🚇 *HarbourFront*
Sentosa
Map 19-A1

Fort Siloso

6275 0388 | *www.fortsiloso.com*

The British Government, well aware of Singapore's commercial and strategic value in its colonial empire, decided to built a number of coastal gun batteries in the 1880s. One of these was Fort Siloso which was built on the island then known as Pulau Blakang Mati (which means 'island behind which lies death' in Malay). Unfortunately, when it came to testing Singapore's defences against the Japanese in WWII, the gun emplacements meant the guns were all facing the wrong way.

Nevertheless, a tour of the fort today is worthwhile, providing you with quite an entertaining glimpse of the past (although serious historians may not entirely approve). You can work your way through the tunnels and networks, look at interactive displays and even try out an obstacle course. The fort is open from 09:00 to 18:30 daily and entry costs $5 for adults, $3 for kids.

1 Fullerton Square
Chinatown
🚇 *Raffles Place*
Map 17-D2

The Fullerton Singapore

6733 8388 | *www.fullertonhotel.com*

Named after Robert Fullerton, the first governor of the Straits Settlements, the Fullerton used to be the General Post Office. When it was built in 1928, it was the largest building in Singapore and cost over $4 million. The Post Office occupied three floors, and its counter, at 100m, was reputed to be the longest in the world at that time. The revolving beacon was added to the roof in 1958 and its beams could be seen up to 29 kilometres away. This lighthouse is now an Italian restaurant. The General Post Office moved in 1996, and after a $340 million restoration the Fullerton opened in 2000 as a landmark hotel. While its exterior is very 'old Asia', its interior of marble and shining surfaces is very much new Asia of the modern Shanghai kind. Have a drink in the deluxe Post Bar, then take the underpass to the One Fullerton waterside complex.

22 Scotts Rd
Orchard
🚇 *Orchard*
Map 14-A4

Goodwood Park Hotel

6737 7411 | *www.goodwoodparkhotel.com*

Tucked into a hillside on Scotts Road, Goodwood Park was designed by J Bidwell, the architect most famously known for Raffles Hotel. Originally known as the Teutonia Club, a club for German expatriates, its construction and landscaping began in 1900. Its tower is now a national monument. Not nearly as grand as the restored Raffles complex, Goodwood nonetheless gives you a feel for the original colonial hotel.

The Istana

Orchard Rd
Orchard
🚇 **Dhoby Ghaut**
Map 14-C4

6737 5522 | *www.istana.gov.sg*

The President of Singapore's official residence, this national monument is open to the public on selected public holidays. The neoclassical building was completed 1869 and, originally named Government House, was the official residence of Singapore's colonial rulers. The architecture's Victorian and Roman influences are complemented by Gothic, Malay and Chinese features. Lush grounds of over 100 acres are cared for by the Singapore Botanic Gardens and include several rare species of plants and an exclusive nine-hole golf course. A visit here is a chance to step briefly back in time to the colonial days.

Johore Battery

Cosford Rd
Changi
🚇 **Tanah Merah**
Map 8-D4

6546 9897 | *www.visitsingapore.com*

During WWII the British believed, given the strength of the Japanese navy, that any attack on Singapore would come from the sea. They built fortifications all around the south, west and east coasts of the island, the pride of which was the Johor Battery. Built in 1939 in the then remote area, the site consists of a labyrinth of tunnels used to store ammunition. The battery comprised three 15 inch guns, the largest calibre weapons the British had. Johor Battery was the largest outside of Britain during WWII, and was kept a secret until it was rediscovered in 1991.

Katong Antique House

208 East Coast Rd
East Coast
Map 15-D4

6345 1220

Katong Antique House, which is linked to the local Peranakan heritage association, has a fascinating collection of goodies ranging from antiques and traditional ceramics, to beaded slippers and wedding costumes. And if you call in advance you can arrange for a Peranakan tea or a meal to be served to you. Open from 11:00 to 18:00.

Lau Pa Sat

Boon Tat St
CBD
🚇 **Raffles Place**
Map 17-C3

www.visitsingapore.com

The Telok Ayer Market, better known as Lau Pa Sat ('old market' or, in Malay, 'iron market') is a must-visit for its atmosphere, wafting aromas and the wide variety of hawker food, particularly the satay sticks. The attractive octagonal cast iron structure was made in Glasgow and reassembled in Singapore in 1894. The historic building housed Singapore's second central market, and originally extended over the sea, selling a lot of fish. As land reclamation took place, it became a general market until the 1970s, when the area around it began to change into a commercial district. In 1986, it became a hawker centre. It offers entry from different sides, attractive surroundings and constant ventilation. See also Hawkers Centres on p.427 in the Going Out chapter.

Little India Arcade

Campbell Lane
Little India
🚇 **Little India**
Map 14-C4

www.visitsingapore.com

On Campbell Lane you'll find the Little India Arcade, a narrow pathway through a cluster of restored shophouses, each of which is filled to the brim with Indian clothing, accessories and incense. There's also a rather good Indian sweet shop near the Serangoon Road entrance. The Indian Cultural Corner within the Arcade, which will give you a bit of an introduction to the area, is open from Mondays to Saturdays and admission is free.

Malay Heritage Centre

85 Sultan Gate
Colonial District
🚇 **Bugis**
Map 14-E4

6391 0450 | *www.malayheritage.org.sg*

Once the Istana Kampong Glam, this former palace was built between 1836 and 1843 for Ali Iskander Shah, the last Sultan of Singapore. The family stayed on in it until 1999,

209

after which it was renovated and reopened in 2004 as the Malay Heritage Centre. While there's little in the museum, you will find a replica kampong house upstairs, an example of the dwellings the first Singaporeans lived in, as well as daily performances of Malay dance and music. Open from Tuesdays to Sundays from 13:00 to 18:00 and from 10:00 to 18:00 on Mondays. Fees vary from free entry to the compound, to $8 for adults and $4 for children to attend a cultural show.

Beach Rd ◀
Colonial District
🚇 *City Hall*
Map 17-D1

Raffles Hotel

***6337 1886** | www.raffleshotel.com*

Arriving at the half-circle driveway at Raffles Hotel still feels like an occasion, as the finely dressed and turbaned bellman – something of a celebrity in Singapore – opens your door. Especially when the frangipani trees are in bloom, the landmark Raffles facade remains one of the most attractive and evocative sites in the island-state. Opened originally as a 10 room bungalow in 1887 by the Sarkies brothers, immigrants from Armenia, Raffles soon became a home away from home for far-flung travellers, its ambience documented in the works of writers like Joseph Conrad and Somerset Maugham.

From 1970 though, Raffles began to look distinctly forlorn. It was given a new lease of life when the property was declared a national monument in 1987. An extensive $160 million restoration project was begun and the long-awaited reopening took place in 1991. Raffles is once again a must do for travellers, even if all you do is have a Singapore Sling in the relocated Long Bar or a civilised high tea in the Tiffin Room.

What's impressive about the new-look Raffles Complex is the amount of public space – and the fact that it's not at the expense of the sort of exclusivity that guests will pay several hundred dollars a night for. The secret lies in the fact that the three-storey complex and the addition added during the renovation now also function as a national monument. Its small but fascinating Hotel Museum (free of charge, open daily from 10:00 to 19:00), Bar and Billiard Room (where Singapore's last tiger was shot), and Jubilee Hall are all open to the public, as are 70 shops and restaurants within the complex (a dress code does apply – so no shorts and sandals). The public can also enjoy the well-groomed courtyards and gardens, but the area beyond the lobby is reserved for hotel guests. As an island in the storm of commercial Singapore, Raffles is well worth a visit – better still if you can splash out for an overnight stay.

> ### Telling Tales
>
> For some famous guests, the genteel ambience of the Raffles Hotel wasn't the only attraction. It was said that Somerset Maugham used to sit in the lobby, eavesdropping on guests' conversations to get some new scoop for his next story or a morsel of inspiration for his latest novel.

Heritage Sites – Out of City

Other options **Tours & Sightseeing** p.217, **Museums – Out of City** p.213

Outside the city, the majority of heritage sites fall into three categories. Religious sites include the historic Kong Meng San Phor Kark See Monastery (p.20) and the Siong Lim Temple in Toa Payoh. War-related sites include Kranji War Memorial, Changi Chapel and Museum (p.213) close to where the allied prisoners of war were held captive during the Japanese Occupation, Fort Siloso (p.208) and the Johor Battery (p.209). Another war-related site from an earlier time is the Sun Yat Sen Nanyang Memorial Hall in Balestier. Built between 1900 and 1902 it was used as the headquarters for anti-Manchurian activities outside China. Finally, the most prominent of the country's natural heritage sites is the Bukit Timah Nature Reserve (p.229). A tract of primary rainforest that lies a short distance from the city, it's reputed to host more plant species than you'll find in North America.

Museums – City

Other options **Mosques** p.204, **Heritage Sites – City** p.207, **Art** p.325

Good museums are a relatively recent phenomenon here, but the development of new interactive elements is adding depth to the telling of Singapore's story, which does represent an extraordinary cross-stitching of cultural influences. Unfortunately, many of Singapore's museums do lean rather too heavily on their themes, in particular the importance of racial harmony, sometimes lending the impression that you are getting a good dose of politics with your history. Singapore's stand-out museum is the Asian Civilisations Museum, which traces the roots of Singapore's various Asian cultures in a restored colonial building. The bringing together of these cultural strands is Singapore's

Asian Civilisations Museum

'unique selling proposition', after all. The new-look National Museum of Singapore (previously the Singapore History Museum), which re-opened in late 2006, has redefined the direction for Singapore's museums, while the new Peranakan Museum in the Colonial District promises to be worth watching too. Singapore Art Museum showcases regional artists and hosts regular travelling shows. In a nation that has been a republic only for the last 40 years, history too is a work in progress.

Asian Civilisations Museum

1 Empress Place
Riverside
🚇 ***Raffles Place***
Map 17-C1

6332 7798 | *www.nhb.gov.sg/ACM*

The Asian Civilisations Museum is the pride of Singapore's museum scene and pleasantly devoid of wax figures. Located in the Empress Place Building, a colonial government office built in 1865 and named in honour of Queen Victoria, its three floors house 10 themed galleries that cover the history, religions, cultures and arts in Asia. Behind some of the heaviest doors in this part of town, you'll learn about the spread of rice cultivation in the region and check out the 1,300 artefacts which include the head of an 18th century Burmese Buddha, Javanese shrines and processional palanquins, Islamic art, elaborate jewellery and textiles from the region.

Free tours are available in English, Japanese and Mandarin. Entry fees are $8 per adult, $4 per child and halfprice on Fridays. The Museum is open from 09:00 to 19:00 from Tuesday to Thursday, from 13:00 to 19:00 on Monday and from 09:00 to 21:00 from Friday to Sunday. Up until 2005, the museum had another branch at Armenian Street. This is closed for renovations and is scheduled to reopen in 2008 as the Peranakan Museum.

The Battle Box

51 Fort Canning Rise
Colonial District
🚇 ***Dhoby Ghaut***
Map 17-C1

6333 0510

An interesting stop-over for history buffs and World War II veterans, the Battle Box was the British Malaya Command's underground operations centre during the war. You may only enter as part of a guided tour but fortunately these are conducted every half hour. For 30-40 minutes you'll be taken nine metres underground to a bunker that was the Allied Forces' largest military operations complex in Singapore. You can listen to narratives on headphones and gaze through binocular-like lenses at hi-tech holographic displays of soldiers sending and receiving Morse code. Some of the restored rooms feature slightly creepy life-sized wax-figures of the British commanders who were responsible for Singapore's defences in the days before its surrender to the Japanese forces in 1942, and you'll find Japanese codes still scratched into the walls.

The tours through the 26 rooms and tunnels of the complex are conducted by a tour guide who certainly knows his stuff – he'll tell you how the British were defeated and hand out WWII trivia at the pace of a horse racing commentator. Tours cost $8 for adults, $5 for children and for an extra cost you can also arrange to have a meal at the nearby Legends Garden (formerly the British Army Far East Command Centre). The Battle Box is open from Tuesdays to Sundays, from 10:00 to 18:00 (the last tour is at 17:00).

40 Cable Car Rd
Sentosa
🚇 *HarbourFront*
Map 19-B2

Images of Singapore
6275 0426
An award-winning attraction, Images of Singapore begins with a short video of how the country's four main ethnic groups have contributed to one of the world's busiest trading ports. Then you walk through the exhibits filled with wax figures (some mechanised), documenting Singapore's history from its fishing village days, through WWII hardship to independence and on to the present. Visitors can learn about some of the festivals and customs of the Indians, Chinese, Eurasians and Peranakans. The museum has an overwhelming emphasis on inter-racial cohesiveness. Not a must, but an interesting break from the heat.

93 Stamford Rd
Colonial District
🚇 *Dhoby Ghaut*
Map 17-C1

National Museum of Singapore
6332 3659 | *www.nationalmuseum.sg*
Previously the Singapore History Museum, this cultural attraction reopened in December 2006. The new museum offers a more interactive look at Singapore's history, with light and sounds displays and the telling of Singapore's story from different cultural perspectives, perfect for hands-on kids and information-hungry adults alike. Alongside its exhibition programme, the museum also offers year-round activities and festivals, plus a 230 seat 'black box' auditorium, an education centre and seminar rooms.

45 Maxwell Rd
Chinatown
🚇 *Tanjong Pagar*
Map 17-C3

The Singapore City Gallery
6221 6666 | *www.ura.gov.sg/gallery*
Run by the Urban Redevelopment Authority, the City Gallery boasts a 100 square metre architectural model of the city, as well as two floors of exhibits detailing the country's transformation to the bustling and economic powerhouse it is today. Well worth an orientation visit when you first arrive in Singapore. Admission is free.

510 Upper Jurong Rd
West Coast
🚇 *Boon Lay*
Map 9-D1

Singapore Discovery Centre
6792 6188 | *www.sdc.com.sg*
There's some interesting cutting-edge fun and technology on display here, including interactive robots, a motion stimulator ride, a five-storey movie theatre that screens three-dimensional films and paintball using replica M4 Carbine guns. The Singapore Story also features some vivid historical reconstructions of the island state's history but the military's self-aggrandising version of events and selective interpretation of history and nationhood doesn't make for too many repeat visits. It has been renovated and at the time of writing it had reopened, and most of its exhibits were complete. Tickets cost $9 for adults, $7 for children, and the centre is open from 09:00 to 19:00 from Tuesday to Sunday.

23B Coleman St
Colonial District
🚇 *City Hall*
Map 17-C1

Singapore Philatelic Museum
6337 3888 | *www.spm.org.sg*
Housed in the former Methodist Book Room Building and dating from around 1895, this may not have broad appeal but it is an interesting stop for those keen on stamp collecting. The museum has rare stamps, interactive displays and stamp designing activities for kids. Entry is $2 for adults, $1 for kids.

15 Science Centre Rd
Jurong East
🚇 *Jurong East*
Map 10-A1

Singapore Science Centre
6425 25 | *www.science.edu.sg*
Great for kids, the interactive learning at Singapore Science Centre offers special exhibits, such as the Lord of the Rings and Art of Star Wars, in addition to over 850 regular exhibits. It's easy to spend an entire day here, especially with things like The Millennium Stimulator, which takes you through the heart of an active volcano. Of course, it's a popular excursion spot for school groups too. Visitors can also catch both

Omnimax movies and Planetarium shows on a five-storey high screen that's set at 30° to the horizon. The centre is open from Tuesday to Sunday, from 09:00 to 19:00.

Museums – Out of City

Other options **Tours & Sightseeing** p.217, **Heritage Sites – Out of City** p.210

The Changi Chapel and Museum is the main museum out of the city limits, and it's also a heritage site. Other specialist museums reserved strictly for enthusiasts include the Republic of Singapore Air Force Museum at Payar Lebar Airbase; the Republic of Singapore Navy Museum at Sembawang Camp (bring your passport for entry) and the Singapore Mint Coin Gallery in Boon Lay.

1000 Upper Changi Rd North
Changi
🚇 *Expo*
Map 12-D1

Changi Chapel & Museum

6214 2451 | www.changimuseum.com
This evocative museum commemorates the Allied prisoners of war, and Singapore's experience of World War II through the eyes of different groups and races. The small but well-stocked museum features the remarkable Changi Murals, made by imprisoned women to secretively let the men know they were alive. There is also a replica of the original Changi Prison chapel here, as the original site is still used for mainstream prison activities.

Festivals

Singapore sinks a great deal of time and effort into its festivals. The core religious and cultural events bring iconic parts of the city into chaotic and colourful life. Festive 'light-ups' are held to mark the various events important to the different nationalities in Singapore's cultural mix.

In late October to November, the Hindu Festival of Lights or Deepavali is symbolised by the lighting of small lanterns. A visit to Little India now will give you the chance to enjoy the beautiful Deepavali Light-Up, as well as cultural performances, flowers, sweets and scents. Hari Raya Puasa or Hari Raya Aidilfitri (late October-December) is the first of two major religious dates celebrated by Muslims, this one to mark the end of a month of fasting, Ramadan. In the 44 days leading up to Hari Raya Puasa, Geylang Serai is a bustling market of lights and illuminated arches. One of Singapore's most popular times for visitors is at the end of the year. First the streets, particularly Orchard Road, come alive with the extravagant Christmas Light-Up. Then in January, in line with the lunar calendar, Chinatown becomes awash with red lanterns, the scent of incense and the ever-present buzz of shoppers preparing for their Chinese New Year feasting.

Other cultural events worth watching include Singapore's Chingay Parade in February, a home grown event that has evolved into a world class show. It started out in 1973 as a Chinese street parade to coincide with the Chinese New Year. Over the

years though, it's become a multicultural event that now takes place at night and incorporates stilt walkers, lion and dragon dances, floats and lighting and pyrotechnic displays. In September the Mid-Autumn Festival sees coloured lanterns being released into the night sky, making it glisten with distant lights. Thaipussam in February marks a deeply spiritual day of penance for Hindus: devotees walk the three kilometres between two famous temples in Singapore and male Hindus, as a sign of piety, practise self-mortification, after careful preparation through prayers and fasting. Friends and family cheer the devotees along the way, chanting prayers and singing songs.

Beaches

Other options **Beach Parks** p.214, **Outer Islands** p.201, **Swimming** p.297

Considering Singapore is the world's largest port for container traffic, you soon realise why it no longer has beaches of the same class as Malaysia's east coast or Thailand. Out to sea lies a carpark of sorts for container ships. This and the fact that Singapore continues to reclaim land means that its waters are often murky. Yet the Lion City does boast some beaches, and while swimming may not be at the top of the list, it has extensive watersports options.

Sentosa has by far the best beaches in Singapore, with imported sand and palm trees, and a good range of activities (see Sentosa's Beaches on p.196). The East Coast Sea Sports Club (map 12-B3) likewise is a good place to try out laser sailing or kayaking. Further east, Changi Beach (map 8-E3) is fine for a picnic or a stroll after your fish and chips – and has spectacular views of thunderstorms out to sea. Punggol Beach holds more historic significance, as it commands a view of Johore, and the site of a World War Two massacre in which 300 Singaporeans were killed by Japanese soldiers.

Beach Parks

Other options **Parks** p.214

Parks that combine the best of green spaces and a beach are a good place to make the most of a light coastal breeze. They offer a wide range of facilities, from rollerblading and cycling tracks to barbecue pits and seafood restaurants.

All along the
East Coast
🚇 *Paya Lebar*
Map 18-C1

East Coast Park

1800 471 7300 | *www.nparks.gov.sg*

Built on reclaimed land, the East Coast Park is one of Singapore's best and most enjoyed parks, with an 11 kilometre stretch of seafront where people swim, cycle, rollerblade, windsurf, sail and eat. Popular at weekends, there are several bird sanctuaries, a popular sea sports club where you can take laser class sailing lessons and hire windsurfers, and nice breezy bars, hawker centres and restaurants. You can rent bikes and rollerblades for the car-free asphalt track marked with biking lanes. It runs around the park's perimeter and is at least 20km long, so definitely a worthwhile workout. Along the way you'll find a waterpark; the Big Splash complex, and The Marine Cove Recreation Centre; an outdoor leisure complex offering tenpin bowling, squash and mini golf. In the evenings the East Coast Seafood Centre is a great place to enjoy fresh pepper crab alfresco.

Pasir Panjang
West Coast
Map 10-C3

West Coast Park

1800 471 7300 | *www.nparks.gov.sg*

The 50 hectare West Coast Park was earlier a victim of land reclamation, but has subsequently been redeveloped. It has a number of features and facilities, including an adventure playground, bicycle obstacle course, fitness corner, an exercise garden that offers a workout for the grey matter in the form of a chess garden, a large dog run, a bird sanctuary and even foot reflexology facilities. Those seeking the beachfront within the park should enter via the West Coast Ferry Road or off the West Coast Highway and head to the north western corner of this long and narrow park.

Parks

Other options **Beaches** p.214

Perhaps a legacy of his time spent at England's leafy university campuses, Lee Kuan Yew was the driving force behind Singapore's greening programme and the result is some wonderfully scenic parks. The National Parks Board manages 1,763 hectares of green and open spaces, including 44 regional parks and over 300 community parks and playgrounds. Their website (www.nparks.gov.sg) provides detailed information on which parks you can camp in overnight, opening hours and the activities you can take part in.

Bishan Park
Central Singapore
🚇 ***Bishan***
Map 7-B3

Bishan Park

1800 471 7300 | www.nparks.gov.sg
Situated in the central area of the island, north of city, this is one of the country's biggest parks at 52 hectares. With its lakes and bridges, colourful shrubs and lush greenery it's also one of the most popular. It has a cycling track, children's playground, lake and shaded lawn and it's often the venue for live music events. People enjoy fishing, walking and picnicking in the grounds here.

Fort Canning Park
Colonial District
🚇 ***Clarke Quay***
Map 17-C1

Fort Canning Park

6332 1200 | www.nparks.gov.sg
The only elevated park in the area, Fort Canning was once known as Bukit Larangan – the Forbidden Hill. Stamford Raffles built a thatch-roof residence at the top of this scenic hill in 1822, a building that later became the Government House. In 1860, this was replaced by Fort Canning, named after the first viceroy of India, Viscount Canning. For families and history and nature lovers, Fort Canning is an easy place to spend a pleasant afternoon. It features the Battle Box (see p.211), and the shrine to Sultan Iskandar Shah, the last ruler of the ancient kingdom of Singapura. You'll also find gothic gateways and gravestones from the old Christian cemetery embedded in the brick walls. Fort Canning's fragrant Spice Garden was built on the site of Raffles' former botanical garden – the area where an archaeological dig uncovered Javanese artefacts from the 14th Century Majapahit empire.

The Fort Canning Centre is home to the At-Sunrice Cooking academy and the park is the venue for periodic rock concerts such as the annual international world music festival, World of Music and Dance (WOMAD). Singapore Dance Theatre, Singapore's own ballet troupe, is based at Fort Canning, and holds its annual Ballet Under the Stars here. Outdoor movie screenings are another frequent event.

Off East Coast
Parkway
Marina Bay
🚇 ***Marina Bay***
Map 17-E2

Marina City Park

1800 471 7300 | www.nparks.gov.sg
Marina City Park is a 26.2 hectare park right at the bottom of the city, which means it's well-sited to offer good views of the sparkling skyline. Catch the MRT to Marina South. Set on reclaimed land, it has a two-tiered pond with a fountain that spouts water to a height of 18m. There are three large open spaces where major events can be held, and you can wander among sculptures ranging from the contemporary (Soaring Vision and Spirit of Youth) to the historical (Chinese Legendary Heroes). A Constellation Plaza helps to trace the constellations in the night skies, while the Sundial Plaza at the seafront facing the Promenade is meant for kids to learn how to tell time.

Opp Sentosa Island
Telok Blangah
www.nparks.gov.sg
🚇 ***HarbourFront***
Map 16-F3

Mount Faber Park

1800 471 7300 | www.nparks.gov.sg
Covered in secondary rainforest, Mount Faber is another of Singapore's fabulous green spaces. For 105 metre high panoramic views of the island – particularly good at night – you can visit the collection of restaurants and bars on Faber View, the hill opposite Sentosa Island. Recent redevelopments have seen a number of the bars become very stylish although the service is still rather lacking. Nevertheless, sitting on a breezy elevated hillside, overlooking 140 acres of forest, makes for a pleasant evening. The hill is also the starting point for the scenic cable car that serves Sentosa.

215

**St Andrew's Rd &
Connaught Drive**
Colonial District
📍 **City Hall**
Map 17-D1

The Padang
6736 6622
This patch of grass in the middle of Singapore now plays host to everything from the annual festive Chinggay Parade to Linkin Park concerts, but it has witnessed some memorable moments in Singapore's history. During World War Two, Japanese occupying soldiers herded the island's Europeans to the Padang, before marching them on foot to Changi Prison – half an hour away by car today. Post-independence, the Padang hosted the first ever National Day Parade, and is still used for this every few years.

Its use for more frivolous activities is still an important part of Singapore life: in the colonial days people would gather here to walk and swap gossip (at a corner of the park quickly named Scandal Point), and today it's still the place to watch those old colonial pursuits, football and rugby. The Singapore Cricket Club, which dates to 1852, is the oldest leisure and sports club in Singapore. Since it's members only, you'll need to befriend a member but it's really quite casual and friendly inside, with particularly good food and inexpensive beer.

Pasir Ris
📍 **Pasir Ris**
Map 8-B4

Pasir Ris Park
1800 471 7300 | *www.nparks.gov.sg*
Pasir Ris Park in the north-east spans 71 hectares, including six hectares of preserved mangroves. Boardwalks lead into the mangrove forests, where you can view mud crabs, mudskippers and, yes, mangrove trees. A three-storey high bird watching tower gives you a great vantage point for spotting the many bird species to be found in Singapore. The park shaves the beach, and has a number of facilities like playgrounds, a cycling track, barbecue pits and seafood restaurants.

1 Cluny Park Rd
Tanglin
Map 13-E4

Singapore Botanic Gardens
6471 7361 | *www.sbg.org.sg*
Founded in 1859, the Botanic Gardens' grounds were originally used as a testing area for cash crops. A few blocks from the top or western end of Orchard, they now make up a fine 52 hectare expanse of landscaped tropical gardens and established trees. The gardens boast a collection of over 3,000 species of orchids, a mini rainforest trail and a spice garden, making them a superb place to walk, jog, explore and picnic. With several lakes and a hillside amphitheatre, the gardens are the venue for many concerts, including the free Singapore Symphony Orchestra events. There are a number of restaurants within the grounds, including Au Jardin and Halia. The gardens also house the National Parks Board's headquarters.

The Istana

Botanic Gardens

Tours & Sightseeing

Other options **Weekend Break Hotels** p.234

Explore Singapore
Singapore Explorer –
love the name, but no
relation to this
Singapore Explorer! –
offers a couple of
variations on the usual
touristy themes such as
their trolley tours, the
bumboat and glass-top
boats, the Labrador
Secret Tunnels tour and
the Suntec Summit
Tour that offers you a
bird's eye view of
Singapore from the top
of a 45 storey tower in
Suntec City. Check out
www.singapore
explorer.com.sg.

Tourism is one of Singapore's key service industries and while it's largely due to the Singapore Tourism Board's efforts that this is so, the country also recognises the need to keep growing the sector. Where this is of interest to you as a resident and to your visitors, is the resulting range of activities and tours that awaits you.

Most of the popular tours of the city are offered by a number of tour operators, but there are options too numerous to mention here – you can go on tarot reading tours, nature walks, chocolate trails and just about whatever you fancy. Many of the tour operators will be more than happy to tell you all that they offer, or to tailor make a tour for you.

The Singapore Visitors Centres are excellent resources: they'll give you information, make bookings and sell you tickets, but most major hotels, travel agents and the operators we have listed here can help you with bookings too. STB also publishes The Official Guide & Map which lists individual operators and

Singapore Visitors Centres

The Singapore Visitors Centres are well-equipped to answer your tour queries and make bookings or find out where you can join up with a tour. There are a number of the centres around the island.

Name	Address	MRT Station
Changi Airport	Terminals 1 and 2	Changi Airport
Cruise Centre	1 Maritime Square	HarbourFront
Liang Court	177 River Valley Road	Clarke Quay
Orchard	Cnr Cairnhill and Orchard Road	Orchard

www.visitsingapore.com is also useful. Companies like City-Discovery.com (www.city-discovery.com/singapore) offer you a central online booking centre, which means you don't need to decide between the various operators, as they've done it for you. In general it's useful to try and book a tour two or three days in advance and you may be asked to pay a 50% deposit.

If you've lived in Singapore for a while but now have guests to entertain, treat yourself to joining them on the tours. Residents often forget that tourism applies to them too and you might find yourself discovering a different side to your new country of residence. If you think you're all out of ideas, this section will provide you with plenty of inspiration. When you do go out, remember to dress comfortably with good, 'sensible' shoes for any walking that may be done. Hat, sunglasses and sunblock will be essential, especially on any boat or open-top bus rides. And don't forget your camera.

Faber Tours
Among the guided
excursions that Faber
Tours offers are the Port
Discovery Tour (see
Boat Tours p.219) and
Traditionally Chinese, a
tour of Chinatown that
includes a trishaw ride
and information about
its history. If you
wanted guided tours of
WWII sites Faber has
Surrender Years of
Singapore and a
Singapore Battlefield
guided trips, and they
also cover Sentosa
Island and
its attractions.
Call 6377 9649
for more information.

City Sightseeing Tours

City in Transformation Tour

This covers the Financial District, Boat Quay, Chinese temples on Waterloo Street, a Hindu temple, a synagogue, a Catholic church and Arab Street. The three and a half hour tour costs $28 for adults and $14 for children. A number of tour operators offer this tour. See Tour Operators on p.224.

Round Island Tour

A full day tour that takes you to the outskirts of the city to places like the Haw Par Villa, Kranji War Memorial, Bright Hill Temple and Johore Battery. Singapore Visitors Centres and major hotels will be able to help you book a place. Pick-ups from your hotel are from 08:30 and tickets cost from $74 for adults and $37 for children under 10. For companies offering this tour, see Tour Operators on p.224.

Shop & Eat

Combine the twin obsessions of all who live in Singapore. This tour takes you through some of Chinatown's most famous shops and eateries. Find some brilliant buys, stock up on silk pyjamas and Chinese arts and crafts and sample a variety of delicacies and snacks. Tours cost around $45 for adults, $25 for children and last about three-and-a-half hours. Tour companies like Holiday Tours & Travel offer variations on this theme. For their contact details, and for other tour companies, see Tour Operators on p.224.

Transit Tour

Singapore Visitors Centres
Singapore Changi Airport Arrivals & Transit Halls
🚇 *Changi Airport*
Map 8-D4

www.visitsingapore.com

If your friends transit in Singapore and have at least five hours to spare, be sure to let them know about this free two-hour sightseeing tour of the city. They can register at the Singapore Visitors Centres at the Departure/Transit Halls at Changi Airport's two terminals. Counters are open from 08:00 to 16:25 and seats are allocated on a first come first serve basis. If your friends hold passports that require visas for Singapore they will need these in order to do the transit tour.

CityCab

They'll collect you!

6542 5831 | www.citycab.com.sg

On the Singapore Cabby Tour, trained drivers operate tours around Singapore including a Round Island Tour, Singapore by Night Tour, Local Foods and Attractions Tour and Eastern and Western Heartland tours. You get to see the island in the comfort of a taxi with a Singaporean (and a real-life taxi driver at that) showing you the way. Call 6542 5831 to book and your driver will pick you up from anywhere. Prices start from $105 per car for a three to six hour tour. Visit the website for more information.

Boat & Yacht Charters

Other options **Boat Tours** p.219, **Dinner Cruises** p.397

Despite its often murky waters and busy shipping lanes, Singapore can be a fun place to hop on a boat and go for a trip. Most expats don't have their own boats, so hiring a charter is the way to go. Quite a few outfits offer day trips, while some go on extended voyages. Day trips usually involve an early morning start and can include activities like kayaking, relaxing with a beer in a boom net or wakeboarding. The day usually ends with a quiet view of the sunset before heading back to shore. Beyond day trips, some of the companies listed below also do overnight trips or longer charters, or if you're flexible, you could catch a yacht in transit and get yourself on a one-way trip to Thailand or Malaysia.

Boats, Boats & Boats

Raffles Marina
Tuas
Map 5-A4

6861 6965 | www.bbboats.com

Boats, Boats & Boats has two 48ft luxury motor cruisers with crew available for charter. Based out of the Raffles Marina, they offer day trips to the Southern Islands and Johor Straits. Overnight trips can also be arranged. A popular option is the Sunset BBQ, where the yacht anchors off the west coast for a sunset-and-grill session. You can BYO or arrange a barbecue package. Each yacht takes a maximum of 10 passengers. For more details contact the Boats, Boats & Boats office or call Bernard Ho at 9626 8083.

Four Friends

Changi Sailing Club
Changi
🚇 *Simei*
Map 8-D3

6747 3105 | www.schoonerfourfriends.com

The Four Friends is an attractive 60ft schooner skippered by the charismatic Warren Blake. Your options include a day cruise, a sunset tour or an extended multi-day trip to explore far-away islands in Malaysia, Thailand or further afield. The boat can sleep 12 in three cabins, space for four in the main deckhouse and the additional option of sleeping up on deck under the stars. Four Friends is equipped to support diving trips, and also has three sit-on-top kayaks and a 21ft motor launch. Delicious Thai and Vietnamese food and cold beer is available, and a boom net lowered into the water can provide hours of relaxing fun. Call 6747 3105 or 8161 1911.

Raffles Marina
Tuas
Map 5-A4

Maxout Hydrosports

6869 2291 | www.maxouthydrosports.com

Maxout Hydrosports is located in the far west of Singapore, at the Raffles Marina. They have three motor yachts for rent for day trips, mainly around the western side of the island. The Carpe Diem is a 60ft yacht, the Oriental Dream is 40ft and Molly is 36ft and each comes with a skipper and crew. The boats rent for $180, $150 and $120 respectively and the minimum rental period is six hours. Each boat can take a maximum of 12 people and a popular option is to do a combination rental with a yacht and a ski boat, using the former as a home base on the water and the latter for waterskiing or wakeboarding. Call them for details on packages, longer trips and catering.

Nr Ferry Terminal
Changi
Expo
Map 4-C1

SAF Yacht Club

6389 3776 | www.safyc.org.sg

The SAF Yacht Club's corporate sailing programme is a great way to do some relaxing team building. You can choose from a two-hour sunset cruise, a halfday experiental sailing session or a fullday programme. There are two boats available, a 36ft keelboat that can take up to 10 people or an 80ft boat that takes 20. Costs range from$70 -$200 per person and include a packed lunch. For more details call Jamie or Bud at the Programme & Activity Department.

1 North Bridge Rd
Colonial District
City Hall
Map 17-C2

Singapore River Cruise

6336 6111 | www.rivercruise.com.sg

The 90ft yacht Fantasy is available for day and dinner cruises on the waters around Singapore and to the Southern Islands. Built for comfort and pleasure, it can take up to 60 people and has a professional crew of eight. Fantasy is fully air-conditioned, has fishing equipment and board games and even boasts a comprehensive sound system with karaoke. Other boats for rent include the MV Falcon Princess, a catamaran capable of taking 300 people on its three decks, the Cheng Ho III, a Chinese-style vessel with a 200 person capacity, and the Harbour Queen, which takes up to 86 passengers in two air-conditioned saloons on the main deck.

Boat Tours

Other options **Boat & Yacht Charters** p.218, **Dinner Cruises** p.397

109 Mount Faber Rd
Telok Blangah
HarbourFront
Map 16-F4

Faber Tours

6377 9640 | www.fabertours.com.sg

Faber Tours' Port Discovery Tour explores the southern tip of the island for a glimpse of Singapore's ports, Pasir Panjang Wharf, Pasir Panjang Terminal, Keppel Terminal, Tanjong Pagar Terminal, and Mount Faber. The tour includes a cable car ride and a pick-up service from hotels in the city. A three and a half hour tour, tickets cost $49 for adults and $39 for children.

Various locations

Singapore DUCKtours

6338 6877 | www.ducktours.com.sg

With their trademark bright yellow amphibious craft, it's hard to miss the DUCK crew. They offer a combination city and harbour tour in a military craft that dates back to the Vietnam War. Kids will love it. The 'Ducktainers' take you through historical landmarks around the Civic District before you splash into the water for views of the Merlion Park, the Esplanade and Clifford Pier. You'll board at the DUCKcounter at Suntec City Mall and tickets cost $33 for adults, $17 for children and $2 for children aged 1 to 2 years.

Various locations

Singapore Explorer

6339 6833 | www.singaporeexplorer.com.sg
Singapore Explorer offer tours by both bumboat and glass-top boat. Taking a bumboat along the Singapore River is an excellent way to get a feel for the city and get a different perspective of the godowns, shophouses and the colonial government buildings. Or if you prefer your sightseeing in air-conditioned comfort, you can take in the fabulous views from the Singapore River in a glass top boat. The boats leave from Clarke Quay and Raffles Place MRT Jetty daily from 09:00 to 23:00 and the glass top boat is also available for corporate events.

Harbourfront Centre
Telok Blangah
HarbourFront
Map 16-F4

Watertours Pte Ltd ▶ p.221

6533 9811 | www.watertours.com.sg
Start or end your day of sightseeing sailing down the Singapore River on the Cheng Ho, a replica Chinese junk boat dating from the Ming Dynasty period. Boats depart daily at 10:30, 15:00 or 18:00 for the various routes, each one exploring different sites and islands. All cruises include light refreshments and/or high tea or dinner and prices start at $25 for adults and $12 for children. Cruises last around two hours. Boats are also available for charter for a capacity up to 200 persons.

Brewery Tours

St James
Power Station
Telok Blangah
HarbourFront
Map 16-F4

TigerLIVE ▶ p.223

6376 9339 | www.tigerlive.com.sg
Since Singapore is the home of Tiger beer, fans of the golden stuff make sure The Tiger Brewery Tour is on their itinerary. Tours will take you through the whole brewing process, from the history of the beer through to the tapping process and ending with a few all-important tasting sessions. Open to visitors Monday to Friday (except Public Holidays). Tours take place daily – the first at 10:00 and the last at 18:00. The tour is conducted in English. Advance booking required. See website for directions and further details.

Bus Tours

Various locations

SH Tours

6734 9923 | www.asiatours.com.sg
The SIA Hop-On Bus is a special tourist bus service that offers a hop-on, hop-off service at designated stops around the city. The bus stops at a number of hotels – for a complete list you can visit www.singaporeair.com. You can buy a day pass from the driver and enjoy unlimited air-conditioned bus rides around the city's shopping, dining, cultural and entertainment areas, stopping at major shopping malls, hotels and landmarks, as well as the ethnic districts of Chinatown, Little India and Arab Street. The Hop-On runs daily from 09:00 to 18:00 at 30 minute intervals. Day passes are free for Singapore

> **Junk Rider**
> Cruise around Singapore waters on a traditional Chinese junk and catch a glimpse of the past. The two and a half hour tour includes a stop at Kusu Island and costs $23 for adults and $11 for children. Several of the tour companies offer junk cruises, see Tour Operators on p.224 for contact details. One company worth checking out is SH Tours (6734 9923).

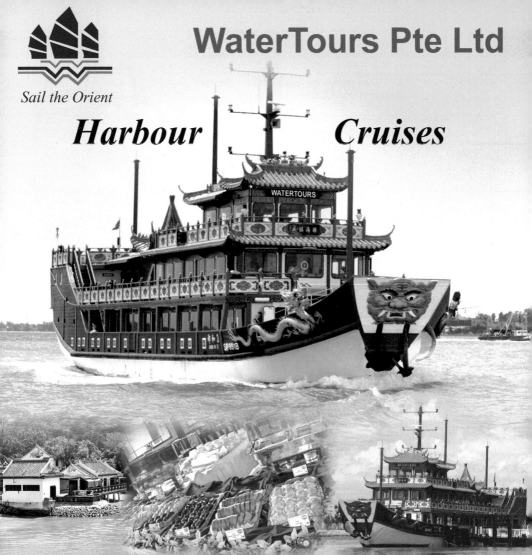

WaterTours Pte Ltd

Sail the Orient

Harbour Cruises

TYPE OF CRUISES	DEPARTURE	TIME DURATION
Morning Glory	1030hrs	2.5hrs
High Tea	1500hrs	2.5hrs
Dragon Cruise	1500hrs	2.5hrs
Imperial Dinner	1830hrs	2hrs

For Reservation or Private Characters
Please call 65339811 or email sales@watertours.com.sg
Website www.watertours.com.sg

Stopover Holidays passengers, $3 for SIA and SilkAir
Passengers and $6 for other passengers.

Various locations

Singapore DUCKtours

6338 6877 | *www.ducktours.com.sg*

Your topless option in Singapore, the HiPPOtour takes
you around the city on an open-top double-decker. ,
cruising Orchard Road, Little India, Kampong Gelam,
Chinatown, and the Historic District. It's a hop-on kinda
thing; pick it up at the DUCKTours office on Orchard
Road or at Suntec City. It has three types of tours, a city
tour, a Sentosa tour which only takes you up to
Sentosa and the heritage tour. The tour cost $23 for a
one day pass. You can also buy a two-day unlimited
Singapore Sightseeing Pass that includes a city tour, a
heritage tour, a river cruise, a Moonlight City Adventure as well as their famous Red
Lantern Tours for $13 for adults, $7 for children. Each of these tours is available
separately too. DUCKtours also run amphibious tour option (see Boat Tours, p.219).
You'll find a DUCKtours counter at Suntec City Mall and you can buy tickets or find
out more at the various Singapore Visitors Centres too.

Various locations

Singapore Explorer

6339 6833 | *www.singaporeexplorer.com.sg*

Straight from the 1920s, the Singapore Trolley offers you a chance to amble through
the colonial, cultural and art districts of Singapore at a gentler pace. The Trolley travels
from the malls of Orchard Road to the colonial district and on to Clarke Quay with a
narration of the sights you're passing. It takes about an hour to complete the 17 stop
route and you can hop on and off as you please.

Helicopter Tours

Other options **Flying** p.264

Seletar Airport
Seletar
Map 4-F4

ST Aerospace

6481 0546 | *www.staero.aero/hfs*

ST Aerospace operates a helicopter charter service that offers flights for commercial
purposes as well as tours. Up to four passengers and one pilot can take the 60
minute flight around Singapore. You'll get to see about two-thirds of the island, but
won't be allowed to take any pictures as there are some concerns about national
security. A flight costs $2,500, with a regular service offered during office hours on
weekdays. If you want to fly on the weekend you'll have to pay a premium. To book
a flight, call the office and have your passport details at hand so that you can be
cleared to access the airport.

Heritage Tours

Changi Tours

Created by the Changi Chapel & Museum, the Battlefield Tour and Changi WWII are
dedicated to the memory of all who fought and suffered during World War Two. The
tours offer you insights into battle strategies and losses and life during World War Two.
The Battlefield Tour covers Mt Faber, Labrador Park, Alexandra Hospital and the Kranji
War Memorial. The Changi WWII tour offers a glimpse of life as a prisoner of war and
visits the Changi Chapel and Museum, Changi Beach, which was the site of the Sook

Tiger
LIVE

THE ULTIMATE BREWERY EXPERIENCE

Thrill your imagination at TigerLIVE, a multi-sensory experience that will bring the magic of Tiger Beer to life. Discover a spectrum of electrifying Tiger experiences with state of the art 3D-technology and sound FX that will leave you thirsty for more!

Experience TigerLIVE at

St James Power Station
3 Sentosa Gateway #01-02
Singapore 098544

Open daily from 10AM to 8PM.
Last admission at 6PM.

Visit www.tigerlive.com.sg
call +65 6376 9339
or fax +65 6376 9376 for more info.

Ching Massacre, Changi Village, the Johore Battery and the Selarang Barracks (a Japanese POW camp). The Battlefield Tour costs $25 per adult, $20 per child, and the Changi WWII tour costs $40 per adult, $20 per child. Journeys and Malaysia and Singapore Travel Centre are among the tour operators who offer these tours. For details of these and other tour companies, see the Tour Operators table below.

Invasion Tour

Follow the footsteps of Japanese soldiers as they launched the invasion of Singapore during the World War II. Starting from the North, the four-hour tour covers the Japanese War Memorial built by Australian POWs, Kranji River, Kranji War Memorial, Bukit Chandu, Pasir Panjang and Labrador Park, and Alexander Barracks. Tickets cost $49. One of the companies that offers this tour is Malaysia and Singapore Travel Centre. For their contact details, and for other tour companies, see the Tour Operators table below.

> **The Rising Tide**
>
> In April 2006 Singapore saw an increase of 16% in visitor numbers from the same time the year before. Which means how many visitors exactly? A staggering 815,000.

Peranakan Trail

Discover the history, culture and lifestyle of the Peranakan babas and nonyas. You'll be taken on a walk through a spice garden, see a fascinating display of Peranakan costume and jewellery, look at the rich architecture and finally enjoy some nonya delicacies. Tours start at 08:30 with a hotel pick-up and cost $39 for adults, $19.50 for children under 10. For details of tour companies in Singapore, see the Tour Operators table below.

Rags to Riches Tour With Trishaw Ride

This tour allows you to pretend to be an old-fashioned towkay (a Chinese tycoon) for the day. The tour starts at the Chinese Heritage Centre and takes in a traditional teahouse, a trishaw ride through Chinatown, and on to Boat Quay where you'll see the legacy of some of the Singaporean towkays. This three-and-a-half hour tour starts with pick up at 13:30 and cost $75 for adults, $37 for children under 10. A number of operators offer this option – you can book through www.city-discovery.com, an online central reservations site that will choose from a number of operators and make your arrangements for you.

Tour Operators

Club Med Singapore ▶ p.235	6830 0889	www.clubmed.com.sg
Faber Tours	6377 9640	www.fabertours.com.sg
Holiday Tours & Travel	6738 2622	na
Journeys	6325 1631	na
Malaysia and Singapore Travel Centre	6737 8877	na
RMG Tours	6220 1661	www.rmgtours.com
SH Tours	6734 9923	www.asiatours.com.sg
Siakson Coach Tours	6336 0288	na
Singapore DUCKtours	6338 6877	www.ducktours.com.sg
Singapore Explorer	6339 6833	www.singaporeexplorer.com.sg
Singapore River Cruise	6336 6111	www.rivercruise.com.sg
Watertours Pte Ltd ▶ p.221	6533 9811	www.watertours.com.sg

Various locations ◀ Singapore Explorer

6339 6833 | www.singaporeexplorer.com.sg

Labrador Park was once a fort and on this hourly guided tour you'll be able to visit its imposing gun posts and then venture into the maze of wartime bunkers beneath it. The tours run from 10:00 to 19:00 daily and cost $8 for adults, $5 for children. While you can get to Labrador Park on your own steam and take time to enjoy its natural beauty too, Singapore Explorer takes you into the secret tunnels on this tour as well.

Island Resorts

Marina Country Club Ubin Resort

600 Ponggol
Seventeenth Ave
Pulau Ubin
🚇 *Punggol*
Map 1-E2

6388 8388 | *www.marinacountryclub.com.sg*
The MCC Ubin Resort is a quick getaway that's ideal for familis or a group of friends. Located on the edge of the Ketam Channel on Pulau Ubin, in a mangrove setting, it's just 30 minutes by ferry from the Marina Country Club at Punggol on the mainland. The resort consists of one or two-roomed air-conditioned chalets with a colour TV, a fridge, a kettle and two skate scooters. What more could you want? Well, there's also a recreation centre that offers abseiling, kayaking, guided trekking and plenty of gear that you can hire if you fancy trying your hand at fishing, tossing a frisbee or an energetic game of volleyball.

The Sentosa Resort & Spa

2 Bukit Manis Rd
Sentosa
🚇 *HarbourFront*
Map 19-C2

6275 0331 | *www.thesentosa.com*
An elegant Beaufort Hotel property on the cliffs in Sentosa Island, this property is the most recently renovated of the Sentosa resort hotels and boasts 214 suites, rooms and villas. It's also home to Spa Botanica, Singapore's first true destination spa where you can wander through a meditation labyrinth, have a steam bath or wallow in a mud pool!

Shangri-La's Rasa Sentosa Resort

101 Siloso Rd
Sentosa
🚇 *HarbourFront*
Map 19-A1

6275 0100 | *www.shangri-la.com*
Singapore's only beachfront resort, the Rasa Sentosa is perfect for a painless getaway with the kids, thanks to its Kid's Club… and a number of quieter pursuits for parents; from a stroll through the extensive tropical gardens, to spoiling yourself at the Health Club & Spa. If you're feeling energetic there's also a climbing wall and beach volleyball on offer. The Rasa Sentosa has 459 rooms, a swimming pool and two outdoor Jacuzzis.

Sijori Resort Sentosa

23 Beach View
Sentosa
🚇 *HarbourFront*
Map 19-C2

6271 2002 | *www.sijoriresort.com.sg*
Housed in an original pre-war building right beside the Merlion, the Sijori Resort Sentosa has 64 rooms with private balconies that overlook lush greenery, the sea or the Merlion itself. There are plenty of dining options to choose from and a well-equipped Health & Recreation Club means you're guaranteed to work up an appetite. There's also a a pool table, video arcade and karaoke lounge to keep you entertained (or entertaining, as the case may be).

Walking Tours

Singapore Tourism Board offers good free walking tour maps at the airport, various hotels and Singapore Visitors Centres. These allow you to take yourself on a self-guided tour through the riverside district, Chinatown and Little India. The Raffles Hotel Museum also has a Civic District Trail walking tour map and heritage enthusiasts will enjoy the sketches and historical descriptions in Singapore – A Walking Tour by G Byrne Bracken, available at Kinokuniya.

Sentosa Luge and Skyride

Part go-cart, part toboggan, the luge is easy to manoeuvre and a quick ride downhill on a 650m track. It's not quite the X-Games, but it's enjoyable and definitely a rush for kids. To get to the top, you take a trip on the Skyride, a chairlift which takes you over the treetops of Sentosa. All rides include the Skyride and are priced at $8 for a single, $15 for two rides and $24 for a family pass of four rides. Children aged 3 to 6 can ride tandem with an adult and if you don't fancy hurtling down on the luge you can do just the Skyride. Consider doing it in the morning or later part of the afternoon, unless you fancy catching a fair amount of tropical sunshine on your way up the hill. For more details log on to www.sentosa.com.sg.

225

Other Attractions

The cable car ride from Mt Faber Park to Sentosa is worthy of a spin to enjoy the spectacular virgin rainforest view, and the sight of the cruise terminal below and the ships out to sea. During the Food Festival meals are served onboard the cable car. Once you reach Sentosa itself, the Carlsberg Sky Tower also commands spectacular views of Singapore. Other popular attractions are listed below.

Tan Quee Lan St
Bugis
🚇 *Bugis*
Map 14-D4

DHL Balloon

6338 6877 | *www.visitsingapore.com*

For an aerial view of Singapore, try out the DHL Balloon. The world's largest tethered balloon, it's been cleared by the Civil Aviation Authority to take people 40 storeys up, where they can photograph or video the 360° view of the city below. The viewing platform is sturdy and you're able to walk around it easily. Tickets (with warnings that children and baggage are 'not allowed' to fall off the balloon – which, rest assured, does have mesh safety barriers) cost $23 for adults, $13 for children, and a ride lasts for 10 minutes. The balloon 'flies' every 30 minutes from 11:00 to 22:00 daily, weather permitting.

5 Temasek Blvd
Suntec
🚇 *City Hall*
Map 17-D1

Fountain of Wealth

6295 2888 | *www.suntec.com.sg*

While Suntec City's visitors are mainly there for business, retail and convention purposes, the Fountain of Wealth is a drawcard for many tourists. The world's largest fountain, it occupies the centrepiece of the traffic island in Suntec City, although most of it is underground, and accessible via the mall. Made of bronze, it has a ring of 66 metres and a base area of 1,683 square metres. Suntec City's design, like much of Singapore, is built in accordance with feng shui and the buildings represent the fingers and thumb of a left hand poking out of the ground, with the fountain forming the hand's palm. While the water is low, visitors walk around the fountain for luck and at night it's lit up with a laser show.

3E River Valley Rd
Riverside
🚇 *Clarke Quay*
Map 17-C1

G-Max Reverse Bungee

6338 1146 | *www.gmax.com.sg*

With a scarcity of suitable structures to bungee from in Singapore, the G-Max Reverse Bungee ride solves the problem. The G-Max capsule is anchored to the ground with bungee cords stretched to the top of two poles like a slingshot. The capsule is then released with you inside it - sending you hurtling into the sky at amazing speed, and some significant G-force. The thrilling high-speed ride gives you not only an instant rush

DHL Balloon   *Fountain of Wealth*

of fright, but also a scenic view of the gaudy paintwork, lily pad umbrellas and gum drop railings of Clarke Quay below. Rides cost $35, $25 for students, and there is a height requirement of 1.2m. Your launch is filmed from an in-capsule camera so for $15 you can take home a DVD of the experience and laugh at yourself for years to come.

Snow City

**21 Jurong
Town Hall Rd**
Jurong
🚇 *Jurong East*
Map 10-A1

6560 1511 | *www.snowcity.com.sg*

This hangar-sized fridge contains a three-storey high slope for those who would like to experience the cold (it's a chilly -5°C inside). You and the kids can spend half an hour at a time sliding down the slope on a tube. While the place is really quite gimmicky, it's fun when it's too hot outside or when the malls' appeal has worn thin.

Extra sessions are put on during school holidays and ski and snowboarding lessons are also available. Opening hours are from 10:30 to 18:30 Tuesday to Sunday and from 09:00 to 20:00 on public and school holidays. Entry is $6 for adults, $3 for a child.

Amusement Centres

Other options **Amusement Parks** p.227

Singapore's range of indoor amusement centres are a mixed bag. But if you choose carefully they will provide the kids with a few good air-conditioned afternoons of fun, and may even double up as an interactive history or science lesson. The highlight is the Singapore Science Centre (see p.212 in Museums - City) which hosts some world-class travelling exhibitions and puts on some entertaining science exhibits. There's also the enjoyable but rather dated Cinemania and Snow City (p.227), and the worthy but over-stated military museum, Singapore Discovery Centre (p.212). As these are all clustered together, a good plan is to do two or three attractions at once, skipping over less absorbing exhibits (and maybe revisiting them another time when they might prove more interesting to the kids).

The Battle Box (p.211) and Fort Siloso (p.208) recreate Singapore's war-time history in an interesting fashion. At Sentosa (p.196) you can supplement the indoor attractions with an afternoon at the beach, while if you head to Jurong you can take in the Bird Park (p.248) and still catch a movie afterwards.

Amusement Parks

Other options **Water Parks** p.229, **Amusement Centres** p.227

When they open in 2009, Singapore's two new Integrated Resorts at Marina and Sentosa will include theme parks, theatres and museums. For the time being, there are a numerous other options for a family's day out (see below for more details), and even if some of these could do with a bit of an update, there's still plenty of fun to be had in various forms. For the main theme parks in Singapore, see below. For other attractions listed elsewhere in the chapter, see the Singapore Discovery Centre (p.212), Singapore Science Centre (p.212), Jurong Bird Park (p.230), Snow City (p.292) and the Singapore Zoo with its Night Safari (p.230).

Escape Theme Park

1 Pasir Ris Close
Pasir Ris
🚇 *Pasir Ris*
Map 8-B3

6581 9112

If it's a traditional family theme park you're after, then Escape Theme Park delivers a good few hours of family noise, fun and splashes. It's an old school attraction with reliable favourites like a haunted ride, rollercoasters, a waterpark, ferris wheel, plane ride and bumper boats. Open on weekends and over school and public holidays from 10:00 to 20:00. Tickets cost $16.50 for adults, $8.30 for children or $40 for a family pass.

227

262 Pasir Panjang Rd
Pasir Panjang
Map 16-A2

Haw Par Villa

6872 2780

Built by the brothers behind the Tiger Balm company, Haw Par Villa is an Asian mythology theme park, which is currently pretty run down. For kitsch and novelty value though, it's probably worth a visit. The park includes nightmarish scenes of the 10 courts of hell within the stomach of a giant dragon. Not for the squeamish, the rides do depict very graphic torture scenes awaiting sinners in hell before reincarnation. Open daily from 09:00 to 19:00.

Dragon Boat Races

A great spectator sport even for those who think excitement comes in horsepower and high-octane fuel. The annual dragon boating festivals are held on Boat Quay in November and Esplanade each June. With races in men's, women's and mixed categories, the national events are hotly contested, with victory often a matter of just fractions of a second. For details of how to get in on the action, see Dragon Boat Racing on p.260 in Activities.

Horse Racing

Other options **Horse Riding** p.271

A day at the races is an enjoyable change of scenery and a good way to appreciate the social phenomenon that is gambling in Asia. Horse racing here dates back to 1842 when the Singapore Sporting Club was formed. Always prepared to multitask, the racecourse grounds have also been used for polo matches, and even the country's first aircraft landing. In 1924, the Singapore Sporting Club became the Singapore Turf Club. The club is now based in Kranji, and the highlight of its calendar is the $3 million Singapore Airlines International Cup in May which is part of the World Series Racing Championship.

1 Turf Club Ave
Woodlands
Kranji
Map 3-E4

Singapore Turf Club ▶ p.305

6879 1000 | *www.turfclub.com.sg*

Why not live it up with a day at the races? Racing is conducted on selected Fridays, Saturdays and Sundays every month and starts at 13:45. You can watch all the action on a large outdoor screen or take your pick from vantage points with or without air conditioning. Admission to the Lower Grandstand, the non air-conditioned public level, is $3, while the air-conditioned Upper Grandstand costs $7. You can gain admission to special areas like the @Hibiscus, which also allows access to the restaurant for $20 or the Gold Card Room for $15. Dress is smart casual and entry is restricted to those 18 or over. It's a fun day out, especially during the annual Singapore Airlines International Cup. Holidays Tours & Travels and Travel East offer packages to the races (see Tour Operators on p.224).

Natural Attractions

Singapore's best natural attractions are not just good, they are world class. Singapore Zoo (p.231), Singapore Night Safari (p.230) and the Jurong Bird Park (p.230) are must-dos and even seasoned residents visit them every now and then for the ambience, the animals and the superb design of each attraction. If you're have guests in town these will be some of the attractions you'll readily take your visitors too.
Other attractions in this category include Underwater World (p.229), which makes for an excellent, if rather short, afternoon out. The Dolphin Lagoon and Butterfly Park fall a little short of the mark as mainstream attractions and are mainly for real enthusiasts.

Powerboat Racing

For one weekend in September each year, as the F1 Poweboat Racing circuit hits town, Marina Bay comes alive with the mighty noise of jet-propelled racing. The noisiest of the Marina Bay area's array of events, the F1 Powerboating is great to watch and spectators gather all around the bay, particularly at Marina South, One Fullerton and Esplanade for a vantage point.

Water Parks

Other options **Amusement Parks** p.227

1 Pasir Ris Close
Pasir Ris
🚇 *Pasir Ris*
Map 8-B4

Wild Wild Wet

6581 9112

The king of water parks in Singapore is Wild Wild Wet, which is part of the Escape Theme Park (p.227). The highlight is Ulah-Lah, billed as the first raft slide in South-East Asia and the closest thing to white water rafting that Singapore can offer. It lets you and five others race other rafts on an exciting flume ride. The Waterworks is a high speed, twisty flume ride with distinctive angles. The Shiok River is a leisurely ride of 335 metres through lush landscape and younger children can play in the Professor's Playground with its slides, ladders, water cannons and fountains. Tickets cost $12.90 for adults, $8.80 for children and the park is open from 13:00 to 19:00 on weekdays and 10:00 to 19:00 on weekends.

Aquariums & Marine Centres

80 Siloso Rd
Sentosa
🚇 *HarbourFront*
Map 19-B1

Underwater World

6275 0030 | *www.underwaterworld.com.sg*

One of Sentosa's most popular sights, this attractive aquarium houses some 250 species of marine life from around the region. The highlight is the travelator – a 83 metre moving walkway that takes you through a tunnel filled with shoals of fish, rays, sharks and massive grouper that swim alongside and above you. The aquarium is particularly entrancing after 19:00, when they turn off the lights and equip visitors with torches to spot the critters with. The Dolphin Lagoon is part of the aquarium and you can watch the pink dolphins (Indo-Pacific humpback dolphins) do their thing at regular shows during the day. You can also dive with the sharks or the dugongs and the aquarium hosts corporate dinners on the travelator if you're wanting a different sort of experience for your colleagues or clients.

Nature Reserves

Singapore manages 3,326 hectares of nature reserves, and in the absence of an opportunity to go for a soothing drive in the countryside, escaping to a scenic reservoir or a tract of virgin forest is not only for the birds, but also for stressed out office workers. Highlighted by the Bukit Timah Nature Reserve, Singapore's range of nature reserves include the Mandai Lake Nature Reserve and the popular MacRitchie Reservoir with its superb 250 metre Treetop Walk. Sungei Buloh Wetland Reserve is the newest reserve, while Chek Jawa on the eastern tip of Pulau Ubin is unique for its natural isolation. Yet even in the more built up areas, the Pierce Reservoir Park and Seletar Reservoir make for scenic spaces in which to walk, run or just pass the time. They're also popular with dragon boating and kayaking clubs.

177 Hindhede Drive
Bukit Timah
Map 6-D3

Bukit Timah Nature Reserve

6468 5736 | *www.nparks.gov.sg*

Singapore and Rio de Janeiro are the only two cities in the world to include a significant area of primary rainforest within their boundaries. Just 12 kilometres from the city, the Bukit Timah and Central Catchment Nature Reserves are home to more than 840 flowering plants and over 500 species of animals, including butterflies. The 164 hectare reserve is said by world-renowned ecologist Dr David Bellamy to contain more plant species than the entire North American continent. This includes a tree that is centuries old. You have the choice of taking the North View, South View or Fern Valley paths. Each

229

is well-marked so you can wander on quietly, keeping a lookout for butterflies, monkeys and flying lemurs or the unique insect-eating pitcher plant. At the centre of the park is Bukit Timah Hill, Singapore's highest point at 164 metres above sea level. Considering the prime real estate that lies alongside Bukit Timah, its preservation is impressive, but should not be taken for granted.

There are two mountain bike trails; one that cuts through the jungle and abandoned quarry sites and another that runs through the neighbouring Central Catchment Nature Reserve to MacRitchie Reservoir.

Central Catchment
Nature Reserve
Central Singapore
🚇 ***Marymount***
Map 7-A4

MacRitchie Reservoir Park
1800471 7300 | www.nparks.gov.sg

The Catchment Nature Reserve includes more than a square kilometre of primary rainforest, most of it around the MacRitchie Reservoir. Used as a rubber plantation in the 19th century, there remain some rubber trees in the area too. Boardwalks surround the scenic reservoir, and at lengths of between 3 and 11km, they make for a great nature walk. Enjoy good views of the water and aquatic wildlife, and some unique flora including pitcher and ant plants. Also try out the 250m aerial free standing suspension bridge that spans Bukit Piece and Bukit Kallang. Twenty-five metres above the ground at its highest point, it's a great place to enjoy the view and watch the birds in the nearby canopy. Another way to enjoy the reservoir is to rent a kayak and go for a paddle.

Zoos & Wildlife Parks

2 Jurong Hill
Jurong
🚇 ***Boon Lay***
Map 9-E2

Jurong BirdPark
6265 0022 | www.birdpark.com.sg

A must-see, this park consists of 20 or so serene hectares on the western slope of Jurong Hill. With 8,000 birds from 600 species, it is among the largest bird parks in the world, and its presentation makes it a must-see, even if you're not a bird enthusiast. Built at a cost of $3.5 million in 1971, the park features The Waterfall Aviary, the world's largest walk-in aviary which is home to over 1,500 free-flying birds. The Jurong Falls within the aviary is said to be the tallest man-made waterfall in the world at 30 metres high. The World of Darkness is Asia's first nocturnal bird house, while Pelican Cove features seven species of these beautiful birds, including a unique underwater viewing gallery, where the birds scoop for fish at feeding time. There are also daily live performances including the All Star and Birds of Prey Shows.

Singapore Zoo
Seletar
🚇 ***Ang Mo Kio***
Map 6-D1

Singapore Night Safari
6269 3411 | www.nightsafari.com.sg

Possibly the best attraction Singapore offers, Night Safari at Singapore Zoo (see the separate entry below) makes the zoo experience a serene and haunting one, taking advantage of the cooler night air and the fact that this is when many of the animals are awake and active. The 40 hectare forested park is only open at night and features 120 species. It's worth the extra price to pay for the tram that takes you along the eight geographical zones, and within inches of strolling antelopes and hyenas menacingly sniffing the air. Well-planned feeding times and thoughtful food placement together with bright but non-harmful lights make for perfect animal viewing, often surprisingly close to you. As most of the animals are bred in captivity they are used to people, and seldom take much notice of your presence. But you are asked not to use flash

Zoo-Safari Combo

There are combined zoo and night safari tickets to be bought, but do make sure it's clear whether you're supposed to view both parks on one day or different days when you buy them.

photography and it's definitely worth choosing a tram without a large group on it. The quieter the guided tour, the more captivating it is. Once the tram ride is done it's time to walk the trails, which are well marked and lit, and allow you to stop and take your time at your favourite enclosures. These include the Mangrove Walk, where bats flap past frighteningly close to you.

80 Mandai Lake Rd
Seletar
🚇 *Ang Mo Kio*
Map 6-D1

Singapore Zoo
6269 3411 | www.zoo.com.sg

One of the best known and most popular attractions in Singapore, the Singapore Zoo has over 3,000 animals, representing 410 species housed on 28 hectares of greenery. To date, 60 acres of land remain for future projects. Opened in 1973 beside the Upper Seletar Reservoir, the zoo's many programmes include the popular 'breakfast with the animals' where you can feed yourself and the animals at the same time, and the incredible experience of the Night Safari (see above). The zoo prides itself on its captive breeding projects, education programmes and open-style exhibits that use hidden barriers rather than the traditional cages. There are also some new interactive activities, including elephant rides. The zoo is a good two to three-hour meander – go in the early evening and take in Night Safari after dinner. But avoid it on school holiday weekends in particular. With over a million visitors each year the park carries the flag for conservation, stressing the preservation of the world's remaining forests.

Singapore Zoo

MacRitchie Reservoir

Singapore Zoo

Jurong BirdPark

231

You're spoilt for choice when it comes to spending a weekend away in Singapore. Not only are the Sentosa and the outer islands a great option for a change from the city buzz, but Singapore is also ideally situated for a quick escape to foreign shores. In fact, with Malaysia accessible by road, and Indonesia only a 45 minute ferry ride away, it's perfectly feasible to hop over to a different country for a day. A weekend is better of course, and a holiday even better still. For information about more of Singapore's neighbours that make good weekend destinations too, turn to Holiday Hotspots on p.236. For a list of travel agents that can help you make arrangements, see p.224.

For information about more of Singapore's neighbours that make good weekend destinations too, turn to Holiday Hotspots on p.236. For a list of travel agents that can help you make arrangements, see p.224.

By Rail

Relaxed and inexpensive, if not entirely punctual, Malayan Railway (www.ktmb.com.my) has regular services that connect Singapore to major cities and towns like Johor Bahru and Kuala Lumpur on the western seaboard of Peninsular Malaysia.

If the train journey itself is part of the adventure, The Eastern & Oriental Express (www.easternorientalexpress.com) allows you to live the life of the rich and famous. This luxury train is a glimpse of what life was like in the bygone era of train travel. Starting out from Singapore's Tanjong Pagar Railway Station, E&O journeys include sightseeing tours in Penang and River Kwai and can take you as far as Bangkok and Chiang Mai. Tickets start at $1,120 but keep an eye out for their special promotions at various times of the year.

By Cruise Ship

A major cruising port of call, Singapore offers a superb range of regional cruises from the affordable to the premium. Some of the lines such as the SuperStar Virgo (www.starcruises.com), Silversea Cruises (www.silversea.com) and Star Clippers (www.starclippers.com) take you to destinations including Australia, Mumbai, Phuket, Malacca, Laem Chabang, Hong Kong and Penang.

By Coach

A good way to get to Malaysia if you would prefer not to fly is with the coaches that connect Singapore with Kuala Lumpur and beyond. It's cheaper than flying, and a first-class seat together with an air-conditioned view of the landscape makes it a hassle-free and atmospheric way to travel. Some of the coach companies are Hasry Express (www.hasryexpress.com), Transtar Travel (www.transtar.com.sg) and Aeroline Bus Shuttle (www.aeroline.com.my).

Bintan, Indonesia

Just a 45 minute ferry ride from Singapore and an hour behind in time, it's quite possible to find yourself on the beach in Bintan on a Friday evening, at precisely the time you left the office! Run as a joint venture between Singapore and the Riau Province of Indonesia, Bintan is an easy and hassle-free weekend break, that scores big for convenience, breezy white sand breaches and resort activities, and lacks only in the fact that you'll pay Singapore prices for most things except beer. For more information see www.bintan-resorts.com or call 6389 3899 (Singapore office).

Malaysia

There are a variety of destinations in Malaysia that make a suitable weekend break. The capital city, Kuala Lumpur, is a 45 minute flight or a five-hour drive away, while Johor Bahru with its mosques, shops and museums, is just across the causeway. North of Johor Bahru, and about a 90 minute drive from Singapore, is Kota Tinggi. Site of the Kota Tinggi Waterfalls, it's a good place to picnic, swim and go for jungle

---

Keep it Legal

If you decide to drive to Malaysia for your weekend or holiday, remember that the Malaysian police enforce their speed limits strictly - and your Singapore car is easily picked out because of its license plates. Singapore law also requires that your car's petrol tank is at least three-quarters full when you leave Singapore and you'll be fined if it's not.

walks. Three hours from Singapore by car is Malacca, which was once the ancient kingdom's capital, is a three-hour drive from Singapore and a good stopover if your ultimate destination is KL, especially if you fancy some antique shopping en route.

Malaysia's Islands

About an hour and a half away from Singapore by air, you'll find great diving, good food, indulgent spa treatments and, of course, all the beach and watersports you could dream of, Langkawi makes an excellent weekend getaway. For more information about Langkawi check out www.langkawi.com.my, or try www.islands.com.my for other island escapes in Malaysia.

Singapore's Islands

Singapore's outer islands are great for day trips or weekend breaks, particularly if you're happy to be self-sufficient and camp or stay in bungalows. The Lazarus and Sisters Islands don't have any facilities but offer a good day's snorkelling and chilling out on the beach. Kusu or Turtle Island is run by the Sentosa Development Corporation and is an 8.5 hectare holiday resort, but overnight stays are not allowed.

Pulau Ubin's traditional village life feel makes it a real attraction for urbanites wanting to chill out for a couple of days (see p.251). Marina Country Club Ubin is the main accommodation option here and provides a variety of activities, or you can arrange camping through the National Parks Board at eitherthe Noordin, Mamam or Jelutong campsites. (Each campsite has toilet facilities, but water is not suitable for drinking or bathing. Only Jelutong has campfire pits.) See www.nparks.gov.sg or call 1800-471 7300.

St John's Island is a hilly island that offers swimming in lagoons and shaded walks. You can arrange accommodation in the Holiday Bungalow (sleeps 10) or in dormitories at the Holiday Camps through the Sentosa Development Corporation (6275 0388, www.sentosa.com.sg). For more information, see Outer Islands in Singapore - Main Areas (p.201) and Island Resorts (p.225).

Sentosa Island ▶ p.197

This must be about the only weekend destination you can get to by taxi. But crossing over to Sentosa Island will give you an immediate sense of getting away from (almost) all of it. Sentosa (see p.196 under Singapore – Main Areas) has such a wide range of entertainment and leisure options that if you're part of a group or a family, this is great

Travel Agencies

AB Mohamed Travel	6297 5041
Abbey Aviation Pte Ltd	6324 1488
Air Services International Pte Ltd	6298 7855
Airelated Travel	6532 5686
American Express Travel	6880 1111
Anglo-French Travel	6222 4222
Carlson Wagonlit Singapore	6220 2228
Chan Brothers Travel	6212 9686
Club Med Singapore ▶ p.235	6830 0889
Creative Tours	6225 0866
Diners World Travel	6298 8988
Dynasty Travel International	6338 4455
Farmosa Holiday Tour	6534 1133
Fortune Travel	6738 0622
Gasi Holidays Pte Ltd	6733 2228
GC Nanda & Sons	6220 2020
Global Travel	6226 2866
Holiday Tours & Travel	6734 7091
Hong Thai Travel Services	6532 3223
Imperial Tours & Travel	6339 1866
Lotus Travel	6323 1188
New Shan Travel	6221 9333
Reliance Travel Agencies	6334 2227
RMG Tours	6220 8722
Scenic Travel	6226 3611
SIME Travel	6416 6716
Singapore Explorer Pte Ltd	6339 6833
Sino-America Tours	6535 2611
STA Travel	6737 7188
Star Cruise Travel Service	6226 1168
Tradewinds Tours & Travel	6419 2222
Travelex Singapore	6534 3211
Travelways	6735 1544
Universal Travel Corporation	6533 3922

Mini Marvel

Hong Kong is just a four-hour flight from Singapore, and currently one of the hottest holiday destinations on the planet. Luckily for you, the Mini Hong Kong Explorer makes sightseeing easy, boasting all the need-to-know info on about the city on its little pages. Stick it in your back pocket and get on that plane!

for finding that rare thing – a destination that suits everyone. From rides and tourist attractions, to beach bars and destination spas, it's a weekend escape without the travel time. Sentosa boasts three resorts: the Shangri-La's Rasa Sentosa Resort, the Sijori Resort Sentosa and The Sentosa Resort & Spa. For more details on these hotels, refer to their entries in Island Resorts on p.225.

Weekend Break Hotels

Marina Country Club & Resorts	6388 8388	www.marinacountryclub.com.sg
The Sentosa Resort & Spa	6275 0331	www.thesentosa.com
Shangri-La's Rasa Sentosa Resort	6275 0100	www.shangri-la.com
Sijori Resort Sentosa	6271 2002	www.sijoriresort.com.sg

The premium all-inclusive
family holiday

www.clubmed.com.sg

Club Med

Holidays from Singapore

Singapore is the perfect place from which to explore Asia and the Pacific Rim. Take advantage of cheaper flights and advantageous time zones and explore the wonderfully diverse regions of the south and east.

South-east Asia & the Indian Ocean

Flight time: 4.5 hours
Time difference:
Three hours behind
Best time to visit:
Year round

India

India is a land of contrasts, from Goa's beautiful beaches to the vibrant city of Mumbai and the imposing mountains of Kahsmir. Goa is probably the top holiday spot with its palm-fringed beaches and luxurious hotels. Alternatively, travel to Agra for architecture, handicrafts and jewellery, as well as to visit the legendary Taj Mahal or the rose pink city of Jaipur. Daily flights from Singapore.

Flight time: 2.5 hours
Time difference: None
Best time to visit:
Aug - Sep

Indonesia

The main destination for most visitors to Indonesia is Bali, the Island of the Gods. Bali's tranquillity has been horribly disrupted in recent times, but it is still one of Asia's best destinations. For its remarkable culture, fascinating temples, chill out beaches and the number of reasonably priced hotels, Bali remains unmatched in the region for a relaxing and absorbing holiday. There are numerous options for daily flights to Jakarta and Denpasar.

Flight time: 1 hour
Time difference: None
Best time to visit:
Mar - Sep

Malaysia

Only an hour away if you fly, 'KL' is a great city to explore, especially when you're feeling a little jaded by Singapore. Cheaper by far, friendly, relaxed and even more culturally mixed, Kuala Lumpur is also a little more crowded and chaotic than Singapore, but perhaps more 'Asian' as a result. A city that offers culture, food and nightlife in abundance, KL is a good tonic from the Lion City, but it also makes you appreciate home on your return. Take your pick – you can reach Malaysia by air, rail, sea or road.

Flight time: 4.5 hours
Time difference:
Three hours behind
Best time to visit:
Year round

Maldives

While south-east Asia tops it for culture, few destinations in the world have coastal resorts as stunningly beautiful as the Maldives. It is worth falling in love in Singapore just for an excuse to travel to the Maldives. Unrivalled for its pearl white sand and spectacular diving, Maldives is not as inexpensive as south-east Asia, but it is soothingly spectacular. Singapore Airlines flies to Male five times a week.

Flight time: 4.5 hours
Time difference:
Three hours behind
Best time to visit:
Year round

Sri Lanka

The beauty of Sri Lanka is that whether your budget ranges from basic to luxurious you'll find ways of having the holiday of a lifetime. Capital city Colombo has its attractions, but most holidaymakers head for the beautiful beach resorts. Daily flights on Singapore Air are available.

Flight time: 2.5 hours
Time difference:
One hour behind
Best time to visit:
Aug - Feb

Thailand

Bangkok is a favourite weekend stop for many Singaporeans, but if you're from outside the region Thailand is well worth a longer stay. The islands offer great watersports and everything from marine to nightlife. Moving away from its seedy reputation, and unmatched for its great food and shopping, interesting Buddhist culture, and a swathe of upmarket bars, clubs and cafes, Bangkok is one of Asia's most fun and engaging cities. You'll have a range of options on bargain travel deals to Thailand.

Not big, but very clever…

Perfectly proportioned to fit in your pocket,
this marvellous mini guidebook makes sure
you don't just get the holiday you paid for
but rather the one that you dreamed of.

Hong Kong Mini Visitors' Guide
Maximising your holiday, minimising your hand luggage

Vietnam

Flight time: *2 hours*
Time difference: *Two hours ahead*
Best time to visit: *Dec - Apr*

Thanks to a number of budget carriers, access to Vietnam from Singapore is easier than ever. While Ho Chi Minh City (formerly Saigon) is perhaps a little more modern and less exotic than the capital city Hanoi, it is also much more fun and spirited. Here you'll find food, culture, historic buildings and the wonderful floating markets of the Mekong Delta. Daily flights from Singapore to Hanoi and Ho Chi Minh.

Far East & The Antipodes

Australia

Flight time: *7.5 hours*
Time difference: *Two hours ahead*
Best time to visit : *Year round*

Australia's got a bit of everything: beaches, amazing underwater life, hip and trendy culture to soak up in Melbourne and wine districts such as the Barossa and Coonawarra. Most of the cities offer a wealth of cafes, bars, clubs and year-round events. Sydneysiders may suffer from knowing their city is the coolest place around, but give it a week before you really argue with them. Singapore Airlines flies to various Australian cities daily.

China

Flight time: *6.5 hours*
Time difference: *None*
Best time to visit: *Apr - Oct*

In the grip of its pre-Olympics frenzy, Beijing is worth visiting now before it loses too many of its more visible signs of the past. A bustling and frantic holiday destination, the Forbidden City, terracotta warriors and the Great Wall are nevertheless all wonders to behold. Shanghai is one of the world's fastest growing cities too and the buzz has to be experienced. Daily flights on Singapore Airlines to Shanghai, Beijing and other cities.

Hong Kong

Flight time: *3.75 hours*
Time difference: *None*
Best time to visit: *Oct - Nov*

Gateway to China and a city of great towers and unrivalled shopping, Hong Kong is a scenic and vibrant destination, with perhaps a little more soul than its rival Shanghai. But when it comes to better prices and greater awareness of how important leisure travellers are, it definitely has the edge. People flock here for Hong Kong's food, nightlife and new attractions like Disneyland. Singapore Airlines flies to Hong Kong daily.

Japan

Flight time: *6.5 hours*
Time difference: *One hour ahead*
Best time to visit : *Spring and autumn*

In contrast with the 'Asia-lite' of Singapore, a visit to Japan is like being thrown in the deep end. From the buzzing vast metropolis of Tokyo to the tranquility of Kyoto's atmospheric old quarters or the beauty of its countryside, Japan is a hit with everyone who visits. Not a cheap destination - accommodation can be wallet-draining, but well worth a trip. Direct flights are available with Singapore Airlines and Japanese airlines such as JAL.

New Zealand

Flight time: *10 hours*
Time difference: *Four hours ahead.*
Best Time to Visit: *Dec - Mar for summer, Jul - Sep for skiing*

The North Island's bubbling mud pools, hot water beaches and the Bay of Islands' many scenic inlets and coves are well-worth summertime exploration. Wellington is the country's arts capital and a year-round destination, and a short trip by ferry takes you to the winelands of Marlborough. The South Island offers plenty for nature lovers in the way of whale watching, hiking through Milford Sound or the glaciers of the West Coast. Indigenous Maori tribal attractions are to be found everywhere and there are adventure sports to be had too. In winter New Zealand's ski slopes in Queenstown are a real drawcard. Daily flights are available from Singapore to New Zealand.

Flight time: *5 hours*
Time difference: *None*
Best Time to Visit:
Apr - Sep

Taiwan

The drive and determination of Taipei (with the world's tallest building) rapidly gives way to the serenity of deep-green mountainsides and tea plantations in this remarkable country. Hot springs, marvellous rock formations, strange and beautiful lakes, temples and even a Spanish fort are some of the many aspects of Taiwan that make it well worth a visit. Spring is when the weather is good and the cherry blossoms and azaleas compete for attention. Singapore Airlines offers daily flights to Taipei.

Middle East & Africa

Flight time: *11 hours*
Time difference:
Six hours behind
Best time to visit:
Year round

South Africa

Whether you choose the vibrant, cosmopolitan city of Johannesburg, the tropical coastal beauty of Durban or the stylish, Mediterranean-influenced Cape Town, South Africa is a fantastic holiday destination. Often referred to as a 'world in one country', the list of things to do and see here is almost endless: why not start with whale watching, surfing, spotting some big game on a wildlife safari or wine tasting in the Cape? Singapore Airlines fly to South Africa daily.

Flight time: *7.5 hours*
Time difference:
Four hours behind.
Best time to visit:
Nov - Apr

United Arab Emirates

A gleaming city in the desert, Dubai is the Singapore of the Arab world, a gateway to the Middle East that offers travellers spectacular hotels, vibrant nightlife and great leisure options. Further afield there are many opportunities to explore the deserts and rich cultural heritage of the United Arab Emirates and its neighbours. There are daily flights from Singapore to Dubai on Singapore Airlines.

Dubai

Sydney

Hong Kong

239

Catch all the exciting racing action @Hibiscus

Head to where the action is!

A day at the races guarantees fun, glamour and the excitement of winning. Located on Grandstand Level 3 of the Singapore Racecourse, @Hibiscus is the perfect place to entertain and view the races up close.

With its chic décor and full-service in-house bar, @Hibiscus caters to the trendy-set who are out to have a good time. For a whole day of fun and excitement, join us @Hibiscus!

Click www.turfclub.com.sg for more details today!

SINGAPORE

TURF CLUB

IT'S MORE EXCITING WITH HORSES !

- The Singapore Racecourse is open to those 18 years old and above.
- For more information, please call 6879 1000 or visit the Club's website: www.turfclub.com.sg.

Activities

Sports & Activities

Singapore may not strike you as a sporting nation when you first arrive to the skyscrapers at Raffles Place and the shopping malls of Orchard Road, but dig deeper and you'll find a full complement of activities, facilities, clubs and teams.

The government has recognised the importance of a sporting culture to the development of a vibrant society, and has become actively involved in increasing participation in sport and improving sports infrastructure. From world-class events and local leagues to community fitness days and individual classes, there's bound to be an activity for you here. Singapore's tropical climate means it's possible to play most sports year-round. The rainy season (November to February) can turn field sports into muddy affairs and the heat and humidity in the middle of the day will drive many indoors in search of air conditioning, but you learn to work around these problems and once you acclimatise they fade into the background. There's even the opportunity to participate in winter sports, with a thriving ice hockey scene and an indoor snow centre.

Singapore's main limitations lie in its small size: airborne activities (flying, gliding, hot air balloons) are curtailed by airspace issues; cycling around the island and dodging traffic get a bit tiring after a while; and field sports teams or clubs occasionally have

Activity Finder

difficulty securing an appropriate venue. Luckily, it's possible to take daytrips to Malaysia and Indonesia for many of the activities that can't be done in Singapore.

Aerobics & Fitness Classes

There's no shortage of aerobics options in Singapore and classes run the gamut of styles from body combat and MTV dance through to body balance and ABT (abs, butt and thighs). Almost every health club – and most country clubs – offer classes to help you trim down and tone up. Studios are generally bright, clean and air-conditioned. Watch for new classes, as it doesn't take long for the latest miracle workout to make its way here from the US or Europe. For more information on what you can find where, see the table opposite.

Aerobics & Fitness Classes

Name	Area	Phone	Type of Class
Amore	Park Mall	6733 7333	ABT, Body Bar, Hi-Lo, Kardio Sculpt,
	Parco Bugis Junction	6336 6822	Kickboxing, Step
California Fitness	Orchard	6834 2100	ABT, Body Combat, Body Jam, Body Pump,
	Raffles	6524 0900	Boxercsise, Hi-Lo, Indoor Cycling, Jacky Chan
	Bugis	6337 2577	Boxercise (Bugis only), Step
Fitness First	Paragon	6737 7889	ABT, Body Balance, Body Combat, Body Jam
	CBD (George St)	6538 7666	(Paragon & George Street only), Body Pump,
	CBD (Capital Tower)	6536 5595	Body Step, Cardio Step (Paragon & George
	Raffles	6534 4333	Street only), MTV Dance, Rpm
Planet Fitness	Far East Square	6438 3833	Body Attack, Body Balance, Body Combat,
	Suntec City	6820 9000	Body Jam, Body Pump, MTV (Great World
	Caltex House	6438 3000	City only), Power Step
	Great World City	6235 962	
Takashimaya Fitness Club	Orchard	6739 9314	Boxercise, Hi-Lo, Step
The American Club	Orchard	6739 4312	ABT, Body Combat, Body Pump, Body Step,
			Boxercise, Indoor Cycling
The Hollandse Club	Bukit Timah	6464 5225	Cardio Sculpting, Low Impact, Step

American Football

Other options **Football** p.264

American Football in Singapore is arranged by the Singapore American Community Action Council (6363 6454) and is for kids only. SACAC runs three leagues for grades 5-6, 7-8 and 9-12 between August and October each year. All equipment is included in the league registration fee. A non-competitive, instruction-based Flag Football league for third to fourth grade kids is run in September and October. Practices and games take place at the Singapore American School in Woodlands (map 3-F4).

Aqua Aerobics

Aqua aerobics is a popular form of low-impact exercise in Singapore – any excuse to get in the water is welcomed when the sun is out and humidity reaches 90%! Be sure to wear waterproof sunscreen though, as being underwater does not stop the sun's rays from getting to your skin.

Aqua Aerobics

The American Club	Orchard	6737 3411
The British Club ▶ p.307	Bukit Timah	6467 4311
Fitness First	CBD (Capital Tower)	6536 5595
	CBD (George St)	6538 7666
The Hollandse Club	Bukit Timah	6464 5225
Takashimaya Fitness Club	Orchard	6739 9314

Oops!

Did we miss anything out? If you have any thoughts, ideas or comments for us to include in the Activities section, drop us a line, and if your club or organisation isn't here, let us know and we'll give you a shout in the next edition. Visit www.explorer publishing.com and tell us whatever's on your mind.

243

Archery

SAFRA Tampines
Tampines
🚇 *Tampines*
Map 12-A1

DM Archery
6346 4788 | www.dmarchery.com

For the aspiring Robin Hood, DM Archery operates a 30 lane indoor archery range at the SAFRA Tampines facility. Half of the targets are set at 18m, the other half at 9m. DM offers courses, corporate programmes and sells equipment at its pro-shop. The range is open from 14:00-22:00 every day and drop-in rates are $8 per hour, including equipment and instruction. If you have your own equipment you may want to look at one of the monthly or yearly packages to reduce your costs.

Art Classes
Other options **Art Galleries** p.203, **Art & Craft Supplies** p.326

26A Pagoda St
Chinatown
🚇 *Chinatown*
Map 17-C2

Chankerk Fine Arts (My Art Space)
9690 5775 | www.chankerk.com

A variety of classes are offered here, with everything from oil painting and portraiture, to landscape painting and sculpture, and more. Fees go from $170 for the four week introductory class to $320 for the eight week creative drawing class, but note that material is not included. In addition to teaching the techniques of each medium, instructors (including the eponymous Chankerk) try to give students an introduction to art history and encourage the development of their individual style. They also run corporate workshops which are ideal for getting your team working together and thinking creatively.

Red Sea Gallery
River Valley Road
🚇 *Somerset*
Map 17-B1

Creating Waves
6732 6711 | www.redseagallery.com/cwaves.html

Creating Waves is an art school within the Red Sea Gallery. Children's classes are segmented by age group and are themed to cover a wide range of media, from drawing and painting to sculpture and ceramics. Classes are 90 minutes long and each theme runs for six to eight weeks. Adult ceramics courses introduce students to a variety of techniques and styles. Other courses include a creative art workshop and contemporary watercolour. For more information contact Charlie Churcher at creatingwaves@redseagallery.com.

23 Emerald Hill
Orchard
🚇 *Somerset*
Map 14-B4

Instinc
6735 9867 | www.instinc.com

Instinc's classes are taught in a beautiful shophouse, a minute's walk up Emerald Hill from Orchard Road. A wide range of two-hour workshops offers everything from giftwrapping, papermaking, soft sculptures to collage and paper mache. Each workshop costs $50 and includes all materials. Longer five or eight week courses are also available on silk-screen printing and portrait techniques with other workshops run on request. A full list can be found on the Instinc website.

COMO SHAMBHALA

COMO SHAMBHALA,

A CENTRE OF PEACE AND
HARMONY, EMBODIES THE HOLISTIC
WAY OF LIFE, INNER PEACE, A BALANCE
OF THE SENSES AND ONENESS OF
BODY, MIND AND SPIRIT.

LEVELS OF CLASSES
BEGINNERS I
BEGINNERS II
GENERAL
ASHTANGA(LED)
INTRO TO YOGA
INTRO TO ASHTANGA

STYLES OF YOGA
HATHA
ASHTANGA
HATHA-VINYASA

SPECIAL
PRE-NATAL
POST-NATAL
INTEGRATED YOGA THERAPY
PILATES
PRIVATE CLASSES

COMO SHAMBHALA URBAN ESCAPE
583 Orchard Road #06-05 Forum Singapore 238884
Tel: (65) 6735 2163 Fax: (65) 6735 2993
www.comoshambhala.bz
email: singapore@comoshambhala.bz

Studio Miu

6733 0917 | www.singaweb.net/studiomiuart

Studio Miu is tucked away in the back corner of Takashimaya Shopping Centre's Fourum (located on the fourth floor, of course). They also have a new studio at Chip Bee Gardens in Holland Village (Map 13-C4), but as it's run out of a private house all telephone inquiries are routed through the main branch. The studio runs art classes for kids aged two and a half or older. They regularly have exhibitions of well-known local artists at the gallery around the corner and many of these exhibiting artists then conduct courses at the studio, offering you an unique opportunity to learn from a range of experts. They even hold regular Manga workshops. Class costs vary, but are around $50 for a two to three hour session and are usually held in a series of six or eight classes. Studio Miu is Japanese-run and tuition is in English and Japanese.

The Substation

6337 7535 | www.substation.org

The Substation is a happening cultural hub in the centre of town. Among its wide variety of classes it offers a four-week course on batik painting, one of the oldest traditional arts in South East Asia. Course fees are $120 and materials cost an additional $40.

UniqArts

6344 1670 | www.uniqarts.com.sg

UniqArts offers just about everything for just about everyone at its main studio in Katong. It also runs classes from the function room of the Seletaris Condo in Sembawang (513 Sembawang Road, Map 4-C3). Your options range from sculpture and Manga drawing to Chinese calligraphy and customised fine art classes. The creativity-juice workshop allows adult students to explore the creative process and unleash their ideas, while the interactive online art class lets kids learn techniques from the comfort of their home. Fees vary but expect to pay between $200-350, including materials, for courses running for 8-10 weeks.

Astronomy

The Astronomical Society of Singapore

6567 4163 | www.tasos.org.sg

Probably the best way to get involved in astronomy is to drop by the Astro Scientific Centre (www.astro.com.sg) or give them a call on the same number as The Astronomical Society of Singapore, listed above, as owner Albert Lim is also the president of TASOS. The society regularly has outings around Singapore and occasionally goes to Malaysia to get away from Singapore's urban lights for a darker, less light-polluted view of the night sky. Informational talks and observatory sessions are held throughout the year and you'll find the schedule on the TASOS website. You must become a member of the society in order to participate in activities.

Australian Rules Football

Singapore Wombats

6733 1215 | www.anza.org.sg

The Wombats are Singapore's only Aussie rules football team. From March to November they practise every Saturday at 16:00 and regularly host teams from the Australian Navy. The team also travels to tournaments in Jakarta, Kuala Lumpur, Hong Kong and Tokyo and there's a junior programme for children aged 4 to 16, with coaching provided by the Wombats' players.

Badminton

Badminton is a popular sport in Singapore, where you'll often see people playing in parks and near housing estates. The Singapore Badminton Association (SBA) manages badminton's development here, runs the national team and oversees the various competitions held here each year. Casual players can simply look for the ubiquitous badminton courts at most community centres, or join one of the many clubs afflllated with the SBA. Many of these clubs are run as part of corporate recreation programmes with some of the larger companies in Singapore; others are connected to country clubs or community centres. There is a list of these clubs on the SBA website (www.singaporebadminton.org.sg) under the membership link.

Baseball

Various locations

Typhoons

www.baseball.sg

The Typhoons offer a friendly, multicultural environment for playing baseball. The team is made up of enthusiastic players from Canada, USA, Japan, Taiwan, the Philippines, Malaysia, Australia and Singapore, giving it a truly international flavour. They practise on Saturdays at 10:00 and play on Sundays during the National Baseball League season. Beginners are welcomed at the training sessions to get a feel for the game. Email Ronnie Ha at haronnie@starhub.net.sg.

Various locations

X-Men

www.eteamz.active.com/xmen

The X-Men are all about serious baseball and serious fun. They hold regular practices throughout the year and organise games with other local teams. For more details on practices, games and joining the club, send an email to xmenbaseballclub@yahoo.com.

Basketball

From a casual shoot-around to organised league games, there's plenty of basketball action to be found here. Check out the Kallang Community Centre on Friday nights, the Singapore American School on Wednesday nights and Cairnhill Community Centre which has games from 18:00 on Monday, Wednesday and Friday and during the day on weekends. There's also the National Institute of Education on Evans Road, off Bukit Timah Road, the American base at Sembawang and a game at 07:00 on Sundays at the Anglo-Chinese School on Barker Road. A number of leagues run throughout the year, all administered by BBAXN (that's the company's name not an acronym). You can register on www.bbaxn.com or simply show up at one of the pickup games and do some networking.

Beauty Training

Other options **Beauty Salons** p.310

Paradiz Centre
Colonial District
🔲 *Dhoby Ghaut*
Map 14-C4

Cosmoprof Beauty, Make-up & Spa Academy

6339 3325 | www.cosmoprof.com.sg

Cosmoprof has separate academies for make-up and for beauty and spa treatments. The make-up academy offers range of courses including personal, bridal, stage and drama make-up. The beauty and spa academy offers courses leading to internationally recognised accreditations including CIDESCO and CIBTAC diplomas. Short courses in Thai and Swedish massage, hot stones therapy and body contouring are also available.

247

Raffles City ◀
Colonial District
🚇 **City Hall**
Map 17-D1

SPAcademy

6883 2308 | *www.spacademy.com.sg*

SPAcademy, based at the Convention Centre in Raffles City, offers a full range of courses for those aspiring to enter the spa industry. Some of these lead to CIBTAC and ITEC accreditation and diplomas and certificates in spa operations and management. The academy's Learning for Life programme also offers individual classes in traditional Chinese medicine, homeopathy, aromatherapy and other disciplines.

Birdwatching

Other options **Environmental Groups** p.261

Singapore offers birdwatchers opportunities to see a huge variety of birds in a relatively small area. One day could easily comprise a morning in jungle, followed by a late afternoon outing to a wetland area – and it's not unheard of to see over 100 species in that time. Singapore has recorded over 350 species sightings, of which about 150 are resident birds. Species include the red-crowned barbet, chestnut-bellied malkoha, long-tailed parakeet and copper-throated sunbird. Recommended sites are Bukit Timah Nature Reserve (p.229), one of the last remaining patches of primary forest, and the Central Catchment Nature Reserve (Map 6-F2). The Botanic Gardens (p.216) in the heart of town are convenient, but birdwatching is more difficult given the crowds. Offshore options include the Semakau Landfill site (Map 1-C4) and Pulau Ubin (p.251). Jurong Bird Park (see below) is also worth visiting as you're guaranteed sightings of an impressive variety of birdlife in a relatively compact area. If your interest is in photographing birds, the Nature Photographic Society holds dedicated bird photography outings once a month led by experienced bird photographers, with beginners also welcome, see p.284 for more information.

2 Jurong Hill ◀
Jurong
🚇 **Boon Lay**
Map 9-E1

Jurong BirdPark

6265 0022 | *www.birdpark.com.sg*

A dizzying array of over 9,000 birds from 600 species inhabits this 20 hectare park and its four aviaries. Regular bird shows are held, demonstrating the birds' unique characteristics. Special attractions include the Lory Loft, Pelican Cove, Penguin Parade and the World of Darkness. The park is great for families and kids, but also worthwhile for serious bird enthusiasts.

Various locations ◀

Wildbird Singapore

www.nss.org.sg/wildbirdsingapore

Wildbird is a special interest group of the Nature Society of Singapore. Experts on the avian fauna of Singapore lead a number of birdwatching outings every month. Regular destinations include Sungei Buloh Wetland Reserve, Bukit Timah Nature Reserve and the Semakau Landfill site. Outings are meant for members only but visiting birders should contact the relevant outing leader through the website (www.nss.org.sg/wildbirdsingapore) or email wildbirdsingapore@yahoogroups.com to inquire about going along. Wildbird also conducts the annual bird census, now in its 20th year, and puts out a quarterly newsletter Singapore Avifauna.

Boules

Swimming Complex ◀
Toa Payoh
🚇 **Toa Payoh**
Map 14-C1

Sports Boules Singapore

6356 5093 | *www.sportsboules.org.sg*

Boules has a small but enthusiastic following in Singapore, and courts can be found at many local community centres. The Sports Boules Singapore training centre at the Toa

248

Payoh Swimming Complex is primarily a training centre for youngsters and national players, but social games also take place at the courts there. A number of competitive events are organised by the association throughout the year.

Bowling

Other options **Boules** p.248

It's evident from the number of bowling alleys on the island that this is a popular activity. Many country clubs have their own lanes, including the American Club (8 lanes, see p.295), Singapore Island Country Club (12 lanes, p.268), Singapore Recreation Club (10 lanes, 6430 7563) and Orchid Country Club (36 lanes, p.267). The Hollandse Club (p.296) adds a twist with its glow-in-the-dark bowling alley – great for children's birthday parties. Commercial bowling alleys also abound, with some of the larger ones having upwards of 30 lanes. While most of these are some distance from downtown, the area around Marina South has close to 70 lanes within about 200m of each other. Equipment is generally modern and facilities are clean and well-maintained. A game costs between $2-4 depending on the time of day.

Various locations

Cathay Bowl
www.cathaybowl.com.sg

The four Cathay Bowl locations at Ang Mo Kio, Yishun, Tampines and Boon Lay boast a total of 84 lanes. All branches have modern flat screen scorers and 36 inch overhead display units. Cathay have introduced a number of fun twists to the game including Cosmic Bowling, Bumper Bowling and a Bowling Ramp to help small children towards their first strike. The Cathay Bowling Academy also offers bowling instruction.

Various locations

Superbowl
www.superbowl.com.sg

Superbowl has 162 lanes of bowling excitement across six locations. Marina South (6221 1010, 36 wooden lanes) and Marina Square (6334 1000, near Suntec City, 18 wooden lanes) are the most central of the six. The newest facility is the one at SAFRA Mount Faber (6276 5225), which has 34 state-of-the-art synthetic lanes, and hosted the Bowling World Cup in 2004.

7 Marina Grove
Marina Bay
🚇 **Marina Bay**
Map 17-E3

Victor's Superbowl
6223 7998 | www.victorssuperbowl.com.sg

Victor's Superbowl has 32 wooden bowling lanes and computerised scoring. For your bowling equipment needs you can turn to the in-house Ken Pro Shop, which also offers services such as ball resurfacing, while a small cafe offers food and refreshment. A number of leagues run throughout the week and the occasional major tournament is also hosted here.

Boxing

110 Mountbatten Rd
Kallang
🚇 **Kallang**
Map 14-F3

Kadir's Boxing School
9843 3009 | www.sgboxing.tripod.com

Kadir's Boxing School offers training for women and men of all ages. Members take part in competitions, and the more competitive boxers go to overseas tournaments. The gym is located at the Singapore Martial Arts Instructors Association near the National Stadium and is open from Monday to Thursday, 19:00-21:30, and Saturday mornings from 09:30-12:30.

249

101 Balestier Rd
Toa Payoh
🚇 Toa Payoh
Map 14-D3

U2Can

6293 9225

Run by an IOC-qualified coach, U2Can provides a gym, training and the occasional tournament for boxing enthusiasts. The club has a ring and a number of boxing bags set up at the Ceylon Sports Club. Memberships for-men and women cost $50 per month, $40 for students. The club is open on weekday evenings from 19:00-21:00 and on Saturdays from 15:00-16:30.

Bridge

51 Bishan St 13
Bishan
🚇 Bishan
Map 7-B4

Singapore Contract Bridge Association

6356 8540 | www.scba.org.sg

The Singapore Contract Bridge Association offers introductory bridge courses at its Bishan clubhouse every month and regular bridge games every day except Wednesdays. All are welcome but non-members will have to pay a small fee. The SCBA also organises the Singapore Inter-Club Bridge League which runs from April to October and during which games take place on Saturdays at clubs around Singapore. Call the SCBA for the latest information on social games or the league.

5 Stevens Rd
Orchard
🚇 Orchard
Map 14-A4

Tanglin Club

6739 4128 | www.tanglinclub.org.sg

The Tanglin Club's bridge section holds regular sessions for beginner to intermediate level players. Members and their guests meet in the club's Card Room for duplicate bridge on Monday, Wednesday and Friday afternoons. Duplicate and social bridge is played on Wednesday evenings and novice sessions are run on Tuesday afternoons. One-on-one instruction is available on request. The club also arranges the occasional luncheon and BGB Sims game.

Camping

Other options **Outdoor Goods** p.348

Singapore's hot and humid climate (with the occasional torrential downpour) make camping slightly uncomfortable, although setting up camp near the ocean can offer a refreshing break from the heat. In addition, camping here is not exactly a true wilderness experience, as you'll most likely be pitching a tent on a manicured lawn under some trees. But if you're set on experiencing the great outdoors, there are five parks for you to head to: Changi Beach Park (map 8-F4), East Coast Park (p.214), Pasir Ris Park (p.216), Sembawang Park (map 4-D2) and West Coast Park (p.214). Details can be found on the National Parks website at www.nparks.gov.sg. While there are no camping fees, permits are required for weekdays and, conveniently, park rangers will come by your tent to issue these. Pulau Ubin and the Southern Islands are other camping destinations that are just a short boat trip away (see below for Pulau Ubin). The Southern Islands, consisting of Kusu, St. John's, Sisters' and Pulau Hantu, are administered by the Sentosa administrative authorities (www.sentosa.com.sg, 6275 0388) and you will need prior approval for overnight camping. A ferry service runs from the Sentosa Ferry Terminal to Kusu and St. John's, but speak to the boat operators at Jardine Steps (Harbourfront MRT station) or Clifford Pier (Raffles Place MRT station) to get to Pulau Hantu or the Sisters' Islands. For more details on these islands, see Outer Islands on p.201 in the Exploring chapter.

Get Out There

You'll find Singapore, with its large international community that welcomes newcomers, an easy place to get involved in sports. If what you're looking for is not offered in an organised league or club, it's likely to be played in an informal fashion at the pitch or community centre around the corner. Ask around and you'll find what you're looking for.

North east of ◀
Singapore
Map 8-C2

Pulau Ubin

6542 4108 | *www.npark.gov.sg*

A $2 bumboat ride from Changi Point Ferry Terminal will get you to Pulau Ubin, a large island off the north east coast of Singapore. The developed parts of Pulau Ubin are said to be like a trip back to the Singapore of the 1960s, with kampong-style life still eking out a small existence. There are a number of grocery stores where you can pick up food and any supplies you might have forgotten. Tents can be pitched at the beach campsites of Noordin, Mamam or Jelutong, all of which have toilet facilities, although only Jelutong has designated fire pits. No permits are required. For more information on what there is to do on the island, see Pulau Ubin in Outer Islands on p.201.

Canoeing

Other options **Kayaking** p.273

Tanjong Beach ◀
Sentosa
🚇 *HarbourFront*
Map 19-D3

Singapore Paddle Club

9748 3441 | *www.singaporepaddleclub.com*

The Singapore Paddle Club, which operates off Tanjong Beach on Sentosa, is south-east Asia's first outrigger canoe club. They have two six-man and a number of one-man outriggers, and they will soon have a purpose-built boathouse on the beach too. The SPC regularly attends competitions in Guam, Saipan, Hong Kong and Hawaii among other places. Beginners and serious athletes are welcomed. Beginner training sessions take place on weekend mornings, while experienced paddlers hit the water throughout the week, going to Singapore's Southern Islands, along the East Coast and occasionally to the Riau Islands in Indonesia. Paddlers frequently encounter sea turtles, rays and other marine life. For more information email info@singaporepaddleclub.com or call the coaches: Nick Yap at 9748 3441 and Albert Santos at 9423 7092.

Chess

Other options **Scrabble** p.291

1 Goldhill Plaza ◀
Novena
🚇 *Novena*
Map 14-C3

Intchess Asia

6258 0100 | *www.intchessasia.com*

Intchess Asia, which incorporates the Asean Chess Academy, is the only FIDE-accredited chess academy in Asia. They hold classes for all levels of player and provide FIDE-approved certification courses for chess instructors. (FIDE by the way is the acronym for the World Chess Federation's official name in French.) With over 100 members, Club Intchess meets on Tuesdays and Saturdays for practice sessions. Membership fees start at $72 and include a subscription to Intchess Magazine. The Asean Chess Academy also organises tournaments and workshops.

Climbing

Singapore has a well-developed climbing scene for such a small country. For information on sport climbing competitions contact the Singapore Mountaineering Federation (6220 9505) or see their website at www.smf.org.sg. Natural outdoor climbing is possible in the Bukit Timah Nature Reserve's Dairy Farm Quarry and on Pulau Ubin and the best information on these areas is in the guidebook *Climb Singapore* by the folks at Climb Asia. SAFRA and a number of the schools have outdoor climbing walls in varying states of repair. The school facilities are generally only for students, but the public can access SAFRA's facilities for a fee. Once you've pushed the limits of what Singapore has to offer, the Batu Caves in Malaysia and the limestone cliffs of Krabi, in Thailand offer some spectacular and more challenging climbing

251

opportunities. Regardless of where you go, make sure your chalk bag is full – the heat and humidity make for sweaty hands and a slippery grip!

Climb Adventure

10 Hoe Chiang Rd
Tanjong Pagar
Tanjong Pagar
Map 17-B3

6220 3305 | *www.climbadventure.com*

Located in the centre of town, Climb Adventure is a great place to get in a climbing session during your lunch break or after work. And with 5,400 square feet of climbing space and climbing routes that are usually changed monthly, you'll always have a new challenge waiting for you. An adult day pass costs $10, shoes, belay devices and harnesses can be rented and a snack bar ensures you're well-fuelled for a full day of climbing. Climbing courses for all levels are offered by certified staff from the Singapore Mountaineering Federation.

Climb Asia

117 Rangoon Rd
Newton
Farrer Park
Map 14-D3

6292 7701 | *www.climb-asia.com*

Set up in a pre-war shophouse that now houses a 7.5m climbing wall and Singapore's largest bouldering area, Climb Asia is run by some of Singapore's top climbers. The pro-shop carries equipment from all the top brand names as well as Climb Asia's climbing guidebooks to Singapore and Malaysia. A half-day fun climbing course costs $25 and SNCS sport climbing levels 1 and 2 are $70 and $115 respectively. Entry fees are $10 for non-members, $4-6 for members depending on the day. A lifetime membership costs only $20.

SAFRA Adventure Sports Centre

60 Yishun Ave 4
Yishun
Yishun
Map 4-D4

6852 8200 | *www.safra.sg*

SAFRA Yishun doubles as the national climbing centre, and has the largest and most diverse facilities in Singapore. With 15, 18 and 25m walls, an artificial ice climbing wall and an indoor bouldering gym it offers something for everyone. Members of the public can spend a full day here for $32 during the week and $46 on weekends and public holidays. Equipment rental is also available for standard and ice climbing.

Cookery Classes

at-sunrice

Fort Canning Centre
Colonial District
Dhoby Ghaut
Map 17-C1

6336 3307 | *www.at-sunrice.com*

at-sunrice is a full-service culinary academy offering everything from tips on how to select fresh herbs and spices to professional chef training. Those hoping to wow friends and family in the kitchen can start with the spice garden walk, tea reception and spice paste demonstration ($30) and progress to the week-long Taste of Asia course ($1,288). Unique interactive sessions include birthday parties where the kids learn to bake their own cake and workshops where the family gets together in the at-sunrice kitchens to cook its own selection of recipes that are then put into a cookbook.

Bentfork Cooking School

Block 43 Jalan
Merah Saga
Holland Village
Buona Vista
Map 13-C3

6475 4961 | *www.bentfork.sg*

Bentfork Cooking School is associated with a group of well-known Singapore restaurants including Michelangelo's Italian Restaurant, Original Sin and Sistina Ristorante. Chef Angelo Sanelli and his team teach a variety of classes for all cuisines and then some. Particularly interesting are offerings such as 'The men do get it' course aimed at getting men into the kitchen and the after-dinner delights of 'Cigars & Port'. Bentfork is also available for corporate bookings where you and your colleagues get to improve your teamwork by creating a gourmet meal together.

Cookery Magic

Off Haig Rd
Geylang
🚇 *Paya Lebar*
Map 15-B3

6348 9667 | *www.cookerymagic.com*

Cookery Magic cooking courses are taught by Ruqxana Vasanwala who, after 14 years of work as an engineer, decided that she preferred the kitchen to the office. Classes are taught at her home kitchen, although larger groups can be accommodated at other venues. Instruction is available in all types of Asian and European cuisine as well as baking, and trips to the local wet market to shop for ingredients before the class can also be arranged. Cookery Magic also offers a unique opportunity to learn how to cook traditional Malay dishes in a 200 year old kampong house on Pulau Ubin and visits to an organic farm.

Coriander Leaf

3A River Valley Rd
Riverside
🚇 *Clarke Quay*
Map 17-C1

6732 3354 | *www.corianderleaf.com*

The Coriander Leaf provides instruction in south Asian, south-east Asian, Middle Eastern, Mediterranean and fusion cooking styles. The recipes taught are intended to give students an understanding of each cuisine – and to be able to recreate the dish at home. The venue is lovely: classes take place on the bright and attractive second floor of a riverside shophouse. You can get a group of up to 10 friends together and make it a social event, or simply sign up and use the opportunity to meet like-minded aspiring culinaires.

Palate Sensations

1 Westbourne Rd
Queenstown
🚇 *Buona Vista*
Map 16-C1

6479 9025 | *www.palatesensations.com*

It's all about having fun, making a bit of a mess and cooking up a storm at Palate Sensations. Its team of instructors will guide you through the preparation and presentation of a wide variety of light and healthy dishes in both local and international cuisines. Set in a quiet and attractive colonial estate, the cooking studio sports the latest appliances and gadgets to help you along the way. Group classes are limited to a maximum of 15 participants and private lessons are also available. The studio can also be hired out for corporate team events, private functions and dinner parties.

Shermay's Cooking School

43 Jalan Merah Saga
Holland Village
🚇 *Buona Vista*
Map 13-C3

6479 8442 | *www.shermay.com*

Part cooking school and part retail store, Shermay's is a great place to pick up new recipes and new kitchenware. Shermay, the school's owner, is a successful cookbook author and chef who creates everything from traditional Nonya dishes to fine French cuisine. He and a number of celebrity chefs from some of Singapore's top restaurants teach the classes which can either take the format of step-by-step demonstrations, or hands-on work by students with guidance from the chef.

Cricket

Being a former British colony, cricket is a popular game in Singapore and there are numerous clubs and pitches around the island. Between training sessions, social games and Singapore Cricket Association (SCA) competitions, there's plenty of action to be had.

253

One of the most prominent clubs is the Singapore Cricket Club at the picturesque Padang. Expat clubs such as the British Club and ANZA also field teams in the SCA's competitions and hold regular friendlies.

200 Turf Club Rd
Bukit Timah
Map 13-C1

ANZA Cricket Club

9615 0290 | www.anzacc.org.sg

The ANZA Cricket Club is open to ANZA members and has its home grounds at Turf City. The club fields teams in all three divisions of the Singapore Cricket Association, with the Firsts playing 50 overs at 10:00 on Sundays; the Seconds playing 40 overs at 13:00 on Sundays; and the Thirds playing 30 overs at 13:30. For the slightly less serious, the Dream Team plays a social game from 11:00 to 16:00 at Turf City on Saturdays. To get involved give Clive Tilbrook a call at 9615 0290.

73 Bukit Tinggi Rd
Bukit Timah
🚇 *Bukit Batok*
Map 6-E4

The British Club ▶ p.307

6467 4311 | www.britishclub.org.sg

Members of the British Club's cricket section play in the third division of the Singapore Cricket Association league and organise social games whenever possible. Matches are played on Saturday afternoons and a group of 7-12 year olds meets on Sunday afternoons for training at the club's nets on the corner of Dunearn Road and Swiss Club Road. For more information call the club or email sports@britishclub.org.sg.

Connaught Drive
Colonial District
🚇 *City Hall*
Map 17-C2

Singapore Cricket Club

6338 9271 | www.scc.org.sg

Founded in 1852, the Singapore Cricket Club is the city's second oldest sports club, and one of its most prestigious. With its clubhouse set on the Padang, the cricket pitch commands an impressive view of the Singapore skyline and the colonial buildings nearby. The club fields teams in three divisions, as well as a more casual Saturday XI and a programme for younger players. For details on membership, call the number above.

Cycling

Other options **Mountain Biking** p.280, **Cycling** p.51

Various locations

ANZA Cycling

6733 1215 | www.anzacycling.com

While affiliated with the Australian and New Zealand Association, ANZA Cycling is open to anyone. This well-organised club has group rides happening almost every day of the week, catering to a wide range of abilities. So it's just up to you to decide how early you want to get up and whether you want to tackle the hills at Mount Faber, ride with the pace lines at Changi or go for a nice rolling loop at Kranji. Rides range from the relaxed weekend cruise to 200km sessions in Malaysia or Indonesia for the fanatics. Ad hoc rides are arranged via the email list, which you can join on the website. For up-to-date information visit www.anzacycling.com or email membership@anzacycling.com.

Dance Classes

Other options **Music Lessons** p.282

70 Palmer Rd
Tanjong Pagar
🚇 *Tanjong Pagar*
Map 17-C3

Attitude Dance Studio

6226 2381 | *www.asiasalsa.com*

Attitude Dance Studio, headed by its highly qualified artistic director Gūpson Pierre, specialises in teaching salsa. Ten salsa courses spanning different skill levels and styles means you're sure to find something to fit your needs. For only $70 you can enjoy five lessons in the beginners' module, but be warned: there's a good chance you'll become addicted to salsa! Check out the studio's website for a list of all the courses, a class schedule and to register online.

Various locations

Belinda Tan

9625 8385 | *www.saharasundance.com*

Performer and instructor Belinda Tan promotes bellydancing as a way for women to gain self-confidence and become comfortable with their bodies. And you get a full-body workout and improve your flexibility at the same time. Group classes are taught at four different skill levels, and courses consist of eight weekly classes of one hour each. Private lessons can also be arranged. For more information email sambalatino@yahoo.com.

Various locations

Belly Dance Discovery

9879 9960 | *www.bellydance.com.sg*

At Belly Dance Discovery students are encouraged to 'bring out the goddess' in them through physical expression. Classes range from beginner to advanced and gradually introduce more complex elements such as incorporating the veil and fan and Middle Eastern rhythms. You can also branch out into styles such as Saiidi Cane, Turkish, Pop and Flamenco. Classes are held at venues in Tanjong Pagar and Orchard. Fees for eight weekly sessions are $120-130 for members and $160-170 for non-members.

153 King's Rd
Bukit Timah
Map 13-E2

Claribel's Raks Sharki Studio

6476 2292 | *www.claribelstudio.com*

Claribel's Raks Sharki Studio offers bellydancing classes and also sells all the necessary accessories such as costumes, scarves, shoes, CDs and videotapes. Classes are run for beginners through to more advanced dancers and are capped at a maximum of 12 students. Fees are $150 for eight sessions. Tuition in Japanese is also available.

Far East Square, 70
Telok Ayer St
Chinatown
🚇 *Raffles Place*
Map 17-C2

Country Line Dance Association

www.cldas.com

For a taste of the west in the Far East, you can head down to Far East Square every Friday and Sunday night to watch, or join in, the line dancing fun. Sessions are held in public so you can just wander by and scope it out if you're a bit shy. Association members pay $1 per session; non-members pay $3. Song lists are published on the website so if you know your line dances you can practice ahead of time. One-off events are also held regularly and you'll find details of these on the website.

Bukit Timah Plaza
Bukit Timah
Map 6-D4

Forms Ballet and Dance Centre

6467 2589 | *www.formsballet.com*

Forms Ballet offers classes for all ages from three years up in its clean and bright studio at Bukit Timah Plaza. Classes follow the internationally recognised Royal Academy of Dance syllabus and students can take annual RAD exams. A trial class is recommended

255

as it gives newcomers the opportunity to see if they like it, and allows the instructor to place students in an appropriate class. Trial classes cost from $10-20.

Hard Rock Café

50 Cuscaden Rd
Orchard
🚇 *Orchard*
Map 14-A4

6235 5232 | www.hardrock.com.sg
So you've taken your salsa class and now you're ready to test out your new moves. The Hard Rock Café holds occasional salsa nights with instructors on hand to help if you've forgotten a step or two since taking a class. The salsa music starts around 20:30 and ends late. Call the Hard Rock Café to find out when the next salsa night is scheduled.

Jitterbugs Swingapore

9 Raffles Blvd
Millenia Walk
Colonial District
Map 17-D1

6887 0383 | www.swingapore.com
Jitterbugs Swingapore is a one-stop shop for just about every style of dance you can imagine, from lindy hop, salsa and merengue to hip-hop, ballet and tap dancing. They even throw in a bit of yoga and pilates for good measure. Classes are for adults and kids and a course usually runs for eight weeks. There's no need to have a partner before enrolling – in fact, rotating partners is encouraged so you'll meet and dance with a lot of new people. Although membership is not required, it does reduce the cost of a class quite significantly. An annual membership costs $50, or make it a lifetime membership for $350.

JJSalsaRengue@DanceHub

24A Murray St
Chinatown
🚇 *Chinatown*
Map 17-C3

9671 8985 | www.jjsalsarengue.com
JJSalsaRengue@DanceHub specialises in salsa and merengue. Jackson and June, the studio's founders, have extensive performance and teaching experience and have travelled overseas to learn advanced salsa techniques. A variety of classes are available, from beginner to advanced salsa rueda casino classes. Fees start at $90 for a six week course of 90 minute classes.

John & Josephine Dance Creative

Parklane
Shopping Mall
Colonial District
🚇 *Dhoby Ghaut*
Map 14-C4

6334 6230 | www.johnjosephinedance.com.sg
Dust off your dancing shoes; with a full range of lessons for all levels, John & Josephine Dance Creative will teach you to waltz, tango, samba and more. Classes are held every afternoon and evening of the week. Group classes cost $100-120 for eight one-hour sessions and private and semi-private classes are also available. You can buy shoes, clothing, CDs, DVDs and anything else you might need to dance the night away from a store on the premises. John & Josephine Dance Creative also organises the Singapore Millennium International DanceSport Championships, one of the most established dancesport events in the region.

Singapore Dance Theatre

Fort Canning Centre
Colonial District
🚇 *Dhoby Ghaut*
Map 17-C1

6338 0611 | www.singaporedancetheatre.com
In addition to performing extensively throughout the year, the Singapore Dance Theatre runs a series of adult dance classes, including ballet, jazz ballet, modern dance and classical Japanese dance, in its attractive home at Fort Canning Centre. Terms run for eight weeks and are taught by SDT performers. Fees range from $120 to $200 and trial classes can be arranged for $20, subject to availability.

St. Andrew's Society of Singapore

Various locations

6465 4459 | www.standrewssociety.org.sg
Prepare to be transported to the highlands of Scotland with some traditional Scottish dancing in a fun and social atmosphere. The St Andrew's Society of Singapore holds

gatherings every Thursday evening at the Republic of Singapore Yacht Club for $5 per session. Advanced dancing and children's classes are also on the programme, but they are held less frequently and take place at the ISS International School. The society holds several functions that include Scottish dancing throughout the year, the highlight of which is the annual ball in November.

45 Armenian St
Colonial District
🚇 *City Hall*
Map 17-C1

The Substation

6337 7535 | *www.substation.org*

The Substation offers a wide variety of classes in a range of artistic disciplines, including one on contemporary dance, at its convenient downtown location. You'll get a chance to explore your body language in relation to music and energy while learning a series of bounces, jumps and floor works. Eight weekly sessions cost $160.

Diving

Other options **Snorkelling** p.293

Scuba diving in Singapore is limited and a rather poor alternative to the world-class diving to be had in the rest of Southeast Asia. Due to the land reclamation projects that stir up huge amounts of silt, the waters around Singapore are relatively murky and at a depth of 3m you'll need a torch to read your gauges. Pulau Ubin and the Southern Islands may be worth a visit – but be aware that there can be strong currents near the Sisters Islands. If you do make the trip to the Southern Islands you could see resident sharks and a sea turtle or two. For more details you can contact the dive centres listed below, but they will most likely tell you that a quick and reasonably priced trip to Malaysia or Indonesia will offer better sights and experiences than anything on offer in local waters. The Tanglin Club and British Club have active dive groups, but you'll need to become a member of the club before you can participate in the group activities.

33 Mohamed
Sultan Rd
Tanglin
🚇 *Somerset*
Map 17-B1

51 Scuba

6732 5751 | *www.51scuba.com*

51 Scuba has all the bases covered for diving in Singapore and the region. They offer courses from introductory Discover Scuba sessions to dive master and everything in between. The initial training is usually done in a pool with the open water component of the course involving a weekend trip to Tioman or Dayang off the east coast of Malaysia. 51 Scuba also organises diving trips around the region and sells the gear you'll need once you're hooked on scuba.

20 Upper Circular Rd
Riverside
🚇 *Clarke Quay*
Map 17-C2

Friendly Waters Seasport Services

6557 0016 | *www.friendlywaters.com.sg*

Friendly Waters is a true one-stop shop for all your diving needs. They sell equipment, teach courses, organise trips and have three of their own vessels, including the 75ft liveaboard Samudera Quest. To top it off, Friendly Waters even has its own dive resort, The Diver's Lodge on Pulau Aur in Malaysia. And when you're stuck on land you can head to Narcosis Bar, right next to the Friendly Waters dive centre at the Riverwalk, where they run occasional dive nights, with diving videos playing and the drinks flowing.

184 Telok Ayer St
Colonial District
🚇 *Tanjong Pagar*
Map 17-C3

Orpheus Dive

6223 2190 | *www.orpheusdive.com*

Orpheus Dive is a full-service PADI 5 Star Dive Centre, offering courses, equipment and dive trips throughout the region. Most of their courses involve a pool session in Singapore, followed by a trip to Malaysia to gain open water experience. They also

257

arrange regular environmental trips under the Project AWARE banner, where divers conduct underwater and beach cleanups and collect broken corals for replanting.

Scuba Corner

809 French Rd
Little India
Lavender
Map 14-E4

6338 6563 | *www.scubacorner.com.sg*

Scuba Corner has been providing dive training and trips for over 10 years and is a PADI 5 Star Instructor Development Centre. They offer courses, a full range of top-quality equipment and dive trips around the region. Trips can be from two nights up to a week long and go to Pulau Aur and Pulau Tioman in Malaysia, Koh Phi Phi in Thailand and many other destinations. Scuba Corner also carries PADI products and has a fully-equipped workshop to service and repair your scuba gear.

Waikiki Dive Centre

298 Beach Rd
Arab Street &
Kampong Glam
Nicoll Highway
Map 14-D4

6291 1290 | *www.waikikidive.com*

Waikiki Dive at The Concourse is a PADI 5 Star Dive Centre, as well as a National Geographic Dive Centre. It offers a full range of PADI dive courses and new and used scuba equipment from well-known brands for sale. Waikiki also organises diving trips around the region, including many of the Malaysian islands and dive locations in Thailand, the Philippines and Indonesia.

Dog Training

Other options **Pets** p.350

A Good Dog

Various locations

9754 7621 | *www.agooddogtraining.com*

Certified by the Australian Association of Professional Dog Trainers, Tan Teck Woon's approach is to teach owners how to train their dogs, rather than training the dogs for them. By establishing a strong owner-dog relationship, owners are able to continue with their dog's training even after they have completed the classes. A Good Dog holds classes for puppies, basic and intermediate levels. Group classes usually take place at Katong Park, but private or semi-private lessons can be held at your home or a location of your choice.

Awesome Pawsome

Various locations

9003 5644

Who knew your dog could get a PhD? Awesome Pawsome offers courses ranging from puppy kindergarten up to formal and competitive courses which, when completed, will allow your dog to put a designation after its name. 'Canine good citizens' is the general obedience and behaviour course offered, while there are also sports-oriented courses for jumping and agility. Group and individual lessons are available, as is canine behavioural counselling, canine temperament profiling and pet bereavement therapy should your dog pass away. Awesome Pawsome also participates in 'Pets are Therapy', a programme where owners and their dogs visit hospitals and homes to provide pet-based therapy for patients.

Mitchville K-9 Kennels

T-92 Seletar West
Farmway 1
Yio Chu Kang
Map 7-C2

6482 0084 | *www.mitchville.com.sg*

Mitchville K-9 Kennels will teach your dog five commands to follow in its basic obedience course. Classes are taught on a one-on-one basis, and initially the instructor works directly with the dog without the owner being present. Once the commands have been learned and the dog is trained, the owner is brought in to learn how to give the commands. Instruction can take place at your home or at Mitchville K-9's kennels. The cost is $1,300 and it generally takes about a month for your dog to be trained.

Fashion Boutiques p.123
Financial Advisors p.95

Written by residents, these unique guidebooks are packed with insider info, from arriving in a new destination to making it your home and everything in between.

Explorer Residents' Guides
We Know Where You Live

Dragon Boat Racing

Dragon boating is popular among expats and locals alike. While some teams can get very serious and competitive, most remain laidback and friendly, with as much attention paid to the paddling as to the beers consumed afterwards. Beyond the boat and paddles, there's not much gear required. Make sure to wear old clothes, bring a waterbottle, footwear, a towel, sunscreen and a hat. It's also a good idea to have a plastic bag for your valuables to keep them dry. The Singapore Dragon Boat Association organises a number of events throughout the year, and the international teams occasionally hold friendly events as well.

Stadium Rd
Kallang
🚇 *Kallang*
Map 14-F4

American Association Dragon Boat Team

6738 0371 | *www.aasingapore.com*

The American Association Dragon Boat Team, based at the Kallang Water Sports Centre, is open to anyone interested in putting a paddle in the water, training and having fun. The only requirements are that you can swim and that you're a paid-up member of the American Association. The team trains every Saturday from 16:00-18:00 and each session costs $10 to cover coaching and the rental of the boat. For more information email aasdragonboat@yahoo.com.

Kallang Riverside
Park
Kallang
🚇 *Kallang*
Map 14-F4

AustCham Dragon Boat Team

www.ozdragon.org

The AustCham Dragon Boat Team practises on Saturdays at 15:30 on the Kallang River. Despite the name, you don't have to be Australian to join team. They make sure to get in a good hour or so of paddling before they head back to shore for the all-important socialising and rehydrating. However, things do get fairly serious in the build-up to important races, when additional training sessions are added to the schedule. The AustCham team had a good 2005, winning their category in all three major races they entered. For more information email info@ozdragon.org.

Kallang Riverside
Park
Kallang
🚇 *Kallang*
Map 14-F4

BritCham Dragon Boat Team

www.britishdragonboat.com

The BritCham Dragon Boat team takes part in most of the events held in Singapore, including the Singapore Dragon Boat Regatta, Singapore River Regatta, SAVA Sprints and other fun events. You don't have to be British to join the team; there's a healthy international mix represented and everyone is welcome. More than just a bunch of paddlers, there's a distinctly social aspect to the team, and apres-paddle sessions are regularly held at Wong's, near where the boats are put in for training (in the Kallang Riverside Park near the Police Coast Guards HQ). Each training session costs $10, covering coaching and some refreshments. Check the website for the latest training schedule or email mail@britishdragonboat.com.

Kallang Riverside
Park
Kallang
🚇 *Kallang*
Map 14-F4

Canadian Dragon Boat Team

6734 5954 | *www.canadians.org.sg*

The Canadian Dragon Boat Team is one of the top teams in Singapore, and competes in all the local races as well as annual overseas competitions. The team is open to anyone, but to participate in competitions you must be a paid-up member of the Canadian Association. While experience and fitness are welcomed, enthusiasm and a desire to compete are a good start. The team trains on Saturday afternoons and Sunday mornings, and adds in Thursday evening sessions in the lead up to competitions. Participation costs $10 per session, which covers rental of a paddle, coaching fees and a few drinks afterwards.

260

Drama Groups

Singapore's a great city of experiencing the cutting edge of Asian theatre. The drama scene here is vibrant, with many top-notch performances being staged every year at a variety of venues. While there's only a limited number of amateur theatre companies, most groups – be they amateur or professional – will be happy to take on volunteers for backstage or administrative positions.

23-24 Whitchurch Rd
Queenstown
Map 16-C1

The Stage Club

9382 6255 | *www.stageclub.com*

Established in 1945, The Stage Club is Singapore's oldest theatre company. It's a non-profit, amateur theatre company providing anyone who is interest in contributing with both on and off-stage opportunities to do so. The club puts on about five productions a year across a wide range of genres. They've just moved into a newly renovated clubhouse in a beautiful old colonial house off Portsdown Road. Social gatherings are usually held on Thursday evenings, often coinciding with rehearsals for upcoming performances.

45 Armenian St
Colonial District
🚇 *City Hall*
Map 17-C1

The Substation

6337 7535 | *www.substation.org*

Acting workshops are among the many courses offered at the Substation. Experienced actors teach some of the more technical aspects of acting, such as projection, articulation, physical language and phrasing. The course runs for four weeks with two sessions per week and costs $200. Participants should be over 14 years old.

Environmental Groups

Other options **Voluntary & Charity Work** p.85

It's not for nothing that Singapore is known as the Garden City. Over 5% of its land area is reserved for nature and it manages to be an incredibly green city despite its small size and high population density. New environmental groups pop up regularly and most are only in the very early stages of development. The best way to find out what's happening on the green scene is to get in touch with the Singapore Environmental Council at www.sec.org.sg.

Nr Singapore
Power Building
Orchard
🚇 *Somerset*
Map 17-B1

Environmental Challenge Organisation

9147 4541 | *www.eco-singapore.org*

With its headquarters in an old double-decker bus in Youth Park next to Orchard Road, Environmental Challenge Organisation (Singapore), or ECO for short, is at the forefront of Singapore's youth environmental movement. ECO aims to promote awareness of sustainable living and environmental issues and to provide opportunities for youths to take action for environmental causes. ECO puts out a regular newsletter highlighting issues and projects going on around Singapore and the world. They are always looking for volunteers and hold a monthly open house cum recruitment drive, aptly named Buzz the Bus, at their headquarters.

261

Green Volunteers Network

Various locations

6337 6062 | www.gvn.com.sg

The Green Volunteers Network is the volunteer arm of the Singapore Environment Council. It organises a variety of activities and programmes that allow volunteers to turn their environmental awareness into action. Projects include reforestation, park and coastal cleanups, fundraising activities and educational initiatives. You can sign up via their website, over the phone or by dropping into their office at 52A Duxton Hill.

Nature Society (Singapore)

510 Geylang Rd
Geylang
🚇 *Aljunied*
Map 15-B3

6741 2036 | www.nss.org.sg

The Nature Society is a non-profit group dedicated to the appreciation and conservation of Singapore's natural environment. In addition to frequent nature walks and educational talks, the society also conducts conservation projects and community outreach activities. As a member of the Nature Society you'll receive a bi-monthly newsletter and quarterly magazine and you can participate in guided nature outings and contribute to conservation projects. A single membership costs $50; family membership is $85.

Society for Prevention of Cruelty to Animals

31 Mount Vernon Rd
Hougang
🚇 *Bartley*
Map 7-D4

6287 5355 | www.spca.org.sg

The Society for Prevention of Cruelty to Animals aims to improve the plight of animals in Singapore through education, care and the placing of strays or abandoned pets in new homes. It runs regular public awareness campaigns to promote responsible pet ownership. Volunteers are needed in all areas from animal shelter reception to public relations. Simply fill out the form on the website and drop it off at the SPCA's office or fax it to 6287 5997.

Fencing

Fencing Masters

177 Ubi Ave 4
Ubi
🚇 *Eunos*
Map 15-C1

9451 1835 | www.fencingmasters.com

Fencing Masters at the Pan Malayan Warehouse offers a wide range of courses covering foil, épée and sabre fencing at all levels and for all ages over 6. Individual lessons can be arranged to fit your schedule, while group lessons are held on Saturdays. Open nights run alongside training sessions on weekday evenings, giving those with more experience a chance to square up against other fencers from around Singapore. Group classes start at $200 for four lessons, while individual classes start at $75 for adults, but are cheaper when bought in blocks of up to 20 sessions.

Z Fencing

271 Bukit Timah Rd
Newton
🚇 *Newton*
Map 14-B3

6295 1432 | www.zfencing.com.sg

Z Fencing gives you the opportunity to imagine you're Zorro or one of the Three Musketeers as you develop your swordsmanship in their classes. Z-keteers is a programme for children aged 4-12, Z Youth Fencers caters to 13-20 year olds and Z Die Hard is for adults who are still young at heart. Besides the main salle at Balmoral Plaza, there are also two other facilities, one at United Square near Novena MRT and one at Parkway Parade on the East Coast.

First Aid

PRATIQUE Emergency Care

275 Beach Rd
Colonial District
🚇 *City Hall*
Map 17-D1

6297 8123 | www.firstaidtraining.com.sg

PRATIQUE Emergency Care, Training and Consultancy offers first aid and cardio-pulmonary resuscitation (CPR) courses for the general public as well as in the workplace, schools and other organisations. PECTAC can help you to put together a comprehensive first aid kit and offers a course on using an automatic external defibrillator (AED), a device that is increasingly showing up in public spaces to help prevent death by heart attack.

Singapore Red Cross Society

6336 0269 | *www.redcross.org.sg*

In addition to blood donation drives and running homes and hostels for the disabled, the Red Cross Society offers both standard and occupational first aid and CPR courses. Courses can be taught over a longer period of short sessions, or you can try to cram it all in to fewer, more intensive classes. You can also do a refresher course if the skills you've learned have gotten a bit rusty. Fees range from $50-130 which includes bandages and a face shield but not necessarily the workbook.

Fishing

Other options **Boat & Yacht Charters** p.218

Singapore has many opportunities for fishing, from shore casting and stocked fish ponds to charters in coastal waters and deep sea fishing. The fish ponds dotted around the island are usually stocked with barramundi, mangrove jack, golden pomfret and snapper. Shore casting is possible along Singapore's rivers, coastline and at designated areas in most reservoirs. Fishing charters can be arranged from most marinas. There are a couple of good resources: one is the Sport Fishing Association (Singapore) with a website at www.sfas.net; and the other is a large online fishing community you'll find at www.fishingkaki.com. Both websites are a good start for information on how and where to fish in Singapore. A cluster of fishing tackle shops in the streets off Beach Road, between the Plaza Park Royal Hotel and Sultan Mosque (map 17-E1) should meet your equipment needs.

Ah Bee Charter

9616 8895

Veteran fisherman Ah Bee will take you and four other anglers for day charter trips into the coastal waters around Changi. The trip lasts from 07:00-16:30 and costs $350, which does not include food, bait or tackle, although water and ice are provided. With a focus on bottom-fishing, you're likely to catch grouper, snapper and barramundi.

Anglers Hut

6298 1015

Anglers Hut is a full service tackle shop that also offers fishing charters. In addition to day trips in Singapore waters, extended trips to Malaysia can be arranged. An evening van ride will take you up to Rompin in Pahang province in three and a half hours, where you'll stay overnight in a hotel. In the morning the boat heads for the open water where you'll get a chance to do battle with sailfish that can weigh in at over 30kg! Most trips give two days on the water. Contact the Anglers Hut for details on costs and the next scheduled trip.

Night Anglers

9154 0722

Based out of the SAF Yacht Club, Night Anglers provides day and night charter trips in the waters around Tanah Merah and the Johor shore. Day trips cost $350 and run from 08:30-18:00, while night trips cost $390 and last from 19:30-07:00. The price of the trip includes ice, water and hot drinks, but not food, bait or tackle. Trips can accommodate up to six anglers and the boat has a toilet and a proper wheelhouse for shelter. Daylight will see you catching smaller fish, like diamond trevally. At night you'll be reeling in snapper, grouper, stingray and baracuda.

263

Flower Arranging

Other options **Flowers** p.336, **Gardens** p.339

702A Geylang Rd
Geylang
◎ **Paya Lebar**
Map 15-C3

June Floral Art School

6848 4500 | www.junefloral.com

June Floral Art School offers courses with a focus on Singaporean, American and modern European floral design. Basic floral design is a 20 lesson course that will provide you with a solid foundation in handling techniques and the principles of arranging. Other courses cater to those who want to make it a career, people who want to arrange flowers for weddings and more. Group and individual instruction is available, with groups limited to six students per instructor.

2-57 Roxy Square
East Coast
Map 15-C4

Novel Floral & Gift Ideas

6449 3695 | www.novelfloral.com.sg

Whether you want to be a professional floral designer or just take up flower arranging as a hobby, Novel Floral has a course to fit your needs. The six-lesson basic course teaches you the basic concepts of floral design as well as how to make a centrepiece, hand bouquet and fruit basket. The more intensive 'wedding works' course stretches to 18 lessons.

Flying

Other options **Helicopter Tours** p.222

Seletar Airbase
Seletar
◎ **Yio Chu Kang**
Map 4-F4

Republic of Singapore Flying Club

6481 0200 | www.singaporeflyingclub.com

If you're keen to take to the skies over Singapore, the Republic of Singapore Flying Club is the place to go. It provides Private Pilot Licence (PPL) courses for a price of between $20,000 and $30,000. While the limited airspace in Singapore precludes trainees from completing their Pilot Navigation Training, this can be done at an affiliated club in Malaysia, so you'll be awarded an unrestricted PPL. The club has one aircraft, a Socata Tampico TB9 as well as an instrument flight simulator.

Football

Singaporeans are truly football-crazy, be they playing the game, watching it or discussing the latest fixtures. The most prominent European teams have a large local following, especially teams from the English Premier League. On weekday evenings and weekends most open spaces and football pitches see enthusiasts trying to emulate their favourite players' latest moves. There are a couple of leagues that cater to expats and offer some good competition, as well as football academies for children and an indoor football centre for five-a-side games.

38 Jalan Benaan
Kapal
Kallang
◎ **Nicoll Highway**
Map 14-F4

The Cage

6344 9345 | www.thecage.com.sg

The Cage, behind the Singapore Indoor Stadium, is Singapore's first indoor football centre. It has two artificial turf pitches, each measuring 15m by 25m, for five-a-side football. The turf is UEFA and FIFA approved, so that you'll be able to make all your moves without the ball bouncing off in the wrong direction, as can happen on an uneven outdoor pitch. Bookings can be made via the website once you register. Fees range from $50-100 per hour, depending on the time of day and it's open 24 hours a day. Package deals are available.

Various locations ◄

Cosmo League

www.cosmoleague.com

The Cosmo League is the most popular and competitive league in Singapore and has a number of teams based on country affiliation, but also some club teams. Games are played on weekends on pitches around Singapore. The best way to join in is to go on to their website where all the teams are listed and their full contact details are available. Pick a team that looks appropriate and give them a call to see if they're looking for new players.

Various locations ◄

ESPZen Leagues

6420 2103 | *www.espzen.com*

This is the largest amateur football league in Singapore, with seven divisions in the Sunday league and one division in the midweek league that takes place on Wednesday and Thursday nights. To get on a team go to www.espzen.com and register as a player looking for a team. You'll also find a list of teams looking for players here.

51 Broadrick Rd ◄
Kallang
🚇 *Nicoll Highway*
Map 15-B4

JSSL Arsenal

6348 5780 | *www.jsoccerleague.com*

Affiliated with Arsenal FC in the UK, JSSL Arsenal offers football coaching and an organised league for children under 12. Coaching staff from Arsenal FC come to the school throughout the year to provide training to the kids as well as to the local coaching staff. Fees are $350 for a 10 session term and there's a one-off $80 registration fee that includes a jersey, socks and shorts. Training sessions of 90 minutes each are held weekly.

Frisbee

Various locations ◄

Freakshow Ultimate

www.freakshow.sg

Freakshow is one of Asia's top Ultimate clubs and regularly participates in regional tournaments. The team is mixed, and made up of a mix of locals and expats. Training is held on weekends and sometimes on weekday evenings throughout the year. If you're interested in playing Ultimate at a high level, you can contact the captains through the website and they'll get back to you with the schedule for upcoming practices.

Various locations ◄

Singapore Ultimate

6835 3856 | *www.singaporeultimate.com*

Singapore has a vibrant and rapidly growing Ultimate Frisbee community. Singapore Ultimate runs two leagues per year, usually starting in January and July and lasting for two to three months each. It also organises the annual Singapore Open, Asia's largest international Ultimate tournament. Pickup games occur most nights of the week and on weekends at fields around Singapore. See www.singaporeultimate.com for a schedule and the locations. They also have a set of disc golf targets that are sometimes set up in an 18 hole course in Marina City Park.

Gaelic Games

21 Evans Rd ◄
Bukit Timah
🚇 *Newton*
Map 13-F2

Gaelic Lions

www.gaeliclions.com

The Gaelic Lions have brought some of the Emerald Isle to Singapore in the form of regular Gaelic football sessions. They train on Thursdays at 19:00 and Sundays at 17:00 at the School of Physical Education running track, just off Bukit Timah Road near the

Botanic Gardens. Separate men's and women's sessions are held at the same time, so feel free to bring your partner with you. A great way to learn the game, improve your skills and get in shape, practices are also used to prepare for the Asia Gaelic Games that the club attends annually.

Gardening

Other options **Gardens** p.339

One of the first things people notice upon arriving in Singapore is how green it is. The city-state didn't receive its Garden City moniker by accident either: the National Parks Board, or NParks for short, maintains a vast amount of greenery in the country's parks, nature reserves and other public spaces. The popularity of gardening is constrained to some extent by the prevalence of apartments and condos with no garden space, but there's still a significant community of gardening enthusiasts here. A useful online resource is www.greenculturesg.com, a Singapore-based gardening website and forum.

37 Beach Rd
Colonial District
🚇 *Lavender*
Map 17-D1

Singapore Gardening Society
6338 2709 | www.gardeningsingapore.org

Established in 1936, the Singapore Gardening Society has significantly influenced the development of horticulture here. The society holds talks, workshops and home visits (usually on the third Saturday of each month). The Grapevine, the society's monthly newsletter, keeps members updated on scheduled events and includes articles about gardening. To become a member you'll need to pay a $20 joining fee and a $30 annual subscription.

Golf

For such a small land area Singapore has a great number of golf courses. Many of the courses have seen the touch of prestigious designers and multi-million dollar renovations, and it shows in the quality of the experience you'll have. Top end courses can be found at the Laguna National Golf & Country Club, Tanah Merah Country Club and Sentosa Golf Club. Most courses have country club facilities at their clubhouses, including pools, restaurants and lounges. You also usually have to be a member or a member's guest, although some clubs allow walk-ons during the week.

Overseas Golf Courses Near Singapore

Bintan, Indonesia

Ria Bintan	www.riabintan.com	6433 7714
Bintan Lagoon	www.bintanlagoon.com	6223 3223

Batam, Indonesia

Indahpuri	www.indahpuri.com	(62) 778 323720
Palm Springs	www.palmsprings.com.sg	6276 1027
Tering Bay	na	6225 0833
Southlinks	www.southlinksgolf.com	6278 7079

Johor, Malaysia

Legends	www.legends-resort.com	(02) 07 652 4388
Palm Resort	www.palmresort.com	6222 9388
Palm Villa	www.palmvilla.com.my	(607) 599 9099
Pulai Springs	www.pulaisprings.com	6762 5655

Overseas Golfing

If you feel limited in your choice of courses in Singapore you can always take a day-trip to Malaysia or Indonesia for a round of golf. There are numerous quality courses within 30-45 minutes travel by car or ferry. Singapore golfers regularly make the trip to the islands of Bintan and Batam in Indonesia or Johor, just across the causeway in Malaysia. A venture off the island is sure to be a worthwhile trip for a day of golf at one of the fantastic courses listed in the table to the left. The Ria Bintan course is considered to be the best in the area, while Bintan Lagoon has courses designed by Jack Nicklaus and Ian Baker Finch. The Legends course is one of the better ones in Johor. Most of the courses have sales offices in Singapore and offer online bookings.

Don't forget your passport – you are heading overseas, after all. Indonesia offers a visa on arrival for most nationalities, but it's worth checking when you book to see what is required. These courses cater to large numbers of golfers from Singapore and staff will be well versed in the procedures for entry.

20 Netheravon Rd
Changi
🚇 *Pasir Ris*
Map 8-D3

Changi Golf Club

6545 5133

The Changi Golf Club is a hilly nine hole, par 34 course. A second set of tee-boxes allow for your second round to have a different feel from the first. It's open to walk-on golfers on weekdays, but weekends are reserved for members and guests. There is a small chipping area, but no driving range.

60 Fairways Drive
Bukit Timah
Map 13-C1

Green Fairways

6468 7233

Green Fairways is another nine-hole course that is primarily an option if you want to get in a few holes but haven't secured a booking anywhere else. You can walk on at any time and get a tee time fairly quickly. The course is a par 33 and plays 1,660m long. Costs are $42 for nine holes during the week and $52 on the weekend.

9 Science Centre Rd
Jurong
🚇 *Jurong East*
Map 6-A4

Jurong Country Club

6568 5186 | *www.jcc.org.sg*

The 18 hole Jurong Country Club course is a 6,306m par 72 course. The front and back nine have a distinctly different feel. The front is set among rolling wooded hills with one major water hazard, while the back nine is laid out on a flat plain where Jurong Lake comes into play. Lights are installed around the course, so you can enjoy a cooler game of night golf. There is a five-hole executive course for beginners, a short game practice area and a 54 bay driving range.

10 Bukit Chermin Rd
Telok Blangah
🚇 *HarbourFront*
Map 19-A1

Keppel Club

6375 5528 | *www.keppelclub.com.sg*

Set at the southern tip of Singapore, the Keppel Club golf course offers golfers 5,987m of undulating terrain. The par 72 course has numerous bunkers and hazards to challenge golfers of all levels. There is a two-level 56 bay driving range where resident golf professionals provide lessons for beginners and seasoned golfers alike. Golfers are required to have an official handicap before playing the course – handicap tests can be arranged by calling the office.

**11 Laguna
Golf Green**
Changi
🚇 *Tanah Merah*
Map 12-C3

Laguna National Golf & Country Club

6542 6888 | *www.lagunagolf.com.sg*

The two 18 hole courses at the Laguna National Golf & Country Club offer distinctly different golfing experiences. The Masters Course is a par 72 course designed in the old Scottish tradition of pronounced fairway mounds and prominent water features. The Classic Course, also a par 72, has more of an American feel to it, with large bunkers and a premium on the short game. A three tier, 70 bay driving range, and a short game area for chipping, putting and bunker practice allow you to hone your skills.

1 Orchid Club Rd
Yishun
🚇 *Khatib*
Map 4-D4

Orchid Country Club

6750 2111 | *www.orchidclub.com*

Three distinct nine-hole courses make up the 27 hole international championship course at the Orchid Country Club. The three courses – Aranda (par 36, 3,037m), Vanda (par 36, 3,051m) and Dendro (par 37, 3,262m) – are named after orchids. At 590m, the Dendro course's third hole is one of Singapore's longest par fives. The 160 bay driving range, here the lower deck's 80 bays have computerised automatic tee-up, is considered one of the best in the city. There's also a four-hole practice course with two par fours and two par threes. If you're keen to try out a slightly heftier ball, the clubhouse also houses a 36 lane bowling alley.

Raffles Country Club

450 Jalan Ahmad Ibrahim
Jurong
🚇 *Choa Chu Kang*
Map 9-B1

6861 7655 | www.rcc.org.sg

The Raffles Country Club has two 18 hole courses, both designed by Robert Trent Jones Junior. The par 72 Lake Course has 5,819m of rolling fairways set along the shores of the Tengeh Reservoir. The 6,081m par 72 Palm Course is a challenging mix of strategically placed bunkers and water hazards, and hosted the Asia PGA Championships in 1997 and 1998. The club also has a driving range and a number of restaurants for a relaxing post-game meal. There's a handicap requirement and Saturday afternoons are reserved for members only.

Seletar Base Golf Course

244 Oxford St
Seletar
🚇 *Khatib*
Map 7-C1

6481 4745 | www.seletarbaseclub.org.sg

The Seletar Base Golf Course was built in 1930 as a golf club for the British Royal Air Force. It has since changed hands and is now a public nine-hole course. There is also a chip-and-putt course for practicing your short game and a driving range for the long game. The club has full facilities, including a swimming pool, tennis and squash courts, billiards, a restaurant and karaoke rooms.

Sembawang Country Club

249 Sembawang Rd
Sembawang
🚇 *Khatib*
Map 4-B4

6751 0320 | www.sembawanggolf.org.sg

Managed by the Singapore Armed Forces, the Sembawang Country Club is sometimes referred to as the Commando Course. Known for its narrow fairways and large greens, it can be a challenging course for even the most seasoned golfer. Despite being short by international standards at 5,900m, it still rates as a par 72. There's a covered driving range managed by Golfer's Place.

Sentosa Golf Club

Sentosa Golf Club
Sentosa
🚇 *HarbourFront*
Map 19-D3

6275 0090 | www.sentosagolf.com

The Sentosa Golf Club is one of Singapore's most exclusive and magnificent golfing venues. The two 18 hole championship courses offer challenging holes among rolling hills at the eastern end of Sentosa Island and stunning views of the Singapore Harbour and South China Sea. The Serapong course was voted one of the top five in Asia by Asian Golf Monthly. The Tanjong course was renovated in 2006. Its last four holes are floodlit for night golf, so you can still complete your round if you have a late tee time. The club also boasts a driving range and a David Leadbetter Golf Academy.

Singapore Island Country Club

Nr MacRitchie &
Peirce Reservoirs
Central Singapore
🚇 *Braddell*
Map 6-F3

6459 2222 | www.sicc.org.sg

The Singapore Island Country Club (SICC) boasts four 18 hole courses set along MacRitchie and the Peirce Reservoirs. The Bukit Course is SICC's par 72 championship course. The New Course is also par 72, and both of these courses have limited access for non-members – see the website for details. The Island Course is a hilly par 71 offering pleasant views of the Lower Peirce Reservoir. The Sime Course is a par 71 in a treed park-like setting. There is also a driving range and a nine-hole executive course for aspiring golfers to work on their stroke. The Bukit and Sime courses share a clubhouse, while the Island and New courses share a clubhouse at another location. There's also a 12 lane bowling alley for rainy days.

25 Changi Coast Rd
Changi
🚇 **Expo**
Map 12-D2

Tanah Merah Country Club

6542 3040 | www.tmcc.org.sg

The two 18 hole courses at the Tanah Merah Country Club are arguably among the top courses in Singapore. The 6,402m, par 72 Garden Course is set right next to Changi Airport and is a walking course (no buggies allowed). The beautiful Tampines Course (6542 4256) is just down the road on Xilin Avenue and plays at 6,421m and par 72. The Garden Course has a floodlit 30 bay driving range so you can practice your long game even after the sun sets.

23 Folkestone Rd
Clementi
🚇 **Dover**
Map 10-C2

Transview Golf and Country Club

6773 8000 | www.transviewgolf.com.my

Formerly the premises of the Warren Golf & Country Club, the Transview course now offers some of Singapore's more affordable golfing. It's one of the few courses where you will be able to walk-on on a weekend and get a tee time right away. The nine-hole is not among Singapore's elite courses, but it's a good option if you've failed to get a booking time elsewhere and need to get your golf fix for the weekend.

81 Choa Chu Kang Way
Northwest Singapore
🚇 **Choa Chu Kang**
Map 6-A2

Warren Golf and Country Club

6586 1244 | www.warren.org.sg

The members and guests-only Warren Golf and Country Club has an 18 hole, par 71 course that plays at 6,022m. It's a relatively flat, American-style course with some challenging bunker placements. A number of holes cross the PUB canal that runs through the course. There is also a 53 bay driving range and the clubhouse has a pool, squash and tennis courts and a billiards room.

Hashing

Other options **Running** p.289, **Pubs** p.433

Hashing has turned into a wildly popular activity in Singapore and you can see hares and other hashers roaming around the island on most days of the week. Since the formation of the original club in Kuala Lumpur in neighbouring Malaysia in 1938, hashing actually has a surprisingly long history in Singapore and several groups have evolved over the years, including a kids' hash, dog hash and bike hash (see Mountain Biking, p.280). Joining one of these groups of 'drinkers with a running problem' can be a great way to explore some of the less-visited areas of Singapore, and a good way to get set with a social circle.

Various locations

Hash House Harriers Singapore

9831 5662 | www.hhhs.org.sg

The Hash House Harriers Singapore is a mens-only chapter. They run every Monday at 18:00 but check their website (which also has links to other hashes) for any changes. Guests should bring $20 for the run and beer and if you've worked up an appetite on your run bring an extra $10 for food.

Various locations

Hash House Horrors

http://horrors.hash.org.sg

The Hash House Horrors is a hash for children. Check out the website (complete with 'horrorble' songs) for updated information, but it usually runs every second Sunday at 16:30 and it takes about 30 minutes to complete the course. Quarterly membership fees are $50 for the first child in a family, $40 for the second and $30 for each child thereafter. Visitors and guests are charged $15 but there's no charge for parents or accompanying adults.

Various locations

Kampong Hash House Harriers
http://kampong.hash.org.sg

The Kampong Hash House Harriers run on the third Saturday of every month. It is a mixed chapter, and couples are especially encouraged to come out. You can register on their website, which also has an entertaining quick guide to the history of hashing and rules if you're a newcomer to the sport.

Various locations

Lion City Hash House Harriers
6462 2180 | *www.lioncityhash.com*

A good opportunity for a run before getting to the usual Friday night drinks, the Lion City Hash House Harriers is a sociable, mixed hash. Quarterly subscriptions costs $20 and while plenty of running happens, the emphasis is on having a good time and the hash's rules make sure to cover the logistics of getting the beer wagon to thirsty runners. If you log on to the website you'll also find links to regional hashing events. The Lion City harriers meet on Friday evenings at 18:00.

Various locations

Saturday K9 Hash House Harriers
9658 5868 | *www.doghash.com*

Singapore's dog hash is a great way to give you and your dog a workout, get to know other dog owners and let your dog make some new friends. Despite the canine focus the hash is open to anyone, dog owner or not. The hash is run on the first Saturday of every month, with registration at 16:30 and the start at 17:00. Membership fees are $80 for a half year, $60 if you don't drink beer. Guest fees vary, so check the website for the details on upcoming hashes or call Lily Loo at 9658 5868.

Various locations

Seletar Hash House Harriers
9634 8403 | *http://seletar.hash.org.sg*

The Seletar Hash House Harriers, a men-only chapter that has been active since 1980, run every Tuesday at 18:00. To get in touch with them visit the website where you can download an application form or email onsec@hash.org.sg.

Various locations

Singapore Hash House Harriets
9151 5421 | *www.singaporeharriets.com*

The Hash House Harriets go down in history as the first ever women's hash, having held their first run in 1973. They have since evolved into a mixed chapter that runs on Wednesday evenings at 18:00.

Various locations

Sunday Hash House Harriers
8100 0326 | *www.sundayhash.org.sg*

The Sunday Hash House Harriers is a mixed hash that runs on alternate Sundays. Hashes start at 17:30 sharp but they invite members to arrive early and get a head start on the socialising. Membership fees for six months are $130 for drinkers and $60 for non-drinkers. Guests pay $20 if they will be drinking and $10 otherwise.

Hiking
Other options **Outdoor Goods** p.348

Various locations

Nature Trekker
9255 2555 | *www.naturetrekker.org*

Nature Trekker is a group of adventurers dedicated to exploring and appreciating nature. Joining is quite simple: sign up on their website (membership is free) and you'll be added to the mailing list and kept informed of upcoming adventures and hikes.

270

Most treks take place in Singapore, but the group does make occasional forays into Malaysia. Treks and nature trips are led by experienced volunteer trainers and guides.

Various locations ◄

Singapore Adventurers' Club

6749 0557 | www.sac.org

The Singapore Adventurers' Club brings together nature-loving individuals who enjoy experiencing the outdoors through hiking, climbing and other exciting activities. The club runs regular activities around Singapore including hikes at Bukit Timah Nature Reserve and Pulau Ubin, and the Choo Choo Trek, which follows an abandoned rail line from downtown out to Jurong. To become a member of the club download the membership form on their website.

Hockey

Other options **Ice Hockey** p.272

22 Camden Rd ◄
Bukit Timah
Map 13-E1

The Hollandse Club

6464 5225 | www.hollandseclub.org.sg

The Hollandse Club fields men's, women's and youth hockey teams. The teams are open to anyone, although a higher fee is levied if you are not a Hollandse Club member. The men's and women's team play in the national league and practice on Wednesday evenings at the School of Physical Education at 21 Evans Road, off Bukit Timah Road. Games against local and international school teams are organised for the youth team, which trains on Sundays at the Delta Sports Complex in the Tanglin Area.

88 Boon Lay Place ◄
Jurong
🚇 *Lakeside*
Map 5-F4

Tornados Hockey Club

9824 4735 | www.tornadoshockey.org.sg

The Tornados Hockey Club is Singapore's only fully fledged hockey club. While it is competitive, the club maintains a strong social component too. It fields a number of different teams, some of which – the men's, veterans and under 21s – play in the national league. There are also plans to develop a women's and an under 12 team. Fun hockey sessions are organised to introduce the game to young children. Training takes place on Sundays, and since May 2006 the team's new home pitch and clubhouse is at Hockey Village, a facility with five pitches. For more information contact Gordon Wright on the above number or visit the website.

Horse Riding

Other options **Polo** p.285

51 Fairways Drive ◄
Bukit Timah
🚇 *Clementi*
Map 13-C1

Bukit Timah Saddle Club

6466 2782 | www.btsc.org.sg

The Bukit Timah Saddle Club was established in 1951 to promote horseback riding in Singapore and to provide a home for retired racehorses. The club has both horses and ponies available for riding. It provides a popular beginners' course, coaching in dressage and jumping and stabling for horses. The club is affiliated with the Equestrian Federation of Singapore and leading instructors sometimes conduct clinics here.

80 Mount ◄
Pleasant Rd
Toa Payoh
🚇 *Toa Payoh*
Map 14-B1

Singapore Polo Club

6854 3999 | www.singaporepoloclub.org

Besides the sport of polo, the Singapore Polo Club also offers group and private lessons to its members. Special attention is given to matching the rider with an appropriate horse and riding fundamentals such as proper posture and communication between horse and rider. Lessons start as early as 07:00 so you can get in a ride before heading off to work. The Polo Club also has an affiliation with the UK Pony Club and provides a good opportunity for young children to become comfortable with ponies and horses.

Ice Hockey
Other options **Ice Skating** p.272

There's a growing ice hockey scene in Singapore and, perhaps surprisingly, it includes a reasonably large number of locals. Games are played at the Fuji Ice Palace (see Ice Skating, p.272) – the only ice rink in town. There are two leagues for adults and one for kids. The best way to get on a team is to contact the league organisers and they can point you to a team that is looking for players.

Various locations

National Ice Hockey League
www.singaporeicehockey.com
The National Ice Hockey League is one of the best organised leagues in Asia, with eight teams playing in two divisions. The level of play is higher than you might think for a league in the tropics, but as long as you have a moderate level of skill you should fit in without a problem. Note that games are played four-on-four due to the small playing area at the Fuji Ice Palace. Games are played on Monday and Thursday nights and costs per player for the season are about $450. For more information on teams and the league, you can email icehockey@singaporeicehockey.com.

Various locations

San Miguel Sunday Night Hockey League
9170 1282
The San Miguel Sunday Night Hockey League is Singapore's newest ice hockey league and was created to fill a gap in the weekend schedule. In its first year the league had approximately 60 players spread over four teams and played a 20 game schedule. The cost per player is about $400 and games are played on three Sundays a month. For information on the league and joining a team, contact Anthony Blass on the above contact details.

Various locations

Singapore Ice Dragons
6738 9772 | www.canadians.org.sg
Run through the Canadian Association of Singapore, the Singapore Ice Dragons is a youth development club that caters to kids from 5-17 years of age. Weekly practice sessions, split by age group, are designed to help kids learn new hockey skills and a six-team youth league plays on Sundays. The season runs from September to April each year. There are currently almost 120 kids in the league and it costs approximately $400 per child. Skill levels range from complete beginners to some of the older kids being good enough to play in the adult leagues. For more information you can visit the website or send an email to Buffy Duke at singaporekidshockey@yahoo.com.

Ice Skating
Other options **Ice Hockey** p.272

2 Jurong East St 13
Jurong
🚇 *Jurong East*
Map 10-A1

Fuji Ice Palace
6565 1905 | www.fujiice.com.sg
It seems odd to lace up your skates and hit the ice in tropical Singapore, but it can be done. The 22m by 40m rink at the Fuji Ice Palace in the Jurong Entertainment

Centre is open to the public from 10:00 to 22:00 most days, except when the hockey leagues take over later in the evenings. Public skaters can gain entry in two-hour blocks, each block costing $10.50 for adults and $8.40 for children and students. Skates can be rented for $2.10 and skate sharpening costs $6.30 per pair.

Jetskiing

Jetskiing is not a big activity in Singapore, despite its apparently conducive situation as an island in the tropics. The problem lies in the licencing requirements imposed by the Singapore government. Anyone wanting to rent a jetski will have to produce a powered pleasure craft driving licence. Obtaining such a licence requires a two to four day course, which is enough to put off those who are just looking for a one-off experience. But if you're determined to get your licence, the course is offered by the Republic of Singapore Yacht Club, SAF Yacht Club and the People's Association. You will probably have to buy your own jetski as no clubs currently rent them out.

Karting

Yung Ho Rd
Jurong
🚇 **Lakeside**
Map 9-F1

Kart World
6266 2555 | www.kartworld.com.sg

Start your engines! Kart World offers 500m of outdoor track for you to pretend you're Michael Schumacher on, as you tear around hairpins and scream down the straights. If you have your own kart, full-day access to the track is $50 on weekdays and $60 on weekends. You can also rent a kart in 10 minute blocks for $35 for a single-engine kart and $40 for a more powerful twin-engine beast. Prices come down if you take up a membership. It could be reassuring to know that Kart World also offers engine rebuilding and repairs.

Various locations

Karting Club of Singapore
9667 9695 | www.kartfreaks.com

The Karting Club of Singapore is a group of karting enthusiasts that enjoy tinkering with engines and zooming around a track at breakneck speeds. At the time of writing the KCS was without a home track, as the National Stadium carpark where it used to operate was shut down by construction. However, the group expects to find a new home soon and get back to regular gatherings and racing. For an update on the situation or upcoming events, call Jeff Keng on the number listed above.

Kayaking
Other options **Canoeing** p.251

Kayaking in Singapore takes place in two environments: out on the ocean, or in the inland reservoirs. Sea kayaking is not heavily regulated, and anyone with a kayak can put in and head out to sea. Popular trips include Pulau Ubin, the Southern Islands, Seletar Island or just paddling along the coast. Kayaking in the reservoirs is supposed to be limited to organised groups and public rental from appointed clubs that run a centre at the reservoirs. You can kayak in most of the reservoirs in Singapore, including MacRitchie, Bedok, Upper and Lower Seletar, Pandan and the soon to be completed Marina reservoirs. The largest and best equipped centre is the Paddle Lodge at MacRitchie reservoir, run by the Singapore Canoe Federation (SCF).

273

902 East Coast
Parkway
East Coast
Map 18-D1

Paddle Culture

6884 4553 | *www.paddleculture.com*

Paddle Culture at the Big Splash Aquatic Centre offers a full range of kayaking programmes. Beginners can get their first taste of paddling with one, two and three star courses taught by certified instructors and corporate teams can sign up for the team building programme. You can also give canoe polo a bash, where you and a bunch of other kayakers chase a ball around the pool and try to score goals. Paddle Culture also organises excursions and rents out kayaks at $8 per hour. If you've taken a course at Paddle Culture, the rental rates can be significantly less. Excursions are typically four-hour trips along the coast and offer a great opportunity for you to brush up on your skills.

MacRitchie Reservoir
Central Singapore
🚇 *Braddell*
Map 7-A4

Paddle Lodge

6258 0057 | *www.scf.org.sg/Facilities/PLDetails.html*

The Paddle Lodge at the far eastern end of MacRitchie Reservoir is the Singapore Canoe Federation's main facility and the waters of the MacRitchie are used a-competition course for canoeing and kayaking events. You can rent two types of kayaks from the Paddle Lodge. Sit-on-top kayaks, $10 per hour, are available to anyone and come in one or two-seater versions. Conventional kayaks (where you sit with your legs on the inside) are available at $15 per hour, but only to paddlers with a one star certification – which can be obtained through courses with the SCF.

Various locations

People's Association Sea Sports Club

6340 5335 | *www.seasports.org.sg*

The People's Association runs a number of paddle centres where you can rent kayaks, get instruction and try out sea kayaking. Locations are at Changi (6545 1140), East Coast (6444 0409), Kallang (6296 6883) and Pasir Ris (6582 4796). There is also an outlet called Paddlezinc (6340 5335) at the Bedok Reservoir that gives you the option of slightly calmer water in pleasant surroundings.

Kids' Activities

Contrary to what you might think when you see the number of children tagging along behind their parents in Orchard Road's shopping malls, Singapore has plenty to offer kids. From junior sports teams to art and dance classes, there are heaps of things to keep your kids interested, active and having fun. The Canadian Association organises the Singapore Ice Dragons, a junior ice hockey team, and the Singapore American Community Action Council runs an American football league for kids. The international schools have extensive extra-curricular programmes and most clubs have junior section with an activities room, teen lounge and activities for kids. There are also some good children's activity centres and parks with impressive play structures.

East Coast Park

Tanglin Shopping
Centre
Tanglin
🚇 *Orchard*
Map 14-A4

ANZA

6733 1215 | *www.anza.org.sg*

ANZA runs a number of activities specifically for kids. The ANZA Athletics Group is for kids aged 5-16 and meets once a week from September to March at the Clementi Stadium. Field and track competitions are frequently held. There's also the 1st ANZA Scouts (see entry on p.291) which, with the focus firmly on fun, meets every Thursday at the Australian International School.

274

Bouncy Castles & A Whole Lot More

1-204A Acacia Court
Clementi
Map 13-A3

6465 6006 | www.bouncy-castles.com.sg

Bouncy Castles & A Whole Lot More delivers just that. The company hires out a huge range of all things fun, providing you with the makings of a memorable party for your children – what kid can resist inflatable castles and slides, a floating dinosaur for the pool or even (non-inflatable) magicians and snake charmers? Check out the company's website for a full listing of products and services, including useful information on space requirements for inflatable structures.

Ch'i Life Studio

Orchard Hotel
Shopping Arcade
Orchard
🚇 *Orchard*
Map 14-A4

6735 8812 | www.chi-life.com

Ch'i Life Studio is a wellbeing centre conveniently located in the Orchard Hotel Shopping Arcade. It offers classes for kids and teens, including yoga, wushu, kickboxing, akido, kung fu and tae kwon do. Classes are usually held on weekends and weekday evenings. See the website for a full list of programmes.

Explorer Kids

1 Pasir Ris Close
Pasir Ris
🚇 *Pasir Ris*
Map 8-B4

6589 1668 | www.explorerkids.com

Explorer Kids is a giant playground and fun centre. It's a great place to hold a birthday party, or just to let the kids loose for a romp. The centre also runs baking sessions or 'how to be a pop star' workshops, among other things. The fun doesn't end when you leave – Explorer Kids' website has games, contests and a member's section with online activities for kids. Entry to the play centre is $3-7 depending on time of day and if you are a member.

Genius R Us

75B Tanjong
Pagar Rd
Tanjong Pagar
🚇 *Outram Park*
Map 17-C3

6221 4561 | www.geniusrus.com

Genius R Us strives to bring out the genius in every child through its enrichment workshops. Activities include baking, crafts, pottery and yoga. The workshops target kids aged 2 to 12 and cost around $60 for a three-hour session. For a full calendar of workshops, see their website.

KinderGolf

Various locations

6441 3383 | www.kindergolf.com

Are you certain your child could be the next Tiger Woods? If so, KinderGolf can help your young golfer develop strong fundamental skills in a fun environment. Founded by Donna Lee, a certified staff instructor with the United States National Association of Golf Coaches and Educators, KinderGolf specialises in teaching golf to children aged 2 to 7 years old. There are six KinderGolf schools in Singapore, so visit the website to find the one nearest to you.

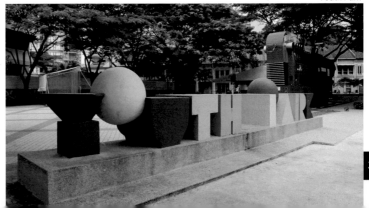

Youth Park

275

Turf City
Bukit Timah
Map 13-C1

KindyROO

6466 0339 | *www.kindyroo.com.sg*

KindyROO is part of a regional network of early childhood development and learning centres for kids aged 1 month to 5 years old. Based on an Australian-accredited syllabus, the centre provides development activities that will stimulate your child's senses and motor skills. While there is a fun gym, KindyROO is meant to be more than just a playground and its sessions are intended to benefit your child's coordination and sensory development.

Various locations

Spartacus Developments

6467 6210 | *www.spartacuscamps.com*

Since 2001 Spartacus has been organising parties and camps for children in Singapore. Their mission is to provide fun, safe and entertaining activities for kids and Spartacus staff members have extensive experience in working with children and qualifications such as teaching experience, first aid training and life guard certification. Parties can be arranged for any number of kids aged 5 and older, at a venue of your choice. Fees range from $300 for one hour to $500 for two hours. Face painters, photographers and other extras can be arranged at an additional charge. Spartacus also runs camps during the school holidays, usually from 9:30-14:30 on weekdays. Camps cost $370 per week, including lunch, snacks, a DVD with photos from the camp, a t-shirt and a cap. With themes like 'Jedi training', 'sports crazy', 'art attack' and 'Nutty Professor 2', your kids will be thrilled!

Kitesurfing

Other options **Windsurfing** p.302

You might think that with Singapore being surrounded by water, it would be a great place for kitesurfing. And it would be if it weren't for the fact that all the good wind is off the East Coast near Changi Airport. The authorities have decided that airplanes win out over kites and kitesurfing is banned. So if you're in need of a fix, your best bet is to take the 45 minute ferry ride south to Bintan, Indonesia, or a longer trip up north to Kuantan in Malaysia. For details on the regional kitesurfing scene, contact Nazir at xtreme board sports by email at nazir@xbsports.com.sg or at 9662 0354.

Language Schools

Other options **Learning Mandarin** p.158

1 Sarkies Rd
Newton
⊕ **Newton**
Map 14-B3

Alliance Française

6737 8422 | *www.alliancefrancaise.org.sg*

If you fancy a bit of French then the Alliance Française is undoubtedly the place to go. Following a tape-based conversational learning process, terms run for two months at a time with one or two classes per week depending on your schedule. A five-day crash course is also an option. The centre caters to everyone from children to advanced speakers as well as those wanting to specialise in translation and business French. Free placement tests can also be taken here and private lessons are offered.

Wheelock Place
Orchard
⊕ **Orchard**
Map 14-A4

Berlitz

6733 7472 | *www.berlitz.com*

Berlitz offers good selection of language and cross-cultural training. You can learn English, Spanish, Italian, French, Mandarin, Portuguese, German, Malay and Japanese in group or one-on-one classes. Their 'total immersion' programme allows you to really sink your teeth into a language with 7.5 hours of instruction per day for between two and six weeks. Corporate courses can be arranged for cross-cultural and business language instruction – useful if you're travelling around the region for work.

British Council

30 Napier Rd
Tanglin
Map 13-F4

6473 1111 | *www.britishcouncil.org.sg*

The British Council offers a full range of English courses, from kindergarten up to junior college level and business English as well as preparation for internationally recognised exams. Most courses are held at the main centre on Napier Road, but there are three other centres, including a Professional Development Centre on Cecil Street, near Raffles Place (6223 3767). Registered students can access online learning tools, a lending and reference library and over 70 qualified expatriate teachers and trainers. Courses can be taken on a full-time or part-time basis.

inlingua School of Languages

1 Grange Rd
Orchard
🚇 *Somerset*
Map 17-B1

6737 6666 | *www.inlinguaasia.com/singapore.htm*

With instruction in over 10 different languages, inlingua probably has a course to fit your needs. Their flexible system offers programmes of 15, 25 or 35 hours of instruction per week so you can decide on the pace at which you want to learn. Class sizes are capped at 15 for most courses and six for others to ensure an intimate and personalised learning environment.

Linguaphone Language Centre

Centrepoint
Orchard
Map 17-B1

6235 1855 | *www.linguaphoneasia.com*

Linguaphone provides English and Mandarin instruction using their simple and proven listen-understand-speak approach. Courses in both languages range from beginner level to advanced, and a placement test will be administered to see where you fit in. Linguaphone also offers a preparatory course for the International English Language Testing Service (IELTS) exam. The staff to student ratio is usually 1:15 and classes run for two months at a time.

Libraries

Other options **Books** p.328

The National Library Board (NLB) runs Singapore's network of public libraries, of which there are four types: reference libraries for researchers and academics; regional libraries with extensive collections covering a broad range of interests; community libraries with fiction and non-fiction ; and community children's libraries that cater to children aged 10 and under. Expats need to supply their passport and employment pass (or dependant's pass, student pass, etc.) when applying for a library card. There is a $10.50 registration fee plus a $10.50 annual membership fee for a basic membership that entitles you to borrow four books or magazines at a time. Premium membership costs $21 each year, and entitles you to borrow eight items, including multimedia materials such as DVDs and CDs. Many of the social clubs, sailing clubs and country clubs in Singapore have their own small library too. These private libraries often cater to a specific interest; the collection at the Republic of Singapore Yacht Club's library and chart room has an emphasis on nautical-related publications, while the library at the Hollandse Club has a sizeable collection of Dutch books. However, these libraries are generally for club members only.

Alliance Française

1 Sarkies Rd
Newton
🚇 *Newton*
Map 14-B3

6737 8422 | *www.alliancefrancaise.org.sg*

The Alliance Française has an extensive library with over 10,000 books, 54 periodicals (including kids magazines), and plenty of DVDs, CDs, videos, CD-ROMs

277

and audio tapes. Most materials are in French, although travel and tourism books about France are available in English. The library is open to the public but you must be a member of the organisation to borrow an item. The library has a multimedia resource centre where you can use audio tapes, CDs and CD-ROMs for free: there's a small charge if you wish to take a DVD or video home with you. The library has a special kids' area with pillows and chairs, and story-telling sessions are held at 15:30 on Fridays.

100 Victoria St
Colonial District
🚇 *Bugis*
Map 17-D1

Lee Kong Chian Reference Library
6332 3255 | www.nlb.gov.sg

Also called the National Library, this new venue is the centrepiece of the National Library Board's network. Not only does it house countless books, periodicals and multimedia items, but it also has an impressive arts facility where dramatic and musical performances take place. A pleasant outdoor atrium on the ground floor means you can enjoy a coffee from the cafe and start reading the books you've just borrowed. Information about this and other NLB libraries can be found on the website or by calling 6332 3255.

Esplanade
Marina Bay
🚇 *City Hall*
Map 17-D2

library@esplanade
6332 3255 | www.nlb.gov.sg

Located on the third floor of The Esplanade Theatres on the Bay facility, library@esplanade has the most extensive collection of audio-visual items and musical scores of the various NLB libraries. It is dedicated to the performing arts, including music, dance, theatre and film. Information about this and other NLB libraries can be found on their website or by calling 6332 3255.

Ngee Ann City
Orchard
🚇 *Orchard*
Map 14-A4

library@orchard
6332 3255 | www.nlb.gov.sg

Conveniently located in the heart of the Orchard Road shopping belt, library@orchard has a reasonable collection of fiction and non-fiction. Billed by the NLB as 'the ultra cool and sexy place to be', what sets this library apart is its location and the small cafe at the one end of the library where you can munch on a sandwich while reading. Just don't spill your lunch on your book in view of the librarians! For more information about this and other NLB libraries visit www.nlb.gov.sg or call 6332 3255.

Martial Arts

Various locations

Aikido Federation
9669 2851 | www.aikidofederation.com

The Aikido Federation offers classes for children and adults of all levels at its seven dojos. Classes last for an hour and are held on weekday evenings or weekend afternoons. Course fees are between $25 and $35 per month depending on which dojo you register with. The federation also conducts workshops and public demonstrations.

Various locations

Aikikai Singapore
6474 4621 | www.aikikaisingapore.com

Aikikai Singapore has been around in one form or another since 1958. It now provides aikido instruction at a number of locations (dojos) around the island. Check the website for details on class times for each dojo. Fees vary, but range between $25 and $40 per month. Most classes are for adults, but the Tampines dojo (6785 8800) offers a wider selection of courses, including one for kids and one for instructors.

JH Kim Taekwondo Institute

114 Middle Rd
Colonial District
Bugis
Map 17-D1

6299 0495 | *www.tkd-singapore.com*

The JH Kim Taekwondo Institute is a branch of the original institution in Boston, USA. The school has two training rooms, including an Olympic-sized court for competition training, six kicking bags and weights. Programmes include traditional and sport Taekwondo, T-kids for children aged 3-16 and 'kick like a girl' for women. Monthly fees range from $100 for a weekends-only membership to $150 for unlimited access. Student and children's rates are slightly lower. A one-off registration fee of $40 is required when you sign up and a uniform costs $60.

Ki-Aikido

Various locations

6466 2503 | *www.ki-aikido.com.sg*

Ki-Aikido teaches a different kind of aikido from that of other aikido schools in Singapore and you can do a preview class at one of their four dojos to see what it's like and whether you want to go ahead and enrol. Classes cost around $50 per month, depending on which location you sign up at. For more information or to enrol email ki-aikido@ki-aikido.com.sg.

Shitoryu Karate Association

94 McNair Rd
Kallang
Boon Keng
Map 14-E2

6299 5740 | *www.ska.org.sg*

The Shitoryu Karate Association was the first karate school in Singapore and it's still a great place to train. It has a gym, training bags, a reference library and a large open air dojo (don't worry, it's covered!) set across the street from an attractive row of terrace houses just outside of Little India. Classes are taught on weekday nights and during the day on weekends. Monthly fees are $35 for adults and $25 for children under 16.

Taekwon Singapore

324D King George's Ave
Little India
Lavender
Map 14-E3

9387 1214 | *www.taekwonsg.com*

Taekwon Singapore runs classes for all ages and you can also use the facilities here to train on your own. On offer is a large studio, kicking bags, sparring gear and training equipment like hand-mitts, kicking pads and head protectors. Classes run from Monday to Saturday and are segmented into children, youth and adult sessions. A yearly membership costs $80. For individual course fees and other details, contact Noi on the number above.

Mother & Toddler Activities

ANZA Mums and Under 5's

293 Lorong 6
Toa Payoh
Toa Payoh
Map 7-B4

6475 4408 | *www.anza.org.sg*

ANZA's Mums and Under 5's group holds regular play sessions at the Adventure Playground at SAFRA's Toa Payoh club. Your kids will enjoy swimming through huge rooms of plastic balls and clambering around the structures while you meet with mothers of similarly aged children. For more information contact Donna McWilliams on the above number.

Mums & Tots Group

The Hollandse Club
Bukit Timah
Map 13-E1

6469 5211 | *www.hollandseclub.org.sg*

The Hollandse Club's Mums & Tots Group offers a chance for children aged 3 and under to run around and participate in planned activities. Organised activity days include jump & tumble gym, playdough and wallpaper painting. Costs are $5 for club members, $12.50 for non-members and a small fee if you're accompanied by more than one child. The group meets on Tuesday mornings in the club's Rotterdam Room.

Various locations

New Mothers' Support Group

www.nmsg-singapore.com

Contrary to what the name might suggest, the New Mothers' Support Group is in fact for mothers and fathers. The volunteer-run organisation aims to provide new parents with the opportunity to share information on raising young children in Singapore. The group meets one Friday a month at St George's Church, near Tanglin, to socialise. A doctor from the International Medical Clinic is also on hand to answer medical questions. Monthly educational talks are held on topics related to parenting and the group also puts a useful bi-monthly newletter.

Motor Sports

With land at a premium in Singapore, there's limited space for motor sports and thus no permanent circuit. However, there are plans to build a motor sports racetrack in the western part of the island. If all goes as planned, the Tuas International Speedway will have a 3.37km circuit and will be able to accommodate 20,000 spectators. Keep your eyes on the press for details of when, and whether, it is to go ahead.

In the meantime though, you can still satisfy your need for speed to some degree by joining the Singapore Motor Sport Association – visit www.smsa.org.sg or call 6227 7889. About once a month SMSA transforms the carpark of the National Stadium in Kallang into a motor sports facility. The association organises various events for cars and motorcycles, such as auto tests, rallies, sprints and super motards. Due to the space constraints, these tend to emphasise skill and technique over speed and power. In addition to the car and motorcycle events, SMSA also oversees go karting in Singapore, which takes place at the circuit in Jurong (see Karting, p.273). There is paperwork to be filled out before you can take part in any events, so be sure to check with the association before driving your rally car out to Kallang.

Motorcycling

280 Kampong
Arang Rd
Tanjong Rhu
🚇 Kallang
Map 18-C1

BMW Motorcycle Club

6344 1332 | *www.bmwmcs.org*

The club organises several events in Singapore each month, such as breakfast rides, sunset rides, chill out nights and product talks. Longer trips in south-east Asia and beyond are also arranged and members enjoy discounts at several of Singapore's bike shops. You can join the club as an ordinary member (if you own a BMW motorcycle) or an extraordinary member (if you do not own a BMW motorcycle); both types of membership cost $80 per year and require a one-off joining fee of $150. Membership is open to individuals over 18 years old.

Various locations

Storm Riders Motorcycling Club

http://storm-riders.org

Singapore's first official motorcycling club holds informal rides and gatherings on Saturday nights, meeting at the LC Food Court in Tanjong Katong, between Dunman and Mountbatten Road (opposite Chelsea Lodge). The club fosters the community spirit of motorcycle enthusiasts and promotes motorcycle touring, with trips in Singapore, Malaysia and Thailand held throughout the year. Annual membership costs $48.

Mountain Biking

Other options **Cycling** p.51, 254

Although Singapore lacks mountains, mountain biking enthusiasts make the best of the hills and jungle trails that this island has to offer. The Singapore Amateur Cycling

Association is the umbrella organisation for bike-related sports here and organises the annual Cross Country Mountain Bike Series – four to eight races per year covering a variety of categories. Check out SACA's website, www.cycling.org.sg, for info about mountain biking in Singapore, including tips on where to ride and news about local and regional events. Another good internet resource is http://togoparts.com, a Singapore-based online community focused on all things cycling where you will find plenty of mountain biking related information. The volunteer-operated website has a forum, equipment reviews, an electronic marketplace, events listings and contact details for local bike shops. If you want a regular group to ride with – and a fresh angle on your mountain biking activities – check out the entry on the bike hash below.

Various locations

Bike Hash
9617 0047 | www.twa.com.sg/sbh

If you're looking for a fairly regular group to ride with and prefer your mountain biking with a good dose of socialising, Singapore's Bike Hash is for you. It rides on Sundays, but not on a weekly basis, so check the website for details on upcoming rides. Annual fees are $60, or $10 for individual rides.

177 Hindhede
Drive
Bukit Timah
Map 6-D3

Bukit Timah Nature Reserve
6468 5736 | www.nparks.gov.sg

Bukit Timah Nature Reserve is your best bet for feeding your mountain biking desire. The park has a 6km mountain biking trail, although riders should beware of hikers who occasionally stray onto the path. There's no charge to ride on the trail, which winds through the jungle and up and down a few hills, and the best time to hit it-is on a weekday, as weekends can be quite busy. Keep your eyes open during your ride and you're likely to spot monkeys, lizards and birds hiding in the undergrowth. For more information about the reserve call the National Parks Board at 6471 7808 or check out www.nparks.gov.sg.

North-east of
Singapore
Outer Islands
Map 8-C2

Pulau Ubin
1800471 7300 | www.npark.gov.sg

A short boat ride from the north-east coast of Singapore, Pulau Ubin (Granite Island) is a fun alternative to mountain biking on the mainland. The island has a small network of trails that takes mountain bikers through coconut and rubber plantations and past granite quarries. The boat ride to the island from Changi Point Ferry Terminal costs $2 one-way (plus an additional $2 for your bike) and takes 10-15 minutes. There are several shops on the island at the end of the jetty that rent bicycles for $3-10 per day. Rental bikes range from one-gear grandma numbers to basic mountain bikes, with a variety of sizes available to accommodate children and adults. There's no charge for getting on to the island's trails. Pack a lunch and spend the day out there! For more information about the park call the National Parks Board Information Kiosk on Pulau Ubin at 6542 4108 or check out www.nparks.gov.sg.

Music Lessons
Other options **Dance Classes** p.255, **Singing** p.292

Various locations

Cristofori Music School
6338 0009 | *www.cms.edu.sg*
Cristofori has an extensive network of music centres around Singapore, the most central of which is at the Funan Mall on North Bridge Road (6338 0009). Classes range from 'music for little Mozarts' and music theory to guitar and violin instruction. The UK-based Associated Board of the Royal Schools of Music (ABRSM) syllabus is used for course work and exams. Cristofori is also a dealer for leading piano brands and guitar and violin accessories.

26 Clive St
Little India
Little India
Map 14-D4

Indian Classical Music Centre
6291 0187 | *www.sitar.com.sg*
Lessons at The Indian Classical Music Centre are an interesting opportunity for exposure to a different cultural and musical tradition than you may be used to. Tuition is given on instruments such as the sitar, tabla, sarod and flute and vocal lessons are also available. You'll attend one hour-long class once a week and fees are $100 per month or less for groups. The centre also sells instruments, books and CDs.

9 Portchester Ave
Serangoon
Map 7-C3

MIDIWorld
6858 0123 | *www.mymidiworld.com*
MIDIWorld provides music lessons for all ages from 12 months and up, with a focus on integrating technology into the learning process. This alternative learning approach is meant to speed up the pace of learning and may also be a good option if you've been labelled tone-deaf or feel like you've got no rhythm. Classes are offered in various styles of piano, guitar, violin and flute and there are courses geared specially towards kids. MIDIWorld also has a second location at Marine Parade (6342 0700).

Various locations

Yamaha Music School
6747 4374 | *www.yamaha-music.com.sg*
Yamaha Music School has many locations around Singapore, the most central of which is at Plaza Singapura on Orchard Road (6338 6772). Part of the Yamaha Music Foundation network, which has schools in over 40 countries, YMS offers courses for young children, a Contempo Pop Music School and guitar, organ and piano instruction. The Junior Original Concerts programme encourages children to develop and perform their own compositions in front of an audience.

Netball

Tanglin Shopping
Centre
Tanglin
Orchard
Map 14-A4

ANZA
6733 1215 | *www.anza.org.sg*
With an emphasis on having fun while developing netball skills, the ANZA netball programme is open to all girls aged 6 years and older (ANZA membership is required). This is a great place for your daughter to make friends and develop sports skills in a team environment. The group meets on Saturday mornings throughout the season, which runs from September to March, at the Australian International School. There is a $50 registration fee for the season and a $40 fee for a uniform. For more information on ANZA itself, see its entry under Social Groups on p.294.

Various locations

Bedok Kings Rugby Football Club
www.bedokkings.com

Although primarily a rugby club, Bedok Kings RFC has an active netball section that usually enters two teams in the leagues organised by Netball Singapore. The club trains every Tuesday from 19:00-21:00 at the Singapore Netball Centre in Kallang (map 15-B4). The team also travels to overseas tournaments, with three tours in 2006. It isn't all serious netball though, as the club also holds social events each month. Annual membership fees are $300, which includes training costs, uniform and a discount card from the club's sponsors. For more information you can contact Katy McLean at k.mclean@worldsportgroup.com.sg.

Various locations

Bucks Rugby Football Club
www.bucks-rfc.com

The Bucks generally enter one or two teams in the top division of the Netball Singapore leagues. Although open to local players, the club's netball section is made up almost entirely of expat women. The team occasionally takes part in overseas tournaments, often at the invitation of a foreign club. Annual membership dues are $120, which covers entry fees for leagues and entitles you to a discount card for Brewerkz Restaurant and Microbrewery. For more information you can email the Bucks at bucksrfc@gmail.com.

The Padang

6 Stadium Blvd
Kallang
Kallang
Map 14-f3

Netball Singapore
6346 5063 | www.netball.org.sg

Netball is huge in Singapore with about 80,000 players, mostly women, participating in the sport. Netball Singapore organises various leagues throughout the year spanning six divisions. Their website is a great resource for information about netball events taking place in Singapore and where you can rent netball facilities. There is also an online forum that helps to match new players with clubs. The Netball Super League is a semi-professional league of six teams of elite players from different clubs. Although open to expats, the Super League consists primarily of local players.

Orchestras/Bands
Other options **Music Lessons** p.282, **Singing** p.292

Braddell Heights
Community Club
Serangoon
Serangoon
Map 7-C4

Braddell Heights Symphony Orchestra
6288 1258 | www.bhso.com

Formed in 1986, the Braddell Heights Symphony Orchestra is led by music director and conductor Yan Yin Wing. The orchestra primarily plays classical orchestra music and has more than 90 members. BHSO is active internationally, initiating a music exchange program with Korea Symphony Orchestra in 1999 and attracting foreign guest musicians on an ongoing basis.

Singapore Wind Symphony

www.swsym.org

The Singapore Wind Symphony is a non-professional ensemble that welcomes locals and expats. In addition to the main group, SWS has a youth band and several mini-ensembles that play on an ad-hoc basis. The symphony is always on the lookout for competent musicians who are willing to make the time commitment; auditions are held every two to three months.

Paintballing

Other options **Shooting** p.291

Paintball guns are considered firearms in Singapore so you're not allowed to own one. But that's not to say that you can't enjoy a game of paintball. Singapore has two facilities where you can shoot it out with your friends and family. However, some local regulations intended to ensure the safety of participants mean there are variations on the international paintball rules. For example, players are not allowed to cross into their opponents' half of the field during the game, and players must be 14 years old or older to play.

Crossfire Paintball

6792 6188 | www.crossfire.com.sg

Crossfire Paintball offers participants a landscaped playing field with a maze, flying fox and castle for added interest. Crossfire is open by appointment only and closed on public holidays. Two-hour long games cost $300 for 10 players and $35 for each additional player. The price includes equipment rental and 40 paintballs per player. Additional magazines of 40 paintballs can be purchased at $10 for one or $15 for two. A $100 deposit must be paid three days prior to the game. Participation is limited to players 18 years old and older, except for minors aged 15 to 17 years with a waiver form signed by a parent.

TAG Paintball

6324 0038 | www.paintball.com.sg

TAG Paintball boasts top-quality equipment and trained marshals who guide players through game scenarios. The facility is open by appointment only and you need to book two days in advance. Night games from 17:00 to 00:00, where the limited lighting results in more challenging combat conditions, are also an option. Participation is limited to players 18 years old and above, except for minors aged 14 to 17 years with a waiver form signed by a parent. Costs per player are $55 for a day game, $60 for a night game. This includes two hours of play, equipment rental and 100 paintballs per player.

Photography

Nature Photographic Society

www.naturephotosociety.org.sg

The Nature Photographic Society holds regular outings to explore Singapore's natural environment and develop members' skills in nature photography. Outings generally focus on a specific technique (macro or telephoto) or subject (birds, insects or plants).-Beginners are welcome and many sessions are held with beginners in mind. Longer outings include multi-day trips to Malaysia and further afield. Sessions usually take place early in the morning to take advantage of the light. An annual membership costs $50 and just $10 for enthusiasts under 21.

Selegie Arts Centre
Colonial District
📍 *Little India*
Map 14-C4

The Photographic Society of Singapore

6334 3361 | www.pss1950.org

The society offers a wide range of courses covering everything from fashion photography to black and white techniques, studio lighting, travel and creative photography, wedding photography and artistic nude photography. Prices range from $20 for a three-hour workshop to $300 for a six-lesson course and members of the society enjoy a considerable discount. The society also organises outings, competitions and exhibitions that are held in its fantastic gallery at the Selegie Arts Centre.

Polo

Other options **Horse Riding** p.271

80 Mount
Pleasant Rd
Toa Payoh
📍 *Toa Payoh*
Map 14-B1

Singapore Polo Club

6854 3999 | www.singaporepoloclub.org

If you're wild about polo, this is the place for you. Chukkas are played four times a week: on Tuesdays and Thursdays (17:30-19:00) and Saturdays and Sundays (17:00-19:00). There are two main events on the club's annual competition schedule, namely the men's tournament in June and the women's tournament in October. Heavy rainfall in Singapore in July and December limits polo action during these months. To play at the club you must become a member. This costs an initial $15,500 (valid for your lifetime) plus monthly dues of $83.75 (individual) or $89 (family). Additional fees for playing polo are $75 per chukka on weekdays and $120 per chukka on weekends.

Pottery

10 Claymore Hill
Orchard
📍 *Orchard*
Map 14-A4

The American Club

6737 3411 | www.amclub.org.sg

Pottery classes are available for members of The American Club on Fridays from 10:30-13:00. The cost is $135 for four sessions. For more information on The American Club, see its entry under Social Groups on p.294.

Funan The IT Mall
Colonial District
📍 *City Hall*
Map 17-D1

Clay Cove

6338 7769 | www.claycove.com

Clay Cove specialises in pottery classes for kids, offering basic, advanced and themed classes. Basic courses cost $110 for four 90 minute classes, inclusive of all materials. Parent and child classes are held every second month and for $120, you and your child can take part in a two-session class. Clay Cove also offers pottery sessions as a team building activity and holds pottery appreciation workshops.

Powerboating

The Singapore Power Boat Association is the governing body for powerboating in Singapore. The association conducts powered pleasure craft driving licence (PPCDL) courses (a licence is required for operating a powered pleasure craft in Singapore). The course consists of a one-week theory course concluding with a multiple choice exam, a medical examination (to ensure you are not colour-blind or physically handicapped), and a practical boat handling test. The course fee is $300, which includes 20 hours of classroom and practical instruction, a course handbook and trial test questions. The theory and practical tests cost $41.20 and $103 respectively for non-Singaporeans, while there is a further $10 fee for the PPCDL (valid for five years). For more information about the Singapore Powerboat Association, check out the association's website at http://singaporepowerboat.com or call 6344 4244.

Most of the major marinas and sailing clubs have facilities to accommodate powerboats and/or powerboat courses. These include the Changi Sailing Club (p.289), Marina Country Club & Resorts (p.289), Raffles Marina (p.290), SAF Yacht Club (p.290) and Republic of Singapore Yacht Club (p.290). However, you generally have to be a member of a club in order to rent one of its powerboats. For more information about these marinas and sailing clubs, see their entries under Sailing on p.289.

Public Speaking

YWCA Hostels
Colonial District
📍 **Dhoby Ghaut**
Map 17-C1

Toastmasters Club of Singapore
9247 2656 | www.toastmasters.org.sg
Eager to improve your public speaking skills? Singapore has an active chapter of the US-based Toastmasters International. The local club, which has about 40 members from a broad range of backgrounds, meets on the first and third Monday of every month from 19:30-22:00. Guests can join a meeting for a modest $6 guest fee – which includes a light meal. Annual club membership costs $300. Step up and speak out!

Roller Hockey

Various locations

Association Inline Hockey Singapore
www.inlinehockey.com.sg
The Association Inline Hockey Singapore organises the National Inline Hockey League and other roller hockey events throughout the year. There are about ten teams that train and play regularly. Although the teams are made up mostly of local players, expats are welcome. Contact AIHS for more information about how to find a team to join or to set up one of your own. Most roller hockey events take place at the Tampines Millennium Court, Singapore's first purpose-built hockey rink.

Various locations

Skateline
6289 0021 | www.skateline.com.sg
Skateline offers a course in rollerblading technique specifically for roller hockey. It's an introductory course that focuses on hockey skating, stick handling, passing and shooting. They have sponsored the National Inline Hockey League in the past and continue to support it in various ways. Skateline also offers retail services and an online community where you can meet member of roller hockey teams.

Rollerblading & Rollerskating
Other options **Beach Parks** p.214, **Parks** p.214

East Coast
📍 **Paya Lebar**
Map 18-C1

East Coast Park
1800471 7300 | www.nparks.gov.sg
East Coast Park is Singapore's largest and most popular park for good reason. Whether you're after some leisurely cruising or a good workout, the park's paved paths that extend over 20km are perfect for rollerblading. And when you're ready for a break the park's beach, restaurants and other amenities offer plenty of options. For more information about the park call the National Parks Board at 6471 7808 or check out www.nparks.gov.sg.

Various locations

Skateline
6289 0021 | www.skateline.com.sg
Skateline promotes inline skating (rollerblading) and the company is both a school and retailer of rollerblades and skating accessories. They also have rentals at some of their

six locations. Skateline offers a learn-to-skate programme as well as instruction in specialised disciplines such as speed and slalom skating and roller hockey. There are two flexible fee structures for Skateline's open classes: a skate-all-you-can plan for up to 16 classes in one month (ranging from $89 to $168), and a coupons plan ($90 for four coupons, one coupon per class). They offer private or group classes for $25 to $80 per person per session depending on the number of people, and corporate and school classes. Skateline puts out a fortnightly electronic newsletter and you can join their mailing list to receive regular updates on rollerblading news and events.

Area C3 East
Coast Parkway
East Coast
🚇 Kembangan
Map 18-C1

SkateSports

6442 9506 | *www.skatesports.com.sg*

SkateSports is involved in all things rollerblading. Rentals (with free socks!) are available at both their East Coast venue and at Tampines Central Community Centre. The skate shops offer a broad range of rollerblades and accessories and free trials of any of the products so that you can make sure your new set of blades suits you before purchasing. You have several options when it comes to lessons: there are a 'learn 2 skate' programmes for beginners, 'unlimited' packages that allow you to pick which lessons to attend from an extensive schedule, private lessons customised for you and your friends, and corporate and institutional classes. SkateSports also organises the Skatefest series, a mini rollerblading Olympics held monthly at the Tampines Millennium Court.

Rowing

249 Jalan Buroh
Clementi
🚇 Clementi
Map 10-B2

Singapore Rowing Association

6873 5889 | *www.sara.org.sg*

The Singapore Rowing Association is Singapore's one-stop rowing shop. In addition to organising regattas, SRA operates the Singapore Rowing Centre (where it is based), runs training programmes for competitive athletes and coaching for beginners. Beginners' programmes are held year-round on Saturday and Sundays, usually from 8:30 to 11:30. You must be 16 years or older and able to swim 50m in light clothing to participate. The Pandan Reservoir, home to the SRA and a 2km rowing course, is dedicated to rowing, so you need not worry about weaving through traffic from other boaters. Major regattas are normally held at the Seletar Reservoir. SRA associate membership costs $300 for a once-off entrance fee and $200 in annual dues. Associate members have access to the association's boats in eight sessions per month (with rental charges for additional sessions) as well as the gym and other facilities.

Rugby

The Singapore Rugby Union is home to the national rugby teams. SRU also organises the major annual rugby events here, including the National Rugby Championship, the

The Padang

Singapore Cup Championship, the Women's National Rugby Championship and the Singapore Sevens. To achieve its goal of developing Singapore into a top rugby-playing nation, SRU conducts courses for coaches and referees and to get kids involved in rugby from a young age, SRU organises competitions at school level. For more information call 6469 5955 or check out www.sru.org.sg.

Various locations
Bedok Kings Rugby Football Club
www.bedokkings.com

Bedok Kings is one of Singapore's top rugby clubs, with support from national team coaches and players. The club is made up of several teams across a range of skill levels and age groups, attracting top local and expat players alike. Aside from playing in the local leagues, the club also sends teams to regional tournaments and has a touch rugby section that fields teams in the mixed, men's, women's and master's divisions and competes in Singapore's two annual touch leagues. The touch teams, made up predominantly of expats, train at the field inside the National Institute of Education track along Bukit Timah Road (map 13-F3, see Running on p.289) on Tuesdays and Thursdays at 19:00. When they are not out on the rugby pitch, members can often be found enjoying a beer at the Kings' adopted clubhouse, BB's Bungy Bar at Clarke Quay (map 17-C2). For more information email contactus@bedokkings.com.

Various locations
Bucks Rugby Football Club
www.bucks-rfc.com

Competitive men's rugby is the first order of business for the Bucks, but friendship and camaraderie is a strong second. The team trains twice a week and plays games on Saturdays during the season. They also occasionally play in overseas tournaments. Membership is a mix of about 75% expats, 25% locals. Annual membership dues are $400 for adults and $150 for students.

The Bucks' touch section is a little different, with 'social first, competitive second' being its official line. Nevertheless, the teams are strong and both the open and masters' men's teams finished second in their divisions in the 2005 National Touch League. The club's 50 or so members meet for training runs on Wednesday evenings and games or practice sessions on most Saturday afternoons. Membership fees are $150 per year. For more information on the club's activities email bucksrfc@gmail.com.

Various locations
Touch Rugby
www.touchsingapore.org

There's a big touch rugby community in Singapore, with about six clubs and 15 schools regularly fielding teams in women's, men's, mixed and master's divisions. Most of the rugby clubs boast a few touch rugby teams as well. Touch Singapore runs two main leagues annually: a summer league starting in February and a national league starting in July. League games are held on Saturday afternoons at Turf City. For more information email Touch Singapore at info@touchsingapore.org or visit www.touchsingapore.org.

Various locations
Wanderers Rugby Football Club
9871 9742 | www.wanderersrfc.com

Wanderers welcomes players of all skill levels, and even if you're more interested in watching rugby and socialising on the sideline, you can still join as a social member. Widely recognised as the dominant touch rugby club in Singapore, Wanderers consistently lead the local touch scene in three divisions and regularly competing in overseas events. The club has a good mix of locals and expats playing on men's, women's, mixed and master's teams (affectionately called 'The Wrinklies'). The club's training ground is at the Overseas Family School (25F Paterson Road, map 17-B1) which is also the venue for regular social nights held on Tuesdays and Thursdays from 19:00-21:00. Membership fees are $150 for competitive players, $50 for students and $50 for social players. For more information about both their rugby and touch rugby teams email info@wanderersrfc.com or call CJ Torrance at 9871 9742.

Running

Other options **Hashing** p.269

Running is popular in Singapore, although a lot of the local running clubs are made up mostly of locals. Expats keen on running with a group often join one of the many hashing clubs (see p.269).

Various locations

MacRitchie Runners 25

www.mr25.org.sg

The name says it all… sort of. You have to complete a 5km trail run in under 25 minutes to become an official member of the club, but official membership is only required for some of their events. All runners are welcome to join this registered running club, which organises runs and time trials almost daily. Most events take place at MacRitchie Reservoir although there are also track sessions at the National Institute of Education track on Bukit Timah Road. Check out the club's website for a schedule. Membership is free, so grab your running shoes and join up!

Nr Singapore
Botanic Gardens
Bukit Timah
Map 13-F2

National Institute of Education

6790 3888 | *www.nie.edu.sg*

Centrally located and free (just off Evans Road), this is a popular spot for track training. While the track is only partially lit there's usually enough light spilling over from the lit end to make running around the entire track possible, unless there's an event happening on the inner field. There are changing rooms with toilets and showers. Watch for the man on a bike with a black garbage bag in his basket – he sells cold drinks to thirsty runners.

Sailing

Other options **Boat & Yacht Charters** p.218

Being an island nation, Singapore has a lot to offer sailors. It's perfect place to take off from for a short daytrip around the Strait of Singapore or for a longer sailing voyage to some of the beautiful islands of Malaysia to the north or Indonesia to the south. The Singapore Sailing Federation is the governing body for sailing here and its website (www.sailing.org.sg) is a great resource for news and information on regattas and national rankings.

32 Netheravon Rd
Changi
🚇 *Pasir Ris*
Map 8-D3

Changi Sailing Club

6545 2876 | *www.csc.org.sg*

The club offers sailing courses for several craft types (keelboat, dinghy, catamaran and optimist), as well as a powerboat driving licence course. Various competitive and social races are held throughout the year. Onshore facilities include a swimming pool, library, restaurant, lounge, cafe, chalet rooms and BBQs. Members can also make use of moorings and land storage facilities with fees based on the size of the boat. Ordinary membership fees are $2,625, plus monthly dues of $63 for single members or $78.75 for families.

600 Ponggol
Seventeenth Ave
Punggol
🚇 *Punggol*
Map 7-E1

Marina Country Club

6388 8388 | *www.marinacountryclub.com.sg*

Situated in Punggol on the north-east coast, this sailing club has extensive facilities. If you have your own boat, the marina has wet and dry berths, fuelling facilities, and various service providers to see to the maintenance and repair of your boat. There are also all of the amenities that you would expect at a country club including a pool, fitness centre, children's play area, restaurants and bars, and a sea sports centre where a number of wakeboarding companies are located.

Various locations

People's Association Sea Sports Club

6340 5335 | www.seasports.org.sg

This club is operated by the People's Association, the government agency that encourages social cohesion through grassroots organisations. It has four locations around Singapore, each offering a different range of courses and equipment for rent. Although the club targets Singaporeans, expats are welcome. Fees are modest: adult membership costs $40 for one year or $80 for three years, while basic sailing courses cost between $240 and $290 for three seven-hour sessions. The four branches are the Changi Sea Sports Club (map 8-E3), East Coast Sea Sports Club (map 12-B3), Kallang Sea Sports Club (map 17-F1), and Pasir Ris Sea Sports Club (map 8-B3). When visiting the website click on the 'Sea Sports Club online' link.

10 Tuas West Drive
Tuas
🚇 *Boon Lay*
Map 5-A4

Raffles Marina

6861 8000 | www.rafflesmarina.com.sg

One of the only marinas in the region with the Yacht Harbour Association's 5 Gold Anchor Award, the club offers various skipper and keelboat courses and first-class facilities. These include 165 walk-on berths, a boathouse with dry stack storage space for 300 boats, and a clubhouse with a pool, gym, tennis courts and bowling alley.

52 West Coast
Ferry Rd
Pasir Panjang
🚇 *Clementi*
Map 10-C3

Republic of Singapore Yacht Club

6768 9288 | www.rsyc.org.sg

Founded in 1826, RSYC is Singapore's oldest club. It offers numerous courses to help you brush up on your sailing and boating skills. With everything from keelboat sailing to night navigation and outboard engine maintenance, there is something for every sailor here. The club also provides full marina facilities, with plenty of wet and dry berths and concessionaires providing marine repair services and rescue and salvage services. The club also has a host of non-sailing facilities, including a gym, swimming pool, library and chart room, children's playroom, jackpot room, two restaurants and a bar.

Sembawang
🚇 *Sembawang*
Map 4-C1

SAF Yacht Club

6758 3032 | www.safyc.org.sg

With a fleet of more than 200 craft, the club offers aspiring sailors a wide variety of options. A six-session basic sailing course taught in a Laser Pico costs $189 for club members or $231 for non-members. The club also runs a four-day sailing course for kids aged 7-17 using Optimists, Toppers and Picos ($73.50 for members, $105 for non-members). The club has two clubhouses (Changi Clubhouse, east of map 12-F3, and Sembawang Clubhouse, map 4-C1) and one sea sports centre (map 12-D3). Members can rent boats for $5 to $40 per four-hour session, depending on the type of craft.

Mini Explorer

Don't be fooled by the size of this little star – it's full of insider info, maps, contacts, tips and facts about this vibrant city. From shops to spas, bars to bargains and everything in between, the Mini Explorer helps you get the most out of your stay in Singapore, however long you're staying.

Scouts & Guides

There's an active Scouts and Guides scene here, with many schools hosting a local unit and events held both in Singapore and abroad. You can contact the Singapore Scout Association at 6259 2858 (www.scout.org.sg) or Girl Guides Singapore at 6259 9391 (www.girlguides.org.sg). There are also a couple of international Scout units such as the Boy Scouts of America (BSA) Troop 07 and the ANZA Scouts. See entries below.

United World College
of South East Asia
Clementi
🚇 **Buona Vista**
Map 13-A4

ANZA Scouts

6733 1215 | www.anza.org.sg

This Australian Scout Group has three sections: Joeys (6-8 years), Cubs (8-10 years) and Scouts (10-12). The group has over 40 members and boys and girls are welcome. Meetings are held on Saturday afternoons at the United World College. For more information contact Lydia Astill at astills@singnet.com.sg.

Singapore
American School
Woodlands
🚇 **Marsiling**
Map 3-F4

BSA Troop 07

http://bsa.startingpoints.org

Troop 07 meets on most Tuesdays at 18:15 in room H301 at the Singapore American School. The troop is open to boys aged 11-17 and you can find more details on how to join the group on the website. Each month has a theme, such as sports, environment, camping/outdoor and first aid. For more information email Tom_Hartberger@citratubindo.com.

Scrabble

Other options **Chess** p.251

10 Anson Rd
Tanjong Pagar
🚇 **Tanjong Pagar**
Map 17-C3

Scrabble Association

www.toucanet.com

Scrabble is regularly played by groups around Singapore, so check out the 'venues' link on the Scrabble Association's website to find a location near you. The most important annual events for the local Scrabble community are the National Scrabble Championship, the Singapore Open and the Lim Boon Heng Cup, which are all two-day competitions. Players from Singapore also regularly go to overseas competitions such as the King's Cup in Bangkok in June. Membership costs $24 per year.

Scrapbooking

92 Zion Rd
Tiong Bahru
🚇 **Tiong Bahru**
Map 17-A2

Scrapbooking Cove

9822 3497 | www.scrapbookingcove.com

Scrapbooking Cove is an online store specialising in scrapbooking materials and products. Although it's a relatively new hobby in Singapore, the small community of scrapbooking enthusiasts is growing. Julie, the proprietor of Scrapbooking Cove and an avid scrapper, is always happy to offer tips and advice. She also conducts classes for small groups. Contact her at julie@scrapbookingcove.com.

Shooting

Other options **Paintballing** p.284

73 Bukit Tinggi Rd
Bukit Timah
🚇 **Bukit Batok**
Map 6-E4

The British Club ▶ p.307

6467 4311 | www.britishclub.org.sg

The British Club's shooting section is affiliated with the Singapore Rifle Association, allowing members to take part in regular training, practices and competitions. Shotgun, pistol and rifle events take place at the National Shooting Centre where participants can make use of international-standard facilities. For more information on The British Club, see its entry under Social Groups on p.294.

Old Choa Chu Kang Rd
Northwest Singapore
🚇 **Choa Chu Kang**
Map 5-D3

Singapore Shooting Association

6795 3760 | www.singaporeshooting.org

The association operates the National Shooting Centre, the only shooting range in Singapore open to the public. It offers international standard facilities, including two trap and skeet ranges, a sporting clays range, three open 50m ranges, 16 lanes of 50m ranges and 20 lanes of 25m ranges (10 of which can be converted to 10m ranges). It's open 09:00-18:00 daily, except on Mondays. Range fees vary by type of target for registered shooters (members of affiliated clubs); guest shooters pay $20 on weekdays and $25 on weekends. In addition to operating the National Shooting Centre, the association also provides shooting and coaching courses throughout the year. The Singapore Gun Club and Singapore Rifle Association also have offices at the National Shooting Centre.

Singing
Other options **Music Lessons** p.282

Kallang Theatre
Kallang
Map 14-F4

The Philharmonic Chamber Choir
www.tpcsnet.com
Formed in 1994 by accomplished Singaporean conductor Maestro Lim Yau, this 30 member non-professional a capella group strives to challenge its singers and provide Singapore with world-class choral performances. The choir takes part in overseas competitions and festivals, having previously brought home awards from events in the US, Italy and Hungary. The group has also ventured into recording and has four CDs to its name. Music reading and good pitch are prerequisites for prospective members. The choir has a once-off joining fee of $100 and a monthly membership fee of $20. Regular rehearsals are held on Wednesdays from 19:30-22:30 in the Kallang Theatre Orchestra Room.

Various locations

Singapore Symphony Chorus
9734 2244 | www.symphonychorus.sg
The Singapore Symphony Chorus is a non-professional choir of about 120 members, many of whom are expats. The choir performs mainly symphonic works with the Singapore Symphony Orchestra, collaborating on three to four performances each year. Prospective members must be able to read music and have good rhythm and pitch, which you will have to demonstrate at an audition. Regular rehearsals are held on Monday evenings from 19:30-22:15, with additional rehearsals scheduled closer to performances. Rehearsals are held either at the Victoria Concert Hall (map 17-D2) or at the Esplanade – Theatres On The Bay (map 17-E2).

Skiing & Snowboarding

21 Jurong Town
Hall Rd
Jurong
🚇 Jurong East
Map 6-B4

Snow City
6560 1511 | www.snowcity.com.sg
While it's not exactly the Alps, Snow City is your best bet for some cool action without hopping on a plane. The centre's Snow Chamber has a 60m long slope (with a 14 degree gradient) with artificial snow that is maintained at -5°C. The main activity is snowtubing, although there are sessions dedicated to skiing and snowboarding on Tuesdays to Saturdays from 20:00 to 22:00. In addition to the slope, there's also an area where younger children can frolic in the snow among tunnels, slides and an igloo.
Snow City appeals primarily to kids and teenagers, but adults are welcome to join in the fun. Entry fees are $12 for a single session (one hour) or $18 for a double session. Admission includes rental of a jacket and boots, helmets for children and the use of the snowtubes. You need to book in advance for the snowboarding or skiing sessions. Entry fees are $58 for two hours and include rental of a jacket, boots and skis or a snowboard. Snow City is closed on Mondays.

Skydiving

In its measured way, Singapore has begun to embrace skydiving in recent years, and more opportunities are being created for people to jump. Since 2004 Singapore has put on an annual Singapore Skydive Festival in August, attracting rookie and experienced skydivers from Singapore and around the world to jump in a unique setting. Held at Marina South Park, the event sees about 300-400 tandem jumps and 1,000-2,000 regular jumps take place over four days. Jumping from 12,000 feet, skydivers can see an entire country below them as they soar through the sky, enjoying incredible views of Singapore's impressive skyline on the way down.

Oops!

Did we miss anything out? If you have any thoughts, ideas or comments for us to include in the Activities section, drop us a line, and if your club or organisation isn't in here, let us know and we'll give you a shout in the next edition. Visit www.explorerpublishing.com and tell us whatever's on your mind.

Snooker

Like any city, Singapore has plenty of pool and snooker facilities ranging from bars with a table tucked in the back to dedicated billiards halls with numerous top quality tables. Pool and snooker enthusiasts may want to check out www.poolfanatic.com, an online forum catering to Singapore's billiards community. Login and you will find discussions about all things billiards, including information on tournaments, techniques and equipment for sale. If you are looking for a special snooker experience, check out the Bar and Billiard Room at the historic Raffles Hotel. For $16 per hour, you can play snooker in a setting that will transport you back to colonial times. For a more casual atmosphere, check out Brewerkz Restaurant & Microbrewery at Riverside Point. Although the restaurant has only two pool tables ($2 per game), you won't mind waiting your turn while enjoying one of their tasty microbrews.

02-01 Clarke Quay
Riverside
🚇 **Clarke Quay**
Map 17-C2

Baize

6339 0280 | www.baize.com.sg

This upmarket pool hall is just the place to start a Friday evening on the town. With 11 pool tables in a trendy setting on Clarke Quay, Baize attracts novices and pool sharks alike. Drop by after work for a few games before heading out for dinner or hitting the clubs. You can also grab a bite to eat here, choosing from a small menu of finger food that includes a tasty club sandwich. There's a dress code in effect at night, with no shorts or sandals (for the guys) allowed. Tables cost $12 per hour.

Snorkelling

Other options **Diving** p.257

The waters around Singapore are not conducive to snorkelling but there are plenty of destinations in Malaysia, Indonesia, Thailand and Philippines with excellent fish-gazing. Some of the best options close to Singapore are Pulau Tioman, Pulau Rawa, Pulau Sibu, Pulau Dayang and Pulau Aur, all Malaysian islands off the east coast of peninsular Malaysia. Except for Tioman (which is still excellent), these islands are part of the Marine Park of Johor, an area known for its phenomenal diving. With clear waters and plenty of underwater life to enjoy, these islands make for great long weekend getaways. The waters are alive with everything from blue spotted rays and boulder corals to whale sharks and butterfly fish, so bring along your underwater camera. This area is best between April and October, as the monsoon season from November to March makes for rougher seas become and many of the accommodation providers close down for the period.

293

1-20 The Riverwalk
Riverside
🚇 *Clarke Quay*
Map 17-D2

Living Seas
6435 0436 | *www.livingseas.com.sg*

Although primarily a diving operator, Living Seas accommodates snorkellers on its trips to Pulau Tioman and Pulau Aur. Packages cost around $350 per person (twin sharing) for a trip that departs from Singapore on Friday evening and returns on Sunday night. You can either stay cooped up in your apartment for the weekend or snorkel in warm, clear waters with breathtaking underwater life – the choice is yours!

Social Groups
Other options **Support Groups** p.149

With the long history of expatriate presence in Singapore, there is no shortage of social groups waiting to welcome newcomers with open arms. A well-developed network of clubs and associations caters to just about any and all expat needs and can provide a comforting sense of community for those feeling homesick. These organisations also provide an avenue for expats to take a more active (and often rewarding) role in the community by organising and sponsoring events or establishing charitable initiatives. Major clubs that have established facilities, such as The American Club, The British Club and The Hollandse Club (see the entries below), are open to all and have a diverse membership. In some cases though, the type of membership and the applicable fees vary depending on your nationality, and sometimes there are quotas to ensure that a minimum proportion of the club's members are of a particular nationality. In addition to these, other organisations have been

Other Social Groups	
The American Association of Singapore	6738 0371
Association of Women for Action & Research	6779 7137
Belgian & Luxembourg Association of Singapore	6328 7062
British Association of Singapore	6339 8229
Chinese Women's Association	6276 9746
French Association of Singapore	6887 0256
German Club-Deutsches Haus	6467 8802
Goethe-Institut	6735 4555
Indian Women's Association	6235 1449
Italian Women's Group	6469 0532
International Researchers Club	6826 6194
Japanese Cultural Society	6338 3428
The Japanese Association, Singapore	6468 0066
Korean Association of Singapore	6299 8966
Kowloon Club	6440 9237
Mensa Singapore	6345 5288
Netherlands Charity Association	6775 5546
PrimeTime Business and Professional Women's Association	6234 0973
Royal Society of St. George	6733 1872
Scandinavian Women's Association	6775 5546
Singapore American Community Action Council	6733 9249
Singapore Business & Professional Women's Association	6220 6867
Singapore Council of Women's Organisations	6837 0611
Singapore St. Andrew's Society	6465 6248
Spanish Speaking Women's Association	6466 9534
St. David's Society of Singapore	6472 2826
St. Patrick's Society of Singapore	6339 8229
Swiss Club, Singapore	6466 3233
Toastmasters Club of Singapore	9839 0857

included in the Other Social Groups table (above) that have a specific national affiliation, such as the Italian Women's Group or The Japanese Association, membership tends to consist of citizens of that particular country. Most groups have a good mix of individuals and families joining, welcoming those with common interests or backgrounds.

The American Club

10 Claymore Hill
Orchard
Orchard
Map 14-A4

6737 3411 | www.amclub.org.sg

The American Club is a full-service members club located in the heart of Singapore, just off Orchard Road. Member services include dining, sports and recreation facilities, a concierge, travel desk and more. The club has a large pool, tennis and squash courts, fitness programmes from aerobics and swimming lessons to karate and yoga and even an eight lane bowling alley. Arts and culture classes such as elementary Mandarin, pottery and calligraphy are available. Social events are also organised including fashion shows and holiday celebrations and dinners.

American Women's Association of Singapore

The American Club
Orchard
Orchard
Map 14-A4

6733 6170 | www.awasingapore.org

The American Women's Association of Singapore was established in 1935 and has become a favourite with expat women here. AWA offers everything from social gatherings and sports activities to overseas trips and volunteer opportunities. The association usually holds a meeting on the second Tuesday of each month in the Colonial Room at The American Club. Regular membership costs $125 per year and is open to female citizens of the US and Canada. Citizens of other countries may join as associate members. Meet and greet sessions are held regularly to welcome new members.

ANZA

Tanglin Shopping Centre
Tanglin
Orchard
Map 14-A4

6733 1215 | www.anza.org.sg

A social organisation rather than a club with facilities, ANZA has contributed greatly to the thriving Australian and New Zealand community in Singapore. It organises everything from pub nights, sports groups and tours to classes and volunteer efforts. ANZA also supports charities such as the Dover Park Hospice, the Salvation Army and the Little Sisters of the Poor. ANZA's various groups hold regular meetings and events, and all the details can be found on their website or by contacting them directly at their office.

The British Club ▸ p.307

73 Bukit Tinggi Rd
Bukit Timah
Bukit Batok
Map 6-E4

6467 4311 | www.britishclub.org.sg

Situated in a park-like setting next to the Bukit Timah Nature Reserve, the British Club offers members the chance to relax in a comfortable and elegant environment. A busy social calendar is available to members, including arts and language classes, activities and special events. The sporting life is also fully catered to with facilities for tennis, squash, billiards, swimming and more. Dedicated football and cricket pitches are just a two-minute drive from the club. Dining and leisure round out the offerings, with five different restaurants, a library and children's play centre.

Canadian Association of Singapore

Various locations

6734 5954 | www.canadians.org.sg

The Canadian Association is a volunteer-run group that aims to bring Canadians and friends of Canada together for social and sports events. It has regular coffee mornings, pub nights and children's playgroups. For over 50 years the highlight of their annual social calendar has been the Maple Leaf Ball. The Canadian Dragonboat and the Singapore Ice Dragons youth hockey teams are both organised through the Canadian Association. The association also puts out *The Maple Leaf Times* which keeps members up to date on social events, news about the Canadian community in Singapore and volunteer opportunities.

295

22 Camden Rd
Bukit Timah
Map 13-E1

The Hollandse Club

6464 5225 | *www.hollandseclub.org.sg*

The Hollandse Club offers its members a full range of facilities and services. From social groups to sports, there's not much they don't cover. A newly built tennis pavilion includes a gym, glow-in-the-dark bowling alley and the Garden Spa, managed by the Aspara Group. (see Health Spas listings on page 311) With a mums and tots group and a teens' room, members of all age groups are catered to. There are plenty of dining options on the premises and there's a wine club that meets once a month to learn more about wines from around the world.

Squash

Other options **Leisure Facilities** p.304

73 Bukit Tinggi Rd
Bukit Timah
🚇 **Bukit Batok**
Map 6-E4

The British Club ▶ p.307

6467 4311 | *www.britishclub.org.sg*

The British Club has four squash courts and a shop where you can rent rackets and balls. Various squash social nights and leagues are held here throughout the year. For more information about the club see its entry under Social Groups on p.294.

52 Stadium Rd
Kallang
🚇 **Kallang**
Map 15-A4

Kallang Squash & Tennis Centre

6348 1291 | *www.ibook.ssc.gov.sg*

Operated by the Singapore Sports Council, this centre near the national stadium has seven air-conditioned squash courts, six singles and one doubles, open daily from 07:00-22:00. Court rental costs $10 per hour on weekends and after 18:00 on weekdays, and $5 per hour before 18:00 on weekdays (the doubles court costs $15/10 per hour). Reservations can be made over the phone or through the website; payment is required immediately for internet reservations, while payment for phone reservations can be made at the centre 15 minutes before your reserved timeslot. The centre has changing rooms, water fountains and a sports shop where you can rent rackets and buy balls.

Connaught Drive
Colonial District
🚇 **City Hall**
Map 17-C2

Singapore Cricket Club

6338 9271 | *www.scc.org.sg*

Situated on The Padang, this club has recently renovated its sports facilities, including two squash courts. The squash section is active throughout the year, holding leagues and inter-club competitions with other country clubs in Singapore as well as touring abroad. You will need to be a member, or a guest of a member to access the squash courts. For more information about the club see Country Clubs on p.306.

45 Tanjong Rhu Rd
Tanjong Rhu
🚇 **Kallang**
Map 18-A1

Singapore Swimming Club

6342 3600 | *www.sswimclub.org.sg*

Among its many facilities, the Singapore Swimming Club also has four squash courts. The courts are open from 07:00 to 22:00 (with the last booking on Saturdays being at 19:00) and cost $2.50 per court for 45 minutes. Non-members can go in as a member's guest for $5. For more information about the club see the entry under Swimming on p.297.

5 Stevens Rd
Orchard
🚇 **Orchard**
Map 14-A3

The Tanglin Club

6737 6011 | *www.tanglinclub.org.sg*

The Tanglin Club boasts six singles and one doubles squash court. The club's squash section has over 60 members who take part in the club nights, social squash and tournaments that take place throughout the year. Individual coaching is also available by request. The club's facilities are for members and their guests only.

Surfing

Other options **Kitesurfing** p.276, **Windsurfing** p.302

If you're packing your bags for Singapore and wondering whether to bring your board, do. While there are no breaks in Singapore, there are plenty of good spots in the region that are easily accessible for a short (or long) surfing holiday. The closest is the Indonesian island of Bintan, which is about 45 minutes by ferry from Singapore's Tanah Merah Ferry Terminal. Big waves roll in off the South China Sea, particularly during the north-east monsoon season (November to March), giving surfers plenty of action. With pleasant beaches and accommodation ranging from rustic to luxury, a weekend of surfing in Bintan will have you returning to work feeling fully recharged. If you have a bit more time, the famous breaks of Bali are a short two and a half hour flight away. An enchanting island that has captured the imagination of surfers for generations, Bali does not disappoint.

Swimming

Other options **Leisure Facilities** p.304, **Beaches** p.214

Swimming is popular in Singapore, probably because being in the water is a wonderful reprieve from the equatorial heat. Whatever the reason, Singapore has some excellent swimming facilities and the country boasts some very talented swimmers. If you're simply looking for a leisurely splash in the water, most condominiums have their own pools. But if you're looking for an Olympic-sized pool for laps, you will probably have to go to one of the public swimming complexes or private clubs.

The Singapore Swimming Association is the national organisation for swimming as well as for water polo, diving, synchronised swimming and open water swimming. It focuses on developing Singapore's swimming talent through training programmes for elite athletes and coaching courses. The association also organises numerous events. For more information contact the association at 6258 1011 or check out their website at www.swimming.org.sg.

There are several swimming complexes operated by the Singapore Sports Council that are open to the public although they can be quite busy on evenings and weekends. Most swimming complexes have a competition pool, a teaching pool and a wading pool. Entry fees are generally about 50 cents to $2 per person. See the table below for a list

Swimming Complexes	
Ang Mo Kio Swimming Complex	6456 6821
Bishan Swimming Complex	6353 6117
Buona Vista Swimming Complex	6778 0244
Clementi Swimming Complex	6779 0577
Kallang Basin Swimming Complex	6295 4261
Katong Swimming Complex	6344 9609
Toa Payoh Swimming Complex	6259 4808
Woodlands Swimming Complex	6269 4192

of some of the major swimming complexes and phone numbers, or click on the sports facilities link on the Singapore Sports Council's website (www.ssc.gov.sg) and check out details on all of Singapore's swimming complexes. Also listed are entries for some clubs and organisations offering lessons as part of their programmes.

10 Claymore Hill
Orchard
🚇 Orchard
Map 14-A4

The American Club

6737 3411 | www.amclub.org.sg

The American Club's members have access to the club's aquatics programmes, including swimming lessons, aqua aerobics and swim camps. A popular expat hangout, the club is a great place to unwind on weekends and enjoy a little taste of home. For more information about the club, see the entry under Social Groups on p.294.

297

Various locations

APS Swim School Singapore
6777 5823 | *www.apsswim.com*

Founded by a Singapore Olympic swimmer, the APS Swim School offers lessons for children and adults, from basic skills classes to advanced technical coaching sessions. Lessons are taught at various complexes in Singapore, including the Farrer Park Swimming Complex at 2 Rutland Road. Fees range from $112 to $222 per month, depending on the programme and the number of lessons per week. The Aquatic Performance Swim Club for children interested in competitive swimming is affiliated with the school.

73 Bukit Tinggi Rd
Bukit Timah
🚇 *Bukit Batok*
Map 6-E4

The British Club ▶ p.307
6467 4311 | *www.britishclub.org.sg*

Among its facilities and services, The British Club offers a variety of swimming programmes with professional coaching for beginners, children, adults and competitive swimmers. Facilities include a 25m pool with six lanes, a splash pool and a Jacuzzi. Use of these facilities is reserved for members and their guests. For more information on the club, see the entry under Social Groups on p.294.

45 Tanjong Rhu Rd
Tanjong Rhu
🚇 *Kallang*
Map 18-A1

Singapore Swimming Club
6342 3600 | *www.sswimclub.org.sg*

One of Singapore's top recreation clubs, this club has offers lessons and coaching for competitive swimmers. A one-year family membership costs $2,000, plus $65 in monthly dues. The club also has a gym, tennis and squash courts, a bowling alley and billiards tables, ensuring plenty of diversions for your family while you swim to your heart's content.

Table Tennis
Other options **Leisure Facilities** p.304

Table tennis has a huge following in Singapore, so much so that the Singapore Sports Council has named it one of the city's seven core sports. Top local players fare well on the international table tennis scene, making them minor celebrities at home. The Singapore Table Tennis Association is the national body responsible for grooming top athletes and overseeing the major local and international competitions held here. The STTA offers introductory table tennis courses ($150 for 10 lessons) as well as technical courses for coaches at the STTA Academy (map 14-D1). The SAFRA-DONIC Table Tennis Academy (6352 6865, located at the SAFRA Toa Payoh Clubhouse, map 14-D1) also offers lessons in Chinese. For more information about the STTA call 6354 1014 or visit www.stta.org.sg.

Team Building
From Sailing (p.289) and Dragon Boating (p.260) to Kayaking (p.273) and Skydiving (p.293), team building activities are widely available in Singapore. If you find an activity that you are interested in, chances are any service provider concerned will be more than happy to put on a corporate team building event for you. And for a less intense approach you could always take your colleagues on a spa retreat (see Health Spas on p.311).

Tennis
Other options **Leisure Facilities** p.304

Most social and country clubs have tennis courts, and many have social tennis nights or regular club competitions. Refer to the Club Facilities table on p.309 for a listing of clubs with tennis courts. The Singapore Tennis Association is the governing body for tennis and as such it organises tournaments and runs coaching programmes for juniors and adults. Fees depend on the number of sessions per week; a session per week over three months for juniors costs $210, while an eight-week module for adults with one session per week costs $160. For more information call 6348 0124 or go to www.singtennis.org.sg.

Kallang Squash & Tennis Centre

52 Stadium Rd
Kallang
🚇 *Kallang*
Map 15-B4

6348 1291 | www.ibook.ssc.gov.sg

This facility is operated by the Singapore Sports Council and has 14 floodlit outdoor tennis courts that are open daily from 7:00-22:00. Court rental costs $9.50 per hour on weekends and after 18:00 on weekdays, and $3.50 per hour before 18:00 on weekdays. Reservations can be made over the phone or through the website; payment is required immediately for internet reservations, while payment for phone reservations can be made at the centre 15 minutes before your reserved timeslot. The centre has changing rooms, water fountains and a shop where you can rent rackets and buy balls.

Ladies Tennis Singapore

Various locations

6465 2646 | www.ladiestennissingapore.com

This competitive ladies' doubles tennis league, sanctioned by the Singapore Tennis Association, is open to women of all skills levels. The league has two seasons per year: February to May and September to December. Teams play one match a week at the various teams' home courts, which may be at private clubs, condos or public facilities. Fees are $200 per team of six to eight players. In 2006, over 25 teams were registered in the league.

Savitar

Raffles The Plaza
Colonial District
🚇 *City Hall*
Map 17-D1

6837 3705 | www.savitargroup.com

Savitar is a private sports management company specialising in tennis. The company runs programmes at a number of prestigious clubs and hotels in Singapore, offering courses and private instruction for players of all skill levels. Private instruction fees start at $60-70 per hour, while fees for multi-week courses range from around $180 to $390. The main office is on the sixth floor of Raffles the Plaza.

Singapore Tennis Centre

1020 East Coast
Parkway
East Coast
🚇 *Kembangan*
Map 18-F1

6241 8070

This centre near the McDonalds on East Coast Parkway has 10 floodlit outdoor courts located just a short distance from the beach. Court rental costs $14 per hour during peak times (weekends, public holidays and weekday evenings) and $10 per hour at other times. The centre offers individual and group lessons for all skill levels and age groups.

Waterfront Sports

7 Japanese
Garden Rd
Jurong
🚇 *Lakeside*
Map 10-A1

6449 9034 | www.waterfrontsports.com.sg

Opened in January 2006, Waterfront Sports boasts six floodlit tennis courts, a wall court and a large clubhouse. Everyone from beginners to competitive players can take lessons here, with packages starting at $100 per month. On Saturdays the centre hosts Saturday Night Fever match play from 19:00 onwards: you can take part in the friendly matches and socialise for $10. Courts can be rented for $15 per hour during peak times (Saturdays, Sundays, public holidays and weekday evenings) and for $10 per hour at off-peak times.

Triathlon

Singapore has an active triathlon community in part because Singapore's tropical climate means that outdoor training and competitions are possible year-round. The Triathlon Association of Singapore organises two triathlons, one duathlon and one aquathlon per year, while other triathlon clubs also hold their own informal events. Of the three disciplines, cycling is the most challenging as it's difficult to find roads that have few traffic lights (cyclists are not allowed on the freeways). However East Coast Park and Sentosa, the two most popular training locations for triathletes, both offer roads with less traffic, beaches for swimming and great running paths.

Synergy Multi-Sport

365 Clementi Ave 2
Clementi
🚇 *Clementi*
Map 10-C2

6777 0664 | *www.synergymultisport.com*

Synergy Multi-Sport has clinics, workshops and training camps tailored to novice and elite athletes. Courses are designed to improve athletes' performance by developing both their physical and mental skills. Fees range from $30 for short clinics to $200 or more for multi-day training camps. Synergy is a good option for beginners seeking their first taste of triathlon and for pros looking to fine-tune their performance.

Triathlon Association of Singapore

19 Aroozoo Ave
Serangoon
🚇 *Kovan*
Map 7-D4

6227 7577 | *www.triathlonsingapore.org*

TAS organises two triathlons, one duathlon and one aquathlon per year. Aside from its role in promoting the sport at a national level, TAS also holds training sessions on alternate Saturdays at either East Coast Park or Sentosa (refer to the TAS website for a schedule) and offers more formal training programmes for adults, juniors and kids. Fees range from $88 to $150 per month for kids and adults and from $100 to $150 per month for juniors.

Triathlon Family

Various locations

www.triathlonfamily.com

An established triathlon club in Singapore with about 1,000 members, Triathlon Family attracts both veterans and novices. With four training sessions per week, the club emphasises group training as a way for members to make new friends and push each other to excel. And best of all, membership is free!

Tribob

40 Saunders Rd
Orchard
🚇 *Orchard*
Map 14-C4

6734 1594 | *www.tribob.com*

Popular with expats, Tribob provides high-quality triathlon training services to its 100 plus members. Individual membership costs $1,200 for six months ($1,000 to renew) or $2,000 for a year ($1,700 renewal). This gives you access to seven training sessions per week, qualified coaches, free talks by the in-house sports doctor and preferential prices for race packages and overseas training camps.

Volleyball

The Volleyball Association of Singapore oversees both indoor and beach volleyball in Singapore. They hold plenty of events, including tournaments and courses for coaches and referees. Many of the indoor volleyball teams are from polytechnics, universities or other local organisations. The best way to get involved is to provide VAS with your contact information and volleyball background, which the association will then forward to the clubs to see if any of them have an opening. For more information about VAS call 6259 2786 or visit www.vas.org.sg.

Beach Club
Sentosa
🚇 *HarbourFront*
Map 19-B3

Sunset Bay

6275 0668 | www.sunsetbay.com.sg

This unassuming bar on Sentosa's Siloso Beach is home to hot beach volleyball action all year-round. If you have a group of five or more people, you can pay $5 per person for all-day access to one of the seven courts and the use of a ball. And if that's not enough of a bargain the fee also includes the use of the bar's sea kayaks, several games of pool and a few bottles of mineral water for the group. The courts are busiest on weekends so groups take turns using them, challenging others to friendly matches. Even if you show up alone you're sure to find a team willing to let you join them. With the bar right there for post-game drinks you'll be hard pressed to find a better way to spend your weekend.

Waterskiing & Wakeboarding

Other options **Water Polo** p.302

The Singapore Waterski & Wakeboard Federation is the governing body for waterskiing and wakeboarding and organises competitions such as the important National Wakeboarding Championships and various waterskiing competitions. Contact the federation at 6348 9943 or check out www.swwf.org.sg. Wakeboarding has caught on in the past few years and has eclipsed waterskiing in popularity – for the time being anyway. However you will find operators cater to enthusiasts of both sports and most of these are clustered in three locations: off Punggol at the north-east end of Singapore, the Kallang River, and the East Coast Lagoon.

Operators generally offer lessons as well as boat and equipment rentals. Rates are usually hourly per boat (rather than per person) and usually include rental of life jackets, helmets and wakeboards or waterskis. The following table lists some of the main operators. While below that, is an entry for Ski 360°, Singapore's first cableski park.

Waterskiing & Wakeboarding Operators

Name	Area	Phone	Website / Email	$ per hour per boat (weekends)	Wake boarding	Waterskiing
Extreme Sports & Marketing	Kallang	6344 8813	www.extreme.com.sg	120	Yes	Yes
Launch Wakeboard School	Ponggol	6581 2202	www.launch2002.com	100-120	Yes	No
Maxout Hydrosports	Tuas	6869 2291	www.maxouthydrosports.com	100	Yes	No
Ponggol Sea Sports	Punggol	6386 3891	www.pssa.com.sg	90	Yes	Yes
Pro Air Watersports	Punggol	6756 8012	www.proairwatersports.com	95-105	Yes	No
Ten Eighty Wakeboard Academy	Punggol	6257 5859	www.1080wakeboard.com	85-100	Yes	No
Waketime	Punggol	6387 1997	www.waketime.com.sg	90-120	Yes	No

1206A East Coast Parkway
East Coast
🚇 *Bedok*
Map 12-A4

Ski 360°

6442 7318 | www.ski360degree.com

Ski 360° near the East Coast Seafood Centre opened in January 2006 and is Singapore's first cableski park. It can accommodate eight wakeboarders or water skiers at a time, averaging 140-150 riders per day on weekends. Passes cost $40 for one hour on weekends or $30 on weekdays, with a 50% discount for a second hour. The fee includes rental of a life jacket, helmet and wakeboard or water skis. The park is lit at night, allowing enthusiasts to ride the waves until 22:00. The park has toilets, lockers and showers as well as a restaurant and pro shop.

Water Polo

Other options **Polo** p.285

Water polo falls under the auspices of the Singapore Swimming Association. The association organises numerous tournaments throughout the year at school and club levels, although these primarily target locals. Expats interested in playing recreational water polo should try the Chinese Swimming Club at East Coast (see the entry below). For more information about water polo events contact the Singapore Swimming Association at 6258 1011 or check out www.swimming.org.sg.

21 Amber Rd
East Coast
Paya Lebar
Map 18-A1

Chinese Swimming Club

6345 1221 | *www.chineseswimmingclub.org.sg*
Recreational water polo is played on Sundays at 12:30 by an informal group of players at the Chinese Swimming Club. About 15 to 20 players show up each week, mostly men in their late 30s to 50s. Don't expect high intensity water polo – this group is more focused on having a good time on a Sunday afternoon. The group welcomes expats, so grab your costume and hit the pool!

Windsurfing

Other options **Kitesurfing** p.276

Singapore has two monsoon seasons a year, which means good winds for windsurfers. The north-east monsoon season from November to March is generally the best time to windsurf, although the south-west monsoon season from June to September comes a close second. Despite the monsoons, the winds in Singapore are not overly strong, making it a good place for beginners to get started. The main windsurfing spots are the waters off East Coast Park and off Changi Beach Park, although the latter is more isolated. A short 45 minute ferry ride from the Tanah Merah Ferry Terminal, the Indonesian island of Bintan is a popular destination for windsurfers. With roaring winds during the north-east monsoon season, you'll go for a weekend and call in sick on Monday just to have an extra day on the water. Be sure to check out the Mana Mana Beach Club in Bintan (www.manamana.com), host of the Amslam windsurfing event held every January as part of the Asian Windsurfing Tour.
Windsurfing equipment is generally cheaper here than in Europe and North America, so if you're planning to buy it makes sense to do so here.
A handful of windsurfing competitions are held here with the main ones being the Singapore Open Windsurfing Championship, the Singapore National Windsurfing Championship, the People's Association Windsurfing Championship and the Pasta Fresca Windsurfing Championship. Races are usually held fairly far off-shore, so they are best observed from a boat. Check out the Boardsailing Association Singapore website (www.singaporewindsurfing) for more information.

1212 East Coast
Parkway
East Coast
Bedok
Map 12-B3

Pasta Fresca Sea Sports Centre

6449 1855 | *www.pastafrescaseasportscentre.com.sg*
The Pasta Fresca Sea Sports Centre hires out windsurfing equipment and has storage space for windsurfers with their own equipment. Windsurfing course are offered throughout the week. Importantly, it also provides reliable and prompt rescue services.

Various locations

People's Association Sea Sports Club

6340 5335 | *www.seasports.org.sg*
This club is operated by the People's Association, a government agency that encourages social cohesion. Each of its four locations offers a range of windsurfing

and sailing courses and equipment for rent. Although the club targets Singaporeans, expats are welcome and it's not expensive: adult membership costs $40 for one year or $80 for three years, while basic windsurfing courses cost $60 for two three-hour sessions.

Nr Woodlands Ind Est
Sembawang
🚇 *Sembawang*
Map 4-C1

SAF Yacht Club

6758 3032 | www.safyc.org.sg

The Singapore Armed Forces Yacht Club offers a wide range of options for aspiring windsurfers. A basic windsurfing course costs $60 for club members or $90 for non-members. Sailboards can be rented for $6 to $10 per hour. The club also has two clubhouses and a sea sports centre.

Wine Tasting

Block 43 Jalan
Merah Saga
Holland Village
🚇 *Buona Vista*
Map 13-C3

Bentfork Cooking School

6475 4961 | www.bentfork.sg

Affiliated with some of the top Italian restaurants in Singapore, Bentfork Cooking School offers several wine-related courses that will appeal to the wine fanatic in you. Wine appreciation, wine and cheese pairing, and wine and food pairing classes will leave you feeling confident as a sommelier. Contact Bentfork for the latest class schedule or gather your friends and arrange a class at a time convenient for you.

01-07 Riverside Point
Riverside
🚇 *Clarke Quay*
Map 17-C2

Wine Garage

6533 3188 | www.winegarage.com.sg

Located at Riverside Point next to its sister restaurant Brewerkz, Wine Garage boasts a massive collection of wines with over 300 labels available. The restaurant regularly showcases selected wines through its tastings and wine dinners. These events are a great opportunity to socialise and sample, and the fees are very reasonable (a two-hour tasting session costs $35). Seats are limited, so it's best to make a reservation.

Crazy Horse Cabaret

The Istana

Leisure Facilities

Between its health clubs, country clubs and various sports centres, Singapore has a fairly modern and comprehensive sports infrastructure. The government recognises the importance of a sporting lifestyle and is pursuing a number of projects to increase the quality and range of sporting facilities. The planned Singapore Sports Hub will provide state-of-the-art facilities near the centre of town, including a stadium, aquatic centre and a multi-purpose indoor arena. What you may find lacking is space for field sports such as football, frisbee and rugby – understandable, given Singapore's limited land area. While fields are available, they are often expensive to rent or of poor quality. Using a park is an option, but you'll be competing with kite flyers, club gatherings and pedestrians. International schools though generally have excellent facilities.

Health Clubs

There is a good selection of health clubs, most of which have modern, well-maintained equipment and a wide range of classes, to choose from here. Many of them are clustered around the Raffles Place area to cater to busy executives and young professionals wanting to fit in a workout during lunch or after work. Orchard Road also has its fair share of clubs and there are a couple of smaller gyms in business parks at either end of the island catering to employees of the industrial companies located there. Competition is fierce and clubs change their prices and packages every couple of weeks depending on what their competitors are offering so it's worth shopping around to find the right deal. Many hold recruitment drives on Orchard Road and near Raffles Place.

Clubs prefer you to take out a membership to use the facilities, if for no other reason than to avoid any liability if you have not taken the required gym orientation. However some do have day-use deals of around $25 to $35. Memberships range from $60 to $120 per month, depending on how much patience you have when dealing with the sales staff and whether you want access to one or all of the gym's branches. Most gyms charge a joining fee of $100 to $300, but if you make a bit of a fuss they might drop it. Mornings and weekdays are the quietest times, with 17:00-21:00 being the busiest period. See the Club Facilities Table on p.309.

Sports Centres

There are two networks of sports centres in Singapore. The Singapore Armed Forces Reservist Association (SAFRA) runs five centres, some of which have bowling alleys, archery ranges and climbing walls. While membership to SAFRA is not open to expats, access to some of the facilities is available. This access may be limited to certain hours and days, but rates are modest – such as the $3.15 entry fee for the swimming pool at SAFRA Mount Faber Club. For details of the centres see the table on the right, or for more information see www.safra.sg.

SAFRA Centres		
SAFRA Mount Faber Club	Telok Blangah	6278 6011
SAFRA Tampines Club	Tampines	6785 8800
SAFRA Toa Payoh Club	Toa Payoh	6259 4000
SAFRA Town Club	Clarke Quay	6236 7700
SAFRA Yishun Club	Yishun	6852 8200

Singapore's community centres, or CCs as they are commonly called, are run by the People's Association (www.pa.gov.sg). There are over 100 centres spread across the island and facilities vary from a simple auditorium to basketball and badminton courts and swimming pools. For details and locations of some of the most convenient of these, see the table on the next page. Although CC members are mostly locals, expats are

Catch all the exciting racing action @Hibiscus

Head to where the action is!

A day at the races guarantees fun, glamour and the excitement of winning. Located on Grandstand Level 3 of the Singapore Racecourse, @Hibiscus is the perfect place to entertain and view the races up close.

With its chic décor and full-service in-house bar, @Hibiscus caters to the trendy-set who are out to have a good time. For a whole day of fun and excitement, join us @Hibiscus!

Click www.turfclub.com.sg for more details today!

SINGAPORE
TURF CLUB

IT'S MORE EXCITING WITH HORSES !

- The Singapore Racecourse is open to those 18 years old and above.
- For more information, please call 6879 1000 or visit the Club's website: www.turfclub.com.sg.

welcome to join and fees are minimal – you may pay as little as $20 for three years.

Country Clubs

Most country clubs in Singapore have extensive sports facilities. Some clubs have everything from swimming pools and squash and tennis courts to bowling

Community Centres		
Bukit Merah CC	Bukit Merah	6474 1097
Buona Vista CC	Holland Village	6778 5163
Cairnhill CC	Newton	6737 9537
Kim Seng CC	Tiong Bahru	6272 3878
Marine Parade CC	Marine Parade	6346 7703
Siglap South CC	Siglap	6241 1925
Tanglin CC	Bukit Timah	6251 3922
West Coast CC	West Coast	6779 1098
Woodlands CC	Woodlands	6368 9938

alleys and gyms. Most golf clubs have additional facilities at their main club house, so you can get in a game of tennis or a few laps after your round of golf. See the Club Facilities table (p.308) for details.

All these clubs require you to take a full club membership (not just a gym membership) – which can be a significant investment. Pricing structures vary and membership options can be complex, so it's best to contact the clubs directly. Generally, clubs have a one-off joining fee for a lifetime membership but some offer an annual fee pricing plan for expats.

Lifetime memberships can set you back anywhere from $8,500 to $30,000, while annual membership fees range from $3,500 to $7,000. Before signing up, check whether membership is transferable should you move out of Singapore. Some clubs allow this for a hefty fee, while others do not allow it at all. In addition to the joining fee, there's a monthly membership fee of $100 to $200. Some clubs also impose a monthly minimum of around $100-$200 that you must spend at the club's food and beverage outlets.

Clubs do encourage prospective members to drop by for a tour of their facilities and you may be able to negotiate trial use of the facilities for a day before making a decision. Members can usually sign in guests for free, although guests (and members) will be charged for the usual things such as food and beverages.

DISCOVER A QUINTESSENTIALLY-BRITISH SLICE OF LIFE
IN THE HEART OF SINGAPORE.
CALL US ON 6467 4311 FOR A CLUB TOUR.

LOG ON TO www.britishclub.org.sg OR EMAIL membership@britishclub.org.sg

THE BRITISH CLUB, 73 BUKIT TINGGI ROAD, SINGAPORE 289761
CRICKET AND SOCCER FIELDS - 4 TENNIS COURTS - 4 SQUASH COURTS
2 FULL SIZE SNOOKER TABLES - AEROBICS STUDIO - FULLY EQUIPPED GYM - SWIMMING POOL
3 BARS, 1 PUB - 4 RESTAURANTS RANGING FROM FINE DINING TO REAL FISH AND CHIPS
OUTSIDE CATERING - FUNCTION ROOMS AND EVENTS

Club Facilities

Country Clubs	Location	Area	Map	Tel
American Club	10 Claymore Hill	Orchard	14-A4	6737 3411
British Club ▶ p.307	73 Bukit Tinggi Road	Bukit Timah	6-E4	6467 4311
Fort Canning Country Club	11 Canning Walk	Fort Canning	17-C1	6338 1212
Hollandse Club	22 Camden Park	Bukit Timah	13-E1	6464 5225
Laguna National Golf & Country Club	11 Laguna Golf Green	East Coast	12-C3	6542 6888
Orchid Country Club	1 Orchid Club Road	Khatib	4-D4	6755 9811
Raffles Marina	10 Tuas West Drive	Jurong	5-A4	6869 1800
Republic of Singapore Yacht Club	52 West Coast Ferry Road	West Coast	10-C3	6768 9288
Singapore Island Country Club (Island location)	180 Island Club Road	Lower Peirce Reservoir	6-F3	6459 2222
(Bukit location)	240 Sime Road	MacRitchie Reservoir	6-F4	6466 2244
Singapore Polo Club	80 Mount Pleasant Road	Bishan	14-B1	6854 3999
Singapore Recreation Club	B Connaught Drive	City Hall	17-C2	6430 7557
Singapore Swimming Club	45 Tanjong Rhu Road	Tanjong Rhu	18-B1	6342 3600
Tanglin Club	5 Stevens Road	Orchard	14-B3	6739 4128

Health Clubs				
Amore	Park Mall	Orchard	17-C1	6733 7333
	Parco Bugis Junction	Bugis	14-D4	6336 6822
	The Amara	Tanjong Pagar	17-C3	6223 3822
California Fitness	Orchard Building	Orchard	17-B1	6834 2100
	Republic Plaza II	Raffles Place	17-C2	6534 0900
	Bugis Junction	Bugis	14-D4	6337 2577
Fitness First	Paragon	Orchard	14-B4	6737 7889
Fitness First Plus	Capital Tower	Tanjong Pagar	17-C3	6536 5595
	OUB Centre	Raffles Place	17-C2	6534 4333
	One George Street	Chinatown	17-C2	6538 7666
Fitness-Plus	International Business Park	Jurong	10-B1	6567 4788
	Changi Business Park	Changi	12-C2	6588 3393
Planet Fitness	Far East Square	Chinatown	17-C3	6438 3833
	Great World City	River Valley	17-A1	6235 9622
	Suntec City	City Hall	17-D1	6820 9000
	Caltex House	Raffles Place	17-C2	6438 3000
Takashimaya Fitness Club	Ngee Ann City	Orchard	14-B4	6739 9314

Club Facilities

	Gym						Activity				Relaxation				
Treadmills	Exercise bikes	Step machines	Rowing machines	Free weights	Resistance machines	Tennis courts	Swimming pool	Squash courts	Aerobics/Dance Exercise	Massage	Sauna	Jacuzzi	Plunge pool	Steam room
✓	✓	✓	✓	✓	✓	4FL	✓	2	✓	✓	–	✓	–	✓
✓	✓	✓	✓	✓	✓	4FL	✓	4	✓	–	✓	✓	–	–
✓	✓	✓	✓	✓	✓	1FL	✓	–	✓	✓	✓	✓	–	✓
6	4	1	1	✓	✓	5FL	✓	2	✓	✓	–	✓	✓	✓
4	3	1	–	✓	✓	6FL	✓	–	✓	✓	–	–	✓	✓
✓	✓	–	–	✓	✓	3FL	✓	1	✓	✓	✓	✓	–	–
2	2	1	1	✓	✓	3FL	✓	–	✓	–	✓	✓	–	–
✓	–	✓	–	✓	✓	–	✓	–	✓	✓	✓	✓	–	–
✓	✓	–	✓	✓	✓	–	✓	–	✓	✓	✓	✓	–	✓
✓	✓	✓	✓	✓	✓	7FL	✓	4	✓	✓	✓	✓	–	✓
2	3	✓	1	✓	✓	2FL	✓	2	✓	✓	✓	✓	–	–
✓	✓	✓	✓	✓	✓	2FL	✓	–	–	–	✓	✓	✓	✓
✓	✓	✓	–	✓	✓	4FL	✓	4	✓	–	✓	✓	–	✓
✓	✓	✓	✓	✓	✓	8FL	✓	7	✓	–	–	–	–	✓
6	5	4	3	✓	✓	–	–	–	✓	✓	–	✓	–	✓
6	5	4	3	✓	✓	–	–	–	✓	✓	–	–	–	✓
6	5	4	3	✓	✓	–	–	–	✓	✓	✓	–	✓	✓
50	16	22	4	✓	87	–	–	–	✓	–	✓	–	–	✓
40	28	31	5	✓	78	–	–	–	✓	–	✓	–	–	✓
26	16	19	5	✓	73	–	–	–	✓	–	✓	–	–	✓
31	53	11	2	✓	45	–	–	–	✓	–	✓	–	–	✓
12	26	3	4	✓	25	–	✓	–	✓	–	–	–	✓	✓
10	31	4	2	✓	17	–	✓	–	✓	–	✓	–	–	✓
15	12	5	3	✓	19	–	✓	–	✓	–	✓	–	–	✓
5	4	5	–	✓	2	–	✓	–	✓	–	✓	✓	–	–
5	4	1	–	✓	2	–	✓	–	✓	–	✓	–	–	✓
50	40	15	15	✓	✓	–	–	–	✓	–	✓	–	–	✓
35	25	20	10	✓	✓	–	–	–	✓	–	✓	–	–	✓
50	40	25	15	✓	✓	–	–	–	✓	–	✓	–	–	✓
50	40	25	15	✓	✓	–	–	–	✓	–	✓	–	–	✓
✓	✓	✓	✓	✓	✓	–	✓	–	✓	✓	✓	✓	–	✓

Well-Being

Well-being is an important part of life in Singapore. From the local seniors practicing tai chi in the parks to the young professionals flocking to spas for massages and beauty treatments, everyone is interested in taking care of themselves and looking their best. There is a strong Asian influence in many of the services offered, with Indian, Japanese and Chinese cultures leaving their mark on massage, yoga, meditation and more. There has been a huge increase in the number of yoga studios and health spas in recent years and you'll find facilities ranging from the most modern and cutting-edge to the more traditional. Wherever your inner peace lies, you're sure to find it in Singapore.

Beauty Salons

Other options **Beauty Training** p.247, **Health Spas** p.311, **Perfumes & Cosmetics** p.349

Singapore being the modern and stylish city that it is, there's no shortage of beauty salons to make sure you're looking your best. Your hair, nails and skin can be rejuvenated, coloured, straightened, hydrated, waxed, peeled… you name it, you can find it. In short, you can pamper your body no end and spend the rest of your days trying out the treatments dreamed up by the leading minds of the beauty world. The latest technologies and styles don't take long to arrive in Singapore after they've been created elsewhere, so you won't feel like you're losing out by being away from home.

With literally hundreds of salons across Singapore, finding the right one for you can be a bit tricky. The best strategy is to ask friends for a recommendation or just to walk into the salon you see every day on your regular routes. A quick look around their facilities and read through their brochures should give you an idea of whether it's the place for you. At the very top end a couple of places worth considering are Passion (6733 5638) at Palais Renaissance and Le Salon (6738 8006) at Ngee Ann City, both on Orchard Road. Passion's David Gan is the current stylist to the stars of Singapore and is in high demand. For something a little less taxing on the wallet but still high quality service, try Backstage Hair Salon (6733 6696) at the Forum on Orchard Road, which offers hair styling, manicures, pedicures and more.

Hairdressers

Singapore abounds with hairdressers who cater to both men and women. A cut can cost anywhere from $10 for a quick trim at a barber shop to $500 and more for a haircut from a top hairdresser with celebrity clients. But an average salon haircut with a wash and head massage costs about $30 for men, $60 for women.

Two popular salons are Shunji Matsuo and Toni & Guy, both upscale establishments that offer excellent hairdressing that's simultaneously cutting edge and sophisticated; see the Hairdressers table below for contact details. Every suburban shopping mall will have at least one hairdresser and there are small boutique salons spread around the island, but you'll find

Hairdressers		
Backstage Hair Salon	Orchard	6733 6696
Fantastic Sam's	Orchard	6737 9925
Le Salon	Orchard	6738 8950
Mahogany Salon	Orchard	6737 0255
Passion Salon	Orchard	6733 5638
REDS Hairdressing	Various locations	6735 5711
Shunji Matsuo	Various locations	6238 1522
Toni & Guy	Various locations	6835 4556
Visage The Salon	Orchard	6733 0933

a lot of the good places are located around Orchard Road. For good children's haircuts, try Fantastic Sam's at Forum the Shopping Mall; for a small fee they'll even provide you with a certificate if it is your baby's first haircut.

Expand Your Horizons
There's no end to the number of activities you can immerse yourself in while in Singapore. Its diverse international population, combined with a growing appreciation for leisure activities and the arts, means you can spend your days learning a new language, dancing or painting technique and still only scratch the surface of what's on offer. The different country associations are always a good place to start searching for information on a hobby or course, see Social Groups on p.294. Numerous local publications also provide information on activities available in Singapore. IS Magazine is a weekly publication covering the social scene in Singapore and has a good coming events and classifieds section that includes workshops and classes. The Substation (see the entry under Art Classes on p.244) is also an important hub for the arts in Singapore and definitely worth visiting if you're looking to connect with the local arts scene.

Health Spas

Other options **Leisure Facilities** p.304, **Massage** p.313

Spas have become increasingly popular in Singapore in recent years, and there's no shortage of soothing ways to help you destress and walk out feeling rejuvenated and revitalised. You'll find a good mix of Asian-inspired spas and those with more of a European influence here but really, you can get massages, scrubs and treatments of almost every kind. Despite spas being perceived as mainly for women, many also offer treatments for men as well as couples' packages. Now that's quality time!

Various locations

Amrita Spa

6336 4477 | www.amritaspa.com

The Amrita Spa has branches at the Raffles Hotel, Raffles the Plaza and Swissotel Merchant Court (6239 1780). The Raffles Hotel spa is exclusively for hotel guests, but the other two take walk-in customers. The spas offer a full range of treatments and special therapies including treatments for couples, golfers, jet lagged travellers and men's Kur and Sundari Ayurvedic spa rituals. Manicure, pedicure and hair salon services are also on the menu. Tailored one to three-day packages are available upon request and you can even buy Amrita Spa products to continue your spa experience at home.

Paragon Shopping
Centre
Orchard
🚇 *Orchard*
Map 14-B4

Andana Spa

6836 9988 | www.andanaspa.com

Set on the top floor of the Paragon Shopping Centre, Andana – which is Sanskrit for paradise – has a full range of spa treatments to bring you relaxation and a renewed sense of mind and spirit. The deluxe spa package includes a 45 minute massage, unlimited food and beverages from their menu and the use of their pools, movie lounges and private rooms. To this you can add on any number of treatments, or just take them on an a la carte basis without the package. Options include massages, facial beauty treatments such as Guinot Hydradermie, Decleor detoxification and body contouring sessions, waxing and hand and foot care.

The Fullerton
Marina Bay
🚇 *Raffles Place*
Map 17-D2

The Asian Spa

6877 8183 | www.cosmoprof.com.sg

Set in the unique Fullerton Hotel, The Asian Spa sprawls over 20,000 square feet complete with rooftop pool. Signature services include hot stones therapy, aroma body massage and Javanese heritage treatments. Your skin will also feel clean and radiant after a body brushing using Dead Sea salts and black mud.

Various locations

Aspara Spa

6879 2688 | www.aspara.com.sg

The Aspara offers fragrant herbal baths, stress-releasing massages or a Tahitian body scrub to do wonders for your sense of wellbeing. And if you've been there, indulged in that, they also do a Javanese lulur which is a seaweed body wrap. Aspara has three branches, one at the Amara Hotel at Tanjong Pagar, another with a serene tropical garden at the Goodwood Hotel just off Orchard Road (6732 3933) and a recently opened Garden Spa at the Hollandse Club (6461 1146).
Hollandse Club members have access to the Aspara Garden Spa's private treatment rooms for a massage, steam bath or hydro massage bath or you can sit in the outdoor pavilion while you get your hands and feet pampered at the Garden Nail Bar.

311

Benjaphan Thai Herbal Spa

559 Bukit Timah Rd
Bukit Timah
🚇 *Newton*
Map 13-E2

6469 7622 | *www.benjaphan.com*

The Benjaphan Thai Herbal Spa in King's Arcade is great for an authentic Thai spa experience. The bright and cheerful facilities include lots of greenery and natural light, so you almost feel like you're getting your dose of indulgence in the great outdoors. Their signature treatments include Thai herbal steam therapy and a herbal compress treatment, but they have a wide selection of packages to choose from. Most of the products used in Benjaphan's treatments are also for sale.

Earth Sanctuary

86 Club St
Chinatown
🚇 *Chinatown*
Map 17-C2

6324 7933 | *www.earthsanctuary.com.sg*

The Earth Sanctuary Spa offers holistic therapies in a rustic and intimate shophouse on Club Street. The diverse menu includes elements of Australian Aboriginal treatments, as well as Hawaiian, Javanese and Balinese therapies. A full range of massages, wraps, scrubs, baths and skin services are available, along with spa-related workshops and classes and a line of Earth Sanctuary private label products.

Estheva Spa

Palais Renaissance
Orchard
🚇 *Orchard*
Map 14-A4

6733 9300 | *www.estheva.com*

Estheva is a women-only spa that takes its cue from the natural thermal spas in southern Italy. Anti-aging therapies such as CelluGie for the body and CelluVie for the face are meant to revitalise your skin, reduce cellulite and enhance your body's contours. If indulgence is your aim, have a look at their spa parties, spa nights or spa brides packages (the latter being a six month 36 session programme for the bride, her mother, the bridesmaid and the groom).

Eucalyptus Day Spa

43A Craig Rd
Tanjong Pagar
🚇 *Outram Park*
Map 17-b2

6324 1338 | *www.eucalyptus.com.sg*

This day spa, located in a 100 year old shophouse near Chinatown, offers therapies based on Eastern remedies (and one or two from the modern-day West). You can relax in the private treatment rooms or the open-air rooftop garden while you are pampered by Eucalyptus Day Spa's professionals. There are more than 10 different kinds of massages, plus Ayurvedic therapies, body scrubs and a treatment for everything from your head down to your feet, including CACI therapy which uses micro-currents to tone and firm targeted areas.

Mayuri Ayurvedic Spa

2 Serangoon Rd
Little India
🚇 *Little India*
Map 14-C4

6737 5657 | *www.mayurispa.com*

As its name would suggest, Mayuri Ayurvedic Spa in Tekka Mall in Little India uses traditional Ayurvedic treatments such as Shirodhara, Marma Massage and Udwarthana to relax tense muscles and ease stress. Specially formulated Ayurvedic products are used to correct imbalances and promote healing and a sense of well-being. Some treatments target specific areas of the body such as the lower back, shoulders or knees to ease pain associated with arthritis or strained ligaments and muscles.

Qi Mantra

83A Club St
Chinatown
🚇 *Chinatown*
Map 17-C2

6221 5691 | *www.qimantra.com*

For a modern take on Chinese acupressure, head to Qi Mantra in China Town. They've taken traditional treatments and ingredients and blended them into therapies that match the modern decor of their spa. Try the 'general health blast', 'herbal punch' or even the 'gingerific blast' to work out the knots in your back, shoulders and neck and get you ready for another week at the office.

302 Orchard Rd
Orchard
🚇 *Orchard*
Map 14-B4

Renewal Day Spa

6738 0988 | www.renewal.com.sg

The decor may be that of the rustic Provencal countryside, but the spa menu at Renewal Day Spa is a blend of East, West and the latest techniques and technologies. This tranquil retreat in Tong Building, just off bustling Orchard Road, is a great place to unwind. Hydrotherapy, body wraps and scrubs and range of massages will have you coming back to try the all the items on the menu.

Various locations

The Retreat

6738 0080 | www.theretreat.com.sg

The Retreat specialises in Thalasso treatments, which involve the use of nutrient rich sea water, mud, algae and sand to stimulate the body. It offers a full range of therapies including exfoliation, massage, facials, waxing and nail work. You can opt for the ground level treatment suites with lush garden surroundings, or go up to the suites on the eighth and ninth floors for spectacular sea views and rooftop showers. There are three branches of The Retreat: at Grand Hyatt (6416 7156), Marriott Hotel (6831 4526) and its flagship spa at Changi Village Hotel (6738 0080).

2 Bukit Manis Rd
Sentosa
🚇 *HarbourFront*
Map 19-C2

Spa Botanica

6371 1318 | www.spabotanica.com

The award-winning Spa Botanica at The Sentosa Resort & Spa is designed to make you forget the stress of urban life in its beautiful setting on Sentosa. Pools, waterfalls and lush gardens help you to relax and get the most out of your treatments and guests are encouraged to take a few minutes to walk the labyrinth to clear their minds before their spa sessions. Methods used here focus on natural ingredients to cleanse and revitalise and signature treatments include the 'galaxy steam bath', 'tropical glow' and 'Singapore flower ritual'.

15 Cairnhill Rd
Orchard
🚇 *Somerset*
Map 14-A4

SPA Valley

6235 4341 | www.spavalley.com

SPA Valley uses a range of soothing European products in a modern and tranquil environment. Skin care, a spa body programme, hydrotherapy, weight loss, hair care and microdermabrasion are all on the menu. The weight loss programme uses Dr Dunner Elderberry Internal Cleansing and Slimming Therapy from Switzerland. SPA Valley also stocks Terme di Saturnia products from Italy.

Massage

Other options **Leisure Facilities** p.304, **Health Spas** p.311

Massage is a great way to combat the effects of a hectic work or travel schedule and it's not unusual for people in Singapore to go for a massage once or twice a week. Every health spa offers massage services (see the reviews for the individual Health Spas on p.311), but some are more focused on massage than others, and there are also a few massage-only establishments. The array of techniques and therapies is mind-boggling, but who's to stop you from trying them all until you find your favourite?

Orchard Hotel
Orchard
🚇 *Orchard*
Map 14-A4

Elements

6737 6466 | www.elements.com.sg

Elements offers a full range of spa and slimming services, but it's best known for its massages and has built a reputation as one of the better establishments in the city. Massage options include Swedish, Shiatsu, Indonesian, Tui Na and Thai. Owned by

313

Olympic swimmer Leslie Kwok, Elements' clientele includes many top athletes and Sports/Remedial massage is one of the more popular items on the massage menu.

Neem Tree Well-Being Sanctuary

58 Circular Rd
Riverside
🚇 *Clarke Quay*
Map 17-C2

6336 5101 | www.neemtreesanctuary.com

Located in the heart of the central business district, the Neem Tree Well-Being Sanctuary is ideally situated for an after-work massage to melt away the day's woes. There's plenty to choose from, including therapeutic sports massage, facelift massage therapy, shirobhyanga massage, abhyanga massage, padabhyanga massage and bastii massage. Other services include hatha yoga, lymph drainage therapy, relaxation sessions, ear candling and reiki. Prices vary for the various services and multi-session packages are available.

Spa Esprit

The Paragon
Orchard
🚇 *Orchard*
Map 14-B4

6836 0500 | www.spa-esprit.com

Spa Esprit is a quality high-end massage and spa outfit with some very experienced masseuses. There are two venues, one at Paragon Shopping Centre on Orchard Road, the other in Holland Village at 18A Lorong Mambong (6468 1292). Both offer a range of massages including a treatment that's half massage and half power stretch, so you'll leave feeling relaxed, supple and a few years younger.

Traditional Massage

5 Tank Rd
River Valley Road
🚇 *Dhoby Ghaut*
Map 17-B1

6737 0147

This is not one of the fancy spas that you'll find along Orchard Road. Rather, Traditional Massage is what it says: a place for a good, affordable massage. Tucked into an older building next to the Sri Donaayuthapani Temple and across from UE Square, it offers a range of quality massage options including deep tissue, Swedish and Thai oil massage. A prepaid package of sessions will lower the price even further, giving you hours of relaxing massage treatment. They have a second branch at 199 Upper Thomson Road (6735 4657).

Meditation

There are many forms of meditation in Singapore, many of which are of Indian and Buddhist origin. Classes in the Samatha and Vipassana methods are widely available but there are others thanks to a growing appreciation of holistic methods aimed at complementing and encouraging a healthy, well-balanced lifestyle.

Samarpan meditation is practised on a weekly basis at various locations around Singapore. All sessions are free of charge and open to anyone interested in learning more about Samarpan mediation which is meant to provide physical, mental, spiritual and even material benefits (by removing mental blockages to satisfaction and success). Sessions are held on Saturday evenings near Boat Quay (email kaursurin@yahoo.com), on Sunday mornings and Wednesday evenings in Toa Payoh (email orient24@singnet.com.sg) and on Monday and Thursday mornings near Balestier Road (email jessng@pacific.net.sg). Separate events and retreats are also held regularly.

Awareness Place (The Well-Being Centre)

Bras Basah Complex
Colonial District
🚇 *City Hall*
Map 17-D1

6336 5067 | www.awarenessplace.com

Awareness Place is a holistic wellbeing store that stocks everything you'll need to foster a peaceful body, mind and spirit. They have inspirational and spiritual books, CDs and products for meditation. Regular workshops, meditation sessions and talks are held at either Awareness Place or the Kong Meng San Phor Kark See Monastery at 88 Bright Hill Road (Map 7-A3).

Small but indispensable…

Perfectly proportioned to fit in your pocket, these marvellous mini guidebooks make sure you don't just get the holiday you paid for, but rather the one that you dreamed of.

Explorer Mini Visitors' Guides
Maximising your holiday, minimising your hand luggage

Vipassana International

9011 9432 | www.sg.dhamma.org

Vipassana is an ancient Indian meditation technique that strives for total liberation and full enlightenment. Ten-day courses are held on St John's Island, 6.5km south of Singapore, with each day's schedule running from the 04:00 wake-up bell to lights out at 21:00. The course is free – the organisation survives solely on the donations of past participants. For a detailed outline of what is involved and how to get there, log on to their website.

Vipassana Meditation Centre

251 Lavender St
Kallang
🚇 **Lavender**
Map 14-D3

6445 3984 | www.vmc128.8m.com

The Vipassana Meditation Centre was set up as a place for Buddhists and non-Buddhists alike to study and practice Buddha's teachings. Weekly activities include chanting, meditation and talks (in English and Burmese). A four-day meditation course for beginners is held once every quarter and there is an annual Metta retreat for those wanting to further their knowledge.

Visuddha Meditation Centre

107 Jalan Langgar
Bedok
Bedok
🚇 **Tanah Merah**
Map 12-B3

9010 1663 | www.visuddha-m-c.org

The Visuddha Meditation Centre is open daily from 07:00-21:00 and entry is free. The centre teaches Samatha and Vipassana meditation, with classes usually lasting 90 minutes with a one-hour interview and walking meditation break between sessions. The centre is currently fundraising for a new meditation hall, so check out the website for the latest update on classes before you go.

Pilates

Other options **Yoga** p.318

The Dance Connection & Pilates Studio

204 Bukit Timah Rd
Newton
🚇 **Newton**
Map 14-B3

6887 3473 | www.pilates-dance.com

The Dance Connection & Pilates Studio offers mat and reformer classes for individuals and groups. New students are required to take an introductory session before moving on to higher level classes. Sessions can be purchased in blocks of five or ten which can be used when your schedule allows within a set period. Fees range from $25 for a mat session to $90 for a private reformer session.

Ivana Daniell Studio

Camden Medical
Centre
Tanglin
🚇 **Orchard**
Map 13-F4

6736 2991 | www.ivanadaniell.com

This studio offers instruction in mat and reformer pilates as well as gyrotonic, all taught by an international team of qualified professionals. Individual, semi-private and group classes are available and the class size is capped at eight. Before you join a class though, you will need to have an assessment done which costs $130. Fees for classes range from $35-120 depending on whether you take individual or group classes and which package deal you select.

Oasis Holistic

Selegie House
Colonial District
🚇 **Little India**
Map 14-C4

6442 2881 | www.oasisholistic.com

Pilates courses at Oasis Holistic are meant to help you develop focus, control, precision and the use of your breathing to facilitate movement. Three different courses are available: pilates orientation (mat), pilates on the ball and pilates 101 (mat and apparatus). Course fees range from $96-160. A drop-in session costs $24.

Well-Being

Forum The
Shopping Mall
Orchard
🚇 Orchard
Map 14-A4

Shambhala ▶ p.245

6735 2163 | http://shambhala.como.bz

Shambhala's pilates classes are meant to be an exercise for both the body and mind. Group and individual mat classes are offered, as well as individual reformer classes. Beginner and general levels are catered to and instruction is also available in Japanese.

Liat Towers
Orchard
🚇 Orchard
Map 14-A4

Sky Pilates

6100 7597 | www.skypilates.com.sg

The range of classes here includes mat, reformer, tower pilates and gyrotonic expansion system. If you're looking to improve your golf swing you can try the golfers' class, which focuses on achieving optimal posture, shoulder mobility and torso rotation. Expectant mothers can attend pre-natal classes and pencil in a few post-natal sessions. Fees are $40-48 per class, depending on the package. Private sessions allow you to up the intensity of your workout, or just to accommodate your busy schedule.

Reiki

128B Telok Ayer St
Chinatown
🚇 Raffles Place
Map 17-C2

My Healing Hands

9831 3433 | www.myhealinghands.com.sg

If you're looking to expand your spiritual horizons, My Healing Hands is the place to do it. It's a holistic centre providing a wide range of therapies and treatments from Usui and Karuna Reiki to tarot card reading and astrology. Reiki attunement courses for both the Usui and Karuna techniques are also taught here.

121 Bedok
Reservoir Rd
Kaki Bukit
🚇 Eunos
Map 15-D1

Reiki Chariot

6748 4119 | www.geocities.com/reikichariot

Reiki Chariot offers classes and treatments. Reiki I and II are taught in an intimate group environment and introductory talks can be arranged for a club or corporate group. Treatments usually last for 60-90 minutes at Reiki Chariot or as a house call. They will even treat you at your office, event or at the hospital but wherever you choose to be treated, you will need to make an appointment first.

6 Marine Terrace
East Coast
🚇 Kembangan
Map 15-E4

Reiki Magic

6876 0624 | www.reikimagic.com

Reiki Magic aim to help you to relax and enjoy a healthier body and inner peace. They provide Reiki therapy customised to your needs, saying that one hour of treatment is the equivalent of three to four hours of deep sleep. Therapists Aleksandar and Marina will make house calls and bookings can be done via their online booking form. Courses are also available including advanced and Reiki master.

5 Boon Tat St
Chinatown
🚇 Raffles Place
Map 17-C2

Sanctum

6225 4381 | www.sanctumsg.com

Reiki is just one of the many therapies on offer at Sanctum, a holistic centre that offers just about every imaginable treatment for spiritual, physical and emotional well-being. Located in a comfortable shophouse in Chinatown, Sanctum has calming, casually appointed rooms for one-on-one sessions and an outdoor terrace that's great for evening sessions when it's a bit cooler.

Stress Management

Other options **Support Groups** p.149

39 Tras St
Tanjong Pagar
🚇 *Tanjong Pagar*
Map 17-C3

Breathing Space

6220 3867 | www.breathingspace.net

Breathing Space is a holistic sanctuary in the centre of town that offers a wide range of healing therapies aimed to help you deal with stress. They also do tailored personal and corporate programmes on stress management and life balance. You can arrange a corporate retreat through them and they have a spa on the Indonesian island of Batam, 40 minutes away by ferry.

Tai Chi

198B Holland Rd
Holland Village
🚇 *Buona Vista*
Map 13-C3

Hsin-I Tai Chi Institute

6276 2527 | www.hsin-i.com

Hsin-I's founder Master Tek believes in teaching both the physical movements of Tai Chi and the philosophy behind them. Through dedicated practice, he says, people can rid themselves of physical and mental stress. Classes are taught in a variety of styles including Tai Chi Yang, Wu Tu Nan's Tai Chi Sword and Ba Duan Jing Qigong. Workshops are also offered if you wish to delve deeper into a particular style. The main studio is in Holland Village, with classes also held at the Esplanade – Theatres on the Bay (p.188) and East Coast Park (p.214).

Various locations

Rennie Chong Tai Chi Training Centre

6258 8543 | www.rchongtaichi.com

Rennie Chong is one of Singapore's most experienced tai chi masters and has written a book and a number of articles on the subject. He teaches classes at various locations around Singapore including at California Fitness (see the Clubs Facilities table on p.309).

Yoga

Other options **Pilates** p.316

Raffles City
Shopping Centre
Colonial District
🚇 *City Hall*
Map 17-D1

Bikram Yoga City Hall

6339 6639 | www.bikramyoga.com.sg

Bikram Yoga City Hall is the only authorised Bikram yoga provider in Singapore. Classes follow the 26 asanas as set out by the style's founder Bikram Choudhury in a studio heated to 40°C. Come with an empty stomach, lots of water, an open mind – and be prepared to work up a sweat. The 90 minute long classes start as early as 06:30. Three, six and 12 month membership packages are available.

30 Bideford Rd
Orchard
🚇 *Somerset*
Map 14-B4

Gaia Yoga

6738 2028 | www.gaiayoga.com.sg

Gaia Yoga is located in bright and sunny studios just off Orchard Road and offers a comprehensive range of classes. Everything from Hatha and power yoga to Tibetan heart and Yin Vinyasa yoga are packed into the busy schedule here. Workshops and private lessons are also available, as are pilates and meditation classes. Overseas retreats are also organised occasionally – give them a call to find out more.

Stamford House
Colonial District
🚇 *City Hall*
Map 17-D1

Inner Yoga

6334 2188 | www.inneryoga.net

Inner Yoga runs classes at its cosy studio in historic Stamford House right near City Hall MRT station. Small groups means you receive personal attention and yoga styles taught include Ashtanga, power, Hatha and Yogilates. Drop-in fees are $28, and range of packages are available. Hugger Mugger yoga mats and Lorna Jane yoga apparel are sold at the studio.

Selegie House
Colonial District
🚇 *Little India*
Map 14-C4

Oasis Holistic
6442 2881 | www.oasisholistic.com
Oasis Holistic offers a wide range of classes including Iyengar, Svastha and prenatal yoga. Speciality classes include yoga for kids and living yoga – a course to help you to integrate yoga practices into your daily life. It's also possible to join their beach and garden sessions which are held outdoors before sunrise. Fees start at $18 per class in a block of 16.

Ngee Ann City
Tower A
Orchard
🚇 *Orchard*
Map 14-B4

Pure Yoga
6733 8863 | www.pure-yoga.com
Pure Yoga is part of a regional network that has studios in Hong Kong, Taipei and Kuala Lumpur. A wide variety of classes are taught including Hatha, Ashtanga, power and Pranayama and they cater to all levels, from complete novice to veteran practitioners. Workshops are also run on a regular basis by well-known yoga instructors to give students a chance to delve deeper into the subject. A range of membership packages are available, including one that gives you access to all the studios in the region – perfect for the busy regional executive.

Forum The
Shopping Mall
Orchard
🚇 *Orchard*
Map 14-A4

Shambhala ▶ p.245
6735 2163 | http://shambhala.como.bz
Shambhala offers a wide range of Hatha yoga classes for all levels, including Hatha-Vinyasa, Restorative, pre and postnatal and Yogakids. Integrated yoga therapy is a session designed to help those suffering from various ailments and is meant to complement medical treatment prescribed by a doctor. Five week courses are also available in Inversions, Intro to Yoga and Intro to Ashtanga.

Pacific Plaza
Orchard
🚇 *Orchard*
Map 14-A4

True Yoga
6733 9555 | www.trueyoga.com.sg
Between its two studios at Pacific Plaza on Scotts Road and Ocean Towers at Raffles Place (6536 3390), True Yoga offers over 350 classes per week in over 25 different types of yoga. Both studios have full facilities including a juice bar, lockers, showers and a store selling yoga accessories. Regular introductory promotions are available as well as a variety of class packages.

157A Telok Ayer St
Chinatown
🚇 *Raffles Place*
Map 17-C3

Yogaffinity
6223 8254 | www.yogaffinity.com
Yogaffinity teaches Bikram yoga (Hatha yoga in a heated room) so bring water to the class, although they sell bottles there too. The thinking behind Bikram yoga is that the heat allows for greater flexibility and promotes sweating – which in turns help you get rid of toxins. Most classes run for 90 minutes but they do a shorter session at 12:15 so you can squeeze a class into your lunch break. You can try a class out for free and thereafter drop-in classes cost $28 each. Package deals are also available.

Oops!
Did we miss anything out? If you have any thoughts, ideas or comments for us to include in the Activities section, drop us a line, and if your club or organisation isn't in here, let us know and we'll give you a shout in the next edition. Visit www.explorerpublishing.com and tell us whatever's on your mind.

319

I  beautiful music

Music now looks as beautiful as it sounds. The new W880i
Walkman® phone with up to 900 songs, it's just as
beautiful on the inside.

sonyericsson.com/walkman

Sony Ericsson

Shopping

Shopping

If retail therapy is your kind of sport, you're in the right place. Singaporeans love a good bargain, and the retail landscape has been engineered to pander to that. There's always one sale or another taking place – pre and post Christmas, pre Chinese New Year, annual sales, seasonal sales... But the major shopathon penned in every true shopper's diary is the Great Singapore Sale – the single most important annual shopping event. It takes place over two months, usually from May to July, during which virtually every department store, small retailer and even spas and car workshops slash their prices. The sale is so eagerly awaited by everyone on the island that on the first day of the sale, it's not uncommon for Singaporeans to take the day off work to be there long before the doors to their favourite store open, in eager anticipation of the bargains that lie within.

Retail Efficiency

If you've got a diverse shopping list that needs to be ticked off quickly, it's probably best to head straight to Orchard Road (p.376).

Orchard Road has the biggest concentration of malls. Here, from 11:00 to 21:30 every day (bar two days over Chinese New Year when most shops and restaurants shut), you can browse through racks of international couture labels and high street brands in glitzy malls like Ngee Ann City and Centrepoint. Seasoned shoppers then take a break at Starbucks for a skinny latte before continuing the quest for the latest plasma screen television or perhaps a diamond ring.

For those with a more adventurous shopping spirit, interesting finds may be found in areas like Holland Village, Chinatown, Little India and Arab Street where you can pick up knick knacks, spices and even cutting edge fashion. In the last two years, young designers and edgy clothing stores have set up shop here, livening up the retail landscape with interesting alternatives to mass market labels.

While big name international brand clothes tend to cost about 10% more in Singapore, there are enough local and regional brands of comparable quality and in the latest styles to satisfy your quest for fashion. Electronic goods here are among the cheapest in Asia and the latest models are generally released here at about the same time as in the rest of the world. Computers and cameras cost 20 to 30% less than they would in the UK – you just have to be prepared to shop around for the best price, and to bargain, of course.

As much of a shopping paradise as Singapore appears to be, there are items that are comparatively costly. One of these is groceries, especially meat (in particular beef, lamb and fresh water fish) and vegetables mostly because most of these are imported. Another is cars. In a bid to curb traffic on the roads, the government has put in a comprehensive public transport system and upped taxes on private vehicles, making owning a car here a luxury. Do note that a 5% goods and services tax (GST) covers almost all goods and services, except for the rental and sale of residential land and buildings in Singapore, and the provision of certain financial services. This charge is reflected on the price tag in big

What & Where to Buy – Quick Reference

Alcohol	325	Clothes	332	Home Furnishings & Acc	342	Party Accessories	349
Art	325	Computers	333	Jewellery & Watches	343	Perfumes & Cosmetics	349
Art & Craft Supplies	326	Costumes	334	Kids' Clothes	344	Pets	350
Baby Items	326	Electronics & Home App	334	Kids' Toys	344	Photographers & Artists	350
Beachwear	327	Eyewear	336	Lingerie	345	Second-Hand Items	350
Bicycles	327	Flowers	336	Luggage & Leather	345	Shoes	351
Books	328	Food	337	Maternity Items	346	Souvenirs	352
Camera Equipment	329	Gardens	339	Medicine	346	Sporting Goods	352
Car Parts & Accessories	330	Gifts	339	Mobile Telephones	347	Stationery	353
Cards & Gift Wrapping	330	Handbags	340	Music, DVDs & Videos	347	Tailoring	353
Carpets	331	Hardware & DIY	341	Musical Instruments	348	Textiles	354
Cars	331	Health Food	341	Outdoor Goods	348	Wedding Items	354

department and chain stores but at smaller stores you should check whether GST is included in the price during your bargaining process.

Online Shopping

Singaporeans generally don't have a habit of shopping online – perhaps because it's easy enough to nip down to the shops. However, there has been a hunger lately for foreign brands that aren't yet available from local retail outlets here. While many of the big online retailers like Amazon and Victoria's Secret deliver to Singapore, many US sites won't accept credit cards without US addresses. To counter this Singapore Post launched a VPost Service (www.vpost.com.sg) where you can shop at numerous eligible US merchant websites at the same time and have your chosen items consolidated and delivered to Singapore. The only snag is that this service is only available for sites that do in fact ship internationally. One of the most useful online shopping services is being able to order your groceries online. Fairprice and Cold Storage, two of the largest chain supermarkets, offer the service for a nominal fee. This is especially useful if you need to stock up on heavy staples like bottled water and canned goods. Fairprice only delivers dry goods but you can order meat and vegetables from Cold Storage. Check out www.fairprice.com.sg or www.coldstorage.com.sg. With Singapore being so close to some of Asia's most beautiful holiday resorts, a weekend spent lying on a beach somewhere is always an option. Flights and holidays are easier and often cheaper when booked online. Budget airlines like Tiger Airways (www.tigerairways.com), Jetstar Asia (www.jetstarasia.com) and Air Asia (www.airasia.com) are fast gaining popularity and you can also buy most tickets on the major airlines' websites. Your best bet for good holiday packages is probably to go to local travel agent, Chan Brother's site (www.chanbrothers.com.sg) where you can book online and then pop into their office to purchase and collect your ticket. Singapore's Yahoo auction site (http://sg.auctions.yahoo.com) and eBay (www.ebay.com.sg) are extremely useful for buying second-hand goods. The sites are crammed with household items, electronics, furniture and clothes for sale.

Beat the Queues

Online shopping is also a blessing when it comes to buying movie tickets. Catching the latest releases is a popular pastime in Singapore and unless you particularly relish standing in line for three hours before the show, it's far easier to check for seat availability and book online. Golden Village which has a comprehensive network of cineplexes here, has the most user-friendly site (www.gv.com.sg).

Refunds & Exchanges

While policies on refunds and exchanges vary from store to store, most do not do refunds. Exchanges and credit notes are more the order of the day. Also, most stores will not allow you to exchange goods unless the original tags are still attached, the products are in their original packaging and a receipt is produced. The window of opportunity to exchange goods ranges from three to 14 days, so do ask before paying.

Some of these rules may be bent but sales staff on the shop floor have no authority to make those judgment calls. If you're met with a blank look when explaining what's wrong with an item, ask for the floor or department manager. In larger stores you could go directly to the customer service desk to get queries and special requests attended to.

Consumer Rights

Over the years the Singapore Tourism Board has prosecuted and black-listed errant retailers. They even list errant retailers on their website! As a result shopping here has become a lot more pleasant.

As a consumer, there are several ways for you to report a problem with a retailer or to have a dispute mediated:

- **Consumer Association of Singapore** – if you have a dispute with a retailer over goods and services and you haven't been able to resolve the matter, visit the CASE office at 170 Ghim Moh Road #05-01Ulu Pandan Community Building (6463 1811) to register your complaint. You can also go online to www.case.org.sg/complaint.plx to file your grievance. However, you do need to become a member before you can file a complaint and the membership fee for an individual is $25 per year.

323

- **Singapore Tourism Board** – visitors who feel they've been short-changed (in terms of customer service or faulty goods) can contact the Singapore Tourism Board (1800 736 2000 – toll-free in Singapore). Or you can fax the board on 6734 9035, or email them at feedback@stb.com.sg.
- **e-Alternative Dispute Resolution** (or the E@DR Centre of the Subordinate courts) – specifically created for the parties in an e-commerce transaction to resolve their disputes on the internet, the E@DR Centre offers a free online dispute resolution service. Both parties to the dispute must have an email account and must consent to the matter being mediated by the Centre. For more information on what the centre offers, visit http://app.subcourts.gov.sg/e-adr/index.aspx.

Shipping

Singapore is a major port and many of the world's major shippers have their Asian headquarters here. Air and sea freight services are widely available; airfreight is faster but if you're shipping a sizeable amount – even the contents of your house – sea freight is generally more economical.

If you're moving large items, representatives of the shipping company will come to your residence, often with complimentary boxes, and give you a free quote. Prices can vary quite greatly, so it's really a good idea to get a few quotes before deciding on a company. Goods shipped to Singapore are subject to 5% GST charge unless the items are personal and 'used'. SingPost also offers air and sea mail services at competitive rates but this service works better for smaller items as you have to bring the boxes to the post office to get them weighed and fill in the necessary forms. International courier services like DHL, Federal Express, UPS and TNT are all present in Singapore.

How to Pay

You won't find it difficult to part with your money here. While cash is still the preferred mode of payment (and ATMs are everywhere), all the major stores accept credit cards too. While some of the smaller outlets won't accept credit cards, virtually every retailer accepts the popular NETS (Network for Electronic Transfers Singapore) card, a direct debit card linked to your bank account. You can use NETS to pay for just about everything – groceries, utility bills and even your income tax. When you're bargaining at smaller stores and intend to pay cash or by NETS, be sure to mention this to the sales staff to get a better price. Credit card companies charge the stores a surcharge for each credit card transaction and, more likely than not, this has been factored into the price you've been quoted for an item. Most shops, department stores, supermarkets and restaurants won't accept cheques.

Bargaining

While the big stores offer goods at fixed prices, the story is different once you venture out of the malls. Take a wander around the ethnic areas of Chinatown, Little India and Arab Street, suburbs like Holland Village and IT malls like Funan Centre and Sim Lim Square. Here, your willingness to indulge in a little haggling will help to get you a great deal. At these places, bargaining is a sport…in fact, it's almost a form of bonding. Just being friendly and conversational will, more often than not, score you a better deal. Language isn't a problem as 90% of the sellers speak English. But if you do have trouble understanding each other's accents, a calculator is always an effective communication tool. You'll punch in your offer, they'll shake their heads in despair and key in their counter offer. This exchange goes on until both parties are happy.

The rule of thumb is to start with an amount 30 to 40% lower than the stated price and then work your way up (or down) until both parties are satisfied. Be careful though: an agreement on price is akin to an agreement to purchase – if you're not serious about buying, it's best not to start the bargaining process.

Alcohol

Other options **On the Town** p.429, **Drinks** p.388

Seriously, Don't DUI
Drink driving is a serious offence here and is harshly punished.

Anyone over 21 can buy alcohol from bars, clubs, most outdoor food centres, supermarkets and convenience stores. As with cars and cigarettes though, the government imposes rather high taxes on alcohol so it's worthwhile stocking up when you come through the airport. Prices at the airport's duty free shop are 40 to 70% lower than at the supermarkets. But you can only bring in one litre of spirits, a bottle of wine and three cans (or one litre) of beer – and only if you've been out of the country for more than 48 hours. Arrivals from Malaysia aren't eligible to buy alcohol from duty free.

Wine appreciation has increased here and to cater to this fast-growing trend, there are several specialty wine stores. Even supermarkets like Carrefour now have wine sections. Australian and New Zealand wines are especially popular and South African, American and European wines are also all available.

Alcohol		
Bacchus	The Paragon	6734 4844
Booze Wine Shop	Various	See p.377
Carrefour	Various	See p.377
Cold Storage	Various	See p.378
Ponti Wine Cellars	Centrepoint Homes	6733 0369
Star Cellars	Colonial District	6334 2320
Tanglin Market Place	Tanglin Mall	6734 0105

As a guideline, a mediocre bottle of wine will cost you upwards of $25 and a bottle of Smirnoff Red vodka in the supermarket sells for $54 (the same bottle costs $21.20 at the airport).

Art

Other options **Art Classes** p.244, **Art & Craft Supplies** p.326, **Art Galleries** p.203

Hot Art
Some of the more prominent artists you might want to look out for are Iskandar Jalil, a well-known potter, Wee Shoo Chiang, a prominent oil painter and the late Chen Wen Hsi, a Chinese ink and oil painter. Chen Wen Hsi's paintings are especially sought-after and they've increased greatly in value over the years.

As Singapore has become more affluent, the interest in art has also grown. There are now about 200 visual arts companies and societies in Singapore including photographic societies, art galleries, art auctioneers and other arts-related business. Reports have put the number of exhibitions held here at about 600 per year. The good news is that prices are relatively reasonable here too, ranging from about $1,000 up. Many specialist galleries have popped up to represent local and regional artists. For example, Utterly Art – one of the more active galleries on the scene – has exhibited established local artists, popular young artists from the region and the photography of Ansel Adams and Robert Freeman. Then there's the Singapore Tyler Print Institute which made a splash when it opened in 2002. Established under the guidance of American master printer Ken Tyler and supported by Singapore's government bodies, STPI collaborates with outstanding artists from around the world to create limited edition prints and unique works on paper.

For original Asian pop art, check out Ketna Patel's multimedia creations. The effervescent Kenyan-born Indian was raised in England and now resides in Singapore. She exhibits her work and that of fellow artists in her own gallery in Singapore's Bohemian neighbourhood of Holland Village. You can find out more on www.ketnapatel.com. Ketna prefers appointments to walk-ins, so please call before you head on over.

The MITA Building opposite Clarke Quay near Chinatown must have the highest concentration of art galleries in Singapore. The

Art		
Gajah Gallery	MITA Building	6737 4022
Instinc	23 Emerald Hill	6735 9867
Ketna Patel	Holland Village	6479 3736
Opera Gallery	Ngee Ann City	6735 2618
Red Sea Gallery	River Valley Road	6732 6711
Singapore Tyler Print Institute	41 Robertson Quay	6336 3663
Soo Bin Art Gallery	MITA Building	6837 2777
Utterly Art	South Bridge Road	6226 2605

old national armoury has been converted into a bit of an art hub and is occupied by some good galleries specialising in Asian art. The Soo Bin Art Gallery and the Gajah Gallery in particular are well established.

If you fancy yourself as a bit of an artist, some galleries conduct weekend classes or short five to six-week courses. For more details, see Art Classes in the Activities chapter on p.244, or check out Red Sea Gallery's website (www.redseagallery.com) for what they offer.

Art & Craft Supplies

Other options **Art** p.325, **Art Classes** p.244, **Art Galleries** p.203

Shops here carry a wide range of art and craft supplies and the range of material available is wide enough to cater to serial hobbyists and serious artists alike.

The majority of art and craft supply shops are concentrated in Bras Basah complex, an old grey (rather drab, considering its tenants) 1960s building opposite the Raffles Hotel. Everyone gets their supplies here – from student artists to hobbyists to mothers looking for goodies for children's birthday parties.

Art & Craft Supplies		
Art Friend	Various	See p.377
Creative Hands	Ngee Ann City	6738 1689
Sagacity Arts and Crafts	Bras Basah Complex	6336 6538
Spotlight	Plaza Singapura	6733 9808
Straits Commercial Art	Colonial District	6338 1710

The fourth floor of Ngee Ann City on Orchard Road has become a bit of a mini hub too. You'll find three art supplies shops here and you should enquire about their workshops for adults and children if you're looking for a outlet for all that creative energy.

Baby Items

The birth rate has dropped in Singapore but you'd never think it from the number of shops that cater to the baby market. Walk into any shopping mall and you'll find at least two baby shops. There's even a mall that focuses on babies and children – Forum The Shopping Mall (p.365) at the start of Orchard Road houses the city's largest Toys R Us store as well as dozens of baby fashion, toys, books, furniture and gadget outlets. Toys R Us has a baby section where you can stock up on nursery basics like baby prams and changing tables.

Baby Items		
IKEA	Queenstown	6474 0122
Kiddy Palace	Various	See p.380
Mothercare	Various	See p.380
Mothers Work	Various	See p.380
OshKosh B'Gosh	Various	See p.381
Robinson's	Various	See p.382
Toys 'R' Us	Various	See p.383

Kiddy Palace, which you'll find in most suburban malls, is the biggest chain store to specialise in baby and children's items. Here, you can get your hands on an extensive range of baby carriages including the ever-popular McLaren car seats, teethers, rattles, diaper bags, breast pumps, clothing and toys.

The department store that probably has the most extensive and affordable range of baby items is Robinson's at Centrepoint on Orchard Road. The UK's Mothercare chain is also here, with six outlets around the island. Before heading in, you can also view their products on www.mothercare.com.sg.

IKEA is a good place to pick up basic children's furniture and toys. Prices here are comparable to, and perhaps even slightly cheaper, than in the UK. You can even leave your children in the playground where they can swim in a room full of plastic balls with babysitters to keep an eye on them while you whiz around the store picking up your essentials.

If you prefer shopping from the comfort of your favourite armchair there's www.babysayang.com which should have just about everything you need. Local e-store www.parenthings.com means organic baby and nursing products are just a mouse click away. You can make appointments to view their products as well.

Beachwear

Other options **Clothes** p.332, **Sporting Goods** p.352

With the world's best beaches on its doorstep and year-round sunshine, it's a good thing that beachwear is readily available here. But with hot weather all year long it's difficult to score a really good deal on swimwear. Still, Tannlines (www.tannlines.com) usually has an annual sale just after Christmas and they've been known to slash their prices by as much as 50%. Most of the good quality swimwear you'll find here comes from Australia and Tannlines carries well-known Ozzie brands like Aztec Rose, Wahine and Moontide.

Ocean Paradise has a good selection of inflatable vests and swimming costumes for children and they have two outlets, one at Tanglin Mall and the other at The Paragon. Homegrown surfwear shop 37 Degrees makes really cute sundresses, tops and bottoms for girls (with a small selection of boardshorts for boys). Catering to the teen market, their sizes are cut a little smaller than European brands.

Flash N Splash owns the franchise to most of the surf brands in Singapore. You can pick up surf and skatewear from brands like Oakley, Quiksilver, Volcom, Ripcurl Roxy, Surf Babe, Surfer Girl, Paul Frank, Stussy, Globe and Gallaz here and they also carry all the accessories from sunglasses, trainers and bags to necklaces and keychains.

If you're a keen surfer though and you want to buy a board, you're in for a disappointment – no one in Singapore sells them. Most surfers order their boards off the internet or pick them up on their travels to Australia and Bali. Another item that's hard to come by is a rash vest to protect yourself from the sun and little stinging creatures in the ocean – most stores have only a very limited supply for adults, so that's another thing you might want to buy on your travels.

Beachwear		
37 Degrees	Various	See p.377
Arena	Various	See p.377
Flash N Splash	Various	See p.379
Ocean Paradise	Various	See p.381
Quiksilver	Pacific Plaza	6735 5636
Ripcurl	Pacific Plaza	6734 3435
Roxy	Pacific Plaza	6734 0113
Seafolly	Suntec City Mall	6339 2632
Stussy	Pacific Plaza	6738 2270
Surfer Girl	Pacific Plaza	6884 9002
Tannlines	Various	See p.383

Bicycles

Lock It or Lose It

It's a little known fact, but bicycle theft is the most common crime here. And the strict penalties (up to two years in jail!) haven't deterred the bike bandits either. So if you own a fancy bike you do need to consider buying a strong lock for it and think about keeping it inside.

Cycling, together with rollerblading, is a popular weekend activity, and the East Coast Park has purpose-built biking and jogging tracks by the sea. Restaurants and bars along this beachfront make the area a popular place for recreational and serious cyclists to converge and show off their skills (and their cool gear). Bicycles and tandem bikes are available for rent by the hour or by the day.

If you're in the market to buy a bike, know that prices vary greatly. Carrefour has bikes for about $100 while serious cyclists can spend $10,000 or more on a top-end Cannondale or Trek. Bike shops here are generally run by cycle

Bicycles		
Bike Haus	Bukit Timah	6468 3908
Carrefour	Various	See p.377
Cycle Craft	Siglap	6345 3600
Cycle Worx	Seletar	6459 9166
Heap Hong	Little India	6293 1286
Hup Leong Company	Chinatown	6532 3700
Rodalink Cycle	Clementi	6873 2300
Seng Chu Hin Trading	Tampines	6260 9121
T3 Bicycle Gears	Siglap	6241 7050
Treknology 3	Various	See p.383
Two Wheel Action	Tanglin	6471 2775

327

enthusiasts and they can often give you good recommendations. Most shops also do repairs. Kids' bikes and seats are available at Toys R Us and at most of the bike shops scattered around the island.

If you're looking for cycle adventures, a few bike shops also organise bike tours to nearby Malaysia and the Bintan and Batam islands in Indonesia. Check out Two Wheel Action who also organise bike hashes. Their website (www.twa.com.sg) lists all the necessary information. Helmets are not mandatory, but they're advisable – especially if you cycle on the road as car drivers in Singapore tend to be blissfully unaware of two-wheelers.

Books

Other options **Libraries** p.277

If you're an avid or eclectic reader, you've landed in the right place. Singapore could be one of the best places in the region to find English books from the US, UK and Australia. In the heart of Orchard Road, Borders is a literary fan's idea of heaven. (And even if you're not, you might find a sudden attack of enthusiasm coming on when you hear that a local women's magazine voted it one of the best places to pick up a girl or guy.) Borders also stocks stationery, mostly from UK's Paperchase, magazines and a selection of music CDs and DVDs. Attached to it is a cafe that serves decent lattes, cakes, pastas and pizzas. The cafe also has liquor license and an alfresco area, so it's a very pleasant place to spend an afternoon sipping on wine, reading your freshly-purchased book or just watching people go by. Kinokuniya is one of the largest chains of bookshops in south-east Asia, and of its three outlets in Singapore, the one in Ngee Ann City is huge. It has over 500,000 book titles in various languages, and being a Japanese chain, it has a large Japanese section including shelves of manga. It also houses a Coffee Bean & Tea Leaf and serves up a wide selection of

Books		
Basheer	Colonial District	6336 0810
Bookaburra	Orchard	6235 9232
Bookcraves	www.bookcraves.com	
Borders ▶ p.ix	Wheelock Place	6235 7146
EMF Bookstore	Holland Village Shopping Centre	6467 5335
Harris	Various	See p.379
Kinokuniya	Various	See p.380
Mama Joe Magazine Corner	Holland Village Shopping Centre	6466 2573
MPH	Various	See p.381
Page One	VivoCity	6272 0822
Popular Book Company	Various	See p.381
San Bookshop	Suntec City Mall	6334 2326
Sunny Bookshop	Far East Plaza	6733 1583
Thambi Magazine Store	Holland Village Shopping Centre	na
Times The Bookshop	Various	See p.383

international and local magazines. You'll also find Page One at VivoCity, a speciality bookshop that carries high quality coffee table books and even music scores.
Times The Bookshop and MPH are the two oldest homegrown chains of bookshops in Singapore. MPH was established in 1895 and Times in 1968. They stock mostly bestsellers, management and self-help books and popular magazines. Other chains that remain firm favourites with Singaporeans are Harris, who have two stores, and Popular, who have outlets all over the city-state as well as a great online shop. Bookaburra at Forum The Shopping Mall specialises in children's books from Australia. The store often holds book-reading sessions for kids and also stocks costumes, games, DVDs and CDs. Another speciality store is Basheer, which is something of an open secret in the advertising and graphic arts industries. Located in Bras Basah Complex and online at www.basheergraphic.com, they also ship worldwide.
Meanwhile, the internet has contributed to a revolutionary concept in reading – an online books rental service that was first invented in Singapore. Log on to www.bookcraves.com and you can rent books at nominal fees, have them delivered to you and collected again. Second-hand bookshops here often function as commercial libraries: they'll give you a date by which you need to return a book in

order to get at least 50% of your money back. The price of a second-hand book decreases each time is it loaned out.

The best magazine shop by far is Thambi Magazine store on the corner of Holland Road Avenue and Lorong Liput just at the mouth of Holland Village where you'll find magazines stacked in towering piles. There's also Mama Joe just across the street from Thambi which has a slightly smaller selection. Pornographic magazines are banned but rules regarding graphic content have been relaxed so you can get *Sports Illustrated*'s swimsuit issue and Singapore *FHM*. Even *Cosmopolitan* was recently allowed to sway into town in its stilettos...even if it does have to be shrink-wrapped and branded with a warning sticker declaring its graphic content.

Camera Equipment
Other options **Electronics & Home Appliances** p.334

Singapore is one of the best places in the world to buy cameras and peripheries. Taxes on electronics are low and if you're just passing through, you can get a rebate off the GST.

Keen shutterbugs should head straight to The Peninsula Plaza, Peninsula Shopping Centre and the Adelphi. They're across the road from one another and most shops in this area are trustworthy. They'll give you a fair price partly because of the keen competition, and partly because they're run by enthusiasts.

Cathay Photo Store (www.cathayphoto.com.sg) at Peninsula Plaza is one outlet in a chain that sells all major brands of cameras and accessories. Over 40 years old, it's a well-known hangout for professional and amateur photographers. Alan Photo Trading (www.alanphoto.com.sg) at Sim Lim Square is also well-established and offers the widest range of photographic supplies including popular brands and models of SLRs and digital cameras. John 3:16 at Funan Centre is another good shop for professional photography equipment.

If a digital pocket camera is what you want, simply head to the nearest electronic chain store. Harvey Norman, Best Denki and Courts consistently quote fair prices and you won't have to haggle for hours to get a good deal. They won't be the lowest price in town, but it will be pretty close. You could also price the object of your desire at an electronics chain store and then call or visit Alan Photo or Paris Silk in Holland Village to compare quotes.

If you're up for a good bargaining session, head down to Sim Lim Square, the electronics Mecca of Singapore. If you do walk away with a prize from here though, be sure to get receipts and the right warranty cards. Some stores offer Singapore-only warranties or no warranty at all. Also be aware that camera models can differ too – certain digital cameras from Sony, for example, are only released in Europe and Asia, so if you're buying a camera to use it in North America, it will be a challenge to get it fixed there.

Photo developing stores are everywhere in Singapore, and because of fierce competition, many offer 30 minute

Camera Equipment

Alan Photo Trading	Sim Lim Square	6336 0922
Best Denki	Various	See p.377
Camera Workshop	Peninsula Plaza	6336 1956
Cathay Photo	Peninsula Plaza	6337 4274
Courts	Various	See p.378
Harvey Norman	Various	See p.379
John 3:16	Funan The IT Mall	6337 2877
Paris Silk	Holland Village	6466 6002
RGB Colour	Colonial District	6334 6146

processing time and reasonable prices. The developing quality though can be mediocre so for high-quality, professional prints go where most of the professional photographers go and head for RGB (www.rgb-color.com).

For repairs, the most reputable shop in town is probably the Camera Workshop at Peninsula Shopping Centre.

Car Parts & Accessories

Your trusty mechanic will usually get you any car parts you need. If you need a tyre change, tyres range from $100 to $500 depending on make and quality. Autobacs, a US chain of stores, is probably the most well known car accessories shop and service centre in town. Here, you can get everything from general repairs and getting your wheels realigned to purchasing car care items, entertainment systems and even motor sports accessories.

Core Technologies offers GPS navigation systems for your vehicle. Forza and ST Powered specialise in motorsport accessories like tachometers, and turbochargers. Chin Hon near Little India claims to carry the largest range of genuine shock absorbers as well as engine bearings, brake pads and brake shoes. AsiaMac will custom make leather seats. On top of all this, you can pick up GPS systems and DVD players as well as bumper care products. For more everyday accessories like engine lubricants, steering wheel and seat covers, you can visit Carrefour (p.377) or Giant (p.379) who have a cheap and cheerful collection.

Car Parts & Accessories		
AsiaMac	Tampines	6781 2088
Autobacs	Bukit Batok	6100 2886
Chin Hon Motor & Trading	Little India	6296 3915
Core Technologies	Tiong Bahru	6295 8408
Forza Enterprise	Yishun	6755 3261
ST Powered	Hougang	6282 0330

Cards & Gift Wrapping
Other options **Art & Craft Supplies** p.326, **Books** p.328

You'll find writing pads, pens, markers, crayons and all your other stationery needs at supermarkets and stationery shops. Gift wrap, tags and English greeting cards are also widely available, although finding something that suits your taste may be slightly more challenging. While Hallmark and American Greetings are popular, if it's cards and gift wrap with a bit more attitude that you're after you could try looking in the home decor stores.

Prints is one of the nicest stationery shops in town. Masterminded by a Swedish designer, it stocks acid-free photo albums, journals, cards where you can mix and match envelopes, boxes and gift wrap so beautiful it should be framed.

If you want custom-designed cards, many of the digital printers in town can help you to design a card (many of them have in-house graphic designers) for a small fee and they'll then print the quantity you need. Turnaround time can be as fast as a day but prices and quality do differ so you might want to shop around. Middleroad Singcrafts (commonly known as MRS Signs) in Raffles Place MRT station does a decent job, and Jireh Digital (www.jireh.com.sg) whose swanky office is behind Boat Quay on Circular Road run a thriving business too.

The widest range of greeting cards in town is to be found in one of Kalm's six outlets in various malls. They also sell gift wrap, teddy bears, paper products,

Cards & Gift Wrapping		
Borders ▶ p.ix	Wheelock Place	6235 7146
Jireh Digital Design	Riverside	6557 2279
Kalm's	Various	See p.380
Middleroad Signcrafts	CBD	6533 1555
MPH	Various	See p.381
Prints	Various	See p.382
Times The Bookshop	Various	See p.383

photo frames, wedding guest books and generic gifts (see gifts on p.339). Bargain hunters can save money by buying gift wrap in bulk at the Concourse Building on Beach Road. On the second floor of this strangely dormant building is a cluster of five or six wholesalers of fake plants, gift wrap, party hats and favours, plastic boxes, bags and party snacks mostly from China. You'll find a sheet of gift wrap here for as little as 20 cents. And if you're particularly conscientious you can always pick up good deals on Christmas cards, ribbon and wrapping paper a day or two after Christmas Day when the price of seasonal paraphernalia is usually slashed by half.

Carpets

Other options **Bargaining** p.324, **Souvenirs** p.352

Going Once . . .
Carpet auctions are a fun way to check out the variety and value of carpets and are good for learning what's good and isn't. Prices at these auctions are generally 20% to 50% cheaper than market rate, although it is also a matter of luck.

A few years ago, Singapore was hit by carpet fever. Carpet shops were conducting free appreciation classes and there were carpet auctions every weekend. The craze has died down somewhat now but Singapore is still one of the best places in Asia to buy hand-woven carpets. Most of these come from Iran, followed closely by their competitors from China, India and Pakistan. Check out the local Straits Times for auction notices in the Classifieds section. Auctions generally take place in hotel meeting rooms. Carpet sellers tend to be very proud of their art, so they'll often allow you to take one or two of their treasured items home on spec. Hassan's

Carpets		
Air	Park Mall	6352 7307
Barang Barang	Various	See p.377
Eastern Carpets	Raffles City Shopping Centre	6338 8135
Hassan's Carpets	Tanglin Shopping Centre	6737 5626
IKEA	Queenstown	6474 0122
Neamati Carpets	Arab Street & Kampong Glam	6297 3432
X-tra Living	Park Mall	6336 0688
X-tra Resort	Park Mall	6339 4664

(www.hassanscarpets.com) for example, is one of the oldest and most reputable dealers in town and they allow exchanges. Don't forget to ask for a certificate of authenticity and a detailed invoice if you plan on insuring your purchase.
When choosing a carpet, look at the sharpness and clarity of the motifs, the number of knots per square inch (the more knots the better) and the colour. A new carpet made with synthetic dyes lacks the richness of colour that you'll find in an old carpet.
For every day use carpets, check out IKEA and local chain retailer Barang Barang. Air and X-tra Living at Park Mall have trendy carpets from about $900 for a 170x240cm cotton rug. Arab Street in the Muslim quarter of town also has a number of shops selling bamboo and rattan mats.

Cars

Other options **Buying a Vehicle** p.162

Cars aren't cheap here and cost between 25% and 100% more than they do in the UK or other parts of the world. Certificates of Entitlement (see p.165) can double the price of the car and prices for COEs fluctuate like the stock market so it's best to use an authorised dealer to bid on your behalf. Even if you catch a taxi every day, you're still likely to pay less than you would if you shelled out for a car. On the upside, you can finance almost the full price of the car and interest rates are very low.
If you want a second-hand car, you can give your requirements – make, size, budget – to a dealer who will then set off to find it for you. Keep in mind that the cost of the car includes the scrap value which is about 10 to 12% of the price you pay.

331

Second-hand dealers can be found in Sin Ming and Ubi. Automobile Megamart in Ubi for example, is a multi-storey car park filled with used car dealers. It's a good place to get an idea of how much to pay for what you want. Another good place to look is in the classifieds section of Saturday's *Straits Times*. Singaporeans have a habit of changing cars every two years, and you'll find a generous selection there. For a complete list of new and used car dealerships see p.162 (Buying a Vehicle)

Size Does Matter ◀
Local clothing
companies cater to the
generally smaller
Asian woman, so
remember to size up
when shopping at
these stores. 'Local'
pants tend to be about
three inches shorter
than the European
brands' models.

Clothes

Other options **Sporting Goods** p.352, **Tailoring** p.353, **Beachwear** p.327, **Kids Toys** p.344, **Shoes** p.351, **Lingerie** p.345

You'll find most of the world's fashion labels along Orchard Road, invariably clustered around Ngee Ann City, The Paragon and the Hilton Shopping Gallery. Thanks to Chanel, Gucci, Hugo Boss, Armani and Chloe you won't be left wanting here… However, do expect to pay higher prices for these brands than you would in their country of origin. A Diane Von Furstenberg wrap dress costs about $780 compared to $600 in the US. During the sales though, prices can be slashed by 50 to 70%, and some lucky shoppers have been known to snap up Gucci heels for $100. Club 21, the exclusive distributors of Vera Wang, Armani, Calvin Klein, Paul Smith, Donna Karan and more, hold a sale twice a year.

European high street labels are popular here – shops like Topshop, Warehouse, Miss Selfridge, Zara and Mango are always packed although their hemlines are always too long for shorter Asians. Because of the 'unfavourable' exchange rate between the English pound and the Singapore dollar, Topshop, Warehouse and Marks & Spencer have cut their prices so that their merchandise is about 20% cheaper than in the UK. Mango and Zara are still cheaper than in Europe by about 20 to 30%.

Homegrown designers are well-supported. GG5 makes good quality and reasonable classic clothes with a twist (like shirts for work at about $59), M)phosis, which you'll find in most major malls, is popular among young working adults who want clothes that take them from work to a night out and Individual Expression makes cool summer clothes with an Asian twist. For 'larger' sizes, Marks and Spencer, British India, Australian brand Country Road, Liz Claiborne, Marina Rinaldi and local label Joan Allen have clothing in sizes up to at least a UK 18. Another place to unearth large sizes as well as really good deals (if you know your fashion labels) is at the overruns and seconds shops. At Factory Outlet Store, Abercrombie & Fitch T-shirts sell for $19.90 and at the Export Shop, one can sometimes bag an Ed Hardy T-shirt for a 10th of the price at the official store.

Club Street and Haji Lane off Arab Street have evolved into trendy fashion areas. Here young designers and entrepreneurs have turned

Clothes		
Baylene	Colonial District	6336 9619
BCBG	Various	See p.377
Blackjack	Forum The Shopping Mall	6735 0975
British India	Various	See p.377
Calvin Klein	Orchard	6735 5790
Celine	Ngee Ann City	6736 0511
Chanel	Ngee Ann City	6733 5120
Country Road	Various	See p.378
Donna Karan	Orchard	6735 8891
Dorothy Perkins	Various	See p.378
Emporio Armani	Forum The Shopping Mall	6734 5766
Export Fashion	Various	See p.378
Factory Outlet Store	Various	See p.378
Gucci	Various	See p.379
The Guerilla Store	Colonial District	6224 3226
Hugo Boss	Ngee Ann City	6735 0233
Individual Expression	The Heeren	6737 5035
Inhabit	Palais Renaissance	6737 6993
Joan Allen	Scotts Shopping Centre	6836 3898
Karen Millen	Wisma Atria Shopping Centre	6333 6870
Liz Claiborne	Scotts Shopping Centre	6738 8830
Louis Vuitton	Various	See p.380
M)Phosis	Various	See p.380
Mango	Ngee Ann City	6736 2027
Marina Rinaldi	Forum The Shopping Mall	6732 9727
Marks & Spencer	Various	See p.380
Paul & Joe	Wisma Atria Shopping Centre	6737 8993
Paul Smith	Orchard	6737 8861
Prada	Various	See p.381
Skin	Various	See p.382
Topshop	Various	See p.383
Warehouse	Various	See p.383
Zara	Various	See p.383

traditional shophouses into hothouses of creative fashion. Venue on Club Street, for example, houses limited edition Puma shoes and clothing. Comme des Garçons' guerilla store is currently located in Haji Lane (but they move it to a new 'secret' location every few months!). For original local designs, check out the winner of Singapore's 'Young Fashion Designer of the Year Award 2005' Baylene at Stamford House (www.baylene.com). Her interpretations are fresh and prices are reasonable (there's nothing over $500).

If premium jeans are your thing, Inhabit at Palais Renaissance stocks Blue Cult, True Religion, Notify and Rock and Republic. Blackjack across the street at the Forum The Shopping Mall stocks Da-Nang, Ernest Sewn, Sass & Bide, and Maharishi. Skin at Marina Square has most of these brands plus Von Dutch. It's quite common to get formal gowns tailor-made here. Wedding shops all offer this service. But if you need tailormade everyday clothes, it may actually be cheaper to fly to Bangkok and get it all made in a day there. Alternatively you could look for home-based seamstresses, whose names are usually spread by word-of-mouth.

Computers

Other options **Electronics & Home Appliances** p.334

Singaporeans love their computers. In 2004, 74% of Singapore households owned at least one computer. While PCs form the bulk of the market here, there are Apple Mac shops in many major malls, such as EpiCentre, which has branches on Orchard Road and in Suntec City. Prices for electronics, including computers, generally beat those of the competition in the rest of the world and the latest models land in Singapore within days of their appearance in the launch markets.

Brands here include the ubiquitous Dell, IBM, Compaq, Toshiba, Sony, Fujitsu and the like, but lower-end local brands like Ranger are also common. Most departments stores – even hypermarkets like Carrefour (p.338) and Giant (p.338) – carry a range of computers, but for the true computer buff, there's only one place to shop and that's at Sim Lim Square. Here you've got over 400 shops in one building and whatever your requirements someone here has what you need. Other than Apple Macs, which are price-controlled globally, prices here are generally lower than in Europe and you can haggle your way to an even better deal.

If you're very clear on what you need, many of the shops in Sim Lim square can build a PC to your specifications. Be careful though as warranties for these machines may be limited to Singapore, the store, or parts only. Most other warranties will be international, but you should check to be sure.

Computers		
Best Denki	Various	See p.377
Carrefour	Various	See p.377
Challenger Superstore	Funan The IT Mall	6339 9008
Courts	Various	See p.378
EpiCentre ▶ p.335	Various	See p.378
Giant	Various	See p.379
Harvey Norman	Various	See p.379
iShop Pte Ltd	Cathay Cineleisure Orchard	6622 8988
mc2	Various	See p.380
PK Computer	Funan The IT Mall	6337 0653
South Asia Computer	Funan The IT Mall	6337 0871

333

All major brands have service centres here and you can shop for your Dell online (www.dell.com.sg).

To get the best deals without haggling, watch out for IT fairs advertised in *The Straits Times*. These occur roughly every quarter and exhibitors often offer rock bottom prices for the latest gadgets. Be prepared to squeeze your way through the crowd though – Singaporeans will queue for hours to get excellent deals before stocks run out.

Costumes

As Halloween and fancy dress parties have become more popular, costume shops have sprouted up all over the city to cater to both children and adults.

Those with clever fingers can head down to Arab Street where you'll find a street full of French lace, gold lame, feather boas, fake fur, sequins and all the gaudy things you need to make a memorable entrance at the next costume party.

For those in need of instant gratification, costume shops will alter their ready-made costumes to your size, and given enough time, will even make one for you to hire (if you ask they'll probably sell it to you). Toys R Us (p.383) stocks costumes for children, and the children in us, over Halloween.

Costumes		
Costume City	Tiong Bahru	6270 1722
Costumes & Mascots	Colonial District	6299 0882
Housez of Costumez	Colonial District	6334 3359
Jewel Costumes	Colonial District	6299 2252
Masquerade	Colonial District	6292 4889
No.1 Costume	Colonial District	6333 9440
Theatre De La Mode	Little India	6293 3581

Electronics & Home Appliances
Other options Camera Equipment p.329, Computers p.333

The easiest place to pick up your electronics and home appliances is at the electronics superstores. Best Denki, Harvey Norman and Courts all stock fridges,

Funan The IT Mall

washing machines, dryers, vacuum cleaners, TVs, stereos and other necessary household appliances. Prices are pretty much the same in all the stores other than when they run the occasional special offer or sale. Surprisingly, you can sometimes get a discount on big ticket items so it's always worth asking. Hypermarkets like Giant sell in-house and local brands like Akira and Enzer. Akira even makes plasma TVs that cost about 30% less than the well-known brands.

Designer or cult brands can be a little harder to find. Smeg fridges, for example, are hard to come by here but Miele has a concept showroom on Orchard Road. Dishwashers here, designer or otherwise, aren't hugely popular so most stores only stock one or two models (and it might be challenging finding dishwasher detergent at your local supermarket).

Stores will deliver and install large items free of charge. If you spend more than a certain amount most stores will deliver even smaller items, or they'll charge you a small delivery fee.

Visit the 1st Apple Premium Reseller store in Asia for the best Apple deals.

epiCentre
Orchard ╏ Suntec

é Best Price in the region

é Worldwide Warranty

é Latest & Widest Range of Products

é Free iPod & Mac Training

é iPod & Mac Trade-in

é AppleCare Service Centre

é GST Tax Refund

iPod	
Music	>
Photos	>
Extras	>
Settings	>
Shuffle Songs	

MENU

epiCentre @ **Orch rd** is the first and biggest Apple Premium Reseller®
in Asia. Our newly renovated, 5,000 square feet flagship store offers the latest and
widest range of iPods, Apple computers, software, games and accessories.
We offer customers a one-stop shop Digital Lifestyle shopping experience. Our friendly
and Apple trained sales professionals provide hands-on coaching on everything
Mac and more. To experience it all, visit our brand new 2nd Apple concept
store at **epi**Centre @ **Sunt c**.

iPod Shuffle   iPod nano   iPod   Mac mini

MacBook Pro   iMac   MacBook

MacPro + Cinema display   Premium Reseller   **15%** off* iPod & Mac accessories *Terms & conditions apply

Wheelock Flagship Store: 501 Orchard Road Wheelock Place #02-20/22 Singapore 238880 Tel: 6238 9378 Fax: 6238 6780
New Suntec City Store: 3 Temasek Boulevard Suntec City Mall #02-179 Singapore 038983 Tel: 6835 8168 Fax: 6337 8246
www.epicentreorchard.com

You could also check out supermarket notice boards for second-hand appliances and websites like Yahoo auctions (www.sg.auctions.yahoo.com) and eBay (www.ebay.com.sg) are also good. Of course, if you're in the mood for treasure hunting, there's always a garage sale being held somewhere on the weekend so keep an eye on the Classifieds in *The Straits Times*, particularly on Saturdays.

Electronics & Home Appliances		
Atlas Hi Fi	Plaza Singapura	6339 0966
Audio House	Various	See p.377
Best Denki	Various	See p.377
Courts	Various	See p.378
Giant	Various	See p.379
Harvey Norman	Various	See p.379
Miele	Orchard	6735 1191
Paris Silk	Holland Village	6466 6002

Most rental accommodation here comes equipped with large appliances, beds, and often even a TV. Voltage is 220, the same as in Europe.

Eyewear
Other options **Beachwear** p.327, **Sporting Goods** p.352

The prevalence of short-sighted people in Singapore is one of the highest in the world; 80% of 18 year old males in Singapore have myopia. So it stands to reason that opticians and eyewear shops do a thriving business here and prices are reasonable. You can expect to pay less than 50% of what you would for prescription glasses in the UK. Every shopping mall houses at least four eyewear shops so it's really easy to compare prices and designs.

Eyewear		
Alexis Eyewear	Ngee Ann City	6735 1697
Capitol Optical	Various	See p.377
The Eye Site	Parkway Parade	6348 6670
Federal Optik	Centrepoint	6733 5222
IC Optical	CBD	6532 4567
Nanyang Optical	Various	See p.381
OPSM Optical Centre	Lucky Plaza	6737 3874
Optic Point	Ngee Ann City	6737 8888
Sunglass Hut	Various	See p.382

Unlike elsewhere in the world, you don't have to have a prescription from an optometrist to buy a pair of glasses. All eyewear shops have in-house opticians who can fit glasses or contact lenses as part of the service, and you can collect your new glasses within three days. Some even promise one-hour collection times. You don't need a prescription when buying disposable contact lenses.

Sunglasses are also available in shops that sell prescription glasses and you can have them make your sunglasses prescription glasses too if you wish.

Brands like LA Eyeworks, Gucci, Fendi, Versace, Alain Mikli and Oliver Peoples are available at most of the bigger chains. If you're more into cheap and cheerful, it's fun checking out the accessories counters at major department stores. Takashimaya, for example has a section devoted to trendy shades under $50 near its costume jewellery section, and there's always the surf shops for Oakleys and other sports-branded eyewear, see Beachwear on p.327.

Flowers
Other options **Gardens** p.339

You'll have no problem finding a florist here – every shopping mall houses at least one. Finding one with your kind of taste though, is decidedly different. Many of the florists are stuck in the floral trends of the 1970s – bright pink plastic ribbons, red roses with baby's breath… That said, things are slowly changing. A greater variety of blooms is being flown in from more temperate countries and designs are improving.
Because of the airfreight costs, flowers can be rather expensive. And the hot weather means they don't last longer than a few days. Tropical flowers like orchids, birds of paradise and sunflowers though cost less than they would in Europe and last a while.

336

Supermarkets like Cold Storage and Carrefour carry an assortment of flowers, some of which are already arranged – very convenient if you need to take something to an impromptu dinner party.

The cost of having a bouquet delivered starts at about $80 and most florists offer Interflora services.

Flowers		
Ahhuay Ahhuay	Raffles City Shopping Centre	6356 7478
Blooming Affairs	Holland Village	6463 1911
Boenga	Telok Blangah	6423 1400
Far East Flora	Toa Payoh	6254 6662
Fluv	Chinatown	6536 8806
Goodwood Florist	Toa Payoh	6254 7722
Greeting Cuts	Arab Street & Kampong Glam	6296 6838
Purple Pots	City Link Shopping Mall	6238 8933

If you're looking for cut flowers, wholesale florists along Thomson Road do a booming business and places like Far East Flora and Goodwood Flora are good bets. They also sell a large variety of pot plants and offer a home delivery service (see also Gardens on p.339).

Food

Other options **Health Food** p.341

You'll never go hungry in Singapore – many food places are open 24 hours a day and supermarkets usually open as early as 08:00 and shut at 22:00 or later (some are also open 24 hours). While you'll find many brands you're familiar with here, don't expect to pay the kind of prices you were used to. Groceries cost more because virtually everything needs to be imported. A small wedge of Camembert will easily set you back about $8 and 100g of rocket (or arugula) costs about $4. And because a lot of vegetables are flown in, it's hard to get them with the freshness and crispness that you would in their countries of origin (usually Australia).

There are four major supermarket chains here. Cold Storage serves the more affluent neighbourhoods while Fairprice supermarkets carry mostly local produce.

Hypermarkets are very popular – at Carrefour, for example, expect to find people using their trolleys to make their way to their targeted aisle.

If you're looking for American brands, head down to Jason's at Orchard Towers. The first gourmet supermarket in Singapore, they stock Kraft macaroni and cheese, half and half milk (semi-skimmed) and Reese's Pieces. Tanglin Market Place probably has the largest selection of Waitrose products – even ice cream! Its wide aisles and huge inventory of hard-to-get goods makes this supermarket one of the best for imported goods. Prices are high, but if you're looking for fresh goat's milk or ricotta cheese for example, this is the place to go.

Japanese food aficionados will appreciate Meidi-Ya at Liang Court. Make sure your Japanese is up to scratch though as most items don't have English instructions. They also deliver, so check out www.meidi-ya.com.sg for details. Also worth a visit is Takashimaya for their supermarket and 'stalls' selling all kinds of Japanese snacks and food.

Favourite delis among aspiring chefs include Culina, The Swiss Butchery and the Brazilian Espirito Santo-Latin which carry a comprehensive selection of gourmet meats, sausages and condiments.

There are several organic food stores. Brown Rice Paradise stocks organic fruit and vegetables, a range of imported organic, and macrobiotic, fresh and dried foods, as well as a variety of drinks and breads (see Health and Organic Foods on p.341).

Vegetarians might have a hard time in Singapore. Although all supermarkets stock tofus of different size, shapes and colour, western veggie products are hard to come by, and those on wheat-free or gluten-free diets may find life challenging. Tanglin Mall is probably your best bet in this case, or the lentils and spices in Little India's dried goods shops.

Oops!

Have we missed out your favourite store in Singapore? If you have any additions, or thoughts, ideas or comments for us to include in the Shopping section, drop us a line and let us know, and we'll include it in the next edition. Visit www.explorer publishing.com and tell us whatever's on your mind.

Carrefour

The first hypermarket to set up shop in Singapore, this remains a favourite with locals and expats. Here, you can pick up everything from furniture to flour and prices are competitive. Just be prepared for long queues especially on weekends when people seem to consider a trip to Carrefour a family outing. For details of branches, see p.377.

Cold Storage

This supermarket stocks most of what you need. It has an organic foods section as well as an aisle or two each of Japanese and Australian produce. Its range of house brand goods extends from food to paper and plastic partyware. Cold Storage's online store is fairly extensive and a lifesaver if you need to stock up on essentials but don't have the muscle to lug it all home. See p.378 for locations of their branches, or check out www.coldstorage.com.sg.

Fairprice

This supermarket chain is located mostly in the suburbs and generally stocks local produce. This is probably the best place for staples as prices are slightly lower than at Cold Storage but the selection of international produce is considerably smaller. Their house brand consists of everything from dried goods to pots and pans. They also have an online store (www.fairprice.com.sg) but don't deliver perishables. For locations of their branches, see p.379.

Giant

Originating in Malaysia, Giant offers a wide range of local merchandise and a wet market environment. Fresh local fruits, vegetables and seafood are on offer here. Muslims will enjoy Giant's extensive selection of halal meats, frozen delicacies, canned foods, desserts and snacks. Like Carrefour, Giant also has a ready-cooked food section and you can buy whole barbecued chicken, pizza, fresh bread and cakes here. See p.379 for locations.

Marketplace

Marketplace supermarkets are all located in the downtown area and target expatriates. They specialise in imported produce from the US and UK, with a smaller selection from Japan.

Food		
Anchorpoint	Queenstown	6472 1193
Brown Rice Paradise	Tanglin Mall	6738 1121
Carrefour	Various	See p.377
Causeway Point	Woodlands	6894 1236
Centrepoint	176 Orchard Rd	6737 9000
Chancery Court	Newton	6253 6747
China Square	Chinatown	6438 5262
Cold Storage	Various	See p.378
Compass Point	Sengkang	6384 9303
Culina	Various	See p.378
Eastwood	Bedok	6244 4530
Espirito Santo-Latin Deli	Parkway Parade	6235 5937
Fairprice	Various	See p.379
Funan The IT Mall	Colonial District	6338 9983
Giant	Various	See p.379
Great World City	River Valley Road	6735 4730
Guthrie House	Bukit Timah	6463 3411
Harbourfront Centre	Telok Blangah	6274 9112
HDB Hub	Toa Payoh	6253 4757
Healthy Planet	Ngee Ann City	6834 2688
Holland Village Shopping Centre	Holland Village	6468 5566
Hougang	Hougang St 21	6383 0323
Jasons Market Place	Raffles City Shopping Centre	6336 2676
Jasons The Gourmet Grocer	Orchard	6235 4355
Jelita	Holland Village	6469 3877
Katong Mall	East Coast Road	6346 4736
King Albert Park	Bukit Timah	6462 1255
La Tanglin Boulangerie	Tanglin Mall	6235 1470
Meidi-Ya	Riverside	6339 1111
Ngee Ann City	Orchard	6733 0337
Northpoint	Yishun	6756 7100
Novena	Novena	6352 7223
Paragon Market Place	The Paragon	6738 2798
Parco Bugis Junction	Colonial District	6334 8831
Parkway Parade	80 Marine Parade Rd	6345 4665
Peace Centre	Colonial District	6337 9866
Rail Mall	Bukit Timah	6763 1639
Siglap	Siglap Road	6449 2791
Swiss Butchery	Bukit Timah	6468 7588
Tampines Community Complex	Tampines	6786 5600
Tanglin Market Place	Tanglin Mall	6734 0105
UE Square	River Valley Road	6733 3054
United Square	Novena	6251 5885
Valley Point	River Valley Road	6732 3147
Village Centre	Pasir Panjang	6777 1781

Expect to pay premium prices though. A tub of Waitrose ice cream costs just over $10. But they do have a large selection of organic and health food unavailable in most other supermarkets. The Marketplace group includes Jasons The Gourmet Grocer, Tanglin Market Place, Paragon Market Place and Jasons Market Place.

Gardens
Other options **Hardware & DIY** p.341, **Flowers** p.336

More than 80% of Singaporeans live in government subsidised apartments or HDBs so it's no surprise that most of the plants sold at nurseries are small and suited to indoor life. The larger nurseries though do offer landscaping services and stock larger plants, outdoor furniture, garden sheds and all the paraphernalia that goes inside them. Most of these outlets are clustered around Thomson Road, about 10 minutes from Orchard Road, and in Lim Chu Kang in the far west of the island.

Colourful flowering plants like bougainvilleas, hibiscus and birds of paradise thrive in the hot, humid climate here. Orchids need plenty of direct sunlight and care, but treated right they can do very well in your garden. For others whose thumbs are not as green, money plants are hard to kill and most species of palms and ferns also do well with very little effort. Nursery staff will be able to advise you on the best plants for your lifestyle.

Gardens		
Bedok Garden & Landscape	Bedok	6246 0511
Carrefour	Various	See p.377
Chenwa Landscape	Northwest Singapore	6565 8622
Far East Flora	Toa Payoh	6254 6662
Fukai Environmental	Sembawang	6754 5530
Goodwood Florist	Toa Payoh	6254 7722
IKEA	Queenstown	6474 0122
T&M Outdoor Furniture	Pasir Panjang Road	6273 8116
Tai Kwang Garden	Northwest Singapore	6793 7779

There are several landscapers who will design and install water features in your garden or balcony. Fukai Environment,for example, has a fairly large selection of fountains and most nurseries also stock a range. Alternatively, you could look out for fountains and water features on yahoo auctions (www.sg.auctions.yahoo.com). And don't forget that garage sales are another good source of plants and garden items as expats pack up to leave Singapore.

Most nurseries sell a selection of garden furniture and the furniture shops around Dempsey Road are good for antique or contemporary teak garden furniture. For easy-care outdoor furniture, check out Carrefour and IKEA. IKEA also sells potted plants and a small selection of gardening tools.

Gifts

Gift shopping can be either a chore or a treasure hunt, but it really is entirely up to you. You'll find plenty of gift ideas in Singapore, from run-of-the-mill to quirky and off-the-wall. Places that sell greeting cards usually also have generic gifts and little things too. Shops like Precious Thots and Kalms stock plush toys, picture frames, jewellery boxes and knick-knacks. The Loft at Centrepoint stocks an eclectic mix of home accessories, jewellery, gift wrap and cards as well as small items of furniture. You'll feel as though you're browsing through an antiques store.

The museum shops, which are run by the Banyan Tree (yes, of resort fame), are a great place to look for unusual gifts. At the Singapore History Museum, you'll find Singapore-centric toys and games from the 19th and 20th centuries – chateks, five-stones, pickup sticks and wooden tops. Over at the Asian Civilizations Museum you can pick through ethnic crafts from the region: hand woven carpets from Nepal, silver bowls from Cambodia, ikat weavings from Sarawak. The store also sells apparel, jewellery, spa products, stationery and evening bags. The museum shop in Armenian street is dedicated to the history and culture of the Straits Chinese community and you can buy stationery and porcelain

Gifts		
Kalm's	Various	See p.380
The Loft	Centrepoint	6738 7687
Museum Shops by Banyan Tree	Various	See p.381
Precious Thots	Various	See p.382
Raffles Hotel Gift Shop	Raffles Hotel	6412 1143
Royal Selangor	Various	See p.382
Tiffany & Co.	Various	See p.383

pieces that reflect the more conventional Chinese, Malay and colonial aesthetics here. The shop at the Art Museum is full of gifts inspired by the region's modern art scene. The shop also showcases local paintings, art books and stationery.

Personalising a gift is always a nice touch. At Tiffany % Co. you can have a pen or a piece of jewellery engraved and at Royal Selangor (www.royalselangor.com), the well-known pewter artists, they'll engrave gifts for you if you give them a bit of time. If it's Singapore-specific gifts you're after, the Raffles Hotel Gift Shop offers a wide range – from quality clothing, gifts and souvenirs to sundries and provisions bearing the famous name.

Asians don't usually open their gifts in front of the giver. Many, especially the older generation consider this to be rude, so if you want your friends to open their gifts immediately, ask them to do so.

Handbags

If you're a handbag fanatic, a walk through Ngee Ann City is guaranteed to tantalise your senses: Gucci, Louis Vuitton, Celine, Fendi and Loewe, all the latest styles, all under one roof – it's heaven. Takashimaya Department store in the same building also houses a large selection of bags for all budgets including Coach and Kate Spade. Anya Hindmarch, Calvin Klein and Jean Paul Gaultier are across the road at The Paragon and Prada is at Palais Renaissance further down Orchard Road.

In the last year or two, specialist shops have popped up carrying lines from emerging designers from the US and Europe. Clodette at Shaw Centre and Quintessentials at Mandarin Shopping Gallery are musts for the handbag fiend. You're not going to find cheap knock-offs on the streets of Singapore, but you will find designer-inspired versions in most shops in town. Cheaper versions are usually made of polyurethane (the label might say PU) though. High street stores like Topshop, Warehouse, Mango and Zara also carry handbags.

True handbag buffs will love the opportunity to trade in last season's Gucci must-have, or to pick up past seasons' favourites at stores like

Handbags		
Anya Hindmarch	The Paragon	6836 3881
Clodette	Shaw Centre, Orchard Rd	6887 5882
Coccinelle	Raffles City Shopping Centre	6339 6214
Designer's Exchange	Orchard Plaza	6734 5717
Fendi	Various	See p.379
Gucci	Various	See p.379
Guess Accessory Store	Raffles City Shopping Centre	6334 3121
Louis Vuitton	Various	See p.380
Oppt Shop	The Heeren	6733 9406
Potion	The Paragon	6734 9618
Prada	Various	See p.381
Quintessentials	Orchard	6738 4811
Secondo	Lucky Plaza	6733 2108
Takashimaya	Ngee Ann City	6738 1111
The Vintage Place	Pacific Plaza	6738 9280

Vintage Place, Secondo or Designer's Exchange. And if you're a lover of all things vintage you have to check out www.dustbunnyvintage.com, Oppt Shop and Potion.

Hardware & DIY
Other options **Outdoor Goods** p.348

If you're a DIY fanatic, Singapore may disappoint you. There are no big DIY shops because 'getting things done' is comparatively cheap and if you live in rented accommodation, the landlord usually takes care of small repairs around the house. So if you're an avid do-it-your-selfer, you may want to consider bringing your own tools with you.

The biggest chain of DIY shops is Home-Fix DIY. Here, you can pick up basic equipment like drills, nails and screws, bulbs and the like. You will also find local handyman stores in suburbs like Ang Mo Kio, Toa Payoh and Marine Parade.

If you're considering a change of scenery, Home-Fix DIY stores will custom mix paints on the spot and match colours to a pantone chart if you bring one in. (If you're renting, first check with the landlord whether you're allowed to repaint.) Timber is hard to find but IKEA has a small selection (see Home Furnishings & Accessories on p.342) and there are a few plywood wholesalers in town. But carpentry services are relatively reasonable and most carpenters can help you to design or replicate an item of furniture. Electricians and handymen are also affordable – a house call usually starts at $30.

Hardware & DIY		
Ah Decor Design	Chinatown	6222 1702
Allplus Traders and Services	Home service	6293 6096
Handy-man Centre	Orchard	6737 9592
Handyhouse	Central Singapore	6466 7800
Home-Fix DIY	Various	See p.379
Mr DIY	Bukit Timah Plaza	6467 1546
Nin Services	Home service	9844 1641
Visual ID Carpentry service	Home service	6346 0797

Health Food
Other options **Food** p.337

As Singaporeans get more health conscious, organic food stores and health shops have started sprouting up everywhere. Even Cold Storage has an organic dried food section now. But of all the mainstream supermarkets, Tanglin Marketplace has one of the largest selections of specialist foods including gluten-free and lactose-free products.

Among the better known organic food stores are: Brown Rice Paradise which is probably the oldest organic supermarket in town; Organic Paradise which imports many of its products from the US and its organic produce from Australia; Fire Flies Health Farms which has organic fruits, dry products and homegrown vegetables and Passion Organics where you can buy organic skincare products, have a meal and even attend a cooking class. There are organic farms out at Kranji where you can pick up the freshest vegetables and Bollywood Veggies out there has a restaurant on its premises. All pharmacies in Singapore stock generic vitamins and at GNC, a large supplements chain store, you'll be able to get all your potions – whether it's sports nutrition, diet and energy tonics or beauty supplements you're looking for. (We've listed a few of their 40 outlets in the Shopping Directory on p.377.) Most fitness centres also carry supplements.

Health Food		
Bee Natural	Novena	6251 0311
Bollywood Veggies	Northwest Singapore	6898 5001
Brown Rice Paradise	Tanglin Mall	6738 1121
Fire Flies Health Farm	Northwest Singapore	6793 7875
GNC	Various	See p.379
Green Circle Organic Farm	Northwest Singapore	6861 9286
Healthy Planet	Ngee Ann City	6834 2688
The Organic Paradise	Various	See p.381
Passion Organics	East Coast	6348 6692

341

Home Furnishings & Accessories

Other options **Hardware & DIY** p.341

While on one hand Philippe Starck and Mark Newson appear to be de rigeur in upscale furniture malls like Orchard Road's Park Mall, the contents of other furniture shops could lead you to the conclusion that Singaporeans have a penchant for shiny plastic home decor. Fortunately, there is a mid-way point with some very tasteful stores that stock well-designed and well-made furniture and accessories.

If your taste is of the ultra-modern genre, check out Space at Millenia Walk. They stock Philippe Starck ghost chairs, Flos Arco lamps and other design favourites. Mod Living in an impressive two-storey gallery has high-end European brands like Molteni & C, Dada, Moroso, Frighetto, Nube, Emmemobili, Artifort, Misuraemme, Bravo, Tecmo and Antonio Lupi. Air is a great homegrown store whose contemporary designs are more accessible to most budgets.

With its proximity to Bali and Thailand, it is no surprise that teakwood furniture is bountiful and affordable here. Connoisseurs of teak generally flock to Dempsey Road where many owner-run stores have set up shop. Gillman Village also houses a few stores like The Shophouse which specialises in Asian contemporary teak furniture.

Prices at IKEA are cheaper than in the US but it's extremely popular and gets really crowded on weekends. There's normally a 10 minute queue to find parking at the two-storey building and cashier lines can snake for as long as 20 metres during the annual sale. Other one-stop furniture places include Furniture Square (6569 6988) in the IMM Building in

Home Furnishing & Accessories

House	Central Singapore	6469 3533
Air	Park Mall	6352 7307
Art Trend Gallery	Central Singapore	6868 3551
Asiatique Collections	Tanglin	6471 1853
Barang Barang	Various	See p.377
Cellini	Various	See p.378
Christopher Noto	Central Singapore	6835 9162
Courts	Various	See p.378
Cream	Colonial District	6333 9115
Expat Furniture Rental	Tiong Bahru	6276 7606
The Furniture Company	Tiong Bahru	6235 2760
Galerie Cho Lon	Holland Village	6473 7922
Gallery 278	River Valley Road	6737 2322
Haier Living	Chinatown	6441 3345
Harvey Norman	Various	See p.379
IKEA	Queenstown	6474 0122
John Erdos Gallery	River Valley Road	6735 3307
The Life Shop	Raffles City Shopping Centre	6338 3552
Lifestorey	Great World City	6732 7362
The Living Tree Gallery	Geylang	6767 4013
Lorgan's the Retro Store	Pasir Panjang	6272 4988
Marquez Living	Pasir Panjang	6738 9589
Mod Living	Colonial District	6336 2286
Moss Living	Riverside	6348 3491
Origin Asia	Various	See p.381
Originals	Telok Blangah	6471 9918
Picket & Rail	Various	See p.381
Plank	Park Mall	6338 6280
The Ploh Group ▶ p.IBC	Various	See p.381
Room Interiors	Colonial District	6333 9239
The Shophouse	Telok Blangah	6334 0100
Skybaba	Orchard	6736 1879
Space Furniture	Colonial District	6415 0000
The Tomlinson Collection	Various	See p.383
Vintage Palace	Tanglin	6479 2181
Wicker 21	Tanglin	6474 0445
X-tra Living	Park Mall	6336 0688
X-tra Resort	Park Mall	6339 4664

The Life Shop

Jurong and Furniture Mall (6298 1600) on Beach Road, both of which house three or four floors of shops devoted to selling furniture and accessories. For those who are only here for a short term stay, it makes sense to lease furniture, to pick up a bargain at a garage sale or shop at Singapore's Yahoo auctions (http://sg.auctions.yahoo.com).

Jewellery, Watches & Gold

Singaporeans love their jewellery and the tradition of Chinese and Indian goldsmithing here means you'll get good value for your money. At first glance you may not find much to cater to your taste (as designs tend to be traditional and the gold used is often very yellow) but the market is responding to demand from younger women, who are buying jewellery for themselves on a regular basis. As a result there's also a huge selection of European-design jewellery for all budgets to be found. You can pick up a gold trinket for less than $100, or a Tiffany diamond for $100,000.

All malls in Singapore house at least one jewellery store. For really good deals on gold, mosey down to Chinatown, especially to the People's Park Complex or to Little India's Serangoon Road.

If it's commitment you've got on your mind, check out Larry Jewellery for engagement rings. They've created their own Lazare-cut diamonds and they probably have the most impressive range of Lazare diamonds in town. If you're lucky enough to chance upon a sale, take full advantage of it. And remember that if you're buying diamonds of substantial value you should ask for certification so that you can insure them.

You're in the right place to get a competitive price on your timepiece – Asians have a huge appetite for watches. One study found that Asians own an average of 14 watches each and the positive spin-off of this national obsession is that Singapore is probably one of the cheapest places to buy watches outside of Switzerland. Be sure to ask for the best price when you bargain though – you can generally get the price down by about 30%.

Jewellery, Watches & Gold		
Audemars Piget	Orchard	6836 4938
Bvlgari	Ngee Ann City	6735 6689
Cartier	Various	See p.378
Chew Cheong Jewellery & Gems	Orchard	6734 5097
Chomel	Various	See p.378
Chopard	Ngee Ann City	6733 8111
Cortina Watch	Various	See p.378
Emotus	Various	See p.378
Flower Diamond Boutique	Ngee Ann City	6734 1221
Fossil	Various	See p.379
Goldheart Jewelry	Orchard	6735 0689
The Hour Glass	Various	See p.379
Je Taime Jewellers	Ngee Ann City	6734 8211
Larry Jewellry	The Paragon	6732 3222
Lee Hwa Jewellery	Various	See p.380
Loang & Noi	The Paragon	6732 7218
Mondial Jewellers	Ngee Ann City	6734 3479
Poh Kong Chye Jewellry	Chinatown	6226 2266
Risis Boutique	Suntec City Mall	6338 8250
Rolex	Orchard	6830 5100
Sincere Watches	Various	See p.382
Sinma Jewellery	Lucky Plaza	6737 0352
Swatch	Various	See p.382
Tag Heuer	Ngee Ann City	6235 8477
Takashimaya	Ngee Ann City	6738 1111
Tiffany & Co.	Various	See p.383
Watches of Switzerland	Various	See p.383
Xcessories	Various	See p.383

343

For high-end watches, The Hour Glass, Cortina Watch and Sincere Watches have pretty much cornered the market. Collectively, they carry big brands like Baume et Mercier, Omega and Blancpain and their outlets are mostly around the Orchard area.
If you're looking for costume jewellery, start with the department stores. Takashimaya has devoted a huge section of their monstrous store to jewellery for all budgets.

Kids' Clothes
Other options **Clothes** p.332

For babies' clothes and goodies, Mothercare and Mothers Work are always good options. Chateau de Sable sells items that are designed in France but made in Asia and OshKosh b'Gosh, a global favourite, is also in Singapore. All major department stores also have sections for kids' clothes and Robinson's in Centrepoint in particular has a comprehensive and mid-priced range. Forum The Shopping Mall will probably meet all your kids' clothing needs and also houses designer-labels stores like Guess Baby and Kids, Benetton, DKNY and Kids 21, the children's version of Club 21. Toys R Us is good for costumes for birthday parties or for occasions (in the build-up to

Kids' Clothes		
Chateau de Sable	Various	See p.378
Chickeeduck	The Paragon	6735 2103
DKNY Kids	Forum The Shopping Mall	6736 4556
Fairy Go Round	Suntec	6348 8224
Giordano Junior	Various	See p.379
Guess Baby & Guess Kids	Forum The Shopping Mall	6734 3957
Hipofant	Great World City	6238 9138
Kiddy Palace	Various	See p.380
Kids 21	Forum The Shopping Mall	6737 2306
Life Baby	Raffles City Shopping Centre	6338 3552
Marks & Spencer	Various	See p.380
Mothercare	Various	See p.380
Mothers Work	Various	See p.380
OshKosh B'Gosh	Various	See p.381
Party City	Raffles City Shopping Centre	6336 2161
Zara Kids	Orchard	6733 0029
Ziegler Shoes	Tanglin Mall	6835 1226

Halloween the store has several aisles dedicated to kids' costumes). Party City at Raffles City also has a good selection and Fairy Go Round is a home business that will make a fairy costume for your little girl.

Kids' Toys
In addition to Toys R Us, most department stores stock toys. Robinson's and Takashimaya carry Fisher Price, Barbie Doll and other well-known names. But if you're after big items like the latest Little Tikes bicycle or Step 2 vanity, pop into Aprisin.

Kids' Toys		
Aprisin	Colonial District	6336 8311
AZ Gift & Trading	Colonial District	6291 3130
Gurgles	Tanglin Mall	6836 2450
Hill's Swingsets & Trampolines	Pasir Panjang	6733 9405
IKEA	Queenstown	6474 0122
Kiddy Palace	Various	See p.380
Mothercare	Various	See p.380
Mothers Work	Various	See p.380
Nurture Crafts	Forum The Shopping Mall	6734 3610
Robinson's	Various	See p.382
Toy Station	Bukit Timah	6468 3054
Toys R Us	Various	See p.383
Twinkle Thinkers	Forum The Shopping Mall	6733 3143

Prices are about 20 to 30% less here than at the department stores – and they even deliver.
The stores at Forum The Shopping Mall are where you'll find educational toys. Nurture Craft and Twinkle Thinkers, for example, have a good range of educational toys and books. Toy Station at Serene Centre is excellent for brands like Lego and Barbie at almost 25% less than what they sell for in mainstream stores. Toy Station also

sells playground equipment like swings and wooden forts from the UK. You can pick up very cheap toys at the Bras Bash complex, in areas like Marine Parade and Ang Mo Kio and at the Concourse. But be aware that they haven't been subjected to safety standards so they're probably not advisable for small children.

Lingerie

Other options **Clothes** p.332

All department stores carry a number of lingerie lines. But as Asians tend to be more slightly-built than western women, the better-endowed may have more luck at Marks & Spencer and boutiques like Blush which carries luxury label Princess Tam Tam and everyday brands like Berlei and Vanity Fair.

Lingerie		
The Argent	Wheelock Place	6737 8281
Bare Essentials	Orchard	6238 0809
Blush!	Various	See p.337
Chalone	Colonial District	6337 2647
JL Lingerie	Suntec City Mall	6339 8313
Lingerie Galleria	Colonial District	6339 4551
The Lingerie Shop	Palais Renaissance	6732 3091
Marks & Spencer	Various	See p.380
Tangs	Orchard	6737 5500
Women's Secret	Various	See p.383

When Tangs renovated in 2005, they expanded their lingerie section and named it 'The Dressing Room'. The fitting rooms have been the talk of the town ever since! Each one is different and they're all flatteringly lit. The piece de resistance is the room that actually has a round bed and mirrors all round – it makes buying lingerie a real treat! Tangs also carries a Morgan, Kookaï, Calvin Klein, Australian brand Bonds and cult brands like Elegantly Scant.

Lingerie Galleria has plenty of feminine froth from La Perla and Cocoon while The Lingerie Shop, which is probably the oldest high-end lingerie store here, specialises in Italian and Spanish labels. Women's Secret is a Spanish mid-price brand that stocks a cute range of everyday lingerie.

If it's seduction you have in mind, Tangs has an X-otic corner where you can pick up a hot patent leather outfit, fishnet stockings, wigs and various paraphernalia.

Luggage & Leather

It might seem a little odd, but you can buy luggage in some pharmacies. You won't necessarily find a huge range there but if you need a cabin bag in a jiffy you know that you can always pop down to a Watson's (see the Shopping Directory on p.377).

Other than that, Lucky Plaza on Orchard (6235 3294) is perhaps the best place to start your shopping for luggage and leathers. Little shops selling a huge variety of luggage bags abound. Be sure to bargain though as these shops are geared to cater to the hapless tourist who's shopped their way out of their airline weight limit. A good place to do a price comparison is next door at Tangs. While their selection is smaller, they carry stalwarts like Samsonite and Delsey that don't necessarily cost the earth. They also stock Eminent and various Taiwanese brands at even better prices.

Raffles City Shopping Centre

345

If you're a heavy duty traveller whose luggage needs to be able to take a beating, try Tumi at Ngee Ann City. Known as the Volvo of luggage, Tumi also has smaller concession stores at DFS Scotts Walk and at the Departure Hall of Changi Airport. Samsonite recently launched their Black Label store here. Their pieces – created by renowned product designer Marc Newson and inspired by revolutionary dancer Joaquin Cortes – are pricey but you'll definitely make an impression with them.

Robinson's also carries a fairly good range of luggage for most budgets. But if cheap and cheerful is what you're after, pop down to Carrefour (p.338) or Mustafa Centre which is open 24 hours a day and carries a mind-boggling array of goods including luggage and leather.

Luggage & Leather		
Braun Buffel	Suntec City Mall	6333 0209
Bree	Wisma Atria Shopping Centre	6836 6779
Carrefour	Various	See p.377
Guess Accessory Store	Raffles City Shopping Centre	6334 3121
Louis Vuitton	Various	See p.380
Robinson's	Various	See p.382
Samsonite	Various	See p.382
Tangs	Orchard	6737 5500
Tumi	Various	See p.383

Maternity Items

When Topshop launched their maternity section recently, trendy mums-to-be in Singapore heaved a collective sigh of relief. It's only been in the last couple of years that mums have been allowed to look somewhat stylish – before that you could only find tents and leggings in maternity wear departments.

But things are looking up and apart from Topshop there's also a Maternity Exchange. This offers mums-to-be the option of buying or renting from an extensive range that features popular and luxurious overseas brands like Liz Lange, Belly Basics, Japanese Weekend, Arabella B and Duet Designs. Maternity

Maternity Items		
Marton Belle	Centrepoint	6834 0811
Maternity Exchange	Orchard	6100 3924
Mothercare	Various	See p.380
Mothers En Vogue	Orchard	6738 0037
Mothers Work	Various	See p.380
The Natural Source	Various	See p.381
Robinson's	Various	See p.382
Topshop	Various	See p.383

Exchange has plenty of options for casual days, work and special occasions. For all your other maternity and nursing paraphernalia there's Mothers Work, Robinson's and Mothercare. If you're looking for skincare, The Natural Source has a range of all-natural products from Australia and Mothers Work stocks Mustela, made specially for pregnant mums.

Medicine

Other options **General Medical Care** p.137

In Singapore (and Malaysia) doctors not only write prescriptions, but also dispense them. So to replenish a prescription, you'll need to visit a physician. Pharmacies generally sell over-the-counter medications and common medications that can be dispensed by their in-house pharmacists who are available during office hours. Specialist Compounding Pharmacy Pte Ltd is the first pharmacy in Singapore to specialise in compounded medications. They focus on unique and personalised compounding products that aren't readily available in Singapore.

Eu Yan Sang in Chinatown is the largest Chinese medical store and one of Singapore's top ten

Medicine		
Guardian	Various	See p.379
NTUC Healthcare	Various	See p.381
Specialist Compounding Pharmacy	Orchard	6836 1323
Watson's	Various	See p.383

brands – a must-visit if you're interested in traditional Chinese medicine. Many of the medicine halls in Chinatown have in-house physicians who, just by looking at your tongue or feeling your pulse, are able to diagnose your maladies. Also, when in Chinatown, drop into the On Tai Ginseng Traditional Medical Hall where the helpful staff will advise you on what herbal medicine, dried fruit or nut to take for specific ailments.

Mobile Telephones
Other options **Mobile Phones** p.347

To get a good deal on a mobile phone, it's best to sign up with one of three mobile service providers – M1, Starhub or SingTel. However, this does mean that you'll be locked into at minimum of a one-year contract. These providers' outlets also sell phones without lines but they will cost a few hundred dollars more than if it comes as part of a contract.

M1, Starhub and SingTel also sell pre-paid cards which are especially convenient for visiting friends, your children or while you're waiting for your new employment pass (service providers need to see your EP as well as two bills in your name at your billing address in order to give you a contract). You can purchase top-up cards from 7-Elevens and other convenience stores around the island. Small phone shops in Chinatown and Little India may offer you a fairly decent deal on a mobile. Mustafa's caters for the export market while Harvey Norman and Best Denki have small selections of common brands like Nokia, Sony Ericsson and Samsung. Department stores with electronics sections like Tangs also stock phones.

Mobile Telephones		
Best Denki	Various	See p.377
Cherry Mobile	Various	See p.378
CnC	The Heeren	6887 4497
Harvey Norman	Various	See p.379
M1	Various	See p.380
Mustafa Centre	Little India	6295 5855
Singtel Hello!	Various	See p.382
Starhub	Various	See p.382
Tangs	Orchard	6737 5500

Bluetooth is available here and the service providers are promoting 3G heavily. Starhub has i-mode – a mobile internet service that allows subscribers to read email, download ringtones and video clips, access video telephony and monitor subscription content. SingTel's 3LoGy gives subscribers high speed internet access, video streaming and the ability to make video calls. And M1's 3G service allows subscribers to download videos, watch videos as well as video stream mobile drama, news and infotainment.

You can also get a reasonable deal on a new or second-hand phone on www.hardwarezone.com 's marketplace, www.ebay.com.sg, and http://sg.auctions.yahoo.com.

Music, DVDs & Videos
Compulsive collectors of music CDs and DVDs are going to love Singapore. CDs cost $18 or $25 for imports – and you can sometimes pick them up on sale at Gramaphone for as little as $8. A movie DVD costs about $50. Music tastes here are fairly mainstream with a preference for American top 40 music. But you'll be able to get a variety of worldwide music at HMV.

The three-storey HMV in The Heeren shopping mall is the biggest music and DVD shop in town. They claim to stock over 200,000 titles and they have plenty of listening posts, a full-time radio service and even sound-proof rooms for classical and jazz lovers. And if they don't have what you want, you can order it – as long as it passes the censorship laws – at no extra cost. Vinyl record lovers might have a harder time in Singapore. HMV stocks a selection but it's mostly geared to the club music DJs and wannabes.

347

With censorship laws, some albums are unavailable here, although the censors sometimes allow an album to get away with a warning sticker that the music 'may contain offensive lyrics'.

HMV also has a large DVD selection and it's the place to go to for old BBC comedies and last year's blockbusters. Singapore is very strict about piracy so you'll be hard-pressed to find pirated DVDs.

Music, DVDs & Videos		
Borders ▶ p.ix	Wheelock Place	6235 7146
Gramaphone	Various	See p.379
HMV	Various	See p.379
Sembawang Music Centre	Various	See p.382
Video Ezy	Various	See p.383

You can ask around for 'underground' sources if you're really desperate. Videos are near impossible to find here. If they stock them at all, most stores will have only a very small selection.

Musical Instruments

Other options **Music Lessons** p.282, **Music, DVDs & Videos** p.347

Piano For Hire
If you're here for a relatively short term and you don't care to ship your piano over, you can rent one from the Pianoman's Shop.

Just about every woman who grew up in Singapore will have taken piano or violin lessons so you'll be able to find almost everything you need here.

Renner Piano is a bit of an institution in Singapore. For at least the last 40 years, this is the place where most music students have bought their set pieces for their ABRSM (Associated Board of the Royal Schools of Music) exams. They now have a music school as well as an e-commerce site. Synwin sells a variety of classical instruments and manufacture their own string instruments. And if your heart is set on a Stratocaster you've got to go to Swee Lee. They've been around for about 60 years and their shop in the Bras Basah complex is a

Musical Instruments		
Cremona Music Shop	River Valley Road	6238 8440
The Pianoman's Shop	Bukit Timah	6463 0118
Renner Piano Company	Colonial District	6337 0216
Swee Lee Music Company	Various	See p.382
Synwin Enterprise	Geylang	6743 7865
Yamaha Music	Various	See p.383

trove of musical instruments. Their website (www.sweelee.sg) is fairly comprehensive and gives you an idea of the brands and kind of services they provide.

Outdoor Goods

Other options **Camping** p.250, **Sporting Goods** p.352, **Hardware & DIY** p.341

Being a bit of a concrete jungle, camping in Singapore is pretty much limited to parks such as East Coast Park (p.214) or West Coast Park (p.214), or one of Singapore's islands for a slightly wilder experience. This hasn't stopped several camping stores from doing a fairly brisk trade though, possibly thanks to the army boys stocking up for their jungle training, and adventure travellers heading off to Malaysia's many national parks. SNG Arms in Chinatown has reasonably priced camping gear. Agents for Paul London, they stock everything from Steiner binoculars to Barettas knives, tents, coolers and backpacks. The second floor of Golden Mile Food Centre on Beach Road has an entire floor devoted to army requirements – including outdoor goods.

Outdoor Goods		
Camper's Corner	Colonial District	6337 4743
Columbia	Various	See p.378
Hoe Seng Teck Kee	Colonial District	6292 4074
Outdoor Specialist	Colonial District	6334 1818
SNG Arms Camping Holdings	Chinatown	6223 3966
Wild Roses	Wheelock Place	6887 3938
Winning Marketing	Marina Square	6336 8628
X-Boundaries	Colonial District	6333 3136

Buying outdoor clothing for women can be difficult, but Wild Roses at Wheelock Place carry stuff for trekking and travelling that's hard-wearing, lightweight and quick-drying. If fishing is your bag, check out the numerous fishing shops along Beach Road near Arab

348

Street where you'll find all the poles and peripherals you require. Some of the imported equipment may cost a fair bit, especially if it's come in from the US.

Party Accessories

Other options **Parties at Home** p.439

Swish Do

Ruqxana of Cookery Magic (p.253) creates cakes to your specs, offers cookery classes and tours and even caters for small dinner parties. She'll come to your house to prepare the food and provide service staff to wait on your guests if you wish.

If you're throwing a swanky bash, you can find quality goods at Party City. If you're organising a party for 30 kids though, you might want to visit the wholesale party shops on the third floor of the Concourse. Most of the goodies here are made in China and it's a fabulous place to stock up on gift wrap, party hats, streamers and favours. More useful resources for children's party goods are: Bouncy Castles for giant inflatables; Magic Wand which not only sells magic tricks but also hires out a magician; and the costume shops near Arab Street for fancy-dress and costume parties. Art Friend and Spotlight (see Arts & Crafts Supplies on p.326) also have raw materials if you're feeling creative.

Party Accessories		
Angie The Choice	Novena Square	6258 9898
Bakerzin	Orchard	6733 7672
Bouncy Castles & A Whole Lot More	Clementi	6465 6006
Cookery Magic	Geylang	6348 9667
Magic Wand	Novena	6259 4405
Party City	Raffles City Shopping Centre	6336 2161
Yeo GM Trading	Chinatown	6224 0500

Angie The Choice makes generic birthday cakes which you can order online. Bakerzin makes the most heavenly cakes which you can order online and have delivered but unfortunately they don't make kids' cakes. Ruqxana from Cookery Magic creates swish cakes and chocolates for adult and children in any shape – from handbags and shoes to dolls and dinosaurs.

Perfumes & Cosmetics

Other options **Markets/Souks** p.374

Most of the big makeup brands are available in Singapore other than Prescriptives which pulled out a short while ago. For convenience, department stores are your best bet. MAC is carried at Tangs and Centrepoint, Bobbi Brown at Robinson's and Isetan, La Mer at Robinson's and Takashimaya and Stila at Tang's. And all the department stores feature the other big brands like Clinique, Elizabeth Arden and Lancome. These stores are also a sure bet for regular promotions which increase in frequency and variety over Mother's Day, Valentine's Day and Christmas.

Perfumes & Cosmetics		
Basic Beauty	The Heeren	6738 0126
The Body Shop	Various	See p.377
Cosmoprof	Various	See p.378
Dermalogica	Chinatown	6271 4733
DFS Galleria	Orchard	6735 4525
Escentials	Colonial District	6339 7727
I Nuovi Cosmetics	Various	See p.380
Isetan	Various	See p.380
L'Occitane	Various	See p.380
Make Up For Ever	Colonial District	6333 0678
The Make-up Store	Marina Square	6336 6828
Reijuva Skin Technology	Tanjong Pagar	6223 1200
Robinson's	Various	See p.382
Sa Sa	Various	See p.382
Tangs	310 Orchard Rd	6737 5500
True Colours	Ngee Ann City	6756 2973

The Make-Up Store, which was launched in Sweden in 1996, sources the best products from Europe and the US. As demand grew the shop become a centre for personal grooming. Walking into it is like stepping into a big box of crayons. There's also True Colours at Ngee Ann City which stocks 'boutique' brands like Laura Mercier, Nars and Philosophy and you'll find specialist skincare brands like Dermalogica and La Prairie at day spas. For darker skins, Cosmoprof is a firm

349

favourite and Reijuva also concocts custom blends. Sa Sa is a Hong Kong chain that carries budget brands and imports some cosmetics and fragrances.

Fragrances seldom go on sale but you can get them for slightly less at the duty free shops at the airport. For a one-of-a-kind perfume, drop in to Ecscentials at Raffles Hotel Arcade where experts will blend your personal fragrance.

Pets
Other options **Pets** p.129

Importing Your Best Friend
Many expats bring their pets with them. For information on importing pets into the country see p.66. All dogs need to be registered with the Agri-Food and Veterinary Authority of Singapore – check out p.66 and www.ava.gov.sg.

About 80% of the population lives in government subsidised Housing Board Development (HBD) flats and laws limit the size of the pets they can keep. As a result, most pet shops sell hamsters and gerbils, rabbits, birds, pedigree kittens and puppies of smaller dog breeds.

Pet Safari, the largest pet shop in Singapore effectively consists of 12 independent companies grouped together in a 10,000 square foot space. You'll find all manner of creatures and pet

Pets		
Joy Doggy	Bishan	6252 2162
Pet Lovers Centre	Various	See p.381
Pet Safari	Tampines	6788 1016
Pets Kampong	Various	See p.381
Society for Prevention of Cruelty to Animals	Hougang	6287 5355

accessories here and you're welcome to bring your best friend along while you're shopping around. The Society for Prevention of Cruelty to Animals (SPCA) is constantly looking for homes for abandoned animals, so do visit them to give a dog, cat or rabbit a much-needed loving environment.

Portrait Photographers & Artists

While there were numerous photo studios in the 10 or 12 years before digital photography, the trend to immortalise relatives in formally posed photographs is a dying one. Other than graduations and weddings, few Singaporeans make the trip down to photo studios to mark a wedding anniversary or birthday. The professional photographers who are still around today make house calls at a going rate of about $80 per hour. There are also some long-term expats who've made photography their business and use their own beautiful homes as a backdrop.

Portrait Photographers & Artists		
Conchita Photography	www.photo-aqui.com	6466 3453
Eilaroc	www.eilaroc.com	9477 8659
HaKaren Art Gallery	www.hakaren.com	6733 3382
Janine Stow Photography	www.janinestowphotography.com	9180 1871
Sealy Brandt Photography	www.sealybrandt.com	6474 4665
William's Photography	www.williamphotography.com	6256 8556

Finding a portrait artist is a bit more difficult. Caricature artists can be found along Orchard Road – usually on weekends – but if you're looking for something more formal you can commission an artist through the HaKaren Art Gallery at Tanglin Shopping Centre.

Second-Hand Items
Other options **Books** p.328, **Cars** p.331

Thanks to the high turnover of expatriates, there's always a market for second-hand goods here. If you're patient you'll always be able to get a good deal. The best places to look are on supermarket notice boards, on www.sg.yahoo.auctions.com, www.classifieds.singaporeexpats.com or for garage sales advertised in *The Straits Times'* classifieds section.

Other economical places to pick up second-hand clothes and accessories are at the Tanglin Mall Flea Market that takes place on the first and third Saturdays of the month and the Cross Roads garage sale (visit www.crossroads.com.sg to see when their next event will be held).

Second-Hand Items

Clarke Quay Flea Markets	Clarke Quay	na
Crossroads Giant Garage Sale	Newton	9644 4286
Dead-stock Made Good	Colonial District	6334 4073
Export Fashion	Various	See p.378
Factory Outlet Store	Various	See p.378
Granny's Day Out	Colonial District	6336 9774
Oppt Shop	The Heeren	6733 9406
Stuff in Your Attic	Far East Plaza	6732 3459
Tanglin Mall Flea Market	Tanglin Mall	na
www.dustbunnyvintage.com	Tiong Bahru	9691 9305

You can pick up high street brands like Abercrombie & Fitch and Gap at factory outlets like Export Fashion and FOS.

And if vintage is your thing, you've got a number of stores to investigate. Oppt Shop at the Heeren imports a lot of their goods from Australia. Granny's Day Out is another vintage shop with a loyal following. For real fundis, Dead-Stock is a two year old outlet that stocks limited edition merchandise from the US and Japan, along with new and second-hand shoes in good condition like the Nike Mexico SB (only released in the US) and Nike Futura SB (no longer in production).

Shoes

Other options **Sporting Goods** p.352, **Beachwear** p.327, **Clothes** p.332

Whatever your budget, you'll find a huge variety of women's shoes here – unless your feet are bigger than an Italian size 40 or smaller than a 34, that is. Men's shoes in size 44 or bigger are also a bit of a problem. If you fall into these categories then you should probably stock up on shoes before you arrive in Singapore.

There are many local mass market brands like Charles & Keith, DMK, Substance and Pretty Fit which carry reasonably priced trendy shoes. High street brands like Nine West and Aldo are also here but cost slightly more than they do in the US. While you'll have to go without new Manolo Blahniks, On Peddar carries Sergio Rossi, Jimmy Choo and Christian Laboutin.

Of the department stores, Takashimaya probably has the largest range of shoes – everything from Cole Haans, Hush Puppies and Bruno Maglis to local brands like JWest and Substance.

If you're looking specifically for trainers, go to the Queensway or Peninsular Shopping Centres. They each house two floors of stores selling trainers and sports gear. Puma, Nike, Adidas, Reebok…all the major sports brands are here and prices are about

Shoes

Aldo	Various	See p.377
Bata	Various	See p.377
Beetlebug	Various	See p.377
Birkenstock	Various	See p.377
Bruno Magli	The Paragon	6734 4543
Charles & Keith	Various	See p.378
Cole Haan	The Paragon	6736 0326
Hue	Various	See p.379
Hush Puppies	Various	See p.380
Interpax Shoes Enterprises	Holland Village Shopping Centre	6468 1558
Leapin Lizard	Tanjong Pagar	6222 2783
Limited Edt	Various	See p.380
Mirrco Repairs	Colonial District	6339 7316
Mr Minit	Various	See p.381
Nine West	Various	See p.381
On Pedder	Ngee Ann City	6835 1307
Pedder Red	Ngee Ann City	6735 5735
Pretty Fit	Various	See p.382
Shoekey Enterprise Shoe Repair	Lucky Plaza	6738 4646
The Shu Bar	Orchard	6736 2920
Substance	Wheelock Place	6836 0111
Tang + Co	Ngee Ann City	6732 7003
Tod's	The Paragon	6738 3323
Topshop	Various	See p.383
Ziegler Shoes	Tanglin Mall	6835 1226

30% cheaper than in the main stores along Orchard Road, but only if you bargain.

Not many places make custom-designed shoes although Interpax at Holland Village does and Leaping Lizard at International Plaza is a favourite among brides who want shoes in the exact same shade as their wedding gown.

Souvenirs
Other options **Carpets** p.331

There are no quintessential souvenirs from Singapore per se, unless you're looking for the standard 'Merlion' key chains and Singapore Airlines lookalike uniforms in which case head straight to Chinatown, Arab Street and Little India. Here you'll find Merlion caps, pens, lipstick holders, tiger balm and of course, T-shirts including those with the infamous 'Singapore is a fine city' across the front.

If you're looking for something more subtle, stop in at a Risis boutique or counter. Risis use a process that enables them to dip fresh orchids into 24 carat gold and turn them into brooches, necklaces and tie clips. They also carry fashion accessories like charm bracelets that are rhodium and silver plated.

Museum shops in the various museums in town are also good places to hunt for Singapore-inspired souvenirs like old Peranakan tiles that have been made into coasters and pretty watercolour paintings of the Singapore skyline. DFS Galleria also has the ubiquitous tiger balm and chopsticks nicely packaged as souvenirs.

Souvenirs		
Chinatown Heritage Centre	Pagoda Street	6325 2878
DFS Galleria	Orchard	6735 4525
Museum Shops by Banyan Tree	Various	See p.381
Risis Boutique	Suntec City Mall	6338 825

Sporting Goods
Other options **Outdoor Goods** p.348

Golfers will find most of the state-of-the-art equipment they need in this golf-crazy city with a golf shop in almost every mall. Anglers though will have to head to a cluster of shops around Arab Street for their fishing rods, reels, artificial bait and lines. If your game is rugby you'll find gear and accessories at the Canterbury store at the Heeren while soccer supremos will find two floors of shops selling their kind of stuff at Queensway Shopping Centre. This is also the place to have your tennis racquet restrung, your rollerblade wheels souped up and to buy hockey sticks, pucks and most other sports goods.

If your requirements are more general, you'll find Speedo and Arena swim gear including goggles,

Sporting Goods		
Adidas	Various	See p.377
Canterbury	The Heeren	6732 9489
Champion Sports	Colonial District	6446 6276
Golf House	Various	See p.379
Mizuno	The Paragon	6836 9080
Motion Sports	The Paragon	6735 9949
Royal Sporting House	Various	See p.382
Skater's World	Queenstown	6472 0460
Sports Link	Various	See p.382
World of Sports	Various	See p.383

swimcaps and floaties, gym gear and light weights for home use, as well as most of the popular brands of trainers and sports clothing, at the Royal Sporting House.

Stationery

If you're looking for photocopy paper or pens there are stationery shops and book stores that stock stationery everywhere. You'll find basic school and office stationery at supermarkets and bookshops like MPH, Times and Popular.

If it's serious office supplies you need, like plotting paper, arch files, printer toner and binder machines, shops like Mellon Commercial or Evergreen Stationers should fill your requirements. For fancy art papers and art paraphernalia, try the art and craft shops in Bras Basah (see Arts & Crafts Supplies on p.326).

Stationery		
Aesthetic Bay	Orchard	6339 6788
Elephant and Coral	Wheelock Place	6736 1322
Evergreen Stationers	Various	See p.378
Fook Hing Trading Company	Colonial District	6337 3045
The Hour Glass	Various	See p.379
Mellon Commercial	Tanjong Pagar	6222 0883
Mont Blanc	Various	See p.380
Popular Book Co.	Various	See p.381

Elephant and Coral specialise in writing instruments and have high-end brands like Aurora, Mont Blanc, McLaren and Omas. Fook Hing Trading Company is an open secret among pen lovers. You'll find good quality pens from $80 to about $500 here in brands like Caran d'Ache, Krone, Lamy and ST Dupont.

Tailoring

Other options **Clothes** p.332, **Textiles** p.354

Walk into Far East Plaza, Far East Shopping Centre or Lucky Plaza along Orchard Road and, if you look like a tourist, you'll be accosted by shop owners asking if you want a suit made in 24 hours. Most will make you a suit for under $200 or a shirt for $80 (after a little bargaining) and they're good if you are not too choosy or don't have much time. If you're looking for better quality (and don't mind paying more) be prepared to wait as tailors are in high demand. Do keep in mind that fabrics here are all imported so tailoring here is not quite the bargain it is in Bangkok or Hong Kong.

Tailoring		
Anson Tailors	CBD	6224 1572
CYC The Custom Shop	Colonial District	6336 3556
Frederick Li Bridal Studio	Tanjong Pagar Road	6323 4372
Heng Nam Nam	Park Mall	6227 8023
Kingsmen	Orchard	6734 8906
Mode-O-Day	Tanglin Shopping Centre	6235 1418
Snip n Mend	Orchard	6736 4500
Sunny Point Fashion	Orchard	6720 0881

Anson Tailors near Chinatown have been making suits for smartly-turned out clients (like CEOs who need to cut a dash or TV stars) since 1955 and they use excellent fabrics including Zegna wool. A suit will cost from $2,000 to $5,000 here.

CYC is a custom shirt shop that's been making shirts for former Prime Minister Lee Kuan Yew for decades. One of his shirts is even displayed proudly in their shop at the Raffles Hotel Arcade. Customers can choose from more than 1,000 fabrics, 60 collars and ten styles of cuffs. Shirts cost about $75 and take around 10 days to make.

Most women go to one of the speciality wedding shops to have their wedding gowns and fancy evening dresses made. The *Tatler* set, when not wearing Versace and Gucci, go to local designers Francis Cheong, Heng Nam Nam or Frederick Li who also make wedding dresses. Mode-O-Day is also popular with young socialites and apparently Bill and Hillary Clinton had clothes tailored by them when they stepped into town. If you need alterations done, pop into Far East Plaza. From the second floor all the way to the top floor, you'll find places ranging from full-fledged shops with two or three sewing machines or little holes in the wall no bigger than a bathroom cubicle. Taking up a hem can cost you as little as $3, taking in a dress is about $12.

Textiles

Other options **Tailoring** p.353

There are a few main areas you where you can shop for fabric. One is Arab Street which specialises in ornate laces and fancy fabrics from Europe. It's also a good place to pick up materials for fancy dress costumes – fake animal fur, gold lame, plain cotton linings...they're all here. Chinatown, specifically the area around the People's Park Complex, is another good stop. You'll find about two floors of shops bursting with cottons, wools, silks, laces, curtain fabrics, buttons, zips and sewing paraphernalia.

If you're in the city area, pop into Spotlight in Plaza Singapura. This Australian store is well-stocked with a variety of fabrics (including curtain fabric) and sewing accessories and they offer a sewing service.

If your couch needs to be re-upholstered, contact a furniture upholsterer for someone to come to your house with fabric samples and quotations. IKEA also has fabrics that can be turned into cushion covers, bed covers and curtains.

Textiles		
Abitex	The Paragon	6338 7789
Bin House	Ngee Ann City	6733 6789
IKEA	Queenstown	6474 0122
Poppy Fabric	Arab Street & Kampong Glam	6296 6352
Spotlight	Plaza Singapura	6733 9808
Your's Funishing	River Valley Road	6887 3317

Wedding Items

If you're getting married in Singapore, it might be easiest to engage a wedding planner. Most bridal shops offer a package that includes a wedding dress, evening gown, hair and make-up and photography. Hotels offer standard wedding dinner packages that include decor and invitation cards. But if you decide to manage the event yourself, wedding dress shops do offer 'a la carte' services.

The best place to start looking for wedding gowns is on Tanjong Pagar Road near Chinatown. There are at least 10 bridal shops here for you to choose from. They have gowns for rent and many shops will make a dress to your design and rent or sell it to you. You can also get bridesmaids' dresses here.

The doyen of atelier wedding gowns in town must surely be Tan Yoong. His creations are more haute couture than your usual princess gowns and are preferred by many of the fashion set. For 'branded' wedding gowns, check out The Link Wedding which carries international labels including Vera Wang.

If you'd like a pair of shoes that match your gown perfectly, take a trip to made-to-measure shoemakers Interpax at Holland Village or Leapin Lizard at International Plaza with a swatch of your fabric.

Most digital printers in town will help you to design and print personalised invitations (see Cards and Gift Wrap on p.330). Other options are American Wedding Treasures at Palais Renaissance who have a range of cards from the US and Tecman. Borders is good for wedding favours like soap bubbles in the shape of a wedding cake, guest books and little cake boxes.

Wedding venues generally have their own bakers, and they may require the cake be made in-house so look through the food contract carefully if that's not really what you want. Otherwise, most of the bakeries in town will make you a wedding cake.

Wedding Items		
American Wedding Treasures	Palais Renaissance	6834 0662
Bridal Veil	Newton	6738 6152
Francis Cheong	Orchard	6734 9898
Irene's Creations	Orchard	6732 6856
Kai Couture	Chinatown	6238 1550
The Link Wedding	Shangri-La Hotel	6235 4648
Silhouette The Atelier	Colonial District	6733 7197
Tan Yoong Brides	Lucky Plaza	6734 3783
Tecman	Colonial District	6338 6764
The Wedding Gift Shop	Orchard	6337 5512
The Wedding Present	Tiong Bahru	6327 4423

Shopping Malls

The heat and humidity, combined with the fight for prime space means Singapore is bursting with air-conditioned shopping malls. Orchard Road, for example, is a street of malls, one after the other.

Most centres are self-sufficient, with restaurants, food courts, parking lots and shops that cater to all ages and interests and most of the major malls are linked to the city's MRT. The formula most malls follow is a simple one: an anchor tenant, usually a department store or supermarket and loads of popular chain retails stores and boutiques. If you don't enjoy crowds you'll want to stay away from the malls on weekends. This is when most families take advantage of the 'free' air conditioning and plan family excursions. So unless you don't mind getting run over by toddlers, you might be better off saving your shopping until after office hours (most malls shut at 21:30).

Unless you're planning on buying large and heavy items, it's a good idea to take a taxi or the MRT to your shopping destination, especially if it's on Orchard Road. Parking can get expensive – up to $5 an hour depending on where you park, and you may spend half your time circling the parking lot, trying to find a space. The malls try to differentiate themselves by targeting different groups of people. For instance, while The Paragon and Ngee Ann City both house international fashion brands The Paragon carries slightly edgier labels like G-Star, Miss Sixty and Charles David while Ngee Ann mixes high-end luxury brands with high street stores. Forum The Shopping Mall is for mums and kids.

Shopping Malls		
Centrepoint	Orchard	6737 9000
Century Square	Tampines	6789 6261
Far East Plaza	Orchard	6734 6837
Forum The Shopping Mall	Orchard	6732 2469
Funan The IT Mall	Colonial District	6338 9983
The Heeren	Orchard	6733 4725
Junction 8	Bishan	6354 9282
Lucky Plaza	Orchard	6235 3294
Marina Square	Colonial District	6339 8787
Mustafa Centre	Little India	6295 5855
Ngee Ann City	Orchard	6733 0337
Novena Square	–	6358 0700
Pacific Plaza	Orchard	6733 5655
Palais Renaissance	Orchard	6737 6993
The Paragon	Orchard	6738 5535
Parco Bugis Junction	Colonial District	6334 8831
Park Mall	Orchard	6339 8229
Parkway Parade	East Coast	6345 4665
People's Park Complex ▶ p.370	Chinatown	6535 9533
Plaza Singapura	Orchard	6332 9298
Raffles City Shopping Centre	Colonial District	6338 7766
Scotts Shopping Centre	Orchard	6734 7560
Shaw House	Orchard	6235 1150
Specialist Shopping Centre	Orchard	6737 8222
Suntec City Mall	Colonial District	6825 2667
Tampines Mall	Tampines	6788 8370
Tanglin Mall	Tanglin	6736 4922
Tangs	Orchard	6737 5500
Turf City	Central Singapore	6468 8333
Wheelock Place	Orchard	6738 8660
Wisma Atria	Orchard	6821 3668

Pacific Plaza

Shopping Malls – Main

Centrepoint

6737 9000 | *www.centrepoint.com.sg*

This grand dame of Orchard Road malls has seen many renovations and upgrades over the years. It's the home of Robinson's, Singapore's oldest and most venerable department store. Known since 1888 for its value-for-money quality products and excellent service culture, Robinson's is an integral part of the Singapore shopping culture. Their flagship store is at Centrepoint and there's a second, smaller store in Raffles City Shopping Centre.

Centrepoint also houses the city's largest Marks & Spencer store carrying a limited selection of clothing, shoes, household items, food and lingerie.

The mall has a popular 'food street' in the basement. Here you can choose from a Thai restaurant, pizzeria, Hong Kong noodles and congee or Indonesian cuisine. You'll also find hairdressers, a DIY shop, cobbler and key maker, electronics and camera shops, CD shops, a pharmacy, shoe shops and a Cold Storage down here.

There are two ATMs on the first floor of the mall – the local POSB bank as well as an OCBC teller. You can book tickets for various arts shows at the information desk on this floor too. There's a parking complex at the back of the mall.

The Heeren

6733 4725 | www.heeren.com.sg

Here's where you'll find the largest music superstore in south-east Asia. HMV has one of the largest collections of DVDs on sale in Singapore, plenty of listening posts and even an in-house DJ. Vinyl lovers and aspiring DJs regularly come here to hunt for the latest records to sample and exchange notes with fellow aficionados. HMV closes at 23:00 – probably the latest closing time for a retail outlet along Orchard Road.

The ground floor of The Heeren consists of shops like Levi's, URS Shoes, Swatch and City Chain, a watch store selling brands like Adidas, Cyma, DKNY and Calvin Klein. The other two floors are home to brands like Miss Sixty, Flash N Splash, Canterbury of New Zealand for rugby gear and Adidas, as well as streetwear labels like Ed Hardy, Converse, Limited Edition VAULT which offers footwear, active wear and accessories from international sporting brands.

On levels four and five is Annex, a shopping concept similar to Harajuku in Tokyo or Island Beverly in Hong Kong. Shops here average about 200 square feet and are often owned and run by young entrepreneurs and designers. Focusing on the young and young at heart, Annex has everything from street and vintage fashion to accessories, quirky toys and comics, many for those on tight budgets.

The restaurants on the fifth level sell really good Asian food ranging from Peranakan to Japanese cuisine. For casual dining there's Movenpick's Marche in the basement and Balcony Bar, a two-storey bar and restaurant recently opened up next to The Heeren. It's run by the same people who run Ministry of Sound on Clarke Quay. Light snacks and alcoholic drinks are served over high stools and lounge seats. The Moroccan-themed bar is furnished with a roof top mini Jacuzzi, storm lamps and sofas. While The Heeren has no adjoining parking lot, you can park at Cairnhill Place, accessible from Cairnhill Road or at The Paragon shopping centre.

357

Marina Square

6339 8787 | www.marinasquare.com.sg

A huge renovation project meant this entire mall was all but closed for almost two years. The remodelled venue now caters to the unfettered fashionista as well as tourists and families. The 700,000 square foot space has been divided into eight zones including food and restaurants, fashion, hobby, art and living. The walkways are wide and the high ceilings make it all feel light and spacious.

Giant takes up almost a third of the second floor so you can do all your grocery shopping here. Once that's out the way you can start having fun at the mall's 20 bag and shoe shops including Doc Marten, Crocs and Rockport; four kids' fashion and toy shops including Mothercare and Kiddy Palace; four bridal stores; 17 furniture and houseware outlets including Barang Barang, Molecule and a DIY store; 36 men and women's fashion stores including Massimo Dutti, Warehouse, Topshop, Warehouse and Miss Selfridge, and 53 restaurants and food outlets.

There's a food court on the fourth floor and a Cineplex. On level three you'll find six family rooms, each equipped with a baby changing station and a small couch.

Marina Square is easily accessed from Suntec City and is seamlessly linked to Citylink Mall, Millenia Walk and the Esplanade theatres. While it's about a 10 minute walk through City Link mall to Marina Square, the Convention Centre MRT station directly beneath it is scheduled to be ready in 2010. The mall is also flanked by several hotels.

Ngee Ann City

6733 0337 | *www.ngeeanncity.com.sg*

Orchard Rd
Orchard
🚇 **Orchard**
Map 14-B4

Mall Listing
Adidas
Alexis Optical
Alfred Dunhill
A/X Armani Exchange
Best Denki
Bin House
Blue Canopy
Bricks World
British India
Burberry
Camper
Cartier
Chopard
Christian Dior
Country Road
Crystal Jade Kitchen
Ermenegildo Zegna
Fendi
FURLA
Guardian Pharmacy
Kinokuniya
Larry Kewelry
L'Occitane
Loewe
Louis Vuitton
M)phosis
Mango
Massimo Dutti
Mondial
Mont Blanc
Nature's Farm
Nike Women
Opera Gallery
Puma
Seoul Garden
Shanghai Tang
Stadium
Stuart Weitzman
The Hour Glass
Tiffany & Co
Tumi
Watson's

Easily the largest mall on Orchard Road, if not the island, Ngee Ann City is also called Takashimaya by locals after its anchor tenant. Here, you'll find high-end designer stores, fast food outlets, a hardware store, mobile phone centres and Kinokuniya, a bookshop that's about as large as Borders. It's probably the best place to be to avoid being caught in a heavy downpour, or if you need to pick up a variety of things under one roof. The walkways are generous enough so that you're not constantly bumping into people and the variety of stores will probably keep you entertained for hours. Best of all, there's a branch of the National Library on the top floor with a Starbucks in it.

Ngee Ann City hosts a variety of high street labels. On one floor alone you'll find Guess, Zara, Mango, Country Road, The Body Shop, Timberland, Calvin Klein, local favourite M)phosis, Camper shoes, a Tang & Co shoe shop that carries brands like Beverly Feldman. Hong Kong's famous shoe store On Peddar is also here where you can indulge your fetish for Jimmy Choos, Sergio Rossi, Marc Jacobs and Kate Spade creations among others. Peddar Red on the third floor carries On Peddar's house label. The city's only Hugo Boss store is here too, along with Celine, Gucci, Chanel, Loewe, Louis Vuitton, Fendi, Dunhill, Zegna, Kate Spade and most other top designer brands. But if your wallet is taking strain just at the thought of all this, there are plenty of mass market fashion brands here too – Giordano (the GAP of Asia), URS, Hush Puppies, Vivo Shoes and Stadium (part of World of Sports chain).

Art supply shops are on the fourth floor just above Kinokuniya, which is where you'll also find children's clothing stores. The Best Denki on the fifth floor is an electronics superstore for everything from fridges to digital cameras and in the basement is a large World of Sports shop with Puma right next to it.

The basement food court is a great place to sample reasonably priced and tasty local food. The basement also boasts a comprehensive supermarket and at places like Fortnum & Mason's and Crabree & Evelyn you'll find a large selection of English teas. Parking is ample (enter by Orchard Turn) and there are enough bathrooms in the building that you shouldn't have to line up to use one. All restrooms come equipped with changing tables. In essence, you could probably survive in this mall for months without having to leave it.

The Paragon

6738 5535

The Paragon is a haven for fashionistas with its diverse mix of international brands – Gucci, Valentino, Jean Paul Gaultier, Burberry and Versace – and edgier, newer labels. Here you'll find Potion, a local fashion label that reworks vintage fashion into contemporary, edgy pieces, as well as edgy street fashion labels like G-Star, Miss Sixty, Energie and Diesel. If lesser known cult designers are more your thing, multi-brand concept stores like Inez and Pois will be right up your alley. Together they carry an incredibly wide range of French, Spanish, Italian and even Polish labels, like Roccobarocco, Voyage Passion and Gai Mattiolo.

The anchor tenant is homegrown department store Metro which takes up three floors at one end of the mall. There's also a Marks & Spencer and a Marketplace supermarket where you can get a decent variety of Japanese food and condiments.

There's plenty of good international and local food to be found, particularly at The Food Cellar on basement level one. Other features include a fitness centre (Fitness Plus), a few day spas and art galleries and the Singapore Airlines' customer service centre.

But perhaps one of the things this mall is best known for is its washrooms. Large sofas greet you as you enter the bathrooms' motion sensor doors. There are dedicated nursing rooms and areas with flattering lighting where you can 'refresh' before heading back into the air-conditioned mall. The mall's multi-storey car park is accessible by Bideford Road just off Orchard Road.

Oops!

Have we missed out your favourite store in Singapore? If you have any additions, or thoughts, ideas or comments for us to include in the Shopping section, drop us a line and let us know, and we'll include it in the next edition. Visit www.explorerpublishing.com and tell us whatever's on your mind.

Raffles City Shopping Centre

252 North Bridge Rd
Colonial District
🚇 **City Hall**
Map 17-D1

Mall Listing
Adidas Originals
Agnes b.
Aldo
Bikram Yoga
Bakerzin
Blum
Brooks Brothers
Café Cartel
Capitol Optical
Coccinelle
Cortina Watch
Crabtree & Evelyn
Esprit
Furla
Giordano
Harvey Norman
Hue
Indivi
Life Baby
Life Shop
Levi's
Marks & Spencer
Metropolitan Museum of Art
Mexx
Mont Blanc Boutique
MPH
Nine West
Patterns
Robinson's
Sembawang Music Centre
Swarovski
Swatch
The Body Shop
The Natural Source
Tommy Hilfiger
Unity Healthcare
Vertu
Warehouse
World of Sports

6338 7766 | www.rafflescity.com
Designed by renowned architect IM Pei, this shopping mall is attached to the Swissotel, The Stamford, and Raffles, The Plaza hotels as well as the Raffles City Convention Centre. The mall is also linked to City Hall MRT station and to the underground City Link Mall, Marina Square Shopping Mall, the Esplanade and Suntec City Convention Centre and Shopping Centre.

The supermarket Marketplace and Robinson's are the main tenants here. Aimed primarily at working adults because of the offices in the vicinity, this is a good place to run your errands on the way home from work. It even has a newly opened yoga studio, Bikram Yoga to help work off that stress.

UK high street label Warehouse is housed here along with Nine West, Aldo, Indivi, Tommy Hilfiger, Brooks Brothers, Polo Ralph Lauren, Furla, JWest shoes and Marks & Spencer. There are also opticians, electronics stores, sports shops, kids' fashion, toys and a variety of restaurants. Cedele, a deli that bakes 'haute couture' bread fresh every day, serves one of the best sandwiches in town. The Soup Spoon next to it is constantly packed and at Out of the Pan you can pick a filling and the type of crepe you'd like wrapped around it. The food court on the third floor is where you'll find local food at reasonable prices.

Life Shop is a unique lifestyle concept store, offering homeware, furniture and fashion with a touch of New Asian charm. A Life Baby is a few doors down.

All the major local banks have ATMs in the basement of this mall, and parking is ample. Parking charges are $2 for the first hour and $1 for every 30 minutes thereafter from Mondays to Saturdays. After 18:00, charges drop to $2 per entry.

361

Suntec City Mall

6825 2667 | *www.sunteccity.com.sg*

Suntec City Mall consists of about 270 stores in 888,000 square feet of shopping and caters to the many office workers from the five nearby skyscrapers. The complex is feng shui-ed to the hilt and taking pride of place is the Fountain of Wealth in the middle. It's designed to attract prosperity and if these things go on size alone, it's sure to be a winner as the Guinness Book of Records declared it the largest fountain in the world in 1997. Visitors and locals visit this 'monument' daily to try to get their share of good luck. There's also a daily laser show at the fountain and you can request song dedications for free from 19:00 to 22:00. Add a free laser message on weekends and public holidays and you'll really impress your partner!

The mall has been divided into various zones. You'll find shops for golf, office and fashion wear, luggage, furniture, books, electronics, bridal shops, jewellery, children's fashions, and even hearing aids in this vast complex.

Carrefour, Singapore's first hypermart, is the anchor store here and it's a perpetual hive of activity full of families on weekends and harried office workers after office hours on weekdays.

Suntec City's Cineplex is a hidden gem in a country where people regularly go to the cinemas and weekend tickets have to be booked a day in advance. The Eng Wah Cineplex has comfortable seats, great service, gentle air conditioning that won't freeze you to death and, best of all, it's always easy to get a seat here.

When parking at Suntec City, make a note of where your car is. In fact, it might be good to write down exactly which zone you're in (they're named after animals) and which lot number you've parked in. Many a soul has been seen wandering around this huge car park hitting their car remotes in an effort to find their transport home. People have been known to be lost here for hours…maybe even days.

The mall is currently connected to City Hall interchange but there are plans to build a station under the complex as it also houses a large convention centre. It's a 10 or 15 minute walk through City Link Mall to get here.

VivoCity

6377 6860 | www.vivocity.com.sg

Only open fully since December 2006, VivoCity mall has zoomed into the record books as the largest mall in Singapore, with a whopping 1.04 million square feet of retail space, a fleet of outdoor restaurants along the harbourside promenade, a rooftop sky park and ampitheatre, an open-air playground as well as some very attractive water features. An IR (Singapore speak for casino) is forecast to open in 2009, and it already boasts Singapore's biggest Cineplex, with 15 screens and 2,293 seats. Run by Golden Village, every screen has both comfy seats and ample leg room. In short, VivoCity is the big daddy of shopping malls – with the retail-hungry crowds to match. Don't be surprised if you have to tackle three generations of one family using the mall as a weekend

excursion. Fortunately, there's so much space between stores you shouldn't find yourself railroaded by too many charging toddlers. And, of course, family excursions require food. There are two food courts – Food Republic and Kopitiam/Banquet, and on the basement level you'll find a happy kingdom of fast food outlets, including everything from the famous Sarawak Kolo mee to Malaysia's very own The Chicken Rice Shop.

Then, there's the shops. VivoCity houses Singapore's first Gap store, its only stand-alone Principles boutique and Ted Baker store, as well as a River Island, sportswear shops including Nike and Puma and a wealth of kids and maternity wear outlets. It is home to the flagship store for Toys R Us, and has its own hypermarket – Vivomart, which ships in international produce. Alternatively, if you're not even into shopping, Eu Yan Sang, the homegrown Traditional Chinese Medicine empire, has opened a gorgeous concept store at VivoCity - Red White & Pure. It incorporates a spa and 70 seat dining area, spread over two floors. If you need to burn off an over-excited binge in one of the two humungous food courts, you'll find a gym and dance clubs here, as well as regular events and festivals.

Designed by Toyo Ito, a well-renowned Japanese architect, VivoCity is an aesthetic, as well as capitalist beauty. Famous for blending buildings with their natural surroundings, which in this case is a gorgeous waterfront, Ito has moved away from the traditional 'box' mall style to create an airy and futuristic architectural wonder. The directorial signs inside have some catching up to do, and you may find yourself a little lost en route between Mango and Crocs, but fortunately, the exit route is a lot simpler. The mall is linked to The Harbourfront, where there is direct MRT access, and you can hop on a cable car to get across to Sentosa. Harbourfront is also the cruise centre.

363

Wisma Atria Shopping Centre

623 2103 | www.wismaonline.com

Awarded the Superbrands Singapore Status in 2004, Wisma Atria has managed to capture a traditionally demanding and fickle market – young working women. Refurbished just last year, the mall is covered in blue glass and is something of a landmark on Singapore's busiest shopping strip. It houses over 100 trendy mid to high end fashion boutiques and other lifestyle stores on its five floors.

Each floor has its unique identity. The basement, for example, is famous for its floor to ceiling aquarium where a black tip reef shark lives among other sea life. The shops here feature casual wear and accessories for the young and trendy shopper. Prices are reasonable – you might, for example, put together an entire ensemble for less than $200. As the floors progress upwards, the stores become higher end.

Level one houses Wisma's department store Isetan as well as Mango, Nine West and G2000. Indochine Wisma Atria is an upmarket five-in-one dining concept, featuring a restaurant, bar and supper club, a 24 hour alfresco noodle bar or cafe, a beer garden and an oyster bar.

You'll find a variety of fashion labels on the second floor, including Topshop/Topman, Warehouse, Karen Millen, BCBG, bebe, FCUK, Esprit and Paul & Joe boutiques. The third level has activewear, beach wear and casual wear from stores like Nike Women, Surf Babe and Tannlines which specialises in swimwear from Australia. Level four is devoted to lifestyle concept shops like Sony Gallery. It also has a food court where you can choose from self service stalls or have food served to you from one of the pushcarts that do the rounds.

You can buy tickets to performances around town at the ticketing counter on the ground floor and do GST refunds (for tourists only) at the information counter. You can enquire about places of interest in Singapore, book city tours, make flight reservations and confirmations and even request for a limousine to pick you at the nearby concierge counter which is open seven days a week from 10:00 to 22:00.

The mall is linked to Orchard MRT station and is also linked by an underground passage to Lucky Plaza and Ngee Ann City. The attached multi-storey parking lot is accessed by Orchard Turn in the back of the building.

Shopping Malls – Other

Scotts Rd ◀
Orchard
🚇 *Orchard*
Map 14-A4

Far East Plaza

6734 6837 | *www.fareast-plaza.com*

A must for bargain hunters, Far East Plaza on Scotts Road boasts six floors of more than 800 stores and eating places. While there's no anchor department store here, there is a Level One on…you guessed it, level one.

Inspired by the little owner-run shops in Harajuku in Japan, an entire floor at the plaza is devoted to an array of street fashion from Hong Kong, Korea and Thailand, outrageous shoes and a few local fashion designers all targeting teenagers and the young-at-heart. The upper floors are a mixed bag of tailors, photo development shops, pharmacies, instant name-card makers, luggage stores, camera equipment outlets, eyewear places, souvenir shops, tattoo and piercing parlours, clothing alteration places and eat-and-run restaurants.

Despite the hodge podge of businesses, Far East Plaza is becoming a hotbed of trendy local design and experimental retail concepts. Here you can find Ambush, a store selling limited edition trainers and T-shirts, and Surrender which carries brands like 3d, mo'wax and unkle toys. T-shirts are displayed in pull-out cast iron frames while the cool toys are locked up in a brightly lit glass wall display. ZTamp on the third floor stocks a surreal range of charm necklaces and bracelets whose dangling miniature Barbie dolls, old buttons and even dice makes these pieces strangely compelling.

Far East Plaza is also home to Johnny Two Thumbs, Singapore's best-known and longest surviving tattoo parlour. You'll find dozens of clothing alteration shops here, many of whom will deliver within an hour, unless it's a weekend when they're at their busiest.

There's a UOB ATM in the concourse and an OCBC teller at the entrance. There's a 20 cents charge to use the bathrooms and they're not the cleanest. There are no nursing rooms or changing tables either. It's a bit of a walk but you could go to the bathrooms at the Grand Hyatt next door instead. Parking is available at the back of the building with the entrance at Scotts Road.

Nr Orchard ◀
MRT Station
Orchard
🚇 *Orchard*
Map 14-A4

Forum The Shopping Mall

6732 2469 | *www.forumtheshoppingmall.com.sg*

About a 10 minute walk from Orchard MRT station, this shopping mall specialises in stuff for kids. Toys R Us is the anchor tenant here and the many fashion outlets for children include Guess Kids, Esprit Kids, Benetton Kids and Kids 21 which features labels like DKNY, Paul Smith and Comme des Garçons. The shop also boasts a kids' hair salon and several stores with educational books and toys from Australia like Bookaburra.

While children are the focus here, keeping the mothers happy is also an important part of the mall's unique selling proposition. Designer label stores like Song + Kelly 21, Calvin Klein and Max Mara are hugely popular. Blackjack has the hippest streetwear in town – browse through rails of Maharishis, James and Danang, Ernest Sewn, Sass & Bide and Luella.

365

To keep your energy up there's the city's only California Pizza Kitchen, a Coffee Bean & Tea Leaf, a conveyor sushi belt place and a 24 hour MacDonald's here. A 7-Eleven kiosk on the street just outside the mall does the job for a quick 'big gulp' or the day's paper. A special room in the mall has been made available to nursing mothers.

Holland Village Shopping Centre

211 Holland Ave
Holland Village
🚇 **Buona Vista**
Map 13-C4

6468 5334

The heart of Holland Village, Holland Village Shopping Centre is four floors of eclectic shopping. A favourite among expats, this centre is probably about 25 years old. It hasn't yet undergone a facelift and it has some idiosyncracies (the escalators only go up, for instance), which only add to its charm.

Shops here carry popular Balinese teak and Asian style furniture pieces. Lim's Arts and Crafts has Chinese antique furniture as well as decorative items like candles, lamps, tableware, curtains and cushion covers. There's a hardware shop here, a furniture upholsterer, ladies' and kids' fashion stores, a pet shop, florist, hair-dressing salons, nail bars, and second hand book store EMF. Cold Storage here is open 24 hours. Cafe 211 on the top floor is a charming deli with a rooftop seating area where you can while away quiet afternoons, or nurse shop-sore feet.

Mustafa Centre

145 Syed Alwi Rd
Little India
🚇 **Farrer Park**
Map 14-D3

6295 5855 | *www.mustafa.com.sg*

This mall, in the heart of little India is open 24 hours a day, the only one of its kind in Singapore. If you popped in at 02:00 on a weekend, you'd think this was a country of insomniacs: the place will be teeming with life. Perhaps this is because Mustafa's is the only place where just about everything you could possibly need is crammed under one roof. Here, no matter how wee the hour of the morning is, you'll be able to pop into the travel agency, buy gold, do your groceries, pick up a new computer or luggage, a set of curtains or maybe that blood pressure monitor. Your TV has just blown up, it's 03:00 and the World Cup is on? Quick! Get to Mustafa's before half time ends! And yes, even if you need a new car at some odd hour, Mustafa is also home to a Hyundai showroom. Forget aesthetics and little luxuries like changing tables for moms or wide aisles. Mustafa's is strictly no frills – fluorescent tube lighting blazes above you and there's no escaping the supermarket trolley shuffle with other patrons. And to cut down on theft, bags are checked at the door and sealed with plastic taggies, much like handcuffs, once you leave a store. However, Mustafa is still an Aladdin's cave: prices here are about 20% cheaper than down on Orchard Road, and it is the place to go if you need to stock up on all things Indian – spices, Punjabi suits, basmati rice, jewellery, music CDs, DVDs and more. Indian and Bangladeshi workers head to this iconic mall for all the things from home.

There's a very basic car park at the back of the building and multi-storey car parks in the HDBs or housing estates about a 10 minute walk away. However, if it's at night and you're a woman on your own or with children, or if you have heavy shopping with you, rather take a taxi. There are some parts of Little India that, while not dangerous, can be a little unsavoury and you may not be up for a wander into the middle of the brothel district.

Pacific Plaza

9 Scotts Rd
Orchard
🚇 *Orchard*
Map 14-A4

6733 5655

Although it's smaller than most of the Orchard Road malls, Pacific Plaza is one of the trendiest centres. It's also home to the largest branch of That CD Shop, a homegrown chain. Two floors of jazz, R&B, classical, rock, chillout and pop music housed in darkwood interiors, with a top of the range sound system and ample listening booths make this a fabulous place to explore new music at.

Pacific Plaza also houses some of Australia's most popular surfwear lines with Stussy, Mambo, Billabong, Rip Curl and Quiksilver all represented. The Adidas concept store is popular with fashionistas thanks to its limited edition shoes and fashion. If you're into vintage, or want to trade in your designer clothing, you'll enjoy going through the racks of used designer clothing and accessories at The Vintage Place. Last season's Gucci, Prada, Donna Karan and Dolce & Gabanna are all here.

Pacific Plaza's anchor tenant is Pure Yoga which has 16,000 square feet of yoga and pilates studios on the top floor.

Students and young office workers head here at night to go to Chinablack, a club that plays top 40 hits. With a snazzy, dark interior, it's a smorgasbord of eastern and western decor influences but more importantly, the central dancefloor is big enough for those who want to boogie the night away.

Bathroom cleanliness in the mall is average but there are no changing tables or nursing facilities. Parking out the back costs $1.30 per 30 minutes during the day on weekdays and $2.60 per entry after 18:00 or after 14:00 on Saturdays. Entry on Sundays is $2.60.

Park Mall

9 Park Mall
Orchard
🚇 *Dhoby Ghaut*
Map 17-C1

6339 8229

If you're mad about furniture and interiors, this is the place to come to for inspiration. Park Mall is 45 stores' worth of design inspiration. At X-tra Living, you'll find Montis from Holland, Morisa, Alivar and Magis from Italy, and the inimitable Alessi, plus all-chrome designer kitchens at Arclinea's showroom, and beautifully designed wooden and modern steel furniture at homegrown brands Air Division and Plank.

Park Mall also houses lighting shops and stores selling kitchen and bathroom fixtures. Mad Fish Tanks in the basement makes fish tanks to order using mahogany and teak woods. So your living room aquarium can also function as a coffee table or bar counter. There are small food places that serve local fare in the basement, as well as a Watson's 'personal care' store. Heng Nam Nam is a dressmaker whose clientele consists mainly of 'ladies who lunch'.

Situated just across from Plaza Singapura, parking is fairly easy with the entrance to the parking lot accessible from Penang Road. Dhoby Ghaut MRT station is just next door.

Parkway Parade

80 Marine Parade Rd
East Coast
Map 15-D4

6345 4665

The largest mall in the Marine Parade area, Parkway has served East Coast residents for more than 20 years and earned its place as a firm favourite with locals. Even residents who've moved out of the area still venture back to reminisce occasionally.

Parkway consists of over 250 stores on six levels. Unusually, it has several anchor tenants: Japanese department store Isetan, hypermarket Giant, and supermarket Cold Storage. Fitness Centre has also just opened up a branch here with over 120,000 square

367

feet of workout space. The two electronic superstores – Best Denki and Harvey Norman – are here too, as well as what is arguably the best deli in town, Espirito Santo Gourmet and Butchery on the ground floor. The food court in the basement is also very comprehensive with better food (and more generous portions) than in the average food court along Orchard Road.

Don't try to venture here on weekends unless you have to though. Queues to enter the car park snake around the block, and drivers have been known to take 45 minutes to get into the carpark and find a parking space – even though there are almost 1,200 berths. It's better to take the MRT and hop on the free shuttle the mall provides. This is a two-way service that runs every 20 minutes between Bedok MRT station at the cab stand across from the bus interchange and Parkway Parade on weekends and public holidays from 11:00 to 22:00.

1 Park Rd
Chinatown
🚇 *Chinatown*
Map 17-B2

People's Park Complex ▶ p.370

6535 9533

Hailed as a masterpiece of 1970s experimental architecture from the Japanese Metabolist Movement, People's Park Complex is said to represent the significant historical, architectural and development trends that have prevailed in Singapore over the last four decades. In shopping terms, it's a condensed version of a Chinese downtown and is great for bargains of all sorts. Here you'll find extensive ranges of conventional products in everything from electrical and electronic goods, luggage and textiles to bargain-priced clothes and cosmetics, and even antiques.

68 Orchard Rd
Orchard
🚇 *Somerset*
Map 14-C4

Plaza Singapura

6332 9298

One of the last malls on the Orchard Road stretch, Plaza Singapura places the emphasis on fashion, entertainment and food for families and young adults. Its retail outlets are spread over nine themed floors. So the ground floor, with its focus on fashion for young adults, is where you'll find Sense (a local label), Dorothy Perkins, G2000, M)phosis and Forntieer. The stores in the basement feature casual wear for teens and young adults while the fifth floor is for furniture and household essentials. Spotlight takes up much of the space here but other stores include Aussino for bedlinen, Barang Barang and vintage knick knack retailer Eclectic Attic. This is the location of Carrefour's second outlet in Singapore and the supermarket stays open later than most of the other tenants, with the exception of the Cineplex on the top floor. Golden Village Plaza, or the GV Plaza as it's known, is a popular cineplex with seven cinemas.

163 Tanglin Rd
Tanglin
🚇 *Orchard*
Map 13-F4

Tanglin Mall

6736 4922 | *www.tanglinmall.com.sg*

Just a five minute walk away from Tanglin Shopping Centre, the more 'suburban' Tanglin Mall caters to the residents who live in the Grange Road, Tanglin Road, and Nassim areas. Patrons tend to be expat families with small children. The Gymboree on the third floor keeps the kids entertained as they're taught to sing, dance and play instruments like hand-held drums, tambourines and maracas.

The Market Place supermarket in the basement is superb for stocking up on products from the UK, US and Australia. Other tenants include organic health food store Brown Rice Paradise, a World of Sports outlet, That CD shop, a large British India store that stocks clothes for men, women and children and houseware, opticians, a Birkenstocks shop, tailor, Barang Barang and numerous fashion outlets.

The mall is connected to Trader's Hotel next door and parking is accessed from the hotel lobby.

19 Tanglin Rd
Tanglin
🚇 *Orchard*
Map 14-A4

Tanglin Shopping Centre

6737 0840

A short walk from frenzied Orchard Road, Tanglin Shopping Centre is comparatively mellow and laidback. Although in need of a facelift, the mall retains some charm. Chock-a-block with Chinese and Tibetan antiques, Persian carpets, tapestries and curio shops it's like a mini-UN of artefacts.

One of the stores specialises in antique maps of South East Asia while another is one of Singapore's oldest carpet traders, Hassan's Carpets. On the third floor is D&O Video, the first art house video rental shop in all of Singapore which opened about 15 years ago. Its legendary owner was a Russian art house movie buff who was known to turn away patrons if he didn't like them, or if he felt they didn't know enough about movies. When he passed away several years ago *The Straits Times* carried stories about him and customers attended his funeral. His family still runs the store.

Select Books is an independent bookshop that specialises in south-east Asian titles. They also publish and distribute books, supplying libraries all over the world. You can also buy online from them – visit www.selectbooks.com.sg.

Tanglin Shopping Centre is known for its numerous Japanese restaurants on the fourth floor. Tambuah Mas, probably Singapore's oldest Indonesian restaurant, has been here for over 20 years and is a firm favourite.

Department Stores

Shaw House
Orchard
🚇 *Orchard*
Map 14-A4

Isetan

6733 1111 | *www.isetan.com.sg*

The Japanese department store Isetan has four stores in Singapore: its flagship store at Shaw House on the corner of Scotts and Orchard Road, Isetan Wisma on Orchard Road, Isetan Katong in Parkway Parade and Isetan Tampines in Tampines Mall.

Isetan has a cosmetics and fragrance section, shoes, sportswear, women's and men's fashion as well as fashion accessories. Spanish high street brand Mango has also got an outlet within Isetan, as does agnès b, Topshop, Laura Ashley and Ralph Lauren.

Although Isetan Scotts and Isetan Wisma are across the street from each other, they cater to slightly different markets. Isetan Scotts' focus is on younger adults and more mass market brands while Isetan Wisma carries fashion labels like G-star, DKNY, Laundry by Shelli Segal, Emporio Armani, Paul Smith and local-brand-made-good Song + Kelly 21. The supermarket in the basement of Isetan Scotts carries a large variety of Japanese foods.

Various locations

John Little

6737 2222 | *www.johnlittle.com.sg*

Established in 1845 and acquired by Robinsons in 1955, this department store chain has seven stores in Singapore at Specialists' Shopping Centre on Orchard Road, Plaza Singapura, Compass Point, North Point, White Sands, Causeway Point and Jurong Point.

John Little is famous for its value-for-money houseware. Catering to young middle income families looking for contemporary style and good value, the store offers a good selection of mid-price kitchenware, bedding and home accessories as well as the usual array of womens' and men's fashion, toiletries and accessories. The flagship store in Specialists' Shopping Centre has a stand-alone section at the back of the first level that stocks winter wear all year round.

369

珍珠坊

珍珠坊，新加坡第一间综合型的购物中心。数十年如一日，至今仍是旅客与本地顾客向往的购物天堂。

在这里，您可以购买到应时应节，价廉物美的百货。

珍珠坊在七十年代堪称为建筑中的佼佼者，这富历史性的地标，今日的购物天堂本身就是牛车水的缩影。

PEOPLE'S PARK COMPLEX

People's Park Complex

A Singapore retail icon, People's Park Complex (PPC) has withstood the test of time for 40 years. Today, it remains a local shopping haven, where tourists and locals alike flock to for the best buys.

Besides its famous comprehensive selection of Chinese products, People's Park Complex offers bargains galore, from electrical and electronic goods, luggage and textiles, to fashionable yet reasonably priced clothes and cosmetics.

Along with its established name in the retail scene, the architecture heritage of People's Park Complex is a historical landmark. With six-storeys housing 300 shops and offices, it's hailed as a masterpiece of 1970s experimental architecture.

People's Park Complex is a major part of the Chinatown landscape, identified as a mini Chinatown in itself, a three-dimensional hub of modern Chinese shopping, based on tradition.

Whatever you're looking for – watches, jewellery, food, art, tonics, accessories, fengshui readings, tour agencies, fashion and beauty – People's Park Complex has everything you need and much more.

Metro

Various locations

6836 3322 | *www.metro.com.sg*

A stalwart of the department store scene in Singapore, Metro has its flagship store, Metro Paragon, on Orchard Road and outlets in Tampines, Woodlands and Sengkang. There are also Metro department stores in Jakarta and Bandung in Indonesia.

As you'd expect of a department store, Metro stocks everything you could possibly need – from cosmetics and shoes, to frying pans and bed linen. Metro Paragon focuses on fashion and houses Accessorize and Monsoon under its roof. It's well known too for its extensive shoe department. The other three Metro stores in Singapore carry more household items and fashion lines that cater to the budget-conscious.

OG

Various locations

6317 2222 | *www.og.com.sg*

OG has traditionally been seen as a 'Chinese' department store. Most of its goods are local or sourced from the region. Recently though, the store – particularly its Orchard branch – has tried to change its image. It relaunched Hemispheres, an 80s retail concept that sought to nurture local fashion designers by giving them a venue to test the market and showcase their work without the expense of setting up a store, and OG in Orchard also stocks labels like Dorothy Perkins and Guess.

Still, OG remains a favourite among older women who complain that as other stores cater only to younger women it's hard to find classic clothing that doesn't break the budget.

There are three OGs in Singapore: OG Albert next to Bugis Junction, OG Orchard Point next to Centrepoint and OG People's Park in the heart of Chinatown.

Robinson's

Centrepoint
Orchard
🚇 *Somerset*
Map 14-B4

6733 0888 | *www.centrepoint.com.sg*

Founded in 1858, Robinson and Spicer originally sold basic food stuff. It was renamed Robinson and Co in 1859 and today it's simply known as Robinson's. The department store is such a part of Singapore's history that when the company tried to sell off its shares a few years ago the public outcry was so great as to force them to retract the offer for sale. Today, Robinson's also owns John Little and Marks & Spencer. You'll find the flagship store at Centrepoint on Orchard Road with another Robinson's at Raffles City.

The store is best known for its quality bedlinen. The Centrepoint store has almost half a store devoted to linen, pillows, duvets and other accessories for the bedroom and naturally you'll be able to find everything from the everyday stuff to 500 threadcount Egyptian cotton here.

Recently Robinson's has beefed up its homeware department and it now carries a fairly large selection of designer lamps, vases, candelabras and even designer digital radios. On the fashion side, high end labels like Trucco are recent additions and they also carry UK brand Principles.

Perhaps what truly sets this department store apart is the level of service and its employees' loyalty. Floor staff are known to stay on the job for up to 20 years and service is impeccable. The sales team knows its stuff and gives you objective advice. The sales here are also legendary.

Takashimaya

Ngee Ann City
Orchard
🚇 *Somerset*
Map 14-A4

6738 1111 | *www.takashimaya-sin.com*

Open from 10:00 to 21:30 every day bar Chinese New Year, Takashimaya is housed in Singapore's largest mall (for now) Ngee Ann City on Orchard Road. Its seven floors are is chock-a-block with men's and ladies fashions, houseware, a supermarket, cosmetics, toys, luggage, jewellery, drycleaners, restaurants, a hair and beauty salon and even a gym complete with pool and Jacuzzi.

Takashimaya houses branded boutiques like Gucci, Christian Dior, Ferragamo, Bally, Coach, Bottega Veneta, Armani Collezoni , DKNY and Kenzo. The food court in its basement is a veritable feast – you can sample almost every type of Asian cuisine here and then some.

It's a little known fact, but Takashimaya also carries one of the best tea selections in town. In the basement area next to the supermarket you'll find Fortnum & Mason, Crabtree & Evelyn and Taylors of Harrogate.

The store also has a GST refund centre, five ATM machines covering all of Singapore's major banks, and offers overseas delivery services to Japan with charges based on weight, destination, insurance coverage and packing materials. You can also rent prams for free here – all you have to do is leave a form of ID as security.

310 Orchard Rd
Orchard
🚇 ***Orchard***
Map 14-A4

Tangs

6737 5500 | *www.tangs.com*

Tangs, formerly known as CK Tang, was started when a young Chinese immigrant arrived armed with a chest of goods, and tried to hawk them on the streets in Singapore in 1932. He then parlayed his business into a small department store. A hit from the start, Tangs has grown exponentially over the decades and its now an Orchard Road landmark.

In 2004 Tangs was given a facelift and emerged as a high-end department store with boutique fashion, fragrance and cosmetics. It's won two prestigious tourism awards – one for the best shopping experience in a department store, and the other for its lingerie department aka 'Dressing Room'.

Tangs 'beautyhall' is another of the store's highlights. It's easily the largest cosmetics and fragrance department in town, and it carries both well-known and boutique brands.

The houseware department is known for the quality of the brands it stocks, the variety and the fair prices. They'll also deliver bulky items free of charge. You won't find fridges and ovens here, but you will have plenty of small kitchen appliances and cooking utensils to choose from.

The lingerie department is legendary, carrying not only Triumph, Wacoal and Australian brand Bonds, but also French high street brand Morgan and boutique lines like Elegantly Scant. Its dressing rooms are styled like boudoirs.

There are departments for trendy men's wear and workwear, and concessions retailing Levi's, G-Star, French Connection, Seed and streetwear labels from the UK and US. Its Tang + Co department downstairs has women's wear labels like Poleci, 100% linen, Alannah Hill's frothy creations and shoes.

For a bit of a break or a place to park your partner, there's the Island Java Bar on the third floor and an Island Cafe on the fourth. The basement also houses an enticing food hall. While there is nowhere to sit and rest your weary feet here, there are bar tables to stand at.

373

Hypermarkets

Various Locations
See p.377

Carrefour

www.carrefour.com.sg

This well-known hypermarket from France opened its first Singapore store in Suntec City in 1999. Covering two floors, it sells everything from furniture to frozen shrimp, computer and cameras to camisole tops and Corningware. It proudly declares that its prices are the cheapest in town and if you find the same thing cheaper anywhere else, they'll refund you the difference. In 2003, the store opened its second outlet in Plaza Singapura which is equally popular.

The wide range of food stems mostly from European, predominantly French, sources. The Suntec City outlet also boasts an extensive cellar with an emphasis on French wines. Both outlets sell durians. They're sold in Styrofoam boxes clad in layers of cling wrap but you'll always know when you're in the same aisle as this pungent fruit. The aisles are wide enough for the massive trolleys but you want to avoid Carrefour on a Saturday afternoon when the trolley traffic is bumper to bumper. Carrefour also offers delivery services for purchases over $150.

Various Locations
See p.379

Giant

Giant offers a wide range of local merchandise and a wet market environment. Following the successful launch of this format of stores in Malaysia, Giant's emphasis is 'ethnic and fresh'. You'll find Giant in the IMM Building on the west side of the island, at Parkway Parade in the east, in Turf City in Bukit Timah and at the Sembawant Shopping Centre.

Local produce is plentiful here and it's a good place to pick up Asian vegetables, tofus and spices. Tasting stations are plentiful too. Giant also stocks a fair range of mid-priced, mostly Australian, wines.

Like Carrefour, Giant gets packed on weekends – many make a trip to the hypermarket a family outing for kids, parents and the grandparent. Be prepared for a queue of at least 20 minutes at the tills.

Wet Markets

While expats don't really shop at them, you're bound to have heard of the wet markets. Air-conditioned and conveniently situated supermarkets that match the wet markets for price, particularly for bulk buys, mean that wet markets are slowly disappearing from the Singaporean cultural landscape. However, it's worth a trip down there if you want to catch a glimpse of the old Singapore. They're called wet markets because of the melting ice and the fish and meat stalls constantly being washed down.

If you're here to shop rather than to take in the sights, sounds and rather pungent odours, you should head down early in the morning when everything is fresh and you have the most choice. Variety is usually greater and you may score on prices but payment is cash-only. If you shop at the same stall on a regular basis you'll find that prices become even better. The Empress Market in Holland Village is friendly and many of the traders speak English while

Wet Markets		
Chinatown Complex	Smith Street, Chinatown	Map 17-C3
Empress Market	Farrer Road	Map 13-D3
Holland Village Market	Lorong Mambong, Holland Village	Map 13-C4
Tekka Centre	Buffalo Road, Little India	Map 14-D4

Tekka Centre and Chinatown Complex are two of the largest wet markets where you'll find everything from meat and seafood to flowers, spices, toys and decorations.

Streets/Areas to Shop

A shopping paradise, Singapore's prime shopping spot is undoubtedly Orchard Road. It's a street that's crammed with malls and department stores, each targeting a slightly different audience. Even when you venture to other parts of the cities, the malls are essentially a scaled-down version of Orchard Road types with less variety and more children. However there are still a few places that haven't succumbed to the mall culture.

Little India
🚇 Bugis
Map 14-D4

Arab Street

Arab Street is for textiles and fabrics. The entire street is filled with retailers and wholesalers who bring European fabrics in to Singapore. Many local fashion designers source their fabrics here.

Wander down the side streets and you will be surprised by the interesting finds you make. Among the stores selling furniture and art there's a vintage shop with fashion and furniture fittings from the 60s and 70s on Bussorah Street. Wander down sleepy Haji Lane and you'll find artist workshops, stores selling fashion designed by art school students, a shop that sells chandeliers that the owners fashion themselves and a secret Comme des Garçons guerilla store.

Nr Botanic Gardens
Tanglin
Map 13-E3

Dempsey Road

If you're looking for wooden furniture, get yourself down to Dempsey Road. Situated just across from the Botanic Gardens in the old English army barracks, it's a pleasant place to shop for furniture and art under lush trees and warm tropical breezes.

The furniture places stock items from the region, mostly Indonesia, Thailand and China. Many of the stores aren't air-conditioned so you might want to don shorts and a light T-shirt in anticipation of the heat. If you're prone to mosquito bites, spray some repellant on before you head out.

Recently a few wine bars and restaurants have set up shop here too. Most notable of these is PS Café (p.409), a beautiful restaurant surrounded by glass walls that overlook the lush rainforest. Reservations need to be made weeks in advance though.

Holland Village
🚇 Buona Vista
Map 13-C3

Holland Village

Singapore's 'bohemian enclave', Holland Village is a microcosm of life here. It's a curious mix of old and new, although the area is slowly becoming gentrified. Often referred to as 'Holland V', the area is effectively defined by two main streets – Lorong Mambong and Lorong Liput – but has spilt over and now extends across the road to Chip Bee Gardens (specifically Jalan Merah Saga). The stores there are slightly newer but have as much character as the ones across the street. It's about a 10 minute drive from the Botanic Gardens.

Shops and restaurants occupy old two-storey shophouses. In fact, at four floors high, the Holland Village Shopping Centre is the highest shopping building in the neighbourhood. Here traditional coffee shops sit side by side with global coffee houses, ritzy wine bars and fine restaurants. Popular with younger Singaporeans and expatriates it's dominated by, and often visited solely for, its eateries.

In the last few years though, the area's also evolved into a bit of a shopping zone with some specialist shops. Antipodean at Lorong Mambong stocks Australian designers, accessories made by local designers as well as jeans from Paper Denim & Cloth. Galerie Cho Lon has an eclectic mix of Asian and European antiques and houseware and a small selection of art and books. Da Paolo La Gastronomia is an offshoot of the successful chain of Da Paolo Italian restaurants. They sell chef-made pastas, leafy salads, conveniently packed soups and sauces, ready-to-go slices of pizza, freshly made muffins and breads. The area also boasts holistic centres, spas, antique shops, picture framers and hairdressers.

375

Orchard
🚇 *Orchard*
Map 14-B4

Orchard Road

The Champs Elysees of Singapore, Orchard Road rivals all the other areas in terms of sheer volume, quality, and choice. Technically it extends beyond Orchard Road: the shopping actually begins at Tanglin Road and extends up Orchard Road with a detour to Scotts Road where Far East Plaza, Scotts Shopping Centre, the Hyatt Hotel, Pacific Place and DFS Galleria are. It continues all the way up Somerset Road to the Dhoby Ghaut area near Hotel Meridien. Walking from one end to another would take you about 40 minutes if you weren't side tracked by shops and food outlets along the way. Orchard Road is where Singaporeans, residents and tourists shop. If you're looking for the big brand names and the latest fashion trends, you'll be spoilt for choice here, no matter what your budget is. A T-shirt can range from $5 to $5000 along this shopping belt where budget shops sit next to swish boutiques.

Fairs and Bazaars
Other options **Second-Hand Items** p.350

There are several fairs and bazaars run by long-time expats in Singapore. They showcase small businesses and feature mostly babies' fashions, homewares and furniture. Fancy Faire takes place every three months while The Fair takes place once every two months. Both are usually held in hotels around Orchard Road. Check out expat magazines like *The Finder* or *The Expat* for exact dates.
The Shophouse Fair takes place every last Thursday of the month from 9:00 to 18:00. Here about 40 vendors show off their products which are sourced throughout Asia, Europe, Australia and the States. The range includes homeware, children's clothing and accessories, women's clothing, jewellery and more.

Fairs and Bazaars

Absolutely Fabulous Show and Sell	Raffles Place	91872930	na
Fancy Faire	Orchard Road	na	www.fancyfaire.com
THAT Bazaar	Orchard Road	9737 7353	lynnetteee@hotmail.com
The Fair	Orchard Road	6235 3608	na
The Shophouse Fair	Queenstown	9338 8506	www.theshophouse.com

Shopping Directory

37 Degrees	The Heeren (6733 0868), Junction 8 (6258 0572), Jurong Point (6790 1923)
Adidas	The Heeren (6235 8219), Ngee Ann City (6238 0571), Ngee Ann City (6737 0551), The Paragon (6235 1037), Parkway Parade (6345 5629), Pacific Plaza (6238 6388), Suntec City Mall (6334 3107), Tampines Mall (6787 2809), Wheelock Place (6235 2836)
Aldo	Centrepoint (6836 4919), Harbourfront Centre (6376 2141), Raffles City Shopping Centre (6336 2533), Suntec City Mall (6334 2549), Wisma Atria Shopping Centre (6836 2271)
Angie The Choice	Clifford Centre (6236 9393), Novena Square (6258 9898)
Arena	Raffles City Shopping Centre (6334 3308), Tampines Mall (6788 5010)
Art Friend	Bras Basah Complex (6336 8338), Colonial District (6238 6771), Kallang (6345 4182), Ngee Ann City (6733 8482)
Audio House	Liang Court (6338 0388), Sim Lim Square (6333 1651)
Bakerzin	Millenia Walk (6837 2422), One Fullerton (6438 8700), The Paragon (6333 6647), Raffles City Shopping Centre (6336 6006), Takashimaya Food Hall (6733 7672), United Square (6251 5550)
Barang Barang	Geylang (6745 8892), Great World City (6738 0133), Harbourfront Centre (6376 4120), Marina Square (6333 5805), Plaza Singapura (6339 1146), Tanglin Mall (6785 8937)
Bata	Centrepoint (6235 3750), Great World City (6235 9406), Junction 8 (6259 5401), Ngee Ann City (6735 2391), Suntec City Mall (6334 5891), Parkway Parade (6345 0256), Peninsula Plaza (6337 9446)
BCBG	The Paragon (6738 1063), Wisma Atria Shopping Centre (6738 7458)
Beetlebug	Plaza Singapura (6835 7748), Wisma Atria Shopping Centre (6732 7790)
Best Denki	Great World City (6732 8122), Jurong (6564 4022), Ngee Ann City (6835 2855), Parkway Parade (6440 4188), Plaza Singapura (6333 0110)
Birkenstock	Tanglin Mall (6835 2702), Wheelock Place (6887 3136)
Blush	The Paragon (6724 4847), Scotts Shopping Centre (6733 4830)
The Body Shop	Centrepoint (6735 3474), Citylink Mall (6238 8002), Great World City (6238 2248), Parkway Parade (6345 6447), Plaza Singapura (6334 9761), Raffles City Shopping Centre (6336 2551), Scotts Shopping Centre (6735 3407), Wisma Atria Shopping Centre (6734 6050)
Booze Wine Shop	Chinatown (6435 1900), Republic Plaza, CBD (6532 6700)
British India	Millenia Walk (6337 1410), Ngee Ann City (6834 1172), Raffles City Shopping Centre (6333 3536), Tanglin Mall (6735 3466)
Capitol Optical	Far East Plaza (6736 0365), Forum The Shopping Mall (6737 0692), Lucky Plaza (6734 4166), Raffles City Shopping Centre (6339 7030), Wisma Atria Shopping Centre (6732 2401)
Carrefour	Plaza Singapura (6836 6868), Suntec City Mall (6333 6868)

Cartier	Hilton Shopping Gallery, Orchard (6235 0295), Ngee Ann City (6734 2427)
Cellini	Arab Street & Kampong Glam (6296 9140), IMM Building (6425 6278), Park Mall (6837 2208)
Charles & Keith	Amara Hotel (6221 1814), Citylink Mall (6338 0913), Junction 8 (6353 6018), Parkway Parade (6346 9803), Wisma Atria Shopping Centre (6238 3312)
Chateau de Sable	The Paragon (6836 1445), Suntec City Mall (6838 3855), Tanglin Mall (6836 9170)
Cherry Mobile	Funan The IT Mall (6334 5288), Novena Square (6352 7922)
Chomel	Isetan Scotts (6733 1111), Great World City (6734 7595), Shaw House (6734 7067), Takashimaya (6738 2703)
Cold Storage	Centrepoint (6737 4222), Funan The IT Mall (6338 9983), Great World City (6735 4730), Harbourfront Centre (6274 9112), HDB Hub (6253 4757), Holland Shopping Centre (6468 5566), Parco Bugis Junction (6336 1990), Parkway Parade (6344 9011), Peace Centre (6337 9866), Takashimaya (6735 1266), Tampines Community Complex (6786 5600), United Square (6250 9690), Valley Point (6732 3147), Village Centre (6777 1781)
Columbia	Wheelock Place (6733 4058), Wisma Atria Shopping Centre (6733 2691)
Cortina Watch	Lucky Plaza (6734 3668), Millenia Walk (6339 1728), The Paragon (6235 0084), Raffles City Shopping Centre (6339 9185)
Cosmoprof	Colonial District (6339 9118), Esplanade (6336 1269)
Country Road	Isetan Scotts (6836 0848), Millenia Walk (6339 0348), Ngee Ann City (6735 0623)
Courts	Ang Mo Kio (6453 3772), Bukit Timah (6468 1355), Causeway Point (6894 2030), Centrepoint (6733 2131), Compass Point (6315 9249), Funan The IT Mall (6338 6533), Jurong Point (6793 5676), Pasir Ris (6581 1080), Suntec City Mall (6339 6800), Tampines Mall (6788 8027), Tiong Bahru Plaza (6275 4761)
Culina	Bukit Timah (6468 5255), Orchard Blvd, Orchard (6735 8858)
Dorothy Perkins	Plaza Singapura (6238 1539), Suntec City Mall (6336 6180)
Emotus	Isetan Scotts (6735 0574), Marina Square (6336 9757), Parkway Parade (6348 5295), Takashimaya (6735 5068)
EpiCentre	Suntec City Mall (6835 8168), Wheelock Place (6238 9378)
Evergreen Stationers	Centrepoint (6733 5046), Great World City (6235 8801), Parkway Parade (6345 8173), Suntec City Mall (6338 9765),
Export Fashion	Holland Road Shopping Centre (6463 2972), Peninsula Plaza (6337 3661), Tanglin Mall (6235 0692)
Factory Outlet Store	Holland Village (6778 4818), IMM Building (6560 1508), Orchard (6736 3559)

Fairprice Ang Mo Kio Avenue 8 (6457 0930), Bedok North St 1 (6443 8038), Bishan (6353 6036), Bukit Timah (6469 6245), Changi (6449 8611), East Coast (6348 0826), Jurong (6560 8547), Queenstown (6778 6443), Serangoon Central Drive (6289 1647), Siglap New Market (6448 4285), Tampines (6781 9306), Tanjong Pagar Plaza (6224 5703), Tiong Bahru (6273 4325), Toa Payoh (6250 8019), Yishun MRT Station (6755 4233)

Fendi Ngee Ann City (6887 5981), Orchard (6229 8176)

Flash & Splash The Heeren (6734 4029), Pacific Plaza (6738 2270), Plaza Singapura (6238 7868)

Fossil The Heeren (6836 6610), Pacific Plaza (6734 1516)

Giant IMM Bld, 2 Jurong East St 21 (6565 4700), Parkway Parade (6565 4700), Sembawang Shopping Centre (6565 4700), Turf City (6565 4700)

Giordano Junior Ngee Ann City (6735 8265), The Paragon (6238 2306), Raffles City Shopping Centre (6336 5305)

GNC Ang Mo Kio Central (6752 5227), Bedok Central (6446 4355), Bukit Panjang Plaza (6769 6795), Centrepoint (6834 0616), Funan The IT Mall (6339 0155), Great World City (6835 0648), Jurong Point (6790 8956), Novena Square (6255 6047), Parco Bugis Junction (6337 1230), Parkway Parade (6447 6029), Plaza Singapura (6837 0508), Raffles City Shopping Centre (6336 0145), Suntec City Mall (6836 4550), Tampines Mall (6781 8360), Tanglin Mall (6887 4392)

Golf House Ngee Ann City (6355 1111), Raffles City Shopping Centre (6337 6855), Suntec City Mall (6332 1495)

Gramaphone CBD (6538 4828), Centrepoint (6736 1852), Colonial District (6337 6828), International Plaza (6324 1595), The Paragon (6235 3105), Parkway Parade (6348 2848), Scotts Road, Orchard (6235 2011)

Guardian Ang Mo Kio MRT (6553 7378), Changi Airport Terminal 2 (6545 1566), Gleneagles Hospital (6472 1941), Marina Square (6333 9565), Ngee Ann City (6738 8045), Parkway Parade (6344 2101), Suntec City (6338 4377), Tampines Mall (6787 0648), Wisma Atria (6733 5317)

Gucci Ngee Ann City (6735 9188), Orchard (6732 3298), The Paragon (6733 1425)

Harris Great World City (6732 3679), Marine Parade Central (6342 5031)

Harvey Norman Centrepoint (6732 8686), Funan The IT Mall (6334 5432), Millenia Walk (6311 9988), Parkway Parade (6346 4705), Raffles City Shopping Centre (6339 3777), Suntec City Mall (6332 3463), Tiong Bahru (6225 6006),

HMV Colonial District (6238 7218), The Heeren (6733 1822)

Home-Fix DIY Bishan (6457 8038), Bukit Panjang Centre (6769 9550), Causeway Point (6893 1228), Compass Point (6489 2728), Great World City (6235 7308), Harbourfront Centre (6270 7038), IKEA Building (6474 5328), Jurong (6896 3280), Marina Square (6883 2038), Northwest Singapore (6765 1823), Plaza Singapura (6338 9330), Siglap Centre (6443 4541), Tanglin Mall (6738 6086)

The Hour Glass Lucky Plaza (6733 1262), Millenia Walk (6339 4870), Ngee Ann City (6734 2420), Peninsula Plaza (6337 8309), Raffles Hotel Arcade (6334 3241), Scotts Shopping Centre (6235 7198)

Hue Raffles City Shopping Centre (6334 5612), Scotts Road, Orchard (6738 3450)

Hush Puppies
Centrepoint (6734 3635), Great World City (6732 4991), Harbourfront Centre (6275 1963), Ngee Ann City (6735 1746), Plaza Singapura (6238 8029)

I Nuovi Cosmetics
Causeway Point (6891 0252), Century Square (6783 0835), Colonial District (6341 9593), Compass Point (6315 9251), Suntec City (6333 0833)

Isetan
Parkway Parade (6345 5555), Shaw House (6733 1111), Tampines Mall (6788 7777), Wisma Atria Shopping Centre (6733 7777)

Kalm's
CBD (6533 2044), Centrepoint (6734 3263), Century Square (6783 1689), Holland Road Shopping Centre (6468 8429), Ngee Ann City (6733 7093), Parkway Parade (6345 3881)

Kiddy Palace
Causeway Point (6894 2636), Century Square (6789 2848), Compass Point (6315 9323), Junction 8 (6254 3757), Jurong Point (6793 5383), Marina Square (6336 3713), Northpoint (6754 8847), Northwest Singapore (6764 0790), Parkway Parade (6346 2057), Toa Payoh (6352 7781)

Kinokuniya
Liang Court, Orchard Rd (6337 1300), Ngee Ann City (6737 5021), Parco Bugis Junction (6339 1790)

L'Occitane
Centrepoint (6738 0997), Citylink Mall (6238 8426), Ngee Ann City (6737 6312)

Lee Hwa Jewellery
Bukit Timah (6898 2162), Causeway Point (6893 1657), Citylink Mall (6835 9217), Harbourfront Centre (6270 6179), Marina Mandarin (6339 5572), Parco Bugis Junction (6334 2838), Peninsula Plaza (6339 7863), Plaza Singapura (6338 1930), Suntec City Mall (6333 4410), Wisma Atria Shopping Centre (6736 0266), Yishun (6759 4330)

Limited Etd
The Heeren (6836 9095), Queenstown (6476 3835)

Louis Vuitton
DFS Galleria, Orchard (6735 4525), Hilton Shopping Gallery, Orchard (6737 5820), Ngee Ann City (6734 7760), Raffles Hotel Arcade (6334 3876)

M)Phosis
Citylink Mall (6884 4481), Ngee Ann City (6737 2190), Raffles Place (6538 1789)

M1
Great World City (1800 843 8383), Ngee Ann City (1800 843 8383), The Paragon (1800 843 8383), Parkway Parade (1800 843 8383), Plaza Singapura (1800 843 8383), Raffles City Shopping Centre (1800 843 8383)

Magic Wand
The Heeren (6734 4784), Tanglin Mall (6887 3384), United Square (6259 4405)

Marks & Spencer
Centrepoint (6734 1800), The Paragon (6732 9732), Raffles City Shopping Centre (6339 9013), Wheelock Place (6733 8122)

mc2
Funan The IT Mall (6333 0577), Liang Court Shopping Centre (6334 4844), North Bridge Rd (6333 4544), Sim Lim Square (6336 0003), Suntec City (6333 0168)

Mont Blanc
Ngee Ann City (6735 5038), The Paragon (6238 7176), Raffles City Shopping Centre (6334 1903)

Mothercare
Causeway Point (6513 3210), Centrepoint (6513 3218), Newton (6513 3208), Parkway Parade (6513 3216), Plaza Singapura (6513 3213), Suntec City Mall (6513 3212)

Mothers Work
Great World City (6738 5886), Tanglin Mall – Maternity (6887 3571), Tanglin Mall – Mother & Baby (6738 2161)

MPH ◄ Afro Asia Bld (6222 6423), Novena Square (6353 7133), One Raffles Link, Citylink Mall (6835 7637), Parkway Parade (6348 1483), Raffles City Shopping Centre (6336 4232)

Mr Minit ◄ Centrepoint (6336 1138), Great World City (6336 1138), Parco Bugis Junction (6336 1138), Queenstown (6336 1138), Riverside (6336 1138), Siglap Centre (6336 1138), Tanglin Mall (6336 1138)

Museum Shops by Banyan Tree ◄ Asian Civilisations Museum (6336 9050), Singapore Art Museum (6338 1016), Singapore History Museum (6337 1877)

Nanyang Optical ◄ Bishan (6453 5021), Causeway Point (6894 2644), Compass Point (6315 9057), Junction 8 (6353 7828), The Paragon (6737 2908), Parkway Parade (6440 0566), Pasir Ris (6585 1291), United Square (6250 7768)

The Natural Source ◄ Causeway Point (6893 9371), Colonial District (6536 8478), Great World City (6836 9536), Junction 8 (6259 3070), Novena (6258 4065), Parco Bugis Junction (6334 7210), Parkway Parade (6469 0276), Raffles City Shopping Centre (6338 6839), Suntec City Mall (6341 9586)

Nine West ◄ Raffles City Shopping Centre (6336 5488), Takashimaya (6736 4896), Wisma Atria Shopping Centre (6735 6660)

NTUC Healthcare ◄ Great World City (6235 1601), Harbourfront Centre (6271 5100), Raffles City Shopping Centre (6337 1358), Tanglin Mall (6732 1380)

Ocean Paradise ◄ The Paragon (6836 2672), Tanglin Mall (6235 4718)

The Organic Paradise ◄ Chinatown (6220 8148), Orchard (6736 2089)

Origin Asia ◄ Chinatown (6226 2680), River Valley Road (6733 7384)

OshKosh B'Gosh ◄ Forum The Shopping Mall (6884 9597), Newton (6298 2895), Novena (6296 1895), Raffles City Shopping Centre (6334 9565), Suntec City Mall (6513 3367)

Party City ◄ Queenstown (6462 6011), Raffles City Shopping Centre (6336 2161)

Pet Lovers Centre ◄ Bishan (6452 6032), Holland Village (6463 9491), Orchard (6737 1083), Parkway Parade (6346 6413), Plaza Singapura (6336 6728)

Pets Kampong ◄ Great World City (6734 7089), Novena Square (6253 9190)

Picket & Rail ◄ Hougang Mall (6385 5740), Jurong (6561 5707), Marine Parade Central (6348 1076), Specialist Shopping Centre (6235 4169), Suntec City Mall (6836 9688), Woodlands Road (6362 2096)

The Ploh Group ◄ D'Apres Nous, 111 Emerald Hill Rd (6733 5156), Palais Renaissance (6737 7503), SPACE Furniture, Millenia Walk, 9 Raffles Blvd (6415 0000), The John Erdos Gallery, 83 Kim Yam Rd (6735 3307), The Ritz-Carlton Millenia, 7 Raffles Ave (6337 8888)

Popular Book Company ◄ Colonial District (6338 1375), Marine Parade Central (6793 5282), Orchard MRT Station (6838 0823), Thompson Plaza (6459 6167)

Prada ◄ Orchard (6229 8180), The Paragon (6735 5715), Palais Renaissance (6735 6762), Raffles Hotel Arcade (6339 9021)

Precious Thots	Raffles Place (6538 2128), Raffles City Shopping Centre (6332 1494), Parco Bugis Junction (6333 0963), Marina Square (6338 1776), Great World City (6333 6377), Suntec City Mall (6332 1493), Plaza Singapura (6336 6179)
Pretty Fit	Parco Bugis Junction (6337 5812), Plaza Singapura (6835 7749), Wisma Atria Shopping Centre (6836 3580)
Prints	Citylink Mall (6336 3316), The Paragon (6887 3008)
Robinson's	Centrepoint (6733 0888), Raffles City Shopping Centre (6216 8388)
Royal Selangor	Centrepoint (6235 6633), Clarke Quay (6268 9600), Raffles City Shopping Centre (6339 3958)
Royal Sporting House	Centrepoint (6732 5288), Funan The IT Mall (6338 8633), Great World City (6734 2983), Marina Square (6336 4149), Raffles City Shopping Centre (6337 6855), Scotts Road, Orchard (6734 7503), Suntec City Mall (6332 1495), Tampines Mall (6787 5711), Tanglin Mall (6735 5875)
Sasa	CBD (6532 2311), Great World City (6238 0195), Holland Village (6469 1629), Junction 8 (6258 0988), Parco Bugis Junction (6336 9180), Plaza Singapura (6339 0017), Wisma Atria Shopping Centre (6738 8232)
Samsonite	Ngee Ann City (6735 8870), Raffles Hotel Arcade (6334 0955), Shaw Centre (6734 8863), Suntec City Mall (6338 6557)
Sembawang Music Centre	Cathay Cineleisure Orchard (6738 7727), Funan The IT Mall (6339 4238), Orchard MRT Station (6738 2767), Parco Bugis Junction (6837 3128), Parkway Parade (6345 3063)
Shop N Save	Bedok Market Place (6243 5748), Ang Mo Kio (6453 9312), Clementi (6775 4632), Century Square (6789 3420), HDB Hub (6252 3244), Jurong (6560 0246), Serangoon (6481 9730), Tampines (6786 2877), Woodlands (6365 7103), Yishun (6257 5128)
Sincere Watches	Ngee Ann City (6733 0618), Orchard (6738 9971)
Singtel Hello !	Causeway Point (6894 1363), Citylink Mall (6332 2080), Compass Point (6481 8181), Orchard Rd (6395 4313), Parco Bugis Junction (6332 3123)
Sports Link	Novena (6354 9080), Queenstown (6471 2363), Tiong Bahru Plaza (6377 5600), Turf City (6462 6122)
Skin	Marina Square (6334 4492), HNB Tower, Orchard (6733 9520)
Starhub	OUB Centre (1800 782 7482), Plaza Singapura (1800 782 7482), Tampines Mall (1800 782 7482)
Sunglass Hut	Changi Airport Terminal 1 (6542 2110), Changi Airport Terminal 2 (6214 1563), Great World City (6235 8727), Millenia Walk (6333 1635)
Swatch	The Heeren (6737 1917), Junction 8 (6258 8355), Plaza Singapura (6334 8042), Raffles City Shopping Centre (6334 5951), Suntec City Mall (6336 9093)
Swee Lee Music Company	Colonial District (6336 7886), Sims Drive, Geylang (6846 3610)

Shopping Directory

Tannlines	The Paragon (6735 0215), Wisma Atria Shopping Centre (6235 8870)
Tiffany & Co.	Ngee Ann City (6735 8823), Raffles Hotel Arcade (6334 0168)
Times The Bookshop	CBD (6536 9124), Centrepoint (6734 9022), Holland Village (6466 5702), Plaza Singapura (6837 0552), Marina Square (6334 4650), Tampines Mall (6783 3106)
The Tomlinson Collection	Chinatown (6536 7478), Geylang (6744 3551), Raffles Hotel Arcade (6337 1700), Tanglin Shopping Centre (6733 1221)
Topshop	Parco Bugis Junction (6238 7927), Parkway Parade (6345 1750), Suntec City Mall (6336 4571),
Toys R Us	Forum The Shopping Mall (6235 4322), Jurong Point (6791 2252), The Paragon (6836 4865), Novena (6352 9320), Suntec City Mall (6336 3908), Tampines Mall (6787 0662)
Treknology 3	Queenstown (6466 2673), Tanglin Place (6732 7119)
Tumi	Ngee Ann City (6737 8862), Orchard (6735 4525)
Video Ezy	Central Singapore (6467 3438), East Coast Road (6446 1844), Parkway Parade (6440 9331), River Valley Road (6737 3007)
Warehouse	Marina Square (6338 0743), Raffles City Shopping Centre (6338 1062), Wisma Atria Shopping Centre (6836 3953)
Watches of Switzerland	Centrepoint (6738 0900), The Paragon (6732 9793), Scotts Shopping Centre (6737 3708)
Watson's	Centrepoint (6734 5019), Holland Road Shopping Centre (6468 1152), Lucky Plaza (6235 3357), Ngee Ann City (6735 4936), Siglap Centre (6442 0894), Suntec City Mall (6337 2372), Tanjong Pagar (6227 3176)
Women's Secret	Centrepoint (6737 5933), Great World City (6235 6367), Marina Square (6337 2209), Tanglin Mall (6836 8363)
World of Sports	Cathay Cineleisure Orchard (6884 4190), Harbourfront Centre (6275 4840), The Paragon (6735 4187), Plaza Singapura (6337 5094), Takashimaya (6835 1793), Wisma Atria Shopping Centre (6738 2451)
Xcessories	Junction 8 (6354 4909), Novena Square (6352 7225), The Paragon (6836 0886), Parkway Parade (6346 5221), Suntec City Mall (6337 2219)
Yamaha Music	Jurong (6458 3383), Plaza Singapura (6336 3311), Tampines Mall (6788 1336)
Zara	Great World City (6835 9595), Orchard (6733 0029), Ngee Ann City (6735 1018)

The world has much to offer.
It's just knowing where to find it.

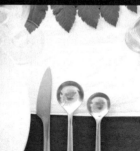

If you're an American Express® Cardmember, simply visit
americanexpress.com/selects or visit your local homepage, and click on
'offers'. You'll find great offers wherever you are today, all in one place.

selects

THE WORLD OFFERS. WE SELECT. YOU ENJOY.

Going Out

Going Out

Singapore's social scene is alive and kicking – and if anything, still improving. Going out here is what expatriates who love the city-state rave about, and what those who leave town often miss the most, perhaps second only to the food. One obvious reason it's nice to go out in Singapore is the evening respite from the heat – either outdoors in the cooler night air or the chilly air-conditioned world indoors. And a more recent arrival is a more cosmopolitan range of dining, socialising and drinking options; wine bars, off-beat film houses, comedy clubs, live music and theatre, late-night coffee houses, cigar bars and a wide array of alfresco options.

While there are places dominated by expatriates, the beauty of Singapore is the easy blend of people of different cultures and backgrounds, both Singaporean and expatriate. Singaporeans are brought up speaking English and studying in a highly urbanised environment. Often they have comparably western' pay levels and exposure to travel and foreign education.

The fact that Singaporeans are often as hip, if not more, than recent arrivals makes nightlife fun here. As does the fact that seeing an ang moh (Chinese for foreigner) is no big deal. This relative equality and anonymity is refreshing for south-east Asia, as is a culture becoming more permissive and accepting of modern vices like alcohol, sex and (more recently) gambling, plus partying until the wee hours. Do note that the dramatic exception to this permissive nature applies to recreational drugs and violent behaviour – where Singapore often practices a zero-tolerance policy, so do take care.

Alcohol is widely available here, increasingly until really late – and drinking is becoming commonplace with the obvious exception of Muslim restaurants or events. You may find it expensive, as alcohol is heavily taxed, so don't be surprised to pay $14 for a pint of beer. But competition in the bar scene is alive and well, so do look out for specials like generous happy hours and 'one-for-one' nights. Drinking a lot and getting rowdy is fine here too, although really 'losing it', so to speak, particularly if you get confrontational, is as frowned upon here as it is in most Asian countries. The upside of this is that Singapore is a relatively safe place to go out, and for women in particular, the ability to move around the well-populated areas at night without feeling at risk is a real plus to living here.

If you like eating out, with a special penchant for Asian cuisine, you have come to the right place. Singaporeans often replace 'how are you?' with 'have you eaten?' – to eat well is by their standards is to be well. And as with Malaysians, there is nothing unusual here about discussing the next meal while you eat the current one. Food here is not only good but it is available at all hours in hygienic surroundings, so experimentation is

Top Picks

Singapore has a vast array of restaurants, cafes, bars and nightclubs, and this section features a wide selection with around 150 reviews. But if the taxi's waiting and you simply don't have time to read every write-up, fear not – for listings of venues with great views, the top posh spots, the best places to eat outside or the ideal location for a romantic meal, check out our recommendations in the Top Picks table on p.388.

Cuisine List – Quick Reference					
American	393	German	401	Mexican	416
Australian	393	Hawker Centres	427	Middle Eastern	417
Brunch	394	Indian	401	Pizzerias	418
Chinese	394	Indonesian	403	Seafood	418
Dinner Cruises	397	International	403	Singaporean	419
European	398	Italian	410	Spanish	421
Far Eastern	398	Japanese	413	Steakhouses	421
Food Courts	428	Latin American	415	Thai	421
French	399	Mediterranean	416	Vietnamese	422

highly encouraged. And while there are named gourmet restaurants, the right local morsel can be almost as fantastic for as little as two dollars.

After work drinks are common here, while dinner time stretches from before dark until reasonably late – with last orders typically around 22:00 at most restaurants. Pubs tend to open until 01:00, while bars and clubs can go until 03:00, and can increasingly apply for all-night licenses, a rarity still in Asia even compared with more famous party spots like Bangkok.

Eating Out

People in Singapore eat out a lot, and the dining scene is developing and changing. From the corner hawker stalls to the finest French restaurants, there is a lot of variety. Understandably, the city-state is best for those who enjoy Asian food – and the variety of localised cuisines, Chinese, Malay, Indian, Thai, Vietnamese and other regional styles is superb – to the extent that local people will refer you to the exact dish or must-try and where to have it. And low and behold, when you arrive, there is a queue for that exact dish.

There is a rich variety of restaurants in the fine dining category, with world class wine selections and some excellent ambience – in garden parks, beside golf courses or with sweeping views of the city or sea. Singapore has a lot of wealthy residents and guests, plus dining is a popular way to entertain clients or business partners – so expect to have to book at the best places, especially if they are new and come recommended.

Probably where the Lion City is most lacking for expatriates in particular is food in the mid-range, from $10 to $20 for a main course. Many expats notice the lack of sandwich bars and cafes, or find them over-priced for what they are. However, seek and you will find; there is usually more diversity than you expect at first.

Asia in general is family friendly, and you will usually find that staff will warm to serving children, no problem. Just be mindful of other guests – during 'maid's day off' (Sundays) when not everyone is as delighted by your screaming darling as you are.

Local Food

Singapore's health and hygiene consciousness is for lovers of Asian food, a mixed blessing. For many, the 'upgrading', that is the government's obsession, leads to a certain 'sterilisation' process when it comes to popular food spots. A common complaint is that the place is 'not the same' following renovations. Yet for foreigners, the obsession with hygiene opens up a new world of Asian cuisine. In most cases, those with a fairly well-travelled stomach can eat most things in Singapore – the occasional upset stomach on arrival will usually not turn out to be anything serious. So while 'street food' in Singapore is seldom served on the street, it is almost always safe if you stick to places with a good turnover that don't leave dishes to sit too long.

'Die Die, Must-Try'

As the local expression has it, Singaporeans are obsessed with finding the perfect dish – the perfect example of hainan chicken rice or katong laksa, for example. While fun to behold, this mania exposes a common difference between local and expat views on dining. For many locals, the dish in front of you is paramount, everything else secondary. For visitors, it is almost the opposite – the atmosphere and experience of the surroundings is almost as important than the meal, if not more so. After all, your first chicken rice usually tastes great no matter whose you try. For this guide aimed at expats, our reviews have taken a holistic approach – there are some places you need to go just for certain dishes, while others are worth it for the experience, as an introduction. After all, you always remember your first! Note that once your following of certain Singaporean dishes reaches cult status, KF Seetoh's guide Makansutra is a must buy (see Recommended Reads on p.57).

Parking

Parking is always a challenge in Singapore, but there are a few car parks around, plus a pre-paid parking voucher system to allow you to park on the street. Fines are easy to get, so it's best to buy the vouchers. Valet parking is also available at the better nightclubs, hotels and restaurants, but be sure to check beforehand if you plan to drive.

Delivery

Delivery is most common for pizza outlets (see Pizzerias p.418), yet increasingly being offered for local hawker food, Indian food and others. Ask your favourite local restaurant or try the internet for starters. Where delivery is not available, the option of a 'packet' or da bao (take-away) is very common for cheap and mid-range outlets. There are also a number of outlets that specifically cater to dinner parties (see Parties at Home on p.439).

Drinks

Other options **Alcohol** p.325

Alcohol is widely available throughout Singapore, outside places of worship and halal establishments. You can buy beer, wine and spirits in supermarkets and 7-Eleven stores until late, and outlets selling drinks range from coffee shops or hawker stalls to world-class bars with a wide selection of international brands.

Service Charge

Most restaurants include a service charge of 10%, so will not automatically expect a tip. A number of restaurants will also charge for moist towels or peanuts.

You must be over 18 to drink, and outlets may request photo ID on admission. Alcohol is heavily taxed as a luxury item. Typically you will pay $10 to $15 for a standard serving of beer, wine or spirits in a bar, more in a restaurant. The more upmarket, the more expensive. Look for the times of happy hours, when half-price or 'one-for-one' promotions are on offer. Drinking cheap can mean taking to the coffee shops or suburban bars, where a $5 to $8 large bottle of beer is more common. Regular travellers commonly stock up on duty free alcohol in the airport (the allowance is one litre each of wine, beer and spirits per person) and drink at home. Or start at home, and finish by hitting the town. The best aspect of Singapore becoming a more cosmopolitan city in recent years has been the advent of outdoor wine bars, classy cocktail bars, and character outlets set in forested areas or parkland – see Bars (p.430) for more details.

Drinking & Driving

Singapore operates a zero-tolerance policy on drink driving with hefty punishments for those found intoxicated. The police put up regular roadblocks late at night to catch offenders, so consider yourself warned. If you've had a tipple (or seven) take a taxi! They are good value, safe and abundant. Fares are very reasonable, though they increase during peak hours, within the CBD, and after midnight. Have a cab number handy for late hours (see Taxi Companies p.52).

Top Picks - Quick Reference

Romantic		Alfresco		Enjoy the View		Posh Spots	
Da Paolo e Judie	410	Da Paolo e Judie	410	Al Dente Trattoria	410	Crystal Jade Golden Palace	394
Epicurious	404	Epicurious	404	BLU	393	Golden Peony	394
Graze	404	Graze	404	Brewerkz	430	Hua Ting	395
Halia Restaurant	406	Halia Restaurant	406	Cross Roads Café	424	Iggy's	398
Ikukan	413	Le Tonkin	422	Epicurious	404	Jaan	399
Jaan	399	Pierside Kitchen	408	Hai Tien Lo	395	Keyaki	413
Le Tonkin	422	Pizzeria Giardino	412	Halia Restaurant	406	mezza9	407
Original Sin	416	Raffles Courtyard	419	Jaan	399	Raffles Grill	400
PS Café	409	Spinelli Coffee Company	426	Pierside Kitchen	408	Rang Mahal	402
Saint Julien	400	Table 108	420	PS Café	409	Saint Julien	400
San Marco	412	Vansh	403	San Marco	412	San Marco	412
The Cliff	404	Via Mar	421	The Cliff	404	The Cliff	404

For non-alcoholic drinks, Singapore offers lots of stalls selling fresh juices from $3 upwards – you choose the mix you want. Water is drinkable from the tap, so go ahead and don't be afraid to request ice water in restaurants. A wide range of foreign and local soft drinks are available. Try the ice teas, sugar canes and barley drinks for something different. Do watch sugar levels though, as Asians typically prefer their drinks very sweet.

Hygiene

People may complain about some things in Singapore, but hygiene is unlikely to be one of them. The city's reputation for cleanliness is well-known, and justified, in such a hot and humid country. All food outlets are carefully inspected for hygiene – one of the best aspects of living here is that it is safe to eat virtually everywhere.

Stomach upsets are not uncommon, especially when you first arrive. But in general, if you choose places with a high turnover of food and where food is not left sitting for long, you are pretty safe. For those with delicate stomachs, the indoor food courts are an even safer bet.

Special Deals & Theme Nights

Most bars run special deals on weekdays to draw in the crowds, while weekends usually take care of themselves. Themes include the standard ladies' nights, a few flight attendant nights (show your flight pass to get deals) and various drink specials. Happy hours usually go until 08:00, and generally the staff are kind enough to alert you to last call for happy hour so you don't miss the cheap beer by five minutes.

Restaurants will often have a lunch buffet during the week, but really pull out all the stops on the weekends, with Sunday brunch being an almost sacred institution for many.

Because Singapore observes the major Chinese, Malay, Indian and Christian occasions, each with a spin-off related to eating or drinking, the cultural calendar is packed throughout the year. In addition to the more traditional festivals, in pubs and expat areas you'll also find celebrations of the boozier kind including St Patrick's Day, Australia Day and 4th of July – not to mention FA Cup Night and the Superbowl.

Tax & Service Charges

Singapore has a 5% goods and services tax (GST), which is charged by most bars and restaurants. The government has announced that the GST is increasing to 7%, but exact details were to be announced in spring 2007. Hotels, restaurants and bars generally also charge a 10% service charge and a 1% CESS tax (a tourist tax collected by Singapore Tourist Board). Prices are generally shown on menus as the base price, with GST, service charge and CESS only calculated on your final bill. Some menus or advertising will show prices followed by three plus signs (eg. $25+++) to indicate the three additional charges added to the base price. Your bill will always state the amounts of the service charge and GST being charged at the bottom of your bill.

Tipping

Tipping is generally not expected, especially in the many restaurants that include a 10% service charge in their bills, but if you want to reward particularly good service, anything from 5% and up is considered generous. As an alternative to tipping Singapore has service awards, so you may nominate someone exceptional. In a city striving to improve its service sector, such incentives do help. Likewise, Singapore Tourism Board is a good place to send feedback on poor service.

Dress

Expats don't dress like tourists in Singapore – the 'hell in the tropics' outfits don't blend in. Residents dress in 'urban cool' when they go out, the biggest consideration is usually whether you are going indoor or outdoors – air conditioning or warm air - and dressing accordingly. Men are usually better off wearing long pants, and short sleeved shirts or smart T-shirts at night are ideal. Women should not be afraid to show a little skin if they choose. Upmarket establishments frown on shorts, sandals or sports shoes – while outdoor eateries are often very casual.

Quick Reference Icons

- 🌐 Explorer Recommended!
- 😊 Kids Welcome
- 🚫 Alfresco Option
- 😄 Have a Happy Hour
- 🎵 Live Music
- 🍺 Serves Alcohol
- 🚚 Will Deliver

Dine in contemporary style, the SQUARE's latest interactive show kitchen. "FOOD" is prepared right in front of your eyes.

Food at the SQUARE is Fresh, Fast & Funky

International Delight

Try signature local SQUARE favourites "Chilli Crayfish"

Chefs performing live in the SQUARE

LOCATED AT LEVEL 7 ▪ NOVOTEL CLARKE QUAY SINGAPORE ▪ OPENS DAILY FROM 6.30AM - 12 MIDNIGHT
177A River Valley Road Singapore 179031 Tel.: (65) 6338 3333 E-mail: fnb@novotelclarkequay.com

Restaurant Listing Structure

The Going Out section features a select 150 venues that will certainly keep you busy for a while. Each review attempts to give an idea of the food, service, decor and ambience, while those venues that really excel earn the coveted 'Explorer Recommended' taq.

Primarily, venues are listed by cuisine type (in alphabetic order) or within the cafe, bar, pub, nightclub sections, but if you want to go out for a specific occassion – such as to dine alfresco, check out a band, treat the kids or indulge in a happy hour, check out the icons for what the place offers (see Quick Reference Icons on the previous page). For recommendations of Singapore's best eating out options, refer to the Top Picks table on p.388 for listings of romantic venues, alfresco eateries, posh spots and places with great views.

If you want to plan your evening around a particular location – maybe you have guests in town and you want to dine in their hotel or a hotel nearby – then simply turn to the index at the back of this book. Each of the hotels (or any other location with restaurants and bars) will have a list of all its outlets and their cuisine category.

Discounts

Singaporeans love a bargain, and there are discounts galore for going out – from happy hours to credit card specials and loyalty cards. Keep your eyes peeled... you won't need to look far!

Vegetarian Food

The best place to start for vegetarians is local cuisine – among Singapore's mix of cuisine styles many Indians are vegetarians, while Thai and Vietnamese cuisines in particular also have a lot of non-meat choices.

On the other hand, Chinese restaurants may tell you that a dish has no meat in it only for you to find a bit of chicken it floating in your dish, so always double check before you order. However, there are some Chinese restaurants that are completely vegetarian, serving a range of mock meat dishes from duck and fish to a whole suckling pig, fairly close in taste and resemblance to the real thing, but made entirely of gluten. Specialist western vegetarian restaurants are less common – but for award-winning Mediterranean food that even non-vegetarians rave about, try Original Sin in Holland Village (p.416). Meantime, enjoy the plentiful fruit stalls, where a selection of cut fruit with ice will only cost of few dollars.

For those who include fish as part as their diet, Singapore has a wide variety of fish and seafood outlets. In Food Courts, try the Yong Tao Foo stalls, where you can load your own plates with fish balls and vegetables.

All You Can Eat & Drink

Other options **Brunch** p.394

All-you-can-eat buffets are popular with expats – not just on Sundays, when brunch is a big thing for many people (see p.394), but also throughout the week. Just about all the major hotels offer buffets at one or more of their outlets, check local press for current deals. Favourites include the Shangri-La's The Line (p.406), Oscar's at the Conrad Centennial (p.408) and Straits Kitchen at the Hyatt (p.409) where you can enjoy buffet style breakfast, lunch or dinner. Over at The Raffles Hotel, the curry buffet at the Tiffin Room (p.410) is a hot favourite. Just remember to wear loose clothing...

Local Cuisine

An incredible international mix and universally popular, Singapore's cuisine is a must-try. Dishes like hainan chicken rice, katong laksa, nasi padang (various dishes with rice), chilli crab and roti prata are closely associated with the culture and for many expats, finding new food favourites is a highlight of their stay. Generally served spicy (piquant) and with a variety of condiments on the side, 'eating local' here is easy, affordable and enjoyable. So get stuck in there, and as they say, 'Let's Makan (eat).'

American

Shangri-La Hotel
Orchard
🚇 **Orchard**
Map 14-A3

BLU

6213 4598 | www.shangri-la.com

With a lovely view high above the Orchard skyline, BLU has a lovely hushed jazz club feel. Amidst Philippe Starck lamps and Wedgewood settings, the menu is one of Singapore's finest – west coast Americana with a twist of French flair – including Maine lobster paella and superb cuts of beef. Sample the degustation menu for a fine selection of dishes. With a cool and sophisticated atmosphere, complete with crisp, white table clothes, the single room that encompasses all of BLU has a touch of the exclusive without feeling stuffy. The perfect place for chic dining.

50 Cuscaden Rd
Orchard
🚇 **Orchard**
Map 14-A4

Hard Rock Café

6235 5232 | www.hardrock.com.sg

Just off Orchard Road, it's not like you're going to miss the Hard Rock Café as there's a whopping 1961 Cadillac sitting above the entrance. Expect continuity, from the friendly smiles and awesome service (the folks that work here really do get into the spirit of things) to the list of good ol' American and Tex-Mex mainstays like the sumptuous burgers and sizzling fajitas. The menu is mainly carnivorous with some seafood thrown into the mix, but there is also a selection of vegetarian alternatives. At around 22:30 the mood moves up a couple of notches, with young people flocking to keep a beat to the DJ (on every night) or the live band (check schedule). There is zero formality and the HRC doesn't normally like taking reservations so just get here and allow yourself some waiting time. And just so you know, you can order food at either of the two great bars.

The Paragon
Orchard
🚇 **Dhoby Ghaut**
Map 14-B4

Lawry's The Prime Rib

6834 9586

First established in Beverly Hills in 1938, Lawry's in Singapore continues their tradition of offering delicious food and exceptional service, all at top-notch value. The decor exudes a feeling of old-world American elegance: magnificent paintings adorn the main dining and private rooms, which are rich with dark woods to reiterate the luxury of a bygone era. Americans will be pleased to know the quality of the food here is as fine as back home. Aside from prime ribs, the menu boasts of beef tenderloin, rack of lamb, boneless chicken breast, lobster, salmon and seasonal fish dishes. Come for the exceptional quality of the meat grilled to perfection because the preparation and presentation is plain, simple and meticulously traditional. The lunch special is a more affordable way to taste the best of what Lawry's has to offer. A special children's menu is available.

Australian

52 Circular Rd
Chinatown
🚇 **Chinatown**
Map 17-C2

The Moomba

6438 0141 | www.themoomba.com

Huge, vibrant Aboriginal paintings and motifs decorate this warm and cosy restaurant converted from a two-storey shophouse. Moomba, translated from Aborigine, means 'let's get together' and the casual, unpretentious and fun-loving spirit of Australians has been well captured here. Characteristic of modern Australian cuisine, the food is not fussy, light, refreshing with a focus on fresh flavours and clever combinations of herbs and vegetables. For an appetiser, try the caramelised figs with blue cheese and for the main, a barbecued kangaroo loin with a white truffle infused soya glaze and wasabi potato mash. You'll soon get the idea why this place is unique. All menu items come with a wine recommendations, mainly an Australian or New Zealand option.

Brunch

Other options **All You Can Eat & Drink** p.392

Sunday brunch is a popular pastime in Singapore, and the variety to choose from is immense. Most brunches are buffets, offering one price for food only and another including free-flowing alcohol, such as champagne or Bloody Marys. The array of food on offer is often staggering, with enough seafood, roast meats, sushi, pasta, dim sum and sinful desserts to overwhelm even the most voracious appetite. The Four Seasons (Orchard, 6734 1110) is widely thought to have one of the best one in town – and also has an excellent a la carte dim sum buffet upstairs – but individual tastes will dictate which becomes your favourite. Other top brunches include The Greenhouse at the Ritz-Carlton (p.406), Cross Roads Café (p.424) in the Marriott, Marmalade Pantry (p.407), Mezza9 in the Grand Hyatt (see p.407) and the Shangri-La Hotel (6737 3644) – with their popularity making reservations a necessity. Some venues, such as Mezza9, offer private rooms for larger groups. Prices start around $70 and can run up to $120 including champagne.

Chinese

Other options **Far Eastern** p.398

The Paragon
Orchard
🚇 *Somerset*
Map 14-B4

Crystal Jade Golden Palace

6734 6866

The Crystal Jade chain of restaurants spread across the island are synonymous with invariably consistent quality, good food and value for money. The Crystal Jade Golden Palace is the flagship and showcases its haute cuisine. It is in a class of its own and ranks among the very best of restaurants in Singapore. The main dining room, with its high ceilings and dark wood running through the restaurant exudes a classy, modern finesse. The regal ambience befits the cuisine which connoisseurs unanimously concur is superlative. The menu is focused on both Teochew and Cantonese dishes such as the signature barbecue pork, crispy prawn dumplings and shredded chicken in spicy sauce. Many of the dishes are expensive because of expensive seafood ingredients such as shark's fin or abalone; however, dig deeper into the thick menu and more down-to-earth and homely fare can be found. Golden Palace is also renowned for its Hong Kong-style congee, hand-made noodles and dim sum.

Conrad Centennial
Suntec
🚇 *Bugis*
Map 17-D1

Golden Peony

6432 7482 | www.conradcentennial.com.sg

Long renowned as a premier Cantonese restaurant, Golden Peony is famous for its unique east-meets-west menus prepared by Hong Kong chefs. The lush interiors reflect this east-west juxtaposition: teak screens and wall sized Chinese paintings set beside modern furniture yielding a contemporary charm that epitomises finesse. Golden Peony is famed for its rare dim sum specialities otherwise unavailable in Singapore. Its Cantonese dishes are delicate, refined and use ingredients specially imported from various parts of China. In response to the increasing demand for western wines with Chinese cuisine, the restaurant boasts a master wine list matched to its menu.

Pan Pacific Hotel
Marina Bay
🚇 **City Hall**
Map 17-D1

Hai Tien Lo

6826 8338 | *www.singapore.panpacific.com*

Encapsulated by full-length glass windows 37 floors above the Marina Bay, Hai Tien Lo is one of Singapore's premier sky dining restaurants. Since its launch in 1986, the restaurant has consistently maintained a reputation for innovative Cantonese dishes of exceptional quality. In tune with the city's more cosmopolitan sophistication, this institution has recently undergone a transformation. The decor, with a crisp, modern Chinese ambience, perfectly complements the culinary creativity of its new chef, the dynamic Lai Tong Ping. With many years of experience under his hat, the end result is a steady stream of regular guests feasting on the immaculately presented signature dishes such as Special Trio of Treasures, Fried Imperial Swiftlet's Nest in Egg White and Fillet of Cod in Japanese Sake Sauce.

Orchard Hotel
Orchard
🚇 **Dhoby Ghaut**
Map 14-A4

Hua Ting

6734 3880 | *www.millenniumhotels.com*

Winner of numerous prestigious awards, this posh restaurant is famous for its intricate Asian delicacies and Cantonese specialities created by master chef Chan Kwok, born in Hong Kong into a long family line of chefs. The extensive menu is innovative yet traditional; its most popular dishes cannot be found anywhere else. To keep customers returning, his team of chefs is constantly creating new dishes. For dim sum connoisseurs, Hua Ting is paradise; expensive ingredients are used to concoct unique blends of flavours. Take for example its steamed or pan-fried carrot cake with dried scallop, or baked mango and chicken tarts. Distinguishing Hua Ting from many other Chinese restaurants is the polished service and staff who can readily explain the menu items in detail. Reservations, particularly for lunch, maybe required days in advance.

30 Victoria St
Colonial District
🚇 **Boon Keng**
Map 17-C1

Lei Gardens

6339 3822 | *www.leigardenrestaurant.com*

Its list of awards reads as long as some restaurant menus. Lei Gardens is regarded as an institution among Chinese restaurants, famed for its superb quality, rigorous standards and innovative Cantonese cuisine. The service standards are on par with the food. The decor, while unmistakably upmarket, is in the style of typical Chinese restaurants. Food tastings among its chefs are conducted regularly to incorporate feedback from customers, always with the aim of perfecting, perfecting and perfecting. The dishes are light, refined and express the best of traditional Cantonese cooking techniques. Catering to the well-heeled or corporate customers on an expense account, the restaurant is not sparing in the use of expensive ingredients (seahorse, exotic herbs), nor the time and effort taken to prepare a dish; the result justifies the means. For those adamant that only Hong Kong dim sum is dim sum, Lei Gardens is the place in Singapore for them.

395

Madam Butterfly

Clarke Quay
Riverside
🚇 *Clarke Quay*
Map 17-C2

6557 6266 | www.indochine.com.sg/clarke

With the entrance flanked by terracotta warriors and a large fishtank amidst bold pinks and blues greeting you as you enter the restaurant itself, one can tell that Madam Butterfly is a theatrical take on ancient Chinese tradition. Housed in Clarke Quay's oldest Chinese building and serving modern Chinese cuisine, this restaurant is an ideal place for big-night-out dinners, complete with colour, drama and the promise of a nightclub atmosphere downstairs. One of a string of Indochine outlets in Singapore opened by Laotian Australian entrepreneur Michael Ma, although this is not his best in terms of culinary feats, the food is tasty and hearty, and it makes for a fun place to dine on modern Chinese food with the perfect atmosphere before you get the party started.

Mushroom Pot

Singapore Indoor
Stadium
Kallang
🚇 *Kallang*
Map 14-F4

6342 3320 | www.mushroompot.com

A first of its kind in Singapore (and possibly the only one of its kind), the Mushroom Pot features over 20 types of imported and wild mushrooms. Apart from being delicious to eat, mushrooms have long been known to contain healing properties and are high in protein, minerals and vitamins. Besides having unheard-of mushrooms in every dish, this restaurant's novel Chinese fusion is unique. Signature dishes include the sliced mushrooms and potatoes covered with fish roe and melted cheese; and the codfish topped with matsutake mushrooms and a tangy sauce with a touch of curry. One must-try dish is the mushroom hot pot (steamboat) which gives you the chance to savour a variety of mushrooms all in one go.

My Humble House

Esplanade - Theatres
on the Bay
Marina Bay
🚇 *City Hall*
Map 17-D2

6423 1881 | www.tunglok.com

This restaurant serves up a completely different experience of upscale Chinese dining: the cuisine is modern Chinese and the decor is neo-classical. Dramatic juxtapositions of fabrics, shapes and furniture design shatter any pre-conceived notions you may have of a Chinese restaurant. Tremendous license has been given to the chefs to express their creativity and the food is not only novel, it's good; with equally aesthetic presentation. Ask for the 'Simple Satisfaction', a prawn dish with unique sauces. If you want noodles, then try 'Tenderness' made of diced beef tenderloin with fish noodles.

Peony Jade

Clarke Quay
Riverside
🚇 *Clarke Quay*
Map 17-C2

6338 0305 | www.quaysidedining.com

Situated by the bank of the Singapore River, Peony Jade simultaneously satisfies cravings for two very popular Chinese cuisines, Szechuan and Cantonese, on one table. The take on the food is modern and uses traditional cooking methods. The restaurant is a converted 'godown', now a contemporary restaurant with a touch of elegance. The chef encourages you to try the traditional Szechuan smoked duck with camphor wood and fragrant tea leaves, and the braised hot and sour seafood in a deep fried beancurd box. A Cantonese speciality is the deep fried codfish with oat cereals, an absolute must-try. The food ranges from classics to the highly imaginative, which all has two things in common: it draws crowds and wins awards.

Shang Palace

Shangri-La Hotel
Orchard
🚇 *Orchard*
Map 14-A3

6213 4473 | www.shangri-la.com

Traditional and ornate, Shang Palace will transport you (or attempt to, at least) to the Chinese dynasties of old. The extensive traditional Cantonese menu is filled with exotic specialities including dim sum, seafood dishes and many imaginatively concocted options. If you are unsure what to order, you can choose from a variety of tantalising signature dishes. There are set menus for couples and groups, and a vegetarian menu is also available. The staff are attentive, formal and can be relied upon to help you navigate your way to satiation. Shang Palace is open for lunch and dinner, and reservations are recommended.

Amara Hotel
Telok Blangah
🚇 **Tanjong Pagar**
Map 17-C3

Silk Road

6227 3848 | *www.silkroadrestaurants.com*

Travellers have journeyed the Silk Road spanning China for trade, adventure or a walk through history. If you wish to travel it for the food, then you need go no further than the Silk Road restaurant. Highly trained chefs recreate the original and unique flavours of the dishes and maintain authenticity by using specially imported spices and sauces. Service staff know the culinary customs and history of the dishes in the menu and are happy to talk you through some of the more mystical choices. Warm, neutral colours and dim soothing lights create a contemporary and dignified mood. The kitchen is showcased and you can see your meal being prepared in front of you. Pair your food with an aromatic eight-treasure tea prepared by a tea master using a copper kettle with a metre long spout, or with a Chinese wine.

Ritz-Carlton, Millenia
Marina Bay
🚇 **City Hall**
Map 17-D1

Summer Pavillion

6337 8888 | *www.ritzcarlton.com*

Ideal for that important business lunch or impressing your in-laws, the Summer Pavilion offers fine Cantonese cuisine. Set among the hotel's lush gardens, the restaurant is filled with suits tucking into some of award-winning Master Chef Fok Kai Yee's exquisite creations such as baked cod fish with champagne sauce or a lavish pacific fish noodle soup with lobster. But anyone would be impressed with the good number of variations on two Chinese restaurant staples – shark's fin soup and bird's nest soup. Non-meat eaters can rest easy as there is a decent vegetarian menu to pick from.

Singapore Marriott
Orchard
🚇 **Somerset**
Map 14-A4

Wan Hao

6735 5800

Wan Hao serves up a great selection of authentic Cantonese dishes by the restaurant's chef from Hong Kong. Take your time here to enjoy the great ambience which fuses eastern and western decor. Sip one of their premium teas with names like Morning Blossom Pearl Tea and Forbidden Dragon Pearl. The restaurant specialises in shark's fin and bird's nest soup, but if you need some advice on ordering, the manager will be glad to help. The place is popular with ladies who lunch and executives – so if you are looking for a good Cantonese lunch on the company expense account, you won't go wrong here.

Dinner Cruises

Other options **Boat Tours** p.219, **Boat & Yacht Charters** p.218

Dinner cruises are popular with many who are new to Singapore (for one popular example, see the review on the next page). Not only do you get to fill your belly with good food, but you also get the chance to enjoy the evening breeze and a view of the skyline from the water, which is massively appealing, even if you already know the city inside out.

397

100 Kim Seng Rd
River Valley Road
🚇 **Outram Park**
Map 17-A1

SH Tours

6734 9923 | www.asiatours.com.sg

SH Tours offer the popular Starlite Dinner Cruise, where you can spend the evening cruising the waters of Singapore aboard a traditional Chinese junk with a Singaporean buffet dinner and live music for extra entertainment. This cruise departs daily from Clifford Pier at 18:00 and costs $39 for adults and $20 for children under 12. Embarkation is 15 minutes before departure.

European

Other options **Mediterranean** p.416, **Italian** p.410, **German** p.401, **French** p.399, **Spanish** p.421

The Regent
Orchard
🚇 **Orchard**
Map 13-F4

Iggy's

6733 8888 | www.regenthotels.com

Acclaimed chef Ignatius 'Iggy' Chan, who has worked in three of the finest kitchens in Singapore, has set up his own restaurant at the five-star Regent Hotel. Serving modern European food, Iggy's has a small, exclusive dining room; space enough for a mere 14 hungry diners, as well as a Japanese-style counter for another 16 people to feast. There is no menu, instead you'll be presented with three differently priced set menus to choose from, each changes at the chef's whim and according to his mood and season – it is his place after all. However, he is happy to modify dishes to suit individual palates. Iggy's has a few signature dishes that include Wagyu Beef Hamburger, Trio Foie Gras and Squid Ink Risotto. As expected of an artist and perfectionist, the restaurant is beautiful and subtly chic.

25 Church St
Chinatown
🚇 **Chinatown**
Map 17-C2

Oosters Belgian Brasserie

6438 3210

This place is popular with the Raffles Place crowd, and there is a whole section on the menu dedicated to the mussel. Take heed from this and try them, as they are truly not to be missed. The Belgians eat them by the kilo, and you can order yours here in 500g or 1kg increments. You can have your mussels in a variety of ways, topped with gruyere cheese or served in tom yam soup. Other items worth checking out on the menu are cold Belgian sausages with cheese, bitterballen, boeuf brabancon – a traditional beef stew, and kriek magret - a tender duck breast served with croquettes. To complete the experience, Oosters offers Leffe beer on tap, in addition to an extensive range of Abbey beers, Trappist beers and artisan beers.

Far Eastern

Other options **Vietnamese** p.422, **Thai** p.421, **Singaporean** p.419, **Japanese** p.413, **Chinese** p.394

3A River Valley Rd
Riverside
🚇 **Clarke Quay**
Map 17-C1

Coriander Leaf

6732 3354 | www.corianderleaf.com

The restaurant scintillates the senses with its unpredictability - from the casual yet stylish ambience of east and western influences in the decor to the piped-jazz music accompanying Middle Eastern, south Asian, south-east Asian and Oriental cuisines prepared with western techniques and sauces. The menu features both traditional and interpreted dishes moving from the essence of Asian cooking towards modernity. Take for example this appetiser: Vietnamese five-spice chicken confit, asian greens, extra virgin olive oil & balsamic reduction. Or for a main course, try the ginger-butter prawn with cherry tomato & mint relish, and coriander rice. Food presentation is inspired by French traditions albeit the cuisine is Asian. Or is it? Hard to tell, sometimes… you just have to try it because it's unique.

Asian Civilisations
Museum
Riverside
🚇 **Raffles Place**
Map 17-C1

Siam Reap II

6338 7596 | www.indochine.com.sg

Tucked in one corner of the Asian Civilisations Museum, right beside the waterfront and under a canopy of trees, Siem Reap II makes for one of the most magnificently romantic, alfresco dining experiences on the island. In the evenings, the dazzling backdrop of lights formed by Singapore's tallest skyscrapers, the live jazz band accompanying a spicy range of popular Cambodian, Laotian and Vietnamese dishes will invariably get you in tip-top spirits. Best of all, the cost of dining here is very affordable. After dinner, continue the night lounging in huge, comfortable sofas under the open sky. Siem Reap II is also renowned for its hugely popular sandwiches, available for lunch.

French

37 Duxton Rd
Tanjong Pagar
🚇 **Tanjong Pagar**
Map 17-C3

Creperie Ar-Men

6227 3389 | www.creperie-armen.com

This authentic French creperie from Brittany, a first in Singapore, gets appreciative nods from the French expats living here. Both food and ambience transport you to a cosy diner on the coast of Brittany where cuisine is marked by simplicity, a lack of pomp, and high-quality ingredients shipped in from France. The crepes are made on traditional cast iron griddles using a technique that dates back five hundred years. Bretons eat crepes like Italians eat pizza, and similarly what goes into a crepe is really up to the person making it; there are no rules to the combination of ingredients. There are savoury crepes as there are sweet varieties; some are as simple as butter, honey and lemon and others as elaborate as the Croix Alpine comprising potatoes, onion and bacon cooked in white wine sauce, with reblochon cheese sauce; or the Ty Breizh made from mussels, prawns, squid and clams cooked in white wine sauce, garlic, fine herbs and cream. A visit is made all the more worthwhile by the modest prices.

Swissôtel The
Stamford
Colonial District
🚇 **City Hall**
Map 17-D1

Jaan

6837 3322 | www.equinoxcomplex.com

There are less than a handful of restaurants in Singapore offering as spectacular a view of the city as Jaan. Perched atop the highest hotel on the island, the view, day or night, from the 70th floor is inspiring. Lining the floor-to-ceiling windows are tables for two; yes, Jaan is irresistibly romantic. The centrepiece of this intimately small and sumptuously decorated restaurant is the Murano crystal and silver chandelier running the length of the ceiling. The cuisine is modern French and the menu changes seasonally or according to the irrepressibly creative flair of Chef Michael Muller from Alsace. In him you'll find a chef who loves to mingle with diners and is happy to personalise his creations to individual palates. When it comes to matching wine to the food, you'll be wise to ask for their recommendations: they've done their homework and the matching is splendid.

501 Bukit Timah Rd
Bukit Timah
Map 13-E2

La Cuisine

6468 8850

La Cuisine is a small gem of a restaurant in an unassuming location with just eight tables inside and two out front. It has the cosy feel of a living room, while the elegant furnishings and framed haute couture ads on the walls give it a chic edge. From the warm crusty bread at the start of the meal to dessert at the end, dining here is a treat for your taste buds. Dishes are deceptively simple, but the flavours speak of authentic French food made with fresh, top quality ingredients. Choose from the excellent value, daily set menu or order a la carte. The wine list hosts an impressive selection of French wines, which the restaurant staff will be happy to help you pair with your food. If you don't live nearby, La Cuisine is well worth making a special trip down to try it out; if you live in the area, you may soon find it to be your favourite neighbourhood jaunt.

Raffles Hotel
Colonial District
🚇 *City Hall*
Map 17-D1

Raffles Grill

6337 1886 | *www.singapore-raffles.raffles.com*

Restored to its resplendent glory with most careful attention paid to detail, at the heart of this grand hotel is the Raffles Grill - the mother of French haute cuisine in Singapore. This formal restaurant, where a dinner jacket is highly appropriate, exudes the elegant luxury that lent the old world its charm, and where this cuisine is truly at home - traditional, classic French-style cooking. The service is immaculate and the wine list offers classic vintages from as far back as 1900.

3 Fullerton Rd
Riverside
🚇 *Raffles Place*
Map 17-D2

Saint Julien

6534 5947 | *www.saintjulien.com.sg*

The husband and wife team at Saint Julien have succeeded at serving traditional bourgeoise food perfectly enough to win both Restaurant Manager of the Year in 2005 and Singapore Restaurant of the Year in 2006. Chef Julien has presided over kitchens in the finest restaurants in Asia: The Raffles, The Peninsula Hong Kong and The Oriental Bangkok. There could hardly be a more perfect venue for a fine dining restaurant than the Fullerton Water Boathouse, an old landmark adjacent to the Anderson Bridge, with expansive unobstructed views of the river and skyline. The mood inside is luxuriously sophisticated. The a la carte menu caters to a complete French fine dining experience; from three choices of Brittany oysters, caviar, foie gras to shell fish such, also take a minute to pick between the cod a la provencal, lamb, duck, pigeon, a legendary cheese platter, desserts and one of the finest wine lists of any restaurant in the city.

3 Magazine Rd
Riverside
🚇 *Chinatown*
Map 17-B2

Saint Pierre

6438 0887 | *www.saintpierre.com.sg*

Often mistaken for French fusion cuisine, chef and owner Emmanuel Stroobant is quick to point out his technique is absolutely French, the difference is the Japanese ingredients. Highly creative and exceptionally refined in the interplay of flavours, the modern French dishes you find at Saint Pierre are as good as it gets in Asia. The husband and wife team are passionate about not just food but the whole dining experience. The service is warm, relaxed and highly professional. And the wine

matching is exceptional – Emmanuel is completing his second coffee-table book about matching wines, after several years of research. The degustation menu is a magical tour of flavours dancing on the palate. If in season, ask for the ravioli de crabe nageur comprising roasted swimming crab with eggplant, zucchini, herb and olive oil infused with pickled young galangal shoot and myoga espuma. For a memorable main, order the tout boeuf, 200 day aged wagyu beef served with, among other ingredients, poached foie gras, wild mushrooms, red beet braised in caramelised vinegar.

12 Chun Tin Rd
Bukit Timah
🚇 *Bukit Batok*
Map 6-C4

Vis A Vis

6468 7433 | *www.vis-a-vis.com.sg*

Recently renovated for a homely Mediterranean feel, Vis A Vis offers French fine dining in a casual setting where the entire family, kids and all, are welcome. The restaurant is well known for its rack of lamb and the especially tender grilled meltique sirloin, a marbled steak similar to Kobe beef, without the latter's astronomical price. The set lunch is excellent value for money, and the house is often full with local and expats from the nearby suburb and offices taking advantage of the specials.

German

9 Raffles Blvd
Marina Bay
🚇 *City Hall*
Map 17-D1

Paulaner Bräuhaus Singapore

6883 2572 | *www.paulaner.com.sg*

As you walk into Paulander Brauhaus, the focal point is its very ornate, and very German, in-house microbrewery - as well it should be being the only place in Singapore to have one. Paulaner is great for group bookings and a perfect venue for a big party, whatever the celebration. In fact, if you have a group between 10 and 15 people, ask and the resident brew master will take you on a tour of the microbrewery. You will also be guided through a beer tasting session where you will get to indulge on the different types of brew available. When it comes to the grub: well, the menu is split into two sections, Continental and then German specialities such as pork knuckles and Nurnberger Bratwurst with sauerkraut, which are not to be missed!

Indian

76-78 Serangoon Rd
Little India
🚇 *Little India*
Map 14-C4

Komala Vilas

6293 6980 | *www.komalavilas.com.sg*

After a hot morning's walk around Little India's flower markets and temples, one of the archetypal experiences is calling in for vegetarian food on Serangoon Road at Komala Vilas. Komala Vilas has been serving authentic Indian Food on Banana Leaves since 1947. With dishes like onion dosai with sliced onion filling, a snip at $2.40; tomato uttappam (pancake with tomato spread) for $2.50; or a samosa plate-puff

401

with mixed vegetable filling for $1.80, the price and formula work perfectly. Lined with whitewashed walls, sit at simple tables and enjoy people watching at this busy, egalitarian institution. Warning: for maximum effect, don't cheat and try the other outlets first.

Raj Restaurant

76 Syed Alwi Rd
Little India
Little India
Map 14-D4

6297 1716 | *www.rajrest.com*

Can't make up your mind between northern and southern Indian vegetarian food? Then Raj, in the heart of Little India, gives you a spectacular spread of over 200 choices at prices comparable to the other restaurants in the vicinity, but distinctly superior in quality and service. The ambience is warm, relaxed and relatively posh. The chefs are from India, which makes the tastes authentic and more refined than commonly available. You can order a simple plain dosai or chappati meal up to the rich, creamy paneers and kormas of Moghul India. They haven't missed anything and you won't miss the meat. Great value.

Rang Mahal

Pan Pacific Hotel
Marina Bay
City Hall
Map 17-D1

6333 1788 | *www.rangmahal.com.sg*

Rang Mahal takes Indian cuisine to a level you've probably never seen before. Once ranked as one of the top 100 restaurants in the world by Conde Nast Traveler magazine, the restaurant has a solid reputation and is busy most nights of the week, so reservations are recommended. The presentation is very modern, matching the hip interior, with beautiful carvings on the walls, sculptures, water features and smooth down-tempo Indian beats in the background. The open kitchen lets you watch the chefs at work cooking up all sorts of delicious dishes, while private rooms are ideal for more intimate gatherings. There's a choice of a la carte, tasting and gastronome menus, as well as wine or whiskey matched menus and a lunchtime buffet. The food, drinks and service are all top quality, the wine list is impressive and dishes range from traditional Indian to a just a hint of fusion.

Samy's

25 Dempsey Rd
Tanglin
Map 13-E4

6472 2080 | *www.samyscurry.com*

Understandably popular, Samy's delivers the perfect combination of great southern Indian home-cooked style food served on banana leaves in a breezy open colonial building, surrounded by big shady trees. As Dempsey Road becomes a new hip spot, Samy's just continues doing what it has always done – serving delicious morsels from buckets of curry which waiters pass around regularly, as well as tandoori, squid, fish head curry, rice and other treats. No air-con or reservations, but cold beer is available. Sit on the verandah if you get a chance for the best views.

Song of India

33 Scotts Rd
Orchard
Orchard
Map 14-A4

6836 0055

Spurred into action by the stereotypical images of India that have done a disservice to the modern nation today, the owners of Song of India set out to correct this misconception. The result is a stately, formal and luxurious home to refined Indian haute cuisine. The Christofle cutlery, Riedel wine glasses and fine artworks decorating the colonial black-and-white bungalow create an ambience of opulence. The stage is set for nine chefs from India, overseen by celebrated master chef Milind Sovani, to serve up a menu drawn from all over the country, with a special emphasis on Lucknavi cuisine - the food of Lucknow's royalty.

Attention has been made to ensure the food is the finest you'll find and also healthy – ghee is replaced by olive oil, and you're left with an authentic taste without the heavy stomach that often accompanies an Indian meal. The choice of dishes is immense: seafood from coastal Kerala; Luknavi cuisine with its complex and delicately balanced use of spices and marinades; creamy kormas and hot curries; naans and succulent meats from the tandoor… this restaurant sings beautifully a song of India.

Marina Square
Colonial District
🚇 **City Hall**
Map 17-D1

Vansh

6345 4466 | www.vansh.com.sg

While 'modern Indian' is often intererpeted as 'fusion food', this is definitely not the case at Vansh. Making its mark with stylish presentation and some distinctive dishes, the menu remains true to traditional Indian cuisine. Set on the water by the Kallang River, this is a great place to relax with friends. The outdoor area has plenty of space between tables for privacy and the the suitably low volume of the Bollywood music videos playing adds to the atmosphere rather than overpowering conversation. Indoors, Vansh's open kitchen takes centre-stage and you can watch the four chefs working the tandoor and the teppan as they prepare your dishes. The vibe is very funky, with loungy, comfortable furniture and a separate bar area at the back that is ideal for drinks. The attentive staff are happy to guide you through the menu, which is tweaked regularly, and make recommendations. The food is of good quality, making great use of spices and portions are moderate. It is pleasantly quiet during the week, but picks up on weekends, so reservations are recommended.

Indonesian

69 Killiney Rd
Orchard
🚇 **Dhoby Ghaut**
Map 17-C1

Warung M. Nasir

6734 6228

This humble restaurant is home to the Singaporean's dream: food which is cheap, good and convenient! For $5 or less (now that's cheap) you get excellent (it's better than good) Indonesian nasi padang, and it's only a five-minute walk from the centre of Orchard Road... how convenient is that? Hold on, it gets better. Not only is it air conditioned inside the warmly-lit restaurant using old-fashioned marble-topped tables, you get wonderful jazz non-stop to accompany your meal. And the service is unpretentiously friendly. Nasi padang consists of an assortment of spicy dishes (but not spicy 'burn'), pre-cooked and placed in pots behind the counter. Indicate what you want and this will be served up together with a plate of rice. You have a choice of beef, chicken or fish curries with a variety of vegetables to go with. Alternatively, you may simply stop by for a cup of coffee or tea along with some traditional kueh-kueh (desserts).

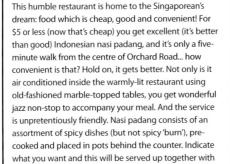

Halal Food

With a mainly Chinese vibe, there are many unusual, tasty treats on offer in Singapore - whether you try them or not is up to you! However, with a large Muslim population and many more tourists, halal food is also widely available and a certificate system is in place to avoid confusion. For extra guidance, get hold of the guide published by the Singapore Tourist Board which lists halal food outlets, from top restaurants to neighbourhood grocery shops.

International

Other options **All You Can Eat & Drink** p.392

Raffles Hotel
Colonial District
🚇 **City Hall**
Map 17-D1

Bar & Billiard Room

6412 1307 | www.raffleshotel.com

Perfect for a skive off work or a particularly long lunch, the Bar & Billiard Room serves up a fabulous buffet with a great selection of salads, fresh seafood, cheeses

403

and stews. Remember to leave space for dessert since the puddings, macaroons, icecream, and cakes are simply delicious. The bar serves up over 70 martinis and a good range of cocktails, including its signature Brass Monkey. In the evenings, there's a live band that plays here and the two antique billiard tables are available for a game. Perfectly old world.

The Cliff

The Sentosa
Resort & Spa
Sentosa
HarbourFront
Map 19-C2

6275 0423 | www.beaufort.com.sg

From the sounds of peacocks to the seabreeze off the ocean nearby, and seated amidst eye-catching decor by Japanese designer, Yasuhiro Koichi, The Cliff is perfect for a hushed and special meal away from the city chaos. Dishes arrive at your table looking superb, and usually interesting creations, like ocean trout confit with macadamia-sesame nougat – or warm chocolate truffle cake with cointreau icecream. Certainly not cheap, but an impressive spot that looks as good as it's food tastes – The Cliff lives up to its reputation of excellence.

The Colbar

9A Whitchurch Rd
Queenstown
Buona Vista
Map 16-C1

6779 4859

The Colbar is a Singapore expatriate institution, and mercifully escaped the developer's jackhammer in 2003 when highway pressures looked like closing it – in the end, it was moved. Wear your singlet and shorts and venture down memory lane for this lovely, casual slice of the past. A former canteen for British soldiers, The Colbar traces its roots back some 58 years. Now declared historically important, its relocation five minutes away from the original location, complete with original building, was thanks to heavy petitioning and is a blessing for those who yearn for classic fare. Dishes such as ox liver with peas and chips or a chicken curry that is the toast even of noted Singapore foodies, all taste refreshingly home-cooked – not such a common quality in Singapore any longer. Their Sunday brunch is done in downscale style and worth a visit.

Epicurious

60 Robertson Quay
Riverside
Clarke Quay
Map 17-B1

6734 7720 | www.epicurious.com.sg

Fancy some gourmet comfort food served at a rustic wooden table overlooking the river? At Epicurious, every delicious bite is testament to the freshness and quality of the ingredients, prepared by folks who obviously care about good food. Mismatched wooden furniture and crockery like grandma used to own add to the charm. The relaxed riverfront setting and friendly, unpretentious service are especially popular on weekends when breakfast is served all day (or until the breakfast items runs out). Families young and old, party people nursing hangovers and the occasional golden retriever share the charming alfresco patio. Excellent custom-built sandwiches and other light bites are available at lunch while dinner features more 'grown up' bistro fare. The intensely flavoured mushroom soup is a favourite, as is the fruit crumble (big enough to share). Take advantage of happy hour deals on the highly drinkable house wines and beers or bring your own bottle ($15 corkage applies). You can also purchase gourmet deli items to take home.

Graze

4 Rochester Park
Queenstown
Buona Vista
Map 13-B4

6775 9000 | www.graze.sg

As the name suggests, Graze is designed for dining at a leisurely pace in relaxed surroundings. Chic, contemporary, fresh and breezy are the motifs running through both the ambience and the country-style gourmet cuisine. The restaurant is located in a black and white colonial bungalow amidst lush greenery with a

Work Visas p.54
Weekend Breaks p.155

Written by residents, the Hong Kong Explorer
is packed with insider info, from arriving in a
new destination to making it your home and
everything in between.

Hong Kong Explorer Residents' Guide
We Know Where You Live

EXPLORER

romantic, warmly lit, alfresco dining area with hugely comfortable sofas under the open sky. Australian Chef Matthew Lawdorn has designed a menu of fine quality home-made cuisine, emphasing a fresh modern style. The creative touches are subtle but with a distinct touch of sophistication. The signature dishes deserve your attention; particularly the 'King Prawns 3 ways' – tempura, chilled and pan tossed with coconut coriander sorbet, and the soy lacquered wagyu ox cheek with coconut rice. Perfect either before or after the meal is the upstairs lounge bar called Mint, with delicious cocktails, cool mellow music, and a sofa bed on the terrace gazing over verdant gardens.

Ritz-Carlton, Millenia
Marina Bay
🚇 *City Hall*
Map 17-D1

The Greenhouse

6337 8888 | www.ritzcarlton.com

Popular with families, children are more than welcome to indulge in the opulence of the buffet selections at The Greenhouse. If you go for the Sunday Champagne Brunch, there's little more you can ask for to begin your week than the free flowing Moet & Chandon as well as lobster, fresh oysters, mussels, 50 types of cheese, foie gras and chocolate souffle. Service is excellent here with the staff making sure that your champagne flute is never dry. If you are here on other days, The Greenhouse kitchen, headed by Chef Benton Toh, offers a menu with Californian, Italian and Asian influences. For the Sunday brunch, be sure to make reservations a day or two in advance.

Singapore Botanic
Gardens
Tanglin
🚇 *Redhill*
Map 13-E3

Halia Restaurant

6476 6711 | www.halia.com.sg

Five minutes from the bustle of Orchard Road are the Botanic Gardens, a beautifully serene oasis of gardens and rainforest, where you'll find Halia (Malay for ginger), surrounded by one hectare of ginger with stunning foliage and colourful flowers. The friendly service, cosy ambience, and sheer peacefulness of the restaurant is a wonderful place to dine, day or night, or for breakfast or afternoon tea. The western-asian cuisine can be described as smart-casual food at lunch and fine dining at dinner. Halia's signature dishes are the crisp black pepper soft shell crab; roasted rack of lamb marinated in Javanese spices; and the seafood stew halia. For dessert, you must try

the cappuccino 'Dunking Pit' made with layers of warm chocolate, cool vanilla cream and iced coffee shavings together with a brownie for dunking.

Shangri-La Hotel
Orchard
🚇 *Somerset*
Map 14-A3

The Line

6213 4275 | www.shangri-la.com

The Line is Shangri-La's bold nod to modernist design and gastronomic play. Designer Adam Tihany is also responsible for big name restaurants such as Le Cirque and Per Se in New York. A departure from the traditional coffee-shop buffet, shining in white and orange under impressive studio spotlights, the all-you-can-eat buffet restaurant features 16 culinary stations offering dishes from over 15 cuisines. Choose from the sushi and sashimi counter, salad station, crustacean counter, noodle shop, western and Italian counter, wood-fired pizza oven, the grill, dim sum kitchen, wok station, tandoori ovens and the bar. One highlight is the ice-cream teppanyaki, hand rolled in nuts on an iced marble slab; and the chocolate fountain, a metre high cascade of melted milk chocolate, waiting for you to dip fat strawberries into. The 410 seater restaurant is popular at weekends, so booking is advised.

Palais Renaissance
Orchard
🚇 **Orchard**
Map 14-A4

Marmalade Pantry

6734 2700 | www.marmaladegroup.com

Located on Orchard Road, the Marmalade Pantry is a favourite stop for the city's trendy shoppers. This uber-stylish bistro serves as an oasis for a good healthy meal before continuing on their way. Set in an airy, light-filled atrium, the steel and mirror decor, and milk chocolate leather sofas make for a chic bistro with a decidedly relaxed and informal atmosphere. The menu, however, is one you'd normally associate with a fine-dining restaurant: salmon teriyaki with chilled soba, soft shelled crab and rocket, foie gras burgers. Dishes are deliciously innovative and cooked to perfection and all ingredients are exceptionally fresh. You'll find the chef accommodating, waiters friendly and the service well polished. The Sunday brunch is hugely popular and reservations are necessary.

**Singapore
Marriott Hotel**
Orchard
🚇 **Somerset**
Map 14-A4

Marriott Café

6735 5800 | www.marriott.com/sindt

With its prime location in the lobby of the Singapore Marriott Hotel, the Marriott Café is a great place to indulge yourself or impress others. The restaurant is best known for its buffets, of which there are four per day: breakfast, lunch, tea, and dinner, all offering sumptuous arrays of international cuisine. The tea buffet (15:00-17:30 daily) is a popular afternoon escape for shoppers taking a break from the frenzied crowds along Orchard Road. In the evening, the restaurant is ideal for dining with clients or in-laws, as the elegant decor is sure to impress. If buffets are not your thing, you are sure to find something to your liking on the extensive a la carte menu. Whatever you order, the freshness of the top quality ingredients used in the kitchen is evident with every bite, from crisp veggies to tender meat and rich desserts.

**Grand Hyatt
Singapore**
Orchard
🚇 **Newton**
Map 14-A4

mezza9

6416 7189 | www.restaurants.singapore.hyatt.com

The mezzanine floor of the Grand Hyatt offers the widest variety of haute cuisine dishes under one roof in Singapore. Nine different areas are set up in one hip and ultra-chic area for you to select from Japanese, Chinese, seafood, grilled meats, or desserts from heaven. You go from area to area and pick up sashimi, deep-fried soft shell crabs, wagyu ribeye, a wine or two, and on to dine in supreme comfort. The open kitchen concept is beautifully employed here, so you don't mind waiting and watching the preparation. With free Moet champagne, mezza9's Sunday brunch is still hard to top. Very much a family affair, the kids can scoot off to the playroom equipped with toys, games and a television and staff to take care of them while your epicurean quest continues unabated.

36 Club St
Chinatown
🚇 **Raffles Place**
Map 17-C2

Mozzaic

6325 3360

Mozzaic's unique selling point is its unusual, eclectic mix of three very different and unrelated cuisines – Japanese, European and Brazilian. While the varied fare is common for many hotel eateries, this 'international cuisine' concept is uncommon

407

for independent restaurants. Mozzaic not only works, but offers patrons more choice without compromising on quality. Their range of seven cuts, including beef, lamb, chicken and pork sausage, for the Brazilian churrasco is good value for money at $38 for unlimited servings sliced straight from the skewers. Recommended from the Japanese menu are an ingenious Japanese-Brazilian hybrid of a meaty chargrilled salmon head churrasco, and the tasty roast kamo - slices of simmered duck served cold with a mushroom and leek salad. The cheery interior with clean lines provides for a slightly up-market, though relaxed, eatery that guests feel comfortable at whether they are in their office smarts or their casual weekend clothes.

Conrad Centennial
Suntec
🚇 **City Hall**
Map 17-D1

Oscar's

6432 7481 | *www.singapore.conradmeetings.com*

Next time you are in the vicinity of Suntec City, head across the road to Oscar's on the sidewalk terrace of the Conrad Centennial Hotel. In contrast to its heavy-concept hotel restaurant rivals, the appeal of the Californian-styled Oscar's is its classy simplicity, with a rich array of cuisine options amidst a breezy and busy, yet friendly, ambience – making it an easy choice for shopping stops and business lunches alike. With three packed buffet offerings a day, this 24 hour cafe is a great choice for those on the run, offering comfortable indoor and outdoor dining options. Favourites to try include its signature caesar salad, prepared in front of you, your parmesan sliced with gusto fresh from the middle of a large round block. Also try the excellent local dishes, including sumptuous laksa with fat king prawns; excellent noodle dishes such as mee goreng and char kway teow, each served with tasty sambal.

1 Fullerton Rd
Marina Bay
🚇 **City Hall**
Map 17-D2

Pierside Kitchen

6438 0400 | *www.marmaladegroup.com*

This stylish waterfront restaurant and bar offers stunning views of the river and bay, and is ideal for a casual fine-dining lunch, a relaxed breezy afternoon coffee, convivial after-work drinks or a dinner rendezvous. Inside or outside, the subdued lighting and music complement the distinctive pared-down decor of modern clean lines - leaving one to focus on the food. Award winning chef Robin Ho presents dishes with delightfully creative touches. The menu, focusing on seafood, is truly international, with an emphasis on the freshest possible ingredients and their suppliers vary according to the season or day of the week! For instance, oysters are picked for the perfect size and flown in on the same day they're eaten. Waiters are well trained, friendly yet formal, accommodating but unobtrusive. The entire dining experience is consistently high: from clever cocktails, to appetisers, main courses and desserts, and the wine list is impeccable.

Singapore Marriott
Orchard
🚇 **Orchard**
Map 14-A4

Pool Grill

6224 1133 | *www.singaporemarriott.com*

Standing on the corner of Orchard Road and Scotts Road... you know what you need? A lift. Take the lift in the Marriott Hotel to the serene Pool Terrace, and the alfresco Pool Grill restaurant. Unknown to many, the Pool Grill offers a great respite from the downtown city beat, as you sit and stare at the aquamarine waters and smart blue of the beach loungers. Together with the rooms available on the Pool Terrace, the aim is to help lend the spot the feel of a resort in the city centre. High on calming appeal, the food is tasty fare – a solid selection of pizzas, pastas and salads at lunch time, and tempting grilled seafood towards the evening. For a reliable meal in a perfect city retreat, head up to the Pool Grill.

408

28B Harding Rd
Tanglin
Map 13-E4

PS Cafe

6479 1588 | www.pscafe.sg

PS Cafe was undoubtedly the 'it' restaurant of 2006. Brainchild of the trendy Project Shop in The Paragon mall, PS was an offshoot of the popular hidden gem, Blood Brothers Café. A much more ambitious project, they have certainly done their homework, with retro furniture, modern 1950s rectangular design, leafy tree view and a casual cool air about it. When you walk in, it feels more like California or Sydney than Singapore. Unfortunately at times, the excessive attitude from the staff reminds you where you are. The food is fresh, inventive and good value for what you get. Never mind the hype, walk in on a Saturday or Sunday for brunch (they don't take bookings), for a refreshingly casual yet quality experience.

Shangri-La Hotel
Orchard
🚇 *Orchard*
Map 14-A3

Rose Veranda

6213 4486 | www.shangri-la.com

This coffee house on the second floor of the Shangri-La is a perfect place to lounge away a lazy afternoon; boasting 101 teas to choose from, and a nice selection of English and Asian appetisers, mains and desserts. Remember to pace yourself with the food, because the brilliant spread includes cheeses, salads, dim sum, sushi and sashimi, roast chicken, curries, laksa, scones, cakes, and pudding. If you don't have the luxury of free time on weekdays, it is advisable to make reservations at the weekend for one of two high-tea slots from midday to 15:00 or 15:15 to 18:00.

Novotel Clarke Quay
Riverside
🚇 *Clarke Quay*
Map 17-C1

The Square ▶ p.391

6433 8790 | www.novotel-asia.com

Conveniently located in the Novotel Clarke Quay, The Square offers tasty, international cuisine served in bright, modern surroundings. You can choose between the buffet and a la carte options, either of which are guaranteed to satisfy. There are three buffet sessions per day - breakfast, lunch and dinner - while a la carte dining is available all day from 06:00 to 23:00. The buffet boasts stations with chefs on hand to prepare sashimi, pasta and local favourites to order. With so many dishes to choose from, it is tempting to fill up quickly on the delicious salads, meats, seafood, pastas, and more on offer; however, wise diners will save some room for dessert. A chocolate fountain and local delights such as durian puffs are only some of the treats that await you at the end of the meal.

Grand Hyatt
Orchard
🚇 *Newton*
Map 14-A4

Straits Kitchen

6732 1234 | www.restaurants.singapore.hyatt.com

Opened late in 2004, Straits Kitchen is a Singapore-inspired restaurant offering a genuine, yet elegant, portrayal of local food in the theatrical environment of a contemporary 'market place' setting – thankfully air conditioned, unlike the real thing. Renowned Japanese designer Super Potato has now matched its success of mezza9 upstairs with the interior, while the restaurant succeeds with its exhibition style in presenting not just the food of Singapore, but also a rich expose of the culture as well. From a menu of Chinese, Indian and Malay dishes, the restaurant serves up local favourites like laksa, fried hor fun, carrot cake, hainanese chicken rice, rota prata, and whole steamed fish. A fun experience, and the perfect buffet for lovers of local food.

Restaurant Timings
Most restaurants in Singapore have last orders at about 22:00. The more lively the neighbourhood, the more likely you are to find something for a late night/early morning nibble.

409

Raffles Hotel
Colonial District
🚇 **City Hall**
Map 17-D1

Tiffin Room

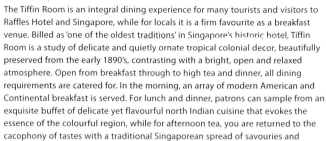

6412 1194 | *www.raffleshotel.com*

The Tiffin Room is an integral dining experience for many tourists and visitors to Raffles Hotel and Singapore, while for locals it is a firm favourite as a breakfast venue. Billed as 'one of the oldest traditions' in Singapore's historic hotel, Tiffin Room is a study of delicate and quietly ornate tropical colonial decor, beautifully preserved from the early 1890's, contrasting with a bright, open and relaxed atmosphere. Open from breakfast through to high tea and dinner, all dining requirements are catered for. In the morning, an array of modern American and Continental breakfast is served. For lunch and dinner, patrons can sample from an exquisite buffet of delicate yet flavourful north Indian cuisine that evokes the essence of the colourful region, while for afternoon tea, you are returned to the cacophony of tastes with a traditional Singaporean spread of savouries and sweets to help while the time away till dusk.

1 Orchard Blvd
Orchard
🚇 **Orchard**
Map 14-A4

Whitebait & Kale

6333 8025 | *www.whitebaitandkale.com*

Whitebait & Kale is a great example of Singapore's dining evolution – a restaurant which has done its homework on people's lifestyles and tastes. From its whitewashed walls and open kitchen, to chalkboard specials and stylish music selection, this is a place you could at eat every day, with smart food choices and a nicely busy atmosphere. Consciously billing itself as a 'food company', Whitebait is also a deli, bar, wine shop and events & parties company. Clearly positioned for the expat market living around the Orchard, Tanglin and Holland Village areas, its appeal to Singaporeans is also evidence that its formula works. Without feeling too pretentious, Whitebait appeals to the design and health-conscious alike – with its menu a tasty and creative selection that mixes classic favourites with inventive food specials and new taste blends.

Italian

Other options **Pizzerias** p.418, **Mediterranean** p.416

Esplanade
Marina Bay
🚇 **City Hall**
Map 17-D2

Al Dente Trattoria

6341 9188 | *www.aldente.com.sg*

Located in the Esplanade Mall, Al Dente Trattoria is the perfect place to grab a bite before or after a performance at the adjacent Esplanade Theatres on the Bay. The best seats in the house are on the roof-top patio, where enchanting views of Marina Bay and the Singapore city skyline unfold in front of you. There is also seating in a more formal, indoor dining room downstairs, if you would prefer to enjoy your meal inside. Tables complete with neat white linen and candles set the mood for a romantic meal in elegant surroundings. From a menu of predominantly Italian food, particularly pastas and wood-fired pizzas, the staff are more than happy to recommend dishes, and help match it with a wine from the extensive wine list from four continents, including a selection of 20 premium wines. There are also some well-priced lunch specials. Al Dente has three other venues around Singapore - check the website for more details.

81 Neil Rd
Chinatown
🚇 **Chinatown**
Map 17-B3

Da Paolo e Judie

6225 8306 | *www.dapaolo.com.sg*

Bring a healthy appetite to Da Paolo e Judie — you'll want to finish every last tasty morsel of the generous portions served. This fine dining establishment offers mouthwatering northern Italian cuisine with a focus on seafood and freshly-made

410

pasta. Fresh, natural flavours and the use of quality ingredients (many of which are sourced directly from Italy) means you can practically taste the sea in their signature seafood dishes. Attentive, knowledgeable staff are quick to provide recommendations when the vast menu selection threatens to overwhelm. Leave room for dessert, the chocolate lava cake is to die for. You may bring your own wine (corkage starts at $35) but why bother when you can choose from a wide-ranging array of very decent wines available in-house, each personally selected by Paolo Scarpa himself?

36 Purvis St
Little India
Lavender
Map 17-D1

Garibaldi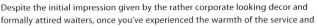

6837 1468 | *www.garibaldi.com.sg*

Despite the initial impression given by the rather corporate looking decor and formally attired waiters, once you've experienced the warmth of the service and the genuine effort to diners feel special and at home, you'll see why Garibaldi is one of the most popular Italian fine dining restaurants. The food is very much the primary attraction, and Chef Roberto, part owner, is completely hands-on in the kitchen. He has also personally selected the 550 plus wines that make up one of the finest lists in Singapore. Dishes are carefully crafted using authentic Italian ingredients, many flown in from Italy, with the flavours and textures beautifully balanced. Signature dishes include the lamb tenderloin with porcini mushrooms and balsamico sauce. If in season, ask for the white truffle pasta – a simple preparation that is a real treat for your tastebuds. Although one may initially feel disinclined to bring children to Garibaldi, they are very often found happily here.

207 River Valley Rd
River Valley Road
Clarke Quay
Map 17-B1

Il Gladiatore by Fuenti

6333 8875

Previously known as Fuenti, Il Gladiatore opened early in 2006 with a Roman theme. The staff fitted in togas and the pseudo roman pillars might not be for everyone but it is well worth getting past, especially for meat lovers. You could also consider embracing your inner gladiator or slave girl by hiring the restaurant for a theme party. Restaurants offering the usual pasta favorites or tiramisu might be dime a dozen but you can count on Il Gladiatore to give you a slightly different take on Italian cuisine. There is a strong emphasis on meat here and specialities worth checking out are the baked artichoke on a slice of delicate air-dried beef and the sizzling grilled meat platter for two. To accompany your meal, the wine list offers a good selection from various regions in Italy, in addition to Australian, French and New World wines.

Sentosa Golf Club
Sentosa
HarbourFront
Map 19-D3

Il Lido

6866 1977 | *www.il-lido.com*

A newcomer to the scene in 2006, Il Lido is a modern Italian restaurant which combines hip surroundings, breezy views of the ocean and golf course and a colourful lounge bar bedecked with modern furniture and smooth music. Young high-flier owner and manager Beppe De Vito has produced a restaurant that

411

matches his personality – sociable, hip and passionate about food. Inspired by Venice's Lido Island, its major advantage lies in its remote and spacious surrounds and ocean views, with the island location offering a ambience that the city restaurants struggle to match. The food is fantastic – soulful ingredients lovingly prepared, with staff well trained to understand food and wine. While not a hushed meal choice, book your table outdoors near the balcony for a more romantic evening; or indoors for more buzz. For a great atmospheric meal that becomes a few cocktails and tunes later, this is a great choice.

27 Tanjong Pagar Rd ◀
Chinatown
🚇 **Tanjong Pagar**
Map 17-C2

Oso

6327 8378 | www.oso.sg

Step inside Oso, and for a moment you are in Italy. The decor, colours, setting, music and cuisine are all authentically and traditionally Italian. With no fusion items, there's nothing exotic about the menu – it's straightforward Italian fine dining, where the magic is created using superbly fresh ingredients, a passion for perfection and a huge dose of Italian zest. The service is first rate and waiters can be relied upon to provide sound recommendations. Dishes such as eight hour oven baked lamb rack 'agnello' with black onions and salsifis, or roasted cod filet 'merluzzo' in balsamico sauce served with rosemary potato puree are perfectly accompanied by rare vintage collector's wines. Reservations are imperative.

Chijmes ◀
Colonial District
🚇 **Lavender**
Map 17-C1

Pizzeria Giardino

6338 8711

If you can picture yourself casually gobbling truffle-laced ravioli amidst lush lawns and fairy-lit trees, then Pizzeria Giardino at Chijmes is your place. Relaxed and friendly, the energetic staff and smooth tunes conspire to create a warm and convivial atmosphere that attracts couples and groups alike. Best known for its delicious wood-fried pizzas, the open air kitchen produces a range of tasty Italian dishes at reasonable prices alongside classic favorites and cheekily-sweet desserts. It does pay to get in a little early as this venue is popular with both residents and visitors who can be forgiven for settling in and enjoying the atmosphere late into the night.

The Fullerton ◀
Singapore
Chinatown
🚇 **Raffles Place**
Map 17-D2

San Marco

6438 4404 | www.sanmarco.com.sg

Situated in the old lighthouse in the majestic Fullerton Hotel, San Marco is an intimate restaurant with stunning views of the sea. The decor is minimalist to say the least; everything is elegantly precise, with anything that could distract the senses removed to leave you at peace to savour the delicately-balanced and beautifully-refined Italian creations of chef Kelvin Lee, protege of celebrity chef Emmanuel Stroobant. The quality of service is rare; you barely notice the waiters, yet plates are cleared before you even realise they're empty; and the pacing of the dishes is faultless. The 10 course degustation menu is well worth trying, portions are just right and despite the number of dishes, you will not be left too full to detract from the pleasure of the experience. If not, try the roasted lamb rack served with vine-ripened cherry tomatoes in mixed wild berries sauce.

21 Club St ◀
Chinatown
🚇 **Tanjong Pagar**
Map 17-C2

Senso

6224 3534 | www.senso.sg

The restaurant provides world-class Italian cuisine to discerning customers in Singapore. You get the complete experience – from the architecture and decor to the service, food and wine. The neo-classical lines of its colonial architecture hint to the fact Senso was once a convent. There are three main areas, each with a completely different ambience. The bar is uber-hip and modern. The main dining area, with fire-red chairs basking in a warm light is at once cosy and corporate. The dining area in the courtyard transports you to a mansion in southern Italy. Formally attired waiters. who know what they are talking about, present a menu of exceptional Italian cuisine that is contemporary in presentation and traditional in preparation. The wine cellar is enviable and the recommendations for food pairing precise. Best of all, in spite of the restaurant being so swanky, it is still a place where you can immediately relax.

Japanese

Other options **Far Eastern** p.398

23 Mohd Ali Lane
Chinatown
Tanjong Pagar
Map 17-C2

Ikukan

6325 3362

This quaint little restaurant is a delight to visit; serving up contemporary Japanese cuisine alongside some of the chef's unique creations that delight the palate. Located in the hip Club Street area, the contemporary but homely interior puts diners immediately at ease. The menu offers items like black winter truffles with mizuna and prosciutto, a wonderfully-done grilled cod, chawan mushi with foie gras or the citrus yuzu, creme brulee with oolong poached pears, and a great yakitori selection. There are some very reasonably-priced lunch sets or you could opt for one of the special set meals which gives you a chance to sample more of the menu.

Raffles The Plaza
Colonial District
City Hall
Map 17-D1

Inagiku

6431 6156 | *www.singapore-plaza.raffles.com*

One of the more spacious high-end Japanese restaurants, Inagiku has a sushi bar, a teppanyaki counter and a tempura bar set in three different parts of the restaurant, as well as a separate main dining area. Private tatami rooms are also available for discrete business meetings or private parties. The decor is surprisingly ordinary for such an expensive restaurant, but the extra-ordinary quality of the sashimi and sushi makes up for it. You'd be hard pushed to find better uni (sea urchin) sushi anywhere. The menu is extensive and the dishes are prepared in a traditional manner. The wagyu beef served teppanyaki style is highly recommended, and another speciality is the whole lobster in golden sauce.

Pan Pacific Hotel
Marina Bay
City Hall
Map 17-D1

Keyaki

6826 8335 | *www.singapore.panpacific.com*

Set in the centre of an immaculate garden is Keyaki, a fine dining Japanese restaurant authentically modelled after a Meiji-era Japanese farmhouse. Tradition and authenticity is assured by Chef Ishii's 30 years of experience in Japanese cuisine. Keyaki offers the full spectrum of Japanese food, from the popular sushi, sashimi, tempura, teriyaki, soba, udon, shabu shabu, sukiyaki dishes to Japanese haute cuisine – kaseki. The spacious restaurant has a sushi bar, teppanyaki counter and is special in its ability to provide a broad Japanese dining experience without compromising on quality in any area. The set-lunches, served post haste, are popular with corporate executives. Dinner is a more leisurely affair with only an a la carte menu available. Saturday and Sunday lunches, where for a fixed price you may order as much as you want from the a la carte menu, are often family affairs where young children are welcome.

413

Kuriya

Great World City
River Valley Road
🚇 *Tiong Bahru*
Map 17-A1

6736 0888 | *www.kuriya.com.sg*

You may be forgiven for thinking the Japanese-French fusion offered at Kuriya is but another faddish concoction aimed at attracting customers by virtue of novelty. However, if you examine the pedigree of its two Japanese chefs, one trained as kaiseki ryori chef in Kobe and the other as a French chef in Geneva, you'll readily understand why Kuriya deserves its reputation as one of Singapore's finest Japanese restaurants. The chefs have found the perfect marriage between classic Japanese cuisine and the innovative, contemporary flair of French cooking. Besides the extremely fresh sashimi and sushi, you can enjoy a table barbecue, claypot and grilled items. There are non-traditional items on the menu, such as foie gras, but the presentation and taste is distinctly Japanese. Try the sushi mosaic, a blend of Italian cuisine and traditional Japanese food delicacies. The French flair makes a tour de force among the desserts: wasabi parfait with pannacotta or tofu with yoghurt and a topping similar to creme brulee.

Nadaman

Shangri-La Hotel
Orchard
🚇 *Orchard*
Map 14-A3

6213 4571 | *www.shangri-la.com/singapore*

Tucked away in the Shangri-La Hotel, if you are looking for a leisurely meal and plan to spoil yourself a bit, you can't go far wrong here. A popular lunch spot with the Japanese community, this restaurant specialises in a traditional form of Japanese cuisine known as kaiseki or a tasting menu. These menus range from $40 for a mini kaiseki lunch to $180 for a Kobe-style steak kaiseki, and feature several small courses of delightfully put-together dishes made from fresh, seasonal ingredients. If you are unsure, feel free to ask the friendly manager for a look at the menu that changes according to what's available monthly.

Shiro

24 Greenwood Ave
Bukit Timah
Map 13-D1

6462 2774 | *www.imaginings.com.sg*

The subdued lighting and zen-inspired decor presents a quiet, cosy ambience marked by finesse and a comforting sense of privacy. There are no distractions. The front door is locked and you need to ring a bell for someone to open up; other than dining customers, no one is allowed to simply wander in. And disturbed you do not wish to be, because the food here needs your full attention. Like other superlative fine dining Japanese restaurants, Shiro's menu is seasonal so diners get to taste the freshest possible ingredients which the chef has sourced from all over Japan. For instance, the monk fish liver tastes like fine foie gras. While the cuisine is modern Japanese and many of the dishes are unique creations of the chef-owner Patrick Tan, the preparation techniques are very traditional. House specialities not to be missed are the Japanese Pacific saury grilled with sea salt, and the sliced wild duck with Japanese special sauce.

Tatsuya

Crown Hotel Orchard
Orchard
🚇 *Somerset*
Map 14-B4

6737 1160 | *www.crownhotels.com.sg*

Acknowledged as one of the city's consummate sushi chefs, owner-chef Ronnie Chia has apprenticed under master chefs in Japan as well as the legendary Yoshio Nogawa in Singapore. He has a loyal following and it behoves you to make a reservation, especially if you want one of the coveted seats by the sushi counter. It goes without saying the sashimi is a must try – it's firm and very fresh, and Tatsuya has a distinctive style of preparing their sushi, which is exceptionally tasty. The ideal way to dine here is to simply leave it to the chefs to orchestrate your meal, degustation style; they will create a perfect symphony of tastes that invariably leave patrons going home with a wonderful sense of well-being. Request what's in season for a pleasant surprise. Other specialities include crabmeat tofu and grilled codfish with a special cod roe sauce.

10 Devonshire Rd
Orchard
🚇 *Somerset*
Map 17-B1

Yoshida

6735 5014 | www.imaginings.com.sg

For a thoroughly authentic Japanese sushi and sashimi bar, Yoshida is where the Japanese in Singapore go. Little is different from what you may encounter in Tokyo, where master sushi chef and owner Hideaki Yoshida comes from. Yoshida has been delighting patrons for over 20 years. The quality of the food is absolutely top-notch. The menu has an extensive offering of grilled and deep-fried dishes. Food prepared is traditional Japanese cuisine, but exquisitely refined and designed to encourage the natural flavours of the ingredients to dance in your mouth. The atmosphere is cosy yet lively; chairs and table settings are tightly packed, the music changes from Japanese classical to western pop, all making for an informal feeling where you just relax and enjoy the food. Dishes are seasonal; so ask for recommendations. House specialities and mainstays include the Kobe beef on hot stone, and the pacific cod and sea urchin in butter sauce.

Latin American

Other options **Mexican** p.416

14 Sixth Ave
Bukit Timah
Map 13-C1

Brazil Churrascaria

6463 1923

With 15 different cuts of meat prepared by five Brazilian chefs, this informal and lively restaurant is heaven for carnivores. A huge salad bar in the centre of the dining area serves as a counterpoint to an incredible selection of meats; ranging from the humble sausage and chicken to a wide variety of cuts of lamb and beef, ribs, ham and exotica like grilled chicken hearts. Skilled pasadors carve the meat directly onto your plate and you are encouraged to devour all the meat you can eat for one fixed price. Whatever your choice, it all arrives succulent, moist, tender and delectably marinated. Meals can be accompanied by some top wines or for a more potent punch, the caipirinha, in lemon, lime or strawberry, is a must-try. Reservations are strongly recommended; even the owners themselves don't automatically get a table!

415

Mediterranean

Other options **Spanish** p.42, **Italian** p.410

Other options **Spanish** p.42, **Italian** p.410

Orchard Hotel
Orchard
🎧 **Orchard**
Map 14-A4

Esmirada

6735 3476 | *www.esmirada.com*

Upmarket and gregarious, this restaurant is full-on Mediterranean in decor, spirit and cuisine. Food-wise you'll get to taste a wide range of Mediterranean styles from grilled meats and kebas to salads, pasta, soups and of course, the wine. Esmirada is perhaps best known for its garlic bread; served upright in a basket, it's moist and soaking with flavour. Other signature dishes include the French bouillabaisse, also known as the fisherman's stew. There is a choice of chicken, beef or prawn kebabs that will have you hankering for more. For dessert, try the tiramisu and close with a cup of rich black coffee - delissimo. The waiters are energetic and friendly, and when night falls they are known to go on Greek-style plate-smashing binges.

Jalan Merah Saga
Holland Village
🎧 **Buona Vista**
Map 13-C3

Original Sin

6475 5605 | *www.originalsin.com.sg*

An award-winning vegetarian restaurant, Original Sin is hugely popular even among non-vegetarians. Flavours are so rich and tasty, you simply don't miss the meat. You have the option to dine alfresco under the stars or in the candlelit interior surrounded by warm earthy tones. The restaurant delights the senses on so many levels. Culinary director Marisa Bertocchi, who worked with various chefs for over 10 years in Adelaide, started off as sous chef in the mother restaurant, Michelangelo's. So popular were her vegetarian creations that Original Sin was born. The menu respects the desires of the most stringent vegetarians; vegans and Jains can be comfortable here. For starters, try the magic mushroom made with oven baked Portobello mushroom with ricotta cheese, spinach, pesto and pine nuts, topped with a tomato basil sauce and mozzarella. For a main course, you can't possibly go wrong with the moussaka consisting of baked layers of chargrilled eggplant, potato, tomato and lentils, infused with Middle Eastern spices, topped with a white sauce. Their pizzas and pastas are also very popular and the wine list is awesome.

Mexican

30 Merchant Rd
Riverside
🎧 **Clarke Quay**
Map 17-C2

Café Iguana

6326 1275

With half-priced house margaritas pretty much all day except between 21:00 and midnight, this place is a fantastic dinner stopover before you head down to Clarke Quay just across the bridge. In addition to boasting over 100 labels of tequila and mezcal, more than 11 types of margaritas, their own Iguana larger and yummy chocolate shooters, this riverside restaurant's drinks counter is pretty damn near perfect, and its solid fare is definitely worth checking out as well. Outstanding items on their menu are the mussels, taco salad, fajhitas, burritos and kahlua glazed sauteed bananas with ice cream. Servings are substantial and their list of mains has something to keep the carnivores, seafood lovers and vegetarians happy. Always, always make reservations if you plan to have dinner.

El Patio Mexican

34 Lorong Mambong
Holland Village
🚇 *Buona Vista*
Map 13-C3

6468 1520

Located along a stretch of popular restaurants in Holland Village, El Patio's generous portions make sure you leave feeling like one of their deep fried jalapeno poppers filled with cream cheese. This seven-year old restaurant offers both indoor and outdoor dining, and a menu filled with Mexican favourites such as chicken, beef, lamb, prawn and salmon fajitas and chimichanga. For those that can't make up their minds, El Patio offers a combinero set of two different mains. Take your time as you begin with a basket of nachos and salsa on the house and wash down all that artery busting Mexican goodness with the restaurant's signature margaritas served in jam jars.

Harry's Mexican Restaurant & Bar

Orchard Parade Hotel
Orchard
🚇 *Orchard*
Map 14-A4

6235 5495 | www.harrys.com.sg

Tucked away at the back of the Orchard Parade Hotel, just off of Orchard Road, Harry's is a good place to satisfy your craving for Tex-Mex cuisine. The art on the walls and tile mosaic on the bar and tables will get you in the mood for tacos and enchiladas, not to mention the mean margarita they mix here. The Mexican music can be a bit much when the restaurant is less busy on weeknights, but it adds to the atmosphere on Friday and Saturday nights when it gets crowded and things are turned up a notch. The friendly staff are happy to guide you through the menu, although it's mostly the usual fare, so you won't need too much help. Catering primarily to hotel guests and Orchard Road office workers, there are vegetarian and kids menus as well, so it's ideal for families too.

Middle Eastern

Al Hamra

23 Lorong Mambong
Holland Village
🚇 *Buona Vista*
Map 13-C3

6464 8488 | www.alhamra.com.sg

Lebanese chefs revive the hearty cuisine of Beirut, considered to be the Paris of the Middle East. The food is skillfully prepared and authentic, and for that extra touch, your meal is accompanied by lively Arabic music. The only modern innovation to this otherwise traditional Middle Eastern fare is the emphasis on satisfying the demands of today's health-conscious customers. There is a separate menu for vegetarians. The house signature dish – assorted mixed grill - gives you a comprehensive tasting of Lebanese food in one plate. This dish applies the finesse of French cooking with herbs and spices to an assortment of grilled lamb chops, minced lamb and chicken kebabs served with grilled vegetables and onions. Enjoy your meal in air-conditioned comfort or alfresco on the sidewalk of hip, trendy Holland Village.

Cappadocia Café Restaurant

11 Unity St
Robertson Walk
Riverside
🚇 *Clarke Quay*
Map 17-B1

6732 2411

Cappadocia's roots are Turkish, Mediterranean and continental cuisine, and you get a rare opportunity in Singapore to taste good Turkish bread, dips, shish kebabs, pizzas and vegetarian dishes. The ambience is casual and you can relax on comfortable sofas and cushions. The food offers bold, robust flavours and must-tries are the grilled prawns in lemon garlic sauce or the rolled fillet of beef stuffed with button mushroom and spinach. There's little to wonder why this cafe/restaurant is a popular hangout. Another branch is located at 390 Up Bt Timah Road.

Pizzerias

Other options **Italian** p.410

People in Singapore love pizza, and while it is a little more expensive on average than in western countries, there is a good variety. For dining out (as well as the Italian restaurants, see p.410), two of the best places for gourmet pizzas are California Pizza Kitchen (6836 0110, www.cpk.com) in Forum The Shopping Mall on Orchard Road, and Spizza (www.spizza.sg), which has branches all over Singapore. Pizza delivery is also common, see the table on the right for the most popular options.

Pizzerias		
California Pizza Kitchen	Orchard	6836 0110
Canadian 2-FOR-1 Pizza	Various locations	6241 0241
Da Paolo Pizza Bar	Riverside	6479 6059
Pizza Hut	Various locations	6235 3535
Pizzeria Giardino	Colonial District	6338 8711
Rocky's Pizza	Tanglin	6468 9188
Spizza	Various locations	6224 2525

Seafood

87 Frankel Ave
Siglap
 Kembangan
Map 15-F3

Blue Lobster
6442 5090

Blue Lobster is a little gem in the heart of Siglap. As the name would suggest, seafood dishes take centre stage in the small but intense menu. Chef Karl Dobler puts his 27 years of experience to work, creating extraordinary dishes with a variety of fish and shellfish that highlight his European, Asian and Australian influences. For the oyster aficionado, Thursday's oyster night is not to be missed, with all oysters priced at $1. To complete the perfect meal, take the time to explore the extensive dessert menu, with decadent creations that will have you lingering over coffee in a state of bliss. The restaurant has a cosy feel to it, with a front patio for relaxed alfresco dining and intimate booths inside. If sitting indoors, ask to be seated towards the back, where colourful, translucent curtains separate the tables.

Clarke Quay
Riverside
 Clarke Quay
Map 17-C2

Fish Tales
6837 3251

Fish Tales is a departure from the typical Singaporean seafood restaurant; with chilli and pepper crab nowhere in sight, the focus is squarely on the stylish presentation of a range of fresh fish and shellfish. Set on the bustling strip of restaurants on Clarke Quay, the outdoor area is not the place for a quiet romantic dinner, with the live music from restaurants next door making a pleasant background for a meal. The small indoor area affords a more intimate and classy setting, pulling off a maritime theme without being tacky. Open every day for lunch and dinner, Fish Tales has a set lunch menu in addition to its regular a la carte selections. And between the type of fish, style of cooking and accompanying sauces, there are over 150 ways to eat your catch. The competent staff can help you navigate through the selections, recommending the freshest fish options, as well as the best shellfish selections.

34 Greenwood Ave
Bukit Timah
Map 13-D1

Greenwood Fish Market & Bistro
6467 4950

Fish markets hardly ever smell good; but for this restaurant, it's worth those five seconds of breathlessness to get to the bistro behind the fresh seafood counter. The service staff are great at offering recommendations and there are hot and cold platters that offer a taste of their seafood selection, perfect to share as an appetiser or between two as a main course. Some mains that are particularly worth checking out are the dory with foie gras and the black cod. If you love oysters, come by on Tuesdays and indulge at $1 a pop, as long as you order a main course. The place does a decent serving of fish and chips at $9.90, only for take away. And if you have space, definitely give the warm chocolate cake a go.

Jumbo Seafood

East Coast Seafood Centre
East Coast
Map 15-F4

6442 3435 | www.jumboseafood.com.sg

Nobody should spend too long in Singapore without having a good seafood meal. A good place to enjoy one of the Lion City's signature dishes, chilli crab, is at Jumbo Seafood, especially because it has a chain of five outlets, including one in the East Coast Seafood Centre and several in the city centre. Signature dishes include red Sri Lankan crab stir fried in rich chilli gravy with deep fried buns; or an even more delicious dish, some would argue, white pepper crab served in a black peppery gravy. Complemented by lobsters, prawns, beancurd and fish, an evening at Jumbo is a messy experience – expect to get your hands enjoyably dirty, and to get some exercise as you crack into the thick crab shells.

Raffles Courtyard

Raffles Hotel
Colonial District
🚇 City Hall
Map 17-D1

6412 1140 | www.raffleshotel.com

Sit under the stars and be serenaded by the jazz band delivering as your seafood dinner sizzles just nearby. You might want to avoid your favourite white shirt here as the restaurant's speciality is its Sri Lankan chilli crab, best tackled with your sleeves pulled up and your hands straight in there. The menu offers a wide selection of other local seafood favourites as well, including fried baby squid, stir fried frog legs and kang kong. To end on the sweet note, or to sooth your burning tongue, have an ice kachang (in a generous serving) or pisang goreng (banana fritter) in icecream. If you still have room for more, adjourn to the Gazebo Bar for yet another local creation – the Singapore Sling.

Singaporean

Other options **Far Eastern** p.398

Blue Ginger

97 Tanjong Pagar Rd
Tanjong Pagar
🚇 Tanjong Pagar
Map 17-C3

6222 3928 | www.guanhoesoon.com

The restaurant gives a sense of being in a wealthy Peranakan home and this is important because the cuisine is no more than common home-cooked fare typical to Peranakans. What distinguishes Blue Ginger is the quality of the food, made possible by the freshest, finest ingredients available. It's best to go in a group of at least four so you can order more dishes; it is a common custom to share the dishes on the table. The perennial favourite is ayam buah keluak, braised chicken flavoured with turmeric, galangal and lemongrass cooked with Indonesian black nuts. Other must-tries are the sambal terong goreng, a deep fried eggplant with fresh chilli paste and sweet soya sauce; and otak otak, a fishcake made with turmeric and lime leaves enriched

Singaporean Chili Crab

419

with galangal, chilli, candlenuts and shrimp paste, often wrapped in banana leaf and barbecued.

Raffles Hotel
Colonial District
City Hall
Map 17-D1

Empire Café
6412 1101 | *www.raffleshotel.com*

Not to be dismissed as just another hotel offering a bourgeois take on hawker favourites, the Empire Café at the Raffles Hotel makes for a good pit stop if you are shopping in the area. Enjoy hainanese chicken rice, roti prata, bak kut teh, spring rolls, beef noodles and chili prawns within the air-conditioned interior of the cafe - built to resemble the kopitiams, or coffee shops, from a few decades back. Although the prices are not lost on the location, the standard of the food here is worth impressing that visitor or your picky grand-aunt. Also remember to check out Ah Teng's Bakery (just next to the cafe) that offers some very good icecream, cakes, cookies and pastries.

214 Joo Chiat Rd
East Coast
Map 15-D4

Guan Hoe Soon Restaurant
6344 2761 | *www.guanhoesoon.com*

For Guan Hoe Soon Restaurant to survive, nay flourish, among the Peranakan community since its opening in 1953, is a measure of its authenticity and quality. The third generation of the original Yap family still own and run this place. Slight modifications to the original recipes have been necessary as today's customers are more health conscious. Thus less salt and oil are used. The food is good, the prices moderate and the decor is as functionally plain as would be expected from a restaurant whose only focus is avoiding the notorious displeasure of a nonya matriarch whose palate has been cheated. Try the ayam buah keluak, babi pong tay, itek tim, chap chye, hee peow soup and beef rendang.

Chijmes
Colonial District
Lavender
Map 17-D1

Table 108
6338 6108

It is not so much the menu but the location that makes Table 108 the perfect choice for visitors to Singapore. With a lively outdoor setting heightened by the buzz of surrounding restaurants and bars, this is a venue best frequented in the evening where you will find yourself dining at the foot of the floodlit Chijmes cathedral. Not content with alfresco excellence, Table 108 also offers a sumptuous red lanterned indoor setting and small but chic martini bar where you can enjoy a drink before or after your grilled stingray or prawn mee soup.

> **Peranakan Food**
> Peranakans, or nonyas, were Chinese immigrants that settle along the Straits of Malaya and inter-married with indigenous Malays. Nonya food has a peculiarly difficult taste to establish and unless spot-on, becomes either Chinese or Malay food or simply unrecognisable. Nonyas are renowned for being insufferably fastidious about how their food tastes and many true-blue Peranakans seldom deign to eat their cuisine in a restaurant, preferring to cook it themselves as most nonya women are expert cooks. For chances to sample this cuisine, try Guan Hoe Soon Restaurant or Blue Ginger (see the reviews in this section).

Chijmes

Spanish

Other options **Mediterranean** p.416

Esplanade
Marina Bay
📷 *City Hall*
Map 17-D2

Via Mar

6423 0900 | *www.wellborn.com.sg*

One of the few authentic Spanish restaurants on the island, Via Mar provides an extensive tapas selection and a good a la carte menu of main courses. Spanish chefs were brought in to train the local staff, and no less than the HRH Queen of Spain visited Via Mar on an incognito visit to Singapore. The indoor dining area is pleasingly decorated in warm but vibrant Spanish style, and lit for a romantic mood. Most patrons, however, opt for the spacious alfresco area. The lunch specials are excellent value, but highlight of the week has to be Tuesday's Senora's Night when ladies pay $35 and men $52 for eat-as-much-as-you-can from the tapas menu plus free-flowing house wines and Carlsberg on draft! Don't miss out on the gambas al ajillo (prawns cooked in olive oil, garlic and chilli) and the baby squid calamares. Another house speciality is the cochinillo asado (whole roast suckling pig) which goes great with wine; advanced orders are necessary.

Steakhouses

Other options **American** p.393

Raffles Hotel
Colonial District
📷 *City Hall*
Map 17-D1

Long Bar Steakhouse

6412 1307 | *www.raffleshotel.com*

While in Singapore you can't miss a visit to the world-famous Raffles Hotel, and a meal at the Long Bar Steakhouse makes your visit even more special. The menu features premium steaks and seafood grilled to perfection, with an Asian touch of local spices. The most discerning taste buds will not go wanting with the variety of starters including seafood, crispy tofu, foie gras and a many exotic soups and salads. For your main course choose from choice seafood, prime rib and steaks served with your choice of unique sauces. There are set dinners for two including surf & turf and the steakhouse grill. For dessert, don't miss the sago coconut jelly with papaya, macadamia, pandan cream, and gula melaka icecream, a true Raffles original.

Thai

Other options **Far Eastern** p.398

899 East Coast Rd
East Coast
📷 *Eunos*
Map 15-E3

Lemongrass

6443 1995 | *www.lemongrass.com.sg*

East Coast Road is a foodie's paradise, where on this single stretch of road you'll get just about any nationality of cuisine to be found in Singapore. Among them is Lemongrass, a mid-priced Thai restaurant with over 60 dishes to choose from its main menu (no pork or lard is used) and another 20 plus dishes on a separate vegetarian menu. The food is tasty, down-to-earth and typical of what middle-class Thais eat everyday. The interior is purposely designed to be simple, old-fashioned and reminiscent of a period that has been all but erased by modernity. There is an alfresco option, and reservations are necessary if you want one of these few tables.

Tanglin Mall
Tanglin
📷 *Tiong Bahru*
Map 13-F4

Patara Fine Thai

6737 0818 | *www.patara.com.sg*

The mission of Patara Fine Thai's two restaurants is to offer home-style cooking as a fine dining experience. The renowned spirit of Thai hospitality is embodied in the aromatic flavours of their cooking and the attentive service as soon as you enter. Carefully selected Thai chefs, using imported ingredients, work hard to replicate the tastes you will find in Bangkok's top-end restaurants. In addition, there are fusion-style dishes for a novel twist. Soft warm lighting and stylish dark-wood furniture produce an ambience of subtle elegance. Patara's specialities include a delectable seafood bouillabaisse in a coconut cream and galangal reduction, and the lemongrass marinated rack of lamb with a chili sauce and sweet rice rolls. Desserts are spread on a buffet and for many Thais, this is the highlight of a meal. Another branch is located in Swissôtel The Stamford on Stamford Road (6339 1488).

Colours By The Bay ◄ | ## ThaiExpress
Marina Bay |
🚇 **City Hall** | *6533 6766* | www.colours.com.sg
Map 17-D2 | Tasty and well-priced for the quality of the food, ThaiExpress is a good, mid-priced option for those who like the option of eating Thai food on a regular basis. A successful chain of restaurants in the region, with 15 outlets in Singapore at last count, the secret of ThaiExpress is excellent recipes and good choices, including a number of relatively nutritious options like mango salads and grilled meat. Excellent for its laksa, curries and street-food inspired favourites, ThaiExpress is in fact relatively regional in its influences. Try the chicken wings, the soft-shelled crab and the black olive rice – all dishes that will keep you coming back for more. Buy a few dishes and share Asian-style. In the city, the most visible outlet is the large one near the sea at Colours By The Way, alongside Esplanade.

Vietnamese

Other options **Far Eastern** p.398

18 Mohamed ◄ | ## Le Tonkin
Sultan Rd |
River Valley Road | *6235 6006*
🚇 **Clarke Quay** | Luxuriously plush, this fine-dining north Vietnamese and French restaurant-cum-
Map 17-C1 | lounge is exquisitely sophisticated, yet completely relaxed, with friendly service and wonderful food. Perfect for a lovely night out, business dinner or simply a drink after work, Le Tonkin is the creation of two well-travelled partners; one Vietnamese, the other French. The restaurant serves mainly north Vietnamese food, with the emphasis on typical and authentic Hanoian fare – prepared by a Vietnamese master chef who personally ensures only the finest and freshest ingredients are used. Indoors, the decor exudes an air of stylish luxury; maroon and deep royal-blue cushions, gold-tinted hand-painted walls, floor to ceiling curtains, all bathed in a warm light from the stage for truly fine dining. Outdoors, the wicker chairs, wide sofas and a gorgeous wall of bamboo trees sequester you from the beat of the city, inviting you instead to simply unwind and enjoy.

1 Old Parliament ◄ | ## Viet Lang
Lane |
Colonial District | *6337 3379* | www.wellborn.com.sg
🚇 **Raffles Place** | Located in the oldest government building on the island, the Empress Place, Viet
Map 17-D2 | Lang's alfresco dining space allows you to soak in both the old and new worlds of this cosmopolitan city. Inside the decor is contemporary, cosy and designed for intimate get-togethers and elaborate parties. The menu has a repertoire spanning north, central and south Vietnam, so you will get popular favourites like spring rolls wrapped in rice paper and pho (noodle soups), to elaborate, fine-dining dishes such as the house speciality of roasted whole fish stuffed with chicken meat and seafood or the steamed crab with beer. Ingredients and condiments are imported direct from Vietnam to guarantee diners a genuine taste of authentic Vietnamese flavours.

Cafes & Coffee Shops

Other options **Afternoon Tea** p.426

Singapore is slowly embracing a cafe culture, but it's not yet a part of day-to-day life as it is in some European countries. There are numerous local and international cafes and coffee shop chains with a presence in Singapore, and with more continuing to pop up around the island, it seems that demand is growing. Most cafes serve hot and cold drinks, both coffee based and non-coffee based, and a selection of cakes and pastries. Some take a step further with their food menus, offering sandwiches and other light meals. Many offer a choice of indoor or outdoor seating, with smoking only allowed in designated outdoor areas (if at all). Most often open early to serve the morning crowds of caffeine-starved office workers, and they some stay open until 23:00 or midnight if they are in popular entertainment districts. Some popular chains with multiple outlets include Spinelli Coffee Company, Starbucks, Coffee Bean & Tea Leaf, Pacific Coffee Company, The Coffee Connoisseur, Dôme... the list goes on.

Fruit Juices

Due perhaps to the warm weather all year-round, juice bars are a very common feature in Singapore. Most indoor food courts in shopping malls will have a fruit stall, making fresh blended juices from a variety of temperate and tropical fruit. In addition, it is not uncommon to see higher-end juice bars in Suntec City or Marina Square for example offering fruit juices with additional energy boosters like wheatgrass, ginger and other vitamin and mineral supplements.

The Paragon
Orchard
🚇 *Somerset*
Map 14-B4

Bakerzin

6333 6647 | *www.bakerzin.com*

This cafe is well known for its French culinary culture, extraordinary east-west fusion food and addictive desserts. Founder-owner Daniel Tay is one of Singapore's foremost pastry chefs and maintains five-star quality standards in his kitchen. The must-try is the Otah Bruschetta; Otah is a fish paste 'cake' full of spicy ingredients wrapped in a banana leaf and barbecued. Locals love to eat it with bread and what better bread than ciabatta for an upper-class take on a local favourite... it works! Another divine creation is the braised escargot in white wine cream sauce served with asparagus and toasted brioche bread. For dessert, don't miss their legendary warm chocolate cake – but be warned, it's positively addictive. Alternatively, for a rainbow of delights, try the dessert tapas that includes lychee espuma, creme camomile, ginger jelly with lychee concasse, just three choices of the 14 available.

Holland Village
Shopping Centre
Holland Village
🚇 *Buona Vista*
Map 13-C3

Café 211

6462 6194

This roof-top restaurant/cafe in Holland Village is decent, but unfortunately not particularly memorable. Having said that, the alfresco setting makes it quite a good option for a cup of coffee or juice or a plate of spicy chicken wings in one of Singapore's nicest outdoor roof gardens. It's also a nice location for a quiet evening beer. Possibly 211 is such a haven because it does not announce itself from the street – take the escalator in the shopping centre to the top floor.

501 Orchard Rd
Wheelock Place
🚇 *Orchard*
Map 17-C1

The Coffee Bean

6887 3743 | *www.coffeebean.com.sg*

Like most of The Coffee Bean's 39 branches, this outdoor instalment of the chain has pretty average tasting coffee, though the cakes and biscuits are good. But in terms of a place to sit and people watch, this spot is probably one of the city's best. Park

423

yourself streetside on the corner of Orchard and Scott's Roads for a view of the large movie advertising screen from the Lido, and one of Singapore's busiest and most international pedestrian crossings. Second best for people watching – the outdoor seats under the tarpaulin at Coffee Bean, Holland Village (6466 4955). See website for more locations.

7 Raffles Place
CBD
🚇 **Raffles Place**
Map 17-C2

Coffee Club

6532 6273 | www.coffeeclubworld.com

The original Singapore-based company for espresso drinks, Coffee Club has some high-visibility locations throughout the city-state, none more so than this one on the lawn beside Raffles Place MRT station, in the heart of the financial district. Emphasising premier pricing and an extensive food menu, Coffee Club takes the cafe theme further towards a restaurant than the others. Yet while their coffee is not bad, it is not quite on the level for other contenders like Spinelli's. There are 17 other outlets around Singapore, see website for locations.

779 Bukit Timah Rd
Bukit Timah
Map 13-C1

Corduroy & Finch

6762 0131 | www.corduroyandfinch.com

This hard-working space on the West Coast lives up to the billing of 'Deli, Cafe, Lounge' probably better than any in Singapore. In a clever piece of interior design, Corduroy & Finch combines in two levels a mouthwatering deli that has gourmet ingredients stacked to the ceiling, together with a cafe-bar that spreads from bench seats and tables downstairs, to traditional and more loungy seating on the mezzanine floor upstairs. Open early until late seven days a week, this is one of the few suburban spots where you're guaranteed superb breakfasts and a light-night wine bar in the same spot. Deliberately European in its approach to good eating, C&F always feels busy without the chaos. Clever and decadent all at once in its menus, the restaurant is billed as comfort food, and arguably best for breakfast and lunch, when the range is impressive, prices reasonable and sunlight flooding through the windows.

Singapore Marriott Hotel
Orchard
🚇 **Somerset**
Map 14-A4

Cross Roads Café

6831 4605

This is great place to take a break from pounding the pavements of Orchard Road and to rest your weary feet for a bit. Get a table next to the sidewalk and watch the world go by as you have dinner or just sip your iced tea. The menu here is a mixture of local dishes and international standards like steak and pasta. However the cafe offers a bit more to keep health conscious diners happy, with its selection of low carb, low fat and low cholesterol dishes. Sugar fans will be pleased to see an extensive dessert menu here too. The special apple strudel and chocolate tiramisu are worth making room for.

9 Penang Rd
Orchard
🚇 **Dhoby Ghaut**
Map 17-C1

Dôme Cafe

6336 8070

Step out of the Dhoby Ghaut MRT station to one side and you're slam-dunked into the frenetic bustle of Orchard Road; step out to the other side of the station and there's Dôme, a cafe offering a breather from frenzied shoppers. You get a

424

wonderful selection of periodicals freely available to accompany your latte, and the reasonably priced menu of items such as Thai chicken salad or chicken mushroom pie. Dôme is ideally located just on the edge of the Orchard shopping belt and the central business district. The spacious yet cosy ambience invites you to take it easy, mingle and enjoy good conversation: perfect for a catch-up with friends or casual business meetings.

Helio Cafe

Marina Square
Colonial District
City Hall
Map 17-D1

6339 9159 | www.heliocafe.com

Created by an interior designer with a passion for food, Helio Cafe delivers beautifully on both counts. The contemporary design plays with warm and dark wood tones, rattan, candles and lots of space for an airy and seductively relaxing ambience. Despite being in a major shopping mall, Helio remains a sanctuary, a hidden secret. The food is a fusion of different cuisines with an emphasis on freshness and authentic ingredients that owner Clement Ronald handpicks on his overseas trips. These ingredients and a certain culinary flair make simple dishes like the creme sauce pasta or mushroom soup distinctive. A popular dish is the signature the kueh pie-tee rice, made from rosemary chicken and rice stuffed into the crispy shell used by Peranakans. There are over 50 blends of teas to choose from and a variety of gourmet coffees to accompany sinfully delicious desserts.

Menotti

Raffles City
Shopping Centre
Colonial District
City Hall
Map 17-D1

6333 9366 | www.garibaldi.com.sg

Picture Italian high fashion applied to a cafe and you've got Menotti, a truly authentic Italian cafe and bar. The decor is slick, modern and chic. The menu is traditional from the coffees, pastries, cakes, snacks to breakfast, lunch and dinner meals. No suprises other than the exceptional quality and authenticity. The cafe offers a 'day & night' customer experience with indoor and outdoor seating capacity from 10:00 to midnight. The set lunch is composed of a main, dessert and coffee, and is excellent value considering you have such choices as tagliatelle with king scallops and mushrooms in pesto sauce, or linguine with blue swimmer crab.

Pitch Black

63 Haji Lane
Arab Street & Kampong Glam
Lavender
Map 14-D4

6392 3457 | www.pitchblack.com.sg

Pitch Black marks another sign of the rapidly growing art and cafe culture in the city. Housed in a two-storey shop house, the ground floor serves as a cafe while upstairs is 20 seater, mini movie theatre, where you can have your food sent up while you're plonked on huge, comfortable sofas surrounded by cinematic quality sound, watching good movies on a Blu-ray ultra high-definition screen. The cafe itself is inspired industrial chic – harsh concrete and steel with bright colours and black. The food is typical cafe fare like homemade salmon or tuna sandwiches, nachos, chicken wings with a few creative exceptions like the wild berries chicken. The cheese brownie is a novelty, and well worth trying. A cool place to hang out.

Bakeries

Bakeries are popular throughout Singapore, but don't necessarily expect the German rye bread you might be used to back home. Asian tastes for breads tend to mean they are high in sugar and additional flavours - with egg tarts being one particular local craze. However specialist western-style bakeries do exist, and are either attached to supermarket chains like Cold Storage and Jason's, or to specialist delis, such as Da Paolo Gastronomia, Corduroy & Finch (p.424) or Whitebait & Kale (p.410).

425

The Heeren
Orchard
🚇 *Somerset*
Map 14-B4

Spinelli Coffee Company
6738 0233 | www.spinellicoffee.com

Of the many chains of cafes in Singapore, Spinelli Coffee Company has some of the best tasting coffee on the island, thanks in large part due to the company having its own Probat-fired roasting plant. Of its 18 outlets, the most memorable is the ground-floor venue at The Heeren, thanks to a fantastic range of made-to-order sandwiches, salads and fresh fruit – and a large outdoor atrium, under which coffee drinkers spill out and inspect their CDs from HMV next door. Spinelli's has a consistently good range – try the ice-blended 'Original Spin' if hot coffee is too much. The cafe has a good cross section of clientele, in large part due to its cheap and healthy lunches.

Afternoon Tea
Other options **Cafes & Coffee Shops** p.423

One of the traditions that Singapore retained from its days as a British colony is afternoon tea, or high tea. While it may be more popular with tourists than locals, the great demand means there are a number of excellent choices. Many locations advertise afternoon teas, but these are often closer to full-blown buffet lunches than the traditional high tea that can be found at the Tiffin Room in the Raffles Hotel (p.410). Just across the street, but 69 floors up, is a truly 'high' tea at Equinox (City Hall, 6837 3322), at the top of the Swissôtel. The Four Seasons (Orchard, 6734 1110) and Rose Veranda (p.409) at the Shangri-La on Orchard also offer popular afternoon teas.

Internet Cafes
In a city with high broadband coverage, offering specialist paid internet access is not such a big draw. Lower quality internet cafes are dotted around the island, appealing to LAN Gamers and backpackers visiting the island. Conventional cafes tend to offer wireless access, either free or as part of a subscriber package.

Hawker Centres

Other options **Food Courts** p.428, **Singaporean** p.419

For all the variety of cuisine to be found in the thousands of restaurants in Singapore, when you want to taste truly 'Singaporean' food, you have to go to a hawker centre. You'll notice a few standard dishes; the local must-haves that form a staple diet such as chicken rice, char kway teow (fried flat noodles), wanton mee (dumpling noodles), roti prata (Indian crepe) and hokkien fried noodles. There are a number of outstanding hawker centres that are famous because of the extensive variety and overall high quality of most stalls (see below for reviews of some of the top places). In addition to those reviewed, you can refer to the table above

Hawker Centres		
Adam Road Food Centre	2 Adam Rd	Bukit Timah
Amoy Street Food Centre	Telok Ayer Street	Chinatown
Chomp Chomp Food Centre	20 Kensington Park Rd	Serangoon
East Coast Lagoon Food Village	1220 East Coast Parkway	East Coast
Hong Lim Food Centre	Blk 531A Upper Cross Street	Chinatown
Tiong Bahru Market	30 Seng Poh Rd	Chinatown
Zion Riverside Food Centre	Zion Road	Chinatown

which lists more centres spread around the island. Chomp Chomp in Serangoon Gardens, in particular, is one smaller hawker centre worth mentioning, as it packs a punch with the food from every stall of a high quality. Getting a table on weekends is a test in patience; just know that those people queuing up are all regular customers and the food is worth the wait.

18 Raffles Quay
CBD
🚇 *Raffles Place*
Map 17-C2

Lau Pa Sat Food Centre

This protected structure is home to a must-try food experience; built in 1894 Lau Pa Sat is the largest remaining Victorian filigree cast-iron structure in south-east Asia. In the heart of Singapore's business district, the former market is struggling a little to get tenants as the rentals are considered on the high side. On the south side, the satay stalls on the street are popular and delicious, and many choose the tables on the street for this reason. One stall in particular, Fatman Satay, is a local favourite. Inside the four armed structure, the Indian food is among the best – you could do a lot worse than a masala dosai set here.

Maxwell Rd
Chinatown
🚇 *Chinatown*
Map 17-C3

Maxwell Food Centre

Chosen by residents as the best hawker centre in a 2003 survey by the National Environment Agency, Maxwell is in the heart of, and among other claims to fame, is heralded by many in the know as having the 'best chicken rice' in the country. Open 24 hours and always busy, Maxwell is not the most comfortable, but the taste, variety and of exotic nature of its dishes makes up for it. Take your pick, but anyone new to must try the local nasi padang (rice and your selection of dishes on top). Go outside of peak lunch hours if possible, and graze amidst the two long aisles of food. Delicious.

Newton Circus
Newton
🚇 *Newton*
Map 14-B3

Newton Food Centre

Probably Singapore's most popular hawker centre, late night at Newton is still a Singapore institution. The 'new Newton' reopened in 2006 to much praise, although it has boosted the traffic to the food centre, especially on weekends. Previously, its detractors had a point – Newton could be bad for touting, and unsuspecting tourists in particular were prone to getting ripped off if not careful. The rule is, avoid the over-friendly people beckoning you to their seats. If you do order from one of them, agree clearly on the price before it is cooked, otherwise it is a seller's market, and rip-offs are not uncommon. Best thing is to sit in a seat of your choice, note your table number, and graze to your leisure, tell them your table number, then pay on the arrival of the food. A huge labyrinth of food stalls and great for local dishes, the beauty of Newton is you can sit under the stars and eat fantastic local fare at relatively low prices. Arrive hungry!

Food Courts

Other options **Hawker Centres** p.427

Similar in concept to Hawker Centres (see the previous page), the basic food court is an indoor, air-conditioned version. Kopitiam has a chain of them, often found in popular shopping centres such as Suntec City Mall; individual stalls are vetted for quality which explains why Kopitiam is popular. Food Junction is a competing chain also found in many malls, and offers a more international choice of food such as Japanese, Dongbei and Thai. Picnic Food Court on Orchard Road is hugely popular because of its superbly central location and excellent choice of food ranging from local, Thai, Korean, Japanese, Taiwanese and Italian.

Food Courts		
Banquet Foodcourt	1 Harbourfront Walk, VivoCity	Pasir Panjang
East Coast Lagoon Food Village	1220 East Coast Parkway	East Coast
Food Cellar	290 Orchard Rd	Orchard
Food Junction	Various locations	–
Food Republic	Wisma Atria Shopping Centre	Orchard
Kopitiam	Various locations	–
Marina Food Loft	Marina Square	Colonial District
Picnic Food Court	Scotts Shopping Centre	Orchard
Raffles Market Place	Raffles City Shopping Centre	Colonial District
Treats Food Court	Parkway Parade	East Coast

Expanding further on the hawker stall concept are the upmarket versions, for example Raffles Market Place, which has a smorgasbord of mini-bistros serving crepes, fancy sandwiches, pastas, pies, sushi and food normally found in a cafe-bistro.

On the Town

Singapore's social scene is popular and diverse. Since the regional downturn, considerable investment went into new bars and restaurants, tapping into the fact that this urban population often eats out all the time. Being in a hot country, the cool of the evening is the right time to socialise. And typically here, you'll be invited out to dinner rather than invited home, though this differs among expats. Dinner is usually from 20:00 until midnight, while most bars serve drinks until 01:00. Licensed premises can apply for all-night licenses now, so bars and clubs do stay open later – the old Singapore 'where to drink after 3am' syndrome is fading fast.

Singaporeans do spend a lot of time on the town and while Fridays and Saturday nights remain the most popular nights, it is not uncommon to see crowds at bars, cafes or clubs midweek, often lured by drink specials or events. Drinking can be expensive in Singapore, with an average drink costing $10 and upwards, but there is aggressive competition for happy hour, especially for the after work crowd. Typical discounts are either half-priced drinks, or two for the price of one. Wednesday night is a popular Ladies' Night in the city, and bars compete to offer the ladies free flowing drinks, usually between for a set time period.

Popular dining and drinking areas for expats include Orchard Road, the Quays along the Singapore River, The Esplanade and Holland Village. The ethnic quarters are also superb for their specialist cuisines and more off-beat bars at great prices – the Chinatown, Little India and Arab Street-Geylang areas are food havens.

Singapore's nightlife continues to be in a state of transition; the city-state's new gaming laws allowing casinos will see two new resorts in place by 2009 and a raft of new nightlife and entertainment changes have accompanied that.

Theme Nights
Wednesday is a popular Ladies' Night, while mid-week Quiz Nights are also fast becoming a hit. Check around for what's going on, or pick up a copy of IS Magazine, which has details of what's happening around town.

Dress Code

Indoor nightspots in Singapore commonly enforce a dress code, although the rules tend to be more flexible for women than for men. In general – shorts, trainers and sandals are frowned upon or banned outright by upscale venues. Some nightclubs take it one step further and don't allow you in if you are wearing jeans. In a few rare cases, bouncers or hostesses at the door will keep you waiting on the sidewalk if you aren't dressed hip enough, even if you technically meet the dress code requirements. Outdoor bars and pubs are more likely to have a relaxed dress code or none at all, so you can usually get away with shorts and sandals.

Boat Quay

429

Bars

Other options **Nightclubs** p.433, **Pubs** p.433

Singapore has witnessed an impressive and welcome upsurge in the number and quality of bars on offer, set mainly in clusters of night spots throughout the city-state. As residents lean towards a more cosmopolitan lifestyle and licensing laws relax, you'll find some great alfresco options near the water and see more daring interior design but on the flipside, there is also a continued fondness for importing popular chain bar concepts from abroad too.

2 Emerald Hill
Orchard
Somerset
Map 14-B4

Alley Bar
6732 6966

A popular yuppy and expatriate bar off of Orchard Road, Alley Bar is true to its name, taking up the narrow space between two old shophouses. The high-ceilinged bar is L-shaped, and it can be tight quarters when it gets packed on weekends. Drinks include good margaritas and all the high-end cocktails you could possibly need to impress a date. The food menu offers some tasty local alternatives to your typical bar snacks, including dumplings and dim sum. This is a cool choice for the first drink or two, but any more might break the bank.

Suntec City
Convention Centre
Suntec
City Hall
Map 17-D1

Balaclava
65339 1600

Long in need of a decent stand-alone after-work bar, Suntec City now boasts one of Singapore's best. Balaclava is large in space and laid back in atmosphere, packed with office workers on Friday evening in particular. The cool interior features lots of red, lamps and divides, mixing timber, leather and silk. With a good indoor and outdoor mix of seating, it's a good bet en route to your transport home, or the next bar.

Asian Civilisations
Museum
Riverside
Raffles Place
Map 17-C1

Bar Opiume
6339 2876

Part of the Indochine chain, Bar Opiume has a spectacular location in the Asian Civilisations Museum, with great views of Boat Quay and the skyline of the business district. One of the premier chill-out bars in town, the comfortable sofas up above the riverbank are great for an after-work drink, but also a convenient launchpad for a big night on the dance floors further down the river at Clarke Quay. Live jazz music keeps the atmosphere smooth and relaxed from 21:30 onwards on most nights of the week.

30 Merchant Rd
Riverside
Raffles Place
Map 17-C2

Brewerkz
6438 2311 | www.brewerkz.com

The best and most inexpensive in-house brewery in Singapore – Brewerkz offers great ale, free wireless broadband (a dangerous combination already) and delicious meals. With around eight different beers, (including strawberry!), and the impressive margaritas at Mexican eatery Café Iguana (p.416) next door (also owned by Brewerkz), this is a large and well-organised operation, which manages to remain friendly. One of the best places to watch sports in Singapore, Brewerkz supports a lot of local sports teams, and bolsters many a pot-belly.

28 Boat Quay
Riverside
Raffles Place
Map 17-D2

Harry's Bar
6538 3029 | www.harrys-bar.com.sg

Harry's Bar is the ubiquitous after-work watering hole for bankers, traders and other white collar workers from Singapore's financial district, which is just a stone's throw from the bar's location at the head of Boat Quay. With other locations throughout the island, and sports regularly screened, Harry's is the ideal place to escape from corporate pressures. A lengthy drinks menu covers every type of alcohol and more; you won't go thirsty here! There is a daily happy hour from 11:00 to 21:00, as well as a Crazy Hour (read: great deals on drinks) on weekdays from 17:00 to 19:00. There's live music seven days a week, and if you fancy a bite with your drink, Harry's offers sizeable portions of western pub food as well as a few local delights or drop by for the Sunday roast and lose your afternoon in good company before returning to work on Monday.

120 Tanjong Beach Walk
Sentosa
HarbourFront
Map 19-D3

KM8

6274 2288 | www.km8.com.sg

Sister club to The Liquid Room, KM8 on Sentosa is Singapore's first beach 'day-club'. Open daily (11:00 to 23:00), but busiest on the weekend (11:00 to 01:00), KM8 boasts a pool, island grooves, jugs of drinks and a sandy dance floor. Bringing in foreign DJs to light things up, this is the place to party on Sentosa. The beach is the perfect excuse for a less-is-more dress code and beautiful people come out in force to heat up this trendy hangout.

Novotel Clarke Quay
Riverside
Clarke Quay
Map 17-C1

Lounge Bar ▶ p.391

6433 8790 | www.accorhotels-asia.com/5993

Located next to the lobby in the Novotel Clarke Quay hotel, Lounge Bar has a modern flair and comfortable ambience. Clusters of couches and armchairs provide a good setting for a cozy gathering with friends to enjoy a cocktail or a hot beverage. The lounge offers a wide range of alcoholic beverages as well as a selection of coffees and loose teas, all at reasonable prices. If you're feeling a bit hungry, order one of the tasty bar snacks - they're a big step up from the clichéd bowl of peanuts.

Grand Hyatt Singapore
Orchard
Orchard
Map 11-A2

Martini Bar @ mezza9

6416 7188

The nice cosy greenhouse feel to this bar encourages many groups to while away the hours here after a large lunch or dinner next door at mezza9. True to its name, the martinis are top notch and the menu is expansive. The lychee martini is a local favourite, and they do traditional as well as more exotic martinis with equally good results. For those that enjoy lighting up, there is a cigar room with an excellent high-end selection to add a bit of decadence to any occassion.

Swissôtel The Stamford
Colonial District
City Hall
Map 17-D1

New Asia Bar & Grill

6431 5672 | www.singapore-stamford.swissotel.com

From its vantage point 226 metres up in The Stamford, this bar offers views over Singapore and the nearby Indonesian islands. With the gleaming skyline in front of you and a chocolate cocktail in your hand you really will be living the high life. With house music, bright colours and even a slanting floor (for optimum views of course), this is a bar experience you'll never forget.

5 Emerald Hill Rd
Bukit Timah
Newton
Map 14-B4

No.5 Emerald Hill Cocktail Bar

6732 0818

A 1910 Peranakan shophouse and part of a trio of popular expatriate bars and pubs in the attractive Emerald Hill area (off Orchard Road opposite Somerset MRT station), No.5 is one of the longer-running bars in Singapore. A sure bet for a good drink any day of the week, it attracts a mix of the after-work crowd, those

431

looking for a relaxing chat, and partiers easing their way into a big night. The outdoor area has a unique feel to it, surrounded by old shophouses and tropical foliage, while indoors has the narrow spaces and crowded atmosphere usually found in shophouses, with a comfortable daybed to lounge on in the back and pool tables upstairs.

The Fullerton
Singapore
Riverside
🚇 *Raffles Place*
Map 17-D2

Post Bar
6877 8135 | *www.fullertonhotel.com*

The place to go to toast that new deal, or when the client is shouting drinks, Post Bar in The Fullerton Hotel is so named because its ceiling was the original ceiling of Singapore's General Post Office. It now looks down on more glamourous proceedings, with uniformed bar staff, comfy couches, and an atmospheric music room. The perfect place for champagne before the opera at The Esplanade.

Empress Place
Op Boat Quay
Riverside
🚇 *Raffles Place*
Map 17-D2

Q Bar
6336 3386

A new addition to the scene in Singapore, Q Bar opened in 2006. While a locally managed spin-off of Bangkok's Q Bar, the bar is quite different in its format, offering an extensive international cocktail menu, generous house pours, generous noise on the outdoor balcony, an indoor bar and an upstairs dancefloor opening later at night. Much friendlier staff than Bar Opium next door, Q Bar is a good addition for Empress Place, and is proving - understandably - popular with a more grown-up crowd.

7 Emerald Hill Rd
Orchard
🚇 *Newton*
Map 14-B4

Que Pasa
6235 6626

Styled after a Spanish provision shop, Que Pasa is a popular wine bar serving a wide range of wines and champagnes at moderate prices. The bottle-lined walls, wooden tables and chairs, and soft music create a relaxing atmosphere for a quiet evening, not a wild night out. The bar is also known for its excellent selection of tapas, which includes calamari, chorizo sausages and other authentic Spanish treats. Regular wine tasting evenings held here are a popular addition to the calendar for those who appreciate a fine vintage. Like No.5 next door, Que Pasa's outdoor seating amidst the attractive historic shophouses is popular in the cool of the evening.

Armenian St
Colonial District
🚇 *City Hall*
Map 17-C1

Timbre Music Bistro
6338 8277 | *www.timbre.com.sg*

Out the back of the Substation Theatre and formerly The Fat Frog Café, Timbre Music Bistro opened in late 2005, to re-establish the tree-lined courtyard as the city centre's coolest spot for live indie music. With the departure of the Fat Frog went the grunge image of the space, replaced by a warmer, more contemporary feel, and more often acoustic bands. Dotted with wooden outdoor tables under the trees and serving a tasty selection of bistro meals, cocktails and cold beer, the more upscale nature of the space reflects the maturity of the artsy crowd, and the new Singapore Management University (SMU) downtown campus across the street.

31 Lorong Mambong
Holland Village
🚇 *Buona Vista*
Map 13-C3

Wala Wala Cafe Bar
6733 9400

Probably Singapore's most successful urban bar, the two-storey Wala Wala is always chock-a-block full of people, inevitably spilling out onto the pavement every night of the week – no doubt the feature bar in Holland V's buzz evening scene. Downstairs, people enjoy good pizzas and bar food washed down with a great selection of beers. Upstairs houses more of a campus atmosphere due mainly to the close proximity of the National University of Singapore (NUS), and has a good selection of acoustic rock covers.

Pubs
Other options **Bars** p.430

Singapore pubs are arguably the most expat-driven of all drinking places, and many have a strange dislocated feel to them. Yet the pubs are generally friendly places to meet and have a good-value pint – though shop around and compare price tags before you settle on a local or favourite.

Crazy Elephant

3E River Valley Rd
Chinatown
Clarke Quay
Map 17-C2

6337 1990

One of Singapore's best established live music venues, Crazy Elephant is the home of loud pub blues, graffitied walls, and a maverick attitude all its own – witnessed by the crude jokes that circulate on the television. Undergoing a renaissance thanks to the resurrection of Clarke Quay, Crazy Elephant is one of those pubs that hasn't changed – and can rightly claim it doesn't need to.

Ice Cold Beer

8 Emerald Hill
Orchard
Somerset
Map 14-B4

6735 9929

Housed in a refurbished 1910 shophouse next to Que Pasar and No.5 (see Bars), Ice Cold Beer is a popular watering hole for those who like cold beer at a good price, playing pool and eating great chicken wings, while singing to rock tunes or watching sport on television. That's about as fancy as Ice Cold Beer gets, and that's what makes it work. It feels like a pub, admittedly more like an Aussie pub catering to a relatively young and mixed crowd. The upstairs bar, nicknamed The Stellar Bar, is the nicest.

Muddy Murphy's Irish Pub

Orchard Hotel
Shopping Arcade
Orchard
Orchard
Map 14-A4

6735 0400

This 500 square metre pub, occupying two storeys of Orchard Hotel Shopping Arcade, is the upstairs creation of a 1900 Dublin City Grocers, with downstairs playing the role of farmyard. Singapore's best Irish pub for atmosphere, Muddy's is especially good when it comes to live music playing downstairs or a football game in progress. Complemented by Irish comfort food items like beef and guinness pie, irish stew, and fish n' chips. this is a good place to chat with friends over a pint.

Next Page

17 Mohamed
Sultan Rd
River Valley Road
Clarke Quay
Map 17-C1

6835 1693

While Mohamed Sultan Road is now well past its heyday as the party epicentre of Singapore, it may still be worth a visit for Next Page, if only to be able to say you've been there for a beer and thrown your peanut shells on the floor. This place has been open for 14 years making it the longest running pub in the area, known for its party atmosphere and relaxed, friendly environment. It used to host a crowd rocking out to 80s music on the weekends, but you're likely to find a somewhat more subdued crowd nowadays, enjoying their drinks and free peanuts.

Nightclubs

Perhaps because of its space constraints and partly due to its fascination with technology, Singapore has a much healthier dance music than live music scene, with regular big name international DJ acts coming through, as well as the fostering of local names internationally like DJ Aldrin, and a good small venue scene, becoming more specialised. Since the opening of Ministry of Sound in late 2005, the dance brand's biggest project so far, competition for the dance dollar in Singapore has been hotter than ever.

Attica

3A River Valley Rd
River Valley Road
🚇 *Somerset*
Map 17-A1

6333 9973

Sexy maverick home-grown house club Attica is popular for its use of different spaces, and attracts a good crowd. Increasingly seen as a bit of a pick-up joint, Attica has lost a bit of its shine, but is still a popular weekend club, and a great place to guarantee a good dance. Its outdoor garden at the back appeals to clubbers wanting a respite from the noise.

Bar None

Singapore Marriott
Hotel
Orchard
🚇 *Orchard*
Map 14-A4

6735 5800

One of the most fun, live cover-band bars, Bar None has long been a favourite for those wanting to dance and sing along to familiar rock tracks. A nice alternative to the many 120 beats per minutes dance clubs around town, it fills up fast on weekends and its close proximity to the late-night Living Room bar upstairs guarantees you can party until the wee hours. Good drinks, friendly and efficient service, and a central location make this a great place for a fun night out.

Butter Factory

48 Robertson Quay
River Valley Road
🚇 *Clarke Quay*
Map 17-B1

6333 8243

As the brainchild of style gurus Bobby and Ritz, Butter Factory is evidence of the popularity of R&B and hip hop in Singapore. The main floor fills up each weekend, while the Art Bar plays a more edgy selection of local DJs. Butter Factory places special emphasis on promoting the promising new DJ talents from across Asia, so this is a great place to catch a new star in the making. A creative and friendly environment, this club is best enjoyed on the dance floor and is fun for a night out when you have too much energy to sit around over a drink.

Coco Latte

Gallery Hotel
CBD
🚇 *Clarke Quay*
Map 17-B1

6736 3208 | www.exitmusik.com

An alternative rock bar, Coco Latte's ground floor has some of the best, edgy interior-decorating of any club in Singapore and its ground floor is a fusion of funky animation artworks. Follow the winding staircase up this unique circular-shaped bar and you'll reach the second

Gay & Lesbian

Technically homosexuality is illegal in Singapore and supposedly punishable with a sentence spanning 10 years to life - technically that is because, although the law, what takes place behind closed doors usually stays behind closed doors. While you can flaunt it at a few places (a few bars around Chinatown are cool for a gay night out - try clubs like Happy and Mox bar, both on Tanjong Pagar Road) it's not advised to shout it from the rooftops. There are Singaporeans who shout it from the rooftops - well, at beach parties to be precise - but that ended with a goverment clampdown late 2005.

floor, which is dedicated to dancing. With hip hop, indie and other genres pumping out fast and furious, the small dance floor gets packed on busy nights.

Robertson Walk
Riverside
🚇 *Clarke Quay*
Map 17-C2

Dbl O
6735 2008

Of the clubs that attract a more predominantly Singaporean audience, Dbl O (pronounced 'double oh') is among the best, with a big crowd on weekends and a mix of music styles leaning towards the commercial. This place is big, with three bars and a spacious dancefloor. Despite the reasonable cover charge and inexpensive drinks, Dbl O puts on a quality clubbing experience, making it a welcome change from the high prices found elsewhere.

Beh Boat Quay
Riverside
🚇 *Raffles Place*
Map 17-C2

Hideout
6536 9445

A very cool 'hole in the wall' club, Hideout is an upstairs space at the Raffles Place end of Circular Road. Tailored like a retro living room inside, it is a good place to catch underground local dance acts and DJs spinning tunes that push well beyond the mainstream. Comfortable couches, pillows and chairs make this a great place to chill out, but still keep a groove going. They even run occassional 'after hours' sessions for clubbers who don't want to go home – starting at 06:00.

Blk 3C, The Cannery
River Valley Road
🚇 *Clarke Quay*
Map 17-A1

Ministry of Sound
6333 4168 | www.ministryofsound.com.sg

The London megaclub's Singapore off-shoot opened in December 2005. Charging $10-25 entry depending on the night and time of entry (including one drink), MOS Singapore is a 40,000 square foot venue with a main dance floor downstairs and a selection of smaller floors upstairs. Appealing to a younger audience than its rival Zouk, MOS has remained popular, and its speciality disco, house and R&B rooms have built a loyal following of their own. Not the complete clubbing experience, but certainly a good addition to the dance card in Singapore. The arrogant attitude of staff early on appears to have eased too.

> ### Integrated Resorts: The New Frontier
> At the time of writing, the buzz in Singapore was over the two casinos under construction, a first in the country's history. In a bid to stay relevant against competing destinations, the country approved these casinos as part of two 'Integrated Resorts' at Marina Bay and Sentosa. In a landmark decision, Las Vegas Sands group was chosen for the first project, while Genting International and Star Cruises won the bid for Sentosa. With 2009 the targeted date for completion, the two projects are expected to include international brand restaurants, theme parks and hotels within each complex - and will no doubt draw in other investors anticipating the additional buzz in the city's nightlife scene.

Goodwood Park
Hotel
Orchard
🚇 *Orchard*
Map 14-B4

Thumper
6735 0827 | www.thumper.com.sg

With free entry and a non-pretentious atmosphere, Thumper provides a good clubbing option for this part of town. The club has an outdoor terrace that is great for taking chilling out with friends in stylish surrounds, but the limited seating means you have to be quick to secure a spot. Inside, a decent house band gets the crowd onto the dance floor with lively covers. Thursday night boasts a popular Ladies' Night, with free vodka for female patrons from 21:00 onwards.

435

17 Jiak Kim St
Riverside
🚇 *Clarke Quay*
Map 17-C2

Zouk

6738 2988 | *www.zoukclub.com.sg*

Still Singapore's best-known club and arguably still its best, Zouk is in fact a complex of four spaces – The Wine Bar, House Club Velvet Underground, breaks room Phuture, and the three storey main space, Zouk. Thanks to an enviable international roster of visiting acts, which included stars like DJ Shadow, Sasha and Groove Armada in 2006, Zouk has maintained a following. In fact, the arrival of MOS was good for Zouk-goers, and the superclub enjoyed a $7 million revamp, including a three-colour RGB mixed lighting concept, new fibreglass cloud forms suspended from the roof, contemporary Gaudi-inspired custom ceramics and a new beer-cooling system. Competition has also improved the service – bar staff at Zouk have even been known to smile now in these new, more competitive, times. While full entry for men to Zouk is high at $35, it covers all four spaces, and two drinks.

Crazy Horse

Aside from risque local drag acts at the 'Boom Boom Room', Singapore had long lacked quality cabaret until the opening in late 2005 of the faked Parisian revue show Crazy Horse, celebrating 'the art of the nude'. Despite fevered talk, especially from puritanical elements, Crazy Horse is only tastefully topless, with glamorous international dancers serving up a show at $65-$600 for a seat. For a cheaper night out, visit Le Bar upstairs for a drink and watch the video screens. You'll find all the fun at River Valley Road, Clarke Quay (6336 1800).

Cinemas

Singapore is a movie-mad city and there are many multiplex cinemas to visit but not always a great selection of films. However, for expatriates needing a Hollywood fix or respite from the mid-day heat, the movies are a good bet.

Book ahead to avoid disappointment; the big chain cinemas have good website booking facilities and automated phone lines that allow you to reserve seats. Aside from the websites, *The Straits Times* carries daily movie listings. Singapore cinemas strictly practise assigned seating, so do check your ticket carefully to avoid being shunted around.

Cinemas

Cathay Cineplex Orchard	Orchard	6235 1155	www.cathay.com.sg	17-B1
Eng Wah Suntec	Colonial District	6836 9074	www.ewcinemas.com.sg	17-E1
Golden Village Grand	River Valley Road	1900 912 1234	www.gv.com.sg	17-B1
Golden Village Marina	Marina Bay	1900 912 1234	www.gv.com.sg	17-E2
Golden Village Plaza	Orchard	1900 912 1234	www.gv.com.sg	17-C1
Lido 8 Cineplex	Orchard	6738 0555	www.shaw.sg	14-B4
Prince & Jade Cineplex	Colonial District	6738 0555	www.shaw.sg	17-E1
Shaw Bugis Cineplex	Colonial District	6738 0555	www.shaw.sg	17-E1

Most movies are in English, often with Chinese subtitles, and listings usually specify the main language and that of the subtitles; dubbing of English movies is rare. Mainstream cineplexes schedule foreign and art house features but these films often have a very limited run. Alliance Française is arguably the most active in its exposure of French films, and holds screenings year round.

Censorship in Singapore has rapidly matured and the days when even kissing scenes ended up on the clipping room floor are long gone. Surprisingly, Asian films appear to be cut more often than their western counterparts; judgements tend to be based on the audience's education level and sensitive content so racially or religiously offensive subject matter is out.

Most tickets cost around $9, with discounts on Tuesdays. The most notable special cinema is GV Grand's Gold Class; for $20 per person you get reclining lovers' seats, blankets, snacks, and waiter service of whatever additional items you wish to buy, including wine. While there are a number of additional suburban cinemas, the table outlines the most the most popular cinemas in town for expats.

Comedy

The comedy scene in Singapore is limited, but there are a few options out there if you enjoy taking in a good comedy act. The Singapore International Comedy Festival is held annually in March, bringing in big-name acts from North America, Australia and elsewhere to amuse local audiences. In previous years, Singapore has also held a buskers' festival featuring street performers that included comedians and although the festival was not held in the past two years, it is scheduled to return in November 2007.

Aside from these two festivals and the occasional comedy act to grace the stage at the Esplanade, comedy enthusiasts are reliant upon The 1Nitestand Bar & Comedy Club (6334 1954), Singapore's only comedy club. Located in the heart of Clarke Quay along the Singapore River, 1Nitestand features comedic talents from around the world, accompanied by a good range of drinks and snacks. For an independent listing of upcoming acts in Singapore, try *IS* Singapore magazine, or visit www.mumtazz.com/singapore.

Singapore International Film Festival

Held every April each year for a little over a fortnight, the Singapore Film Festival is well-loved by film buffs. Set for its 20th year in 2007, recent festivals have included over 300 films from 40 countries. The programme is very diverse, always covering plenty of left-field and back-dated movies, plus a solid base of talked-about indie and arthouse fare from the US, Britain and Europe. Special emphasis is given to showcasing Asian and Middle Eastern films, and the festival highlights interesting sub-genre themes each year. Book early for popular shows. A must for film fans. (www.filmfest.org.sg.)

437

Concerts

Coldplay, the Rolling Stones and Madonna have done shows in Singapore, but big names are generally few and far between – the ones that do make it here often seem to be a bit past their prime; Engelbert Humperdinck and Cliff Richard held concerts recently. The lack of a mega-venue has something to do with this. The MAX Pavilion at Singapore Expo (Changi) and Singapore Indoor Stadium are the main concert venues and both have capacities under 10,000 people.

Singapore also has a reputation for less-than-lively crowds, which may turn off some performers. The Asian pop scene has a slightly better profile, including K-pop, J-pop and Canto-pop (Korean, Japanese and Chinese pop), with major names performing fairly regularly. The occasional interesting international act does come through town and there are a couple of music festivals that continue to improve every year, so it's worth keeping an eye on the local papers for upcoming concerts.

Every August
Fort Canning Green

WOMAD Singapore
www.womadsingapore.com

Held over three evenings for one weekend in August each year, WOMAD Singapore is a well-attended event, showcasing the artists from the travelling World Of Music And Dance festival each year. Utilising three stages, as well as a workshop programme and a strong retail component, WOMAD is a good chance to bring your blanket and some wine, and soak up some world music under the stars in this idyllic park amphitheatre.

Every December
Fort Canning Green

ZOUKOUT
www.zoukout.com

Every year, around 18,000 revellers don swimwear and head to Sentosa for the 12 hour dance music festival, Zoukout. It's the annual beach party of local nightclub Zouk, and has a carnival atmosphere, with four stages, rides and food and games, as well as local and international DJ acts. Zoukout generates a lot of interest outside Singapore, with 35% of the attendees coming from overseas.

Theatre
Other options **Drama Groups** p.261

Singapore is said to host one of Asia's strongest theatre scenes. The government actively pumps money into theatre in a bid to constantly expand the entertainment base, most notably with the launch of the $600m Esplanade - Theatres on the Bay. (For more information on this venue, see p.188.) Expect a constant diet of upscale audience-friendly shows in English; from imported musicals and circus acts, to local adaptations of successful dramatic works. Understandably, the city works hard to showcase new Asian theatre premiers, and the annual Arts Festival is a good time to catch new Eastern works, before they hit Broadway or the West End.

In recent years, small independent theatre has staged something of a mini-revival, as Singaporean and Malaysian works deal with ripe themes of the clash between traditional Asian cultures and modern liberal ways. As Singapore quietly loosens its grip on censorship, favouring the western model of audience warnings, the theatre is fast becoming the testing ground as to how far is too far in terms of sexual, racial or party politics. The current trend is far more daring with nudity, topics of gender and race taking centre stage.

Parties at Home

Other options **Party Accessories** p.349, **Kids Activities** p.274

With expatriates often living in comfortable accommodation in Singapore, and often preferring a drink at home instead of paying inflated bar prices, entertaining at home is popular. While cooking a dinner for friends is a common approach, there are a number of specialist food companies in Singapore offering services for parties at home. These include catering or specialist deliveries, which can mean great food with no hassle, and no washing up afterwards! For some of the most popular companies, see the Caterers table above. Many of the big-name hotels also offer catering packages, ring around for details of what they offer (see the Hotels table on p.32 for contact details). Choices range from a spread of Asian dishes to specialist European gourmet food or a large platter of roast meat with vegetables. A cheaper option can be to ask your favourite local restaurant if they offer home deliveries.

If you are planning a party for kids, a number of companies provide all of the equipment rentals or services that you might need to put on a great party, see the Party Companies table on the right. For information on some places that hold parties for kids, see also the Kids Activities section on p.274 in the Activities chapter. And for details of where to get hold of accessories and costumes etc, see Party Accessories on p.349 in the Shopping chapter.

Caterers

Angie The Choice	Birthday cakes	6258 9898
Bakerzin	Cakes (but not for kids)	6733 7672
Brewerkz	American food & micro brew beer	6438 2311
Cookery Magic	Cakes and catering for small parties	6348 9667
Garibaldi	Italian food	6337 2770
Chilli Padi Nonya Catering	Peranakan food	6247 9531
Purple Sage	Asian & western food, equipment rental, etc	6396 6990

Party Companies

That Magical Party	Party planning & entertainment	9688 5571
Spartacus Developments	Party organising	6467 6210
Bouncy Castles & A Whole Lot More	Inflatable play structures, magicians, etc	6465 6006

439

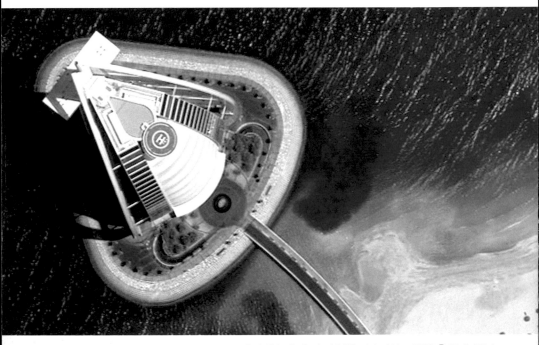

Maps

Maps

User's Guide

This section has a comprehensive selection of maps covering the whole island, enabling you to quickly find your way around Singapore. There's the detailed satellite image maps covering the city centre and surrounding areas, allowing you to pinpoint exact locations (and even see your house!) Then there's two more-traditional vector maps showing the whole city and the country.

More Maps
In addition to the satellite image maps featured in this section, the Exploring section of the book features a vector map on p.176 showing the top areas to explore in Singapore, while on p.102 in the Residents chapter, there's a map highlighting the main residential areas

Mapophobia!
Many people have an irrational fear of all things cartographical, but there's really nothing to be afraid of. The fascinating satellite images in this section are good for getting your bearings - main roads and landmarks are all superimposed to help you work out where you are. If you still can't tell your Katongs from your Kallangs, then turn to p.52 for a list of Singapore's taxi firms!

The overview on the opposite page shows which areas are covered by the image maps, while Map 1 overleaf illustrates the whole of the Singapore (1:175,000) and Map 2 features the city area (1:100,000).

To further assist you in locating your destination, we have superimposed information such as main roads, roundabouts, hospitals, schools, hotels, shopping malls and landmarks on the satellite image maps. Many places listed throughout the book have a map reference - turn to that map to see precisely where you need to go. The overview map on this page is at a scale of approximately 1:330,000 (1cm = 3.3km), all other satellite maps are at 1:40,000 (1cm = 400m) or 1:20,000 (1cm = 200m).

Technical Info

The image maps in this section are based on rectified QuickBird satellite imagery taken in 2005. The QuickBird satellite was launched in October 2001 and is operated by DigitalGlobe™, a private company based in Colorado (USA). Today, DigitalGlobe's QuickBird satellite provides the highest resolution (61 cm), largest swath width and largest onboard storage of any currently available or planned commercial satellite.

MAPS geosystems are the DigitalGlobe master resellers for the Middle East, West, Central and East Africa. They also provide a wide range of mapping services and systems. For more information, visit www.digitalglobe.com (QuickBird) and www.maps-geosystems.com (mapping services) or contact MAPS geosystems on +971 6 572 5411.

Map Legend

Ⓜ Museum/Heritage Site		Expressway	
Ⓔ Embassy/Consulate		Main Road	
Ⓗ Hotel/Resort		MRT --East West Line	
Ⓢ Shopping Mall		MRT --North South Line	
Ⓞ Hospital/Clinic		MRT --North East Line	
ⓘ Tourist Info		MRT (underground)	
🚇 MRT Station		Railway	
KALLANG Area Name		Country Border Line	
— — Restricted Area	(u/c)	Under Construction	
		Marine Lines	
		(u/c) Road	

Online Maps
If you want to surf for maps of Singapore online, www.streetdirectory.com is worth a look, with satellite images and detailed vector maps. Hardcore map fans though are recommended to try Google Earth (http://earth.google.com). This amazing program (you download it from the site) combines satellite imagery, detailed maps, and a powerful search capability, allowing you to fly between various points on the globe and zoom in for incredibly detailed views.

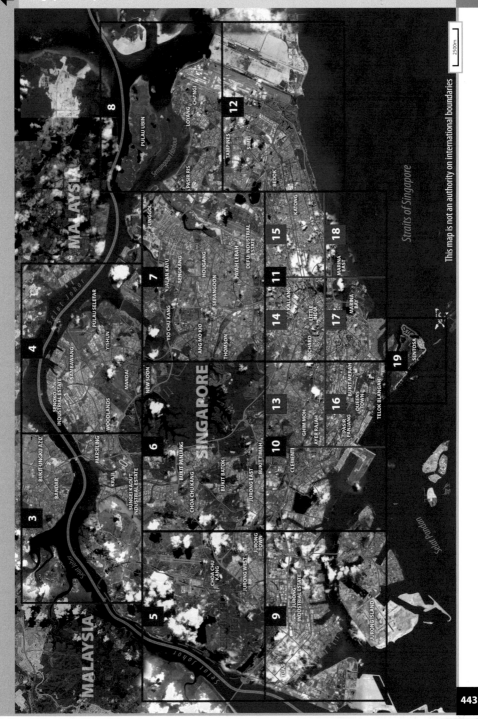

© Explorer Group Ltd. 2007

Image courtesy of MAPS geosystems – Master Reseller for Digital Globe

DIGITALGLOBE

This map is not an authority on international boundaries

2500m

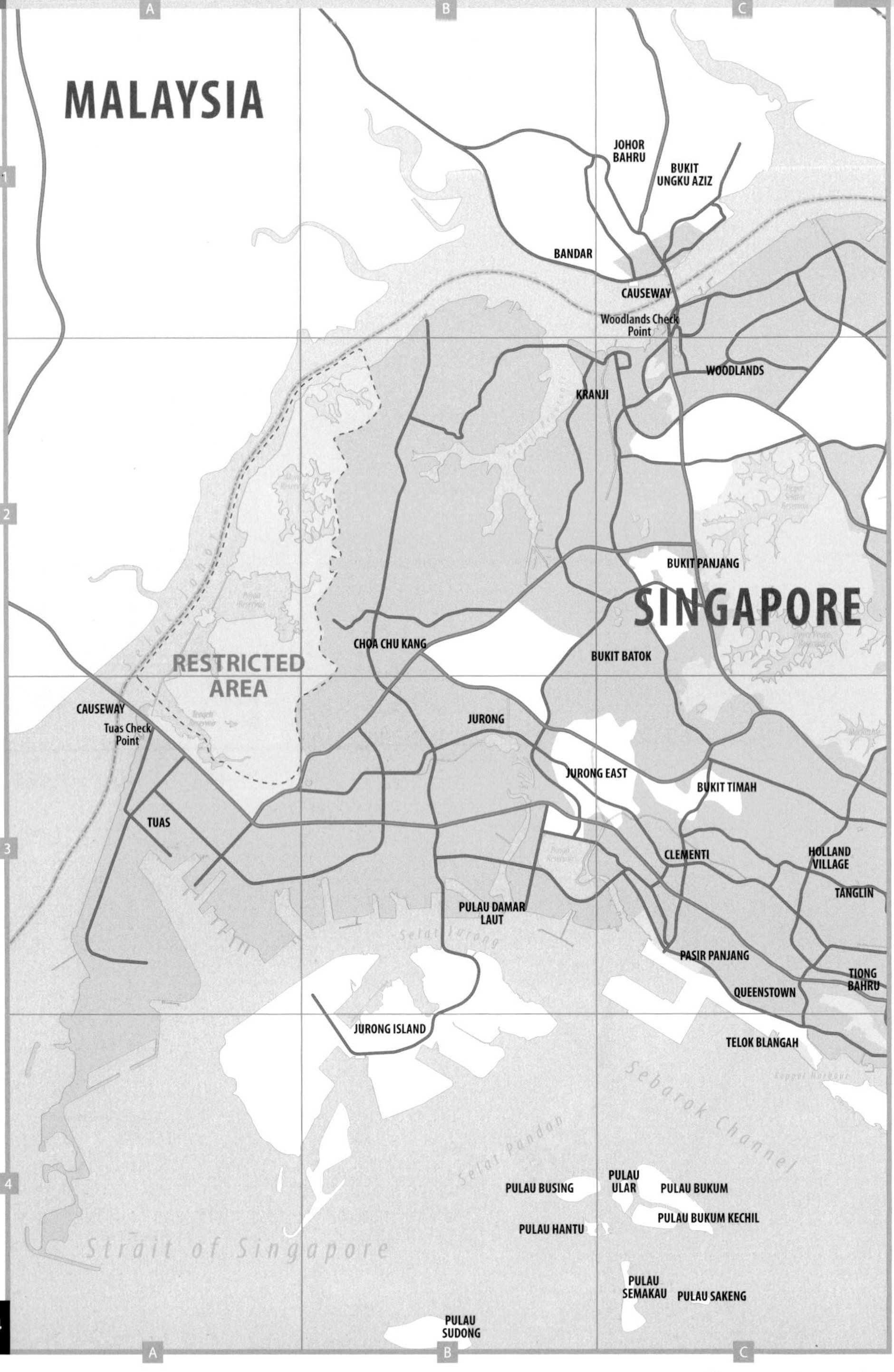

N

MALAYSIA

JOHOR
BAHRU

BUKIT
UNGKU AZIZ

BANDAR

CAUSEWAY

Woodlands Check
Point

WOODLANDS

KRANJI

BUKIT PANJANG

SINGAPORE

CHOA CHU KANG

BUKIT BATOK

RESTRICTED
AREA

CAUSEWAY

Tuas Check
Point

JURONG

JURONG EAST

BUKIT TIMAH

TUAS

CLEMENTI

HOLLAND
VILLAGE

TANGLIN

PULAU DAMAR
LAUT

PASIR PANJANG

TIONG
BAHRU

QUEENSTOWN

JURONG ISLAND

TELOK BLANGAH

Sebarok Channel

Selat Pandan

PULAU BUSING

PULAU
ULAR

PULAU BUKUM

PULAU HANTU

PULAU BUKUM KECHIL

Strait of Singapore

PULAU
SEMAKAU

PULAU SAKENG

PULAU
SUDONG

© Explorer Group Ltd. 2007

MALAYSIA

SEMBAWANG

PULAU
PUNGGOL
BARAT

PULAU
PUNGGOL
TIMER

SELETAR

PUNGGOL

PULAU
SERANGOON

PULAU UBIN

PULAU TEKONG
KECHIL

KAMPONG
SALABIN

SENGKANG

YIO CHU KANG

ANG MO KIO

HOUGANG

PASIR RIS

CHANGI

Singapore
Changi Airport

Changi Ferry Terminal

BISHAN

SERANGOON

PAYAH LEBAH

TAMPINES

TOA PAYOH

MACPHERSON

NOVENA

KALLANG

KAKI BUKIT

BEDOK

TENAH
MERAH

LITTLE
INDIA

GEYLANG

SIGLAP

Tenah Merah
Ferry Terminal

NEWTON

BUGIS

KATONG

MARINE
PARADE

ORCHARD

COLONIAL
DISTRICT

TANJONG RHU

EAST COAST PARK

RIVER
VALLEY

KAMPONG
GLAM

MARINA EAST

FINANCIAL
DISTRICT

MARINA
BAY

CHINATOWN

TANJONG PAGAR

PULAU BRANI

SENTOSA

LITTLE SISTER'S ISLAND (PULAU SUBAR DARAT)

PULAU SERINGAT

KUSU ISLAND (PULAU TEMBAKUL)

LAZARUS ISLAND (PULAU SAKUANG PELEPAH)

ST JOHN'S ISLAND (PULAU SAKUANG BENDERA)

BIG SISTER'S ISLAND (PULAU SUBAR LAUT)

Selat Johai

Serangoou Harbour

Strait of Singapore

This map is not an authority on international boundaries.

2km

Area & Street Index

The table below contains a list of the main areas and streets in Singapore, which are referenced on the map pages.   Many extend beyond one grid reference, in which case the main grid reference has been given.

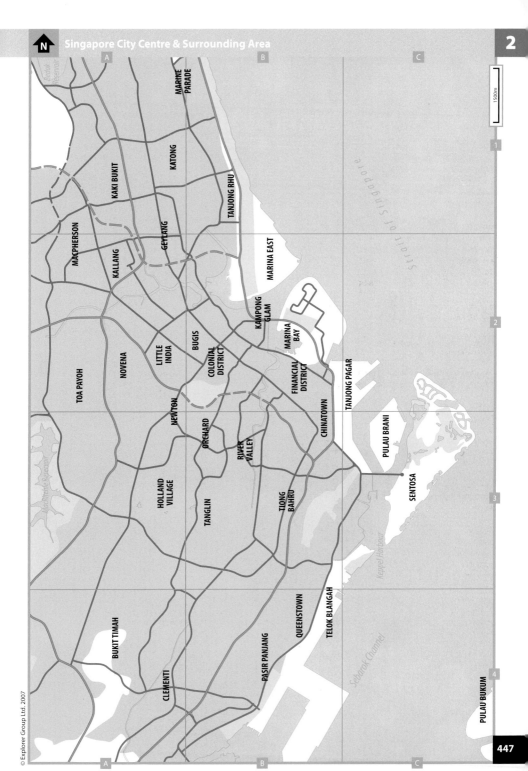

© Explorer Group Ltd. 2007

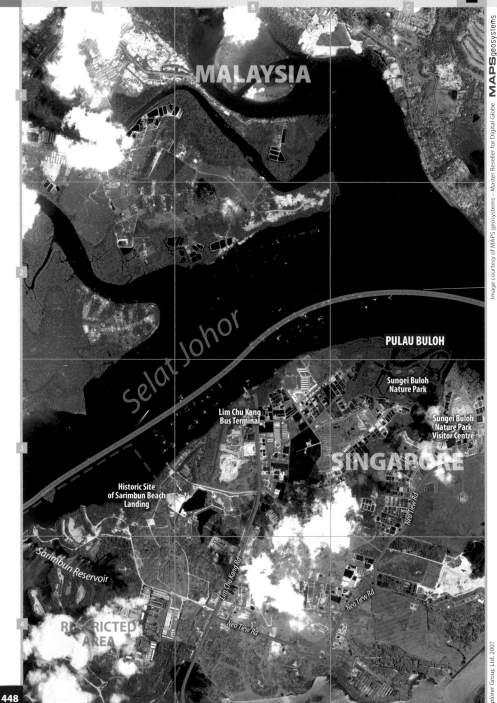

MALAYSIA

Selat Johor

PULAU BULOH

Sungei Buloh
Nature Park

Lim Chu Kang
Bus Terminal

Sungei Buloh
Nature Park
Visitor Centre

SINGAPORE

Historic Site
of Sarimbun Beach
Landing

Neo Tiew Rd

Sarimbun Reservoir

Lim Chu Kang Rd

Neo Tiew Rd

RESTRICTED
AREA

Neo Tiew Rd

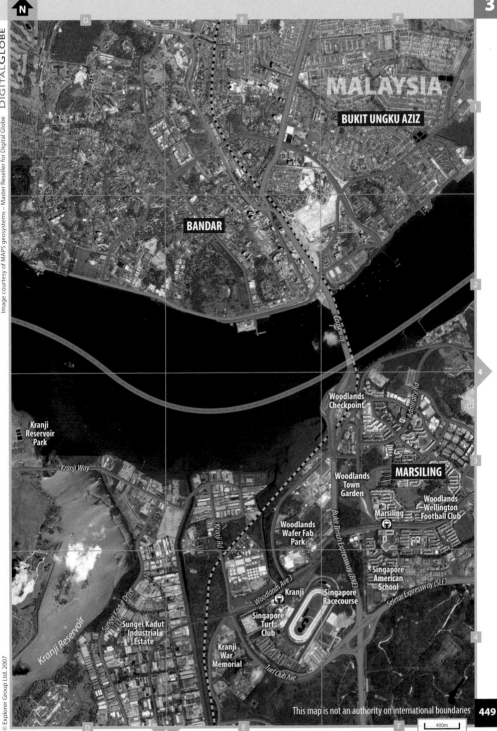

MALAYSIA

BUKIT UNGKU AZIZ

BANDAR

Causeway

Woodlands
Checkpoint

Admiralty Rd

Kranji
Reservoir
Park

Kranji Way

Woodlands
Town
Garden

MARSILING

Marsiling

Woodlands
Wellington
Football Club

Woodlands
Wafer Fab
Park

Bukit Timah Expressway (BKE)

Kranji Rd

Singainji Reservoir

Sungei Kadut Drive

Sungei Kadut
Industrial
Estate

Woodlands Ave 3

Kranji

Singapore
Racecourse

Singapore
Turf
Club

Singapore
American
School

Seletar Expressway (SLE)

Kranji
War
Memorial

Turf Club Ave

This map is not an authority on international boundaries

400m

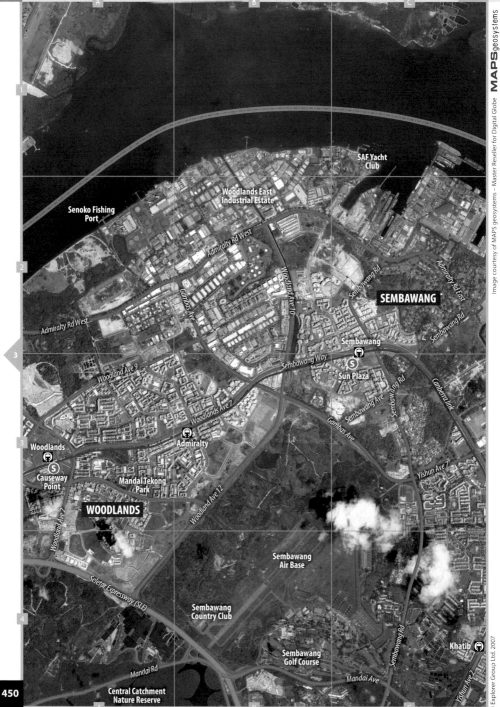

Senoko Fishing Port

Woodlands East Industrial Estate

SAF Yacht Club

Admiralty Rd West

Gambas Ave

Woodland Ave 10

Sembawang Rd

SEMBAWANG

Admiralty Rd West

Admiralty Rd East

Sembawang Rd

Woodland Ave 9

Sembawang Way

Sembawang

Sun Plaza

Sembawang Rd

Woodlands Ave 7

Sembawang Ave

Gambas Ave

Camberra link

Admiralty

3 Woodlands

Causeway Point

Mandai Tekong Park

Woodland Ave 2

WOODLANDS

Woodland Ave 12

Yishun Ave 7

Sembawang Rd

Sembawang Air Base

Seletar Expressway (SLE)

Sembawang Country Club

Khatib

Mandai Rd

Sembawang Golf Course

Mandai Ave

Yishun Ave 2

Central Catchment Nature Reserve

MALAYSIA

Selat Johor

Sembawang
Park

Sembawang
Beach

SINGAPORE

Sungei Simpang

PULAU SELETAR

YISHUN

PULAU PUNGGOL
BARAT

Northpoint
Shopping Centre

Yishun

SAFRA
Yishun
Country
Club

Yishun
Park

Yishun Ave 1

Orchid
Country Club

Golf Course

Yishun Ave 1

Lower Seletar
Reservoir

Seletar
Airport

Piccadilly

SELETAR

This map is not an authority on international boundaries

400m

DIGITALGLOBE

451

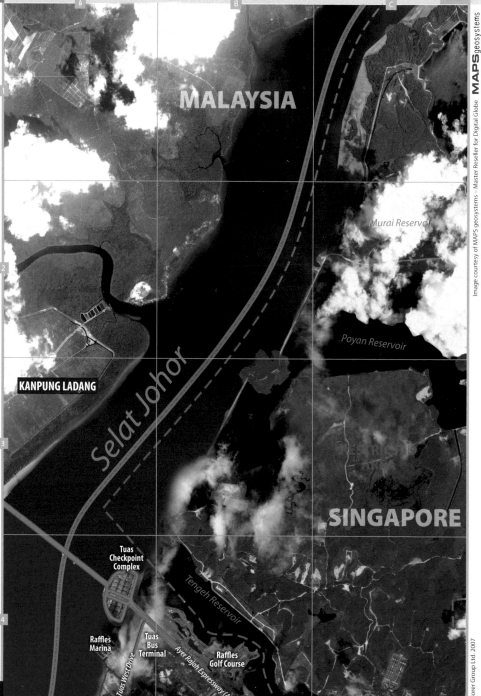

MALAYSIA

Murai Reservoir

Poyan Reservoir

Selat Johor

KANPUNG LADANG

SINGAPORE

Tuas
Checkpoint
Complex

Tengeh Reservoir

Raffles
Marina

Tuas
Bus
Terminal

Ayer Rajah Expressway (AYE)

Raffles
Golf Course

Tuas West Drive

Image courtesy of MAPS geosystems – Master Reseller for Digital Globe

MAPSgeosystems

© Explorer Group Ltd. 2007

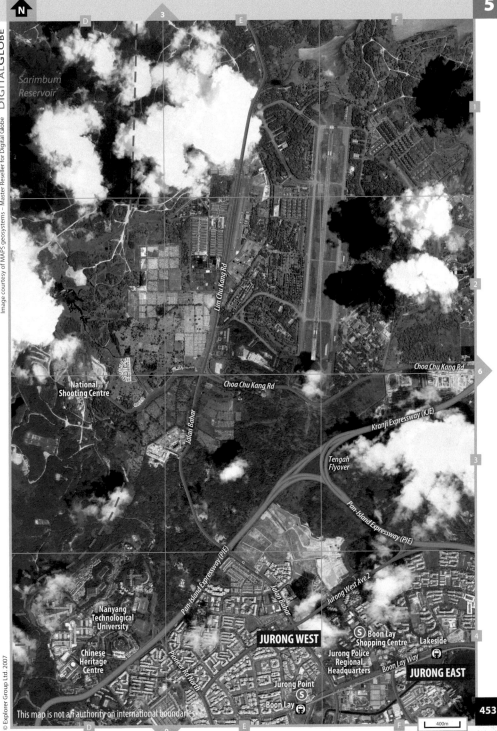

Sarimbum
Reservoir

Lim Chu Kang Rd

Choa Chu Kang Rd

National
Shooting Centre

Jalan Bahar

Choa Chu Kang Rd

Kranji Expressway (KJE)

Tengah
Flyover

Pan-Island Expressway (PIE)

Nanyang
Technological
University

Pan-Island Expressway (PIE)

Jalan Bahar

Jurong West Ave 2

Chinese
Heritage
Centre

JURONG WEST

(S) Boon Lay
Shopping Centre

Lakeside

Jurong Police
Regional
Headquarters

Boon Lay Way

JURONG EAST

Pioneer Rd North

Jurong Point
(S)
Boon Lay

1

2

6

3

4

400m

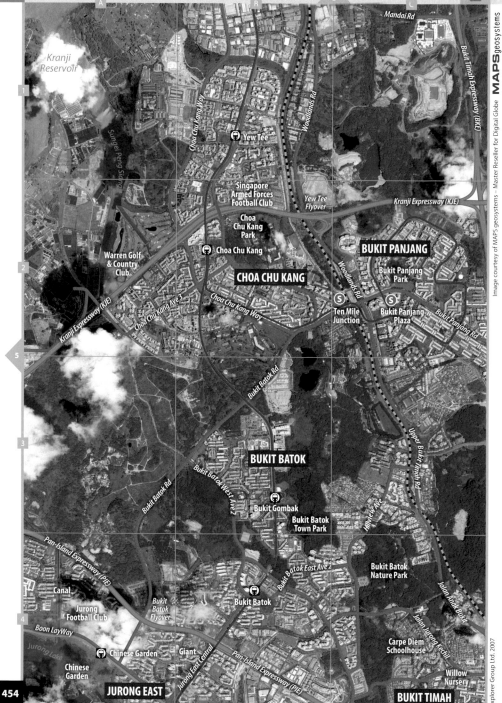

454

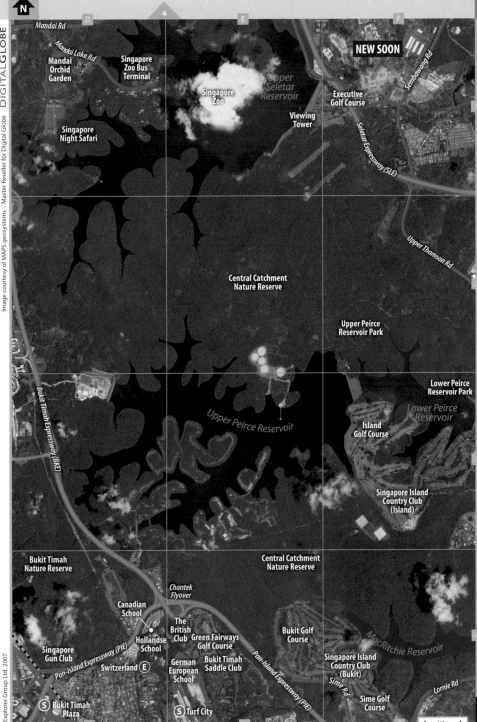

N

DIGITALGLOBE

Mandai Rd

Mandai Lake Rd

Mandai Orchid Garden

Singapore Zoo Bus Terminal

Singapore Night Safari

Singapore Zoo

Upper Seletar Reservoir

Viewing Tower

NEW SOON

Sembawang Rd

Executive Golf Course

Seletar Expressway (SLE)

1

Upper Thomson Rd

Central Catchment Nature Reserve

2

Upper Peirce Reservoir Park

7

Lower Peirce Reservoir Park

Bukit Timah Expressway (BKE)

Upper Peirce Reservoir

Island Golf Course

Lower Peirce Reservoir

3

Singapore Island Country Club (Island)

Bukit Timah Nature Reserve

Central Catchment Nature Reserve

MacRitchie Reservoir

4

Chantek Flyover

Canadian School

The British Club

Green Fairways Golf Course

Bukit Golf Course

Hollandse School

Singapore Gun Club

Pan-Island Expressway (PIE)

Switzerland E

German European School

Bukit Timah Saddle Club

Pan-Island Expressway (PIE)

Singapore Island Country Club (Bukit)

Sime Rd

Lornie Rd

S Bukit Timah Plaza

S Turf City

Sime Golf Course

400m

455

D   4   E   F

D   10   E   13   F

The Complete **Residents'** Guide

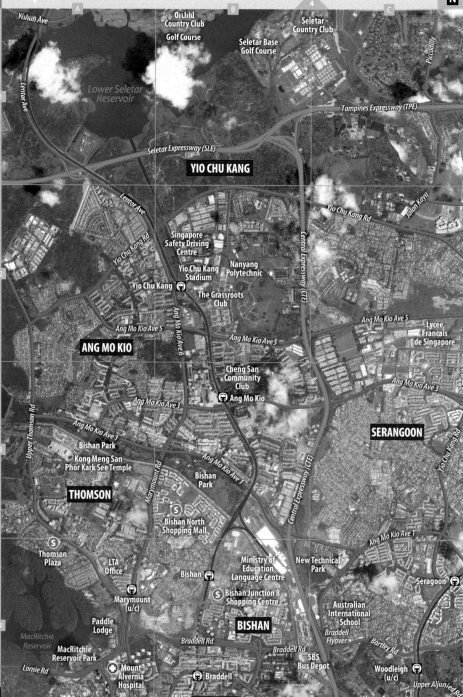

Singapore Explorer 1st Edition

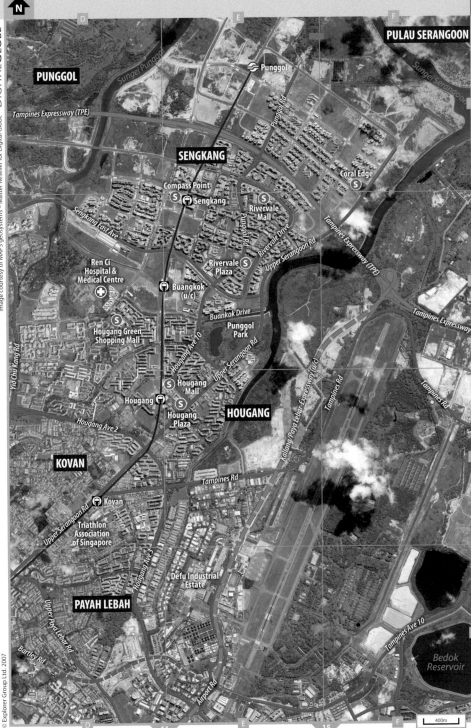

PULAU SERANGOON

PUNGGOL

Sungei Punggol

Punggol

Tampines Expressway (TPE)

Sungei Serangoon

SENGKANG

Compass Point

Sengkang

Coral Edge

Rivervale Mall

Sengkang East Ave

Punggol Rd

Rivervale Drive

Upper Serangoon Rd

Tampines Expressway (TPE)

Ren Ci Hospital & Medical Centre

Rivervale Plaza

Buangkok (u/c)

Buankok Drive

Tampines Expressway

Punggol Park Rd

Hougang Green Shopping Mall

Hougang Ave 10

Upper Serangoon Rd

Kallang Paya Lebar Expressway (u/c)

Tampines Rd

Tampines Rd

Yio Chu Kang Rd

Hougang Mall

Hougang

HOUGANG

Hougang Plaza

Hougang Ave 2

KOVAN

Tampines Rd

Kovan

Upper Serangoon Rd

Triathlon Association of Singapore

Hougang Ave 3

PAYAH LEBAH

Defu Industrial Estate

Upper Paya Lebar Rd

Bartley Rd

Airport Rd

Tampines Ave 10

Bedok Reservoir

N

8

1

8

2

3

12

4

F

D

E

F

11

15

400m

457

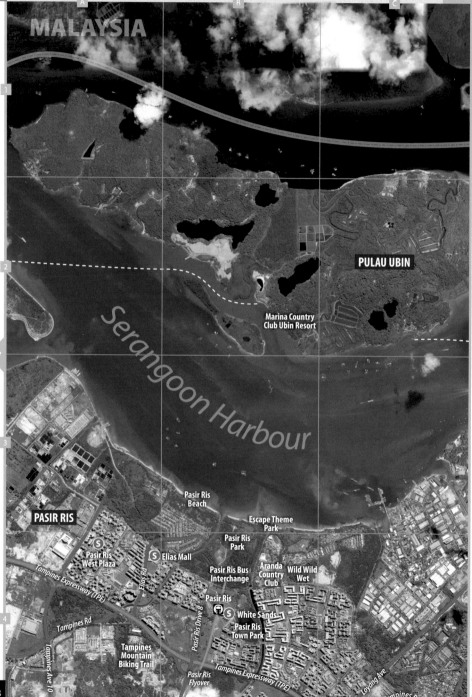

MALAYSIA

PULAU UBIN

Marina Country
Club Ubin Resort

Serangoon Harbour

PASIR RIS

Pasir Ris
Beach

Escape Theme
Park

Pasir Ris
Park

Pasir Ris
West Plaza

Elias Mall

Pasir Ris Bus
Interchange

Aranda
Country
Club

Wild Wild
Wet

Tampines Expressway (TPE)

Pasir Ris

White Sands

Pasir Ris
Town Park

Tampines Rd

Tampines
Mountain
Biking Trail

Pasir Ris
Flyover

Tampines Expressway (TPE)

Loyang Ave

Old Tampines Rd

Image courtesy of MAPS geosystems – Master Reseller for Digital Globe MAPSgeosystems

© Explorer Group Ltd. 2007

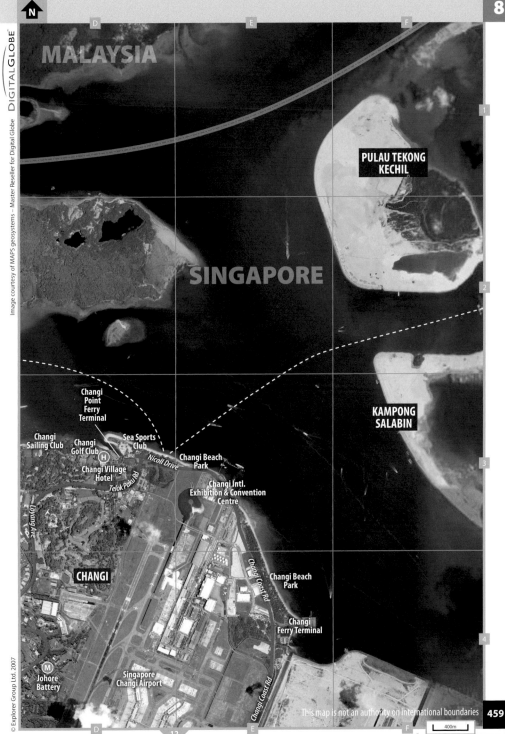

MALAYSIA

PULAU TEKONG
KECHIL

SINGAPORE

KAMPONG
SALABIN

Changi
Point
Ferry
Terminal

Changi
Sailing Club

Changi
Golf Club

Sea Sports
Club

H

Changi Village
Hotel

Nicoll Drive

Changi Beach
Park

Telok Paku Rd

Changi Intl.
Exhibition & Convention
Centre

Loyang Ave

CHANGI

Changi Coast Rd

Changi Beach
Park

Changi
Ferry Terminal

M

Johore
Battery

Singapore
Changi Airport

Changi Coast Rd

Image courtesy of MAPS geosystems – Master Reseller for Digital Globe   DIGITALGLOBE

© Explorer Group Ltd. 2007

This map is not an authority on international boundaries

400m

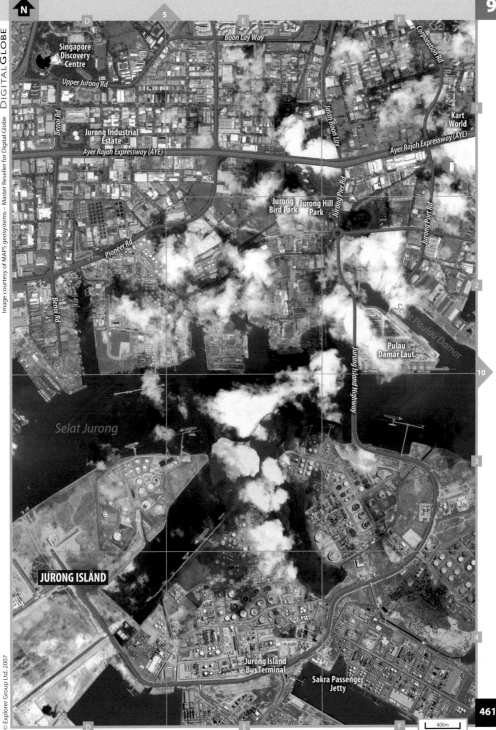

N

DIGITALGLOBE

Boon Lay Way

Singapore
Discovery
Centre

Upper Jurong Rd

Corporation Rd

Kart
World

1

Benoi Rd

Jurong Industrial
Estate

Jalan Boon Lay

Ayer Rajah Expressway (AYE)

Ayer Rajah Expressway (AYE)

Jurong
Bird Park

Jurong Hill
Park

Jurong Pier Rd

Jurong Port Rd

Pioneer Rd

2

Selat Pulau Damar

Benoi Rd

Pulau
Damar Laut

Jurong Island Highway

10

Selat Jurong

3

JURONG ISLAND

Jurong Island
Bus Terminal

Sakra Passenger
Jetty

4

400m

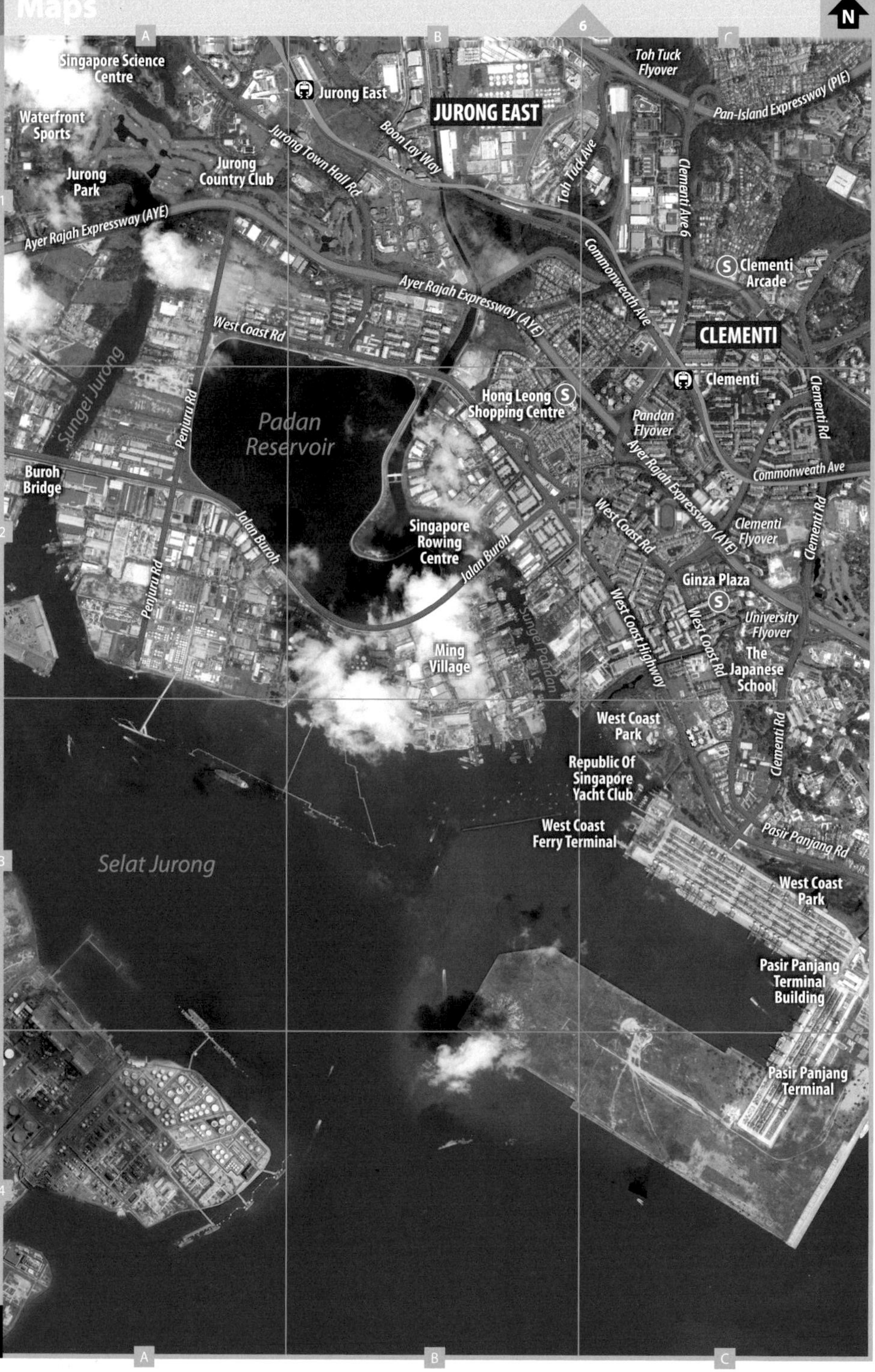

N

Singapore Science Centre

Waterfront Sports

Jurong East

JURONG EAST

Toh Tuck Flyover

Pan-Island Expressway (PIE)

Jurong Park

Jurong Country Club

Jurong Town Hall Rd

Boon Lay Way

Toh Tuck Ave

Clementi Ave 6

Ayer Rajah Expressway (AYE)

West Coast Rd

Ayer Rajah Expressway (AYE)

Commonwealth Ave

Clementi Arcade

CLEMENTI

Penjuru Rd

Sungei Jurong

Padan Reservoir

Hong Leong Shopping Centre

Clementi

Pandan Flyover

Ayer Rajah Expressway (AYE)

Commonwealth Ave

Clementi Rd

Buroh Bridge

Jalan Buroh

Singapore Rowing Centre

Jalan Buroh

Sungei Pandan

West Coast Rd

West Coast Rd

Clementi Flyover

Clementi Rd

Penjuru Rd

Ming Village

West Coast Highway

Ginza Plaza

West Coast Rd

University Flyover

The Japanese School

Selat Jurong

West Coast Park

Republic Of Singapore Yacht Club

West Coast Ferry Terminal

Clementi Rd

Pasir Panjang Rd

West Coast Park

Pasir Panjang Terminal Building

Pasir Panjang Terminal

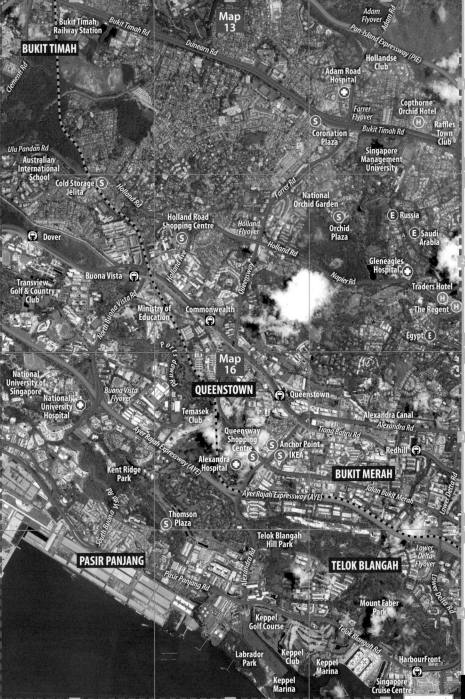

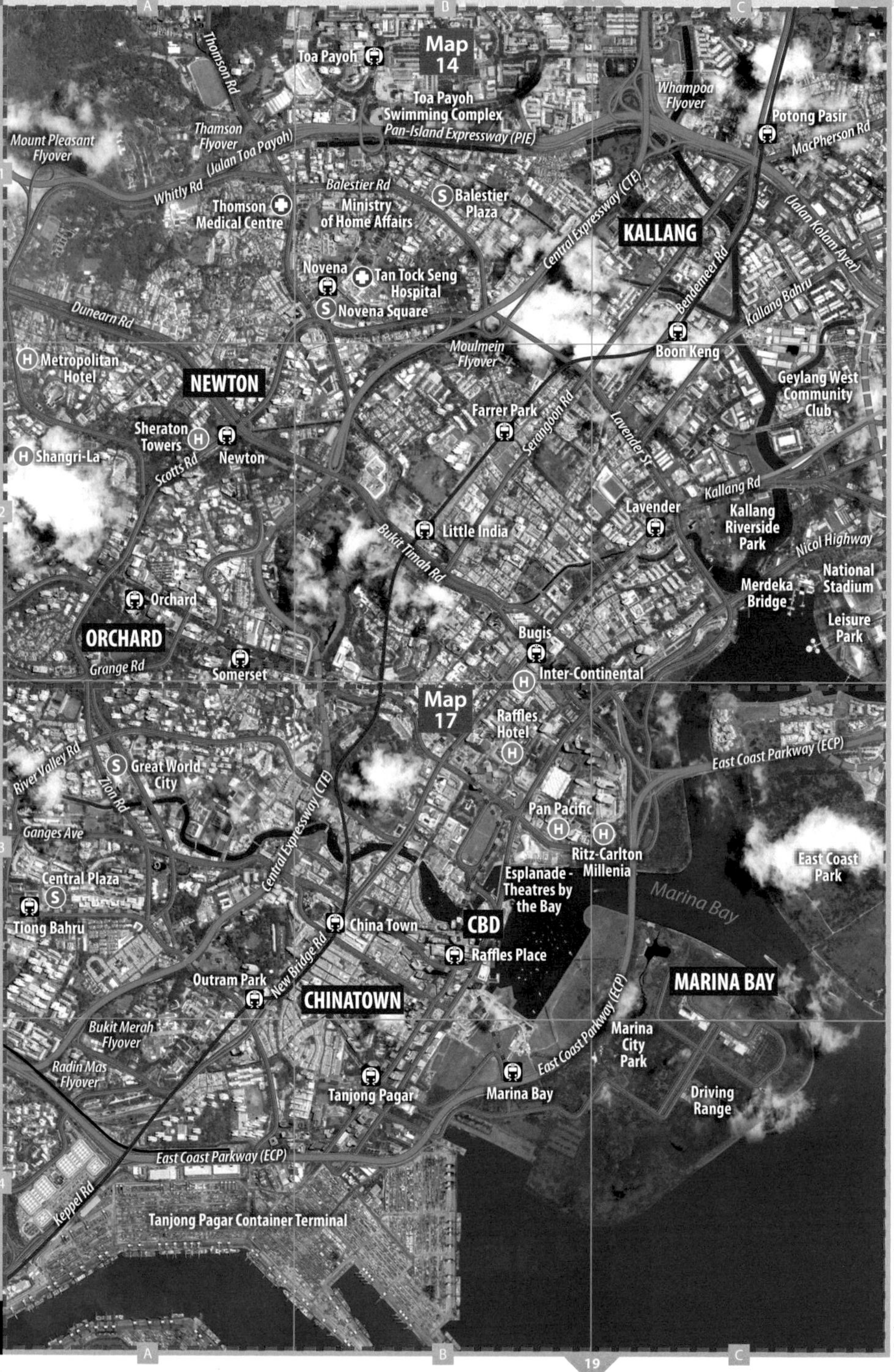
N
A
B
C
7
Map 14
Toa Payoh
Thomson Rd
Toa Payoh Swimming Complex
Pan-Island Expressway (PIE)
Whampoa Flyover
Potong Pasir
MacPherson Rd
Mount Pleasant Flyover
Thamson Flyover
(Jalan Toa Payoh)
Whitly Rd
Balestier Rd
Balestier Plaza
Thomson Medical Centre
Ministry of Home Affairs
Central Expressway (CTE)
KALLANG
(Jalan Kolam Ayer)
Novena
Tan Tock Seng Hospital
Novena Square
Bendemeer Rd
Kallang Bahru
Dunearn Rd
13
Moulmein Flyover
Boon Keng
Metropolitan Hotel
NEWTON
Geylang West Community Club
Farrer Park
Serangoon Rd
Lavender St
Sheraton Towers
Newton
Shangri-La
Scotts Rd
Kallang Rd
2
Lavender
Kallang Riverside Park
Little India
Bukit Timah Rd
Nicol Highway
National Stadium
Merdeka Bridge
Orchard
ORCHARD
Leisure Park
Bugis
Grange Rd
Somerset
10
Inter-Continental
Map 17
Raffles Hotel
River Valley Rd
Great World City
Zion Rd
East Coast Parkway (ECP)
Central Expressway (CTE)
Pan Pacific
Ganges Ave
3
Ritz-Carlton Millenia
East Coast Park
Central Plaza
Esplanade - Theatres by the Bay
Marina Bay
Tiong Bahru
China Town
CBD
Raffles Place
Outram Park
New Bridge Rd
MARINA BAY
CHINATOWN
16
Bukit Merah Flyover
East Coast Parkway (ECP)
Marina City Park
Radin Mas Flyover
Tanjong Pagar
Marina Bay
Driving Range
East Coast Parkway (ECP)
4
Keppel Rd
Tanjong Pagar Container Terminal
19
MAPSgeosystems
Image courtesy of MAPS geosystems – Master Reseller for Digital Globe

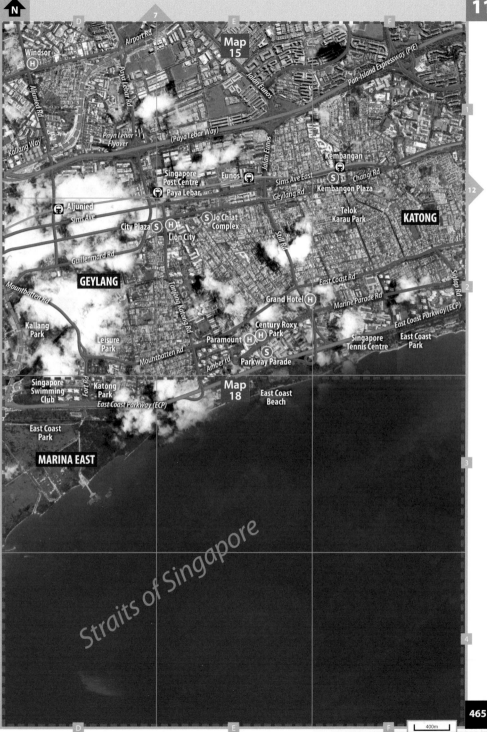

N

Tampines Ave 9

A

Tampines Ave 10

Tampines Ave 7

Changi Chapel & Museum

TAMPINES

Tampines Ave 5

Tampines Ave 1

Tampines

Tampines Expressway (TPE)

Upper Changi Rd North

Century Square

Tampines Mall

1

Tampines Ave 2

Tampines South Flyover

Pan-Island Expressway (PIE)

SAFRA Tampines

New Upper Changi Rd

Pan-Island Expressway (PIE)

Simei

7

Bedok Reservoir

Eastpoint Mall

SIMEI

Changi General Hospital

Changi Business Park

Simei Ave

Park

Pan-Island Expressway (PIE)

Canal

TANAH MERAH

Singapore Expo

Expo

2

Bedok North Rd

BEDOK

Bedok Market Place

Xilin Ave

Tanah Merah Flyover

Gaden Hill Park

Geylang United Football Club

New Upper Changi Rd

Bedok Rd

Tanah Merah

Bedok

Bedok South Ave 1

SIGLAP

Laguna National Golf & Country Club

Canal

East Coast Medical Centre

National Service Resort & Country Club

3

Upper East Coast Rd

East Coast Parkway (ECP)

East Coast Park

Marine Parade Rd

East Coast Parkway (ECP)

East Coast Park

East Coast Sea Sports Club

East Coast Lagoon

Ski 360°

Pasta Fresca Sea Sports Centre

11

S t r a i t s   o f

4

A

B

C

Singapore Explorer 1st Edition

DIGITALGLOBE

Image courtesy of MAPS geosystems – Master Reseller for Digital Globe

Changi Airport

Singapore Changi Airport

Changi Coast Rd

EAST CHANGI

Changi Flyover

Tanah Merah Golf Course

Tanah Merah Country Club

Changi Coast Rd

Tanah Merah Ferry Terminal

Tanah Merah Coast Rd

Singapore

© Explorer Group Ltd. 2007

400m

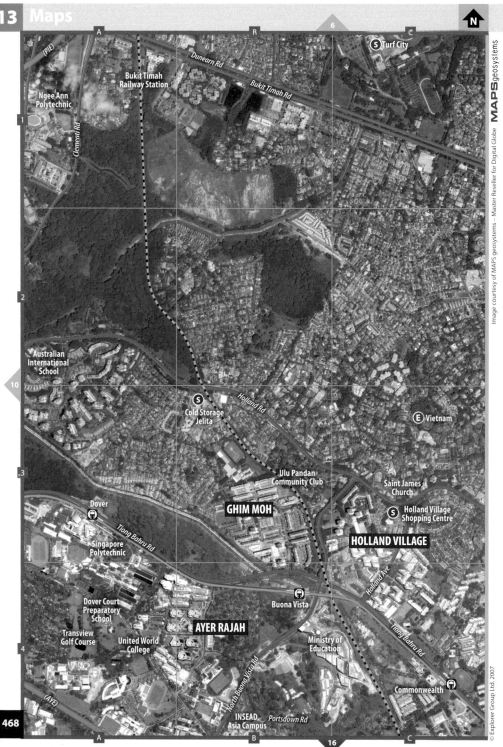

Singapore Explorer 1st Edition

Image courtesy of MAPS geosystems – Master Reseller for Digital Globe

Image courtesy of MAPS geosystems – Master Reseller for Digital Globe

DIGITALGLOBE®

© Explorer Group Ltd. 2007

D 6 **E** **F**

Sime Golf Course

Sime Rd

Adam Flyover

Adam Rd

Hollandse Club

Pan-Island Expressway (PIE)

Dunearn Rd

Hwa Chong International School

Bukit Timah Rd

Adam Road Hospital

(S) Coronation Plaza

Catholic Church of Saint Ignatius

Farrer Flyover

Dunearn Rd

Copthorne Orchid

International Baptist Church

Serene Centre **(S)(E)** France

Bukit Timah Rd

(H) Raffles Town Club

Eco-Lake

Stevens Rd

Farrer Rd

Singapore Management University

I4

Singapore Botanic Gardens

Symphony Stage

(E) Russia

(E) China

National Orchid Garden

(E) Saudi Arabia

Turkey

Holland Rd

Holland Flyover

(S) Orchid Plaza

(E)(E) Japan

Queensway Underpass

Philippines **(E)(E)**

Holland Park

Holland Rd

Swan Lake

Gleneagles Hospital **(H)**

Myanmar **(E)**

Napier Rd

Tanglin Golf Course

British Council

Tanglin Mall

Ridout Tea Garden

Australia **(E)** US **(E)(E)**

UK **(E)**

(S) Traders Hotel **(H)**

(i) The Regent

Ministry of Foreign Affairs

China **(E)**

Camden Medical Centre

TANGLIN

Egypt **(E)**

Brunei Darussalam **(E)**

Indonesia **(E)**

D 16 **E** **F**

200m

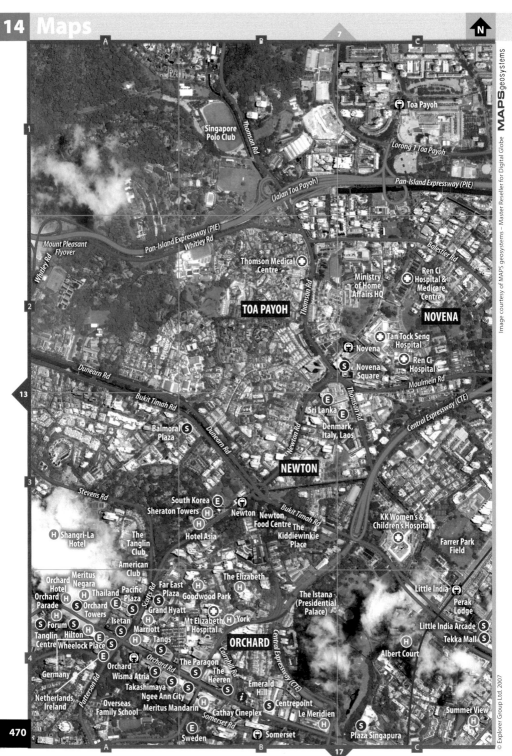

Singapore Explorer 1st Edition

D 7 E F

STTA
Academy
SAFRA
Toa Payoh
Clubhouse

Central Expressway (CTE)

(Jalan Toa Payoh)

Whampoa
Flyover

Upper Serangoon Rd

Potong
Pasir

MacPherson Rd

Pan-Island Expressway (PIE)

1

Central Expressway (CTE)

Serangoon Rd

Serangoon Rd

The
Regent

Kallang Bahru

(Jalan Kolam Ayer)

2

Quality

Boon Keng

Ceylon
Sports Club

Balestier Rd

Bendemeer
Shopping Mall

Bendemeer Rd

Kallang Bahru

KALLANG

15

Climb-Asia

Leong San
See Temple

Serangoon Rd

Sri Srinivasa
Perumal Temple

Farrer Park Sakaya Muni
Buddha Gaya
Temple

Jalan Besar

Lavender St

Kallang

Sims Ave

Geylang Rd

Mountbatten Rd

Kallang/Paya Lebar Expressway

3

Mustafa
Centre

Mustafa

Taekwon
Singapore

Kallang Rd

InnCrowd
Backpackers
Hostel

Dickson Court

Scuba
Corner

Lavender

Kallang
Riverside
Park

Kadir's
Boxing School

LITTLE INDIA

ARAB STREET &
KAMPONG GLAM

Jalan Besar

Victoria St

Immigration and
Checkpoints
Authority

Mirdeka
Bridge

Nicoll Highway

National
Stadium

Tekka Mall

Victoria Street
Wholesale
Centre

Ophir Rd

Malay
Heritage
Centre

Kallang
Water Sport
Centre

Sports
Museum

Leisure Park

4

BUGIS

Golden
Landmark

Bugis

Shaw Bugis
Cineplex

Raffles
Hospital

The
Concourse

The Furniture
Mall

Republic Ave

Oasis
Building

Singapore
Indoor Stadium

471

D 17 E F

200m

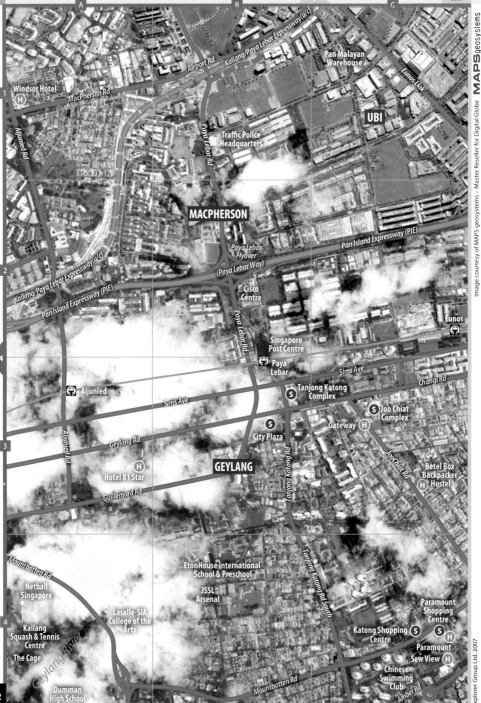

Windsor Hotel

MacPherson Rd

Aljunied Rd

Airport Rd

Kallang/Paya Lebar Expressway (u/c)

Pan Malayan Warehouse

Eunos Link

UBI

Paya Lebar Rd

Traffic Police Headquarters

MACPHERSON

Paya Lebar Flyover

(Paya Lebar Way)

Pan Island Expressway (PIE)

Kallang/Paya Lebar Expressway (u/c)

Pan Island Expressway (PIE)

Cisco Centre

Paya Lebar Rd

Singapore Post Centre

Eunos

Paya Lebar

Sims Ave

Changi Rd

Aljunied

Sims Ave

Tanjong Katong Complex

Joo Chiat Complex

City Plaza

Gateway

Geylang Rd

GEYLANG

Tanjong Katong Rd

Joo Chiat Rd

Betel Box Backpacker Hostel

Aljunied Rd

Hotel 81 Star

Guillemard Rd

Mountbatten Rd

EtonHouse International School & Preschool

Tanjong Katong Rd South

Netball Singapore

JSSL Arsenal

Kallang Squash & Tennis Centre

Lasalle-SIA College of the Arts

Paramount Shopping Centre

Katong Shopping Centre

Paramount

The Cage

Sew View

Geylang River

Chinese Swimming Club

Dumman High School

Mountbatten Rd

Amber Rd

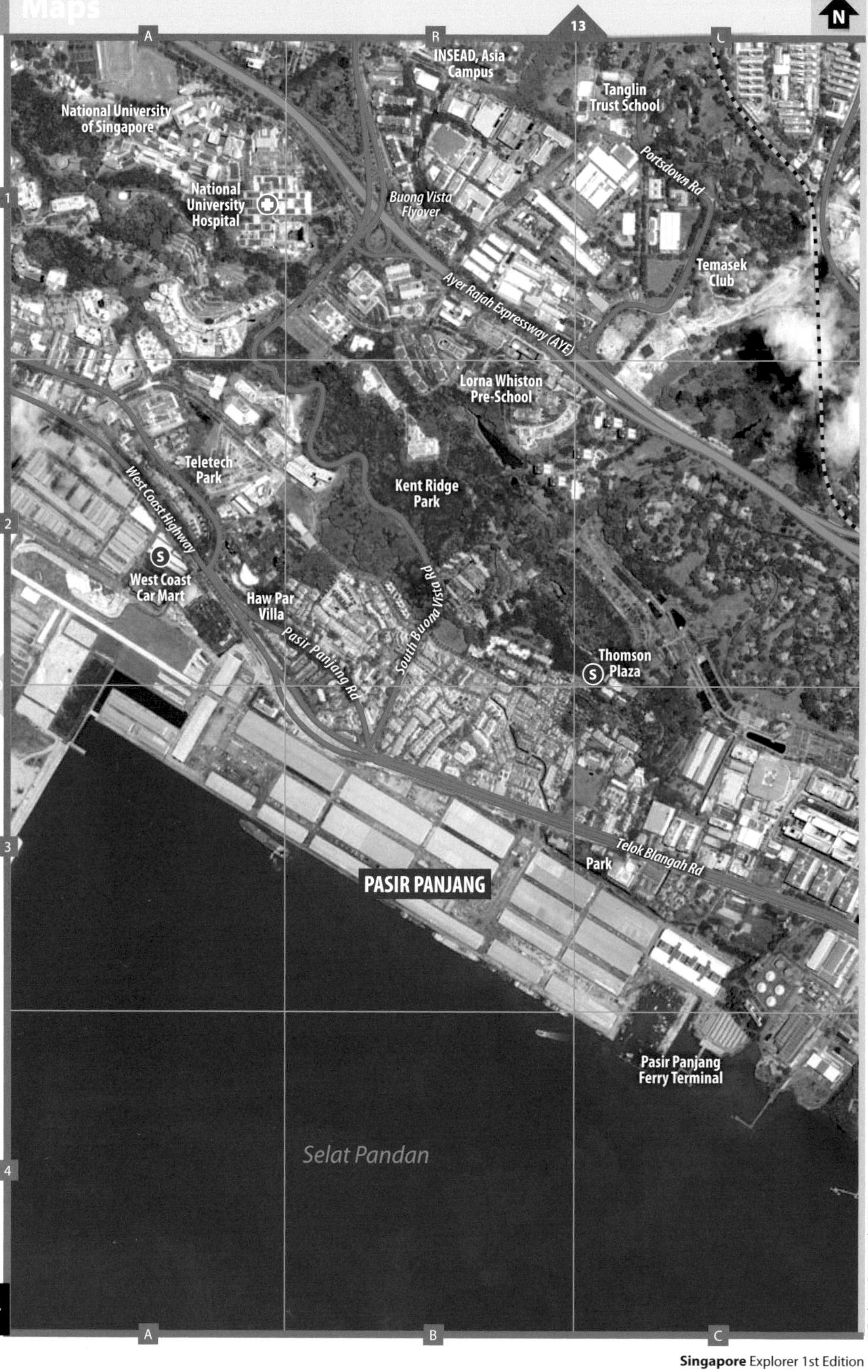

N

13

Image courtesy of MAPS geosystems – Master Reseller for Digital Globe

MAPSgeosystems

National University
of Singapore

INSEAD, Asia
Campus

Tanglin
Trust School

National
University
Hospital

Buong Vista
Flyover

Portsdown Rd

Temasek
Club

Ayer Rajah Expressway (AYE)

Lorna Whiston
Pre-School

Teletech
Park

West Coast Highway

Kent Ridge
Park

West Coast
Car Mart

Haw Par
Villa

Pasir Panjang Rd

South Buona Vista Rd

Thomson
Plaza

Telok Blangah Rd

PASIR PANJANG

Park

Pasir Panjang
Ferry Terminal

Selat Pandan

A   B   C

© Explorer Group Ltd. 2007

Singapore Explorer 1st Edition

N

DIGITALGLOBE

Image courtesy of MAPS geosystems – Master Reseller for Digital Globe

Map labels:

Commonwealth Ave

Queenstown Sports Complex

Queenstown

Queensway

Alexandra Rd

Leng Kee Rd

Alexandra Rd

Alexandra Canal

Tiong Bahru Rd

Redhill

Tiong Bahru Park

Anchor Point

Queensway Shopping Centre

IKEA

Alexandra Hospital

Jalan Bukit Merah

QUEENSTOWN

Gillman Flyover

Ayer Rajah Expressway (AYE)

Jalan Bukit Merah

Lower Delta Rd

Alexandra Rd

Telok Blangah Hill Park

Henderson Rd

Park

TELOK BLANGAH

Mount Faber Park

Cable Car Station

Lower Delta Rd

Keppel Golf Links

Keppel Club

Telok Blangah Rd

HarbourFront Bus Terminal

Labrador Park

Keppel Marina

HarbourFront

HarbourFront Exhibition Complex

Keppel Harbour

Pulau Keppel

HarbourFront Centre

VivoCity

Singapore Cruise Centre

Gateway Ave

200m

16

17

© Explorer Group Ltd. 2007

475

The Complete **Residents'** Guide

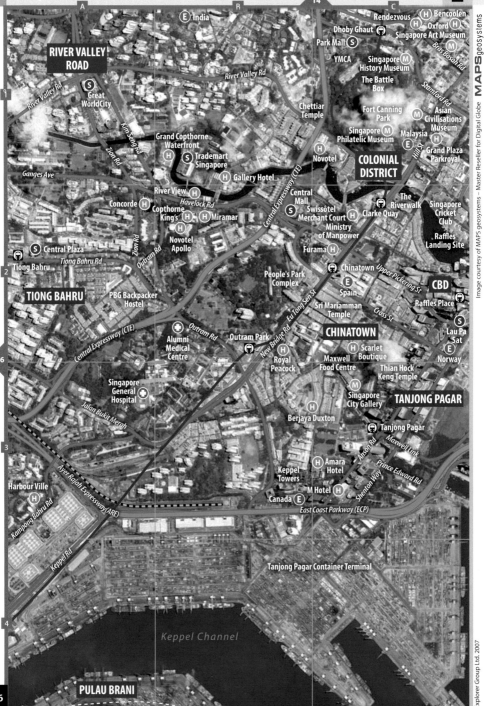

N

Image courtesy of MAPS geosystems – Master Reseller for Digital Globe

MAPSgeosystems

(E) India

Rendezvous (H) Bencoolen

Dhoby Ghaut (H) Oxford

Park Mall (S) Singapore Art Museum

(M)

Bras Basah Rd

YMCA Singapore (M)

History Museum

RIVER VALLEY ROAD

The Battle Box

River Valley Rd

Fort Canning Park

Stamford Rd

(S) Great WorldCity

Chettiar Temple

Singapore (M) Asian

Philatelic Museum Civilisations

River Valley Rd

Malaysia Museum

Kim Seng Rd

Grand Copthorne Waterfront

(H) Novotel

(E) Hill St Grand Plaza

(H) Parkroyal

Zion Rd

(H) (S) Trademart Singapore

COLONIAL DISTRICT

Ganges Ave

(H) Gallery Hotel

River View (H)

Central Mall

The Riverwalk

Singapore Cricket Club

Havelock Rd

Concorde (H) Copthorne King's (H)

(H) Miramar

Central Expressway (CTE)

(S) Swissôtel Merchant Court

Clarke Quay

Raffles Landing Site

Zion Rd

(H)

Novotel Apollo

Ministry of Manpower

Outram Rd

Furama (H)

(S) Central Plaza

People's Park Complex

Chinatown

Upper Pickering St

CBD

(H)

(S)

Tiong Bahru

Tiong Bahru Rd

(E) Spain

Raffles Place (M)

TIONG BAHRU

PBG Backpacker Hostel

Sri Mariamman Temple

Fu Tong Sen St

Cross St

(S) Lau Pa

Sat

Central Expressway (CTE)

Outram Rd

Alumni Medical Centre

Outram Park

New Bridge Rd

Scarlet Boutique

CHINATOWN

(E) Norway

Singapore General Hospital

Royal Peacock

Maxwell Food Centre

Thian Hock Keng Temple

Jalan Bukit Merah

(M)

Singapore City Gallery

TANJONG PAGAR

(H) Berjaya Duxton

Tanjong Pagar

Ansbj Rd Maxwell Link

Ayer Rajah Expressway (ARE)

Keppel Towers

(H) Amara Hotel

Prince Edward Rd

Shenton Way

Harbour Ville

(H)

M Hotel (H)

Kampong Bahru Rd

Canada (E)

East Coast Parkway (ECP)

Keppel Rd

Tanjong Pagar Container Terminal

Keppel Channel

PULAU BRANI

Singapore Explorer 1st Edition

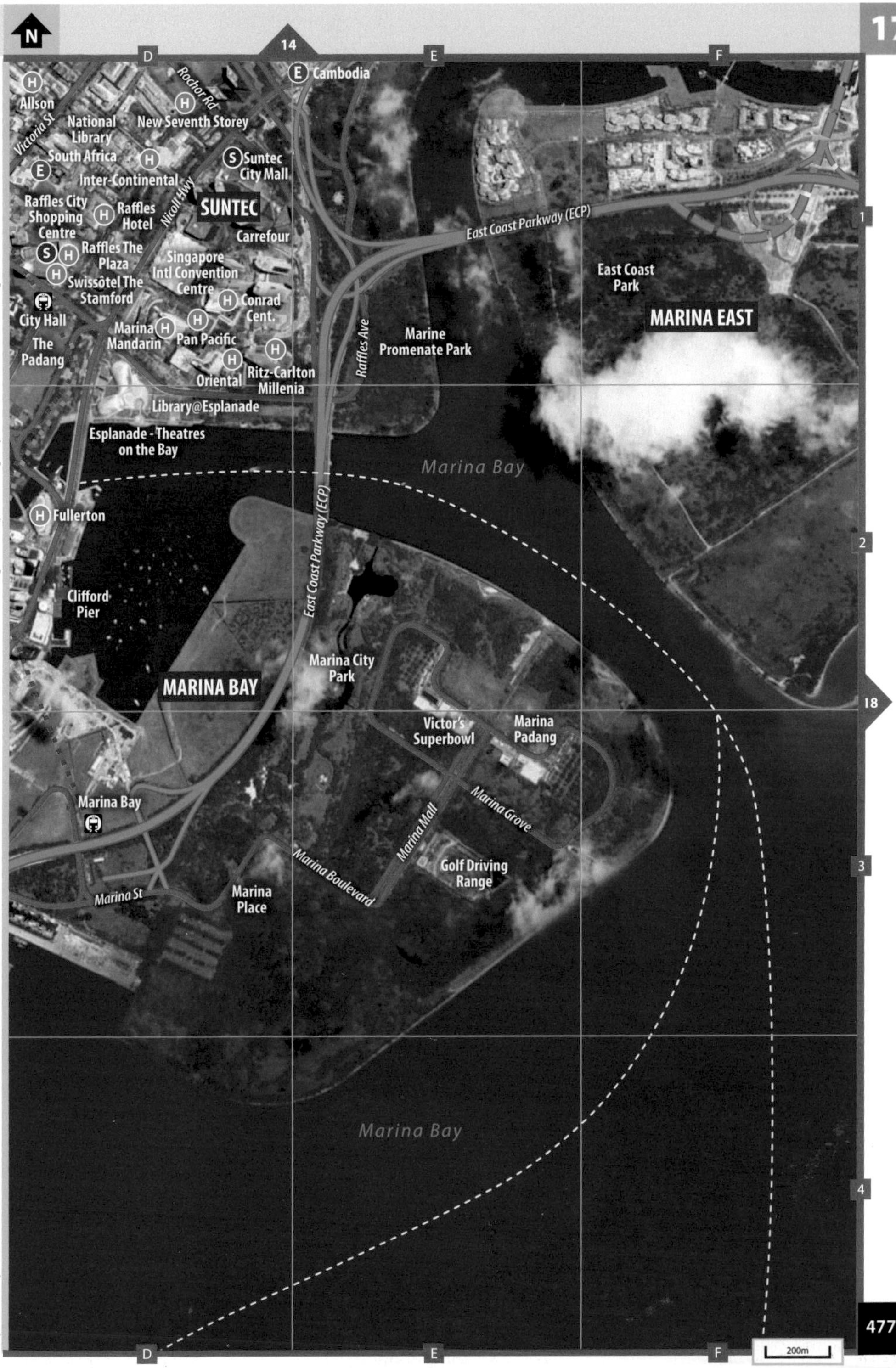

H Allson
Victoria St
National Library
South Africa
E
Inter-Continental
Raffles City Shopping Centre
H Raffles Hotel
S H Raffles The Plaza
H Swissôtel The Stamford
City Hall
The Padang
H Marina Mandarin
Oriental
Library@Esplanade
Esplanade - Theatres on the Bay
H Fullerton
Clifford Pier
MARINA BAY
Marina Bay
Marina St
Marina Place

H New Seventh Storey
S Suntec City Mall
SUNTEC
Carrefour
Singapore Intl Convention Centre
H Conrad Cent.
H Pan Pacific
H Ritz-Carlton Millenia

Rochor Rd
Nicoll Hwy

Raffles Ave
East Coast Parkway (ECP)
East Coast Parkway (ECP)
Marine Promenade Park
Marina Bay

East Coast Park
MARINA EAST

18

Marina City Park
Victor's Superbowl
Marina Padang
Marina Grove
Marina Mall
Golf Driving Range
Marina Boulevard

Marina Bay

1
2
3
4

200m

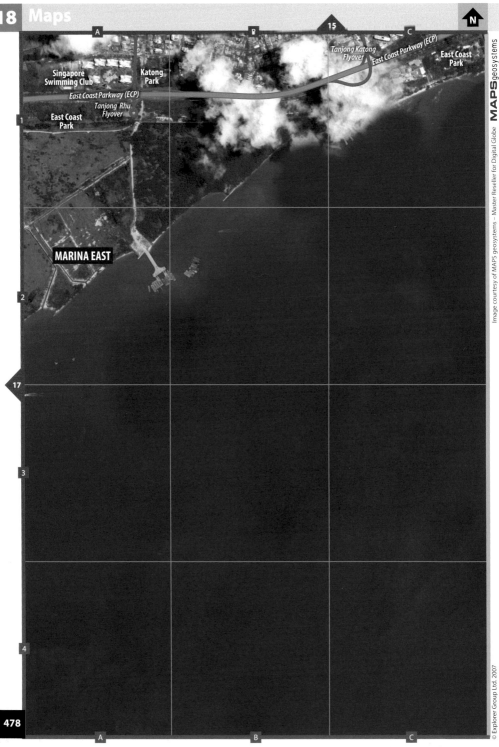

East Coast
Park Beach

Straits of Singapore

200m

16

N

Keppel Harbour

Cruise Bay

Ⓜ Fort Siloso

Underwater World

Ruined City

Lost Civilisation

Sentosa Ferry Terminal

Ⓗ Shangri-La's Rasa Sentosa Resort

Siloso Beach

Ⓗ NTUC Sentosa Beach Resort

Cable Car Station

Dragon Court

Musical Fountains

Cinemania

Volcano Land

Visitor Arrival Centre

Images of Singapore

Scented Gardens

Ⓗ Sijori Resort Sentosa

Maritime Museum

Pulau Palawan

Palawan Beach

Youth Hostel Ⓗ

Southernmost Point of Continental Asia

The Sentosa Resort & Spa Ⓗ

Gateway Ave

Sebarok Channel

MAPSgeosystems
Image courtesy of MAPS geosystems – Master Reseller for Digital Globe

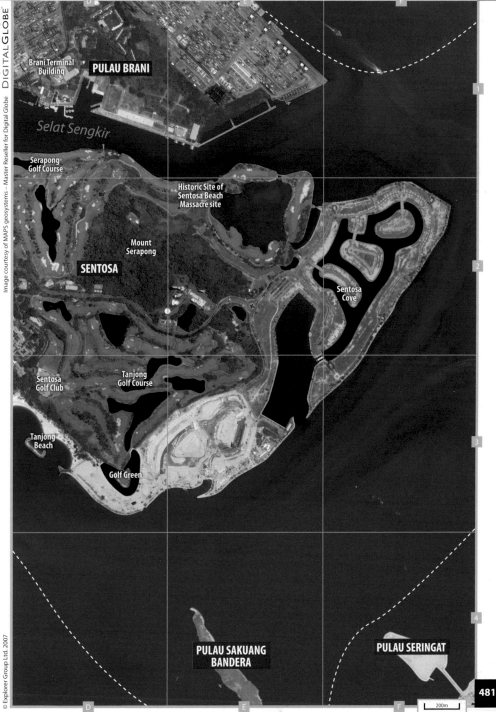

N

Brani Terminal
Building

PULAU BRANI

Selat Sengkir

Serapong
Golf Course

Historic Site of
Sentosa Beach
Massacre site

Mount
Serapong

SENTOSA

Sentosa
Cove

Sentosa
Golf Club

Tanjong
Golf Course

Tanjong
Beach

Golf Green

**PULAU SAKUANG
BANDERA**

PULAU SERINGAT

200m

Basheergraphicb□□ks

At Basheer Graphic Books we specialise in advertising and graphic arts books, as well as covering a comprehensive range of photography, interior design and animation and film titles, among others. Initially set up by Mr Basheer himself in Magazine Road (a purely coincidental street name), we have long since expanded and moved and are now located in the Bras Basah Complex. Basheer books is today a leading supplier of specialist books in its field, supplying Malaysia, Indonesia, Thailand and Hong Kong. Gift vouchers, pre-ordering books, mailing lists and worldwide shipping are just some of the services offered. Check out our website www.basheergraphic.com for forthcoming titles, the latest items in stock and for corporate special deals.

#04-19 Bras Basah Complex (6336 0810) • **www.basheergraphic.com**

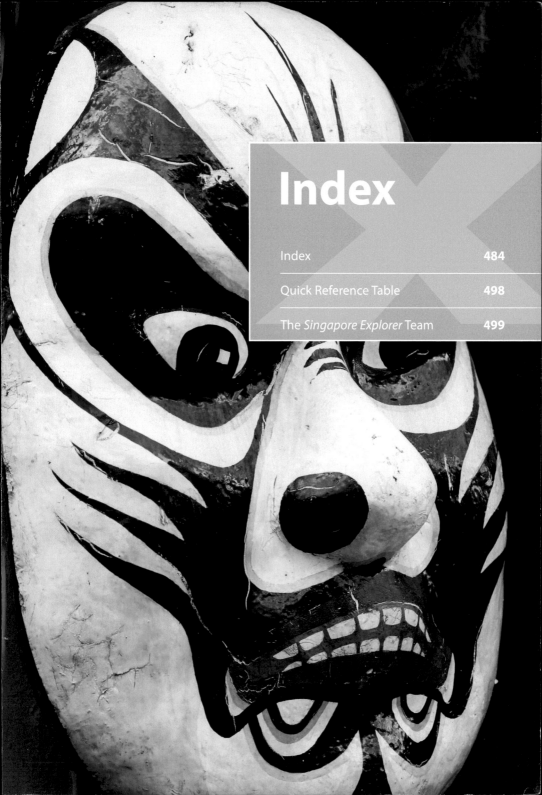

Index

Index

491

Index

Index

Emergency Services

Police	999
Ambulance	995
Fire	995
Electricity Service	1800 778 8888

Pharmacies/Chemists - 24 hours

All hospitals and many clinics have an in-house pharmacy to dispense prescribed medication and to give you advice – for contact numbers, see the table of Hospitals with Emergency Services on the right. For less complex requirements there are pharmacies in most shopping malls – see Medicine on p.346 in the Shopping chapter.

Public Transportation

TransitLink Hotline (Bus, MRT & LRT)	1800 225 5663
MRT Lost & Found	1800 336 8900

Taxi Companies

Citycab	6552 2222
Comfort	6552 1111
Premier/Silver Cab	6363 6888
SMART	6485 7700
SMRT	6555 8888
TRANScab	6555 3333

Singapore Changi Airport

Singapore Changi Airport	6542 1122
Flight Information (24hr Automated)	1800 542 4422
Baggage Services (Lost Property) – Terminal 1	
SATS Lost and Found	6541 8543
CIAS Lost and Found	6511 0459
Baggage Services (Lost Property) – Terminal 2	
SATS Lost and Found	6541 8872
MAS Lost and Found	6541 6815
Meeting Service – Terminal 1	6546 8168
Meeting Service – Terminal 2	6542 2848

Useful Numbers & Country Code

Directory Enquiries	100
International Call Assistance	104
Speaking Clock	1711
Traffic Police	6547 0000
Land Transport Authority (LTA)	1800 225 5582
Automobile Association Of Singapore (AAS)	6737 2444
Samaritans of Singapore	1800 221 4444
STB 24hr Tourist Hotline	1800 736 2000
Singapore Country Code	65
To dial a typical Singapore number from overseas	00 65 XXXX XXXX

Utilities & Services

M1 (Mobile)	1627
SingTel (Telephone & Internet)	1609
SingTel (Mobile)	1626
StarHub (Telephone, Mobile & Internet)	1633
SP Services (Electricity, Gas & Water)	1800 222 2333
Pacific Internet (internet only)	6336 6622

Hospitals with Emergency Services

Alexandra Hospital	6472 2000	Public Hospitals
Changi General Hospital	6788 8833	Public Hospitals
Gleneagles Hospital	6473 7222	Private Hospitals
Mount Elizabeth Hospital	6731 2218	Private Hospitals
Mt Alvernia Hospital	6347 6688	Private Hospitals
National University Hospital	6779 5555	Public Hospitals
Raffles Hospital	6311 1111	Private Hospitals
Singapore General Hospital	6222 3322	Public Hospitals
Tan Tock Seng Hospital	6256 6011	Public Hospitals
Thomson Medical Centre	6256 9494	Private Hospitals
East Shore Hospital	6340 8666	Private Hospitals

Embassies & Consulates

Australia	6836 4100	13-F4
Bangladesh	6255 0075	14-C3
Brunei Darussalam	6733 9055	13-E4
Cambodia	6341 9785	17-E1
Canada	6854 5900	17-B3
China	6418 0224	13-F3
Denmark	6355 5010	14-C3
France	6880 7800	13-E2
Germany	6533 6002	14-A4
India	6737 6777	17-B1
Indonesia	6737 7422	13-F4
Ireland	6238 7616	14-A4
Italy	6250 6022	14-C3
Japan	6235 8855	13-F3
Laos	6250 6044	14-C3
Malaysia	6235 0111	17-C1
Myanmar	6735 0209	13-F4
Netherlands	6737 1155	14-A4
New Zealand	6235 9966	14-B4
Norway	6220 7122	17-C2
Pakistan	6737 6988	14-A4
Philippines	6737 3977	13-F3
Russia	6235 1834	13-F3
South Africa	6339 3319	17-D1
South Korea	6256 1188	14-B3
Spain	6725 9220	17-C2
Sri Lanka	6254 4595	14-B3
Sweden	6415 9720	14-B4
Switzerland	6468 5788	6-D4
Thailand	6737 2158	14-A4
United Kingdom	6424 4270	13-F4
United States	6476 9100	13-F4
Vietnam	6462 5938	13-C3

The *Singapore Explorer* Team
Lead Editor Tim Binks
Deputy Editor Jeanne Davies
Editorial Assistants Ingrid Cupido, John Maguire, Mimi Stankova
Lead Designer Rafi Pullat
Cartographer Noushad Madathil
Photographers Pete Maloney, Pamela Grist
Proofer Joanna Holden-MacDonald

Publisher
Alistair MacKenzie

Editorial
Managing Editor Claire England
Lead Editors David Quinn, Jane Roberts, Matt Farquharson, Sean Kearns, Tim Binks
Deputy Editors Helen Spearman, Katie Drynan, Tom Jordan
Editorial Assistants Ingrid Cupido, Mimi Stankova

Design
Creative Director Pete Maloney
Art Director Ieyad Charaf
Senior Designers Alex Jeffries, Motaz Al Bunai
Layout Manager Jayde Fernandes
Designers Hashim Moideen, Rafi Pullat, Shefeeq Marakkatepurath, Sunita Lakhiani
Cartography Manager Zainudheen Madathil
Cartographer Noushad Madathil
Design Admin Manager Shyrell Tamayo
Production Coordinator Maricar Ong

Photography
Photography Manager Pamela Grist
Photographer Victor Romero
Image Editor Henry Hilos

Sales and Marketing
Area Sales Managers Laura Zuffa, Stephen Jones
Marketing Manager Kate Fox
Retail Sales Manager Ivan Rodrigues
Retail Sales Coordinator Kiran Melwani
Distribution Executives Abdul Gafoor, Ahmed Mainodin, Firos Khan, Mannie Lugtu
Warehouse Assistant Mohammed Kunjaymo
Drivers Mohammed Sameer, Shabsir Madathil

Finance and Administration
Administration Manager Andrea Fust
Accounts Assistant Cherry Enriquez
Administrator Enrico Maullon
Driver Rafi Jamal

IT
IT Administrator Ajay Krishnan R.
Software Engineers Roshni Ahuja, Tissy Varghese

Explorer Publishing & Distribution
Office 51B, Zomorrodah Building, Za'abeel Road
PO Box 34275, Dubai, United Arab Emirates
Phone: +971 (0)4 335 3520, **Fax:** +971 (0)4 335 3529
info@explorerpublishing.com
www.explorerpublishing.com

Contact Us
Reader Response
If you have any comments and suggestions, fill out our online reader response form and you could win prizes. Log on to **www.explorerpublishing.com**

General Enquiries
We'd love to hear your thoughts and answer any questions you have about this book or any other Explorer product. Contact us at **info@explorerpublishing.com**

Careers
If you fancy yourself as an Explorer, send your CV (stating the position you're interested in) to **jobs@explorerpublishing.com**

Designlab and Contract Publishing
For enquiries about Explorer's Contract Publishing arm and design services contact **designlab@explorerpublishing.com**

PR and Marketing
For PR and marketing enquries contact **marketing@explorerpublishing.com**
pr@explorerpublishing.com

Corporate Sales
For bulk sales and customisation options, for this book or any Explorer product, contact **sales@explorerpublishing.com**

Advertising and Sponsorship
For advertising and sponsorship, contact **media@explorerpublishing.com**

MRT & LRT System map

Legend

- **EW** East West Line
- **NS** North South Line
- **NE** North East Line
- **BP** Bukit Panjang LRT
- **SK** Sengkang LRT
- **PG** Punggol LRT
- ◯ Interchange Station
- Ⓑ Bus interchange near Station

East West Line

EW1 Pasir Ris · EW2 Tampines · EW3 Simei · EW4 Tanah Merah · EW5 Bedok · EW6 Kembangan · EW7 Eunos · EW8 Paya Lebar · EW9 Aljunied · EW10 Kallang · EW11 Lavender · EW12 Bugis · EW13 City Hall · EW14 Raffles Place · EW15 Tanjong Pagar · EW16 Outram Park · EW17 Tiong Bahru · EW18 Redhill · EW19 Queenstown · EW20 Commonwealth · EW21 Buona Vista · EW22 Dover · EW23 Clementi · EW24 Jurong East · EW25 Chinese Garden · EW26 Lakeside · EW27 Boon Lay

CG1 Expo · CG2 Changi Airport

North South Line

NS1 Jurong East · NS2 Bukit Batok · NS3 Bukit Gombak · NS4 Choa Chu Kang · NS5 Yew Tee · NS7 Kranji · NS8 Marsiling · NS9 Woodlands · NS10 Admiralty · NS11 Sembawang · NS13 Yishun · NS14 Khatib · NS15 Yio Chu Kang · NS16 Ang Mo Kio · NS17 Bishan · NS18 Braddell · NS19 Toa Payoh · NS20 Novena · NS21 Newton · NS22 Orchard · NS23 Somerset · NS24 Dhoby Ghaut · NS25 City Hall · NS26 Raffles Place · NS27 Marina Bay

North East Line

NE1 HarbourFront · NE3 Outram Park · NE4 Chinatown · NE5 Clarke Quay · NE6 Dhoby Ghaut · NE7 Little India · NE8 Farrer Park · NE9 Boon Keng · NE10 Potong Pasir · NE11 Woodleigh** · NE12 Serangoon · NE13 Kovan · NE14 Hougang · NE15 Buangkok · NE16 Sengkang · NE17 Punggol

Bukit Panjang LRT (BP)

BP1 Choa Chu Kang · Bukit Panjang LRT · Senja · Segar · Fajar · Jelapang · Pending · Petir · Bangkit · Phoenix · Teck Whye · South View · Keat Hong · Ten Mile Junction · Bukit Panjang

Sengkang LRT (SK)

STC Sengkang · Compassvale · Rumbia · Bakau · Kangkah · Ranggung · Renjong · Tongkang · Layar · Fernvale · Thanggam · Kupang · Farmway · Cheng Lim

Punggol LRT (PG)

Punggol LRT · Damai** · Oasis** · Kadaloor · Riviera · Coral Edge · Meridian · Cove · Soo Teck** · Sam Kee** · Punggol Point** · Samudera** · Nibong** · Sumang** · Teck Lee**

Land Transport Authority Singapore